To Tim !

CW01083516

The Oscar Wilde World of Gossip

– NEIL TITLEY –

With Best Wishes
From

Neil Titley

MARCH 2012.

An environmentally friendly book printed and bound in England by
www.printondemand-worldwide.com

www.fast-print.net/store.php

The Oscar Wilde World of Gossip
Copyright © Neil Titley 2011

ISBN 978-178035-073-8

First published 2011 by
FASTPRINT PUBLISHING
Peterborough, England.

SHED PRESS 2009

Dedicated to Winifred Scott-Moncrieff

My warmest thanks for their invaluable aid and advice to Nigel Scott-Moncrieff, Sean Titley, Ann Wroe, Annie Scott, Jason Bevan, AE 'Ege' Parker, Don Mead, Rhoda Koenig, Ken Gleeson, and the staffs of Kensington and Chelsea Library, the London Library, and the British Library.

Born in Inverness, Scotland, Neil Titley is an actor and writer. He has spent his theatrical life concentrating on solo shows and has had considerable success with his Oscar Wilde one-man performance, 'Work is the Curse of the Drinking Classes', which has been seen on four continents. His play on GBS, 'Shaw's Corner', has been televised in over twenty countries. He has one son and lives in London.

THE OSCAR WILDE WORLD OF GOSSIP

Contents:

1

ALPHABETICAL LIST OF CHARACTERS

LYTTON, LORD - English diplomat, Viceroy of India, 321
MACCHETTA, BLANCHE ROOSEVELT - American socialite, 232
MACDONALD, GENERAL SIR HECTOR - Scottish soldier, 474
MACHEN, ARTHUR - Welsh journalist, 506
MAETERLINCK, MAURICE - Belgian playwright, 456
MAHAFFY, SIR JOHN - Irish professor at Trinity, Dublin, 40
MANNING, CARDINAL HENRY - English Catholic prelate, 54
MATA HARI - Dutch dancer and spy, 513
MATURIN, CHARLES - Irish writer, 35
MAUPASSANT, GUY DE - French writer, 232
MAXIMILIAN, EMPEROR OF MEXICO - French Royal family, 84
MAY, PHIL - English artist, 431
McCLELLAN, GENERAL GEORGE - American soldier, 141
MELBA, DAME NELLIE - Australian opera singer, 464
MELLOR, HAROLD - English man of leisure, 470
MENKEN, ADAH - American actress and courtesan, 78
MEREDITH, GEORGE - English writer, 333
MEYNELL, MRS ALICE - English writer, 407
MILES, FRANK - English artist, 85
MILLER, JOAQUIN - American writer, 147
MILNER, LORD ALFRED - English politician, 391
MODJESKA, HELENA - Polish actress, 106
MONTESQUIOU, COUNT ROBERT DE - French aristocrat and poet, 177
MOORE, AUGUSTUS -Irish journalist, 39
MOORE, GEORGE - Irish writer, 36
MORRIS, WILLIAM - English artist and writer, 88
MUNTHE, AXEL - Swedish writer, 451
NAPOLEON III - French Royal family, 83
NESBIT, EDITH - English writer, 230
NEWBOLT, SIR HENRY - English poet, 439
NEWMAN, JOHN - English Catholic prelate, 55
NIJINSKY, VASLAV - Russian ballet dancer, 464
OAKLEY, ANNIE - American markswoman, 224
ODELL, E.J - English actor and clubman, 386
O'REILLY, JOHN BOYLE - Irish-American journalist and rebel, 147
'OUIDA', MARIE DE LA RAMEE - English writer, 231
PARNELL, CHARLES STUART - Irish politician, 257
PATER, WALTER - English professor at Oxford, 59
PATTISON, MARK - English professor at Oxford, 213
PINERO, SIR ARTHUR - English playwright, 316
PINKERTON, ALLAN - Scottish-American detective, 141
POYNTER, SIR EDWARD - English artist, 110
PRINCE IMPERIAL - French Royal Family, 82
PROUST, MARCEL - French writer, 291
QUILTER, HARRY - English art critic, 93
RAFFALOVICH, MARC-ANDRE - French writer, 269
RANI OF SARAWAK, MARGARET BROOKE - Sarawak Royal Family, 190
RHODES, CECIL - South African entrepreneur, 395
RIMBAUD, ARTHUR - French poet and gun-runner, 170
ROBERTSON, W. GRAHAM - English stage designer, 330
ROBINS, ELIZABETH - American actress, 252
RODD, SIR JAMES RENNELL - English diplomat, 80
RODIN, AUGUSTE - French sculptor, 478

INDIVIDUAL TOPICS

FOREWORD

To the Irish author George Moore, he was 'another Dublin jackeen who plagiarised wholesale, without admitting to his thefts'. To the English critic Sir Edmund Gosse, he was 'like Punch on a stick, squeaking, and I don't like the squeak'. To the American author Henry James, he was 'a fatuous fool and a tenth-rate cad'.

The playwright Noel Coward dismissed him with: 'What a tiresome affected sod.' The poet Algernon Swinburne called him 'a harmless young nobody'. His university professor JP Mahaffy claimed: "He was the one blot on my tutorship". The French painter Edgar Degas snorted: 'He looks like an actor playing Lord Byron in a suburban theatre'.

The French diarist Edmond Goncourt noted that he was: 'an individual of doubtful gender, with a ham actor's turn of phrase', while the cartoonist Max Beerbohm described him as: 'an enormous dowager – or schoolboy'.

The American writer Ambrose Bierce said that he was 'twin show to the two-headed calf', and the English journalist TWH Crosland frothed at: 'the complete mountebank, the scented posturer, the flabby Pharisee'.

However, Sherlock Holmes's creator Sir Arthur Conan Doyle declared that: 'he towered above us all and yet had the art of seeming to be interested in all that was said. He took as well as he gave, but what he gave was unique'.

The Irish impresario Dion Boucicault insisted that: 'Those, who have known him as I have, know that this is a noble, warm, kind and lovable man'. The French writer Andre Gide thought that: 'he emitted rays', while the arch bohemian Paul Verlaine admiringly added that he was 'a true pagan'.

The actor Sir Frank Benson called him: 'that savage, irresponsible, talented being', while the American poet Walt Whitman noted: "He is so frank and outspoken and manly".

WB Yeats wrote: 'he was one of our eighteenth century duellists born in the wrong century. He would be a good leader in a cavalry charge. It was the man I admired, who was to show so much courage and who was so loyal to the intellect'.

Sir William Rothenstein, the painter, said: 'He talked as others painted or wrote; talking was his art. I have certainly never heard his equal'; and Sir Herbert Beerbohm Tree, the actor, enthused: 'He turned his words into gems and flung them to the moon'.

His friend Robert Ross recorded that: 'among the fine qualities he showed in his later years, was that he never blamed anyone but himself for his own disasters. He never bore any ill will to anybody'.

Another friend, Robert Sherard, said: "If he had taught me nothing but the great value and happiness of life, I should still owe him an un-payable debt".

The American man-about-town Sam Ward concluded that: "He is one of the few men who gain the more you know him."

When he died in 1900, Oscar Wilde's reputation was at its lowest ebb. Owing to his imprisonment for homosexuality, his writings were ignored, his philosophy regarded as poisonous, his associates scattered or dead, and his life seen as fit only as a moralistic warning on the inevitable result of criminal perversion. His detractors, though, had failed to appreciate one of Oscar's aphorisms: 'Let us remember that art is the one thing which death cannot harm'.

At first, it was through the efforts of a few dedicated friends, (chiefly Robert Ross), that the memory of Wilde remained intact. But, even as early as 1905, certain influential elements of the British establishment were beginning to suffer an uneasy conscience over the treatment he had received. In the wider society, although his name was mentioned only in disapproving whispers or in risqué jokes, the commercial possibilities of his greatest comedies proved irresistible. 'The Importance of Being Earnest' became staple theatrical fare, irrespective of its provenance.

As Wilde's contemporaries died off in the 1930s and 40s, a new generation, unscarred by personal experience of the scandal, took up the story. Foremost among Wilde's champions was the redoubtable British actor Robert Morley, who in 1936 played the role of Oscar in the first, (but by no means last), stage dramatisation of his life, ('Oscar Wilde' by Leslie and Sewell Stokes). It was a heroic, if forlorn, attempt – although produced at a few theatre clubs, the play was banned from public performance by the Lord Chamberlain. Ten years later an appreciative biography by Hesketh Pearson had a significant effect on the reading public, although in the 1950s much of the public reticence and distaste for the subject could still be found in the work of such adversarial biographers as St John Ervine, (Oscar Wilde: A Present Time Appraisal. 1951.)

The year of 1960 proved to be the turning point for Wilde's reputation. Two biographical feature films of his life appeared almost within a week of each other, both deeply sympathetic to his character. One starred the Australian actor Peter Finch, the other, Oscar's long time supporter Robert Morley. After sixty years of popular abuse or silence, suddenly the story of Oscar's life was dominating the local cinema. In the theatre, the Anglo-Irish actor Michael MacLiammoir opened his outstanding one-man show, 'The Importance of Being Oscar', to international acclaim. Wilde was back with a vengeance.

As the Sixties gathered pace, the spirit of rebellion drew some of its inspiration from the 1890s age of decadence. The drawings of Oscar's contemporary, Aubrey Beardsley, matched Che Guevara's poster as obligatory wall decoration across the student world; (Beardsley had the posthumous experience of having a collection of his work taken into police custody on a charge of obscenity – a highly fashionable career move in 1966).

But it was Wilde who became the iconic patron from the past. His photograph appeared on the front cover of the 1967 Beatles 'Sergeant Pepper' album, while in the same year the Rolling Stones celebrated Mick Jagger's release from prison on a drugs charge by making a video called 'We Love You' based, (loosely), on Oscar's own jail experiences. In the style wars of the Sixties, he gave validity to what was assumed to be ephemeral.

Over the following decades, the public attitude to Wilde changed immeasurably. The revival of Oscar's fortunes that began in 1960 had turned into a steady deluge of biographical depiction.

Not surprisingly the theatre led the way. Productions ranged from Peter Coe's 'Feasting With Panthers' (starring Tom Baker), to Moises Kaufman's 'Gross Indecency' (starring, in different productions, Corin Redgrave, then Michael Pennington), to John Gay's 'Diversions and Delights' (starring Vincent Price, and later Sir Donald Sinden). The Canadian actor Maxim Mazumdar played Wilde's lover, Lord Alfred Douglas, in 'Oscar Remembered', and Simon Callow revived the MacLiammoir one-man show in 1997.

Leading playwrights and academics were also drawn to the subject – David Hare in 'The Judas Kiss' (starring Liam Neeson), Tom Stoppard in 'The Invention of Love', and Terry Eagleton in 'Saint Oscar' (starring Stephen Rea).

There have been three major documentaries on television – Irish RTE's 'Oscar Wilde, Spendthrift of Genius' in 1986, Channel 4's 'Indecent Acts' in 1996, and the BBC's 'Omnibus' in 1997. In 1985, the BBC also produced a three-part dramatised biography 'Wilde', starring Michael Gambon.

In addition to the two 1960 films, the cinema has produced the offbeat Wilde-orientated 1995 film 'A Man of No Importance' starring Albert Finney, and the popular Julian Mitchell scripted 1997 film 'Wilde', starring Stephen Fry. The director Oliver Parker has spent part of his career creating films out of Wilde's plays, while Mike Barker directed 'A Good Woman' starring Scarlett Johansson in 2004.

In recent years, several international Oscar Wilde Societies, (especially in Britain, the USA, and Japan), have been established with the purpose of exploring and celebrating every aspect of his life and work. The excellent 'Oscholars' website launched Oscar on to the Internet.

Wilde was finally given his place in Westminster Abbey's Poet's Corner in 1995 and, by the centenary of his death in 2000, statues to his memory had been erected in both London and Dublin.

In the 21st century, a day seldom passes without hearing or reading a Wilde quote somewhere across the media. His work is constantly performed on professional and amateur stages throughout the world. In some European countries he is considered as second only to Shakespeare in the pantheon of English-language literature. In 2007, the Vatican published a collection of Wildean maxims for Christians. His reputation has travelled from obloquy to respectability to virtual deification.

But nowhere has there been such a concentration of attention than in the world of biography. There have been so many books and articles on Wilde and his world that it is pointless even to try to list them, (a glance at the bibliography of this volume will give a partial idea of the range).

In particular, the biography that demands special attention is the brilliant 1988 'Wilde' by Richard Ellman. It remains the benchmark by which all others have to be judged. In some senses, everything else since has been either supplementary or literally academic. (Unfortunately, probably due to Ellman's untimely death, there were some glaring errors in the published text. These however have been amended in 'Additions and Corrections to Richard Ellman's Oscar Wilde' by Horst Schroeder, published in 2002.)

It could be said that if a reader possessed 'The Complete Works of Oscar Wilde', 'The Complete Letters of Oscar Wilde' (edited by Merlin Holland and Rupert Hart-Davies, 2000), and probably the Ellman biography, there would be little need to read anything else on the subject.

Certainly Wilde himself would agree: 'Biographers – those second rate literati, who arrive with the undertaker. The body snatchers of literature. The dust is given to one and the ashes to another and the soul is entirely out of their reach'. His great contemporary Bernard Shaw was even more specific: 'It is a pity that Wilde still tempts men to write lives of him. If ever there was a writer whose prayer to posterity might have been 'Read my works; and let my life alone' it was Oscar'.

Therefore, why on earth write yet another book on Wilde?

The answer lies in another of Wilde's quotes, in 'The Critic as Artist': 'He who desires to understand Shakespeare truly must understand the relations in which Shakespeare stood to the Renaissance and the Reformation, to the age of Elizabeth and the age of James'.

My personal involvement began when I first read Hesketh Pearson's biography, 'The Life of Oscar Wilde', (first published in 1946). It turned out to be a revelation. Some modern biographies, fuelled by the pursuit of exactitude, their authors' occasional aloofness to their chosen subjects, (and the bread-loaf size of the books – to which this volume admittedly is no exception), give the impression that they have all been written by the same person. Pearson belonged firmly to an older school of biography – of devil-may-care, partisan, elbow-nudging verve. Reading his 'Wilde' was like glimpsing an impressionist painting, as opposed to examining an autopsy.

He revealed Wilde as a rebel whose weapon was laughter; an intellectual to whom pedantry was anathema; a man of conspicuous kindness who was capable of annihilating his opponents in a sentence; a sage who declared that most people died of creeping common sense; an amiably boozy, overweight, tragic hero who flew too near the sun, crashed to his ruin, and then, on his deathbed, joked about the wallpaper. He was the ultimate 'lion in a den of Daniels'. To me, he was an intoxicating discovery.

By the onset of the 1980s, I felt that many of the attitudes that Wilde had lampooned so mercilessly one hundred years previously were reappearing. The same predatory commercialism, the same philistine disparagement of culture, the same net curtain-fluttering morality – in short, the same 'Victorian values' that he had despised. In a quixotic effort to defy this trend, I constructed a one-man theatre show entitled 'Work is the Curse of the Drinking Classes'. This fifty-minute monologue was set in a Paris café in 1898, and covered Oscar's comic heyday, his descent into jail, and his last years in exile.

The subsequent tour has taken me from Reno to Reykjavik, from Hong Kong to Harare, from ecstatic highs to humiliating lows, but has never, ever, been dull. No theatrical tour that has included finding that a proposed venue in Jordan has been blown up by religious zealots two days before performance, (resulting in having to recite a show extract in a Roman amphitheatre, wearing a baseball cap, with a Jordanian Army bagpipe band standing to attention behind me); or that included a lost horse wandering on stage during a performance could be described as boring. But what had started as a short theatrical venture turned, almost without my realising it, into an odyssey that has lasted for almost three decades.

In 2001, I set out to compile a small book of Wilde quotes that I thought would be a useful accompaniment to the tour shows. Finding that there were dozens of similar books already available, not to mention the competition from Wilde quotes on everything from calendars to tea towels, I decided to supplement the idea by including some biographical material on Wilde's contemporaries.

It was while doing this research that I soon found that I had stumbled on to a huge topic. Wilde had been acquainted with over three hundred of the most interesting figures of the Victorian age. Some were world famous; others were virtually unknown. My own interest took fire as I became curious as to what connection did Wilde have to such disparate figures as Queen Victoria and Toulouse-Lautrec. What did he think of them – and what did they think of him?

Then again, who were those almost anonymous extras who had darted on to Oscar's stage for a brief paragraph in the biographies and then disappeared – and what had happened to them? People I knew little or nothing about – such as Rennell Rodd or Herbert Vivian or Georgina Weldon? The more I unravelled, the more fascinating it became. As I trawled through the hundreds of memoirs on the period, these characters and the extraordinary stories attached to them became my central theme. Oscar Wilde was the link, but his vast acquaintanceship was the story.

As the years of research ended, I found that, having accumulated almost two million words in biographical notes, the initial small volume on Wilde had expanded into a panorama of the Victorian world. I had largely followed Disraeli's dictum: 'Read no history, nothing but biography, for that is life without theory'.

But I felt that the real value of the gathered information lay, not in the bare bones of biography, (the sort of information that one could acquire easily from the Dictionary of

National Biography or the Internet), but in the flesh and blood detail of their lives. It was the minor but revealing stories, the personal quirks, that gave life and colour to the characters.

As Victor Hugo once wrote: 'This is where, and we insist on this, this is where life is, the throbbing, the shuddering of humanity. Little details are the foliage, so to speak, of big events and are lost in the remoteness of history.'

It had also uncovered a treasury of hilarious, and mostly forgotten, anecdotes. Admittedly, some of them are known and a few are famous, but this was the first time they had been gathered together. More importantly, many of the best stories had not been in circulation since Victorian times.

It was with this exciting sense of re-discovery that I set about reducing the mountain of notes to a manageable book. I found that the best way of organising the material was to use a chronological format and introduce the characters roughly at the time they had encountered Oscar Wilde. Although this gives some figures an anachronistic tinge, (for instance, the pen-portrait of George Moore is slotted into 1864, while he was still an important figure in the 1930s), generally speaking they match their eras.

Another problem was establishing the truth of many of the rumours and assertions current in the 1880s and 90s. Who did what to whom behind closed doors a century ago is always going to be debateable. While giving some leeway to Wilde's argument: 'Legends are often more true than reality', when in doubt I have attempted to provide the most likely interpretation.

While definitely not setting out to write a conventional biography of Wilde, (it having been accomplished so often and successfully before), I have constructed a bare-bones narrative of his life as the link material that holds the 300 character-sketches together. Also, I added some short pieces on various aspects of his life and relevant historical events that seemed of interest – in particular, Oscar's activities in America, his writings, his clubs and restaurants, his life in prison, and such events as the Paris Commune, the Sudan campaign, and the Jameson Raid.

Just as many modern day attitudes would shock a resurrected Victorian, so many Victorian attitudes now shock the 21st century. I decided to refrain as much as possible from personal comment on the sometimes outrageous activities of the characters involved. Oscar wrote: 'I know that there are many historians who still think it necessary to apply moral judgments to history and who distribute their praise or blame with the solemn complacency of a successful schoolmaster' ..... 'Nobody with the true historical sense ever dreams of blaming Nero, or scolding Tiberius, or censuring Caesar Borgia'.

The 19th century was an age of airy prejudice and both sexual and racial generalisation, and now provides a minefield in the use of politically correct terminology. On reflection, I decided to retain the use of the older words, and apologise for any offence in so doing. When such terms as 'Red Indian' and 'Negro' have been used in quotation, I have left them intact. For easier reference, I have italicised the names of those characters whose lives appear in individual sections elsewhere in the book. Also, when referring to Wilde's lover. Lord Alfred Douglas, I have used his familiar nickname of 'Bosie' simply because, with so many of the Douglas family involved in the story, it avoids confusion.

I have to emphasise my huge debt to the hundreds of biographers, archivists and memoirists whose work provided the information in the first place, (most of whom are listed in the bibliography). As the British Prime Minister Arthur Balfour said: 'History repeats itself; historians repeat each other'; and without their efforts over the last 150 years, little of this book could exist. I hope that my work in bringing their magnificent stories back into currency is some small recompense for the fascination and enjoyment they have given me.

I make no apology for the fact that the book is about (almost dedicated to) comic incident and gossip. Oscar was right: 'Gossip is charming – history is merely gossip'. It is the element that injects Technicolor into the sepia view of the past. And if the result is laughter, then what better way to celebrate the greatest wit in the English language?

Because, although this book is essentially about the lives of his contemporaries, the golden thread remains the character and memory of the funniest – the friendliest – the most exhilarating – the cleverest – the most far-sighted – the most courageous – the most forgiving – and the most human of men – Mr Oscar Wilde himself.

Neil Titley, London 2009

MAIN DATES OF WILDE'S LIFE

1854 – Oct 16/ OW born at 21 Westland Row, Dublin.

1855 – June/ The Wilde family moved to 1 Merrion Square North, Dublin

1858-63 – The family spent summer holidays in a variety of Irish resorts and retreats, including Co Wicklow, Co Galway and Dungarvan, Co Waterford.

1863 – May/ OW attended St Columba's College, Dublin

1864 – Feb/ Entered the Portora Royal School, Enniskillen, Co Fermanagh, as a boarding pupil.

1867 – Feb 23/ Death of Isola, OW's nine-year-old sister.
Aug/ Visited Paris with his mother, and brother Willie.

1871 – June/ Left Portora School.
Oct/ Entered Trinity College, Dublin, as an undergraduate.

1874 – Awarded the Berkeley Gold Medal at Trinity.
June/ Visited London with members of family.
July/ Visited Genoa and Paris with his mother.
Oct 17/Entered Magdalen College, Oxford, as an undergraduate.

1875 – June/Travelled to Italy – toured Florence, Venice, and Verona. Stayed at Arona, Lake Maggiore. Returned via Paris to Ireland.
July/ Stayed at family-owned fishing lodge at Illaunroe, Co Galway.
Oct/ Returned for second year at Oxford.

1876 – April 19/ Death of Sir William Wilde, OW's father. OW attended funeral in Dublin.
April/ Stayed for a few days with his uncle at West Ashby, Lincs.
July 5/ Gained a first class Classical Moderations (Mods).
July 9/ Stayed at Bingham Rectory, Notts, with the family of his friend, Frank Miles.
Aug/ Stayed at Illaunroe, Co Galway.
Oct/ Returned to Oxford for his third year.

1877 – March/ Travelled to Italy, including Turin and Ravenna.
April/ Continued trip via Brindisi to Greece, including Corfu and Athens.
April 21/ Sailed from Mycenae, Greece, to Naples
April/ Stayed for several days in Rome
April 30/ Arrived back in Oxford.
May/ Rusticated from college for late arrival back from holiday. Sent down for two terms.
May 1/ Spent a week in London with Frank Miles.
May 7/ Spent a week in Bournemouth recuperating from minor illness.
May 15/ Arrived back in Dublin.
Sept/ OW stayed at Clonfil House in Ireland.
Oct/ Reinstated at Oxford.

1878 – June 10/ Awarded the Newdigate Prize for his poem 'Ravenna'.
July 19/Gained a first class degree in Litterae Humaniores (Greats).
Aug/ Stayed in Dublin.
Oct/ Visited the Sickert family at Neuville near Dieppe, France.
Nov/Returned to Oxford to study for his compulsory Divinity exam.
Lodged over a chemist's shop at 71, (then 66), High Street
Nov 22/ Passed the Divinity exam and took his BA degree.

1879 – Feb/ Moved to 13, Salisbury Street, London, sharing rooms with Frank

Miles.

July/ Toured Belgium with Rennell Rodd; stayed at Laroche and Tournai. 1880 – March/ Applied unsuccessfully for job as Inspector of Schools.

Summer/ Wrote 'Vera', his first play.

June 3/ Involved in producing the 'Agamemnon' by Aeschylus, which was performed at Balliol Hall, Oxford.

July/ OW and Miles rented a new house in Tite St, Chelsea, London.

1881 – June/Published his first collection of poems.

Summer/ Visited the Loire valley, France, with Rennell Rodd; also toured on to Paris, Chartres, and Amboise.

Sept/ After a row with Miles, OW moved to two rooms on the third floor of 9, Charles St, London. This remained his base until he married in 1884.

Dec/ The planned theatre opening of 'Vera' was cancelled.

Dec 24/ Wilde set sail to undertake a tour of the United States.

1882 – Jan 2/ Arrived in New York. Began first leg of his lecture tour that was to last from Jan 9 till May 12. Lectures in the east included New York City, Philadelphia, Washington, and Boston.

Feb 9/ Visited the Niagara Falls.

Feb-Mar/ Lectured in Ohio, Minnesota, Indiana, Kentucky, Wisconsin, Nebraska, Illinois, and Iowa.

March/ Crossed the Rocky Mountains by train to lecture in California, followed by a visit to Salt Lake City.

April 12-13/ Lectured in Denver, Colorado, then in Leadville.

May/ Toured through Missouri, Kansas, Iowa, Ohio, Pennsylvania, arriving back in New York City.

May 13-Aug 26/ Delivered lectures in Canada, including Montreal.

June 11-July 11/ Began tour of the southern USA, starting in Cincinnati. Toured through Tennessee, Mississippi, Louisiana, Texas, Alabama, Georgia, the Carolinas, and Virginia.

July 15/ Began lecture tour of the north-east summer resorts, including Westchester, Saratoga, and Newport, Rhode Island.

Oct 4-13/ Undertook a second tour of Canada.

Oct 14-Dec 26/ Stayed in New York.

Dec 27/ Sailed back to Britain. Stayed for two weeks at 9, Charles St, London.

1883 – Late Jan-mid May/ Stayed in Paris, writing 'The Duchess of Padua'.

May/ Returned to stay at Charles St, London

July/ Began lecture tour of Britain

Aug 2/ Sailed back to New York to witness the opening of his play, 'Vera'.

Aug 20/ Opening night of 'Vera', closed after one week.

Mid-Sept/ Returned to Britain.

Oct/ Resumed his lecture tour of Britain, speaking at over 150 venues.

Nov/ Lectured in Dublin. Became engaged to Constance Mary Lloyd.

1884 – Jan-May/ Continued lecture tour of Britain

May 29/ Married Constance at St James Church, Paddington, London.

June/ Spent first part of honeymoon in Paris, the second in Dieppe.

July/ the couple moved into the Charles St lodgings for six months, awaiting the redecoration of their new home.

Oct/ Resumed lecture tour of Britain and Ireland.
1885 –Jan/ The Wildes move into new home at 16, Tite St.
March 30/ Completed last venue of his British lecture tour.
April/ OW began to concentrate on journalism, including reviews.
June 5/ His first son, Cyril, born.
1886 – /OW spent most of the year writing for various journals.
Oct/ Met Robert Ross, soon to become his homosexual lover.
Nov 5/ His second son, Vyvyan, born.
1887 – / Continued work in journalism.
May/ Appointed as editor of 'Women's World'.
Nov/ First edition of 'Women's World' under OW's editorship.
1888 – / Worked on 'Women's World' throughout the year.
May/ Published 'The Happy Prince and other Tales'.
1889 – July/ After 20 issues of Women's World, OW became bored and drifted
away from the magazine.
July-Aug/ Visited Germany and travelled up the Rhine to Kreuznach.
1890 – June/ Published 'The Picture of Dorian Gray', in magazine format.
Aug/ Visited Bamff, in Perthshire, Scotland.
1891 – Jan 26/ Production of 'Duchess of Padua' opens in New York, renamed
'Guido Ferranti'. Closed on Feb 14.
Feb/ Stayed in Paris and met many French notables.
Feb/ OW's essay 'The Soul of Man Under Socialism' published.
April/ Weekend visit to Taplow Court, near Maidenhead.
April/ 'The Picture of Dorian Gray' was published in book form
May/ OW's collection of essays, 'Intentions' published.
Late June/ OW introduced to Lord Alfred Douglas, ('Bosie').
July/ 'Lord Arthur Savile's Crime and Other Stories' published
July 4/ Spent a weekend at the Crabbet Club in Sussex.
Summer/ Stayed in the Lake District, writing new play.
Oct/ Returned to London, before moving on to Paris for some weeks.
Dec 22/ Returned to London, and spent Christmas with his family.
1892 – Jan/ Took short holiday in Torquay, Devon.
Feb 20/ Opening night of 'Lady Windermere's Fan'.
June/ Rehearsed for his new play, 'Salome', before it was cancelled on
orders from the Lord Chamberlain.
July 3/ Went to Bad Homburg, Germany, for a spa 'cure'.
Aug-Sept/ Stayed at Grove Farm, near Cromer, Norfolk, to write new play.
Oct/ Left Norfolk and visited Reading for leisure weekend.
Oct/ Stayed with Bosie's mother, Sibyl Douglas, at Bracknell, Berks.
Nov/ Visited Paris with rentboys.
1893 – Spring/ Made two trips to Torquay in Devon.
March/ OW lived mostly at the Savoy Hotel, London, during this period.
April 19/ Opening night of 'A Woman of No Importance' in London.
May/ Spent time in Oxford visiting Bosie.
Summer/ Rented cottage at Goring, Berks and wrote new play.
Aug/ Stayed in Dinard, France, to avoid possible Dannay scandal.
Late Sept/ Returned to London and stayed in a hotel at 10/11, St James
Place, London; continued to write 'An Ideal Husband'.
Nov/ Stayed in Paris for a short time.

1894 – Feb/ Published 'Salome', (illustrated by Beardsley).
    March/ Reunited with Bosie in Paris; returned to London on March 31.
    April 1/ Had lunch at the Café Royal with Bosie and his father, the
    Marquess of Queensberry.
    April 27/ Left London to stay in Paris.
    May 6/ Joined Bosie in Florence, Italy.
    June/ Returned to London to find that Queensberry was attacking him.
    June 30/Visit by Queensberry to OW's Tite St home; quarrel breaks out.
    Aug/ Takes family for a holiday in Worthing, Sussex, and writes new play.
    Oct/ Persuaded by Bosie to move to Brighton hotels; they part after
    quarrel.
    Oct 18/ Reconciled with Bosie in London.
    Dec/ Rehearsed new play in London.
1895 – Jan 3/ Opening night of 'An Ideal Husband'.
    Jan 17/ Took a holiday with Bosie in Algeria, visited Blidah.
    Early Feb/ Returned to London to oversee more rehearsals.
Feb 14/ Opening night of 'The Importance of Being Earnest'.
Feb 28/ Received insulting card from Queensberry.
March 1/ Issued writ for criminal libel against Queensberry.
March 13/ Took 10-day holiday with Bosie in Monte Carlo
March 23/ Returned to London; stayed at Avondale Hotel.
    March 25/ Lunch at Café Royal with Frank Harris and Bernard Shaw who advised him
    to flee from England.
Apr 3/ Opening day of the trial of Wilde versus Queensberry.
    Apr 5/ Queensberry acquitted. OW arrested at Cadogan Hotel; remanded to Holloway
    Prison.
Apr 24/ Enforced sale of Wilde family possessions held at Tite St.
Apr 26/ First trial of OW began. Jury decision split after five days.
    May 1/ Released on bail from Holloway. Stayed at mother's home at Oakley St, Chelsea.
    May 18/ Moves to the Leverson's house at 2, Courtfield Gardens, South Kensington.
May 22/ Second trial of Wilde began.
    May 25/ Wilde found guilty on homosexual charges; sentenced to two years prison.
    July 4/ Transferred from Pentonville to Wandsworth Prison
    Sept 25/Taken on first trip to Bankruptcy Court.
    Oct/ Suffered a breakdown; lay ill in the prison infirmary for a month
    Nov 12/ After second visit to Bankruptcy Court, declared bankrupt.
    Nov 21/ Transferred by train to Reading Gaol.
1896 – Feb 11/ First performance of 'Salome' in Paris.
    Feb/ Receives news of the death of his mother.
    July/ Appointment of new governor led to improvements in prison life.
1897 – Jan-March/ Writes his prison letter, 'De Profundis'.
    May 19/ Released from Pentonville Prison. Leaves Newhaven on
    overnight ferry to France.
    May 20/ Arrived in Dieppe; spent next few days celebrating release.
    May 26/ Moved to Berneval, a seaside village near Dieppe.
    July 8/ Began work on 'The Ballad of Reading Gaol'.
    Aug 28/ Met Bosie at Rouen, Normandy.
    Sept 15/ Travelled via Paris and Aix-les-Bains to Italy

Sept 20/ Arrived in Naples for reunion with Bosie. Stayed at the Hotel Royal, then rented the Villa Giudice in Posillipo, north of Naples.

Dec 2/ Bosie left Naples. OW went to stay at Taormina, near Messina, Sicily.

1898 – Jan/ Arrived back in Posillipo; found house had been burgled. Moved to 31, Santa Lucia, Naples.

Feb 13/ Returned to Paris; stayed at Hotel de Nice, rue des Beaux-Arts.

Feb 13/ 'The Ballad of Reading Gaol' published in England.

March-April/ Short of money; spent his time around Parisian cafes. Changed lodgings to the Hotel d'Alsace, rue des Beaux Arts.

Apr 7/ OW's wife Constance died in Italy

May/ Underwent an operation on his throat

Summer/ Still short of funds, spent time in Paris. Made occasional trips to villages outside Paris – Nogent-sur-Marne and, in August, in Chevennieres-sur-Marne.

Sept/ Stayed for a few days with Charles Conder at Chantemerle, near La Roche Guyon.

Dec 20/ Left Paris to visit the French Riviera with Frank Harris; stayed at the Hotel des Bains at La Napoule, near Cannes.

1899 – Jan/ Stayed on the Riviera; visited Nice and Cannes

Mid-Feb/ Left La Napoule; moved to the Terminus Hotel in Nice.

March 13/ Death of OW's brother, Willie Wilde.

March/ Travelled to Italy, stopping at Genoa. Moved on to Gland, Lake Geneva, Switzerland, to stay as a houseguest of Harold Mellor.

April 1/ Stayed at Santa Margherita, near Genoa, Italy; visited Rapallo and Portofino.

May 7/ Returned to Paris; stayed at a couple of small Right Bank hotels.

Summer/ Remained in Paris, grounded by lack of funds.

June/ Visited Le Havre, France.

Aug/ Moved back into Hotel d'Alsace, owned by Jean Dupoirier.

1900 – Jan 31/ Death of the Marquess of Queensberry.

April 2/ Visited Italy as guest of Harold Mellor; toured Palermo, Sicily, then Naples and Rome, before a return visit to Mellor's home at Gland.

May/ Went back to Paris; stayed at the Hotel d'Alsace.

Oct 10/ Underwent operation on his right ear.

Oct 25/ Opening night of 'Mr and Mrs Daventry' in London, a play built around OW'S scenario.

Nov 30/ Death of OW at Hotel d'Alsace at 1.50pm.

Dec 3/ Burial of OW at Bagneux Cemetery, just outside Paris.

1909 – /Transfer of OW's body to Pére Lachaise cemetery in Paris, under new monument by Jacob Epstein

CHRONOLOGICAL CONTENTS

70] SIR RICHARD BURTON, English explorer and writer
74] ALGERNON SWINBURNE, English poet
  78] (ADAH MENKEN, American actress and courtesan
  79] CHARLES HOWELL, English confidence trickster)
79] SIMEON SOLOMON, English artist

<u>1878</u>
80] SIR JAMES RENNELL RODD, English diplomat
  82] WILDE AND CIGARETTES

<u>1879</u>
82] THE PRINCE IMPERIAL, French Royal family
  83] (NAPOLEON III, French Royal family
  83] EMPRESS EUGENIE, French Royal family
  84] EMPEROR MAXIMILIAN OF MEXICO, French Royal Family)
85] FRANK MILES, English artist
86] SIR EDWARD BURNE-JONES, English artist
  88] (GEORGE ELIOT, English writer
  88] WILLIAM MORRIS, English artist and writer)
89] VIOLET HUNT, English writer
90] JAMES McNEILL WHISTLER, American artist
  93] (HARRY QUILTER, English art critic)
93] SIR HENRY IRVING, English actor
  93] (BARONESS BURDETT-COUTTS, English philanthropist)
96] ELLEN TERRY, English actress
98] SIR SQUIRE BANCROFT, English actor
99] LILY LANGTRY, English socialite and actress
  102] (LADY GLWADYS LONSDALE, English socialite
  103] PATSY CORNWALLIS-WEST, Irish socialite)

<u>1880</u>
104] SERGEI STEPNIAK, Russian revolutionary
105] GENEVIEVE WARD, American actress
106] HELENA MODJESKA, Polish actress
108] SIR GEORGE DU MAURIER, Anglo-French cartoonist
  110] (SIR EDWARD POYNTER, English artist
  110] WILLIAM FRITH, English artist)
111] SIR FRANK BENSON, English actor
  112] WILDE AND SPORTS
113] ROBERT BROWNING, English poet
114] ALFRED, LORD TENNYSON, English poet
  116] (JULIA CAMERON, English photographer)

<u>1881</u>
117] SIR WILLIAM GILBERT, English light opera librettist
  119] (SIR ARTHUR SULLIVAN, English light opera composer
  119] RICHARD D'OYLEY CARTE, English light opera promoter
  120] GEORGE GROSSMITH, English singer and writer)
120] SIR EDMUND GOSSE, English critic and writer

24

167] EDGAR DEGAS, French artist
    169] (GENERAL BEN BUTLER, American general)
169] PAUL VERLAINE, French poet
    170] (ARTHUR RIMBAUD, French poet and gunrunner
    174] BIBI LA PUREE, French street thief)
175] VICTOR HUGO, French writer
177] COMTE ROBERT DE MONTESQUIOU, French aristocrat and poet
179] EDMOND DE GONCOURT, French writer
    180] (ALPHONSE DAUDET, French writer)
181] THOMAS EDISON, American inventor

<u>1884</u>
183] CONSTANCE WILDE (First Part), wife of Oscar Wilde
    183] (FABIAN LLOYD, Irish nephew of Constance Wilde
    185] JUDGE 'HANGING' HAWKINS, English judge
    186] HORATIO BOTTOMLEY, English fraudulent businessman)
187] JORIS-KARL HUYSMANS, French writer
188] PRINCESS ALICE OF MONACO, French-American socialite
    189] 'THE LEGEND OF MONTE CARLO'
190] MARGARET BROOKE, RANI OF SARAWAK, Sarawak royal family

<u>1885</u>
192] HENRY LABOUCHERE, English politician and journalist
197] FENWICK DE SALES LA TERRIERE, English soldier
   – AND THE SUDAN
    197] (GENERAL C.G. GORDON, English soldier
    199] COL. VALENTINE BAKER, English soldier
    201] GENERAL GARNET WOLSELEY, Anglo-Irish general
    202] COL. FRED BURNABY, English soldier)
   203] EVENTS DURING THE SUDAN CAMPAIGN
   204] AFTERMATH
206] LORD CHARLES BERESFORD, Anglo-Irish admiral
208] WALTER HARRIS, English explorer
    210] REGGIE LISTER, English diplomat

<u>1886</u>
211] ROBERT ROSS (First Part), Canadian art gallery owner
    211] (THOMAS CARLYLE, Scottish writer and historian)
212] SIR CHARLES DILKE, English politician
    213] (MARK PATTISON, English professor at Oxford)
214] LADY COLIN CAMPBELL, English divorcee

<u>1887</u>
217] WILLIAM T. STEAD, English journalist
219] MARK TWAIN, American writer
    221] (ARTEMUS WARD, American writer)
221] 'BUFFALO BILL' CODY, American scout and showman

26

273] PRINCE EDDY, DUKE OF CLARENCE, son of King Edward VII
    274] (LORD ARTHUR SOMERSET, English soldier
    276] KING GEORGE V, English monarch)
277] HERBERT VIVIAN, English journalist

1890
278] LIONEL JOHNSON, English poet
279] SIR SEYMOUR HICKS, English actor
    280] (WILLIAM TERRISS, English actor)
    281] THE PICTURE OF DORIAN GRAY

1891
282] ERNEST DOWSON, English poet
    283] (LEWIS CARROLL, English writer and Oxford don)
285] HERBERT HORNE, English writer and architect
    286] (JOHN DAVIDSON, Scottish poet and writer
    286] JOHN BARLAS, Scottish poet and anarchist)
286] ARTHUR SYMONS, English writer and critic
    288] (MARIE LLOYD, English music hall artiste)
289] ANATOLE FRANCE, French writer
290] SIR WILLIAM ROTHENSTEIN, English artist
291] MARCEL PROUST, French writer
    292] (GENEVIEVE STRAUSS (Bizet), French salon hostess)
    294] THE SOUL OF MAN UNDER SOCIALISM
295] WILLIE GRENFELL, LORD DESBOROUGH, English aristocrat
296] BOSIE DOUGLAS – (First Part), Scottish poet and Wilde's lover
    297] (THE DOUGLASES (First Part), family of Scottish aristocrats)
303] WILFRED SCAWEN BLUNT, English poet and adventurer
    309] (ALGERNON BOURKE, English clubman
    310] CATHERINE WALTERS, English courtesan
    311] MARQUESS OF HARTINGTON, English politician
    312] HUBERT DE BURGH, Earl of Clanricarde, Irish landlord)
312] GEORGE, VISCOUNT CURZON, English politician
    315] (HARRY CUST, English courtier and journalist)
315] SIR GEORGE ALEXANDER – English actor
    316] (SIR ARTHUR PINERO, English playwright)
317] AUGUSTIN DALY, American theatre impresario
    317] (JUNIUS BOOTH, American actor)
    318] THEATRE FIRES
319] PIERRE LOUYS, French writer
320] ANDRE GIDE, French writer
321] LORD ROBERT LYTTON, English diplomat, Viceroy of India
    323] LADY WINDERMERE'S FAN

1892
324] HENRY JAMES, American writer
    325] (CLEMENT SCOTT, English theatre critic)
    326] SALOME
327] WILLIAM ARCHER, English theatre critic

<u>1895</u>

376] LEWIS WALLER, English actor
377] SIR CHARLES WYNDHAM, English actor
   378] THE IMPORTANCE OF BEING EARNEST
379] BOSIE DOUGLAS – (Second Part)
   379] RENTBOYS
      381] (THE DOUGLAS FAMILY - Second Part)
384] CHARLES BROOKFIELD, English actor
      385] (LORD ROBERT BADEN-POWELL, English soldier
      386] E.J. ODELL, English actor and clubman)
387] SIR CHARLES HAWTREY, English actor
      388] (JIMMY GLOVER, Irish musical theatre promoter)
389] SIR EDWARD CARSON, Irish barrister
      391] (LORD MILNER, English politician)
392] SIR EDWARD CLARKE, English barrister
   393] THE JAMESON RAID
      394] (JOSEPH CHAMBERLAIN, English politician
      395] CECIL RHODES, South African entrepreneur)
   395] THE EVENTS OF APRIL 5TH 1895
397] SIR GEORGE LEWIS, English solicitor
398] GEORGE WYNDHAM, English politician
      400] (CHARLES GATTY, English politician
      400] ARTHUR BALFOUR, English statesman)
   401] ZIONISM
402] HERBERT ASQUITH, English statesman
      403] (MARGOT ASQUITH, English wife of Herbert Asquith
      405] CHARLES WORTH, English couturier
      406] ANTHONY ASQUITH, English film director)
406] MRS HUMPHREY WARD, English writer
407] MRS ALICE MEYNELL, English writer
      407] (FRANCIS THOMPSON, English poet)
409] REV. STUART HEADLAM, English churchman
      410] (CHARLES BRADLAUGH, English politician and free-thinker)
411] WILLIE WILDE – (Second Part)
412] HENRY ARTHUR JONES, English playwright
413] ADA LEVERSON, English writer
      414] (BRANDON THOMAS, English actor and playwright)
414] BOSIE DOUGLAS – (Third Part)
      415] (THE DOUGLAS FAMILY - Third Part)
   416] TO FLEE OR NOT TO FLEE – WHY WILDE STAYED?
   419] PRISON CONDITIONS
420] LORD HALDANE, English politician

<u>1896</u>

422] ALFRED AUSTIN, English poet
      423] (WILLIAM MORE ADEY, English translator)
      424] (SIR EVELYN RUGGLES-BRISE, English prison reformer)
   425] DE PROFUNDIS

<u>1897</u>
425] CONSTANCE WILDE – (Second Part)
   427] (CYRIL AND VYVYAN WILDE, sons of Oscar Wilde)
   428] (MICHAEL DAVITT, Irish politician)
429] JOHN STRANGE WINTER, English novelist
429] CHARLES CONDER, English artist
   430] (FRITZ VON THAULOW, Norwegian artist
   431] PHIL MAY, English artist)
432] LEONARD SMITHERS, English publisher
   434] (REGGIE BACCHUS, English academic and pornographer
   435] ALTHEA GYLES, English illustrator
   435] ALEISTER CROWLEY, English writer and mystic)
  435] THE BALLAD OF READING GAOL
   436] (AE HOUSEMAN, English poet)
436] RUDYARD KIPLING, English writer and poet
   439] (SIR HENRY NEWBOLT, English poet
   439] HENRY RIDER HAGGARD, English novelist)
440] GERTRUDE ATHERTON, American writer
442] JOHN FOTHERGILL, English architect and innkeeper
   442] (ARTHUR CLIFTON, English lawyer)
444] ROBERT SHERARD – (Second Part)
445] BOSIE DOUGLAS – (Fourth Part)
   446] (THE DOUGLAS FAMILY - Fourth Part)
449] ELEANOUR DUSE, Italian actress
   450] (GABRIELE D'ANNUNZIO, Italian writer and adventurer)
   451] (AXEL MUNTHE, Swedish writer)

<u>1898</u>
  452] THE DREYFUS CASE
453] CARLOS BLACKER, English linguist
454] EMILE ZOLA, French writer
456] MAURICE MAETERLINCK, Belgian playwright
457] ALFRED JARRY, French playwright
   458] (AURELIEN LUGNE-POE, French theatre director)
459] HENRI DE TOULOUSE-LAUTREC, French artist
   460] (YVETTE GUILBERT, French music hall star
   461] ARISTIDE BRUANT, French singer and café owner
   462] ERNEST LA JEUNESSE, French journalist)
462] SERGEI DIAGHILEV, Russian ballet impresario
   464] (VASLAV NIJINSKY, Russian ballet dancer)
464] DAME NELLIE MELBA, Australian opera singer
   467] (EDMUND ROSTAND, French playwright)
467] GEORGINA WELDON, English litigant

<u>1899</u>
470] HAROLD MELLOR, English man of leisure
  471] THE FASHODA AFFAIR
471] LORD KITCHENER, Anglo-Irish soldier
   474] (SIR HECTOR MACDONALD, Scottish soldier)

PART ONE

YOUTH

Sir William Wilde to Sir Frank Burnand

34

1854

[On March 28, 1854, the Crimean War broke out between Russia on one side and Britain, France and Turkey on the other. During the ensuing Battle of Balaclava, (fought on October 25), the world witnessed one of the most spectacularly incompetent manoeuvres in military history, namely the Charge of the Light Brigade.]

Nine days earlier, on October 16, Oscar Fingal O'Flahertie Wills Wilde had been born at 21 Westland Row, Dublin. Wilde: 'A name which is destined to be in everybody's mouth must not be too long. It comes so expensive in the advertisements'.

His parents were Sir William Wilde and Jane 'Speranza' Wilde (born Elgee).

SIR WILLIAM WILDE (1815-1876)

(Oscar: 'Whatever was good enough for our fathers is not good enough for us'.)

Wilde's father, a man of great vitality and the possessor of a beautiful speaking voice, was described also as resembling a monkey and derided for his dirt-encrusted appearance. His son Oscar may have been defending the family honour when in later years he said that: 'I know so many men in London whose only talent is for washing. I suppose that is why men of genius so seldom wash; they are afraid of being mistaken for men of talent only.'

Sir William was a renowned eye and ear surgeon in Dublin, who, in his youth, travelled and studied in Egypt and Vienna. He founded St Marks Hospital, Dublin, in 1844 and worked hard to alleviate the sufferings of the 1845 Irish famine. He married Jane Elgee ('Speranza') in 1851, was appointed Surgeon Oculist to Queen Victoria in Ireland in 1863 and knighted the following year.

Not all of his patients were impressed by his skills. The writer *GB Shaw* complained that 'The only occasion I saw Sir William was when he operated on my father for a squint and overdid the corrections so much that my father squinted the other way all the rest of his life'.

In 1864, he was accused of rape by a woman patient, Miss Mary Travers. In a complicated legal suit involving his wife, he was partially vindicated but his reputation (and dignity) suffered. A Dublin ballad about the affair circulated the streets: 'An eminent oculist lives in the Square, His skill is unrivalled, his talent is rare, And if you will listen I'll certainly try, To tell how he opened Miss Travers' eye'.

The incident affected Sir William financially; the court costs were ruinous and, when he died twelve years later, his will provided very little substance for his family.

He sired six known children, three of them, Willie, Oscar and Isola, being legitimate and three, Mary, Emily and Henry, illegitimate. (Oscar: 'A family is a terrible encumbrance, especially when one is not married'.)

Mary and Emily died in their early twenties, when they were burnt to death after their ball gowns caught fire at a party in 1871. Henry, cunningly surnamed Wilson (Will's son), followed his father's career and became a senior surgeon, but died in 1877 aged 39. Isola died of a fever aged nine in 1867, (Sir William: "It made me a mourner for life"). Two sons remained – Willie and Oscar Wilde.

The illegitimacy of three of Sir William's children was quite normal in the 1830s; it was not until the later Victorian period that such a brood would become a matter of scandal. It was said of the great Irish political leader Daniel O'Connell that: 'You couldn't throw a stone in the County Kerry without hitting one of his bastards'.

Sir William also enjoyed other traditional pleasures. When Oscar won the Berkeley Gold Medal at university, Sir William invited dozens of guests to celebrate the event at a party at the Wildes' summer home at Moytura. The alcohol with which they were served, (the infamous 'poteen'), proved so potent that, in case the guests forgot in which bed they were meant to be sleeping, Sir William had to attach nameplates to each pillow.

One of Sir William's mistresses was a teenager called **LAURA BELL** (1829-1894). Laura was a remarkably beautiful, passionate Irish girl, with a cascade of golden hair, large blue eyes and a perfect figure.

In 1849, aged 20, she left Dublin to become one of the most famous courtesans in London. She grew rich, was married to the Bishop of Norwich's grandson, (until he shot himself), and owned a large mansion in Grosvenor Square. She still continued with her professional activities, until she became one of *William Gladstone's* very rare successes in 'saving fallen women'. He persuaded her to give up her promiscuous life style. As a result, she became a zealous Salvationist and moved to a small cottage in Hampstead.

Laura may have had an impact on world history beyond anything that might have been predicted. When he met her during her years as a prostitute in London, the Nepalese Envoy, a young prince called Jung Bahadoor, became infatuated with her. In their time together, she managed to charm over a quarter of million pounds out of him. In the interests of maintaining diplomatic relations, the British India Office was forced to reimburse the prince for Laura's depredations.

However, when the Indian Mutiny broke out in 1857 and Britain was in serious danger of losing control, it was Laura who interceded with her former lover and persuaded him to keep the famed Gurkha troops aloof from the struggle. Nepal stayed neutral and the Raj was saved.

LADY JANE WILDE (SPERANZA) (1826? – 1896)

Oscar's mother was a woman of majestic self-confidence, even in adversity. Tall and broad, she sported over her prominent bosom a collection of dangling brooches, depicting family members; this gave her 'the appearance of a perambulating family mausoleum'. She had a withering distaste for conformity: 'It is only trades-people who are respectable. We are above respectability'.

As a young woman she had been involved peripherally in the 1848 trial of the Irish nationalist Gavin Duffy and later achieved some fame for writing revolutionary poetry. *Bosie Douglas* described her as 'a parlour Fenian'. Her rebel fervour did not extend to rejecting the title of 'Lady', a status that Oscar himself was inclined to emphasise.

During the problems over the rape allegations against her husband, she sailed serenely above what she described as 'the miasmas of the commonplace', an attitude she replicated through the trials of her son. "When you are as old as I am, young man, you will know there is only one thing in the world worth living for and that is sin".

After Sir William's death, Speranza found herself in financial difficulties. One day a friend called at the family home in Merrion Square to find bailiffs pacing the hall. Speranza was upstairs reclining in bed, reciting Greek poetry, and ignoring the situation. She left Dublin in 1879 and moved to London, where she held court over afternoon salons. Some of her less respectful visitors described her as 'looking like a tragedy queen at a suburban theatre' while others thought she resembled her son Oscar in drag.

At one such event, the novelist *Bram Stoker* introduced her to a young woman who he described as 'half English and half Irish'. Speranza replied: "Glad to meet you, dear. Your English half is as welcome as your Irish bottom".

Speranza was particularly proud of her family connection to the writer **CHARLES MATURIN** (1782-1824), author of the Gothic novel 'Melmoth the Wanderer'. He had proved himself to be a suitably eccentric ancestor. Nominally a clergyman, he was far more interested in dancing, a contemporary comment being that 'the ballroom was his temple of inspiration and worship'. Maturin preferred writing in company but, to prevent himself joining the conversation, would seal his own mouth with paste, and wear a cushion on his head to show that he was at work.

(Oscar Wilde used the name of Maturin's fictional hero – (Sebastian) 'Melmoth' – as an alias when he left prison in 1897, although six months later he admitted in a letter that: 'I have re-taken my own name, as my incognito was absurd'.)

1855 - 1864

[After the relatively peaceful period in international affairs following the Battle of Waterloo in 1815, the decade following Wilde's birth saw the rise of a number of serious conflicts.

The Crimean War ended in April 1856, but was quickly followed by the Indian Mutiny, (1857-58).

In China, the Taiping Rebellion, which had been raging since 1850, continued to claim millions of lives. In 1860, Western forces attacked the capital Peking and sacked the Summer Palace.

The American Civil War began in 1861, (a struggle that was to kill almost 700,00 Americans). In South America, an alliance between Brazil, Argentina and Uruguay fought a horrific war against Paraguay between 1864 and 1870, resulting in almost total destruction of the latter country.

In Poland, a nationalist insurrection was crushed by the Tsarist Russian army in 1863.

In Italy, Garibaldi continued his campaign to reunite the country, (capturing Palermo and Naples in 1860).

In Germany, Bismarck also carried out a policy of reunification. In 1864, war broke out between Prussia and Denmark over Schleswig-Holstein, resulting in the incorporation of the disputed province into the expanding German Empire.

(A popular joke circulated about the Schleswig-Holstein Affair that only three people understood what it was all about – Prince Albert who was dead, a German professor who had gone mad, and Lord Melbourne who had forgotten.)]

In June 1855, the Wilde family moved to No.1 Merrion Square, Dublin, where on April 2 1857 Oscar's sister Isola born.

During the next few years, the Wildes spent their summer holidays in the Irish countryside, in such places as Lough Bray Cottage, Vale of Glencree, Co Wicklow, a fishing lodge called Illaunroe, near Killary Harbour, Co Galway, and the seaside resort of Dungarvan, Co Waterford, (where Oscar played occasionally with another child called Edward Carson).

After attending St Columba' School in Dublin for eight months, in February 1864 Oscar followed in his elder brother Willie's footsteps and became a boarding pupil at the Portora Royal School, Enniskillen, Co Fermanagh.

In 1864 Oscar's father William was knighted, but by December both he and Speranza became embroiled in the Mary Travers trial.

Sir William began work on building Moytura House, near the village of Cong, Co Galway, where the Wilde family spent the summer of 1864.

Oscar learned some Gaelic while he was in the west of Ireland – his son Vyvyan later recalled him singing lullabies in the language. He also became acquainted with some of the other local children, among them George Moore.

GEORGE MOORE 1852-1933

On this and other summer holidays, Wilde involved himself in childhood games with George Moore, who lived at the nearby Moore Hall in Co. Mayo. Far from this leading to an adult friendship, the two men loathed each other. When asked if he knew George Moore, Oscar replied that: "I know him so well that I haven't spoken to him for years". For his part, Moore was equally sour: "There was Wilde, another Dublin jackeen who plagiarised wholesale, without admitting to his thefts", and once spluttering: "That man will be eaten by worms".

Moore had an unfortunate physical appearance, which his numerous foes enjoyed emphasising. His yellow thatch of hair was said to look as if it had been pitch-forked on to his head, while the American writer *Gertrude Atherton* described his face as looking like 'a codfish crossed with a satyr'. Even the one person to whom Moore offered hero worship, the French painter Manet, could not create a flattering portrait of him. Manet: "Is it my fault if Moore looks like a squashed egg yolk and if his face is all lop-sided?"

Moore became a considerable literary force and was reckoned to be one of the four great Irish writers of the period, the other three being Shaw, Wilde and Yeats. He was the only one whose star waned with time, although his novel, 'Esther Waters', (among the first to treat the servant class as genuine characters rather than as background), was given the accolade of a Hollywood film adaptation.

He specialised mostly in realist novels, although he ruefully conceded the disadvantages of realism. When travelling with friends on an omnibus to Dulwich, he requested them all to alight at Peckham, explaining: "I've written about Peckham". After inspecting this insalubrious London suburb, Moore groaned: "That is the fate of the realist! He writes about a field and a haystack in Peckham – and there are no fields or haystacks in Peckham".

He attempted to write plays, found that he was incapable of constructing credible dialogue and gave up, admitting that: "You can't fart higher than your arse, that I know".

Some of his best work, though, appeared in his extraordinarily revealing autobiographies, his 'Confessions'. The editor *Frank Harris* recalled that, as a schoolboy, Moore had refused to attend the Catholic confession. Harris: 'He has made up for his recalcitrance since by confessing himself and his fleshly sins in print whenever he could get the opportunity'.

Moore, though hampered by his appearance, possessed enough sexual charisma to provide ample material for these revelations. And, if he ran out of reality, he could always fall back on fantasy. As Sarah Purser of Dublin reported: 'Some men kiss and tell; Moore tells but does not kiss'. *J.E.C. Bodley* described him as 'posing as an homme fatal'.

He spent some of his youth in Paris, aping the excesses of the Decadent movement, and self-consciously playing Gregorian chants on a harmonium while watching his pet python devouring guinea pigs. He returned to London bearing his first book of poems, 'Flowers of Passion', which dwelt at length on incest, lesbianism and cunnilingus, a volume unlikely to attract the approbation of 1870s Victorian England.

In 1874, Moore had a short-lived career in London theatrical management with a producer called Richard Maitland. His choice of partner was his downfall. Maitland had been involved in a production of an Offenbach show which depicted the adventures of a pair of Hussars in a girls' school. The schoolgirls' costumes were exceedingly brief and Maitland was ordered by the Lord Chamberlain's office to add two inches to the length of the skirts. In revenge, Maitland advertised the show as having 'costume design by the Lord Chamberlain.' The resulting rage of this powerful pillar of the establishment meant that any future theatrical projects by Maitland and his associates were doomed.

By 1879, Moore had succeeded to one of the largest estates in Ireland. This coincided however with the rise of civil unrest of the Land League period, during which the estate tenants refused to pay rent and tended to shoot the agents sent to collect it. Moore was forced to take charge; as a self-proclaimed Parisian dandy, it was an unlikely role. He was terrified by his tenants. Even such local customs likely to work to his benefit appalled him. After his father's funeral, one woman arrived to offer two chickens and her daughter as presents for the new squire. After an abortive attempt to enforce payment by hiring twenty cartloads of armed police, he handed the estate over to an agent and fled back to London. As *George Bernard Shaw* commented: 'The only sensible institution in the Emerald Isle was absenteeism.'

Moore did return to his native land around 1900 but stayed in Dublin. He was no more popular in the city than in the country. At his home in Ely Place, he painted his front door in republican green; his neighbours, who favoured white front doors, complained to the landlord. Moore began a law action against them, whereupon they encouraged tomcats to howl outside his windows at night. Moore retaliated by hiring a pipe band to play outside their front doors.

Moore went through six cooks in three weeks. After a row, one cook called the police for protection. Moore led the constable to the dining room shouting: "Is there a law in this country to compel me to eat that abominable omelette?" and demanded the arrest of the cook. One Irish friend, Edward Martyn, said of Moore: "He's a bit of a Bank Holiday sort of fellow, ye know".

Moore's most successful sexual ploy was to encourage female literary hopefuls to co-author new works with him. It was in this fashion that he tried to seduce Pearl Craigie.

[PEARL CRAIGIE (1876-1906), who used the pen name of John Oliver Hobbes, had no doubts about her own talent: "Without vanity I may say that I am the one writer in England who could sign a Wilde comedy and pass unchallenged".

She was the heiress daughter of John Morgan Richards, an American who had amassed his fortune by selling Carter's Little Liver Pills. Her mother proved to be an embarrassment as she had a tendency to chat to unseen Old Testament Prophets while dinner guests were present. Henry James was once spotted ponderously frowning at a large notice at the family home that read: 'What Would Jesus Say?'

On another occasion, she sent a telegram to Rome reading: 'Pope, Vatican. Stop War. Richards.']

In May 1894 Moore, frantic for sex with Pearl, finally ran out of patience while walking in Hyde Park. She told him that she had decided to break off what little there was of their relationship. He later wrote that she 'was enjoying my grief as she might a little comedy of her own invention'. As she walked slightly ahead of him, Moore let lose a mighty kick on her bottom 'nearly in the centre, a little to the right'. He was even more irritated when she seemed pleased that she had forced him to act out of character.

Moore found a more acquiescent lover in Maud Cunard (1872-1948) who he described as 'like a little white ferret' in bed. But again he was denied full intercourse. While explaining that: 'Kisses need not be confined to the mouth', he continued: 'For a whole year I was the lover of an American girl and when she married she was a virgin (technically)'.

This marriage was to Sir Bache Cunard, known as 'Bang Bang' for his love of shooting. After a short interval, Moore and Maud resumed their affair while Sir Bache was busy in on the Scottish moors. Moore said that he thoroughly enjoyed eating the grouse after first enjoying the wife of the marksman. Even this was not the happiest of liaisons, as Maud preferred younger lovers, excusing her absences on the grounds that she wanted to sleep with a youth 'with skinny shanks'. While Moore was staying at the Cunard's house, workmen spotted her in bed with the young conductor, Sir Thomas Beecham.

Moore, despite many women in his life, never seemed to find satisfaction. Once, after visiting a mistress, he arrived at *WB Yeats'* flat and sank down on the sofa, sighing: "God, I wish that woman would wash".

As he grew older his powers waned. In 1913 he was forced to admit to a female acquaintance: "How I regret, for your sake, that I'm impotent". He found his only solace in voyeurism. One evening after dinner, Maud's daughter Nancy Cunard agreed on request to strip off for his perusal. This had an unusual element in that, although it was never proved, it was highly likely that Nancy was his natural daughter.

Moore came to the conclusion that: 'Woman is the sauce to the pudding of life, if you like; but the whole business of love and loving is overrated'. Perhaps one of the few topics on which he might have found agreement with Oscar Wilde was in his toleration of other people's homosexuality: "I see no reason why those who prefer to drink salad oil to champagne should not be allowed to do so".

Living up to the family motto, 'Scratch a Moore and your own blood will flow', George enjoyed savaging his contemporaries. He jeered at GK Chesterton's Catholic faith 'in the power of the priest to turn God into biscuits and wine every morning', and revealed that Chesterton liked belching: "He told me he did". He described Thomas Hardy as 'the villager', Joseph Conrad as 'the sailor' and Henry James as 'the eunuch'. After viewing Claude Monet's water lily pictures he said he found it difficult to find any difference between them and wallpaper. He reviewed a Parisian actress with: 'In Jane Hugard, France has lost a fine concierge'.

His last words were a reaction to a visitor commenting on Joseph Conrad's literary style. Moore jerked up off the pillows and exclaimed indignantly: "What style? Why, it is nothing but wreckage of Robert Louis Stevenson floating in the slops of Henry James!"

Although many people disliked George Moore, they disliked his brother **AUGUSTUS MOORE** even more. His scandal sheet, 'The Hawk', annoyed many Londoners; he had a public fist fight in the foyer of Drury Lane Theatre with the painter *Whistler*, (admittedly not a difficult opponent to provoke); and in 1893, annoyed at finding that the courtesan that he had intended to enjoy was away from home, allegedly raped her maid instead. He was arrested but escaped jail owing to doubts over the true story.

But what upset Oscar Wilde's brother *Willie* most was Augustus's dress sense. Once, when they met at the Café Royal, Augustus was wearing a garish necktie and asked for Willie's opinion. "Well, Gus, since you ask me, I should have thought that only a deaf man could wear it with safety".

One day, Augustus stormed into the office of the editor *Frank Harris* and another partner declaring that they had cheated him over a money deal. Harris refused to reimburse him and Augustus stared at the two men with venom. Harris asked what the hell he was looking at. "I'm looking at you two", said Augustus "and thinking that if you got a cheap Christ and put him between you what a damn fine Calvary you'd make".

1865 - 1871

[The American Civil War ended in 1865, closely followed by the assassination of President Abraham Lincoln.

In 1866, in Chile, the Spanish Navy bombarded the port of Valparaiso, while in Mexico, the French-backed Emperor Maximilian was executed by nationalist forces in 1867.

In 1868, the British Army, under General Napier, invaded Ethiopia and rescued the British envoy Charles Cameron. In Canada, British forces suppressed a separatist rebellion led by Louis Riel in 1869.

The Suez Canal was opened in 1869.

In Italy, Garibaldi's volunteers continued their campaign for unification at the Battle of Salo (1866) against the Austrians, and by capturing Rome in 1870 and incorporating the Papal States into the Kingdom of Italy.

Bismarck's plans for the expansion of the German Empire were aided by the defeat of Austria at the Battle of Sadowa in 1866. In 1870, the Franco-Prussian War broke out, ending in the total defeat of Emperor Napoleon III at the Battle of Sedan. The Germans proceeded to besiege Paris until it surrendered in 1871.

The socialist Commune then took control of the city for two months before being suppressed by bourgeois forces of the Third Republic in the bloodiest week in French domestic history. (25,000 Parisians were killed during the 'Semaine Sanglante', far more than died during the Reign of Terror.)

Oscar Wilde attended Portora Royal School as a boarding pupil from 1864 until in June 1871.

EDUCATING OSCAR

Wilde had an ambivalent attitude towards education: 'Education is an admirable thing, but it is as well to remember that nothing worth knowing can be taught'.

Oscar: 'When I was young I thought the Wars of the Roses were to decide whether a red rose or a white rose was the most beautiful. I learned afterwards that it was just some vulgar dispute'.

His opinion of the teaching profession was equally tepid: 'I am afraid we are beginning to be over-educated. Everybody who is incapable of learning has taken to teaching'.

(One of Oscar's schoolmasters was the Rev. Edward Hardy, who later married one of Oscar's cousins. In 1885, Hardy wrote a handbook on marriage. It included an account of the nuptials of a Hampshire rustic who, when asked if he would take his intended as wedded wife, replied: "Yes, all right, but I'd a sight sooner have her sister".)

Later Wilde commented through one of his characters in 'An Ideal Husband': 'I have forgotten all about my schooldays. I have a vague impression that they were detestable.'

The Wilde family, meanwhile, had been struck by tragedy, firstly in 1867 by the death of Oscar's nine-year-old sister Isola. (Their mother Speranza took Oscar and his elder brother Willie to Paris that summer in an effort to raise their spirits.)

Then in 1871 Oscar's natural siblings, Emily Wilde, aged 24, and Mary Wilde, aged 22, were burnt to death in a horrific accident.

In October 1871, having been awarded a scholarship, Oscar became a student at Trinity College, Dublin, (known by its fellow universities of Oxford and Cambridge as 'the silent sister'). Two of the leading professors were Dr JP Mahaffy and Professor R Tyrrell.

Mahaffy said that the College was: 'the only English foundation that ever succeeded in Ireland'.

Professor the Rev. SIR JOHN PENTLAND MAHAFFY (1839-1919)

JP Mahaffy was Wilde's tutor at Trinity College and had a strong influence on Wilde's early life. Firstly he nurtured the young student's instinctive delight in wit and conversation: 'Never tell a story because it is true: tell it because it is a good story'. Wilde called him 'my first and best teacher. He was a really great talker, an artist in vivid words and eloquent phrases'. Mahaffy recognised that Irish society demanded spontaneous wit almost as a requirement of citizenship. (Wilde: 'If only one could teach the English how to talk, and the Irish how to listen, society here would be quite civilised'.)

Secondly, he helped persuade Sir William to send Oscar to an English university: "You're not quite clever enough for us here at Trinity, Oscar. Better run up to Oxford".

Thirdly, on tours in 1875 and 1877, he introduced Wilde to Greece, thereby steering him away from his interest in Rome and Catholicism. "No, Oscar, we cannot let you become a Catholic but we will make you a good pagan instead".

Later, the friendship dwindled, as the extreme Unionist Tory Mahaffy clashed with the liberal, nationalist Wilde. The professor took particular exception when his former pupil dismissed one of Mahaffy's books as 'arid and jejune'. When Oscar was imprisoned, Mahaffy refused to sign the petition for clemency: 'He was the one blot on my tutorship'. If the topic ever arose again, he would merely remark 'We no longer speak of Mr Oscar Wilde'.

The Rev JP Mahaffy was Professor of Ancient History at Trinity and had a European reputation as one of the great classicists of his era. Once, when he was out with a shooting party, one of the hunters accidentally fired a bullet through the top of Mahaffy's hat. Having examined the damage, Mahaffy grumbled: 'Two inches lower, and you would have shot away ninety per cent of the Greek in Ireland.'

At 6ft 3inches, he was the same height as Oscar, and had the robust looks of an accomplished sportsman. He was a brilliant cricketer who played for the All Ireland team against All England several times, and even acknowledged that WG Grace's views on bowling were 'worthy of attention'. He was not above employing psychological games to upset his opponents. If a batsman managed to hit one of Mahaffy's balls to the boundary, Mahaffy would pace gravely down the wicket to the culprit and congratulate him. He coined the phrase: "That man was morally bowled".

Although he took holy orders aged 25, Mahaffy was an unorthodox clergyman. He once crawled into a roomful of fellow churchmen wearing only a tiger skin rug. If pressed, he admitted to being a cleric: "but not in any offensive sense of the term"; and, when challenged by an evangelist with: "Have you been saved, Dr Mahaffy?" he replied: "Yes, but it was such a very narrow squeak that I never boast about it".

In his official position at Trinity he was sometimes forced to exercise some spiritual authority. One day, he spotted an undergraduate who was not wearing the required academic gown. He beckoned the student over and declaimed: "Boy! Do you not realise that you are imperilling your immortal soul by being without a gown?" He paused then added: "And what is even worse, the fine is three shillings".

When another student attempted to outwit the authorities by stating that his religious denomination was 'sun-worshipper', he found himself woken at dawn the next morning by the college porter with the words: "Dr Mahaffy's compliments, sir, it's time to say your prayers to the rising sun". After a few days of this, the student converted to Christianity.

Mahaffy's real teeth showed when dealing with fellow academics: 'Extreme pugnacity is the essential feature of all true Irish scholars'. At a viva voce examination, he barked at an undergraduate: "Why was Dr Thornton made a Fellow of Trinity?" The confused student replied: "I don't know". "Correct. You get a mark for that. Nobody does".

Another Trinity don announced pompously in the common room that: "They all know I am not for sale". Mahaffy drawled: "Well, you have been a long time in the shop window".

Mahaffy's Achilles heel was that he was a snob. It was said that he only raised his eyes from Homer to examine invitations from the aristocracy. 'Vice-regal tame-cat', 'Tuft-hunter' and 'Castle lackey' were among the milder epithets bestowed upon him by *George Moore*. He was indeed the friend of several monarchs, amongst them the Queen of Spain and Kaiser Wilhelm II. This latter acquaintance led to Mahaffy's worst moment.

When he was introduced to *Queen Victoria* in a line of guests at Dublin Castle, he overstepped the formal greeting by announcing grinningly: "Madam, I met your grandson the Kaiser recently". She moved on, then turned to an aide and asked loudly: "Who is that man?" Afterwards, Mahaffy tried to save face by implying that Victoria was going senile. When that didn't work and he remained the butt of facetious comment, he referred to the Queen as 'having the manners of a badly educated washerwoman'.

42

For many years he had been denied the post of Provost of Trinity, one he regarded as rightfully his. When the office fell vacant in 1904, he had been passed over in favour of a Dr Traill. Wilde himself commented that: "Mahaffy's unpopularity in Ireland, and in Trinity College Dublin especially, is something remarkable". For ten years, he gritted his teeth and waited impatiently, wasting no opportunity to defame the usurper.

At a College dinner, he referred to Traill as 'a beast'. When a colleague gave him a warning cough, Mahaffy added: "But fortunately a deaf beast". In 1914, when Mahaffy heard the news that Traill was feeling unwell, he was heard to mutter: "Nothing trivial, I hope". From then on he took to visiting the ailing provost every day to inquire as to his health; this altruism led to much satiric comment in the common room. Finally in 1914 Traill died, and Mahaffy succeeded to the provost-ship at the age of seventy-five, (a position he occupied till 1919).

Two years later and now seventy-seven, Mahaffy was forced to cope with probably the most exciting incident of his career.

Once before he had had a brush with Irish politics, when on May 6, 1882, he had been due to meet Lord Cavendish, the new Chief Secretary of Ireland, (a friend of the Wilde family who had dined at Merrion Square). Mahaffy was delayed at college, and rushed off to Phoenix Park to keep his appointment. Unable to find Cavendish, Mahaffy went back home. Later he heard the sensational news that the Chief Secretary and his aide Burke had been stabbed to death by assassins in the park. For years afterwards, he would relate with horror how there might have been a third victim.

However, in 1916, Mahaffy found himself commanding the forces defending Trinity College during the Easter Rising. In effect, these forces amounted to a few student cadets, some Australian troops on holiday, and the college porters, under the field command of a Professor Alton, an authority on Ovid. Having locked the gates, they exchanged a few desultory shots with rebels on College Green. Mahaffy decided to continue with the planned exams and provided lunch for the women candidates as the occasional bullet smacked into the wall. By evening, British troops relieved the siege.

The experience heightened his dislike of the Home Rule supporters: 'Patriotism has many curious analogies to alcohol. If taken neat it is a deadly poison'.

Oscar's other great Trinity influence was Professor **ROBERT TYRRELL** (1844-1914). A superb classical scholar, he was chosen in 1901 to be one of the first fifty members of the British Academy. He remained sympathetic to Oscar during the prison years and signed a clemency petition in 1896. Wilde said: "Mahaffy and Tyrrell were Trinity to me". They were not so complimentary about each other. Their mutual dislike had been exacerbated by Tyrrell's criticism of Mahaffy's use of exclamation marks in published work.

Mahaffy at one time was suspended from preaching in the College Chapel after a theological dispute – whereupon Tyrrell complained that, as a result of this, he was suffering from insomnia during the services.

Tyrrell was a convivial man who enjoyed public houses. The sight of the alcohol-free 'Temperance Hotels' sent him into a rage: "There is no such thing; you might as well talk of a celibate brothel". In one pub, he was interrupted during an interesting conversation by someone inquiring the way to the lavatory. Tyrrell said without turning: "It's the first door on the right, marked 'Gentlemen'. But don't let that deter you".

1872-73

[In France, the policy of trials, executions, and deportations of Communards continued with vigour.]

During this period Oscar Wilde inhabited rooms in the Trinity College buildings known as 'Botany Bay'. His academic success was crowned in 1873 when he won the prestigious Berkeley Medal. As well as experimenting by growing a beard, he became influenced by the works of J.A. Symonds.

JOHN ADDINGTON SYMONDS 1840-1893

After Wilde became interested in the writings of Symonds, notably 'The Renaissance in Italy', they corresponded and later exchanged books of poetry. Symonds took the young Oscar seriously, though referring to him as 'Boy'. But by 1889, Symonds was disturbed by the publication of Wilde's 'A Picture of Dorian Gray', saying it was 'very audacious... and unwholesome in tone' – 'If the British public will stand for this they can stand anything'. Symonds was himself homosexual and this judgement on 'Dorian Gray' echoed a previous hypocrisy from his schooldays.

Symonds attended Harrow School in the 1850s – the world partly described by one of its masters, Dean Farrar, in his novel 'Eric, or Little by Little'. What Farrar did not describe was the almost unbridled homosexual antics at the school, where the prettiest boys were bullied into public acts of obscenity, where such characters as 'Cookson, the red-faced strumpet' and 'Bum Bathsheba' Ainslie of the 'opulent posterior' became the prey of the dormitories, and where 'one could not avoid seeing acts of onanism, mutual masturbation, and the sports of naked boys in bed together'.

What finally outraged Symonds was the revelation that the headmaster, the Reverend Dr Charles Vaughan, also was involved. Despite the fact that Vaughan used to stroke Symonds' thigh while reading his essays, it was only when a fellow pupil, Alfred Pretor, disclosed that he had received love letters from the headmaster that the penny dropped. 'I was disgusted to find such desires lurking in a man consecrated by the Church, and entrusted with the welfare of 600 youths'.

On leaving Harrow, Symonds told his father of the situation; Dr Symonds then wrote to Vaughan informing him that he would keep silence only if Vaughan never again attempted promotion in the Church. Vaughan's wife begged Symonds' father to be merciful but to no avail. Vaughan resigned, only to be offered the bishopric of Rochester. Dr Symonds promptly warned him off and Vaughan realised that his career was finished.

Symonds was not the only person to report on the almost unbelievable situation in the English Victorian public schools. An article in the New Review in 1893 claimed that 'the morals of the English public school were comparable with those of Sodom and Gomorrah'. *W.T. Stead* in 1895 wrote: 'Should everyone found guilty of Oscar Wilde's crime be imprisoned, there would be a very surprising emigration from Eton, Harrow, Rugby and Winchester to the jails of Pentonville and Holloway'. Raymond Asquith, the son of the future Prime Minister, reported that, at a mass lecture to Oxford students on the dangers of sodomy: 'We were told that the Headmasters, in league with the Government, were proposing to increase the legal penalty from 2 to 14 years; whereat a perceptible shudder ran through the audience, of whom some 85%, by the lowest estimate, were liable for incarceration on that charge'. Frank Harris also wrote that: 'If the mothers of England knew what goes on in the dormitories of these boarding schools throughout England, they would all be closed, from Eton and Harrow, upwards and downwards, in a day'.

However, Symonds' public-spiritedness in exposing his headmaster was not matched by his own future behaviour. Within a short time of his gaining a chair in poetry at Oxford he was ousted in turn because of his fondness for young boys. He made desperate attempts to conform by marrying and fathering four girls, (one of whom, Madge, carried on the family tradition by becoming one of Virginia Woolf's lovers).

His efforts came to nothing, as he was unable to cure his passion for young guardsmen 'in scarlet uniforms'. In this he was not alone. During the late nineteenth century, many soldiers were part-time male prostitutes – the NCOs vied with each other to break in the new recruits. This phenomenon became known as 'scarlet fever'. The public parks were used for these encounters and one barrister complained bitterly that since the improvement of lighting in Hyde Park, he had lost more than £2000 in fees.

The turmoil of Symond's inner conflicts, resulting in both a nervous breakdown and the onset of pulmonary tuberculosis, led to his retreat from England to the Swiss resort of Davros. Here, he found contentment, his health improved, he became the father of British tobogganing, and, in 1881, found a long-term love with a Venetian gondolier called Angelo. On their occasional travels they behaved as man and valet. (Angelo once found himself alone, to his horror, at the mercy of twenty-five housemaids while staying at Castle Howard, Yorkshire.)

Symonds spent his last years up in the Swiss mountains, where he was visited by *Margot Asquith*, Raymond's young stepmother. She climbed up the steep hillside to his house, handed her letter of introduction to the maid and settled down to wait for the aged writer to emerge. After an hour, no one had come. Then she heard the 'shuffle of slippered feet', someone pausing at the door, and Symonds's querulous voice calling from the next room: "Has she gone yet?" Margot was forced to reply: "No, I'm afraid I'm still here".

By 1900, Oscar Wilde was complaining that all the gondolas in Venice appeared to be staffed by male prostitutes. "Is it due to Symonds?"

1874

[In Britain, Benjamin Disraeli was returned as Prime Minister, having defeated Gladstone at the General Election. Gladstone commented: "We have been borne down in a torrent of gin and beer".
In Spain the Carlist War broke out.
In West Africa, the British Army crushed the Ashanti nation in modern day Ghana and occupied the capital, Kumasi.]

In June Oscar visited London, where he joined Speranza and Willie and heard that he had won a Demyship in Classics to Magdalen College, Oxford.

In July 1874, he went to Genoa with his mother and returned via Paris, where they stayed at the Hotel Voltaire.

On August 24, Oscar was introduced to J.E.C. Bodley at the Dublin Horse Show.

On 17 October, aged 20, Oscar left Dublin to enter Magdalen College, Oxford. Wilde: 'I was the happiest man in the world when I entered Magdalen for the first time. Oxford was paradise to me'. 'It is the capital of romance, in its own way as memorable as Athens, and to me it was more entrancing'.

On 24 November, Wilde failed his Responsions, an exam that was designed to judge whether an undergraduate was suitable for a degree. Only nine other students failed Responsions over Wilde's entire four years at Oxford. What sank Oscar was that the exams included Mathematics, a subject in which he had no interest or ability. Even in 1898, when he was trying to balance his woeful finances, he admitted: "I never could understand mathematics, and life is now a mathematical problem". In his story, 'The Happy Prince', he took a sideswipe at the subject: 'The Mathematical Master frowned and looked very severe, for he did not approve of children dreaming.'

However, Wilde survived the exam and soon he became immersed in college life. J.E.C. Bodley, Prince Leopold and David Hunter-Blair were among his many friends.

JOHN EDWARD COURTENAY BODLEY 1853-1925

One of Wilde's closest friends at Oxford was his fellow student Bodley, a breezy young buck who attended Balliol College. Together they indulged in such antics as invading a performance of Tyrolese singers at the local theatre for 'a grand bally-rag' before being thrown out by 'a rush of affrighted stage carpenters – and curtain'. Afterwards three of the Tyrolese accompanied Bodley and Wilde to the Mitre pub where they attempted yodelling before 'proceeding home erratically'.

Bodley also introduced Wilde to Freemasonry, and initiated him into the Apollo Lodge.

In 1882, Bodley hinted, in a teasingly malicious article, that Wilde had 'assumed a guise which sturdier minds still look upon as epicene'. Oscar felt betrayed by this, although they remained on good enough terms for Bodley to invite him to a Parisian banquet in 1891. Bodley took the opportunity to try to warn him that a book such as 'Dorian Gray' might be misconstrued, advice that Wilde ignored.

In 1899, after prison, Bodley met Wilde in a Paris street and invited him to his family home. Oscar, ashamed in the presence of his old Oxford friend, turned down the offer.

Bodley spent much of his life as amanuensis to prominent men, but was most unlucky in the figures he chose to serve. The first was the politician *Sir Charles Dilke*. Despite Dilke's initial dissatisfaction with Bodley's habits, ('Bodley ought to be in bed by half past twelve – not sit up till five in the morning to dance and flirt.... Nothing on earth can get him up before 9.30am. ... How to get rid of Bodley?'), he steadied his behaviour and became a good secretary. Then Dilke's career collapsed in disgrace, and Bodley was out of a job.

A warm friendship with *Cardinal Manning* should have led to Bodley being chosen to write Manning's official biography, but when Manning died, Bodley was abroad and another writer grabbed the opportunity.

Most prestigiously of all, Bodley was chosen to write the official record of the coronation of *King Edward VII*. Having worked hard on this project, he received only a minor grade of the Victorian Order as recompense. Bodley considered that the Victorian Order had only been created to reward the more obsequious members of provincial public bodies and their ilk. In a fury, he returned the medal by registered post to the King, thus ending any chance of future promotion.

His one real success came after 1890 when he settled in France. Through his books he became an acknowledged authority on French politics and culture. Charles Maurras said of Bodley: "he became almost a Frenchman without ceasing to be an Englishman". One of his more perceptive comments was made on the Franco-Russian treaty: 'The real strength of the Franco-Russian alliance is the complete ignorance which the contracting nations have of each other'.

He finally retired to the south coast of England where he described himself as 'the only Christian in Brighton'.

PRINCE LEOPOLD 1853-1884

The youngest son of *Queen Victoria*, Prince Leopold was a student at Christ Church College, Oxford, and, as a friend of *J.E.C. Bodley*, became well acquainted with Wilde.

Leopold was present, accompanied by Mrs Liddell and her daughter Alice (later of 'Wonderland' fame), when Oscar was deputed to read the lesson in college chapel. Oscar launched into his own choice of 'The Song of Solomon', before being halted abruptly by Dean Bramley hissing: "You have the wrong lesson, Mr Wilde. It's Deuteronomy XVI" – a much less racy Biblical passage. (Wilde: 'I always read the lessons with an air of scepticism').

They were fellow members of the Masonic Apollo Lodge, and later he visited Wilde's London lodgings at Salisbury Street.

Leopold's birth was unusual in that Queen Victoria used chloroform for the first time during a royal delivery. A court wit spread the rumour that, if Leopold had been a girl, he would have been called 'Anaesthesia'.

He had the misfortune to be born with haemophilia, a handicap that he did his best to overcome. Raised in Balmoral and becoming secretary to his mother in 1876, Leopold was a spirited youth who was bored by court life. He enjoyed theatre and built a large library, (with a pornography section acquired under the literary guidance of *Lord Houghton*).

A welcome break came when he met and fell for the society beauty, *Lily Langtry*, although, when he placed her portrait over his bed, it was removed on the orders of Queen Victoria. He managed to persuade Lily to join him on board a yacht off the Isle of Wight. She had to hide below deck until they were out of sight of the imperial telescope at Osborne House.

He escaped surveillance in 1880 when he visited his sister *Princess Louise* and her husband the *Marquess of Lorne* in North America. Together they went to Washington for President Garfield's inauguration, where the brasher American newspapers referred to them as 'Vic's Chicks'. By pure coincidence, Leopold owned a dog called Vic. Unused to such headlines, a puzzled Queen Victoria wrote to Leopold: 'How odd of them to mention your dog?'

Leopold died of internal bleeding in 1884 after a banging his knee while on holiday in the south of France. He was thirty-one.

Right Rev. **SIR DAVID HUNTER-BLAIR** 1853-1939

Hunter-Blair was a fellow student, nicknamed 'Dunskie' by Wilde. He was an intelligent man who saw through one of Oscar's characteristic poses early on. All his life Wilde adhered to the aristocratic opinion that achievements could only be justified if they were accomplished with 'effortless ease'. It was the success of this apparent flippancy that later so exasperated his more pedestrian theatre critics. Wilde: 'Cultivated idleness seems to me to be the proper occupation for man'. But Hunter-Blair said that, behind Oscar's affectation of indolence: 'I knew of his hours of assiduous and laborious reading often into the small hours'.

Hunter-Blair was not impressed by Wilde's Newdigate Prize-winning poem 'Ravenna', which contained the lines: 'On and on/ I galloped, racing with the setting sun'. As Florence Ward revealed in 1876: 'Wilde is a most shocking rider, and tumbles off nearly every time he goes out'. When Oscar declared that he had written the poem 'from the bottom of my heart, red-hot from Ravenna itself', Hunter-Blair spluttered: "Humbug! You went there lounging on the cushions of a stuffy railway carriage". Oscar, for once, was stumped.

Unlike most of Wilde's student friends, Hunter-Blair was a very serious-minded young man. In 1870, by chance he had been in Rome on the day that the King of Italy launched an attack on the Pope. The Papal army was heavily outnumbered and, after a few hours of cannon fire, the Pope surrendered the city. During the fighting, Hunter-Blair volunteered to transport casualties by wheelbarrow from the front line to a nearby convent. Impressed by 'the young Protestant Englishman', the Pope sent for him. Hunter-Blair: 'I found myself invested, much to my surprise, with the Maltese Cross'.

By 1875, he converted to the Catholic faith and set out to persuade Oscar to do likewise. Although he was attracted by the outward forms of Roman religion, Wilde was reluctant, not least because parental opposition would have left him disinherited. When, in 1877, Hunter-Blair sent him the money to visit Rome, Wilde travelled first to Greece under the 'pagan tuition' of *Mahaffy*. When at last he did arrive in the Eternal City, while very impressed by the Holy Father, he was even more impressed by the tomb of John Keats. An irritated Hunter-Blair gradually gave up his efforts at conversion. Wilde: 'Poor Dunskie: I know he looks on me as a renegade'.

Hunter-Blair was a baronet in his own right, came from an important Scottish family, and attended school at Eton. The proximity of the school to the royal castle of Windsor meant that the pupils had some contact with Victoria's court. Occasionally Hunter-Blair and other boys were allowed on to the castle terrace, where, with the Queen and her household, they could listen to the Guards Band playing popular music. After enjoying one piece, the Queen sent a Maid of Honour to find out the title. The Maid returned and answered with embarrassment: "The band master said, Ma'am, the name of the tune is 'Come Where the Booze is Cheapest'."

The Etonians were asked sometimes to provide their own spectacle for visiting dignitaries. On one occasion, during the State Visit to Windsor of the Sultan of Turkey, they presented a military tattoo. Unfortunately, their rifles were old muzzle-loaders, and, when they were ordered to fire a saluting volley, many of the boys were so confused that they forget to remove the ramrods from the rifle barrels. The sky above the parade ground turned into a shower of hurtling ramrods. The Sultan was reputedly 'most impressed'.

At Oxford, Hunter-Blair delighted in college folklore. He particularly appreciated the efforts of an early nineteenth century don who had spent much of his time improving the Anglican rituals of the university. By 1844, the don had reformed the former annual May Day morning ceremony at the top of Magdalen Tower by replacing it with the devout singing of a Latin hymn by a gowned choir. Previously the ceremony had consisted of having a brass band playing while the choristers hurled rotten eggs on the crowd below.

Hunter-Blair had little time for what he considered to be a blemish on Oxford – to wit, Keble College. Oscar entirely agreed: 'In spite of Keble College, Oxford still remains the most beautiful thing in England'.

One of their complaints was Keble's insistence on 'high thinking and low living'. In practice, this meant that the college meals were frugal in the extreme and during Lent positively spartan. One unfortunate undergraduate was hauled up before the Warden for admonishment. "Mr. Wills-Smythe, in this college we provide, at breakfast, fish for those gentlemen who desire to fast; cold meat for those who would like to fast, but do not feel quite equal to it; and hot meat for those who are incapable of abstinence. I observed this morning, Mr. Wills-Smythe, that you partook of all three!"

Another Keble student, this time an American, fell foul of the authorities when he failed to attend Anglican chapel. The Warden was duly upbraiding the man when, to the Warden's horror, the student disclosed that he was a Mormon Latterday Saint. He was immediately evicted from Keble. Hunter-Blair reported that later the man was admitted 'without question into a certain college where, it was said, the presence of a saint of any kind would be a phenomenon absolutely unprecedented'.

In 1878, Hunter-Blair joined the Benedictine Order and later became the Abbot of the Fort Augustus Monastery and College in Scotland. He travelled in Brazil and Canada during his religious duties. For an abbot, he had an unusual relish for horrific anecdotes, of which two of the most gruesome he came across in Canada. Both concerned the British army stationed there.

While on sentry duty at Niagara Falls one bitter winter night, a soldier of a Highland regiment over-indulged in whisky, missed his footing, and slid over the brink of the precipice. Freezing as he fell, his body hit a whirlpool below on which ice never formed. As there was no possible way to recover the corpse, it slowly gyrated round and round in the eddy, still accoutred in bonnet, kilt and plaid, until it slowly disintegrated months later in the spring thaw. It remained a hideous reminder to the rest of the regiment of the dangers of alcohol; they had only to peep over the edge of the rapids to see the revolving remains of their comrade.

The other incident happened to an Irish sergeant who was captured by Red Indian braves, dragged off to their camp and told that he was to die by excruciatingly slow torture. He attempted to gain reprieve by promising his captors that, if they spared him, he would reveal a miraculous plant that he had found in the woods. This plant, if rubbed on any part of the body, rendered the wearer invulnerable to wounds.

Impressed by his claim, the tribesmen agreed. Under escort, the sergeant gathered the plant, then offered to test the miracle himself by rubbing it on his neck and defying the strongest warrior to decapitate him. The offer was accepted, the blow was struck, and the sergeant's head rolled away. The Red Indians then realised that they had nobody left to torture to death, slowly or otherwise.

Among the academics at Oxford, Wilde became particularly friendly with John Ruskin. He was also acquainted with two other renowned Oxford figures, Dr W Spooner and Jowett of Balliol.

PROFESSOR BENJAMIN JOWETT 1817-1893
'First come I, my name is Jowett,
There's no knowledge but I know it;
I am Master of this College
What I don't know – is not knowledge.'

As Master of Balliol College, Oxford (1870-1893) and Vice Chancellor (1882-1886), Benjamin Jowett was not directly involved with Wilde's career, although there was a peripheral connection. In 1876, an acquaintance of Oscar's called William Hardinge, (also known as 'the Balliol Bugger'), was revealed as having written some homosexual sonnets; he also possessed letters from the Oxford don, *Walter Pater*, ending in 'Yours lovingly'. A shocked Jowett expelled Hardinge from the college on a charge of 'keeping and reciting immoral poetry'.

Another link with Wilde was that Jowett was an enthusiastic supporter of College amateur theatre, particularly of the Oxford University Dramatic Society. It was with his direct encouragement that the 1880 groundbreaking production of the 'Agamemnon' of Aeschylus, (with which Oscar was closely involved), was performed in Balliol Hall.

Jowett was famed as an inspirational teacher in Oxford and had a wider reputation for his Greek translations, particularly of Plato. Although popular with the public, his books were criticised for inaccuracy by other scholars. Aware of his failings, he once asked the brilliant but highly unstable poet *Algernon Swinburne*, (who had left Oxford without a degree), to stay at Balliol and correct the proofs of Jowett's new book.

One morning Jowett was conducting a tutorial in his rooms while Swinburne sat working in a small adjoining study; the connecting door between them was open. As Jowett was exercising his powers of sarcasm over the deficiencies of his students' essays, he was interrupted by a roar of laughter from Swinburne next door: "Another howler, Master!" Jowett rose and closed the door, meekly murmuring: "Thank you, Algernon".

Perhaps his great contribution to public life was his belief in choosing and grooming his brightest pupils for future high Imperial office; among those handpicked were such men as *Asquith*, Milner, and *Curzon*. It was to some extent Jowett's work that by 1892, of the two Houses of Parliament, 250 were Balliol men. This practice led to criticism that he was only interested in mass-producing 'prancing pro-consuls and magnificent Viceroys'

To his less favoured students, who nicknamed him 'Little Benjamin', he was a distant and off-putting figure. His faith in the Socratic teaching method – 'lying in wait for you to say something foolish, then snapping you up' – prompted some students to suggest that he should emulate his hero by swallowing hemlock. *Rennell Rodd* complained that: 'Jowett would occasionally invite me to go for a walk with him and scare me to death by his long silences or his monosyllabic replies, which seemed to petrify all attempts at intimacy'.

One day he invited a student to breakfast in his rooms. They ate in total silence. In an attempt to jolly things along, the student remarked that it seemed to be a nice day outside. There was no response and the room fell silent again. At the end of the meal, as the student was leaving, Jowett growled: "That was a very foolish observation".

To another undergraduate, who approached him to confide his doubts as to the existence of a God, Jowett snapped: "If you don't find a God by five o'clock this afternoon, you will be sent down!"

Only rarely did Jowett display a softer side. *Margot Asquith* became friendly with him at the end of his life. She knew by repute that Jowett, in his youth, had fallen deeply in love with Florence Nightingale, the famous Crimea nurse. Her refusal of marriage had broken Jowett's heart and he remained a lifelong bachelor.

One day Jowett asked Margot whether she had ever heard that he had once loved somebody. She did not reveal that she knew about the Nightingale episode but said that she had heard some rumour to that effect. Daringly she asked: "What was your lady-love like, Master?" After a long ruminative pause, Jowett replied: "Violent. Very violent".

JOHN RUSKIN 1819-1900

John Ruskin was a major influence on Wilde's intellectual development and they remained friends long after the Oxford days. As late as 1887, Oscar asked Ruskin to be godfather to his second son, Vyvyan; Ruskin declined on account of his age.

In 1869, Ruskin had become the Slade Professor of Fine Art at Oxford. He was renowned as a Romantic visionary who thought that the role of art should be central to society and who saw the capitalist degradation of the worker into little more than a robot as a destructive evil. Ruskin: 'It is not that men are ill fed, but that they have no pleasure in the work by which they make their bread, and therefore look to wealth as the only means of pleasure'. Oscar approved of Ruskin's stand: 'When commerce is ruining beautiful rivers and magnificent woodlands and the glorious skies in its greed for gain, the artist comes forward as a priest and prophet of nature to protest.'

Although they differed in that Wilde saw art as beyond morality whereas Ruskin thought the two inseparable, Wilde still thought that: 'Ruskin has always seemed to me the Plato of England'.

As a practical demonstration of his theories, in 1874 Ruskin asked for students to volunteer their services to build a road from Oxford to the village of Ferry Hinksey. Oscar, an unlikely labourer, nevertheless was amongst the group that assembled for the task. He received individual tuition from Ruskin himself as to how to wheel a barrow. The scheme was widely mocked, in particular by Punch magazine.

A later comment by Wilde seems to have been based on this experience: "I cannot help saying that a great deal of nonsense is being written and talked nowadays about the dignity of manual labour. There is nothing necessarily dignified about manual labour at all' ... 'Man is made for something better than disturbing dirt".

The road itself was never finished and reverted to swampland. A Ferry Hinksey villager remarked: "I don't think the young gentlemen did too much harm".

As a young man, Ruskin had known the great English artist JMW Turner well and when Turner died in 1851, Ruskin felt the death as a personal bereavement. Turner had bequeathed his paintings to the nation, requesting that they should be placed in an extension to the National Gallery. This request was ignored for almost 150 years and the paintings left in boxes in the Gallery cellars. Ruskin, who had been given some responsibility for the bequest and was becoming concerned over their condition, checked through these boxes.

To his horror, he found that much of Turner's work consisted of pornographic drawings of 'the pudenda of women'. He later told *Frank Harris*: "What a burden it cast upon me! What was I to do? I took the hundreds of scrofulous sketches and paintings and burnt them where they were, burnt all of them. I am proud of it – proud!" He became furious when the incorrigible Harris asked him if he had been tempted to pocket some of the drawings for himself.

Ruskin's fastidious nature may have been partly responsible for his disastrous marital life. His real sexual interest seems to have been young girls, with a corresponding distaste for mature women. When he was fifteen, he fell in love with the 14-year old Adele Domecq, (of the sherry family), who remained indifferent to him. In middle age, he became obsessed with the 10-year old Rose La Touche, and even offered marriage. Rose ended this embarrassing situation by dying. In his old age, when he went partly insane, he was reputed to be a 'liability' with the local schoolgirls.

But his greatest public humiliation came when he married a Scottish cousin called Effie Gray. Although he had met her first when she was aged twelve, she was a young woman of twenty when they actually became man and wife. On the wedding night, Effie was taken aback by Ruskin's refusal to have sex.

It has been assumed that Ruskin's reticence was a result of being shocked by the sight of female pubic hair. Given his artistic schooling in life classes and his involuntary viewing of JMW Turner's efforts, this is unlikely. A more probable cause was that he was repelled by menstruation. This unfortunate impasse was prolonged for five years. Later, a vengeful Effie revealed to the world that Ruskin had contented himself by masturbating while in bed with her.

When they visited Venice so that Ruskin could complete his great work on the architecture of that city, Effie spent the time 'partying with soldiers'. Ruskin, it seems, rather hoped she would elope with an Italian count who was staying at their lodgings. This plan came to nothing when the count eloped with some jewellery rather than with Mrs Ruskin.

Effie's torment ended in 1853 when the artist John Everett Millais, (1829-1896), was asked by Ruskin to paint his portrait. Millais, (eventually to become the most financially successful painter of the Victorian era), became enamoured of Effie's charms.

Ruskin wrote: 'I went to Millais's studio one morning and opened the door quietly, without the faintest suspicion – there they were in each other's arms on the sofa. I was startled and involuntarily stepped back, drawing the door quietly to after me. What was I to do? ... My portrait was not finished and I wanted it finished: I thought it might be one of the great portraits of the world ... I resolved simply to be more ceremonious than I had been'.

Millais and Effie decamped together and later married. Despite this, Ruskin insisted that Millais complete his portrait. Ruskin posed and Millais painted in total, mutually contemptuous, silence until the work was ended.

Oscar Wilde managed to maintain good relations with both disputants. In 1879 he visited the theatre with Ruskin to see *Henry Irving* in 'The Merchant of Venice'. After the show, Oscar bade Ruskin goodnight and continued the evening at the ball held to celebrate the marriage of Millais and Effie's daughter.

He also stayed on good terms with both sides during the even more bitter quarrel in 1878 between Ruskin and *James McNeill Whistler*, when Whistler sued Ruskin for describing Whistler as a 'coxcomb' and his work as 'flinging a pot of paint in the public's face'. The court case ended in a nominal victory for Whistler, (he received one farthing's damages), and Ruskin felt obliged to resign his Slade Chair at Oxford.

He sank slowly into intermittent madness and ended his days being cared for in his house by Coniston Water in the Lake District.

His theories on art had at least one lasting influence. His friend, *Edward Burne-Jones*, used to accompany him on walks around London and would often tease him by pointing out the fake-Gothic design of the new pubs: "That's all your fault, Ruskin!"

REV. WILLIAM SPOONER 1844-1930

Probably the most widely known of Wilde's acquaintance among the Oxford dons was the Dean of New College, the Rev. Spooner, whose unconscious verbal lapses became so famous that his name has entered the English language. His 'spoonerisms' included such legendary transpositions as rebuking a student for 'hissing his mystery lecture' and referring to Victoria as 'our queer old dean'.

In July 1876, Spooner had the misfortune to be Oscar's Divinity examiner. Wilde: 'In examinations, the foolish ask questions that the wise cannot answer'.

Wilde arrived hours late for Spooner's viva voce exam. Spooner, upset by the flippant excuse he offered for his absence, punished Oscar by ordering him to construe the Biblical Judas story from the Greek. After an hour or so, Spooner relented and told him he could stop. Oscar protested that he wanted to keep going as he had become so engrossed in the story he wanted to find out 'whatever happened to the unfortunate man'. Wilde: "I was ploughed, of course".

Spooner's severity over Wilde's behaviour was uncharacteristic of the man, as he was known for his tolerance and kindly nature. The nephew of Archbishop Tait of Canterbury, Spooner had been born an albino; his white hair and pallid appearance led to his Oxford nickname of 'The Silver Spoon'. His vagueness over language was matched by his vagueness over life in general. Meeting a friendly stranger in New College, Spooner invited him to tea the next day: "I'm giving a little party for the new Mathematics Fellow". "But, Dean, I *am* the new Mathematics Fellow". "Never mind, dear chap. Come along all the same".

A Corpus Christi colleague asked him whether the new fashion for Christian Socialism had any supporters at New College. Spooner said he could think of only two adherents – himself and a Dr Rashdall. "But I'm not very much of a socialist and Dr Rashdall isn't very much of a Christian".

One day, he was found roaming the London suburb of Greenwich searching for a pub called 'The Dull Man'. Nobody had heard of it and he returned disappointed to Oxford. His wife told him that the actual address he had been seeking was 'The Green Man' in Dulwich.

One other Wildean link came in 1893, when Spooner's son-in-law, Campbell Dodgson, took on the difficult task of becoming tutor to *Bosie Douglas*, Oscar's later paramour. He accompanied the Wilde entourage on an academically anarchic holiday at Torquay. Oscar, who established the rules of this teaching course, claimed it 'combined the advantages of a public school with those of a lunatic asylum'.

1875

[Benjamin Disraeli purchased the shares that gave Britain the controlling interest in the Suez Canal.]

By 1875, Oscar Wilde was beginning to polish the persona for which he later became known. Having arrived at Oxford as a naïve young man with a lisp and an Irish accent, he now acquired an English public school accent that disguised his true origins so well that even his English contemporaries were fooled. Wilde: 'My Irish accent was one of the many things I forgot at Oxford'.

His flirtations with Catholicism provided another break with his past. At Oxford, the Irish Protestant Wilde almost became the English Catholic Oscar.

52

During the spring of 1875, he met Oscar Browning, who was in Oxford on a visit from Cambridge University.

OSCAR BROWNING 1837-1923

Cambridge was also a rich source of eccentric dons and Wilde greeted one of the best known, Oscar Browning, with the words: "I have heard you so much abused that I am sure you must be a most excellent person". Browning was a Fellow at Kings College, and the two Oscars occasionally fenced over the rival merits of their respective alma maters.

Browning informed him that: "If you had been sent to Cambridge to study science, instead of to Oxford to dawdle over literature, you would know that a hypothesis that explains everything is a certainty". Wilde yawned back: "Yes, I am aware that Cambridge is a sort of educational institute".

They kept a distant friendship for many years afterwards. In 1880, Oscar asked Browning for a testimonial when he applied unsuccessfully for the job of Inspector of Schools. In 1889, Browning supplied a sonnet about Bournemouth for Wilde's magazine 'Women's World'; and he was also the Cambridge tutor of Wilde's protégé, *Robert Ross.*

Wilde's only objection to Browning was that: "I wish he was not called Oscar".

E.F. Benson wrote that: 'Browning was a genius flawed by abysmal fatuity. It was impossible to meet him and not be aware that of his great intellectual force. But it was also impossible not to be aware that he was a buffoon.'

Prior to his arrival at Cambridge in 1875, Browning had been at the centre of a scandal at Eton. He had been a colleague of the famed William Johnson, the author of 'The Eton Boating Song'. Johnson, said to be 'averse to the company of women', had been the mentor of such future luminaries as *Lord Rosebery,* Viscount Esher, *the Marquess of Lorne,* and the *Rev. Stuart Headlam.* After compromising letters to schoolboys were discovered, Johnson was dismissed in 1872, changed his name to William Cory, and abandoned teaching.

Learning nothing from Johnson/Cory's fate, Browning fell into a similar trap when he was accused of excessive intimacy with another schoolboy, the future Viceroy of India, *Lord Curzon.* In fact, he may have been innocent of this charge. Curzon certainly bore him no ill will, remaining a friend for fifty years, and introducing his old schoolmaster to his wife with the words 'Whatever I am, my dear, I owe it all to Mr Browning'.

After his sacking from Eton, Kings College provided Browning with a welcome refuge. At the time the college was reserved for the exclusive use of Old Etonians; they could become Fellows as long as they remained unmarried. While, if they wished to become scholars, no obstacle was placed in their path, it was equally acceptable to do nothing at all.

This policy produced some very strange Fellows. One of them had lived at Kings from his early twenties. Now an elderly man, he was never seen except at twilight when he would emerge from his rooms, shuffle across the college lawn stabbing at the worms in the grass with his walking stick, and rasping: "Damn you: you haven't got me yet".

On Sunday evenings, Browning opened his rooms to an assembly of assorted guests – distinguished notables, selected students, and occasional young muscular sailors. Although the alcohol provided was described as 'a curious pink liqueur tasting of floor polish', Browning would be sufficiently inspired by it to entertain his guests with comic songs.

One undergraduate wrote enigmatically: 'Presently the piano began in the room beyond and we went in to watch our host trolling out 'The Road To Mandalay' with immense gusto. At the close of his performance, the clarinet player gave him a spanking.'

Browning possessed one of the first en suite bathrooms at Cambridge University into which he would invite young working-class men off the street for a bath. During one Sunday soiree, a prankster locked him inside this bathroom with Queen Victoria's grandson (and heir to the British Empire), the hapless *Prince Eddy*. Browning emerged irritated at this lese-majesty, for it might have damaged his intense desire to reach the heights of society.

His snobbery bordered on the heroic. *E.F. Benson* wrote that: 'OB's snobbishness was of a really remarkable order – although already waddling with obesity he took to playing hockey simply for the pleasure of being swiped over the shins by the Prince of Wales'.

After a summer in London, he returned to Cambridge and remarked casually that Wilhelm II of Germany was 'one of the nicest Emperors' he had ever met.

Craving acquaintance with the great, he introduced himself to the renowned poet, *Alfred, Lord Tennyson*. Tennyson seemed not to have the slightest idea who he was, so he announced: "I'm Browning". Tennyson assumed that he was impersonating the poet Robert Browning and grumpily replied: "No, you're not".

> *In June 1875, at the start of the summer vacation, Wilde travelled to Italy with his old Trinity tutor Mahaffy.*
>
> *They stayed in Florence (June 15), Bologna, Venice (June 19), Padua (June 22), and Verona (June 23).*
>
> *On June 25, having run out of money, Wilde left Mahaffy in Milan and stayed alone at Arona on Lake Maggiore – 'a beautiful spot'. He wrote a poem 'Graffitti D'Italia' about the place.*
>
> *Wilde returned via Paris to Ireland, where he visited the family summer home at Moytura, and their small fishing lodge at Illaunroe.*
>
> *In August, he came back to Dublin where he met Florence Balcombe.*

FLORENCE BALCOMBE 1858-1937
and **BRAM STOKER** 1847-1912

Wilde: 'To become wise through love'. How that phrase had stirred me in my Oxford days!'

In 1875, while on summer vacation from Oxford, Wilde met the 'exquisitely pretty' Florence, the 17-year old daughter of Lt. Col. James Balcombe of Dublin. Oscar was so attracted that they became unofficially engaged for three years. He gave her, among other things, one of his very amateur watercolours of Moytura House, and a gold cross with their names entwined. He declared that it was 'the sweetest of all the years of my youth'.

Unfortunately, Florence decided that marriage to a financially unsound student was not wise, and rejected him in favour of the older (and fiscally canny) Bram Stoker. Oscar was genuinely hurt by this rebuff and, even in 1881, wrote: 'She thinks I never loved her, thinks I forget. My God, how could I?'

They remained in occasional contact, Florence attending the first night of 'Lady Windermere's Fan', and Oscar sending her a copy of 'Salome'. After his death, she always referred to him as 'Poor O' and said that her possession of the Moytura watercolour created 'much envy in the breasts of the Oscar cult'.

The marriage to Stoker, although lasting, was not a particularly happy one. Bram, (shortened from 'Abraham'), had been a respectable Dublin civil servant and drama critic until 1878 when he fell under the spell of the famous actor, *Henry Irving*. Throwing up his career in Ireland overnight, he plunged himself into guarding the business affairs of 'The Guv'ner', as he called Irving.

On her honeymoon, also in 1878, Florence was surprised to find herself installed in the Plough and Harrow Tavern in Harborne, Birmingham, with her new husband in the throes of business meetings with the great thespian. She never accepted Bram's neglect of her in favour of his idol.

She was much admired for her beauty. The cartoonist *George Du Maurier* described her as 'one of the three most beautiful women in London', but she had little interest in the physical side of her marriage. Even her son Noel said that she was 'an ornament, not a woman of passion'. The writer Dan Farson (Stoker's great-nephew) claimed that, after Noel's birth, her refusal to indulge in any further sex drove Bram to the use of prostitutes.

Stoker had known the Wilde family in Dublin – (Speranza wrote approvingly: 'He never gets into debt, and his character is excellent') – and, even after the tussle over Florence, Oscar showed no animosity towards his successful rival. They met often through their involvement with the London stage.

For twenty-seven years, Stoker provided the crucial business sense that kept Irving and the Lyceum theatre afloat. He estimated that during this time he had written at least half a million letters on Irving's behalf. Even more importantly, he insisted that he alone held the only key to the financial ledgers' safe, thus stemming the tide of 'The Guv'ner's' profligacy.

Stoker also managed Irving's American tours and became an admirer of the USA: 'Americans have no princes of their own, they make princes of whom they love'. He was very proud of the fact that he managed to keep Irving's theatre open throughout the Great Blizzard of 1887, (when over four hundred deaths were reported and New Yorkers were forced to cut tunnels through the twenty feet high snowdrifts).

On a visit to the American poet *Walt Whitman*, he suggested that, if Whitman removed the sexual references from his famous work 'Leaves of Grass': "then the book undoubtedly would be in every American home". Whitman was not impressed.

Stoker's great achievement was his novel 'Dracula'. This excellent tale of Transylvanian vampirism was written despite the fact that Bram had never been anywhere near Transylvania. Noel Stoker said that the plot came to his father 'in a nightmarish dream after eating too much dressed crab'. Stoker asked Irving to produce 'Dracula' as a play. Having read the manuscript, Irving returned it with a single comment: "Dreadful!"

When they died, both Florence and Bram Stoker were cremated at Golders Green Crematorium, London.

(When this Crematorium was first installed, it was decided to test the workings of the machinery by placing a dead pig into the system. Due to a fault, the body inflated and flew up the chimney. The pig was last spotted drifting away like a bloated balloon over the rooftops of Golders Green.)

In October Wilde returned for his second year at Oxford.

On November 23 1875, he went to hear Cardinal Manning preach at St Aloysius church, St Giles, Oxford. Oscar: 'He was more fascinating than ever'.

CARDINAL HENRY MANNING 1807-1892

From the 1860s onwards, English theological certainties were shaken by the scientific theories of Darwin and by du Chaillu's examinations of the gorilla, an animal too closely resembling mankind for comfort. (Wilde: 'Religions die when they are proved to be true. Science is the record of dead religions'.) Under attack from rationalism, many intellectuals converted to Roman Catholicism.

Although Wilde never joined the Church, (even his 'deathbed conversion' is suspect), he was attracted by the sensuality and beauty of its ceremonies. Occasionally he questioned its aesthetics. In 1898, when he was in the Vatican City, he commented: "I am sorry to say that the Pope has approved of a dreadful handkerchief, with a portrait of himself in the middle, and basilicas at the corners. It is very curious the connexion between Faith and bad art".

However, particularly at Oxford, he was very sympathetic to the faith: 'I look on all the different religions as colleges in a great university. Roman Catholicism is the greatest and most romantic of them'. In his rooms at Magdalen, he hung portraits of the two famed English Cardinals – Manning and Newman.

Both of these men were themselves converts. Manning had been an Anglican clergyman till his late thirties; then, after visiting Rome and talking with the Pontiff, Pius IX, he became a Catholic priest. He enjoyed a meteoric rise through the hierarchy. Within fourteen years, he became supreme in English Catholicism when he succeeded the deceased incumbent, Cardinal Wiseman, as Archbishop of Westminster. By 1875, he had been made a cardinal himself.

(Wiseman, incidentally, had been something of a gourmet. One Lent, his disciples were saddened to see Wiseman devouring four courses of fish for dinner. One of them sighed: 'I am sorry to say that there is a lobster salad side to the Cardinal'.)

Manning was a redoubtable social reformer, (he supported Irish Home Rule, backed the 1889 Dockers Strike, campaigned for teetotalism, and tried to break the White Slave Traffic), but was also an astute and worldly man. Lytton Strachey said that Manning reminded him of the sixteenth century prelate, Cardinal Wolsey.

Manning filled large scrapbooks with all the newspaper cuttings he could find about himself. He also enjoyed pumping his confidential secretary, *J.E.C. Bodley,* for all the latest gossip, after which he would slap Bodley on the back and chuckle: "Well, it's a wicked old world, isn't it?" Bodley: 'In his youth Manning was a terrible converter, but when I knew him he was rather sick of it and never attempted to convert me'.

In 1870, Manning attended the First Session of the Vatican Council in Rome. He told Bodley that, to find out what they had been doing at the Council, the Cardinals always read The Times the next day. It was at this conference that the Pope was declared to be Infallible, a decision that Manning (and Wilde) supported.

It was this decision, among other things, that led Manning to clash with his rival, **JOHN NEWMAN** (1801-1890). 'The Divine Noggs', as he was known, was an important force in Victorian Catholicism. He founded oratories in London and Birmingham, created the new Catholic university in Dublin, and wrote the popular hymn 'Lead Kindly Light' and the poem 'The Dream of Gerontius', (later to become a major musical work by Edward Elgar).

Wilde, though admiring of Newman's 'Apologia Pro Vita Sua' in which he defined the principles governing his life, could not entirely sympathise with him. Wilde: 'The mode of thought that Cardinal Newman represented – if that can be called a mode of thought which seeks to solve intellectual problems by a denial of the supremacy of the intellect – may not, cannot, I think, survive'.

Manning suspected that Newman would lead English Catholicism away from Papal authority. One of Manning's close advisors, Monsignor Talbot, said: "To be Roman is to an Englishman an effort. Dr Newman is more English than the English. His spirit must be crushed".

Beyond doctrinal disagreement, Manning had a personal distaste for his adversary, which he indulged by deliberately choosing as his butler a man called Newman. (When Wilde fell out with his publisher, *John Lane,* he copied this strategy by, in 'The Importance of Being Earnest', naming the butler 'Lane').

For years Manning blocked Newman's promotion but, in 1877, he relented and apologised. Newman was created a cardinal.

Manning showed some prescience when he declared in 1880: 'Europe is rejecting Christianity and with it the reign of moral law. The reign of force is now beginning again as in the early stages, and bloodshed and ruin must be the result'.

1876-7

[In the USA, General Custer made his Last Stand, the American Centennial Exposition was held, and the following year Thomas Edison patented the first telephone.
In Germany Wagner's 'The Ring of the Nibelungs' had its first performance at Bayreuth in 1876.
In Britain Queen Victoria was proclaimed Empress of India in 1876, while
Gilbert and Sullivan's first operetta, 'The Sorcerer', was performed in 1877.
In 1876, the Bulgarian Massacres led to the start of the Russian-Turkish War. By 1877, the Russian army was held at the Battle of Plevna. The British fleet arrived in the area to prevent any further Russian advance towards Constantinople. Peace was declared in December.]

After another term, Wilde spent the spring vacation of 1876 at Magdalen College studying for exams. This was interrupted on April 19th by news of the death of his father, Sir William. Oscar went over to Dublin for the funeral.
Returning to England, he stayed with his uncle, the Rev. John Wilde at West Ashby, Lincolnshire.
On July 5, Wilde gained a first class Classical Moderations (Mods).
On July 9, he was in Nottinghamshire with his friend, Frank Miles, staying at Bingham Rectory where Miles's father was vicar.
In August, Oscar went fishing at Illaunroe Lodge, Co Galway, returning to Oxford in October for his third year.
On November 1, he was fined by the Magdalen authorities for dining out of college at the Clarendon Hotel
On November 27, he was underwent further initiation into the Freemasons.

In 1877, Wilde started serious work on his poetry.

QUEEN VICTORIA 1819-1901

Wilde: 'The three women I have most admired are Queen Victoria, *Sarah Bernhardt,* and *Lily Langtry.* I would have married any one of them with pleasure'.

In 1877, Oscar gave vent to this admiration in his poem, 'Hail Empress', to celebrate Victoria's accession as Empress of India. In 1887, when he became editor of the 'Women's World' magazine, he attempted to inspire a reciprocal response when he asked the palace if the Queen would care to submit some verse for the magazine. She responded in a tart note that she had never written a line of poetry 'serious or comic' in her life, and that any claim that she had done so was 'invention and myth'.

He met her once at one of the Prince of Wales' garden parties – 'looking like a ruby mounted in jet' – and said that it was her personality and 'her exquisite bearing' that struck him most: 'I shall never forget her.' It was an ambivalent position for an Irish nationalist.

His regard wavered only once. While in prison, he grumbled: "If this is the way that Queen Victoria treats her convicts, she does not deserve to have any".

But, on release, he insisted on placing a picture of the monarch on his wall: 'Every poet should gaze at the portrait of his Queen all day long'. He also provided a fete for the local French children to celebrate Victoria's Diamond Jubilee where, as well as the 'Marseillaise', they sang 'God Save The Queen'. Oscar: 'Well, they *said* it was 'God Save the Queen'; and I did not like to differ from them'.

Ascending to the throne at the age of eighteen, Victoria was perhaps the most successful of all British monarchs because her character happened to coincide closely with the British bourgeoisie. She disliked the aristocracy and had the perception to realise that their power had waned; whilst, to her, the working class were virtually a closed book. One of her Prime Ministers, *Lord Salisbury*, said that: 'when I knew what the Queen thought I knew pretty certainly what view her subjects would take, and especially the middle class of her subjects'.

One of the values she shared with this section of society was a belief in frugality. She was annoyed when popular sentiment forced her to indulge in her 1887 Golden Jubilee Day – she wanted to get the whole thing over as speedily as possible and refused to pay for it. She saved a fortune out of her £400,000 a year Civil List pension by banking it almost untouched. This money provides the basis for the wealth of the current Royal Family.

Her views on art agreed with popular philistinism. Having been to see 'King Lear', she gave her opinion that it was: "a strange, horrible business, but I suppose good enough for Shakespeare's day".

Another attitude she shared with her more solid citizens was her insistence on high standards of sexual morality. Whether, in the case of her subjects, this ever rose above vociferous hypocrisy is debatable, but, for her part, it was genuine. She had a real hatred of moral laxity and refused to allow any divorced person at court. Her rigidity was, to some extent, a rebellion against the well-publicised debaucheries of her uncles, led by George IV.

She was fortunate in that the man she married in 1840, Prince Albert, came from a family, the German Dukes of Saxe-Coburg Gotha, whose main contribution to the social fabric appears to have been syphilis. Albert was equally appalled at his upbringing and was happy to join Victoria in her desire for 'a strict court and a high attitude'. Not all her advisors were so keen; her first counsellor and friend, Prime Minister Lord Melbourne, grunted: "Damned morality will ruin us all!"

Although her marriage was not popular at first – Charles Dickens caught the general mood with his jibes at Albert 'Saxe-Humbug-Go-to-Her' – the union was phenomenally successful. Victoria and Albert produced nine children, forty- one grandchildren, and eighty-seven great-grandchildren. *Prince Bismarck* described the Coburgs as 'the stud farm of Europe'.

For twenty years, the royal pair enjoyed a generally idyllic life, becoming involved in all manner of social improvements – the development of the South Kensington museums (known as 'Albertopolis') being a lasting example.

Victoria was never fond of Buckingham Palace as it was overrun by rats, and preferred to stay in the Highland castle of Balmoral. After Albert had improved the building by converting it into a sort of German Schloss and papering the walls in tartan, they settled into a lifestyle that became known as 'Balmorality'. The courtiers were ordered to wear kilts, Victoria learned Highland dancing, and Albert laboriously studied Gaelic.

To avoid unnecessary expenditure, Victoria rationed the fires. As a result, Balmoral proved to be so cold that Albert, who was prematurely bald, was forced to wear a wig.

Occasionally, the Queen returned to Buckingham Palace for official duties, one of which was the reception of debutantes in the State drawing-room. (Wilde's wife, Constance, was presented there in 1887). It was noticed that Victoria seldom stayed longer than ten minutes at these events, leaving the duties to her daughter-in-law, the Princess of Wales. *Robert Hichens* was told that the reason for this was that the endless flow of deeply curtseying women before her made Victoria feel seasick.

Once, on her round of civic duties, she arrived in Cambridge. Until the 1890s, when the city sanitation was modernised, all sewage went directly into the River Cam. The official tour, led by the Master of Trinity, happened to cross over a bridge; Victoria, looking down at the water, noticed some pieces of paper floating downstream and asked what they were. The Master, thinking quickly, replied: "Those, ma'am, are notices that bathing is forbidden".

The state of the Cambridge sewage system might have had some bearing on the fact that in 1861, Albert, visiting Cambridge to upbraid his son Bertie for a misdemeanour, caught typhoid fever and died. Victoria, stricken at the loss, became a semi-recluse. She did not forgive her son for his relatively blameless involvement in Albert's death.

Bertie, otherwise known as the Prince of Wales, constantly suffered from her grudging disapproval of almost everything he did. When the Queen banned smoking in the royal residence, he had to hang a sign reading 'WC' on the door of a small pantry and use it as a secret smoking room.

When he married the Danish Princess Alexandra, Victoria was in a particularly bad mood and ordered that the wedding should take place at Windsor, rather than at the more prestigious Westminster Abbey. The command went out that British sailors should not cheer Alexandra's arrival at Gravesend, and neither should the boys of Eton cheer her arrival at Windsor. Her first morning with her new in-laws was spent being taken on a tour of Albert's illuminated mausoleum.

Even later in Victoria's life, when she returned to some measure of public visibility, the Queen was still in thrall to Albert's memory. When discussing matters of state with ministers, she would often interrupt the conversation to walk away and ask Albert's marble bust what was the best policy. *Disraeli*, on his deathbed, famously declined a visit from his sovereign: "No, it is better not. She will only ask me to take a message to Albert".

Victoria was regarded as naïve. Allegedly, when she signed the Criminal Law Amendment Act in 1885 which severely increased the penalties for homosexuality (the law that was to wreck Wilde), she refused to include a similar ban on lesbians, saying that: "no woman would do such a thing". (In fact, this story appears to have been something of a sub-urban myth.)

In fact, at least six of her major courtiers were themselves homosexual. One of them, Alick Yorke, was the man who provoked the immortal line: "We are not amused", when asked to repeat an indecent anecdote.

Oscar made the observation that courtiers were 'slaves'. 'But they get to like it. It becomes second nature to them. If an old courtier is dismissed from Her Majesty's service, he grows wretched. He often dies of it. You see he cannot breathe in any other air. Courtiers and actors all live other people's lives'.

One courtier who would not have approved of this comment was the Highlander John Brown. After Albert's death, he held an extraordinary position in Victoria's household – partly servant, possibly lover, and definitely drinking companion, (whisky was their preference). There were rumours that they had secretly married, (and even that they had produced a child together, who died aged ninety as a recluse in Paris.)

But what really upset the royal household was Brown's brusque treatment of his social superiors. Sir Arthur Bigge, the Queen's private secretary, rose one morning at Balmoral intending to go out angling. Brown suddenly appeared as Sir Arthur donned his waders, eyed him sternly, and announced: "Ye'll no be going fishing, laddie. Her Majesty thinks it's about time ye did some work".

Victoria's reign lasted sixty-three years and she was acknowledged as an intelligent and – eventually – a beloved monarch. She had been fortunate in her mentors. Lord Melbourne, Prince Albert, Disraeli, even John Brown, had steered her well.

During her Diamond Jubilee in 1898, a British Ambassador, Lord Stair, was asked why affairs ran so much more equably under the rule of a queen than under a king. He replied: "Because a reigning King is ruled by women, and a Queen by men".

From January till March 1875, Wilde stayed at Magdalen College and finally managed to meet Walter Pater.

WALTER PATER 1839-1894

Perhaps the greatest influence on Wilde during his student days was the don, Walter Pater, who he met in his third year at college. Pater's book, 'Studies in the History of the Renaisance', had been Oscar's bible for several years. In an idea borrowed from French writers, it propounded the theory of 'Art for Art's Sake', that modern man should imitate the sensuous life of the Renaissance, while burning always with a 'hard gem-like flame'. Wilde described it as 'my golden book which has had such a strange influence over my life'.

Pater's effect on Wilde may have gone beyond the intellectual. *Frank Harris* reported that, on one occasion, Pater made a pass at Oscar, kneeling down before him and kissing his hand. Oscar rebuffed him, and the embarrassed don muttered: "I had to, I had to – once". *Bodley*, strongly hinting at homosexuality, said that Pater had turned his protégé into 'an extreme aesthete'.

One of Pater's tenets was that 'poetry is only a beautiful stepping stone to prose', and asked Wilde: "Why don't you write prose? It's so much more difficult to write than poetry". Wilde, in a major shift of his literary career, agreed: 'Prose so fascinates me that I prefer to sit at its organ than to play on the pipe or reed of poetry.'

Oscar's early reverence for Pater lessened with age. He disliked Pater's timidity over homosexuality in general and over Wilde's book 'Dorian Gray' in particular: "Oscar is really too bold…. sooner or later he'll come to grief". Wilde – 'Dear Pater was always frightened of my propaganda' – now thought of his ex-hero as 'a vicarage *Verlaine*'.

He especially mocked Pater's habit of whispering his lectures, a habit *Max Beerbohm* called 'a form of self-communion'. Pater asked Wilde after one such address: "I hope you heard me, Mr Wilde?" "We overheard you". For his part Pater, although outwardly civil, came to dislike Oscar, disparaging 'the strange vulgarity which Mr Wilde mistakes for charm'.

In 1894, when Wilde was told that Pater was dead, he replied: "Was he ever alive?"

Soon after graduating at Oxford, where, uncharacteristically, he had involved himself in rowing, (it was said that he would have been a brilliant cox if the riverbanks hadn't kept getting in the way), Pater gained a Fellowship at Brasenose College, where he remained most of his academic life.

As his nickname was 'Judas', he was evidently not a popular figure. One undergrad said that Pater would slink around the college 'as though he had committed a theft'. He lived a hermit-like existence of 'decorous dullness', being cared for by his two colourless sisters, and regularly stopping in bed till noon – 'a man who wore out more sheets than shoes'. Although personally supine, Pater admired male strength and kept a bust of Hercules in his rooms.

He once alarmed a student called Sanctuary by ordering him to report to the senior common room. Sanctuary, expecting a rebuke, was surprised to hear an uneasy Pater stammering: "Oh, Mr Sanctuary…I…I just wanted to say to you…what a very beautiful name you have got".

Pater was known for his refusal to allow any humour at all in his later writings. The novelist Israel Zangwill mischievously told him that his book on Plato contained a bad pun. Pater was mortified and demanded to know where it was; Zangwill refused to tell him. Pater spent weeks irritably scouring the pages for the non-existent witticism.

After Vice Chancellor *Jowett* became worried over Pater's louche reputation and had firmly blocked any further advancement at Oxford, Pater spent much of his time in London. While there, he became a close friend of the eccentric Dr. Lee, the rector of All Saints, Lambeth.

(Lee's main religious crusade was against inappropriate names being chosen at christenings. He was strongly opposed to any name that might 'carry a lascivious sound' and also against long strings of names. He thought it was the duty of all clergymen to alter such mistakes, whether the parents were willing or not. His parishioners complained that the rector named all the girls Mary after the Virgin and all the boys Frederick after himself.

At one christening, he boomed out: 'Name this child'. The mother, unaware of Lee's opinions, whispered: "Archibald Ferdinand De Courcy Paget Reginald". She was astounded when her baby was baptised with the inevitable 'Frederick'. During the understandable row that took place in the vestry afterwards, Dr Lee overrode all objections with the breezy announcement: "Oh, well, it's done now and can't be altered!")

In March 1877 Wilde accompanied Mahaffy to Italy, travelling via Paris, Turin and Genoa to Ravenna (the subject of his later poem). Mahaffy steered Oscar away from Rome and off to Greece – 'from Popery to Parnassus'.

They left Brindisi on April 1st, sailing first to Corfu, ('this sea-tranced isle' and the setting of Wilde's poem 'Santa Decca'), then to Zante (3 April), Katakola, Olympia, then on horseback to Andritzena (7 April), Argos, and Nauplia.

They next took a ship to Athens (13 April) and Mycenae (21 April).

On April 21, Wilde set sail for Naples, experiencing a ferocious 'but exhilarating' storm in passage across the Mediterranean.

He arrived in Rome in late April where he re-met Hunter-Blair and spent ten days with him.

Arriving back in Oxford on April 30, Oscar found himself rusticated for arriving back in college one month late.

He was banned for two terms, from April till October: 'I was sent down from Oxford for being the first undergraduate to visit Olympia.'

On 1st May 1877, the Masonic Churchill Lodge appointed Wilde to the office of Junior Deacon.

On the same day, he came down to visit Frank Miles in London for a week. During this period, he attended the opening of the Grosvenor Gallery with a friend, Lord Ronald Gower, and went to hear the German composer, Richard Wagner, conduct from his work 'The Flying Dutchman'.

LORD RONALD GOWER 1845-1916

By 1877, Wilde's acquaintance began to extend beyond the academic world; one of the first of his new contacts was Lord Ronald Gower, nine years his senior. Gower, another homosexual, was interested in the young Oxford student, whom he declared would be 'the new Byron'. Gower had no patience with what he described as Oscar's 'long-haired head full of nonsense regarding the Church of Rome', and set about vigorously debunking any thought of conversion.

Although refusing the offer of a holiday in Paris, Wilde accepted Gower's invitation in May 1877 to the new Grosvenor Gallery opening.

Despite a bohemian life style, Gower was indisputably aristocratic. He was the younger son of the Duke of Sutherland; his nephew the *Marquess of Lorne* married Queen Victoria's daughter, *Princess Louise,* while his uncles were the Dukes of Norfolk and Devonshire. Cliveden, the magnificent mansion overlooking the River Thames where Wilde was later a guest, was just one of the family homes. Three of Gower's four sisters became duchesses. Oscar was flattered to be introduced to one of them, the Duchess of Westminster, at the Gallery opening; it was his first entrée into the fashionable world.

Gower was a sculptor of some repute, today best known for his Stratford-on-Avon Shakespeare memorial. Wilde was present at the unveiling in 1888 and made a speech at the ceremony proposing the health of the sculptor. He wrote that he had been 'speaking at

Stratford about Shakespeare, but in spite of that enjoyed my visit immensely'. Gower introduced a mischievous addition to his statues by deliberately exaggerating Prince Hal's phallus, an act privately denounced by *J.A. Symonds* as 'moral insanity'.

There is a strong possibility that Wilde had Gower in mind when he created the character of 'Lord Henry Wotton' in his novel 'Dorian Gray'.

Gower had been very good-looking in his youth, a blessing he found to be mixed. In 1866, aged 21, he went off to witness the conflict between Italy and Austria. He was present at the Battle of Salo and met the wounded Italian leader Garibaldi. While staying at an inn after the battle, he was mistaken for a girl by one of Garibaldi's volunteers and spent the night fending the man off with a broom.

Then, in 1870, eager for more battle-tourism, (this time the Franco-Prussian War), he was arrested by German troops who suspected he was 'a Frenchwoman in male attire'.

After his release by the disappointed Prussians, he travelled with an old friend W.H. Russell, the renowned war correspondent, only to be involved in a further incident. The goat (or 'bock') was used commonly in Germany as the sign over a beer-tavern. Russell, who was fond of heraldry, had inscribed his family coat of arms, with the motto of 'Che sara sara', on his travelling carriage. Unfortunately the coat of arms included a prominent goat. Gower and Russell were held at gunpoint as their conveyance was ransacked, to no avail, by thirsty Prussian troops.

One experience that both Wilde and Gower shared, although on separate occasions, was being witness to a public guillotining. They were both shocked by it. Gower described: 'beyond, on the outskirts of the crowd, women shouting in carriages, rouged and painted, and far more horrible than the sight one had just turned away sick at heart from.' Wilde reported: 'I have seen the victim look green with fright. They are kind to him up to the last minute. He may smoke a cigarette as he goes to the Place de la Roquette, but once there, what a change. They are on him like tigers, and his head is thrust into the groove under the knife as if he were not a man at all'.

Gower's sexual taste was mainly for working class 'rough trade' youths, but he finally settled into a form of domesticity with a friend called Frank Hird (in 1898, he made Hird his legal son). Wilde: "Gower should be seen but not Hird".

Gower was never discreet about his homosexual proclivities but his social circle excused or ignored his behaviour. Wilde: 'Civilised society is never very ready to believe anything to the detriment of those who are both rich and fascinating'.

Nevertheless, despite his position, in April 1895 Gower found it expedient to make a rapid exit from England when Wilde's ruin became apparent.

Gower spent much of his life travelling the world; he viewed most of it with a jaundiced eye. He went to Egypt during a cholera outbreak and declared that: 'the native doctors were worse than useless'. It seemed that they would stand as far away as possible from their patients and 'examine them through opera glasses'.

While in Japan in 1884, he attended a sumo-wrestling match: 'I have never seen such grotesquely hideous fat men as these wrestlers were – except at a French bathing-place'.

Stopping in Rome to view the Sistine Madonna, he wrote that he 'noticed that the Child Jesus has a very decided squint'.

RICHARD WAGNER 1813-1883

Wilde: 'I like Wagner's music better than anybody's. It is so loud that one can talk the whole time without other people hearing what one says'.

In the same week as Oscar's visit to the Grosvenor Gallery, he also went to see Richard Wagner conducting excerpts from 'The Flying Dutchman' at the Albert Hall. In common with such poets as *Tennyson* and *Swinburne*, music was not really Wilde's forte. *E.F. Benson* wrote: 'Oscar Wilde, oddly enough, though he had so keen and just a sense of music in spoken or written words, he had absolutely no sense of music itself, being practically unable to distinguish one tune from another'.

The concert itself was not entirely successful. The composer *Ethel Smyth* was present and said of Wagner that he was 'an undersized man with a huge head, apparently in a towering rage from start to finish of the concert – no doubt the performance was insufficiently rehearsed'. Wagner masked any chagrin by going shopping at Whiteley's department store in Bayswater, (where he bought a rocking horse.)

Wagner had a huge influence on the latter decades of the nineteenth century. Although then regarded as a musical revolutionary, his work was more of a culmination of German romantic music than the start of a new form. Debussy said of him: 'Wagner was a beautiful sunset that has been mistaken for a sunrise'. In spite of this, many contemporaries considered his work to be an outrage.

Rossini's famous comment that it had 'lovely moments but awful half hours' was mild in comparison to Tolstoy's fulminations on the 'counterfeit art' and 'nonsensical rubbish' of 'The Ring of the Nibelungs'. *Robert Browning* described him as 'a monster of peacock-like vanity'. *Mark Twain* was more consolatory: 'Wagner's music is better than it sounds'.

Wagner had begun his professional life as a jobbing conductor. By 1848, he had completed three operas, 'The Flying Dutchman', 'Lohengrin', and 'Tannhauser'. He had intended calling the latter work, 'Der Venusburg', until friends pointed out that the title, 'The Mound of Venus', might lead to ribaldry. He hastily renamed it.

His career was interrupted when, in 1849, he joined a revolutionary group called the Young German Movement and became involved in street fighting against the authorities. He was forced into exile from Germany for the next eleven years, much of this time being spent in Zurich and the rest in conducting his work around European cities.

He relied a lot on female company and had numerous affairs throughout his life. His second wife Cosima was the daughter of the composer Franz Liszt; another mistress was Judith Gautier, the daughter of the French poet Theophile Gautier and wife of the French critic Catulle Mendes. He was attacked for his libidinous nature as well as for his art. *Mahaffy*: "Wagner was an unutterable cad and should have been hounded out of all decent society".

His real character lay in his utter egocentricity – a capacity to ignore or overcome any scruples or even common sense if they interfered with his artistic genius. He refused to compromise in any way. The staging of his works required huge expenditure, including building an entirely new theatre to suit their performance. (As Wilde said: 'music is the most expensive of all noises'.) In order to stage 'The Ring', Wagner needed a patron of enormous wealth and doglike faith. Amazingly, such a man existed.

Prince Otto said of his brother, King Ludwig II of Bavaria that, while he himself had lucid intervals: "Ludwig was always mad". Except for servants, Ludwig lived alone in his three castles. Occasionally he would send for musicians but they were not allowed into the buildings themselves – they had to play out in the open. *Gertrude Atherton* reported that once, when Ludwig had violent toothache, even the dentist was not allowed entry: 'Ludwig stuck his head out of a lower window, and the dentist standing out on the terrace pulled the tooth as best he could.'

Ludwig's saving grace was his appreciation of Wagner's genius. By 1864, Ludwig had opened the Bavarian treasury for his friend to spend what he wished on opera. This generosity was not greatly welcomed by the Bavarians. Given the strong rumours circulating that their homosexual young king was actually in love with the aging composer, the burghers of Munich insisted that Wagner leave the country. Broken-hearted, Ludwig was forced to banish Wagner.

However, he still managed to supply most of the money that funded the building of Wagner's dream – a new theatre in the quiet Bavarian town of Bayreuth – and the first production there, in 1876, of 'The Ring of the Nibelungs'.

There was a small design hiccup before the first show. The 'Dragon' used for the combat with 'Siegfried' had been built in sections in London. The neck did not arrive in Bayreuth in time for the show, as it had been wrongly delivered to Beirut in the Lebanon.

Slipping unnoticed into a rehearsal before the first performance of 'Das Rheingold', King Ludwig sat alone in the darkness, breathlessly watching the one great achievement of his life. Ten years later, having gone completely insane, Ludwig drowned himself in the Starnberger See. The body of his psychiatric doctor, with its head smashed in by a heavy stone, was found on the nearby shore.

Wilde: 'There have been two Royal personages really interesting – Rudolph of Austria and Ludwig of Bavaria. The one was murdered by his lover's brother. The other killed his doctor and then himself. They didn't live other people's lives.'

In May 1877, after a week in London, Wilde spent a few days in Bournemouth convalescing from a minor illness.

He returned to Dublin under something of a cloud due to his rustication.

He occupied some of his time by writing more poems, one of which he sent to the leading politician, William Gladstone.

WILLIAM EWART GLADSTONE 1809-1898

The political topic that enthused both Wilde and the former Prime Minister of Britain was the atrocities committed on the Bulgarian people by the Turkish Empire. When war between Russia and Turkey seemed on the point of breaking out, the British government led by *Benjamin Disraeli* favoured an anti-Russian stance and thus were sympathetic to the Ottoman perpetrators. Coming out of retirement, a furious Gladstone attacked Disraeli in the famed Midlothian Campaign of 1879 – 'a pilgrimage of passion'.

Wilde also was moved by the horrors and wrote a sonnet 'On the Massacre of the Christians in Bulgaria': 'Come down, O Son of Man! And show thy might, Lest Mahomet be crowned instead of Thee!' He sent this poem to Gladstone in May 1877; they later met in person and in 1888 Wilde gave him a copy of 'The Happy Prince'.

Together with *Lord Tennyson* and *Queen Victoria* herself, Gladstone embodied the Victorian era. Between 1868 and 1894, he was elected as Liberal Prime Minister four times and championed a number of causes, Irish Home Rule in particular, with evangelical fervour. As a serious and deeply religious man, he consistently made political decisions based on moral purpose. He was the epitome of earnest Victorian respectability.

However, Gladstone was also a wily politician and his colleagues were less respectful than his public. *Henry Labouchere* said that he had no objection to Gladstone always seeming to have an ace up his sleeve, but what he did object to was Gladstone's pretence that God had put it there. *Henry James* called him 'a parson perverted'. Wilde said that whenever Gladstone made a speech to a Scottish audience, he claimed to be a Scotsman.

Wilde: 'In England a man who can't talk morality twice a week to a large, popular, immoral audience is quite over as a serious politician. There would be nothing left for him as a profession except Botany or the Church'.

Gladstone seldom slept for more than four hours a night and found his recreation in splitting logs; his personal axe was a treasured possession. He enjoyed excellent health for almost all of his long life; this was attributed to his habit of chewing every piece of food exactly

32 times. Someone once said to *Lord Salisbury* about Gladstone: "How I wish I had his mind". Salisbury replied: "You can have his mind, if I can have his digestion".

Several people commented on Gladstone's dramatic qualities. *Frank Harris*: 'He was a great actor and could persuade himself of anything'; while *Bernard Shaw* recalled that, when he trained himself as an orator, Gladstone had carefully studied the technique of the actor Charles Kean.

Gladstone always maintained a liking for theatre. He visited a rehearsal of one play that had a stage set of the Paris Opera, with extras leaning from supposed tiers of boxes. He asked to be one of them on the first night and the amused stage manager agreed, warning him to keep out of sight. The audience spotted him and broke out with applause and cries of "Bravo, Gladstone". The play had to be halted while he stood up to take a bow.

On a less flattering occasion, he went backstage to congratulate the actor *Herbert Beerbohm Tree* and asked Tree about the political attitude of the theatrical profession. Tree admitted that they tended generally to be Conservative. Seeing Gladstone's face fall, Tree hurriedly blurted: "But the scene-shifters support you to a man!"

The one great mystery about Gladstone was his attitude over sexual matters. He was very happily married for nearly fifty-nine years, sincerely loved his wife, and exuded rectitude. Yet throughout his life he displayed an obsession with 'saving fallen women'.

He used to patrol the red-light districts of London searching for prostitutes whom he would attempt to reform, sometimes by bringing them back to 10, Downing Street, so that he could recite the Bible to them. He was signally unsuccessful in this, by his own account estimating only twelve converts in sixty years. A street rhyme celebrated this with: 'Eight little whores, with no hope of heaven, Gladstone may save one, then there'll be seven'.

These actions, on the face of it, seemed innocent and even laudable. However, as *Labouchere* pointed out, Gladstone rarely, if ever, chose to save 'an ugly woman'. 'I am quite sure his conception of the Magdalen is of an incomparable example of pulchritude with a superb figure and carriage'. Gladstone also made a point of befriending the prettiest of the society courtesans of the period – such women as Laura Bell and *Catherine 'Skittles' Walters*.

The man-about-town, Algernon Bourke, reported that Gladstone had given one prostitute some odd advice: 'that she should be honest in all her dealings and always to give full value for the money she received'.

The nicknames that were bandied around the 1880s London brothels concerning Gladstone – 'Old Glad-eyes' and 'Daddy-do-nothing' – gave rise to the suspicion that he was, in reality, a repressed voyeur. Although he swore to his son that he had never been guilty of 'infidelity to the marriage bed', in Victorian terms this did not rule out other forms of sexual activity. He disclosed in his diaries that, after meetings with these women, he would flog himself till he had scars on his back. His method of restraint was self-torture.

It was a tribute to his moral authority that the gossip about these activities failed to dent his stature. Perhaps he managed to conceal the truth even from himself.

Gladstone was also a noted scholar who prided himself on his knowledge of Ancient Greek. On a tour of Greece, he gave a public oration in that language forgetting that Modern Greek was quite different. He was bewildered when the Mayor of Corfu thanked him for his speech, but added his regret that Gladstone had had to deliver it in English.

Gladstone had a deep personal dislike for his great political rival Disraeli, with whom Wilde also corresponded in verse.

BENJAMIN DISRAELI 1804-1881

Wilde met the British Tory Prime Minister in 1880. They had a brief exchange. Oscar said politely: 'I hope you are very well', and the aged statesman replied wearily: 'Is anyone ever very well, Mr Wilde'.

Given his Irish nationalist sympathies, the poem that Oscar wrote and sent to Disraeli was simply weird. Called 'Ave Imperitrix', it was a celebration of the British 1879 invasion of Afghanistan – 'The measured roll of English drums, Bear at the gates of Kandahar', etc. – and summoned up the wraith of Cromwell, (of all people), to mourn the subsequent casualties – 'Where is our English chivalry? Wild grasses are their burial-sheet'.

Wilde did have a genuine regard for Disraeli as a fine novelist who could also govern a worldwide empire. He described Disraeli's life as 'that most brilliant of paradoxes'. Perhaps Oscar recognised that Disraeli was the most Wildean Prime Minister Britain had produced.

Both men in their youth, (although separated by fifty years), were dedicated dandies who enjoyed shocking the decorous by their outlandish dress and by their wit. Disraeli's quip – 'I have always thought that every woman should marry, and no man' – could easily have come from Wilde's pen. Both were successful literary figures, and both flirted with social disaster.

The painter Benjamin Haydon (1786-1846) even hinted that Disraeli was bisexual when he said that Disraeli was disposed to excuse the 'infamous vices' of the Orient. Haydon: "I meant to ask him if he preferred Aegypt, where Sodomy was preferment, to England, where it very properly was Death".

Although proud of his Jewish ancestry, (he once told a Jewish boy: "You and I belong to a race which can do everything but fail"), his political career was aided by his family's conversion to Christianity in 1817. This career was almost ruined at the start by his sexual profligacy, (he only narrowly avoided venereal disease), and by some disastrous mining investments which, after the City crash of 1825, left him evading creditors for the next twenty years. He partly bounced back by writing novels, in particular, 'Vivian Grey' (at the age of 24), 'Sybil – or the Two Nations' and 'Coningsby'.

He travelled for three years round the Mediterranean. In Malta, his appearance dressed as a multi-hued Greek pirate led to his being followed by a gaping crowd and the English Governor collapsing with laughter. Disraeli: 'Like all great travellers, I have seen more than I remember, and remember more than I have seen'.

However, by the early 1840s, Disraeli's life changed dramatically. His marriage to the wealthy Mary Lewis cleared his debts, and he was elected to Parliament. At first, his marriage seemed calculating: "When I first made advances to you, I was influenced by no romantic feelings", but he soon became deeply attached to his equally loving wife. He became the owner of a fine mansion in Buckinghamshire called Hughendon Manor.

He also toned down his flamboyant appearance and banter. Disraeli: 'Men destined to the highest places should beware of badinage…. an insular country subject to fogs, and with a powerful middle class, requires grave statesmen'.

In Parliament, where his nickname was 'Beaky', he was soon recognised as a fine orator. His merciless attack led to the destruction of his own Tory leader, Sir Robert Peel. He was no easier on the free trade 'Manchester School' of economics: "If you convert the senate into a counting-house, it will not be long before the nation degenerates into a factory".

He used his talents to mock the Liberal leader, Lord Palmerston, over Palmerston's ambiguous radicalism: "There is no doubt a difference in the honourable gentleman's demeanour as leader of the Opposition and as Minister of the Crown. But that's the old story; you must not contrast too strongly the hours of courtship with the hours of possession".

Palmerston had revenge when, aged 79, he was cited as the co-respondent in a divorce case. (The lady in question was named Mrs Kane – which gave rise to the speculation: 'she was

Kane, but was he Able?'). Disraeli was appalled when he heard the news: "If Palmerston can provide evidence of his potency in his electoral address, he'll sweep the country' – a prediction that proved absolutely correct.

In 1868, Disraeli himself climbed to what he termed 'the top of the greasy pole' and became Prime Minister, despite having always described his own Tories as 'the stupid party'. He lasted long enough to preside over the British invasion of Ethiopia by General Napier, but lost his electoral battle with *Gladstone* within the year. For the next thirteen years, the two were to dominate British politics.

While Disraeli was relaxed about his opponent, Gladstone had a real loathing for the Tory leader. Disraeli found this both puzzling and amusing and reacted with constant teasing. One day, in the House of Commons, while Gladstone was giving a major speech, he found himself distracted by the sight of Disraeli, sitting opposite, earnestly perusing what appeared to be a momentous document, which he finally and very slowly tore to pieces. A curious MP gathered the scraps later only to find it had been a blank sheet of paper.

Disraeli was asked to define the difference between a misfortune and a calamity. He replied that: "if, for instance, Mr Gladstone were to fall into the river, that would be a misfortune. But if anyone were to pull him out, that would be a calamity". He especially annoyed Gladstone when he described Gladstone's inflammatory political pamphlet on the Bulgarian Crisis as being 'the worst of the Bulgarian horrors'.

Disraeli returned to power in 1874 where he was responsible for the proclamation of Victoria as Empress of India, the purchase of the controlling shares over the Suez Canal, and the declaration of two wars in 1879 – one in Afghanistan, the other against the Zulus.

He had a personal misfortune when his wife Mary died of cancer. Aged 70, he fell in unrequited love with another man's wife, Lady Selina Bradford. Disraeli: 'I am certain there is no greater misfortune than to have a heart that will not grow old'. Then he himself suffered bad health.

Once, he felt so ill that he had to leave the Treasury Office and told his secretary: "Don't bother me with the routine work. Please attend to all of it yourself". Walking slowly to the door, he turned and added: "But of course if there is any really important decision to be made…", he paused for a few seconds, "… make it."

The illness became so serious that in 1876 Disraeli had to leave the House of Commons and join the more serene House of Lords as the Earl of Beaconsfield.

His greatest success, though, was still ahead. Facing the twin problems of public moral anger against the Turks for their brutalities in Bulgaria, and the practical necessity of discouraging the Russians from expansion towards the Mediterranean, he managed to avoid British involvement in the Russo-Turkish War imbroglio of 1876-8. Then, in June 1878, he had a chance to display his diplomatic prowess by reconciling the opposing sides at the Congress of Berlin.

Aided by *Lord Salisbury*, (formerly a foe who had talked of Disraeli as 'a Hebrew varlet', but now his right hand man), Disraeli was the outstanding figure of the Congress and managed to persuade all sides to agreement. He was right when he described his achievement as 'Peace with Honour'. In the process, he managed to add Cyprus to the list of British colonies.

Despite this foreign policy triumph, Disraeli lost the following 1880 election due a trade depression, bad agricultural harvests, and two wars. Disraeli on politics: 'Look at it as you will, ours is a beastly profession'.

He never lost his sense of humour though. When a buffoonish Foreign Office Minister named Waddington managed to survive an assassination attempt, Disraeli expressed satisfaction at his escape. Then he added: "It is just as well. Waddington would have made assassination look ridiculous".

One man who admired Disraeli's efforts at the Congress of Berlin was Count **OTTO VON BISMARCK**, (1815-1898), the Minister-President of Prussia from 1862 till 1890. His views of the English were equivocal: "The English have lost their pluck since they ceased to drink" – but his comment on the English Prime Minister was: "The old Jew, that is the Man".

In contrast, Bismarck's own attempts at diplomacy suffered an embarrassing setback while at the same Congress. After he had offered his arm to the very aged Russian Chancellor, Prince Gortchakoff, Bismarck was seized by an attack of cramp and fell to the floor, bringing the old man crashing on top of him. Bismarck's wolfhound, seeing his master apparently fighting for his life, leapt on the helpless Prince and buried his teeth in his neck. It was with difficulty that the dog was dragged off and Prince Gortchakoff escaped a bad mauling.

Bismarck was a big man with protruding eyes and a horseshoe-shaped down-turned moustache. Known in his youth as 'The Mad Bismarck', he was also a man of vast appetites – women, duelling (he fought 28 duels while still at university), gargantuan feasting, and wine (though, when offered German champagne, he said that his patriotism didn't go that far). *J.E.C. Bodley* described him as 'a sergeant-major become company promoter'.

Contemporary accounts of his family were not flattering. Queen Victoria said of his wife Johanna that she was 'a rather masculine lady who had huge feet'. It was reported that his son, Count Herbert, had pushed two foreign diplomats aside at an official occasion, exclaiming: "Pardon, but I am the Count Bismarck". One of them replied: "Well, that explains it. But it doesn't excuse it."

Bismarck spent his life trying to unite a German nation under Prussia, and then a Europe dominated by Germany. He achieved the first by attacking Denmark in 1864, (thus securing the province of Schleswig-Holstein), then by attacking Austria in 1866, (capturing many of the German principalities). He came close to the second ambition by crushing France in 1870. He had a special grudge against the French, as his mother, when a girl, had only narrowly escaped gang rape by Napoleonic soldiers after the Battle of Jena in 1806.

Bismarck showed something of his mentality when he was rebuked by a Frenchman for firing on the Blind Institute in Paris. He retorted that he found nothing wrong in it: "You do far worse; you shoot at our soldiers who are hale and useful fighting men".

Rennell Rodd reported another of Bismarck's diplomatic gaffes. Throughout his life, Bismarck received hundreds of medals from many countries. One day, he was invited to meet a European monarch who had previously presented him with several medals. He hunted through his possessions for the ribbon and star of a particular order, which he presumed he already possessed.

Unable to find his own, he managed to borrow one and arrived, proudly wearing it on his chest, for his audience with the monarch. To his horror, he found that, not only had the medal never been conferred upon him, but also that the monarch was standing ready to present him with it.

Over the summer of 1877, Wilde also wrote to Lord Houghton. Houghton was the centre of an extraordinary group of Englishmen, some famous, others less so, who busied themselves with the production and appreciation of illicit pornography.

RICHARD MONCKTON-MILNES,
LORD HOUGHTON, 1809-1885

It was in Dublin in 1876, (probably through an introduction by *Professor Mahaffy*), that Wilde met the Yorkshire MP, writer, and socialite, Richard Monckton-Milnes (later Lord Houghton). In 1877, they corresponded on the subject of John Keats' poetry. Milnes had written the first biography of John Keats, while Keats had been the subject of one of Oscar's sonnets. Later, in 1881, Milnes gave Wilde a letter of introduction to help him on his American tour.

Lily Langtry said of Milnes that he was 'the most delightful host in all London' and he seems to have been popular throughout society. Florence Nightingale, once a candidate for marriage to Milnes, said that 'he had the same voice and manner for a dirty brat as for a duchess – the same desire to give pleasure and good'. The American writer, Ralph Waldo Emerson, said that Milnes knew everyone from 'the Chartist to the Lord Chancellor', and paid him a fine tribute; 'the most good-natured man in England, made of sugar'.

The only sour note about Milnes came from the poet William Wordsworth. He may have been upset by Milnes' description of him as 'looking like a benevolent wolf'. When, in 1842, Prince Albert planned a State Fancy Dress Ball, Milnes announced that he was going as 'Chaucer'. Wordsworth, aged 75, was annoyed at being summoned to the same Ball and declared that: "if Monckton-Milnes is going as 'Chaucer', I will go as 'Monckton-Milnes' ".

After the death of his father, Milnes became the owner of a country estate six miles from Pontefract, Yorkshire, called Fryston Hall, (when *Tennyson* stayed at the house he called it 'Freezetown'). Milnes himself was less than thrilled by his inheritance, as he hated country pursuits and longed for London or Paris. Friends said that that he was such a good host that he would do anything rather than be left alone in the echoing mansion.

There was a rumour that the building was so rambling that an American guest found himself continually getting lost. He solved the problem by 'blazing a trail' from his bedroom to the dining room by cutting notches in the wood- panelled walls.

Milnes' political career was a languid one at best. He entered Parliament as a country squire Tory after thoroughly bribing the electors of Pontefract. His opponent had taken a principled stand against corruption and, (as Milnes was paying three guineas a vote), lost dismally. Once installed in the Commons, a friend described Milnes as 'being content to be second rate, which very few people are'.

He stayed an inconsequential MP from 1837 till he was given a seat in the House of Lords in 1863 (becoming Lord Houghton). He said that his peerage was 'the token of a half-success in life – a second class degree in politics'. The one interesting point was his slow drift from Tory squire to Liberal MP (in 1846), then to Radical reformer by the time he reached the Lords. The reason for this was his shock at realising the horrific conditions of English working class life; in particular, he equated crime with poverty.

(In this, Oscar Wilde agreed with him: 'Crime in England is rarely the result of sin. It is nearly always the result of starvation' – 'Our criminals are merely what ordinary respectable, commonplace people would be if they had not got enough to eat'.)

Another point on which they found accord was the Elgin Marbles. Wilde was strongly opposed to the removal of this famous statuary from Athens to London and gave a lecture in which he described Lord Elgin as a thief. Milnes was passionately of the same opinion. When he had been to Athens in 1832, he found that Greek anger was running high. Elgin had presented them with a 'hideous' town clock as compensation for the Marbles. It had been destroyed.

On a more grisly note, Milnes found that Elgin's chief agent, a Signor Lusieri, had been so unpopular that he had had to barricade himself into his own home. The house was attacked and Lusieri died suddenly of a broken blood vessel. Popular rumour insisted that, when the citizens discovered Lusieri's body, a large black cat was seen crouching on his face, sucking the blood – presumably a supernatural response to Elgin's actions.

(The writer *E.F. Benson* held a different view. He thought that Elgin had been correct in removing the Marbles as they would not have survived otherwise. While they had been in

Athens, the Turkish soldiers regularly took pot shots 'to see if they could hit the nose of Zeus or the breasts of Athene'.)

Around the early 1860s, Lord Houghton, as he was now known, met a network of like-minded acquaintances and together they built up the largest and most extraordinary collection of pornography in Victorian Britain.

Chief among his aides were the explorer *Sir Richard Burton* and the poet *Algernon Swinburne*; other, more mundane, members of the group were Henry Ashbee and Fred Hankey. Burton became a staunch friend, and christened a mountain in the Cameroons 'Mount Milnes' in his honour. Swinburne was more reserved: "Houghton was a good-natured old fellow but when made into a peer his title might have been 'Baron Tattle of Scandal'."

The Fryston library specialised in pornography (especially works on and by the Marquis de Sade) and in memorabilia of famous murder trials – one prized specimen was a piece of dried skin removed from a notorious murderer. The pride of the Fryston collection was a magnificent Pradier sculpture of two girls performing cunnilingus on each other. An admiring Swinburne wrote: 'It was the sculptor's last work before he left this world of vulgar copulation for the Lesbian Hades. May we be found as fit to depart – and may our last works be like this.'

Before setting out with Lady Houghton for Sunday morning church, Houghton would advise his guests on which books were the most lubricious. His friends were grateful for this literary knowledge. One young man explained: "I have just brought a charming girl within one French novel of being seduced and I need to find a finisher!"

As censorship tightened in Britain, the group had to turn to smuggling from Europe, often by Queen's Messenger in Lord Palmerston's diplomatic despatches. Sometimes the manager of Covent Garden Opera House, Sir Augustus Harris (who had a rare ability to so manipulate his spine as to create a useful recess between his back and his coat) would bring in the goods. In 1876, a bad fire at Fryston destroyed much of the collection and the efforts to douse it rendered the remainder water-sodden.

Houghton's group were involved mostly in collecting pornography but they also wrote it. A favourite format was the round-robin manuscript, in which each member contributed a few pages of a story then passed it on, ('The Romance of Lust', 1873-6, is one such book.)

[There is a strong possibility that, during the 1880s, Oscar Wilde involved himself in a similar exercise, a homosexual pornographic novel called 'Teleny'. Charles Hirsch, a bookseller, reported that Wilde brought a carefully wrapped manuscript to his shop in Coventry St., London, with instructions to issue it only to visitors producing Oscar's calling card. Presumably having peeped inside, Hirsch added that the book was hand written in at least three different scripts. Oscar eventually called again to collect the completed work.]

One of Houghton's less savoury acquaintances was **FRED HANKEY**, (1828 – 1882), the son of the British governor of the Ionian Islands, and a cousin of a Bank of England director. He lived in Paris and devoted himself to the production of erotica. He inspired the Fryston library and was a main supplier to Burton and Swinburne.

The *Goncourt brothers*, not a particularly squeamish pair, were nonetheless shocked by Hankey's activities: 'A madman, a monster ... Through him, as through a torn veil, we had a glimpse of an appalling aspect, a terrible side to the English aristocracy'. While ignoring Hankey's milder activities, such as the organisation of Swiss whores for pornographic postcards, they were upset by reports of his visits to a London brothel, (run by a Mrs Jenkins), which specialised in the public whipping of thirteen-year-old girls. Hankey: 'First we made them sit in class and then whipped – the little ones not too hard but the big ones very hard indeed.'

On one occasion Hankey hired a room so that he could watch a murderess being hanged while having sex with two women during the execution. To his annoyance, the murderess was pardoned.

Even these tastes paled before Hankey's request in 1863 to Sir Richard Burton that the explorer bring back from his travels some skin sliced from the genitals of living girls so that he could use it as covering for Bibles. Burton regarded Hankey's mania with amusement. He wrote that, owing to an unusual scarcity of Dahomey Amazon execution victims that year, Hankey would have to remain disappointed. He suggested that instead Hankey might try intercourse with 'a Muscovy duck while its head was being cut off'.

When Hankey died, much of his collection passed to **HENRY ASHBEE** (1834-1900). Ashbee was a highly respected City businessman, who became Master of the Curriers Company. It is debateable whether he was 'Walter', the author of the well-known pornographic work 'My Secret Life', in which the hero claimed to have bedded 1,200 women and reported the encounters in graphic detail.

Ashbee maintained that the reason that European erotica was so superior to the English attempts was that in Europe good writers had no scruples about writing about sex, whereas in England the job was left to hacks, (he excepted Cleland's 'Fanny Hill).

Ashbee held the theory that one could define variations in sexual habits by race. He declared that, because of corporal punishment in schools, England was top in flagellation; abortion was partly a French speciality, 'but the palm must be given to the Americans'; sodomy was popular in Turkey and Italy; while lesbianism confined itself mostly to France and Turkey ('and nunneries'). Italy was head of the league in necrophilia, and also in bestiality ('in the rural areas').

Although sexually themed books provided his main stockpile, he also had a magnificent collection of works on the Spanish writer Cervantes. When Ashbee died, his will stipulated that the British Museum could have the Cervantes books only if they accepted his entire library as well – all or nothing. The Museum found itself the possessor of over 1000 pieces of pornography. These works now form the core of its 'Private Case of Forbidden Books'.

SIR RICHARD BURTON 1821-1890

Houghton's great friend, Sir Richard Burton, was one of the most extraordinary Englishmen of any age, let alone the nineteenth century, despite the fact that, for a variety of reasons, he failed in almost all of his goals. His personality, seeming to explode beyond the confines of Victorian society, bore a resemblance to the Nietzchean superman – as *Swinburne* described him: 'at once divine and demonic'.

He was a physically tough man – six feet tall, a very powerful build, with a piercing gaze radiating from his scarred saturnine face. A master swordsman, Burton was capable of accurately firing one of the huge old-fashioned elephant guns from his shoulder after downing a bottle of brandy. He could also speak 25 languages (including Icelandic, Hindustani, Hebrew and Amharic), and was to write 43 books. His passion was to explore the world both literally and intellectually.

Burton was a social Darwinist, who believed in racial natural selection, that it was the duty of the white races to rescue the rest from chaos, and that democracy equalled mediocrity. Among the groups he hated were the black races, Jews, Catholics, socialists, Turks, Americans, the Irish, egalitarians, missionaries, Hungarians, and waiters, (who he insulted on every possible occasion). He did have a slight partiality to gypsies as they had once asked him to be their King.

His particular dislike was reserved for women. He accepted the Arab view of the time that women did not understand honour or scruples, were intrinsically more lecherous than men, and were systematically deceitful.

Although he did marry in 1861, his search for an English wife was lacklustre. He scorned the attitude of the Victorian maidens, summed up, for him, by the story that on her wedding night one girl had chloroformed herself and left a message on the pillow reading: 'Mama says you are to do what you like'.

Meeting one decorous mother who demanded to know what his intentions were towards her daughter, Burton snarled: "Alas, madam, strictly dishonourable, I regret to say, strictly dishonourable". After his marriage, he always set off alone on his travels leaving the terse instruction to his wife: 'Pay, pack, and follow'.

Born in Torquay, Burton spent an anarchic childhood accompanying his parents around Europe. All attempts to control him and his brother Edward failed. When a tutor tried to teach Burton the violin, the violin was broken over the tutor's head. In an attempt to instil self-denial, their mother told them to ignore a pile of cakes in a shop window. The Burton children promptly smashed the window, stole the cakes, and ran. By fifteen, the boys had discovered the Naples brothels, mixed with smugglers in the Pyrennees, smoked opium in Pisa, and learnt to drink alcohol. Their father reacted to the latter with a horrified shout at his son: 'The beast's in liquor!' They were refused entry to the German fencing schools because they were too good.

In 1840, Burton was sent to study at Trinity College, Oxford, an establishment that he despised, feeling, as he said, like 'a good man fallen among grocers'. As his only real interest was the study of mesmerism, he decided to have himself sent down. This was achieved by throwing wild parties and by circulating obscene couplets about the dons. He left in a flourish by driving a coach and four horses through the Trinity flowerbeds and then charging down the High Street blowing a trumpet fanfare.

Burton spent the next seven years in the Indian Army, where he soon isolated himself from his fellow British officers. He preferred to live surrounded by his forty pet monkeys, of which he made a close study. He discovered that they had their own language. For instance, that they had three different sounds for 'enemy', one each for python, eagle and leopard. He also took up snake charming and riding on the backs of crocodiles for exercise.

Burton found that the quickest method of learning languages was in the bed of a native-speaking mistress; in this way he learnt Gujerati and Sanskrit. He avoided the fate of another British officer who learnt Hindustani in the same way; as a result, the officer subsequently spoke of himself in the feminine, to the scandalised amazement of his sepoys.

He also developed his extraordinary talent of disguising himself so well that he could pass as a native. Dyeing his skin with henna and with a false beard, he was able to wander among the bazaars to gain important information on local affairs. Despite his affinity with native culture, he was far from sympathetic to it. He believed in an iron British rule over India; liberal attitudes were seen simply as weakness. The method of executing criminals by blowing them from the mouths of cannons he thought was correct, as it was more humane than hanging.

At the same time, he rejected the 'free market' ideas prevalent at the time, whereby India provided the raw materials and had to import the finished product from Britain. Burton: 'The manufacturing mob wishes to buy dirt cheap from India and to make her pay 100% for working her own produce'.

After his investigation into Indian homosexual brothels revealed embarrassingly that both British troops and the Indian Princes were the chief clients, he was sent back to Britain. His enemies had spread the rumour that Burton himself had been intimately involved in the brothel activities.

72

While passing through Goa, he fell in love with a young Portuguese nun, (incidentally learning Portuguese in transit), and planned an elopement. One night, Burton and two servants broke into the nun's convent disguised as Moslems. Burton kept watch while the servants went ahead to carry off the girl. By mistake they entered the wrong room and grabbed a sleeping sub-prioress. Her screams roused the convent and Burton and his men were forced to run for it. Burton had to abandon the idea.

In 1852, he set out on what was perhaps his greatest unalloyed exploratory success. His aim was to be the first unconverted Englishman to enter the holy city of Mecca; the penalty for an unbeliever to do so was execution. Again disguised as a Moslem, he accompanied the haj pilgrimage from the Red Sea port of Yenbo across hundreds of miles of intense desert heat and marauding Bedouin attacks, first to Medina, then to Mecca and the Great Mosque itself. He wrote and sketched his experiences secretly. The trip was a triumph in itself, but it also carved a love of the desert within Burton. He became an Arab at heart and, although scornful of religion, found an emotional bond with Islam.

Returning to Cairo, he went to Shepheard's Hotel to test his disguise. The British officers greeted his appearance with 'Damn the nigger's cheek' comments until he revealed his identity. (Curiously, Lawrence of Arabia was to repeat this incident many years later). Ignoring the plaudits he would have received back in Britain, Burton preferred to rent a house in Cairo where he indulged in orgies that he said 'beat the Arabian Nights all to chalk'.

Helped by his newfound fame, Burton was able to launch his next venture, that of discovering the source of the White Nile. His first attempt began in 1854. Setting out from Aden, ('the coal hole of the East'), where predictably he had learnt Somali from local prostitutes, he managed to travel to the city of Harar. The local Amir held him as captive for a time, but released him when Burton offered to bring back medicine for the Amir's cough. After a gruelling journey through a waterless, lion-infested, desert area, Burton crawled back to the coast.

Acquiring two new assistants, John Hanning Speke and Captain Stroyan, Burton tried again in 1855. This time he only managed to reach Berbera on the Somali coast, before the expedition was attacked. Stroyan was killed, and Burton received the spear wounds that were to disfigure his face for life. Despite Speke being speared eleven times and escaping while his hands were still bound, Burton considered that he had acted as a coward during the action.

The Crimean War offered a brief diversion to Burton's explorations. Eager to win some military laurels, he arrived in Constantinople to find that there was no post for him in the British Army. He was forced to take a command in a Turkish regiment of Bashi-Bazouks. The Bashi-Bazouks were mercenary cavalry from Albania who regarded daily looting and rape as their main recompense. Russian women were seen as legitimate spoils of war. If none were available, the Bashi-Bazouks would turn their attentions to any women at hand. As this often involved Turkish girls, the regular Turkish troops were outraged and the situation veered towards civil war. Burton's support for his men led to accusations of fomenting mutiny and, after four months, he left to resume his search for the White Nile source.

This time, he set off inland from Zanzibar, and, despite their growing animosity, was accompanied again by Speke. After travelling over 600 miles in 134 days, they reached Ujiji, a village near Lake Tanganyika. Burton was ill throughout the trip and was forced to rest while Speke made further explorations. Burton recuperated by learning Swahili in his usual fashion and fathering several children in the process. Speke returned to Ujiji stating that he had discovered that the source of the Nile was not Lake Tanganyika as Burton maintained, but Lake Victoria.

Speke was the first to arrive back in Britain and claimed the honour of the discovery. A furious Burton returned to find his thunder stolen and, in response, bitterly rejected Speke's arguments. The row rumbled on till 1864, when a conference was called to debate the whole topic. The day before it started, Speke, while out shooting, was killed accidentally by his own gun. Later, Burton was forced to admit that Speke had been right; the source of the Nile was indeed Lake Victoria.

Meanwhile, Burton had joined the British Foreign Office, and, in 1861, was posted as consul to the West African island of Fernando Po, known as 'the Foreign Office grave'. He found it intensely boring; even their language was dull. He reported that the natives used so much gesture that they were unable to communicate with each other in the dark.

To relieve the tedium, Burton set out on various trips to the mainland, telling the Foreign Office that he needed the breaks for his health. Though he explored the further reaches of the River Congo and visited Benin City, (where a man was crucified in honour of his arrival), his main intention was to meet the Amazons of Dahomey. He was not impressed: 'The Amazons are bosh…they are mostly old and all fearfully ugly, their officers are apparently chosen for the bigness of their bums… an equal number of British charwomen, armed with the British broomstick would clear them off in a very few hours'.

He found that King Gelele of Dahomey was: 'much addicted to the fair sex, of whom he possesses as many as he likes'. When Burton presented the king with some pictures of naked white women, Gelele asked where he could acquire live specimens. Burton: 'I told him, Heaven forgive me, a fearful fib and said that in my country the women are of a farouche chastity'.

In 1865, Burton was sent as consul to the town of Santos in Brazil, which he called 'the Wapping of the Far West'. Again bored by his assignment he claimed sickness as an excuse and set off to visit the horrific war then raging between Paraguay and its neighbours.

While in Buenos Aires, he met another English explorer, *Wilfred Scawen Blunt*. Although politically the two men were diametrically opposed, in many ways they had an extraordinary resemblance – both brave to the point of insanity, both Englishmen who despised the English, both outsiders who revered Arabia; they could have been described as twin chevaliers of the Right and the Left.

In fact, rather than argue they settled into a drinking session that lasted many nights. Blunt described Burton at this time: 'He seldom went to bed sober and his dress and appearance were those suggesting a released convict… a countenance the most sinister I have ever seen, dark, cruel, treacherous, with eyes like a wild beast's…. caged but unforgiving'.

In 1870, Burton achieved his ideal posting, that of consul to Damascus. On paper, his credentials were excellent, but his ferocious personality led to disaster. Firstly, his refusal to help the local Jewish moneylenders recover their debts, (Burton said that one money-lender had ruined forty villages by sucking them dry), led to the Chief Rabbi of London complaining to the Foreign Office. Secondly, his relations with the Turkish authorities reached such a low ebb that the governor, Rashid Ali, sent a force of three hundred men to assassinate him. Burton was flattered by the number apparently necessary. Thirdly, as usual, he ignored the Foreign Office instructions to stay in Damascus and went wherever he wished, again using the 'sick note' defence.

A year later he was recalled, the Foreign Office making the excuse that Burton might be the target of another assassination attempt. Burton: "I have been shot at, at different times, by at least forty men who fortunately could not shoot straight. One more would not have mattered much".

By 1872, Burton had reached a nadir. Although he did receive a belated knighthood through his wife Isabel's connections, he was now very poor indeed. His pride always stood in the way of easy solutions. He refused an offer to lead the expedition to rescue Dr Livingstone on the grounds that 'was rather infra dig to discover a missionary'.

His manners proved too rough for English social life. When summoned to meet the Foreign Secretary, Lord Salisbury, Salisbury addressed him with bluff familiarity as 'Burton'. Burton promptly called him 'Salisbury' in return. The Foreign Secretary winced and returned to 'Mr Burton', but Burton continued with 'Salisbury' throughout the conversation.

At an important society dinner, a medical doctor asked Burton how he felt after he had killed a man. "Oh, quite jolly, doctor. How do you?"

The Foreign Office eventually despatched Burton to the city of Trieste, an outpost of the Austro-Hungarian Empire where trouble was unlikely. It was a dreary non-job. Burton spent his time trying to invent a hangover cure called 'Captain Burton's Tonic Bitters'. Again he employed his illness as excuse, this time to slide off and explore the Gold Coast. Infuriated to find that 'our man in Trieste' was actually in West Africa, the F.O. ordered him home.

An F.O. memorandum of the time said: 'I believe that as long as there is a river unexplored or a mountain unascended within Captain Burton's reach, his health will always be impaired until he has accomplished both the one or other, though it may be to the detriment of his consular duties'.

Finally cornered, Burton turned to literature. Using his unrivalled knowledge of Eastern texts, he translated the Indian sex treatise, the 'Kama Sutra', the Persian 'Perfumed Garden' (originally from 16th century Tunis), the sex guide, 'The Gulistan', and a collection of Latin erotica called 'Priapeia'. By 1888, Burton produced his uncensored version of 'The Arabian Nights'.

Burton's friend Lord *Houghton* hit on the idea of evading the censors by creating a fictitious publishing house seemingly based abroad. Thus the printing house of the 'Kama Shastra Society of Benares' was actually in Stoke Newington, London.

After the very successful publication of 'The Arabian Nights', Burton commented: "I struggled for 47 years. I distinguished myself honourably in every way I possibly could. I never had a compliment nor a thank you, nor a single farthing. I translated a doubtful book in my old age and immediately made 16,000 guineas. Now that I know the tastes of England, we need never be without money".

His last great obsession was to publish a fully unexpurgated version of 'The Perfumed Garden', to be called 'The Scented Garden'. He died before it was finished. His wife burnt the manuscript together with all of Burton's lifelong literary collections. She claimed, in the face of an appalled reaction, that Burton had appeared in a dream and ordered it.

The irrepressible *Frank Harris* once invented a cod conversation between Burton and another friend, *Lord Lytton*, the Viceroy of India. Lytton expounded at length on the beauty of prepubescent girls – 'the deathless charm of the androgyne', 'slim as a boy with breasts scarce outlined', 'everything rounded to rhythmic loveliness', 'the most seductive creature in all God's world'.

"You make me tired, Lytton," Burton replied. "You cotquean, you! Your oversweet description only shows me that you have never tried the blue-bottomed monkey".

ALGERNON SWINBURNE 1837-1909

The other renowned figure of Houghton's set was Algernon Swinburne. Although he was Wilde's favourite poet at the time, they met only once and Swinburne was lukewarm about the young Oxford graduate. Swinburne: 'The only time I ever saw Mr Oscar Wilde was in a crush at our acquaintance Lord Houghton's. I thought he seemed a harmless young nobody'.

By 1882, he was describing Oscar as a 'mountebank' and, commenting on the poems of Wilde and his protégé, *Rennell Rodd*, wrote: 'Really these fools are enough to make one turn Wesleyan and contribute in future only to The Methodist Magazine'.

Wilde himself became less admiring later on: 'It has been said of Swinburne, and with truth, that he is a master of language, but with still greater truth it may be said that language is his master. Words seem to dominate him…. He is so eloquent that whatever he touches becomes unreal.'

Possibly the greatest influences on Swinburne's life were his school days at Eton, where, in particular, the English public school punishment of flogging caused his latent masochism to flare into a lifelong obsession.

Eton had a flogging tradition that stretched back at least to the 1550s, when the headmaster, Nicholas Udall, (author of the first English comedy 'Ralph Roister Doister'), was imprisoned on charges of homosexual sadism towards his pupils. (He was soon released and Queen Mary I appointed him headmaster of Westminster School instead).

In the 19th century, another infamous Eton headmaster, Dr Keate, charged each pupil a half-guinea for replacement of birches. It was said that he 'knew their behinds better than he knew their faces'. The actor *Sir Charles Hawtry* reported that on one occasion a list of boys who were to be confirmed was sent up to him. He flogged 56 of them before realising his mistake.

In Swinburne's day, the floggings, known as 'executions', were performed in public. One Etonian wrote that: 'Half a dozen boys were flogged each day. They were held down on the block by two seniors. If you kicked or winced you would get six extra cuts…. anyone who chose might drop in. I have sometimes been one of three spectators and sometimes one of a hundred'. The politician *Henry Labouchere* added: 'If a child wept during the flogging, the other boys were encouraged to beat him as well'.

One Eton master told Swinburne that he only really enjoyed beating boys who were from the nobility. This same teacher, noting that Swinburne was very fair, would chose a dark-haired boy and make them hold each other while he whipped them both.

Eton was not alone in these practices. Westminster School also was notorious for flogging, while at Harrow, one master, Edward Bowen (composer of the school song 'Forty Years On'), insisted on stripping the boys in his charge and spanking them over his knees. The journalist *Herbert Vivian* wrote: 'It was against the rules and traditions but some boys preferred it'.

Even the girls' schools were not exempt; one writer (Ivan Bloch) complained about: 'the excessive whipping of young girls in these schools on the naked posterior and the lascivious habits necessarily resulting therefrom'.

Given these conditions, it is not surprising that any flagellant tendency in Swinburne was greatly increased. Nicknamed 'Pepperbottom' by his schoolmates, he took to dousing himself in cologne to heighten his senses during the beatings. He attempted to stop other forms of bullying by appealing to his housemaster Mr Joynes to save him. Joynes ignored the plea and read him the 23rd psalm instead. When Swinburne left Eton, Joynes said of him: "I did my best for that ungodly boy. He was hopeless'.

Later in his life, when he became friendly with the Houghton set, he begged Sir Richard *Burton* to indulge him in these proclivities. Burton agreed to the request and used to thoroughly thrash Swinburne during their mammoth drinking binges. Swinburne also frequented a flagellant brothel in St Johns Wood, London, where 'two golden-haired and rouge-cheeked ladies' consented to chastise gentlemen 'for large sums'.

Swinburne's contribution to the Houghton pornography collection consisted of works with the somewhat repetitive titles of 'Arthur's Flogging', 'Reginald's Flogging', 'Charlie Collingwood's Flogging' and 'A Boy's First Flogging'.

His cousin Mary shared Swinburne's tastes and they co-wrote a flagellant novel called 'The Children of the Chapel'. (Oddly enough, given the title of the later Wilde short story, the main character was called 'Arthur Savile'). Tragically for Swinburne, Mary married a Colonel

Disney Leith in 1864 and the chance of a possibly ideal partnership disappeared. It was the great romantic loss of his life.

Swinburne was an odd-looking man with an over-large head above a puny delicate body. He had fluffy red hair that resembled that of the Pre-Raphaelite girls. Once, on a visit to the theatre with Jane Morris and Lizzie Siddal, both Pre-Raphaelite beauties, a boy selling programmes did a double take at Swinburne and crowed: "Gawd, there's another of 'em".

Having left Oxford without a degree, Swinburne became friendly with the artistic group known as the Pre-Raphaelite Brotherhood. He moved into lodgings at Cheyne Walk, London, with two of the leading literary figures, Dante Gabriel Rossetti and George Meredith.

However, Swinburne's personal habits soon started to grate on his housemates. He had a very high-pitched voice that turned to falsetto when excited. An acquaintance, Mrs Pollen, said that: "when not drunk, his one idea of rational conversation was to dance and skip all over the room, reciting poetry at the top of his voice, and going on and on with it".

Already annoyed at the breakage of valuable china, Rossetti was furious at having his work disturbed by Swinburne and his equally disreputable companion, *Simeon Solomon*, rowdily pursuing each other stark naked all over the house 'like a couple of wild cats'.

Meredith moved out after Swinburne had thrown a poached egg at his head during a literary discussion. He said that he had only resisted kicking Swinburne down the stairs because he realised: 'what a clatter his horrid little bottom would have made as it bounced from step to step'.

By 1866, however, Swinburne had shot to fame as the author of 'Atalanta in Calydon' and of 'Poems and Ballads, First Series'. The impact on literature was as dazzling as that of Byron's 'Don Juan' five decades earlier; Swinburne came to be seen as an international spokesman on political, religious and sexual radicalism. He was abused as much as he was feted. The books were banned by the WH Smith bookstores and there were demands for a public prosecution. The politician John Morley described Swinburne as 'the libidinous laureate of a pack of satyrs', while Thomas Carlyle said he was 'a man standing up to his neck in a cesspool and adding to its contents'.

Another attack came from America, where the poet Emerson called him 'a perfect leper and a mere sodomite'. This particularly annoyed Swinburne. One day he mentioned to the critic *Edmund Gosse* that he had written a letter to Emerson. Gosse replied: "I hope you wrote nothing rash?" "Oh, no, I kept my temper." "Well, yes, but what did you say?" "I called him a wrinkled and toothless baboon".

The French novelist *Guy de Maupassant*, then aged eighteen, offered an insight into Swinburne's domestic life, after he had been among a group of French fisherman who had rescued the drunken poet from drowning at sea. Visiting Swinburne's cottage in Normandy, he said that it appeared that Swinburne and his companion indulged in sex with their servant boys and with their pet monkey. On a second visit, Maupassant concluded that the monkey had been murdered by a jealous servant boy. Lunch consisted of grilled monkey.

The Russian novelist Ivan Turgenev offered another glimpse into Swinburne's state of mind. He asked the poet what would be his ultimate desire, to which Swinburne exclaimed: "To ravish Saint Genevieve during her most ardent ecstasy of prayer – but in addition, with her secret consent!"

Other than flogging, Swinburne's most salient obsession was alcohol. Wilde stated that Swinburne was not a heavy drinker but that he had such a sensitive temperament that even a small glass of wine would leave him crazed.

Swinburne's antics at the Arts Club in London became a scandal. One night, wild with drink, he tried to find his hat in the cloakroom. He tried on all the hats available and, when none of them fitted, he stamped them all flat. Soon afterwards he repeated the offence when he and a companion made two lines of the hats and squashed them all in a one-legged race. *Sir Charles Dilke* visited the club: "A wreck of glasses attests to the presence of Swinburne".

Charles Cameron, (the envoy rescued by Sir Charles Napier from Abyssinia in 1868), and Swinburne caused further outrage by 'using fearful language' and 'actually embracing each other in some indecent fashion'. The Arts Club Committee called on Swinburne to resign. *Whistler* managed a temporary reprieve when he said that: "You accuse him of drunkenness – well, that's his defence", but further 'gross drunkenness' led to his withdrawal.

He even upset his lifelong hero, the writer *Victor Hugo*, when they eventually met. Having been invited to Hugo's house in Paris, Swinburne drank Hugo's health and, in aristocratic fashion, hurled the glass into the hearth. Never having heard of the custom, Hugo was left grumbling at the shattering of one of his best wine goblets.

At one point, Swinburne lived in Great James Street, London, below the flat occupied by the future publisher, *John Lane*, (then a young man newly arrived in the city). One Sunday morning Lane held a small party, attended among others by *Willie Wilde*, where the guests began to sing excerpts from the new *Gilbert and Sullivan* operetta, 'Trial By Jury'. Swinburne, driven mad by a ferocious hangover, hurtled out of his room, ripped all the doorbell wires out of their box, and began shrieking: "This place is nothing but a dirty pothouse – a dirty pothouse, I tell you!"

During the 1870s, the Reform League, knowing their man only by his literary reputation, invited Swinburne to stand as a Member of Parliament. He replied by letter: 'I don't think it is quite my line'.

By 1879, the situation was getting out of hand. Now suffering from delirium tremens, Swinburne took to smashing all the windows in his new lodgings and cutting himself badly in the process. Rossetti wrote: 'I heard of the frightful scenes in Salisbury St…. These became so fervent that all the old lodgers are packing up and leaving.'

Suddenly, a new figure arrived on the scene who was to transform Swinburne's life. Theodore Watts was a solicitor with literary ambitions and a walrus moustache, who later became a best-selling novelist. (Wilde wrote of one of these books 'Aylwin': 'on the whole a capital book to give to one's parents at Christmas time'). Watts's first encounter with Swinburne was not propitious. Bearing an introduction from Rossetti, he found Swinburne's front door open and walked in. Swinburne was stark naked, performing a berserk dance in front of a large mirror. On seeing the intruder, he drove Watts out in a flurry of blows.

Despite this, Watts insisted on removing Swinburne to his own suburban home, 'The Pines' in Putney. There, for the next thirty years, Swinburne lived almost as a convalescent patient under Watts' strict surveillance. Watts laid down the rules: "Much better to have no such songs and no excitement, to have excellent health and unbroken nights with no disturbing dreams, to walk to Wimbledon, to change socks if wet, to rest afterwards, and then to read Dickens aloud".

The result was that Swinburne's health improved but in *EF Benson's* words: 'although he wrote plenty of verse, he never again wrote poetry'. Wilde commented: "Mr Swinburne once set his age on fire by a volume of very perfect and very poisonous poetry…. Then he retired to the nursery, and wrote poems about children of a somewhat over-subtle character. He is now extremely patriotic, and manages to combine with his patriotism a strong affection for the Tory party".

Over the years, Swinburne's spirit seemed entirely crushed. He had always been fond of risqué limericks but now had to consult Watts over their use. When one visitor arrived, Swinburne meekly enquired: "Shall I tell Mr Brown about the man from Peru?" "I think that goes a little too far, Algernon' came the austere reply.

However, the poet *Richard Le Gallienne* was invited to lunch in the 1890s. 'I watched Swinburne tenderly wiping with his napkin the neck of the bottle of Bass which was his only allowance'. Later, Le Gallienne watched as Swinburne took his daily walk on Wimbledon Common. To his surprise, he saw Swinburne slide into a pub called the Rose and Crown as neatly as 'a billiard ball glides into the pocket'. Questioning the barmaid later, he found that Swinburne made a daily practice of taking a bottle of Burgundy to a private room there and sitting 'alone with his thoughts'.

Watts's rehabilitation of Swinburne was resented by many. Wilde said that Watts was a solicitor and that a solicitor's job was the concealment of crime: 'Swinburne's genius has been killed and Watts is doing his best to conceal it'. Watts made the tetchy reply that Wilde was 'a harlequin'. *Frank Harris* used to describe Watts as 'a sick little walrus'.

In 1896, Watts changed his name to the double-barrelled 'Watts-Dunton'. *James Whistler* sent him a mocking telegram: 'Dear Theodore. What's Dunton?'

The two bachelors remained in Putney for the rest of their lives, both brooding on lost love – Swinburne for Mary, his flagellant cousin, and Watts-Dunton for a gypsy girl he had loved in his youth. After Swinburne's death, Watts-Dunton married Clara Reich, a girl forty years his junior.

The actor *Fred Kerr* once told a story that possibly was based on the Putney ménage. The lives of two gentlemen, (who had been inseparable friends through school and college, and then shared a country cottage together for forty years), were suddenly disrupted when one fell in love and married a woman thirty years younger than himself, leaving the remaining bachelor to move out to other lodgings.

After the honeymoon, the bachelor was invited to dinner with the new couple. After the meal, the bride retired and left the gentlemen to their port and cigars. There was a lengthy pause, then the new husband gingerly asked his friend what he thought of the his new wife.

"Do you want my candid opinion?" asked the bachelor. "Indeed, I do, old friend" the husband replied. The bachelor took a deep breath and said: "I don't really like her at all". The husband gazed thoughtfully at the fireplace and sighed: "No, neither do I".

In 1868, Swinburne had a well-publicised liaison with the notorious American actress **ADAH MENKEN** (1835-1868). Adah had become famous as the 'Naked Lady', after she appeared in a stage adaptation of Byron's 'Mazeppa' riding bareback on a horse and dressed only in a flesh-coloured body stocking that gave a convincing appearance of nudity. She had been married four times, as well as taking numerous lovers, and especially favoured boxers and famous writers.

Rossetti introduced them by paying Adah £10 to sleep with Swinburne. The affair was not successful. Adah said that he was impotent and that she couldn't make him understand that 'biting's no use'. She returned the fee. However, gossip spread that Swinburne was going to write a sequel to his most famous work, entitled 'Adalanta in California'.

As a teenager, Adah had been seduced by an Austrian baron, who had taken her from her New Orleans home, then abandoned her in Cuba. She was forced into prostitution in order to fund her passage home. Fifteen years later, and now the toast of Europe, Adah met the baron again in Vienna. He tried to seduce her once more but Adah refused to submit unless the baron gave her an introduction to the Emperor Franz Josef of Austria.

As the Emperor was a severe man with strict views on morality, it was with some difficulty that the baron managed to arrange for Adah to be presented at a palace reception. As she stepped forward to curtsey to Franz Josef, Adah suddenly stripped off her coat and presented herself naked to the astounded monarch. A furious Franz Josef stalked from the room and the baron was ruined in Austrian society.

Another of Swinburne's acquaintances was the plausible blackmailer and forger
CHARLES HOWELL (1837-90). His method of blackmail was to pretend to share his
victim's more questionable tastes and then threaten to reveal them (to this end, he accompanied
Swinburne on his flagellant brothel trips).

Although his actual death was caused probably by pneumonia, on the night it occurred
Oscar Wilde bumped into Watts-Dunton at the Lyceum Theatre and excitedly told him that
Howell had died the traditional blackmailer's death. "He's been found in the street outside a
public house dying, with his throat cut and a ten shilling piece between his clenched teeth".

Wilde was fascinated by the criminal mind – he said of Howell that 'his touch was
paralysis'. Oscar used to recount the story that Howell's victims had clubbed together once and
raised £200 to send Howell to Australia. Howell had accepted the money. A few months later
one of the victims came across him in Piccadilly and demanded to know why the bargain had
not been kept. Howell coolly replied: "My dear chap, if you had two hundred pounds, would
you go to Australia?"

SIMEON SOLOMON 1840-1905

Another of Swinburne's friends was the painter Simeon Solomon. Solomon had been a
teenage prodigy, exhibiting at the Royal Academy when aged only eighteen. He concentrated
mostly on Judaic themes and his 1860 painting 'Moses' brought him fame and the friendship of
many leading artists including Rossetti and *William Morris. Burne-Jones:* "Solomon was the
greatest artist of us all. We are mere schoolboys compared to him". Wilde had Solomon's
picture 'Love Among the Schoolboys' on the wall of his Tite Street home, and was horrified by
its loss during his imprisonment.

Swinburne was a strong influence on Solomon, (he nicknamed Simeon 'The Lamb'), and
was blamed by many for the later collapse of the young painter's life. Although alcohol was the
main agent of destruction, it was his arrest for gross indecency that that caused Solomon's
career to plummet. In 1873, he was discovered in flagrante with a sixty-year-old stableman in a
public lavatory off Oxford Street, London, and received a six weeks prison sentence.

From then on, Solomon descended literally to the gutter. He became an alcoholic
vagrant, selling matches and shoelaces, and sleeping either in the streets or the workhouse.
Opium being as widely available then as tobacco today, Solomon soon became a devotee. He
was also widely known in the homosexual underworld that flourished around Charing Cross
station. Their activities were so prevalent that respectable hotels in the area placed signs in their
windows reading 'Beware of Sods'.

After Swinburne's rehabilitation in Putney he furiously rejected his former protégé: 'a
thing unmentionable alike by men and women, as equally abhorrent to either – nay, to the very
beasts'.

Wilde was also cautious. Solomon, although an obvious tramp, had appointed himself as
a sort of unofficial guide at the National Gallery, where his remarkable knowledge attracted
listeners and tips. *Rennell Rodd* said that he and Oscar had met a man at an exhibition who
impressed them with his views on art. Wilde had told Rodd: "He is most agreeable but you
should know that he is not a man in whose company we could afford to be seen".

Solomon, in some ways, adapted to his reduced lifestyle quite happily. For 21 years he
lived mostly in the St Giles Workhouse, Seven Dials. When worried friends offered him a more
comfortable home he refused, saying: "Thank you but no. I like it here. It's so central".

The highly respectable society painter, Solomon Solomon found that having to share the
same surname with the reprobate Simeon was deeply embarrassing. One day, Lord Swaythling,
an associate of Solomon Solomon, received a message from an 'S. Solomon' saying that he was

in distress and begging for aid. Swaythling hurried off to assist his friend only to find that it was Simeon who had contacted him. As a result, Solomon henceforth signed his name 'Solomon J Solomon'.

However, SJ Solomon was not the only one to feel aggrieved. WB Yeats said that he had met Simeon one night 'fresh from some low pothouse' and very much the worse for wear. Simeon was introduced to someone who mistook him for 'Solomon J.' Simeon staggered to his feet and bellowed with rage: "Sir, do you mistake me for that mountebank!"

> *On June 13 1877, Henry Wilson, Wilde's half-brother, died in Dublin, aged thirty-nine.*
>
> *In September, Wilde stayed at Clonfil House in Ireland, then in October was reinstated at Oxford University.*
>
> *In November, he found himself in the Vice-Chancellor's Court over the enforcement of tradesmen's debts; he owed money to a tailor and a jeweller for Masonic accoutrements. Oscar once described his outstanding bills as 'black and white spectres of dead dissipations'.*

1878

> *[The Russian-Turkish War ended with the Congress of Berlin.*
> *The Second Afghan War (1878-80) broke out on the frontier of British India.*
> *In Rome Pope Leo XIII, (pontiff from 1878 till 1903), succeeded Pius IX, (who had been Pope from 1846).]*

> *In March 1878 Wilde fell ill with 'an unspecified malady' at Oxford.*
>
> *By May 1st he had recovered and attended an all night fancy dress ball given by Mr and Mrs Herbert Morell of Headington Hall, Oxford. (Oscar went as Prince Rupert). He also attended the Magdalen Commemoration Ball.*
>
> *On June 10th Wilde won the Newdigate Prize with his poem 'Ravenna'. (This prize was founded by the antiquary Sir Roger Newdigate (1719-1806) and first awarded in 1806.) On June 26, he read 'Ravenna' in the Sheldonian before the entire university. Mahaffy and Willie Wilde came over to hear it.*
>
> *On July 19, he gained a first class degree in Litterae Humaniores (Greats) and received a rare double first as well. Oscar: 'The dons are 'astonied' beyond words – the Bad Boy doing so well in the end'.*
>
> *He returned to spend August in Dublin.*
>
> *In October, Wilde stayed with the Sickert family at Neuville near Dieppe, France.*
>
> *Then, in November 1878, Wilde went back to study for his Divinity exam at Oxford. This was required in order to receive his degree. For his last term at Magdalen, Wilde lodged over a chemist's shop at 71, (then 66), High Street – his landlady was a Mrs Brewer.*
>
> *Also during November he made the acquaintance of a young student called Rennell Rodd.*

SIR JAMES RENNELL RODD 1858-1941

Although four years younger than Wilde, Rennell Rodd became a very close friend and admirer during his undergraduate days at Oxford. Rodd also won the Newdigate Prize for Poetry and seemed set to become the successor to Wilde as a leading Oxford aesthete. During the summers of 1879 and 1880, they travelled together in France and Belgium, Oscar under the pseudonym of 'Lord Robinson' and Rodd as 'Sir Smith'.

During some bad flooding in London, Rodd accompanied Wilde when he went to offer help to the victims. Rodd was very impressed by Oscar's behaviour towards an elderly and bedridden Irish woman who had lost her possessions. Wilde gave her money and sat with her for some hours, cheering her up with comic tales of their homeland. The old woman blessed him: "May the Lord give you a bed in glory."

However, Rodd came from a distinguished Cornish family who viewed Wilde with great wariness. Rodd himself began to treat Oscar and his poetry with more scepticism: 'I remember finding Oscar Wilde one morning engaged on a long poem, with a botanical work in front of him from which he was selecting the names of flowers most pleasing to the ear to plant in his garden of verse'. Rodd added that: 'his really genial and kindly nature seemed at times in strident contrast with his egotism, self assertion and incorrigible love of notoriety'.

A lasting rift opened in 1882 after Wilde, during his trip to the USA, found an American publisher for Rodd's poetry. Oscar added an unfortunate dedication to Rodd's book: 'To Oscar Wilde – Heart's Brother', etc. Rodd was angered about this over-effusive assumption: 'When Wilde returned dressed in a fantastic suit of red plush, assuming a sort of Olympian attitude as of one who could do no wrong, we parted in anger and did not meet again.'

Wilde reviewed Rodd's poems as 'healthy and harmless' – damning adjectives in the Wilde lexicon.

After a couple of years in London, (during which he shared the sexual favours of a lady called Jenny Patterson with *GB Shaw* – an unlikely rival), Rodd entered into what was to be a very distinguished career in diplomacy.

He spent ten years in the British embassies at Berlin, Athens, and Constantinople. Then, in 1893, he became acting commissioner for British East Africa.

One of his duties was to investigate passing travellers and, in this capacity, he met an extraordinary Austrian lady who had already travelled alone from the Cape to Nyasaland. She was intent on continuing her journey all the way to Cairo. He made every attempt to dissuade her. The country ahead was reputedly cannibal country, (*Richard Burton* had reported that ' the Wabembe tribe of Lake Tanganyika 'prefer man raw, whereas the Wadoe of the coast eat him roasted'); after that was the Sudan, controlled by the equally dangerous Mahdi. She did not have a hope. Nevertheless, she set out north. Rodd kept a watch for her in later years but nothing was ever heard again. He said: "She was the first victim among the pioneers of the Cape to Cairo route".

Rodd himself became involved in military operations when he accompanied British troops sent to suppress a slaver tribe at Witu, 100 miles north of Mombasa. The campaign was harsh. The column had to march in single file through shoulder-high grass under constant attack by snipers, while at night they were overrun by red ants. They besieged the main stockaded town of Pumwali, which eventually they were able to capture after a navy boatswain had crept under the walls with explosives. Rodd: 'I had no definite duties to perform during the assault, so I smoked my pipe'.

Having caught malaria in 1894, Rodd left East Africa to take up fresh duties in Cairo under *Lord Cromer.* In 1897, Cromer sent Rodd as special envoy to Ethiopia to meet Emperor Menelik. At the time, Europeans commonly called the country 'Abyssinia'. Rodd was able to score a diplomatic point by realising that the Ethiopians disliked this name. (It was an Arab word meaning 'mixed' and a derogatory reference to the variety of races there.) But he objected to the local drink, a brew called 'tej': 'a sea-green viscous liquid in whish dead wasps and other debris floated'. He continued that it was: 'no more appetising when your host strained it through the shirt that he was wearing'.

Rodd's visit was quite successful, in contrast to that of the previous British envoy, Admiral Sir William Hewitt, in 1884. Hewitt was clean-shaven, and the Ethiopian emperor had been amazed to see a grown man without a beard. He assumed that Admiral Hewitt was one of Queen Victoria's palace eunuchs.

In 1908, Rodd became the Ambassador to Rome and was later very influential in encouraging Italy to join the Allies during the First World War. The Germans regarded him as the British evil genius in Italy. He was created Baron Rennell of Rodd, for his services.

Rodd was asked once whether he enjoyed his work in Italy. He replied by describing the perfect life to lead: from 20 to 25, to be a reigning beauty; from 25 to 35, a successful French general; from 35 to 50, a wealthy English aristocrat; and for the rest of life, to be a Roman cardinal. As he could not be the last, he wouldn't mind settling for being the Ambassador to Rome.

WILDE AND CIGARETTES

Oscar Wilde made an oblique reference to Rodd and the Cairo Embassy when he commented on some new cigarettes: "They are rather good, I get them direct from Cairo. In fact, the only use of our attaches is that they supply their friends with excellent tobacco".

Oscar consumed eighty cigarettes a day and said that he was unable to write without them. He used to carry a large biscuit tin of cigarettes with him as he moved from room to room of his Tite Street home. Wilde: 'A cigarette is the perfect type of a perfect pleasure. It is exquisite, and it leaves one unsatisfied. What more can one want?'

The cigarette habit had become popular in England after a British soldier, Robert Gloag, had spotted Russian and Turkish troops smoking them during the Crimean War. Gloag started making what he called 'little scorchers' back at his home in Peckham, London. He used straw-coloured paper and filled in the tobacco from a funnel. He introduced the 'Whiff' in 1871, and founded the church of St Stephen, Peckham, from the soaring profits.

On November 22 1878, Wilde passed the Divinity exam at Oxford and received his BA degree.

1879

[In South Africa, the Zulu War led to the battles of Isandhwana, Rorke's Drift, and Ulundi.
In Britain, Gladstone led the Midlothian Campaign in protest against the atrocities committed by the Turks in Bulgaria.]

PRINCE IMPERIAL 1856-1879

Continuing in much the same imperialistic vein that he had used about *Disraeli's* Afghan expedition, Oscar Wilde wrote the poem 'Prince Imperial' to commemorate the death of the young French Prince Imperial Napoleon-Eugene-Louis during the 1879 British campaign against the Zulus. 'Eagle of Austerlitz! Where were thy wings, When far away upon a barbarous strand, In fight unequal, by an obscure hand, Fell the last scion of thy brood of Kings!'

Despite *Disraeli's* comment that it was 'most injudicious', the Prince Imperial, hoping to win military glory, had joined the British army in Africa. Missing the famous encounters of Isandhwana and Rorke's Drift, he was ambushed by Zulus while out on patrol near Ulundi. Attempting to vault into the saddle of his already moving horse, (a trick he had often achieved), unluckily this time his bridle broke and he slipped to the ground. He was struck eighteen times by assegais and his body was mutilated beyond recognition. When the corpse was returned to his mother in Chislehurst, England, he was identified only by his gold teeth fillings.

The Prince Imperial and his parents, Napoleon III and Empress Eugenie of France, had been ubiquitous figures in the English social scene. The Prince of Wales had introduced him into the London social world, where he had fitted easily into the boisterous antics of 'Bertie's' Marlborough House set. He had once ruined a royal séance by climbing through a window into the darkened room and hurling bags of flour over Bertie, the medium, and the rest of the hand-holding participants.

As a trick on Harry Cust, another Marlborough Set member and perhaps the most lecherous of a highly competitive group, the Prince Imperial and the Prince of Wales hoisted a donkey into Cust's bedroom, dressed it in women's clothing, and persuaded it into Cust's bed to await his arrival.

The Prince Imperial's father, Emperor **NAPOLEON III**, (1808-1873), had lived a colourful life himself. A nephew of the famous Napoleon, he had spent his early manhood trying to restore a Napoleonic Empire in France. After several failed attempts, as a result of which he spent six years in a French jail and much time exiled in England, he finally achieved a successful coup in 1851 and established what *Ronald Gower* described as: 'that Empire that smelt half of gunpowder and half of patchouli'.

His 'gunpowder' side, stirred by his wish to emulate his famous uncle, was displayed first by his involvement with the 1854 Crimean War, then by a war against Austria to free northern Italy in 1859, finally by his disastrous clash with *Bismarck's* Prussia in 1870, which led to his collapse and final exile.

The 'patchouli' impression stemmed mostly from the sexual laxity of the Empire period, led enthusiastically by Napoleon himself. While in exile in England he was reputed to have slept with hundreds of women, and even managed to father a child during his imprisonment in France. Once in control of Paris, he availed himself of the endless opportunities.

Though numerically a great lover, his performance was not particularly remarkable. The Marquise Taisey-Chatenoy said that he looked insignificant in his mauve silk pyjamas, that his premature withdrawal left her unsatisfied, and that during the act he breathed so heavily that the wax on the ends of his moustache melted, causing them to droop.

Among his conquests were the Devon-born courtesan, Cora Pearl (daughter of the composer of the song 'Kathleen Mavourneen', Cora's specialities included nude dinner parties, whipping, and orgies); and the 'most beautiful girl in Europe', the Italian Virginie, Countess Castiglione.

Virginie was actually a spy in the pay of Cavour, the prime minister of Piedmont, who had been sent specifically to inveigle Napoleon into the war against the Austrians. Finding that Cavour had not supplied her with sufficient funds, Virginie was forced to accept an offer of £1000 from the hugely rich Englishman, Lord Hertford, to spend a night with him during which she promised to accede to any demand he made of her. These demands proved to be of such perversity that it took her three days to recuperate. At their next meeting, it was said that they had 'an air of mutual respect' and took care to sit well apart.

Virginie succeeded in her mission to persuade Napoleon into war on the Italian side, but she was suspected of involvement in a bungled assassination plot against him and was ordered to leave Paris.

The Prince Imperial's mother, the Spanish born **EUGENIE** de Montijo, (1826-1920), married Napoleon III in 1853. Although their connubial coupling lasted long enough to produce the Prince Imperial, Napoleon soon abandoned her bed for fresh interests. Eugenie reacted rather oddly.

As a girl, she had been disgusted by the excesses of her own mother who, newly widowed and still young, had celebrated her husband's death by gathering together a group of Madrid women and launching an orgiastic spree. The group were known to kidnap attractive young men for sex parties. One game they devised was to ride the youths like medieval knights while tilting at each other with lances. (Eugenie's mother was also a friend of Prosper Merimee. She gave him the story that he turned into his famous novel 'Carmen', the basis of the later opera by Bizet).

Eugenie's dislike of such wild behaviour was shaken by Napoleon's lapse of sexual interest in her. As a result, she began to relate very risqué stories, tried to seduce courtiers and palace sentries, then started to throw kisses to girls. But if her approaches received any response, Eugenie froze.

One incident was indicative of the attitudes prevailing at the imperial court. One summer's night, Eugenie and a girlfriend, Madame de Pourtales, were playing cards together in the gardens. Suddenly, a masked intruder burst upon them and demanded their jewels at gunpoint. He then ordered them to strip. It was only when they were naked that Eugenie realised that actually he was a courtier playing a practical joke. Hearing guards rushing to their aid, instead of being outraged, Eugenie hid the prankster under the heap of clothes. She commented later: "Naughty, wasn't it?"

When Napoleon's Second Empire collapsed amidst the disaster of the Franco-Prussian War, Eugenie fled from the Paris mobs that were searching for her, and escaped in disguise to England. She was to live for another fifty years as an exile, mostly in her house in Kent. Despite the early deaths of her husband and son, she stayed buoyant, became a respected figure, and a confidant of *Queen Victoria*.

Her later neighbour and friend, *Dame Ethel Smyth*, reported an incident at a very grand dinner, concerning the ex-Empress. At that time, Eugenie used to wear immensely long trains to her evening gown, sometimes trailing behind her for twelve feet. Smyth: 'On this occasion, following in her wake, engaged in affable conversation with the lady on his arm, my father gradually marched up the whole length of that train. Being very short-sighted, he was quite unconscious of what was happening, until the Empress was bent backwards in an arc.'

Despite her apparent resilience, Eugenie never forgot the humiliation that the Prussians had brought upon her family and on France in 1870. In November 1918, at the end of the First World War, she walked down the long boulevard to the tomb of Napoleon Bonaparte in Paris. She produced a newspaper and then very slowly read aloud the terms of the German surrender. She was aged 92.

Never very lucky in military terms, Napoleon III's main attempt at foreign adventure also ended in debacle. In 1863, he persuaded **MAXIMILIAN** (1832-1867), the younger brother of Emperor Franz-Josef of Austria, to accompany the French expedition to take control of Mexico. Maximilian was an amiable gentleman who was far more interested in botany than militarism, but he consented.

Napoleon had been a patient of Oscar's father, *Sir William Wilde*, during his exile, and, on Napoleon's advice, Maximilian also consulted Sir William before his departure.

Once installed in Mexico City, Maximilian was declared Emperor. The Liberal party of Mexico, led by Benito Juarez, objected strongly. At first, Maximilian held his ground, and planned various reforms (including freedom for the Indian population). However, with the ending of the American Civil War in 1865, the American government pressured Napoleon to remove his French troops. Maximilian was left stranded and unable to resist the ensuing revolt. He was captured by Juarez's men and executed by firing squad in 1867 – an event immortalised by Manet's famous painting.

Before Maximilian's capture, his wife Charlotte, aged 26, came to Europe to beg for support from Napoleon and the Pope. They refused point blank. During her travels she became convinced that Mexican agents were trying to poison her with locoweed. (There was a strong probability that this was true). Charlotte gradually started to lose her mind and refused to eat any food offered to her. Once, crazed with hunger, she thrust her arm into a cooking pot and suffered serious burns. She never saw Maximilian again and died still insane sixty years later in 1927.

> *In February 1879 Wilde sold the Bray houses that he had inherited. The sale brought him the sum of £2,800.*
>
> *The same month he finally moved to his first address in London – 13, Salisbury Street, off the Strand and overlooking the Thames – where he shared rooms with the young painter, Frank Miles.*

GEORGE FRANCIS (FRANK) MILES 1852-1891

Wilde and Miles had known each other for some time previously. Wilde had visited Miles's home in Nottinghamshire in 1876, where his father was a vicar. Oscar loved the place, ('I am dallying in the enchanted isle of Bingham Rectory'), and greatly admired Miles's four sisters – 'all very pretty indeed'. Miles made a return visit to the Wilde family's fishing lodge at Illaunroe in Co. Galway, where he painted a fresco called 'Tight Lines'.

Although colour blind Miles won the Turner Prize at the Royal Academy in 1880. His disability meant that his work was restricted to line drawings and, in particular, to skilful likenesses of the 'Professional Beauties' of the time; reproductions of these portraits sold in huge numbers. Chief amongst the 'PB's was the remarkably pretty *Lily Langtry*, who Miles claimed to have discovered.

Miles was a serious student of horticulture and pioneered the revival of the herbaceous border; Langtry said that he was a gardener first and an artist afterwards. His enthusiasm was such that later, when Lily was searching for an independent career, Oscar was horrified to hear Miles suggesting that the most beautiful woman in England should devote herself to market gardening.

Miles and Wilde shared a similar sense of humour. They were both overcome with mirth when, on a visit to London Zoo, they overheard a lady staring in disgust at a hippopotamus and muttering to herself: "Horrible! Horrible! Hardly human!"

In 1880, the pair left Salisbury Street and moved into a small house in Tite Street, Chelsea, that Oscar christened 'Keats House'. It was here that Oscar found himself in the position of having to rescue Miles from the consequences of his sexual peccadilloes.

Miles had been a close friend of *Ronald Gower* but, although possibly dabbling in homosexuality, his real taste was for young girls. Despite these activities taking place prior to the 1885 Labouchere Act (that raised the age of consent from 13 to 16), the legal position was already murky and Miles consistently ended up in trouble.

On one occasion, when Miles was being blackmailed by a woman, Oscar invited her to Tite Street to discuss the matter. Pretending sympathy, Wilde found that she only possessed one copy of some incriminating documents. Seemingly won over by her arguments, he told the woman that he would assist her case but needed to see the papers so that he could satisfy himself as to their validity. The woman handed them over and was flabbergasted to see Wilde coolly place them in the middle of his fire and press them into the flames with a poker. She left the house without extracting a penny.

On a more serious occasion, the police were informed of Miles's dalliance with a 13-year-old girl and arrived at Tite Street armed with a warrant. Urging a terrified Miles to make a getaway through a skylight and across the rooftops, Wilde held the door against three detectives. After they broke the lock, Oscar rammed his hefty bulk against the door long enough for the escape to succeed. The police finally pushed their way in. Wilde: "They were furious and spoke of arresting me for resisting the police in the execution of their duty". He explained that he thought the detectives were fellow artists playing a practical joke and that Miles was actually in Europe. It says much for Oscar's plausibility that they believed him.

Their ways parted after Miles's clerical father read Wilde's poetry and, describing them as 'licentious', demanded that his son sever relations with the poet. Miles obeyed, fearful of losing his allowance. Being reprimanded over the morality of his poetry by a paedophile infuriated Wilde. Declaring he would never speak to Miles again, in a rage he packed his belongings, hurling his trunk over the banisters, (where it crushed a valuable hallstand), and departing by cab into the night.

With Oscar's departure, Miles's world seemed to collapse. His father died; he suffered a nervous breakdown on the eve of his marriage, (which was cancelled); finally in 1887 he became insane and spent the rest of his short life in Brislington Asylum near Bristol.

Wilde returned for a week in Oxford in March 1879.
In April, Edward Burne-Jones visited Wilde at Salisbury St.

SIR EDWARD BURNE-JONES 1833-1898

An early visitor to the Salisbury Street household was the well-known painter Edward Burne-Jones. Wilde had admired his work since seeing the Grosvenor Gallery exhibition in 1877, where paintings by Burne-Jones and *Whistler* had dominated the opening day.

Burne-Jones had been raised in the lower middle-class district of the Bristol Road, Birmingham, England, but had proved himself a bright pupil at school. When his son was refused a university scholarship, Burne-Jones's father turned his house into lodgings. Father and son shared one room together and finally scrimped enough to send Edward, (known as 'Ned'), to Exeter College, Oxford – "the poorest student there".

He soon fell under the spell of the Pre-Raphaelite group led by Holman Hunt, Millais, and Dante Gabriel Rossetti; their main artistic creed being that the death of the artist Raphael in 1520 had marked the end of inspired painting. Their task was to re-invent it. While at Oxford Ned also came under the influence of *Ruskin's* socialism and became a lifelong friend of *William Morris.*

Although initially friendly, Burne-Jones fell foul of his most famous artistic contemporary, *Whistler.* Out of a sense of duty, Ned reluctantly appeared in the witness box on Ruskin's behalf when Whistler sued the latter for describing his work as 'throwing a pot of paint in the public's face'. When asked at the trial if he was a friend of Whistler, he ruefully replied: "I was. I don't suppose he will ever speak to me again after today." He was correct. From then on, Whistler referred to Ned as 'that old amateur'; and when Wilde left Britain by ship to lecture in the USA (partly on the Pre-Raphaelites), Whistler commented: 'If you get sea-sick, Oscar, throw up Burne-Jones!'

Oscar remained a friend and their respective families knew each other well. One of Burne-Jones's best-known paintings was 'The Golden Stairs'. It portrayed a bevy of maidens descending a flight of steps (the models included *Margot Asquith*). When *WS Gilbert* composed his satirical opera 'Patience', the target was not just Wilde, but also 'The Golden Stairs'. Ned enjoyed the spoof, as he did theatre in general. He always relished one line that he had heard in a popular melodrama of the day – 'The man who can lay hand on a woman except in the way of kindness is unworthy of the name of a British sailor'.

Burne-Jones and his wife Georgina shared a happy marriage but, despite his fondness for Georgie, very occasionally he strayed into infidelity. His worst experience happened when he became embroiled in an affair with a Greek woman called Mary Spartali. When he tried to end it, Mary suggested instead that they carry out a suicide pact together. Ned was not keen on the idea.

Mary responded by attempting suicide alone and tried to throw herself into the Regent's Canal, London. By chance, this happened to take place outside 19, Warwick Crescent, the residence of the poet *Robert Browning*. Browning owned some pet geese whose loud cackling sounded the alarm. The police arrived to find Ned and Mary struggling around on the ground, as Ned tried to prevent Mary's leap into the canal.

(They were lucky to escape trouble, as at this time the police tended to arrest potential suicides. In 1877, a Mrs Helen Snee had written a letter requesting poison with which to end her life. The letter reached the wrong hands and she ended up in prison instead).

Burne-Jones, chastened by the experience, became much more reserved in his behaviour. When the *Rani of Sarawak* brought the actress *Sarah Bernhardt* to visit him, Sarah greeted Ned by taking half of her posy of flowers and pushing them down her cleavage. The other half she thrust into the top of his waistcoat. Ned, unnerved by this flirtatiousness, cautiously offered the two ladies afternoon tea. Seeing that things were not going well, the Rani deliberately dropped her teaspoon under the table and, when both she and Ned bent to retrieve it, their heads met. The Rani whispered: "Kiss her". A shocked Ned hissed back: "No!" "Her *hand*, I meant", retorted the Rani. Light dawning, Ned did as requested – and a mollified Bernhardt resumed tea.

At one dinner table, Ned was highly amused when the dignified (but short-sighted) grand dame sitting next to him gently patted his thigh and said: "Good dog". Ned: "I didn't know whether it was better to keep still or waggle enthusiastically".

He gradually settled into a contented life with Georgie. Burne-Jones: 'I suppose I have learned my lesson at last…the best in me has been love, and it has brought me the most sorrow, but it has this supreme excellence, that in its sight no mean thing can exist'.

The family moved out of central London and lived for the next thirty years in the then distant suburb of West Kensington. Wilde called it: 'a district to which you drive until the horse drops dead, when the cabman gets down to make enquiries.'

The Burne-Jones's were a hospitable family and delighted in parties. Ned also liked people to visit his studio and view his new work. He sometimes hid behind the studio door so that he could overhear any comments. This habit once led to him being squashed flat against the wall by a visitor hurling open the door in an over-exuberant entrance.

Wilde recounted a story (in 'London Models') that had originated at the Burne-Jones home. Ned hired a Neapolitan maid who only stayed with the family for one month and was almost totally silent during her stay, speaking only on four occasions. At the end of week one, she burst out with: "I was born on a burning mountain!" After the second week, she confided: "I love Fabio". After the third, she went a little further with: "I will kill Maria!" Finally, at the end of the month, as Ned paid her off, she seized his arm and, with a worried frown, whispered: "You are good man. I tell you secret – for your own good. Do not eat the blue ices!!"

Both Ned and Georgie remained staunch Ruskinite socialists, despite their now bourgeois life. Possibly basing her observation on experience, Georgie said that any relationship between masters and servants were: 'either a bloody feud or a hellish compact'.

Ned never forgot his own humble beginnings and when the impoverished Tyneside poet, Joseph Skipsey, who had been a miner since the age of seven, asked for help, Ned got him a job as caretaker at Shakespeare's house at Stratford-on-Avon. Wilde also helped by reviewing Skipsey's work, saying that there was: 'much that is good and fine'.

Burne-Jones's egalitarian principles came under an unusual strain as he became a prominent social figure. He had been born plain Ned Jones, but his son Philip, aspiring to join the Prince of Wales's set, wished for a more impressive surname and demanded that his parents add the double-barrelled 'Burne-'.

An even greater difficulty arose in 1894, when *Gladstone* offered him a knighthood. Ned was reluctant but again Philip insisted that he accept it. Georgie was scornful of the idea and Ned was terrified that his great friend (and proud socialist) *William Morris* would get to hear of it. Ned wondered to a friend whether he could pay the butlers of London £5 a year to announce him as 'Mr Jones'.

When the details of Wilde's life were exposed during the 1895 trials, Burne-Jones was shocked especially by the fact that Oscar had spent money on rent-boys while his wife Constance was short of cash. Ned lent Constance £150 to tide her over. Later, Ned relented in his attitude to Oscar: "Knowing Oscar's many generous actions and the heavy merciless fist of London society ... I shall speak up for him whenever I hear him abused".

Burne-Jones was friendly with one of the giants of Victorian literature, Mary Evans (1819-1880), who wrote under the pen name of **GEORGE ELIOT**. (Wilde was not an admirer; he disliked her scientific realism. Speaking of one of her books, 'Daniel Deronda', he called it: 'that dullest of masterpieces'.)

George Eliot had an oddly long face, framed by flapping bundles of hair. Once described as looking like 'an intelligent horse', she provided hours of amusement to *James Whistler* and his friend Albert Moore. Moore had a dachshund named Fritz, who the pair taught to sit up with folded paws, while looking down his long nose, with his ears flapping forward. This they called 'Fritz's George Eliot impression'.

Eliot was also noted for her vagueness over the practicalities of life. Burne-Jones was a victim of this weakness. He had attended an evening party at Eliot's house, (described as having 'somewhat of the solemnity of a religious function with the religion cut out'). He walked out into the pitch-black night with directions from Eliot to 'turn right to the train station'. Stumbling blindly along a path, he turned right as instructed. Hearing an approaching train he clambered over a fence, then fell thirty feet through brambles to land upside down on the platform, bruised and shaken. Later, he mentioned the incident to Eliot, who replied: "Oh really – hmm, yes – I probably should have said – turn left".

Probably Burne-Jones's greatest friend was **WILLIAM MORRIS** (1834-1896). He was an inspirational figure to many other Victorians, being prominent as a painter, writer, poet, architect, interior decorator, publisher, manufacturer, socialist and conservationist.

Burne-Jones nicknamed him 'Topsy' (after the character in 'Uncle Tom's Cabin'), because of his mop of black hair and generally unkempt appearance. The actor *Frank Benson* called him 'an impetuous poet-craftsman' and 'a jovial, breezy individual in shirt sleeves and slippers, big and strong and hearty, with a bushy beard and hair'. Morris was well known for his disregard of his personal appearance. During his experiments in the art of dyeing, he was introduced to the composer *Richard Wagner* in London. Wagner was utterly perplexed as to why Morris's hands were bright blue.

Richard Le Gallienne attended a meeting at the London house of the Duke of Westminster and reported that Oscar Wilde, the Duke, and other notables were on the platform preparing to speak when Morris: 'blundered in, like a huge bumble-bee…and making a hurried, rather embarrassed attempt to mount the platform, stumbled and almost fell with an uncouth clatter, which provoked a titter of irreverent laughter'.

Wilde and Morris became well acquainted, Oscar describing him as: 'Morris, our sweet and simple Chaucer's child'. Morris's initial judgement of Oscar – 'Not but what he is an ass; but he certainly is clever too' – mellowed considerably and he later told *GB Shaw* that Wilde was: "such uncommon good company and such a superb raconteur".

Morris was a considerable poet; on Tennyson's death, he was suggested as the new Poet Laureate, an idea he quickly turned down. Inspired by a trip to Iceland and his reading of the Norse sagas, he composed a lengthy series of poems called 'Earthly Paradise', consisting of over fifty thousand lines. He was in the habit of visiting the Burne-Jones's to read the latest extracts; Georgie Burne-Jones said that she had to stab herself with a hatpin to keep awake.

Morris had a particular dislike of modernism, commercial mass-production, and the soulless industrialisation of the new cities. (Wilde agreed with him: 'I would give Manchester back to the shepherds and Leeds to the stock-farmers'.)

On his last visit to Paris, a friend noted that Morris spent much of his time in the restaurant of the newly erected modernistic Eiffel Tower. On being asked why he liked the structure so much, Morris snorted: "The only reason that I spend so much time here is that because it's the only place in Paris that I can avoid seeing the damn thing!"

While he was a fine speaker and publicist for English socialism, sometimes his efforts at public relations failed. Morris: "A dreadful woman has been asking me what is my message to the people of Hackney Wick. I was very nice and did my best. I said I hoped they were pretty well and that I was pretty well and – that was all I could think of. But she wasn't pleased".

After Florence Balcombe rejected him, Wilde was reputed to have proposed unsuccessfully first to Charlotte Montefiore, the sister of a fellow Oxford undergraduate, secondly to Violet Hunt. ('Men often propose for practice' – Gwendolen in 'The Importance of Being Earnest'.)

VIOLET HUNT 1862-1942

Also among the visitors to the Salisbury Street household was the 16-year-old Violet Hunt. Wilde was attracted to her and attended afternoon teas at her parents' home at Tor Villa in Campden Hill, Kensington. He quickly abandoned his efforts to discuss Socialism with her – "It is like talking to a daffodil about political economy" – and instead suggested that they went off to explore Africa. Violet demurred, taking the view that that probably they would be eaten by lions.

Nothing marital transpired from their meetings and when they met again in 1883, she said that Oscar was: 'not nearly so nice'. In her memoirs she wrote that she 'as nearly as possible escaped the honour of being Mrs Wilde'.

Violet was a Pre-Raphaelite beauty, described by the actress Ellen Terry as "out of Botticelli by Burne-Jones". She was a vivacious, flirtatious, tactless and impulsive woman, who created an artistic salon when she inherited Tor Villa from her parents. She worked as a journalist, going on to become a popular, if not a respected, novelist.

The French writer *Andre Raffalovich* said of Violet that her epitaph should read: 'a woman made for irregular situations' – a description given some truth by the fact that she attempted to marry Raffalovich himself (calling him her 'little Russian masher'). Raffalovich was profoundly homosexual.

Violet rejected the sexual conventions of the time and, tiring of various unfulfilled affairs, plunged into a relationship with a 57-year-old married libertine, (and ex-British Consul to Oporto, Portugal), named Oswald Crawfurd. He vastly expanded her sexual horizons, taking her to Hyde Park after dark to observe prostitutes at work. After seven years of fights and reconciliation, during which time she contracted syphilis from Crawfurd, the couple parted.

Violet continued her pursuit of unlikely lovers, including Somerset Maugham and HG Wells, and was herself pursued by the well-known lesbian, Radclyffe Hall. Violet said that she rebuffed the lady but 'found it titillating'.

In 1907, she began a long relationship with the writer Ford Madox Hueffer (1873-1939), later to change his last name to 'Ford'. He was eleven years her junior.

Ford had also been acquainted with Wilde, but had a much more severe attitude to him than Violet. Ford: "I always intensely disliked Wilde, faintly as a writer and intensely as a human being...when I knew him he was heavy and dull. I only once heard him utter an epigram." Ford met Wilde in Paris after Oscar's downfall: 'He was a truly miserable spectacle, the butt usually of a posse of merciless students. Of course, the sight of the young people, like starlings, tormenting that immense owl had a great deal to do with my revulsions'.

The fact that Ford was still married blighted his long affair with Violet, who, with age, now wished for some dignity in her life. Attempts at divorce failed and Ford spent two weeks in jail after refusing a court order to restore conjugal rights to his wife. After ten years of cohabitation, Ford discovered that Violet was syphilitic and left her for another woman.

The scandal caused by their irregular marital status was not helped by an incident involving the poet Ezra Pound. Pound had asked a friend, the sculptor Henri Gaudier-Brzeska, to create a bust of himself, specifying that it should be phallic. Using a half-ton block of marble, Gaudier-Brzeska sculpted what looked like an enormous circumcised penis. It was entitled 'The Hieratic Head of Ezra Pound'.

After it was first exhibited, it was found to be too large and too heavy for the galleries to accept, so Pound left it at Violet's house. The sight of a huge marble phallus on the front lawn did not help Violet's attempt to gain respectability. She said that: 'it had been useful for scaring away burglars'.

The sculpture was deported eventually. Violet wrote that: 'Ezra's sexual organ in extenso has been sent at enormous cost' to a hotel in Rapallo, Italy. Even there it caused trouble, being banned from the hotel terrace as it was thought that the building could not support it. It ended up on loan to the Tate Gallery in London.

In July 1879 Wilde stayed at the Hotel Meunier, Laroche, Belgium, then at Tournai with Rennell Rodd.
During the summer he met James Whistler in London.

JAMES MCNEILL WHISTLER 1834-1903

One of the most famous relationships of Wilde's life was his friendship, followed by enmity, with the American painter James Whistler. Recognising each other as fellow wits, they immediately sprang into a teasing battle of banter.

Their most renowned clash ended in a Whistler victory. At a party, a man had remarked: "It's a good thing that we can't see ourselves as others see us", to which Whistler had replied: "Yes, isn't it. In my case, I'd grow intolerably conceited'. Wilde, off guard, sighed: "How I wish I had said that". Whistler thrust in his verbal rapier: "You will, Oscar, you will".

Just before his wedding, Wilde received a telegram from Whistler. It read: 'Fear I may not be able to reach you in time for the ceremony. Don't wait.'

Oscar was happy to fence back. Although he had a genuine admiration for the American's work: "In my opinion, he is one of the very greatest masters of painting", he could not resist adding: "And I may add that in this opinion Mr Whistler himself entirely concurs".

Wilde inscribed one of his poems on a piece of flimsy tissue paper and handed it to Whistler for his opinion. Whistler read it and handed it back. Wilde asked: "Well, Jimmy, what do you think of it?" Whistler nodded judiciously: "It's worth its weight in gold".

While visiting Whistler's studio, Wilde saw a freshly painted portrait hanging on a wall. Seeing Wilde about to touch it, Whistler barked: "Don't touch that, Oscar! It's still wet". Wilde replied soothingly: "Oh, it's all right, Jimmy. I'm wearing gloves".

At first, the English public tended to bracket the two together as fellow leaders of the aesthetic movement. *WS Gilbert's* light opera spoof 'Patience' was aimed at Whistler even more than Wilde. Some of their behaviour provided the satirists with an easy target for comedy.

Lily Langtry commissioned the architect Edward Godwin to design her intended home in Tite Street, London. When Whistler, Wilde, and *Frank Miles* all appointed themselves as advisors, Godwin attempted to incorporate the flood of their ideas. Lily pulled out of the project when it was found that the triumvirate had forgotten to leave room for a staircase.

However, by the 1880s, Whistler's attitude towards Wilde started to sour. He suspected that Wilde was a poseur whose knowledge of art was limited. He was not alone in these suspicions. The artist *W. Graham Robertson* wrote that: 'despite his attitude as the Apostle of Art, Wilde did not really either care for or understand pictures, a fact that painters very quickly found out.'

Even more infuriating to Whistler was his belief that Oscar was taking his ideas and re-hashing them as his own. He regarded Wilde's essay 'The Decay of Lying' as outright theft. When Whistler said that: "Oscar is an imitator, not an artist', a friend suggested: "He might outgrow that". Whistler snorted in reply: "The sponge is always sponging!"

Oscar defended himself – "It is only the unimaginative who ever invents. The true artist is known by the use he makes of what he annexes and he annexes everything" – and hit back with: "Mr Whistler always spells Art with a capital I".

By the 1890s, their friendship was in ruins and Whistler developed an almost obsessive jealousy for his former ally. He tried to destroy Wilde's reputation in the Parisian artistic circles, advising the writer *Mallarme* to 'hide your pearls', and sneering: "Oscar, the bourgeois in spite of himself".

When Wilde was imprisoned, Whistler refused to sign the clemency petition and, hearing that the newly released Oscar was trying to write a new work, made the scornful comment that the title should be 'The Bugger's Opera'.

Although a short man, with his carefully curled black hair (with one frontal white lock), his monocle, and his cane 'the size of a darning needle', Whistler was a striking dandy. He was well aware of his own merits and rarely missed an opportunity to emphasise them.

When some blank canvases went missing, he was asked whether they were of great value. He replied jauntily: "Not yet, not yet". An admirer said that he only knew of two painters in the world: "yourself and Valasquez". Whistler gave him a basilisk stare and asked: "Why drag in Valasquez?"

He was born in Lowell, Massachusetts, USA, and spent some of his childhood in St Petersburg, Russia, where his father worked as a railway engineer. Returning to America, he attended the military academy of West Point, but in 1854 was expelled for failing his chemistry exam: "If silicon had been a gas, I would be a major-general". Then, in Oscar's words: "Like all true Americans, Jimmy Whistler gravitated towards England".

He was not immediately successful as a painter. One day, he noticed *Benjamin D'Israeli* sitting alone in St James Park. He saw his opportunity and asked the aged statesman whether he would sit for a portrait. D'Israeli gazed back wearily and muttered: "Go away, little man".

Whistler turned to the River Thames for inspiration and spent some time amongst the poor in the East End of London. A friend once advised him that his portrait of a prostitute with the top of her blouse unbuttoned would not be accepted by the Royal Academy. Whistler vowed to repaint it and open another button each year: "until I am elected to the Academy and can hang it myself".

As his fame grew, he turned to portraits. He was commissioned to paint a life-size nude study of the French actress, Cleo de Merode. Cleo arrived with her mother as chaperone and, wearing only a headband, draped herself on a sofa. Whistler was not happy that the headband concealed her ears and stepped forward to rearrange it. Her mother rose with a squawk of indignation: "Oh, no, no, monsieur! Cleo's ears are for her husband alone!"

Aside from his acknowledged artistic genius, the characteristic that struck most of his contemporaries was Whistler's extreme pugnacity. He said himself that: "My nature needs enemies". "A friendship is no more than a stage on the way to a quarrel".

As a younger man this aggression took a physical form. The poet Rossetti composed a limerick: 'There was a young artist called Whistler, Who in every respect is a bristler, A tube of white lead, Or a punch in the head, Come equally handy to Whistler.' It is possible that one cause of his notorious conduct was that he felt guilty over his absence from the American Civil War, (his brother William had a distinguished career in the Confederate Army).

For whatever reason, Whistler could not resist a fight, knocking his brother-in-law through the plate-glass window of a Parisian café, punching the Slade artist Alphonse Legros to the floor of his studio, and being banned from the Burlington Fine Arts Club on the grounds that a club could not survive: 'if a member cannot enter except under fear of being subjected to an assault'. When a labourer dropped some spots of plaster on him from a ladder, Whistler knocked him out cold; he was fined for this offence.

In 1866, he visited Valparaiso, Chile, hoping to paint battle scenes from the Spanish-Chilean War. The only event that took place was the shelling of the city by the Spanish Navy; the only casualty of the action was one donkey. Deprived of more stirring scenes, on the return voyage Whistler took exception to eating at the same table as a black Haitian and punched him in the face. He was confined to his cabin, where a ship's officer came to complain about his conduct; Whistler promptly hit the officer as well. On arrival back at Victoria Station, Whistler got into yet another fistfight with a porter.

As he grew older, his capacity for physical attack lessened and instead he channelled his aggression into legal and verbal challenges. The writer *George Du Maurier* and the painter *Walter Sickert* were among the victims of Whistler's litigious activities, while his action against *John Ruskin* became world famous. But it was in the area of gratuitous insult that Whistler specialised. It was noted by at least two contemporaries that the difference between Wilde and Whistler was that Wilde used his wit to entertain, while Whistler used his wit to damage.

When he was told that the meek, diffident husband of a particularly stately American lady was dead, Whistler replied: "No, not dead – but gone behind". One man who bored Whistler approached him jovially and said: "You know, Mr Whistler, I passed your house last night". Whistler drawled back: "Oh, thank you".

If Whistler held a grudge he was relentless. When the painter William Stott of Oldham exhibited a new canvas entitled 'The Birth Of Venus', Whistler realised with fury that the model was his own mistress, Maud Franklin. During an ensuing argument at the Hogarth Club, Whistler slapped Stott's face. In Whistler's own words: 'I am grieved to add that the first slap was followed by a second one, and the incident closed by a kick upon a part of Mr Stott of Oldham's body that finally turned towards me, and that I leave to specify'.

Stott died at sea. On hearing the news, Whistler grunted: "So he died at sea, did he? Just where he always was."

The only man who intimidated Whistler was the French artist *Edgar Degas*, who a mutual friend described as 'sitting on Jimmy like anything'. In Degas's presence, even Whistler's verbal powers failed. Degas: "His conversation was characterised by brilliant flashes of silence". Once, when Whistler strutted into a Paris café dressed immaculately in top hat and frock coat, Degas shouted across: "Hey, Whistler, you've forgotten your muff!"

Whistler achieved the artistic fame he desired and also, after a series of mistresses, in 1888 settled into a happy marriage with Trixie, the widow of the architect Edward Godwin. He became a renowned denizen of the London suburb of Chelsea and helped found the Chelsea

Arts Club. The club members were amused when one of their fellows, who had reputedly attempted to seduce a servant girl, entered the premises leaning on a stick. Whistler commented to his fellow founder Wilson Steer: "Housemaid's knee, I presume".

Whistler spent a lot of time in Paris; an art school known as the 'Academie Whistler' opened there in 1898. He prided himself on his knowledge of the French language but came to grief when he insisted on ordering a meal at a fashionable restaurant. His companion tried to intervene, but Whistler snapped: "I am quite capable of ordering a meal in French without your assistance!" The friend replied: "Of course you are. But I just distinctly heard you ordering a flight of stairs."

Both Wilde and Whistler agreed on their dislike of one mutual acquaintance, the art critic **HARRY QUILTER** (1851-1907). Quilter epitomised the muscular English philistinism both men loathed. His critical reaction to the vogue for Japanese fans and china was that it would 'turn decent Englishmen into prigs and milksops'. Whistler derided the 'fatuous' Quilter's appearance in checked trousers and bright jackets as resembling a bookmaker's tout and always referred to the critic as ' 'Arry'.

Wilde was no admirer either. Quilter worked mostly for the Spectator magazine. This publication had once described Oscar's sonnet on Keats as blasphemous; noting this, an editor of 'Sonnets of the Century' removed Wilde's work from the book. Oscar responded: 'this is, I believe, the only instance of the Spectator influencing anybody on anything'. Quilter predictably rejoiced over Wilde's downfall: "The fall of the High Priest of aestheticism has struck the public imagination'.

After his 1878 libel case against *John Ruskin* produced only one farthing in damages, Whistler, in great financial difficulties, was forced to retreat to Venice and to sell his beloved Tite Street home, the White House. It was Quilter who bought the house and infuriated its previous owner by redecorating it.

Quilter, fresh from what Whistler described as this 'vandalism', now arrived in Venice to do some sketching of his own. He discovered a beautiful Renaissance doorway and, hiring a gondola, spent five days drawing it. On the fifth day, an incandescent Whistler arrived, also in a gondola, angrily shouting that Quilter had got 'his' doorway. Quilter refused to budge and the row raged on.

Finally, Quilter buckled and, seeing that the canal was too small for two gondolas, invited Whistler to join him in the first one. A still disgruntled Whistler climbed aboard, and the pair spent the next few days sitting in the boat, each silently and sulkily sketching the same doorway.

On 28 Nov 1879 Wilde went to see Henry Irving's performance as 'Shylock' in 'The Merchant of Venice' at the Lyceum Theatre, London.

SIR HENRY IRVING 1838-1905

Despite the rejection of both Wilde's early plays, ('Vera' and 'The Duchess of Padua), Wilde had a great deal of respect for the actor Henry Irving whom he described as 'a marvellous and vivid personality'. He admired the way that Irving had risen above commercialism in order to raise the status of theatre: 'At first he appealed to the few; now he has educated the many'.

They clashed only once. When Oscar's play 'Salome' was banned in 1892, Irving, wishing to maintain the newly won respectability of the stage, supported the censor. Wilde was annoyed that no actor had protested against the ban: 'not even Irving who is always prating about the art of the actor'.

However, during Wilde's downfall, Irving expressed his contempt for the actors who had attacked Oscar; and when Wilde left jail, Irving was one of the few people who sent him an encouraging message.

Henry Irving was without question the dominant figure of Victorian theatre. His great achievement was to restore the stage to the position of being an acknowledged art form, as opposed to the degraded popular entertainment that it had become since the eighteenth century.

He accomplished this feat mostly through his superb acting talent and his single-minded perfectionism. His self-centredness sometimes made him a difficult man with whom to work. *Bernard Shaw* wrote that: 'One thing that is almost beyond conception is the ignorance of theatrical people of any world besides their own, however important. But Henry's single-mindedness reached new realms, even for theatre'. He was a proud and lonely man, but also courteous and extremely generous; many people, including his business manager *Bram Stoker* and his leading lady *Ellen Terry*, revered him enough to forgo their own ambitions to aid Irving's dream.

Physically, Irving did not appear to be well suited to the stage. He was derided for his skinny legs and odd walking gait. (Wilde defended him over this: "Irving's legs are limpid and utter. Both are delicately intellectual but his left leg is a poem"). *Shaw* called Irving's voice 'a highly cultivated neigh'. He was also very short sighted and found his way around stage by guesswork. Nevertheless, the critic *William Archer* wrote: 'This man, who could neither walk nor talk, was yet incomparably the best actor in England'.

Born in Somerset under his real name of John Henry Brodribb, he started his career as a solicitor's clerk. For fifteen years he worked his gradual way upwards in the theatre until in 1871 he triumphed in the London production of 'The Bells' and 'woke to find himself famous'.

His main talent lay in his re-interpretation of famous Shakespearian roles, for instance, playing 'Hamlet' as a gentleman scholar and 'Macbeth' as an indecisive man living on his nerves; both radical departures from previous readings. His most famous break with convention was his performance as 'Shylock' in 'The Merchant of Venice'. Many Jewish people had been offended by the usual villainous portrayals; Irving made 'Shylock' the most sympathetic and dignified figure in the play, an act of imagination that won the gratitude of the Jewish community.

Irving once asked his aged dresser what the man considered to be Irving's greatest Shakespearean role and got the answer, 'Macbeth'. He replied that the general opinion favoured 'Hamlet'. The dresser shook his head: "No, Guv'nor. It was Macbeth. You sweat twice as much in that".

By 1878, his rising theatrical success enabled him to take over the lease of the Lyceum Theatre, (originally the English Opera House), just off the Strand in London. The Lyceum partnership of Irving and his new leading lady, *Ellen Terry*, led to a string of successes that lasted for twenty years. He was aided financially by 'the richest heiress in all England', Baroness Burdett-Coutts.

[Heiress to the Coutts Bank fortune, **BARONESS GEORGINA BURDETT-COUTTS** (1814-1906) became a philanthropist on a huge scale. Wilde was not impressed: 'Philanthropy seems to me to have become simply the refuge of people who wish to annoy their fellow-creatures'. Her wealth attracted a siege of suitors. Unfortunately for her, the one love of her life was Sir James Brooke, the founder of the kingdom of Sarawak, (and father-in-law of the *Rani of Sarawak*), who turned down her proposal. In 1881, aged 68, she married William Ashmead-Bartlett, an American aged

27. A joke circulated in the British press: 'An arithmetic problem – How many times does 27 go into 68 and what is there left over?']

In 1883, Irving took his company abroad for the first of eight tours of the USA. It was another triumph. On the first night in New York, however, he was shocked by the complete lack of applause after the first act. He stumped off stage muttering: "It's a damned frost! Those Yankees are icebergs. I might as well play to a churchyard!" He did not realise that Americans reserved their applause till the end of the play and was delighted by the eventual storm of approval.

Irving introduced some new elements to the theatre, being the first producer to keep the auditorium darkened throughout the play. Also, the Victorian public loved to see sparks flying during the stage sword fights. Tiring of his usual trick of attaching flints to the weapons, Irving tried to adapt electricity to produce the same effect, (aided by Colonel Gouraud, *Thomas Edison's* partner). Before one fight scene in 'Romeo and Juliet', Irving had the swords wired up. As his sword clashed with 'Tybalt's' sword, they connected themselves to the mains supply. They lived to fight another day – but returned to flints.

Irving was fascinated by music hall technique and was particularly fond of the great music hall comedian Dan Leno. Leno, on the other hand, longed to perform a tragic role and became determined to give his own serious rendition of Irving's famous performance as 'Richard III'.

As the times of their performances clashed so often, it was only very rarely that Irving managed to see his favourite comic. One day, they were both booked to appear at Drury Lane Theatre on the same variety bill for a hastily constructed charity show. Irving stood in the wings eagerly awaiting Dan Leno to rush on stage and burst into such gems as his hilarious 'Do You Know Mrs Kelly' routine.

Leno, having no idea that his hero was on the same bill or even in the same theatre, strode onstage in 'Richard III' makeup and costume, and launched into the famous opening soliloquy – 'Now is the winter of our discontent', etc.

Irving's initial surprise turned to annoyance when he remembered that he himself was about to follow Leno onstage with the same speech. Leno, innocently unaware of the gaffe, continued to perform his excruciatingly bad 'imitation' of the great actor. The audience sat aghast, while Irving grew livid with rage in the wings.

Finally Dan Leno realised the situation. He advanced to the footlights, hissed at the orchestra conductor to play some music and, to a storm of laughter from the audience, 'Richard III' danced offstage to the sound of a sailors' hornpipe.

Irving's long quest to gain respectability for the theatre finally bore fruit. Although the previous social stigma attached to the stage had gone, (mostly due to the craze for amateur dramatics among the aristocracy), society still did not regard actors as equals. Even in the 1890s, *George Du Maurier* was reluctant to allow his son Gerald to enter on a theatrical career. This attitude began to dwindle after Irving was knighted on 25 May 1895; ironically the same day that Wilde was convicted.

Irving was less lucky in his private life, not that this upset him particularly. His obsessive relationship with the theatre left him emotionally self-sufficient. His disastrous marriage to Florence O'Callaghan, (who secretly disliked the stage), ended on the night of his triumph in 'The Bells'. As they rode home in a carriage with the cheers of the audience still ringing in Irving's ears, Florence sneered: "Are you going to go on making a fool of yourself like this all your life?" Irving stopped the carriage, climbed down, and walked off. He never returned home and never spoke to her again.

His one concession was to offer Florence a theatre box at his first nights. Florence, nursing a raging bitterness, accepted each time just so that she could unnerve him by glowering with fury throughout his performance. She taught their two sons, Lawrence and Henry, to refer to Irving as 'the antique' and to Ellen Terry as 'the wench'. When Edwin Booth played Hamlet in London she asked Irving for tickets so that: "the two sons of Henry Irving can see a real actor". She was furious when the sons later became reconciled with their father.

Shaw said of Irving that: "he would not have left the stage for a night to spend it with Helen of Troy". Despite the probable truth of this observation, Irving did have some later love affairs. According to Ellen Terry, they became lovers after the first night of 'Hamlet', and towards the end of his life he was close to a Mrs Eliza Aria, a fashion writer who owned several bonnet shops. But, as Ellen stated ruefully: "Were I to be run over by a steamroller tomorrow, Henry would be deeply grieved: would say quietly 'What a pity' and would add, after two minutes' reflection, 'Er…Who is there to go on for her tonight?' "

Most of his affection was lavished on his pet dog, Fussie. On one American tour, Fussie was left behind accidentally in New York. Irving stopped the train and found Fussie plodding along the rail tracks following him to California. On another occasion, Fussie was left in Southampton when the company sailed off to the USA. He walked the seventy miles back to the Lyceum Theatre in London. Irving was distraught when Fussie was killed by falling through an open stage trap door.

As the 1890s came to an end, Irving's theatrical empire began to crumble. Although he produced and performed in some of *Tennyson's* plays, modern drama did not interest him. Shaw attacked him as: 'an actor who thought himself superior of any dramatist, who ordered a play as another man would order a glove'. The extraordinary charisma that he and Terry had produced on stage waned.

Never allowing for any illness on his own part, when he injured his knee on the first night of 'Richard III', there was no understudy ready to take over and the theatre closed with losses of £10,000. Then his immense but uninsured stock of scenery was destroyed by fire. His health was struck by pleurisy.

Most of all, his legendary generosity had left him little financial leeway. One day, he overheard his business manager Bram Stoker refusing to hire an elderly woman for a job at the Lyceum. Irving suggested that she could take care of the theatre cats. Stoker answered that they already had three women taking care of the cats. Irving was not deterred: "You must find her something. Let her look after the three women that are looking after the cats".

In 1902, he was forced to sell the Lyceum. After a performance of 'The Merchant of Venice', he led Ellen Terry out for their last curtain call. The Lyceum closed down in 1904 and became a music hall.

Irving kept touring to stave off bankruptcy and died after giving a performance in Bradford, Yorkshire. The news reached Ellen Terry while she was in a play at Manchester. Shaw reported that: 'the next night she ordered the curtain to go up as usual; she managed to act almost to the end, when she came to the lines – "It's summer gone, autumn begun. I had a beautiful husband once, black as the raven was his hair……. " Then she broke down in grief for her old love and friend and partner, while stagehands quickly lowered the curtain, and the audience filed out of the theatre in silence.'

DAME ELLEN TERRY 1847-1928
Ellen Terry was one of the first famous women to be a recipient of Oscar Wilde's extravagant admiration. After seeing her as 'Ophelia' in Irving's 1878 'Hamlet', he wrote a poem to 'Our Lady of the Lyceum', describing her as: 'like some wan lily overdrenched with

rain' – a metaphor she loved. They became acquainted through the architect Edward Godwin and always remained on friendly terms.

In 1889, when Ellen sat for a Shakespearean costume portrait by the Tite Street based painter John Singer Sargent, Oscar was delighted. "Tite Street, on a wet and dreary morning that has vouchsafed the vision of Lady Macbeth in full regalia magnificently seated in a four wheeler, can never again be as other streets: it must always be full of wonderful possibilities".

Even as late as 1894, she was ignorant of Wilde's sexual inclinations. When he sighed to her actress friend: "Aimee Lowther, if you were only a boy, I could adore you", Ellen was puzzled until *Irving* explained to her. It made no difference to Ellen's regard for Oscar.

During his trials, a veiled lady delivered violets to Wilde's house with a note reading: 'To bring you good luck' – Irving's son Lawrence let slip that it was Ellen Terry. In 1899, she was in Paris with Aimee Lowther, and came across Oscar in the street, 'gazing longingly in the window of a pastry shop'. They gave him dinner and he repaid them with sparkling conversation but 'we never saw him again'.

Terry's acting partnership with Henry Irving made them the pre-eminent theatrical couple of the age. It also brought her great fame, (her photograph was on sale all over Britain), and during the 1880s she earned more money than any other woman in England.

Although very good-looking, like many famous beauties she was careless about her personal appearance; *Max Beerbohm* said that she looked like: 'a Christmas tree decorated by a Pre-Raphaelite'. One observer said that though Ellen was soft and yielding on the surface, beneath she had an ego of steel.

One of her qualities was her sense of fun. The actor *Frank Benson* wrote: 'I have seen Ellen, in one of her irresponsible moods, catch hold of a bit of scenery that was being hoisted to the flies, hanging on with her lithe strong arms and graceful figure till she was some forty feet above the stage. The crew would hastily lower her to the stage. She would then dance an Irish jig to show how much better she felt for the flight'.

When she acted opposite *Herbert Beerbohm Tree's* 'Falstaff', one night she slid a pin into his inflated costume padding and gleefully watched his stomach collapse.

Her light heartedness even infected the serious Irving. They once found a small girl hanging about backstage and asked her what role she was playing. They collapsed in laughter when the girl replied: "Please, mum, I'm a water-carrier, then I'm a little page, and then I'm a virgin".

She also aided Irving over his production research. When researching 'Macbeth', the pair visited Scotland and looked for the 'blasted heath'. They discovered that it was now 'a flourishing potato field'.

Terry once had to deal with a presumptuous young director who spelled out every move and intonation he wished in her performance. She listened carefully, did as he ordered, then said: "Now, if you don't mind, I'll just do that little extra something for which I am paid my enormous fee".

Earlier in her career, she did meet her match. When playing Portia in 'The Merchant of Venice', she had to act with a Mr Sykes in the role of Bassanio. During rehearsal, Sykes, a notorious lecher, advanced on her obviously intent on taking full advantage of the stage direction to 'embrace Portia'. Ellen blanched at the prospect and stuttered: "Oh no, Mr Sykes, all you should do is – er – kiss my hand. It's more Venetian". Sykes leered salaciously. "Come on now, Miss Terry, come on. You're cuttin' all the fat out of me part".

Terry had a tempestuous private life that included, not only her relationship with Henry Irving, but three husbands, one long term lover, and two illegitimate children.

Even as a child she had attracted male attention, being a favourite of the Rev, Charles Dodgson ('Lewis Carroll' of 'Alice in Wonderland' fame) who claimed: "I can imagine no more delightful occupation than brushing Ellen Terry's hair".

In 1864, aged sixteen, she married the successful painter G.F. Watts (1817-1904), thirty years her senior, and according to Shaw, 'a middle-aged, lukewarm gentleman'. The marriage lasted less than a year, as Ellen was bored stiff. According to a very unreliable rumour, she burst in on a dignified dinner party at Watts' home and danced naked on the table.

Three years later, and still legally married to Watts, she eloped with the architect Edward Godwin (1836-1886) to live as his mistress. (Godwin was described by Wilde as 'one of the most artistic spirits of this century in England' and he designed both of Oscar's Tite Street houses.) They produced two children out of wedlock, but by 1874 the family was desperately poor. Ellen left Godwin to return to the stage. Terry: 'He loved me, and I loved him, and that, I suppose, is the reason we so cruelly hurt each other'.

(Godwin may also have been an unsatisfactory bedmate. His wife Beatrice (Trixie), who later married *Whistler*, reported: 'He had an affliction that caused him to wake up in the middle of the night shaking with chills that rocked the bed. He insisted on sleeping under six pairs of blankets and, as we were too poor to afford two beds, I was forced to swelter beside him. One night he demanded a fire and I had to go out and chop wood; this caused me to end up in hospital for three months'.)

In 1878, Ellen married an actor, (in her words, 'a manly bulldog'), called Charles Kelly; they separated in 1881. Then, in 1906, she married a young American actor called James Carew; they separated in 1908. Carew said: "The only way to get on with Nell was not to live in the same house'.

In a comment that also reflected Irving's character, Ellen's son Edward Gordon Craig said that: 'great actresses can rarely make successful wives because they are already married to the stage'.

SIR SQUIRE BANCROFT 1841-1926

Squire Bancroft was one of Henry Irving's friendly rivals in the effort to legitimise the Victorian theatre. Occasionally they acted together, though not often. This was perhaps as well, as they were both very short sighted. When called upon by a play-script to fight a duel, a friend said: "I felt that one or both of the combatants would not leave the stage alive".

Together with his wife, the actress and comedienne Marie Wilton (1839-1921), Bancroft achieved a new refinement both in the profession and in their audience. They managed to bring 'Society' back to the theatre.

Although Squire was not a great actor, he was meticulous over the detail of his productions. The actor *Charles Brookfield* wrote in his memoirs that in rehearsal for one play, Bancroft asked him what age he intended to play his character. Brookfield replied: "I don't really know. Maybe about 55?" Bancroft thought hard for a moment, then suggested: "Or – 56?"

The Bancrofts knew Oscar Wilde in the 1880s. He wrote to Lady Bancroft: 'Dramatic art in England owes you and your husband a great debt' and she wrote an article for his magazine, 'Woman's World'. She told a friend that Wilde: 'once congratulated us, when we wrote some memoir of ourselves, on not having waited, as most people do, until they have lost all memory'. (Oscar made a similar comment in an essay: 'I dislike modern memoirs. They are generally written by people who have entirely lost their memories, or have never done anything worth remembering').

In 1885, after twenty years in the theatre, and now in their early forties, both the Bancrofts retired, having amassed a fortune of £180,000. They spent the next thirty-five years as social figures and as respected theatrical elders.

Brookfield recalled that during the interval of a first night at the Haymarket, (a theatre that Bancroft had once run), *Willie Wilde*, hoping to gain an informed opinion to include in his press review, sat down behind Squire and asked his opinion of the play. Squire frowned then carefully inspected the plush material that covered the stall in front of him. Turning to Willie, he observed: "It was in 1879 that I had these stalls covered – just about eleven years ago. They're as good as new. It shows the advantage of going to a really good firm."

After his wife died, Squire moved into the Albany chambers in London. Each morning he would walk to his bank and check his balance carefully, then stroll on to lunch at the Garrick Club. In spite of changing times, he did not change with them.

After seeing *James Barrie's* new play, 'The Admirable Crichton', a friend asked him what he thought of it. He gave a melancholic shake of his head: "It deals, my dear chap, with the juxtaposition of the drawing room and the servants' hall – always to me a very painful subject'.

Wilde's increasing popularity in social circles stemmed mainly from his extraordinary abilities as a conversationalist. The older fashion for convoluted wit, such as espoused by Dr Johnson, had faded; the flashing rapier of retort was now in vogue and, combined with his 'wonderful golden voice', Oscar's style was ideal. Wilde: "Conversation should touch on everything, but should concentrate itself on nothing'. He was becoming a welcome addition to sophisticated London life.

During the winter of 1879, Lily Langtry visited Salisbury Street on many occasions, often accompanied by her fellow 'Professional Beauties', Lady Lonsdale and Patsy Cornwallis-West.

LILY LANGTRY 1853-1929

Despite his engagements and his lavish homage to many famous women, probably Wilde's only real infatuation was for the magnificent 'Jersey Lily' Langtry. It is likely that they were lovers in the physical sense for a short time. In her old age, Lily always kept an empty chair at her dining table 'in memory of dear Oscar'. When a guest commented that Wilde was a homosexual, she bridled: "You fool, you don't understand. Oscar was a very versatile man'.

Langtry had some reservations about Wilde's personal habits, complaining that his fingernails were often dirty and that 'to me, he was always grotesque in appearance'. However, she added that he had 'a remarkably fascinating and compelling personality' and found his voice 'one of the most alluring that I have ever listened to'. She said that Oscar possessed 'what, in an actor, would be termed wonderful stage presence'.

Wilde, for his part, was besotted, describing Lily as: 'Helen, formerly of Troy, now of London'. Later in his life, Oscar gave a possible glimpse of his true feelings when he said that, while he had never felt jealousy over his wife, he had about Langtry. In his poem, 'Quia Multum Amavi' there is a line that seems an echo of their affair: 'Ah! Hadst thou liked me less and loved me more'.

Lily became irritated by Oscar's obsession with her. One morning, her husband found Wilde curled up on the Langtry doorstep fast asleep. He had waited there overnight on the chance of seeing her. Lily: "I am afraid that often I said things which hurt Oscar's feelings in order to get rid of him".

When she became the mistress of the Prince of Wales, Langtry moved beyond Wilde's milieu. He remained a friend, teaching her Latin and, when her royal lover withdrew leaving her in need of an income, persuading her to become an actress – an ideal career move. His literary influence was obvious in the style in which she wrote her only novel, 'All At Sea'.

Wilde was by no means the only man bowled over by Langtry's radiance. Even the French writer *Victor Hugo*, when aged 78, greeted her with: "Madam, I can celebrate your beauty in only one way – by wishing I was three years younger." She was said 'to move like a beautiful panther'. But, while she certainly enjoyed it for its own sake, she saw sex mainly as her passport to fame and riches.

Her flamboyant sensuality and indifference to gossip was a probable inheritance from her father. He was Dean of the Channel Island of Jersey and, in spite of his position, fathered many of the island's illegitimate children. There was an unsubstantiated story that one one Sunday morning he emerged from church with a woman on each arm. Their jealous husbands, who had been lying in wait, charged out to attack him. Their fury was so great that, when he sidestepped them and slipped away, they continued to blindly cudgel one another in the delusion that the other was the Dean.

Lily grew up as a tomboy, albeit a very pretty one. It was claimed that she once stripped naked and ran up the Deanery lane for a bet; on another occasion she helped tar and feather the King George statue in St Helier, to the outrage of the Jersey islanders.

In 1873, she made her first move into society by marrying Edward (Ned) Langtry, a playboy yachtsman with a moderate but rapidly dwindling fortune. Once installed in London, her beauty was soon recognised and most of the major artists vied for her to become their model and, in some cases, bed partner. This sudden fame soon attracted the attention of Bertie, Prince of Wales.

By 1877, she was his lover and for a period he became besotted by her. He once complained: "I've spent enough on you to buy a battleship!" Lily replied: "And you've spent enough in me to float one!" Their mutual sexual appetite was a standing joke to insiders.

On one occasion, they were the guests abroad HMS Thunderer, captained by Bertie's great friend, *Lord Charles Beresford*. All the cabins were below deck and had to be supplied with oxygen through airshafts. One afternoon, while Bertie and Lily were dallying below, Beresford shut off the air supply. In a state of half dress and gasping for breath, the pair were forced to scramble on deck. An innocent-faced Beresford disclaimed all knowledge.

When Lily became pregnant, the list of her lovers was too long to be able to pick out the father. A story circulated that Bertie and Prince Louis of Battenburg tossed a coin to decide the paternity – Prince Louis won. But whoever the true father might be, Lily knew it was not her husband. Worried that Ned might divorce her over such visibly blatant adultery, Lily asked Bertie to help.

Ned was despatched on a bogus mission to the USA to get him out of the way, (two men were stationed at the port to make sure he boarded the ship). Lily was sent to Paris to give birth. Bertie paid the bills. The baby was born in 1881 and Lily claimed her to be the orphaned daughter of her brother. Ned never realised that his wife had become a mother.

(This episode led to an odd sequel. In 1891, Wilde wrote 'Lady Windermere's Fan' in which the character of 'Mrs Erlynne' had been through a similar experience. He offered the role to Lily who indignantly rejected it. Lily: 'It was for me that he wrote Lady Windermere. Why he ever supposed that it would have been at the time a suitable play for me, I cannot imagine, and I had never contemplated him as a possible dramatist'. In reality, it was far too close to the bone for Lily's comfort.)

The affair with Bertie faltered when he met the French actress *Sarah Bernhardt*. Then, when an over-exuberant Lily pushed a spoonful of ice cream down his neck at a crowded ball, Bertie ended their attachment.

Nothing daunted, Lily continued her conquests, once remarking, "Men are born to be slaves". She preferred to entertain simultaneous lovers, rather than to have consecutive affairs. One of her ploys when an unattended male was available was to swoon gracefully to the floor; a condition that necessitated much loosening of clothes, etc. The brothers-in-law of *Jennie Churchill* offered her riding lessons. One lifted her on to the horse, where she promptly fainted into the arms of the other on the far side. Needless to say, she was actually a superb horsewoman.

She ignored any adverse comment on her behaviour and was amused by such newspaper snippets as: 'We have heard that Mrs Langtry has lost her parrot. That the lady possessed such a bird we were unaware, but we knew she had a cockatoo.'

However, her partial banishment from court circles left her financially embarrassed and out of necessity she decided on a theatrical career. Her fame attracted large audiences in spite of bad reviews. Lily: 'I was never a great actress. But I really loved the stage. I took it very seriously'.

Despite being dislodged from the Prince of Wales's bed by Sarah Bernhardt, Lily studied and admired her French rival; they soon became friends. Sarah's young son Maurice was very keen on boxing and once persuaded the two actresses to try the sport in a New York hotel bedroom. Lily: 'We entered into it with great gusto, Maurice giving timely aid to one or other as it was needed, and we were both much the worse for wear at the finish'.

Lily's theatre tours of the USA underpinned her financial success. They also provided her with many more lovers, including a long-term affair with the young millionaire, Freddie Gebhardt. Wilde often joined the pair for dinner at Delmonico's restaurant in New York during the autumn of 1882.

During the next two decades, Lily's mercenary streak became more pronounced and her life even more wild. She bought a London house at 21, Pont Street, (now part of the Cadogan Hotel), where visitors – including guardsmen, young aristocrats and, occasionally, Bertie – were accustomed to ignore the front door and enter the house via a plank that stretched over the basement well from pavement to dining room window. A besotted admirer hired rooms opposite and trained a gun on all male callers.

Not content with Gebhardt's millions, in 1891 Lily became the mistress of a hugely rich Englishman called George Baird. Known as 'The Squire', Baird was thuggish heavy drinker. He surrounded himself with a coterie of horseracing touts and pugilists who amused him by beating up public houses. He had been ostracised from society after shoving the Marquess of Hartington out of his way at a race meeting. When challenged, Baird drawled idly: "Beg pardon, my lord, I thought you were a bloody farmer".

Lily herself became part of the debauched lifestyle, once being ordered by Baird to come downstairs from her bedroom to witness a drunken orgy. She was the victim of several beatings at his hands, her only consolation being Baird's insanely extravagant presents by way of apology. On one occasion he hurled a bundle of paper in her head – the bundle consisted of fifty thousand pounds in notes. On another, after hitting her in the face, he bought her a 220ft yacht named the 'White Ladye', (it was popularly renamed the 'Black Eye'). In 1893, Baird died suddenly in New Orleans after a massive drinking spree.

Her experiences with Baird gave Lily a knowledge of and love for horse racing. She became a very successful gambler, (her criminal contacts from the Baird days introduced her to a gambling trick whereby provincial race results could be obtained by telegraph before the betting had closed in London).

She became acquainted with the famed Bob Sevier, a man who had won £40,000 at chemin de fer in three days at Monte Carlo, and £57,000 in one Ascot Week. Once during a court case, a counsel described Sevier as 'a gambler, pure and simple'. He snapped back: "Gambler, yes. Pure, perhaps. Simple – No!"

Lily was now wealthy enough to compete in the male-dominated world of racehorse ownership, where her stable ran under the colours of 'Mr Jersey'. In 1897, she became the first woman to own a winner, (Merman'), of the Cesarewitch race.

It was ironic that the press reportage of her racing triumph was coupled with news of her husband's death. Ned, with the constant humiliation of his public cuckoldry, had become an alcoholic. He finally reached the stage of visiting railway stations where she was expected, then disappearing before her arrival, being unable to bear the sight. Later he would question the porters about her appearance and demeanour. On the night of the Cesarevitch win, Ned died insanely drunk in Chester asylum.

Lily had become confident and hard, intolerant of weakness, and particularly scornful of other women. Once, having given a lift to a young member of her cast, she threw the girl out into the stormy night, miles from home, after she had made a flippant remark about Lily's sex life. Although she later claimed to have supported Oscar Wilde verbally during his trials and financially afterwards, she did neither.

After a fleeting marriage in 1899 to Hugo de Bathe, (twenty years her junior), Lily continued to go her own way, collecting lovers, racehorses, and money. She gave up the stage and retired to a house in Monte Carlo.

In 1925, she wrote a bowdlerised autobiography called 'The Days I Knew'. When criticised for its blandness, Lily replied: "You don't really think I would ever do such a thing as to write my real reminiscences, do you?"

In one passage she did make a revealing comment: 'Life has taught me that beauty can have its tragic side. It is like great wealth in that respect. It promotes insincerity, and it breeds enemies. A really beautiful woman, like a very rich man, can be the loneliest person in the world. She is lucky if she knows her friends.'

Lily Langtry's fellow 'Professional Beauty' was Lady **GLWADYS LONSDALE** (1859-1917 – born Herbert), the daughter of the Earl of Pembroke. Very beautiful and over six feet tall, she was married to the Earl of Lonsdale in 1878. When he died in 1882, Wilde's mother *Speranza* suggested that Oscar himself might marry Glwadys, but instead she chose Lord de Grey, (later to inherit the title of the Marquess of Ripon). Oscar remained friendly and in 1894 he dedicated his play 'A Woman of No Importance': 'To Gwladys, Countess de Grey'.

EF Benson said of her that: 'At heart she was a Bohemian, while socially a great lady on a pinnacle'. Her husband Lord de Grey, nicknamed 'the shooting machine', was the best shot in England but, apart from that accomplishment and his luxuriant moustache, was an uninspiring husband. Glwadys relieved the tedium of married life by teasing him with such tricks as dropping trays of cheap crockery behind his back so he would think his best dinner service had gone.

When this amusement palled she turned to lovers, among them the Russian dancer Nijinsky and the *Prince of Wales's* friend Harry Cust. When she found that she was sharing Cust's favours with Lady Londonderry, she stole her rival's love letters and read them aloud at tea parties, before posting them on to Lord Londonderry.

By the 1890s she found her true interest in music and opera, and held sway as the main patron of the Royal Opera House, Covent Garden. She was instrumental in promoting the English debuts of the opera star *Nellie Melba*, the Russian ballet impresario *Sergei Diaghilev*, and the singers Jean and Edouard de Reszke.

Jean de Reszke was the cause of some amusement at Glwadys's musical soirees. He had a long beard that he tried to improve by rubbing paste into it to increase the sheen. The paste actually stiffened the beard so that when he smiled his beard would open into two parts exactly like the claws of a lobster.

Glwady's main musical associate was a prominent London solicitor called Harry Higgins who became Chairman of the Covent Garden Opera Syndicate and the manager of Covent Garden for 33 years. He was known for his brusque manner when dealing with the demands of prima donnas.

After one diva had given him endless trouble during a concert season, he asked her to walk with him to the front of the stage. Gesturing at the Covent Garden auditorium, he exclaimed: "Isn't it beautiful". When she agreed, Higgins went on: "I want you to have a good look at it because it is the last time you are ever going to see it from where you are standing".

When another singer demanded an absurdly large fee for her performance, Higgins stared at her perplexedly and said: "But we only want you to sing!"

Another of the 'Professional Beauties' who visited Wilde's Salisbury Street home was **PATSY CORNWALLIS-WEST** (1858-1920). Born Mary Fitzpatrick, (but nicknamed 'Patsy), she was described by her future mother-in-law as 'merely a beautiful Irish savage'. Her mother, Olivia Taylour, in her youth had been the partner in a rare extra-marital fling by Prince Albert. A furious *Queen Victoria* banned Olivia from court.

Patsy continued the family tradition of service to the throne by becoming a mistress of *Bertie, Prince of Wales*, and, by the age of 21, giving birth to two daughters and one son. Significantly the latter, George, was raised with the help of Bertie's money.

To avoid obvious scandal, Bertie married Patsy off to a complaisant husband, the 35-year-old William Cornwallis-West, Lord Lieutenant of Denbighshire. Patsy proved to be a turbulent bride, who enlivened his home, Ruthin Castle, by tobogganing down the staircases on tea trays.

During a dinner party for the Langtrys, Lily commented on the absence of their host. Patsy explained that she had had an argument with her husband and locked him up in the wine cellar. (This incident may have been the origin of the remark by Lady Bracknell in Wilde's 'The Importance of Being Earnest': 'It would put my table completely out. Your uncle would have to dine upstairs. Fortunately he is accustomed to that'.)

Patsy was among the 'professional beauties' who posed unpaid for photographs in dresses by the couturier Monsieur Worth. They were the first fashion models. Oscar Rosenberg, the editor of the magazine 'Town Talk', attacked the practice as moral turpitude. Unfortunately for him, he went too far in his innuendo by adding that the model: 'returns home to assume fresh positions, put on other costumes, and be taken backwards, full face, in profile'. Patsy and Lily Langtry promptly sued him. Rosenberg was arrested and sentenced to two years imprisonment by the notorious Judge 'Hanging' Hawkins.

Patsy had many affairs, including with the *Beresford* brothers, but none brought her more trouble than that with Sergeant Barratt. When the First World War began, Patsy, now in her fifties, nursed and seduced the young soldier while he was convalescing near her North Wales home. When a neighbour threatened to expose 'the debauching of our fighting men', Patsy used her contacts to return Barratt back to the army.

The press caught scent of the affair, questions were asked in the House of Commons, and the politician David Lloyd George, (hoping to use any evidence of aristocratic misdoing for his own ends), took up the case against her. In 1916, an Army Court of Enquiry branded Patsy's conduct as 'highly discreditable' and the press hounded her as 'The Wicked Woman of Wales'.

Things did not go entirely Lloyd George's way, as Patsy's evidence revealed her sex life with the now late King Edward VII (Bertie), that the Prime Minister *Asquith* had a lover, and that Lloyd George himself maintained several mistresses. Lloyd George ordered that the relevant papers be sealed for 100 years.

1880

[In Britain, Gladstone became Prime Minister for his second term.
In Ireland, the Land League agitation began.
In South Africa, the First Boer War started in the Transvaal. The Boers defeated the British at
Majuba Hill and Gladstone withdrew the army. The Convention of Pretoria in 1881 granted independence to
the Boers, but Britain still claimed suzerainty.]

In March 1880, Wilde applied unsuccessfully for a job as Inspector of Schools (a post previously held by the poet Matthew Arnold).

He finished writing his first play 'Vera: or The Nihilists'. This work was heavily influenced by events in Russia; he gleaned inspiration from several sources including the Russian revolutionary Stepniak.

'Vera' has been described by the critic Terence de Vere White as 'a drama of unique inadequacy', and its author as 'a charlatan and wholly an amateur' (New York Times in 1883). However, in the character of 'Prince Paul', Wilde created the first of his dandy-heroes, with such lines as 'My dear count, life is much too important a thing ever to talk seriously about it'.

SERGEI STEPNIAK 1852-1895

The play 'Vera' was based loosely on a real incident in 1878 when one Vera Zasoulich attempted to assassinate the St Petersburg police chief. It must have appeared a relatively safe subject when Oscar began writing it. However, his efforts to have the play produced were dogged by real life events – nature irritatingly mirroring art.

Assassination became a difficult topic when in 1881 both the American President Garfield and the Russian Tsar Alexander II were killed. The latter's assassin had made seven previous attempts and finally succeeded by throwing a primed bomb hidden in an Easter cake into the Tsar's sleigh; her name happened to be Vera. Tsar Alexander was the brother-in-law of the Prince of Wales.

When Sergei Stepniak succeeded in assassinating General Mezentsev, the Russian chief of police, reality had definitely strayed into Wilde's dramatic territory. Oscar postponed his attempts to stage the play.

Wilde became acquainted with Stepniak when the anarchist arrived to live in exile in London. An aristocrat by birth, Stepniak (born Sergei Mikhailovich Kravchinski) had sympathised with the sufferings of the Russian peasantry under Tsarist repression and spent time in prison because of his views. He escaped to fight against the Turks in 1876, and then to attempt an anarchist uprising in northern Italy. He used these military experiences to compose a book on guerrilla tactics.

After his successful stabbing of General Mezentsev, Stepniak escaped firstly to Switzerland, then to England. He settled into a mellow existence in Bedford Park, Chiswick, and wrote books on nihilist politics; *Bernard Shaw* described him as 'an amiable middle-aged gentleman'. His experiences proved useful to other writers; Joseph Conrad gained much information for his novel 'The Secret Agent' from Stepniak.

Despite the gentle pace of his later life, Stepniak also died violently when he was hit by a railway engine as he tried to cross the tracks at Chiswick station.

Wilde made a later reference to Stepniak in his short story 'Lord Arthur Savile's Crime', renaming him 'Rouvaloff, a young Russian of very revolutionary tendencies'. When 'Lord Arthur' explains that he needs an explosive clock, 'Rouvaloff' replies: "So you are taking up politics seriously, then?"

Having completed his play 'Vera' and before events made production difficult, Wilde approached some of the leading actresses seeking their participation in the production; Genevieve Ward and Helena Modjeska were among them.

DAME GENEVIEVE WARD 1838-1922

Although friendly towards Wilde and appreciative of his compliments about her 'noble acting', the American born actress Genevieve Ward turned down the offer of appearing in 'Vera'. She did consent to have tea at Wilde's home in Salisbury Street.

Ward was the granddaughter of the mayor of New York and had enjoyed a wealthy upbringing until her father, Colonel Ward, lost most of his money on bad speculations. While she was eighteen, a Russian aristocrat, Count Constantine de Guerbel, proposed marriage, only to disappear when he found that she was not the moneyed heiress he had expected.

The Ward family immediately travelled to St Petersburg where Genevieve's father used his contacts to inform the Tsar of the situation. The Tsar then ordered Count Guerbel to marry Genevieve or face exile. During the ceremony Colonel Ward stood behind the wedding pair with a shotgun as the vows were exchanged. Genevieve wore black. The Archbishop offered his congratulations to the newly married couple, whereupon the bride and her family marched out of the church to a pre-arranged carriage and left for the border. Guerbel was left standing on the church steps, never to see his wife again. She refused a divorce and abandoned all notions of marriage.

Ward started her career as a soprano singer and found some success at La Scala and Covent Garden before a bout of diphtheria destroyed her voice. She was forced to turn to acting: 'It was a bit of a feat, though I say it. I had to seal up all the music cells of my brain and refit with new office furniture of memory, quite another thing'. With the aid of *Bram Stoker*, in 1879 she found a play, 'Forget-Me-Not' that turned her into an established theatre star.

Her fame was such that it attracted a backstage visit by *Bertie, Prince of Wales*. Genevieve had a small but bad-tempered dog called 'Tek'. Bertie entered her dressing room accompanied by the Duke of Edinburgh and the Duke of Teck. When her dog hurled itself, barking and snapping, at the newcomers, Genevieve screamed: "Down, Tek! Down! Basket, Tek!!" The Duke of Teck stared at her astounded. Bertie was vastly amused and went off chuckling: "Basket, Teck, basket!"

Ward toured the world performing plays and wrote entertainingly of her travel experiences. She was impressed by the winter townscape of Minneapolis, USA, where: 'the inhabitants build, out of blocks of ice, large castles and statues before many of the shops. The ice is shaped with red-hot knives. The cold is so persistent that the things last for months, and are quite an ornament to the city'.

She played in India, Australia, and then New Zealand where she wrote that: 'Wellington must surely be the windiest place in the world. They say a man has to hold his hat on, except when he turns a corner of the street, and then he has to hold his head on'.

In South Africa, she met the Boer leader, President Kruger, but found him an unattractive character. 'The first thing he did was to use the back of his hand as a pocket handkerchief. Then he opened his cavernous mouth in a gargantuan yawn'.

As an actress who had previously been a singer, Ward was well placed to judge some of the more bizarre practices of her fellow performers. She played opposite the greatest tenor of her day, Sims Reeves, in an adaptation of Walter Scott's book 'Guy Mannering'. Half way through the play, under Reeves's instructions, two stage villains carried on a piano, then departed with a cry of: "I hear footsteps – let us disappear".

At this, Sims Reeves walked onstage and remarked: "Ah; here is a piano; let us have a little music". He then proceeded to regale the audience with 'Come Into the Garden, Maud', before himself departing. The villains reappeared exclaiming: "Ha, ha, they have gone; let us take the piano with us" and, suiting action to words, trundled the instrument off into the wings. None of which had any relevance whatever to 'Guy Mannering'. As Genevieve wrote: 'Sims Reeves had no sense of the ludicrous'.

HELENA MODJESKA 1840-1909

Wilde also approached a well-known Polish actress called Helena Modjeska over the possibility of starring in 'Vera', praising her 'graceful fancy and passionate artistic nature'. She was puzzled by Oscar: "What has he done, this young man, that one meets everywhere? He has written nothing, he does not sing or paint or act – he does nothing but talk".

While turning down the play, it was reported that she allowed Wilde to translate her poem 'Sen Artysty' (The Artist's Dream') into English – something of an achievement, as he did not speak Polish.

Modjeska (born Helena Ophid), while a fine actress, was even better known for her devotion to Poland and her detestation of its triple occupation by Austria, Prussia and Russia. In 1848, aged eight, she had witnessed the killing of her countrymen when the Austrian army bombarded her native city of Cracow.

In 1863, while she was acting with a travelling theatre company, an insurrection broke out across Poland. In old age she recalled the sadness and guilt she had felt when, after her company had performed 'grand, inspiring and heart-rending' patriotic songs and speeches to a regiment hastily recruited from the boys of Lemburg, these same boys were slaughtered fighting hopeless odds.

She endured tragedy in her own life when, after her infant daughter died, her husband Gustave Modrzejewski left her.

By 1868, things started to improve when she married the man who was to be her lifelong companion, Karol Chlapowski, and she had a theatrical triumph at the Warsaw Imperial Theatre.

Although Poland was now peaceful, the theatre was subject to strict censorship. A production of Shakespeare's 'Hamlet' was refused a licence because it concerned the murder of a king. An influential friend of Helena managed to have the ban revoked by explaining that: 'the murder was a family affair, and therefore perfectly harmless'.

Then the phrase 'he was a slave to his passion' had to be rewritten in case the word 'slave' provoked the audience. 'Negro' was deemed less offensive by the censor. The resulting line 'he was a Negro to his passion' caused bewilderment.

Helena had her share of stage mishaps. In one show, she had to stand on the battlements of a stage castle and fire a pistol that 'killed' a man below. While the scene was in rehearsal, the supposed victim of the gunshot sent along a substitute. At the following rehearsal the substitute sent along his own substitute. This last extra proved unsatisfactory, so the director replaced him with an elderly stagehand. On the first night, the original extra, the two substitutes and the stagehand charged on stage together. Helena fired her pistol and all four fell dead from the single shot. Helena wrote: 'The public was put into a hilarious mood'.

The Warsaw Theatre box office was run by a man called Zalewski. He was knowledgeable about Warsaw society and enjoyed putting this knowledge to use when allocating the seating. Therefore, deadly enemies would find themselves in adjacent seats, as did recently divorced couples or jealous wives with their husbands' mistresses. He would also arrange for entire rows of bald men or use them to create patterns; during the show he would sit in the gallery and gleefully survey his handiwork.

Helena and Karol's house became a centre for liberal thought and, as such, came under constant police surveillance. The pressure grew so great that eventually the couple decided to leave Poland to try their luck in the USA. In 1876, together with four friends, they arrived in New York.

Helena thought the city to be 'a monstrous, untidy bazaar', but what really upset her was the New York habit of men sitting in rocking chairs and putting their feet up on the windowsills. 'You can see and admire the size of their shoes in the hotel lobbies, the barber shops, the clubs, and even in some private residences. Wherever you turn, these soles stare at you'.

They left the East Coast and made for San Francisco with the intention of farming orange orchards. One of the first people Helena met was a fellow Pole called Captain Piotrowski, a hugely fat old soldier. Helena assumed that he also was a refugee from repression, but Piotrowski told her the real story.

It transpired that his wife had been French and extremely fond of garlic. The captain was allergic to garlic. "I suffered agonies when I saw that pretty, refined wife of mine smacking her lips after each spoonful, for I knew I had to avoid contact with her for at least twenty-four hours". Piotrowski, on the other hand, adored cheese, which his wife hated. When a cheese dish arrived at the family table, she would leave it; while the captain would do likewise when the garlic came.

They lived in a state of compromise until their first child was born. Then garlic appeared incessantly. Piotrowski: "It was an open war and I, who had stood bravely in the ranks against the Russian army, succumbed in this domestic battle and like a miserable coward ran away and stopped only when I reached the USA".

The farming venture failed completely and Helena realised that the family could be saved only by her return to the stage. As she did not speak English, she settled down and memorised one hundred words a day.

Soon she felt able to approach a Californian manager and request an audition. Unfortunately she had kept no press cuttings of her former career and the manager assumed she was simply a stage struck amateur. Dismissively, he gestured for her to start her audition speech. At the end of it, he approached her with tears in his eyes and promised to promote her in any way possible.

With her name now changed to Modjeska, her debut in San Francisco was sensational; soon New York acclaimed her as well. With stardom came American press advertising. She was astonished when she was billed as 'Helena Modjeska, Countess Bozenta' and soon stopped it. "In this free and republican country people are crazy for titles".

Her press agent insisted that she carry a pug dog around with her as "all prominent stars have pet dogs". She was also surprised when she was reported as having lost her stage jewels, until the agent told her that: "every great star always loses hers at least once a year".

(On a Mid West tour, she took a production of 'Hamlet' to one theatre. The company was amused to find the instruction – 'Do Not Spit In This Trough' – written on every wall around the stage. Unable to resist, 'Polonius' finished his famous advice to 'Laertes' with the sotto voce addition of: "And please do not spit in this trough".)

When she arrived in London in 1880, her reception was equally enthusiastic. She was puzzled that her voice intonation in her recitals of Polish poetry could reduce English women to tears even though they could not understand the language. Modjeska: "Or, as that cynical person Mr Oscar Wilde remarked, to have tickled with my voice the tendrils of their nervous system".

When she met her fellow countryman, the violinist Henry Wieniawski, he told her that the most annoying thing about the English was their habit of chatting during musical recitals at the soirees. One night, he got revenge.

108

He had noticed that, when the National Anthem was played, the English went silent and rose to their feet. When he started his piece the conversation level rose, so he slid into the Anthem and everybody stopped speaking; as he finished it and returned to Brahms, the racket increased, so he returned to the Anthem. This happened again and again and he managed to gain a measure of attention. When he stopped playing no one realised what he had been up to. They simply wondered at this odd piece of music in which the National Anthem had been repeated eleven times.

Despite her success in Europe and the USA, Modjeska remained conscious of the plight of her native land. She told one Londoner that she was a Pole: 'He looked as if he wondered whether from the North or South Pole'. She was dismayed at how little anyone cared about the situation. " 'Poland? Where is it?' they ask. We are not on the map any more – and therefore we do not exist'.

In 1884, Helena gave a return performance in Warsaw. At the time the Polish language was forbidden. A 16-year-old schoolboy, the only son of a widow, threw flowers onstage to Modjeska. They were bound by a ribbon in Polish colours and bore an inscription in Polish. For this act, on orders from the Minister of Education, the boy was expelled from his school and forbidden entry to any other school. The boy returned home and shot himself through the head.

Nine years later, in Chicago, Modjeska allowed her rage to explode and gave a fiery speech denouncing the Prussian and Russian governments. Reports of this speech reached the European press and thence the Tsarist authorities. When she returned to Warsaw in 1895, she was advised to leave immediately and police escorted her on to the next train. An imperial decree, (which was never rescinded), was issued barring Modjeska from entering any part of Russian territory.

She settled in California for the rest of her life. When she died her body was buried back in her hometown of Cracow.

The cartoonist George Du Maurier began to lampoon Wilde in Punch magazine.

GEORGE DU MAURIER 1834-1896

Wilde was not the first of the aesthetes to be satirised by the brilliant cartoonist George Du Maurier. In fact his first attacks had begun back in 1873 and had been aimed specifically at the fad for blue and white china initiated by Rossetti and *Whistler.* Du Maurier always insisted that his target was 'not one person at all, but a whole school'. The fact that these cartoons predated Oscar's growing fame proved that Wilde had borrowed a persona that had been established already.

Nevertheless, when Oscar did emerge as the best known of the aesthetes, he was a wonderful subject for Du Maurier's caricature. An 1880 example showed a young couple gazing in rapture at a china teapot. The (Wildean) man: 'It is quite consummate, isn't it?' The (even more Wildean) woman: 'It is indeed! Oh, Algernon, let us live up to it!'

Wilde and Du Maurier were useful to each other in that Du Maurier needed the comic subject while Oscar needed the publicity. Oscar certainly bore no resentment over his treatment; perhaps he did not feel it necessary. It was *Edward Burne-Jones* who commented about Oscar: "Say what you like, there is more wit in that man's little finger than in du Maurier's whole body".

Du Maurier (nicknamed 'Kiki') had been a talented art student working in the Parisian Latin Quarter and Antwerp when, aged 23, the loss of his left eye due to a detached retina forced him to stop painting.

In 1860, he returned to London and acquired a job on Punch. For the next thirty years he drew weekly cartoons for the humorous magazine, skewering the foibles of upper and middle class life. His pictures had a wide circulation and much influence. It was said jokingly that Du Maurier's partiality for tall women and his penchant for elongating their skirts in his drawings raised the height of the average English girl by several inches.

He created a permanent English joke when he drew the cartoon still known as 'The Curate's Egg'. A bishop: 'I'm afraid you've got a bad egg, Mr Jones'. Ingratiating young curate: 'Oh no, my lord, I assure you. Parts of it are excellent!'

He was not impartial in his observations and often indulged his personal dislikes. He especially abhorred the sensationalism of bad women novelists. (Wilde shared this distaste and reviewed one book, 'Astray' by Charlotte Yonge and three other writers: 'It has taken four people to write it, and even to read it requires assistance'.)

Other targets included the self-consciously aristocratic. Grateful but beggarly recipient of a handout: 'Bless you, my lady! May we meet in heaven!' Haughty donor: 'Good Gracious! Drive on, Jarvis!'

Also, elderly spinster ladies came under scrutiny. Miss Priscilla (who lives on the coast): 'Yes, it's a beautiful view. But male tourists are in the habit of bathing on the opposite shore, and that's rather a drawback.' Fair Visitor: 'Dear me! But at such a distance as that…surely….?' Miss Priscilla: 'Ah, but with a telescope, you know!'

His precarious eyesight, (and therefore precarious income), was always a trial to Du Maurier. After he married in 1863, he remained devoted to his wife Emma and his five children and chose to settle in the middle-class London area of Hampstead. Both the family and Hampstead provided him with the security he craved.

(Two of his daughters had difficult marriages. Isabel married the drama critic Clement Scott but, after producing four children, they separated acrimoniously. Sylvia married a young barrister called Arthur Llewelyn Davies; the marriage was unhappy and they both died very young. Their children were brought up by *Sir James Barrie* and were the inspiration for his play 'Peter Pan'.)

By the 1890s, Du Maurier grew bored with cartoons. With the encouragement of *Henry James*, (who described Du Maurier as 'a delightful little fellow'), he turned to writing novels. One of them, 'Trilby', was a nostalgic remembrance of his early art student days in Paris. It was influenced by Henri Murger's book 'La Vie de Boheme', which also provided material for Puccini's opera 'La Boheme'.

'Trilby' was a triumph both in Britain and the USA and sold over 200,000 copies. It was adapted to become a highly successful play and gave *Beerbohm Tree* one of his greatest roles as 'Svengali'.

However, the novel also brought trouble to its author. Many of the characters in 'Trilby' were based on real people whom he had known in the Parisian ateliers. One of them was *James Whistler* who, objecting to his portrayal as the character 'Joe Sibley' and spoiling for a fight as usual, tried to prevent further publication.

Du Maurier agreed to remove the character from his book and, tongue in cheek, replaced 'Sibley' with a new character called 'Bald Anthony' – 'a touching and beautiful character…. a yellow-haired Switzer, son of a respectable burgher of Lausanne, who is tall, stout, strikingly handsome and rather bald' – the antithesis of the American painter. Whistler, not realising that he was being sent up, crowed: "Never was humble pie to such a sickening extent as has been gobbled by the miserable Du Maurier!!!"

Du Maurier himself commented on the incident: "I shall tell Jimmy in the most abjectly fulsome terms of adulation I can invent that he's the damned'st ass and squirt I ever met".

Now ill, Du Maurier found himself and his book the subject of ruthless commercial exploitation. 'Trilby' songs, shoes, sausages, ice-cream moulds, kitchen ranges and, famously, the Trilby hat flooded the market. Deeply disillusioned, he died in 1896, an event his friends claimed was precipitated by the stress.

During the 1880s, the Punch staff went for a holiday to Paris. Du Maurier wanted his colleagues to see the house where he was born. Well fortified with wine, they set off by carriage, till they came to a small house that Du Maurier indicated as his birthplace. No sooner had they alighted and toasted the cottage than Du Maurier said with a puzzled frown: "Ah, no, it was that one over there", and pointed to a larger house opposite. Trooping off in other direction, they duly toasted the new residence.

Ten minutes later, as they drove back, Du Maurier suddenly stopped the carriage with the words: "My apologies. It was that one over there. That's where I was born". This time he waved to an even larger house. As this building was next door to a hostelry, the Punch group climbed out and spent the next hour celebrating the new birthplace.

After they had staggered back to the carriage, the journey home was interrupted yet again by Du Maurier's spotting of a magnificent mansion in the distance: "Heavens above. I've been absolutely wrong. *That* was the place!! Come on".

At this his companions rebelled, declaring that he had been born in three places already and they were not budging again until he had made a final decision. They returned to their Parisian hotel with Du Maurier grumbling that he couldn't remember where he 'had bloody well been born'.

As well as Whistler, the artist **EDWARD POYNTER** (1863-1940) was another of Du Maurier's student companions in Paris. They stayed in touch during their later years of success in London. Du Maurier said of him: "When his stomach is in order, and he has got out of bed the right way, and the wind is in the proper quarter, and there are no dukes or duchesses within hail, he can be one of the most delightful companions in the world".

Wilde was not an admirer of Poynter's work, even after Poynter had been knighted for his efforts. When he was imprisoned in Reading Gaol, the Governor sent for Oscar to inform him of the death of a relative, then added: "It may interest you to know that Mr Poynter has been made President of the Royal Academy".

Wilde replied: "I am grateful to you for your kindness in telling me about my poor aunt, but perhaps you might have broken Poynter to me more gently".

Another of Du Maurier's artistic acquaintances was **WILLIAM FRITH** (1819-1909). He specialised in large-scale realistic canvases such as 'Derby Day' and rejected other contemporary schools of painting. He dismissed both the Pre-Raphaelites and the Whistler Impressionists: 'The Pre-Raphaelites offer overwrought details, the Impressionists no details at all' – and predictably acted as witness against Whistler in his 'pot of paint' court action against *Ruskin.*

In his painting 'Private View of the Royal Academy, 1881', he unwisely made Wilde the butt of an attack. Oscar was portrayed as a tall man in a top hat surrounded by acolytes. Frith: 'I wished to hit the folly of listening to self-elected critics in matters of taste whether in dress or art. I therefore planned a group, consisting of a well-known apostle of the beautiful, with a herd of eager worshippers surrounding him'.

Wilde struck back with a comment on Frith and his ilk: 'If they have not opened the eyes of the blind, they have at least given great encouragement to the short-sighted'. When Frith's 'Derby Day' (first shown in 1858) was bought for the nation, Oscar concocted a scene where: 'a lady gravely asked the Academician if his celebrated picture of 'A Spring Day at Whiteley's' or 'Waiting for the Last Omnibus' was really all painted by hand?' – 'And was it?'

On 3 June 1880, the 'Agamemnon' by Aeschylus was performed by the amateur dramatic society at Balliol Hall, Oxford. This important theatrical event had been suggested by Wilde. Amongst those students involved were Rennell Rodd as scene painter, and Frank Benson who produced the show and who played 'Clytemnaestra'.

SIR FRANK BENSON 1858-1939

Frank Benson had become acquainted with Wilde in 1879. Although never a disciple of the increasingly famed aesthete, Benson thoroughly enjoyed his company. One day, while chatting to Wilde in a London street, Benson heard a passer-by call out: "There goes that bloody fool Oscar Wilde!" Benson was delighted when Oscar blithely remarked: "It's extraordinary how quickly one gets known in London".

In later years, Benson kept his respect for 'that savage, irresponsible, talented being'. 'Wilde was something much more than a needy drawing-room society jester or decadent gaol-bird'.

At Oxford, Benson was known as an outstanding athlete; he shone at football, rowing, cricket, and running (winning the three mile race against Cambridge University). On an unofficial level, he was involved in the 'Alpine Club', the object being to climb all the chimneys and spires of the Oxford colleges. An especially dangerous feat, that of jumping the four foot, six inch high, spiked iron railings of the Main Quad was named 'Benson's Leap' after his performance.

However, Benson's real interest lay in the theatre and the success of the 'Agamemnon' shaped his future. After *Henry Irving* saw the production, he suggested to Benson that the English theatre needed a trained mind to build a company capable of achieving genuine intellectual stature. Benson accepted the challenge and, on *Ellen Terry's* advice, joined the world of touring theatre to gain experience.

For several years he had a worm's eye view of just how degraded the Victorian theatre, and its conception of Shakespeare, had become. Once in Dundee, (a town, Benson said, that: 'regarded the Tay Bridge disaster as a judgement against travelling on the Sabbath'), he came across a travelling theatre that gave versions of the classics. The producer asked Benson if he could borrow six muskets for 'Hamlet'. Benson discovered to his amazement that they gave nine performances of the play between six and ten each evening. The producer explained: "But then, you see, we cut out most of the words and get on with the combats".

During his own touring performance as 'Hamlet', Benson was in the middle of 'To be or not to be' when he heard a loud growl behind him. Turning round, he found himself face to face with a large black dog that eyed him critically. He proceeded with the soliloquy, punctuating the speech with the odd back kick at the animal. Benson: 'Certainly the house was breathless with excitement. Bets were being offered and taken on the result of the man-and-dog fight now proceeding.'

Benson backed up and kicked the dog into a corner, hoping that a stagehand might seize the hound. Because of its evil reputation, all the stage staff in the wings had fled. Benson threw his cloak over the dog, gave it a thundering kick, and proceeded with his soliloquy. To the delight of the audience, the dog crawled out from under the cloak and charged at Benson. 'The excitement rose to fever-heat. "Two to one on Hamlet!" – "Three to one on the pup!" were now to be heard in all parts of the house.'

Benson drew his sword and warded off the dog's attack with the flat of the blade. 'Still reciting Shakespeare at my loudest, I beat, pushed and kicked the snarling spawn of Satan into the prompt corner.'

Seeing the prompters running for the exit, the dog hurtled after them into the wings, where a courageous doorman rammed a fire bucket over its head and hurled it into the street.

Sometimes even Benson could upset the dignity of a theatrical event, albeit accidentally. The actress *Elizabeth Robins* once witnessed Benson's performance as 'Shylock'. At the end of the play, thinking the curtains were closed, he executed a flying leap over the furniture, 'Jewish gaberdine clutched about him and long legs in the air', before landing 'greatly astonished before an equally astonished audience that was giving him an extra curtain call'.

In 1886, his reputation had grown so much that he was invited to take over the annual Shakespearian spring festival at the Memorial Theatre, Stratford-on-Avon. During the next thirty-three years he provided the plays for twenty-eight festivals. He offered one of the greatest pieces of advice for budding actors – they must develop: 'hearts of fire, heads of ice'.

Also in 1886, he married an actress called Gertrude Samwell; they produced a son and a daughter. (Gertrude knew Wilde but was less admiring than her husband. She said of him: 'Unfortunately, when Wilde made a witty remark, he always repeated it, and dished it up on many occasions'.)

In 1916, after an evening performance and still dressed in the bloodstained robes of 'Julius Caesar', Benson was knighted by George V. It was the first time that the ceremony had been carried out in a theatre, and probably for the first time with a stage prop sword.

At Stratford, Benson drove his actors, (the 'Old Bensonians'), and his staff hard. He once rehearsed 'Macbeth' for seven hours without a meal break. When Benson reached 'Macbeth's' line: 'They have tied me to a stake', 'Banquo' was heard to mutter: "I wish they'd tie me to one".

One of the main aims of the Memorial Theatre was that every play of Shakespeare should be performed on its stage. Year by year, Benson pushed on single-mindedly towards this goal. A stage carpenter, after spending two solid days and nights preparing scenery, growled: "Thank God! That's another bloody king gone".

WILDE AND SPORT

Benson always remained interested in sport, especially cricket, and was well known for placing advertisements for new actors such as: 'Fast bowler to play Laertes'. Wilde, on the other hand, refused to play cricket on the grounds that: "the attitudes assumed are so indecent".

Oscar relished teasing the athletically minded. When a school sports master praised the teaching of football, Wilde replied: "Football is all very well as a game for rough girls but it is hardly suitable for delicate boys". He enjoyed presenting an effete image: "I am afraid I play no outdoor games at all. Except dominoes. I have sometimes played dominoes outside French cafes".

The truth though was quite different. Frank Benson said that Oscar was 'possessed of an extraordinary muscular strength that you often find in big, loosely built Irishmen'. He added that only one man, (who rowed number seven in the Varsity Eight), had 'a ghost of a chance in a tussle with Wilde'.

There were many occasions on which Wilde showed his liking for field sports, including 'capital hare shooting' at Clonfin in Ireland, fishing at Illaunroe and with the fishing boats at Torquay, and lawn tennis at Bingham Rectory with *Frank Miles.*

Although his horsemanship was not good, he did manage to negotiate the difficult mountain paths in Greece. He practised some boxing while at Oxford, and was a first rate swimmer. He admitted that 'mountain climbing is not my forte'.

Robert Ross said that Oscar was 'an enthusiastic if indifferent golfer'. Wilde himself said that he liked golf because he could talk while playing. When his possessions were sold off in 1895, a set of golf clubs was amongst the items.

Also present in the audience for the Balliol 'Agamemnon' were the two great poets of the age – Robert Browning and Alfred, Lord Tennyson.

ROBERT BROWNING 1812-1889

Wilde was introduced to the poet Robert Browning at Balliol, and later sent him a copy of his poems with a comment on the 'delight and wonder' that Browning's work had given him since boyhood.

Browning himself had translated Aeschylus's 'Agamemnon' in 1877, but there had been some complaints over obscurities in his text. *Professor Tyrrell* of Trinity, Dublin, said that when he read Browning's version he needed to read the Greek original to find out what the English meant.

Browning's later work often met similar criticism. Once, when he attended a meeting of the Browning Society, he was asked what he had been trying to convey in a particular work. Browning was unable to remember.

He became known originally for less taxing poems, such as those ubiquitous fixtures of future poetry anthologies, 'How They Brought the Good News from Ghent to Aix', 'Home Thoughts from Abroad', and 'The Pied Piper of Hamelin'. His later work included the monumental 'The Ring and The Book' (1869), of which Wilde wrote: 'Browning used poetry as a medium for writing prose'.

Browning's appearance belied his position as a leading poet. The American *Sam Ward* said that he looked more like 'a bank president in Boston', while another American described him as 'a perfected butler'. Wilde (in 'Dorian Gray') wrote: 'Good artists exist simply in what they make, and consequently are perfectly uninteresting in what they are. A great poet, a really great poet, is the most unpoetical of all creatures. But inferior poets are absolutely fascinating. They live the poetry that they cannot write'.

Yet Browning's romantic disposition found expression in 1846 with his famous courtship and elopement with his fellow poet Elizabeth Barrett of Wimpole Street, (the subject of many later films and plays). Elizabeth wrote a superb series of poems about this episode called 'Sonnets from the Portuguese', (changed on Browning's advice from her original title 'Sonnets from the Bosnian').

They lived a happy life mostly in Florence, Italy. One of their few disagreements concerned Elizabeth's involvement with spiritualism and a Scottish-American medium called Daniel Dunglas Home. Browning loathed the man and referred to him as 'Mr Sludge'.

(Home's other devotees included the *Empress Eugenie* and *Napoleon III* of France. At one séance, Napoleon asked the medium to summon both Napoleon Bonaparte and King Louis Phillippe from the spirit world. During the session, Napoleon III received a mighty kick on the bottom. He was unable to discover who had delivered the spectral rebuke.)

When Elizabeth died in Browning's arms in 1861, he left Florence forever. On his return to London, Browning was bathed in sympathy and was enshrined in the public mind as the tragic romantic, mourning his dead lover. The American writer, *Gertrude Atherton*, reported that, although Browning was now desperate to marry a young girl, he dared not shatter his public image.

Instead, he purchased a house in Warwick Crescent, Maida Vale, where he lived for the next 25 years. Becoming, in *Le Gallienne's* words, 'an indefatigable diner-out', Browning was taken to task by *Tennyson* over his love of London society. Tennyson: "I once told Browning that he would die in a white tie, and he rather liked it".

Wilde had an embarrassing dinner experience in the company of Browning. He had accepted an invitation to dine with a Lady Delarey. A few days later, having been invited to another dinner party where he would have the opportunity of meeting the great poet, Oscar cancelled the Delarey party on the excuse that he had to 'go north'. (This anticipated the future Wilde quip: 'I am prevented from attending by a subsequent engagement').

Unfortunately for Oscar, an unsuspecting Lady Delarey cancelled her own party and also arranged to attend the Browning dinner. Just as he was deep in conversation with Browning, Oscar was horrified to see the door open and Lady Delarey appear. Fixing him with a stony glare, Lady Delarey rasped: "So this is what you mean by 'going north'!" She never spoke to him again.

ALFRED, LORD TENNYSON 1809-1892

Together with *Queen Victoria* and *Gladstone*, Tennyson was one the three great public figures of Victorian society. Wilde met and liked the poet: "Grand old man. I spent a delightful afternoon with him. He is not only a poet, but a poem".

Describing him as the 'Homer of the Isle of Wight', Wilde was puzzled by Tennyson's ability to rise above domesticity: 'How can a man be a great poet and lead the life of an English country gentleman? Think of a man going down to breakfast at eight o'clock with the family, and then writing 'Idylls of the King' until lunchtime'.

Tennyson entered Trinity College, Cambridge, in 1828, but left without a degree. While there he became a close friend of another student, Arthur Hallam. One evening, Tennyson was present at one of Hallam's wine-parties at his rooms in the New Court of Trinity. Suddenly an angry Senior Dean entered the room and demanded: "Mr Hallam, what is the meaning of all this noise?" Hallam replied: "I am very sorry, sir, we had no idea we were making a noise". The Dean snorted back: "Well, gentlemen, if you will all come down into the Court, you will hear what a noise you are making!"

Tennyson slowly built his reputation as a first-rate English poet with such works as 'Locksley Hall' and 'Morte d'Arthur', but it was the death of Hallam that inspired his great poem, 'In Memoriam'. This work made him the obvious choice to be the next Poet Laureate following Wordsworth's death in 1850.

In the same year, he married Emily Sellwood, a marriage that proved to be both enduring and extremely happy. Tennyson wrote: 'the peace of God came into my life when I wedded her'. They spent their honeymoon in the Lake District, which prompted one American newspaper to comment: 'We hope, now that Mr Tennyson is married and has returned to his native lakes, that he will give up opium'. They had confused him with the notorious Samuel Taylor Coleridge.

In 1853, the family moved to Farringford, near Freshwater on the Isle of Wight, where Tennyson wrote some of his most famous poems, including 'Maud', 'Idylls of the King' and 'Enoch Arden'. During the Crimean War, he read a press report about the Battle of Balaclava: 'The Times account had the line – 'someone had blundered' – and the line kept running in my head, and I kept saying it over and over till it shaped itself into the burden of the poem'. The result was the famed work 'The Charge of the Light Brigade'.

Despite the huge popular success of this poem, Tennyson always said that, out of all his poetry, he was most proud of the line: 'The mellow ouzel fluted in the elm'.

Tennyson delighted in reading his poetry aloud to awed guests, although things did not always go to plan. He told *Margo Asquith* that on one occasion he had sat a young lady on his knee while he read to her from 'Maud'. When he reached the lines: 'Birds in the high Hall-garden, When twilight was falling, Maud, Maud, Maud, Maud, They were crying and calling', he asked the girl which bird she thought he had been describing. She answered: "A nightingale?" Tennyson: "This made me so angry that I nearly flung her to the ground. 'No, fool! Rook! Rook! Rook!'"

In addition to his poetry, Tennyson wrote several plays, such as 'Queen Mary', 'The Promise of May', and 'Becket'. *Henry Irving* staged several of these dramas, and visited Tennyson's home to discuss the work.

One evening after dinner, the butler filled their glasses with port and then left the decanter beside Tennyson. Intent on talking, Tennyson kept refilling his glass but totally forgot to replenish his guest. When the decanter was finished it was replaced with another, but the same thing happened and Irving's glass was left empty. Next morning, Irving awoke to find his host bending anxiously over him, asking him if he was well. "Pray, Mr Irving, do you always drink two bottles of port after dinner?"

Tennyson was a popular literary figure but he did have some detractors. *Frank Harris* wrote that 'The great social movement in favour of the poor and disinherited, which is the glory of the nineteenth century, never touched Tennyson'. Yeats's patron, Lady Gregory, claimed that 'Tennyson had the British Empire for God, and Queen Victoria for Virgin Mary'.

Tennyson was an unusually tall man who never lost his native Lincolnshire accent. He was so powerfully built that he once picked up a donkey and carried it across his lawn. Far from being an austere intellectual, his favourite reading included murder mysteries and the lightweight novels of *Marie Corelli*. Although Tennyson was a rigidly moral man over sexual matters, the Archbishop of Canterbury, Edward Benson, was astounded when, during a walk together, Tennyson suddenly asked: "Shall I tell you a bawdy story?" "Certainly not!" snapped the Archbishop.

Tennyson was sometimes awkward in social situations. At one garden party he was introduced to a shy young girl who was tongue-tied at meeting the great man. For a few minutes they sat in embarrassed silence. Finally, Tennyson spoke: "Your stays are too tight". The girl stammered out: "I – I don't think so, sir". "Yes, indeed" insisted Tennyson, "I can hear them creaking". Red-faced with confusion, the girl leaped up and scurried away to mingle with the other guests. Half an hour later she was mortified to see Tennyson lumbering towards her again. When he spotted her, the poet bellowed across the heads of the garden party: "Young lady, my apologies! I was wrong! It was not your stays. It was my braces!"

As his fame grew, Tennyson became an object of public interest. He had an ambivalent attitude towards his admirers. When an American lady accosted him in his own garden to ask if he had seen 'Mr Tennyson', he replied that he had seen him about an hour previously walking off towards the beach. She left hurriedly in pursuit.

However, *William Morris* reported walking with Tennyson when they spotted two cyclists approaching in the distance. Tennyson started to grumble that they were sure to stop and demand autographs. When they swept past without halting, Tennyson turned to Morris and indignantly exclaimed: "They never even looked at me!"

Henry Irving had a similar experience when walking with Tennyson in London. After some passers-by had turned back to stare at them, Tennyson grunted: "You see, that's why I seldom come to London. It's very unpleasant being pointed at". In truth, while very few people knew what Tennyson looked like, Irving was known to thousands, and it was the actor who had been the object of interest. Irving said later: "A good fellow, Tennyson, a great man and all that, but a little vain, eh?"

One evening at the Oxford and Cambridge Club, after dinner with friends, Tennyson put his feet on the table and tilted his chair back in the American style. The friends complained but he ignored them, saying he was comfortable with the position. "Everybody's staring at you", insisted one of the friends. "Let 'em stare", retorted Tennyson. Then, one man had an idea. "Alfred, people will think that you are Longfellow." The feet descended.

In 1883, he was given a peerage. *EF Benson* said of the event: "the House of Lords was more honoured by his entering it than he was by entering". Tennyson regretted one aspect of this fame: "I am sorry that I am turned into a schoolbook at Harrow; the boys will say of me 'That horrible Tennyson'."

His death was almost theatrically appropriate. As the full moon shone on his deathbed, he called for a copy of Shakespeare. He turned the pages till he reached 'Cymbeline', then expired, his hand still holding the book.

At his funeral in Westminster Abbey, the pallbearers included two Prime Ministers, (*Lords Rosebery* and *Salisbury*), *Benjamin Jowett* of Oxford, the Master of Trinity, Cambridge, and the United States ambassador. The nave was lined by men of the Balaclava Light Brigade.

One of Tennyson's neighbours on the Isle of Wight was the photographer **JULIA CAMERON** (1815-1879). She had not taken up photography until she was aged 48 but thereafter followed her interest ruthlessly. She came to be regarded as a menace.

George Du Maurier said that: "she pursued her subjects, camera in hand. I find her delightful, but don't think she would suit as a permanent next door neighbour for the next 30 years or so unless one could now and again get away".

Tennyson had little option. Julia not only demanded his photograph but also insisted he signed them all. She would arrive with so many copies that she needed a carriage to carry them and personally brought a fistful of new pens so that Tennyson would have no excuse.

Her great niece, the writer Virginia Woolf, once described a visit to her aunt's house: 'The coalhouse was turned into a dark room. The hen roost was turned into a glasshouse. Boatmen were turned into King Arthur, village girls into Queen Guinevere. Tennyson was wrapped in rugs. Sir Henry Taylor was covered in tinsel. The parlour maid sat for her portrait and the guest had to answer the bell'.

In July 1880, Wilde and Miles moved into a new house in Tite St, Chelsea, London. Wilde: 'The address is horrid but the house very pretty'

Chelsea and South Kensington had been a highly undesirable area for centuries. It lay below the level of the Thames and therefore was subject to floods. Freddie Cadogan said that the family property was a 'sort of morass fit only for vegetable gardens'. But when the Underground railway was built, the ground was drained and the land became fit for building, (incidentally bringing a large fortune to the Cadogan family.)

1881

[In Norway, Hendrik Ibsen published his play 'Ghosts'.

In Britain, Disraeli died, and the Savoy Theatre was built to house the operettas of Gilbert and Sullivan. Their play 'Patience' opened in April.

In France, Vicomte Ferdinand De Lesseps argued the concept of a Canal in Panama. The plan was later to founder in a huge scandal in 1890.

In Russia, Czar Alexander II was assassinated on 13 March

In the USA, President James Garfield was assassinated and died 19 September.]

Wilde spent January 1881 in London. Another link with Ireland was lost when he mortgaged his inherited fishing lodge at Illaunroe.

SIR WILLIAM SCHWENK GILBERT 1836-1911

Although both were humorists and iconoclasts by nature, Wilde and Sir William Gilbert were never natural allies. Gilbert's jovial humour confirmed the English middle-class prejudices. Using the weapon of sadistic ridicule, he championed their liking for 'common sense' and their distrust of the new. Oscar, on the other hand, thought 'sound English common sense' was simply 'the inherited stupidity of the race'. Oscar: 'To disagree with three fourths of the British public on all points is one of the first elements of sanity'. They were entirely out of sympathy with each other.

Gilbert greeted the news of Wilde's Newdigate Prize at Oxford with a graceless sniff: "I understand that some young man wins the prize every year". But he did spot the satiric possibilities of the aesthetic set. Dropping the idea of using curates as targets for his new light opera libretto 'Patience', he chose instead the artistic group that included *Swinburne* and *Burne-Jones*, (the opera opens with twenty love-stricken maidens in the same pose as the girls in Burne-Jones's painting 'The Triumph of Love'.) The main character, 'Reginald Bunthorne', was intended to be *Whistler*.

Oscar had arrived rather late to be a leading member of this group but Gilbert seized on his public persona with glee: 'Though the Philistines may jostle, you will rank as an apostle in the high aesthetic band, If you walk down Piccadilly with a poppy or a lily in your mediaeval hand'. By the time the show reached America, 'Bunthorne' was definitely based on Wilde.

Gilbert had started his career as a junior barrister but failed dismally. After one particularly inept defence (that had earned his client an eighteen-month sentence with hard labour), the client removed her shoe in the courtroom and hurled it at his head. After four years at the bar, Gilbert had averaged five clients a year and had totalled £75 in fees.

He enjoyed amateur acting during this period but proved no more successful on the stage than in the courtroom. One critic wrote that watching Gilbert acting 'Harlequin' gave him a good idea of how Oliver Cromwell might have played the role.

Gilbert's real talent lay in his mastery of language, though success in this field came slowly. By the age of 24 he had written fifteen plays, some of which were performed. The publication of his comic poems, the 'Bab Ballads' of 1869, (and so called because Gilbert's childhood nickname had been 'Bab'), secured recognition.

By 1875, on the suggestion of the promoter Richard D'Oyley Carte, Gilbert joined forces with the composer Arthur Sullivan to produce 'Trial By Jury', the first of a long series of comic opera hits. Gilbert's task was to provide the libretto, as he had no ear for music. He used to say that he only knew two tunes – one was 'God Save the Queen' and the other one wasn't.

'H.M.S. Pinafore' (1878) was the first major success of their collaboration; part of the comedy stemmed from satirising a real life situation. The Prime Minister, *D'Israeli*, had appointed a bookseller, WH Smith, as First Lord of the Admiralty when Smith had never actually been to sea.

(It was during rehearsals for 'Pinafore' that Gilbert asked a sixteen stone tenor, Rutland Barrington, to "cross the stage and sit on the skylight pensively". Barrington did so, but his weight buckled the skylight and he crashed through it. Gilbert commented dryly: "I think that's – ex-pensively".)

'Pinafore' proved as popular in the USA as in Britain but the work was pirated ruthlessly by American producers. D'Oyley Carte lost a copyright action in the US courts, the judge stating that: "no Englishman possesses any rights which a true-born American is bound to respect".

One American impresario suggested that Gilbert could write an American version of 'Pinafore'. Gilbert, still smarting from the court case, responded by fitting a new lyric to his song, originally 'He is an Eng-lish-man – And it's greatly to his credit', etc. The new version was: 'Though he himself has said it – Tis not much to his credit – That he is A-mer-i-can'. The idea was dropped.

The success of Gilbert and Sullivan continued with productions of 'The Pirates of Penzance' (1879), the afore-mentioned 'Patience' (1881), and 'Iolanthe' (1882). Their 1884 opera 'Princess Ida' was a satire aimed at the education of women, and partly referred to the first women's college of Girton.

(Girton, founded at Hitchin in 1869, had been moved to Cambridge in 1873. Among the rules of the college was one that, while men were allowed entry to the building, they had to stand up for the entire length of their visit.)

The partnership reached its peak in 1885 with 'The Mikado', but the next show, 'Ruddigore' (1887) was not well received. 'The Yeoman of the Guard' (1888) and 'The Gondoliers' (1889) saw a return to popularity. (The latter opera was based on an incident in Gilbert's infancy. Aged two, Gilbert had been kidnapped and held for ransom in Naples; his parents paid up and he was returned.)

By 1890, boredom with work they both considered beneath them, combined with quarrels over finances, cracked the relationship between Gilbert and Sullivan. Although they reformed to produce 'Utopia Unlimited' (1893) and 'The Grand Duke' (1895), their collaboration and their friendship ended.

During one revival in 1898, Gilbert and Sullivan emerged from different sides of the stage to bow to the applause, but did not speak to each other and left the theatre separately. They never met again.

Beneath the hearty Tory squire persona, in essence Gilbert was an anarchist. His contemporaries noted that, despite the breezy fun, there was, in the words of the Times in 1907, 'an underlying note of anger'. There was also an element of schoolboy pleasure in the misfortune of other people. The critic Arthur Quiller-Couch wrote: 'The man was essentially cruel and delighted in cruelty'.

No profession roused his contempt more than the press. One day a reporter arrived at his home and asked Gilbert's butler if he could have an interview. In a voice that resounded through the house, Gilbert thundered: "Tell the man to go to hell!!" The butler returned to the front door and announced: "Mr Gilbert is extremely sorry but he wished me to state that extreme pressure of work precludes him from the pleasure of seeing you this morning."

One obese woman reporter did manage to get as far as Gilbert's study and, hoping to impress him, gushed over his dogs. She smiled winsomely at Gilbert and lisped: "It's marvellous how all dogs seem to take to me straight away". Gilbert grunted back: "Not at all. It's just that it's not often they find a bone with that much meat on it".

Despite a happy marriage to Kitty Gilbert, his lack of gallantry toward women was notorious. When someone said that: "Mrs Jones was very pretty once", Gilbert retorted: "Yes – but not twice".

A girl in his opera company complained that a man had made advances to her, putting his arm around her waist and calling her 'a pretty little thing'. Gilbert consoled her with: "Never mind, he couldn't have meant it". A lady of advancing years told him that she 'couldn't remember the Crimean War'. Gilbert's reply was: "Don't you? I'm sure you could if you tried".

Occasionally his quips had a Wildean ring, such as his reply to an invitation to attend an exhibition in America. 'Sir, I view the proposal to hold an international exhibition at San

Francisco with an equanimity bordering on indifference.' But his usual wit was more crudely robust. He said of a theatre impresario who had cast his mistress in a leading role and papered the press for advertisements on her behalf: "The fellow is blowing his own strumpet".

After his retirement, he felt unleashed from a lifetime of writing works of impeccably good taste. This new freedom found expression in dozens of unprintably filthy limericks and a pornographic play in typescript that delighted the West End clubmen.

Gilbert's lack of social grace offended the court circle. In 1890, 'The Gondoliers' was presented at a command performance before Queen Victoria at Windsor Castle. Although even the wig-maker's name was printed in the programme, Gilbert's name was omitted.

He was wounded by this snub and retaliated by writing a satire on the Court, 'Utopia Unlimited' – it was the most bitter of his lampoons. The result was, that while Sullivan was knighted in 1884, it was another 24 years before Gilbert received his knighthood.

Gilbert died in 1911. Two girls had got into difficulties while swimming in a lake at his home and Gilbert dived in to rescue them. The girls survived but Gilbert suffered a heart attack and drowned.

Gilbert loathed his middle name of 'Schwenk', but did not mind his initials of 'WSG'. His musical partner, **ARTHUR SULLIVAN** (1842-1900), on the other hand, while quite happy with his middle name of 'Seymour', thoroughly disliked his initials of 'ASS'.

From childhood, Sullivan was a favourite in influential circles, being praised by Charles Dickens over his youthful compositions and, as a Royal chorister, popular with the Court.

His first entry into the world of operetta came when the magazine Punch organised a benefit performance of 'Box and Cox' for the families of deceased staff members. Sullivan wrote the music, the editor *Francis Burnand* wrote the libretto, and *George Du Maurier* sang the lead part.

His real interest though lay in more serious music; he wrote the hymn 'Onward Christian Soldiers' and 'The Lost Chord' (composed as he sat by his brother's death bed).

Sullivan always felt that he was the disciple to the masterful Gilbert, though Gilbert was conscious of Sullivan's worth. Gilbert: 'We always saw eye to eye, the same humour always struck us in exactly the same way. With Sullivan I never had to do that fatal thing – explain a joke'. It also allowed Sullivan to develop comic ideas within his music.

When the partnership failed, Sullivan felt himself released from 'this slavery' of light comedy and attempted his life's ambition of composing a serious grand opera. The result was 'Ivanhoe' (1891). Given his freedom, Sullivan simply wasn't good enough and the work failed. *GB Shaw*: 'Music in petticoats from the first bar to the last'.

Sullivan spent his last years as an intimate of the Prince of Wales's set, indulging in the regal pursuits of hunting and shooting. *JEC Bodley* recorded that one day, Sullivan set off with a rifle and a servant. Much firing was heard from the woods. At dinner that evening, Sullivan stated that he had not had his usual luck that day; he had only bagged fifteen birds. His servant let slip later that, after 150 rounds had been fired, Sullivan had winged two pheasants and downed one woodcock.

It was a strange fact that neither Gilbert nor Sullivan realised that their operettas had any merit beyond their immediate popularity. Sullivan remained convinced that his botched attempt to write grand opera rendered him a failure. Gilbert said: "I fancy that posterity will know as little of me as I shall of posterity".

Their business manager, **RICHARD D'OYLEY CARTE** (1844-1901), felt no such qualms over his own success. While Gilbert died worth £110,000 and Sullivan worth £50,000,

Carte left over £250,000 at his death. It was felt to be proof of the superiority of business acumen over talent.

The son of a London woodwind instrument maker, (and agent of the Belgian Adolphe Sax, inventor of the saxophone), Carte left his father's firm to become a concert promoter. In 1875, he realised that the combination of Gilbert with Sullivan could be mutually beneficial and persuaded the pair to agree.

At the suggestion of friends, he also arranged for Oscar Wilde to do a speaking tour of America in 1882. The satire on aesthetes, 'Patience', was suffering slightly as the English conception of an aesthete was unknown in the USA. Carte decided to give American audiences a chance to see one in action so that they could appreciate the lampoon. The idea worked far beyond its original remit and Wilde became a star in his own right.

During the run of 'HMS Pinafore', Carte had a business partner, the Dublin impresario Michael Gunn, who once told him the unfortunate story of how Gunn's father had met his death. It appeared that Gunn senior used to travel daily to his office in Dublin on an omnibus that crossed a canal bridge. One morning the horses took fright and dragged the bus down into the empty lock. A lock keeper quickly resolved on a plan to rescue them by floating the bus. He proceeded to open the sluices, thereby filling the lock and drowning the passengers including the unlucky Gunn senior.

The man who played 'Bunthorne', (the 'Patience' character partly based on Wilde), was the singer and entertainer **GEORGE GROSSMITH** (1847-1912). Far from bearing any resentment for the spoof, Wilde asked Grossmith to reserve a three-guinea theatre box for the show, with the words: "I look forward to being greatly amused". Grossmith mimicked Oscar's mannerisms but, as he was a small man, (*Frank Harris*: 'Grossmith looked like a gnat'), his characterisation more resembled Whistler.

Grossmith had a long career with Gilbert and Sullivan, playing leads in all their main shows. However, Gilbert's drill sergeant methods of rehearsal almost brought Grossmith to a nervous breakdown. The company were appalled to see puncture marks on his arms; he was relying on drugs to keep himself going.

He recovered enough to co-author, (with his brother Walter Weedon Grossmith), the excellent comic novel, 'The Diary of a Nobody' (1894).

At the start of his contract, Grossmith met D'Oyley Carte to discuss wages. Carte invited him to a magnificent banquet of oysters and fine wine. Under the influence, Grossmith acceded to Carte's request not to press his claim for the extra £3 a week that he had wanted. Eleven years later, Grossmith glumly calculated that the lunch had cost him over £1,800.

Wilde met Edmund Gosse in the spring of 1881.

SIR EDMUND GOSSE 1849-1928

For such a touchy man as Sir Edmund Gosse, Wilde struck entirely the wrong note when they met in 1881. When Oscar said that he was pleased to meet the critic, Gosse replied that: "I was afraid you'd be disappointed". Oscar answered flippantly: "Oh no, I am never disappointed in literary men. I think they are perfectly charming. It is their works I find so disappointing".

Gosse never forgave him for this impertinence. He reviewed Wilde's book of poems as 'a curious toadstool, a malodorous parasitic growth', and referred to Oscar as being 'like Punch on a stick, squeaking, and I don't like the squeak'.

In return Wilde suggested that Gosse would be recognised by posterity as holding 'a high place among British Poetesses', admitting later: "Well, I think you must give me the credit for never having discussed Gosse except in the most unfair terms".

Gosse had a paternalistic fondness for Wilde's great friend *Robert Ross* but, even eight years after Wilde's death, he wrote to Ross that: 'I am afraid I shall always feel instinctively hostile to Wilde'. He considered that Wilde's only real writing achievement had been his 'sad, noble' letters to a newspaper about prison conditions. Gosse: 'What I principally hated about him, poor creature, was not at all his vices, but his unreality'.

Gosse was a classic Victorian man of letters; in addition to his work as a critic, he wrote poetry, biography, and translated two Ibsen plays. He has remained known mostly for his semi-autobiographical book 'Father and Son' and for one poem 'Tusitala' about his friend Robert Louis Stevenson. He worked as a civil servant for 29 years, a job that gave him: "peace to write, a lovely view of the Thames, and unlimited stationery".

Gosse began his career as a clerk in the cataloguing section of the British Museum. At the time, the clerks were treated rather like errant schoolboys under the control of a superintendent, the Rev. Frederick Laughlin, 'a man who ruled with an iron hand and an uncontrollable temper'.

One day, when Laughlin was absent for an hour, discipline relaxed and the clerks chatted and told jokes. On his surprise return, instant decorum was restored. One clerk, though, had left to fetch a book from an upper gallery. Not noticing Laughlin's return, he leant over the balustrade, spread his arms wide, and boomed out to the workers below: "Am I or am I not the Department's darling?"

Gosse: 'Laughlin turned his head slowly and looked upwards – one look. The clerk fled, and the sound of his footsteps was heard echoing up the metal stairways till they seemed to fade away into infinity.'

One of Gosse's close friends at the British Museum was the poet Arthur O'Shaughnessy (1844-1881), an illegitimate brother of *Lord Lytton.* Arthur was an expert on reptiles and worked in the Natural History Department. On one occasion, he broke a valuable exhibit and repaired the accident by uniting the head of one fish with the skeleton of another. He thus created a new species that baffled the authorities for months.

Gosse's literary reputation grew steadily and, after declining a professorship at Harvard University, he succeeded Sir Leslie Stephen as Clark Lecturer at Cambridge. In 1886, he was the subject of a damaging article by John Churton Collins that denounced Gosse's carelessness over facts.

Given his prickly nature and acute sensitivity to public opinion, this accusation deeply upset Gosse. His domestic staff did not help matters by giving him notice, on the grounds that they had entered his service under the impression that he was a man of letters and now they had learnt from the press that he was a charlatan.

Through the intervention of the socialite *Lady Ettie Desborough,* (who wrote to the Prime Minister: 'Could not the House of Lords library possibly be got for Gossekins?'), later in his life Gosse acquired the job of Librarian to the Upper Chamber.

The library became his personal domain where he sat watching for misdemeanours through 'gleaming gold-rimmed spectacles'. One lord reported that: 'the mishandling of a book would bring him hurtling in a trot across the floor to the side of the offender with a bitingly civil request to know if he could be of any assistance'.

Gosse's temper was tested occasionally by printing errors. He said: "When *Robert Browning* died I wrote in his obituary that 'to the end of his life he was faint, yet pursuing'. The printer's reader queried this, and being angry about many things, I scribbled 'Rats!' at the side. They printed that the venerable poet died 'faint, yet pursuing rats'."

Some of his contemporaries regarded Gosse as a snobbish and prissy example of the 'governess' type. *George Moore*, when writing in favour of the tavern as opposed to the club, commented: 'The tavern gave the world Villon and Marlowe; the club and its leather arm chairs have begotten Mr Gosse'. When Gosse received his knighthood, *Frank Harris* said that it was 'for services to mediocrity'.

In 1898, Wilde and Robert Ross knew a rent-boy in Rome called Ormero. Ormero asked Oscar what he should do if he ever visited London and wanted to see Ross whilst there. Oscar advised him that Ross's real name was 'Signor Edmundo Gosse' and that he lived at the Savile Club. Ormero should appear in person and make enquiries at the Club.

Gosse's predecessor as Clark Lecturer at Cambridge, **SIR LESLIE STEPHEN** (1832-1904), besides being a dedicated scholar, was an enthusiastic mountaineer.

He once returned from on Alpine trip in 1870 and, by pure chance, happened to be the first person to bring back fresh reports of the Battle of Sedan to London. Not that his fellow clubmen would have known it as, on arrival at the club, he became involved in an animated theological discussion. It was three hours before he remembered to mention the news that France had fallen.

Sir Leslie's great achievement was his founding editorship of the Dictionary of National Biography. The strain of such a huge work of scholarship forced his resignation in 1891. His efforts were not always appreciated. When *Bertie, Prince of Wales,* attended the dinner held to celebrate the final publication of the Dictionary, he was unimpressed by the company.

Looking at the assembled scholars, he pointed sourly at a Rev. Ainger, (who had composed the entries on Charles and Mary Lamb), and hissed: "Why is that vicar here? He's not a writer." It was explained that the Rev. Ainger was a major authority on Lamb. Bertie put down his knife and fork and gasped in bafflement: "On *lamb?*"

Gosse reported that in an American Dictionary of Biography he had once looked up the title: 'Highcock – Laurens Persius'. The entry read simply: 'The style of Laurens Persius Highcock lacks distinction'.

Sir Leslie was the father of the writer Virginia Woolf.

Gosse was a life-long friend of the author **ROBERT LOUIS STEVENSON** (1850-1894), the creator of such classic tales as 'Treasure Island' (1881), 'Kidnapped' (1886), and 'The Strange Case of Dr Jekyll and Mr Hyde' (1886). The latter book may have influenced Wilde when he wrote 'Dorian Gray' three years later. Oscar paid tribute to Stevenson, calling him 'that delightful master of delicate and fanciful prose'.

Stevenson sometimes had a foolhardy compulsion to mingle fantasy with real life. In 1879, he went to the USA to marry Fanny Osbourne, a divorcee. (The marriage, though lasting, had some rocky patches, prompting Stevenson to comment: "To marry is to domesticate the Recording Angel".) While in the Far West one day, he was seized with a desire to impersonate an outlaw gunman.

Although a frail, almost wispy man, Stevenson assumed an air of menace and strode down the main street. On the approach of a stranger, Stevenson stopped and glared, then moved his hand sharply to his hip as if about to draw a (non-existent) revolver. The stranger turned pale and held up both hands over his head. Stevenson growled imprecations at him then swaggered on to repeat the process. The actor *Charles Brookfield*, to whom Stevenson told this story, said that: "It was by the mercy of God that he was not shot dead".

Dogged by ill health, in 1880 Stevenson went to Davos, Switzerland, to find a cure for lung consumption. It was in Davos that he wrote much of 'Treasure Island'. A friend, Horatio Brown, left an account of Stevenson's writing methods: 'He had made a mud map of the island all over the floor of a chalet, and would lie there all day, moving dolls about to represent his characters as he wrote'.

In 1888, Stevenson left Europe to settle in Samoa in the Pacific. Another Davos friend, *JA Symonds* commented that Stevenson, 'having the chance to lounge around in palmy coves wearing only a few hibiscus flowers, with the most beautiful people in the world', had instead decided to 'build himself a sort of Scotch manse in a wilderness'. Stevenson died in Samoa in 1894 – Gosse was devastated by the news.

In 1875, Gosse married Ellen Epps, the sister of the second wife of the artist **SIR LAWRENCE ALMA-TADEMA** (1836-1912). Alma-Tadema, (nicknamed 'Tad'), was a Dutchman who specialised in paintings on Graeco-Roman subjects, usually with a background of bright blue sky. In 1870, after the death of his first wife, and encouraged by the favourable British response to his slightly kitsch artwork, he moved to London and took British nationality in 1873.

Alma-Tadema's artistic success was matched by his social popularity and his sumptuous house in St John's Wood was the setting for many parties and for his famous 'Tuesday' soirees. Famous musicians were encouraged to carve their autographs on the lid of his grand piano. His dining room was decked out as an imperial banqueting hall where Alma-Tadema would preside over amateur dramatics dressed as an Ancient Roman in toga and monocle.

In 1881, Alma-Tadema invited Wilde to a masked ball at the house, though Oscar refused to wear the proffered mask. While he offered to advise Alma-Tadema on all things Greek, Oscar insisted that 'Tad' could not draw. Wilde: "I and *Lord Ronald Gower* and Mr *Ruskin*, and all artists of my acquaintance, hold that Alma-Tadema's drawing of men and women is disgraceful".

George Du Maurier was another friend and, as the two men strongly resembled each other, often was mistaken for Alma-Tadema. On one occasion, a lady rushed up to Du Maurier and burst into praise for his 'wonderful paintings of Old Rome'. Du Maurier clasped her hands, looked soulfully into her eyes and, imitating Alma-Tadema's Dutch accent, breathed: "Gom to me on my Chewsdays." He often wondered what had been the result.

Although not a habitual drinker, Alma-Tadema's social life sometimes meant that he imbibed more than his norm. When a friend became the father of twins, Alma-Tadema made a visit to congratulate the new parents. Unfortunately he arrived after drinking several bottles of wine. Casting a bleary look in the direction of the twins, he hesitated for a bit, then announced confidently: "What a lovely baby!"

On June 4 1881, Lily Langtry invited Bertie, Prince of Wales to a thought-reading séance at Wilde's new house in Tite Street.

THE PRINCE OF WALES, later KING EDWARD VII 1841-1910

The Prince of Wales, known as 'Bertie', had several meetings with Wilde. He arranged for Oscar to be a guest to a dinner party where an alleged wit, the courtier Bernal Osborne (whom *D'Israeli* described as 'a clown'), was also present. Osborne displayed his talent by asking if Oscar was related to the eighteenth century criminal, Jonathan Wild. His insinuations grew coarser until Wilde finally stood up and left the room. Bertie was furious with Osborne and apologised to Wilde.

Later, Bertie became a delighted fan of Oscar's plays and attended several first nights. After he had commanded Oscar: 'Do not alter a single line', Wilde mused: 'What a splendid country where princes understand poets'.

In 1898, after Wilde's disgrace, Bertie was in Cannes on the French Riviera. One day, he spotted Wilde in the street and, leaning out of his carriage, removed his hat. Oscar seemed not to comprehend what was happening – he just stared. The Prince settled back and remarked to his companions: "Poor devil. What can we do?"

It is possible that Wilde's rebellious streak struck a chord with the future monarch of the British Empire. Born 'Albert Edward' and the eldest child of *Queen Victoria* and Prince Albert, he was subjected to a deeply repressive upbringing that had the effect of turning him into a resolute rake in adult life.

There is some evidence that his parents did not really like Bertie, and certainly Victoria was an unsympathetic matriarch. When it was suggested that he must be a great comfort to his mother, Victoria snapped: "Comfort! Why, I caught him smoking a month after his dear father died!"

Gladstone said that Bertie 'was kept in childhood beyond his time', and Victoria made a point of excluding him from affairs of state. When Bertie was sent on a royal visit to India, on his outgoing voyage the newly opened Suez Canal was French owned; on his return voyage it was British territory. Victoria had not bothered to tell him.

When his 'eternal' mother finally died in 1901 and he succeeded to the throne, it was significant that he dropped his first name of 'Albert' and ruled as 'King Edward VII'.

After the moral austerities of his mother's court, Bertie was a welcome relief. It was said that the English loved him because he had all the aristocratic vices, (as opposed to his son, King George V, who was disliked because he embodied all the middle-class virtues). The writer *Wilfred Blunt* wrote of Bertie: 'he has certain good qualities of amiability and a Philistine tolerance of other people's sins which endear him to rich and poor'.

This popularity enabled him to influence British social life long before he actually reigned. If the Victorian age intrinsically lasted from 1845 till 1865, the Edwardian age could be said to have lasted from 1880 till 1914.

Another of Bertie's nicknames was 'Tum Tum'. Being only five feet, six inches tall and as plump as his mother, there was something of the gluttonous infant about him that seemed to be part of his charm. He enjoyed five full meals a day and was profoundly addicted to cigars.

Henry James described him as 'an arch vulgarian'; in particular this applied to opera, where he irritated many music-lovers by chatting when he should have been silent. One of Wilde's quips appealed strongly to him: 'Musical people are so absurdly unreasonable. They always want one to be perfectly dumb at the very moment when one is longing to be absolutely deaf.'

His regard for social standards found expression in minor matters such as the strict observance of dress codes. When *Lord Rosebery* arrived at Windsor wearing ordinary trousers instead of court dress, Bertie observed testily: "I presume that you have come in the entourage of the American Ambassador?"

Bertie did possess a genuine common touch. When a Victoria Cross medal winner was invited to have tea at Buckingham Palace, the man used the working class method of pouring his tea from the cup into the saucer to cool and then drinking it. Court officials were shocked, but Bertie displayed the utmost good manners by copying him and also drinking from the saucer.

Excluded from State affairs, Bertie turned his attention to pleasure in various guises. Racing was one of them, and his horses won the Derby three times. He turned Sandringham into a royal residence mostly because of its proximity to the Newmarket races.

He installed a series of cod 'Vanity Fair' erotic portraits in the Sandringham billiard room. *JEC Bodley*: 'Lord Shaftesbury is represented as kissing a nymph, *Matthew Arnold* lolling languidly among a bevy of Cyprian beauties, and Mr Gladstone and *Lord Salisbury* spying on some naked bathers.'

Bertie enjoyed betting as did many of his companions. One associate had a mania for gambling on every conceivable topic. Once, when the Royal chaplain announced during a service that: "There is one God", the man was heard to mutter softly: "I'll take six to four on that".

Another sport that Bertie enjoyed was that of salmon fishing. On one occasion in Scotland, Bertie was aided by a ghillie who spotted a fine fish in the stream and explained where best to hook it. After the Prince's first cast, the excited ghillie called out: "Magnificent, Your Royal Highness…….. Another yard, Your Royal Highness……….Perfect, Your Royal Highness…….. A wee bit to your right, Your Royal Highness…….You're over him, Your Royal Highness ………..Now then, Your Royal Highness………..Och! You've missed him, ye stupid bastard."

Bertie was democratic in his choice of companions. Wealth was rapidly replacing birth as the basis for acceptance, and Bertie dropped the usual social and religious royal prejudices in favour of choosing people that he actually liked. Men such as Lipton the grocery magnate and Maple the furniture king became intimates.

Visiting Americans, (fresh from the upper classes of United States society which strictly excluded Jews), were amazed to find such prominent Jewish families as the Rothschilds and the Sassoons at the heart of the court circle.

Occasionally, this new tolerance stumbled, as on the occasion of the visit of the Shah of Persia to England. The Shah casually asked Bertie whether, for safety's sake, he was going to have his brother executed when he came to the throne. Bertie blanched but recovered to say that there were so many great lords in Britain that it would be difficult to carry out such a cull.

The culture clash of the Shah's visit seemed to affect both sides. For his part, the Shah could not stomach the apparent dominance of western women over their husbands and said: "It seems to me that an English or American husband is nothing better than a sort of butler".

(While in London, the Shah was impressed by the new invention of the bicycle and ordered one made entirely of gold inlaid with jewels. Hearing that even the saddle was to be encrusted with emeralds, a London newspaper commented: 'this must be the converse of the line – 'Uneasy lies the head that wears the crown'.)

Sex was another area in which Bertie rebelled against his parents. He became a fervent libertine but had the sense to conceal the fact as much as possible from his middle-class subjects. By tacit agreement, Bertie and many of the aristocracy could indulge in virtually any sexual misbehaviour, with the one strict proviso that it did not become public knowledge. The Eleventh Commandment of this world was 'Thou Shalt Not Be Found Out'.

To an extent, the essence of Wilde's play 'An Ideal Husband' was based on this very idea. (It is ironic that Oscar, along with such characters as *Charles Dilke* and *Charles Parnell,* was ruined not by his actions but by the fact he failed to keep them from the public eye.)

In effect, Bertie practised droit de seigneur among his married friends; it came to be regarded a something of an honour to offer their wives for his enjoyment. Known as 'Edward the Caresser', he had little interest in young unmarried girls, as they were too inexperienced. Instead, he concentrated on actresses, married women, and the famous beauties of his day. Among hundreds, possibly thousands, of women, *Lily Langtry,* Alice Keppel, and Daisy Warwick were among the most prominent.

Even in old age, Bertie retained a remarkable sexual stamina, although his increasing stoutness inspired a Parisian brothel to install a special chair for him that facilitated fellatio.

When Bertie was on his deathbed, his long-suffering but indulgent Danish wife, Queen Alexandra, remarked: "At least now I know where he is".

DAISY BROOKE, Countess of Warwick (1861-1938), was one of the aristocratic wives who offered themselves to Bertie. Her husband, Lord Brooke, was endlessly complacent; among her other lovers were *Lord Charles Beresford*, (by whom she had a child), and the future First World War Field Marshal, a youthful Earl Haig.

Bertie fell deeply in love with the seductive and beautiful Daisy and especially enjoyed her country house parties. In practice, these events were discreet orgies, where gongs were sounded at 6am to enable bed-hoppers to return to their original rooms.

Oscar Wilde did visit Warwick Castle but was unlikely to have been involved with the extra-curricular action. (Although, in 'An Ideal Husband', he wrote: 'I don't think any one at all morally responsible for what he or she does at an English country house'.

In an unlikely turn of events, Daisy suddenly converted to socialism. In spite of her irritation at being called 'Comrade Warwick' by *Margot Asquith*, she joined HM Hyndeman's Social Democratic Federation, a semi-revolutionary group.

At first, Bertie was so infatuated that he acquiesced and was seen accompanying her on visits to workhouses and workingmen's clubs. On accession to the throne, however, his advisors told him that it was not a good idea to have an obvious socialist so close to the monarchy and he dropped Daisy.

Owing partly to her philanthropic ventures, by 1914 Daisy was £90,000 in debt and Warwick Castle had been let to an American. Growing increasingly desperate, she contacted *Frank Harris* and between them concocted a scheme to blackmail Buckingham Palace with the public exposure of the late King Edward's love letters. The Palace settled £100,000 on her in return for their destruction.

Bernard Shaw recalled arriving at a Socialist conference at a hotel, where, he said, the leaders were standing around the foyer, 'looking as if the social revolution had come and left them all far behind'. For once, they were silent, and the only noise came from the rumbling of their stomachs. Finally, the chairman, HM Hyndeman, spoke up. "The Countess of Warwick has invited us to dinner, and has forgotten all about it".

In her old age, Daisy said of her spectacular sex life: "I could not help it. They were there. It was all a great game".

In June 1881 Wilde published his first collection of poetry in London, (Wilde: 'So you are a rhymer! We all are when we are young'.) Wilde actually made very little money from this book as he had paid the publisher to print it.

The poetry was attacked by many critics; Punch called it 'Swinburne and water' – 'The poet is Wilde, But his poetry's tame'. Although Oxford University library requested a copy, the student assembly, led by the future historian Oliver Elton and the poet Henry Newbolt, voted to reject acceptance. The future politician George Curzon was angered by this discourtesy.

In July 1881, Wilde sent a copy of his poems to the poet Matthew Arnold.

MATTHEW ARNOLD 1822-1888

Wilde and Arnold met later at a dinner party held by Frank Harris and were mutually impressed. At a time when Oscar was still regarded as a poseur, Arnold said of him that he had 'a fine intelligence and was a most wonderful talker'. Wilde, for his part, felt that 'Arnold is a real poet, an English saint in side-whiskers'

Matthew Arnold was the eldest son of the famous headmaster of Rugby School, Dr Thomas Arnold. As a result of such poetry as 'The Scholar-Gypsy' and 'Sohrab and Rustum', and his work as a literary critic, he was elected Professor of Poetry at Oxford in 1857.

Although thirty years older, Arnold had some similar experiences to Wilde. Both won the Newdigate Prize, and both applied for the post of Inspector of Schools, (Arnold successfully, while Oscar was turned down). Also, they both gave lecture tours across the USA arranged by *D'Oyley* Carte, Arnold arriving in 1883, the year after Oscar's relatively effective performances.

Arnold's tour, though, was something of a disaster. He repeated Oscar's mistake of announcing to a disapproving public that his main reason for touring was the money. Arnold himself was disconcerted when he saw that the train set aside for the tour bore a large banner proclaiming 'The Matthew Arnold Troupe', which someone remarked made him sound like a performing seal trainer.

While in England people were used to his style, (*JA Symonds* called it 'that touch of arrogance which nobody minded in him'), in America it was not appreciated. But what really upset his audience were the lectures themselves. The poetess *Julia Ward Howe* was particularly censorious, describing Arnold as: 'stooping to read his notes at a lectern like an elderly bird pecking at grapes on a trellis'.

Having listened to Arnold's lecture on Ralph Waldo Emerson, Howe wrote: 'Arnold does not in the least understand Emerson, I think. His elocution is pitiable and when, after his lecture, Wendell Phillips stepped forward and said a few graceful words of farewell to him, it was like the Rose complimenting the Cabbage'.

Arnold's death in 1888 was very sudden and shocked his friends. Wilde reported that when Robert Louis Stevenson heard about it in Samoa, he said: "How dreadful!" – and then added: "He won't like God".

Arnold's exact contemporary and fellow schoolmate at Rugby was **THOMAS HUGHES** (1822-1896), who later wrote the hugely popular novel 'Tom Brown's Schooldays' (1857), in which he created the character of 'Harry Flashman', the school bully.

Despite this one literary triumph, the rest of Hughes's career was one of relentless mediocrity. His attitude of robust patriotism seemed almost calculated to attract Wilde's jibe attacking those 'who would hoist the Union Jack on the pinnacles of thought'. Nor was Oscar enthusiastic about Hughes's attempt to propagate 'muscular Christianity' by, (in his 1879 book, 'The Manliness of Christ'), presenting Jesus as an idealised English public school prefect.

Although conscientious to a fault, Hughes was described as 'a dismal failure' as a Member of Parliament, while his attempt to construct a cooperative farming community in Tennessee ended in financial collapse. When he became a county court judge in 1882, his judgements became a byword for constant reversal on appeal.

On the strength of his novel, Hughes regarded himself as an authority on boys. The journalist *Herbert Vivian*, when aged 14, was introduced to the author by his parents. This seems to have been something of an ordeal, as Hughes insisted on a semi-regal procedure for such meetings. Hughes would insist that all available boys be presented to him.

Although they had been coached to tell him that their greatest desire was to shake his hand, this was not a pleasant experience. Hughes had a theory that character could be assessed through handshakes. As his hand muscles were like iron, the result could prove extremely painful. Any boy who winced was immediately suspected of lack of manliness.

Hughes would then put a number of questions to the child. Vivian recorded that the interrogation followed the pattern of: "Where are you at school? Like it? Any good at cricket? Fine game, cricket. Makes boys manly. Do your duty, always speak the truth, and then you needn't be afraid of anybody."

Then Hughes would close the conversation with a pat on the head and, if the boy had proved especially manly, the presentation of a copy of 'Tom Brown's Schooldays'. Vivian himself did not receive that ultimate accolade as he had replied that cricket bored him.

During the summer of 1881 Wilde visited the Loire valley, France, with Rennell Rodd. Then went on to Paris, Chartres, and Amboise

By 1881, Wilde was coming under satirical attacks, not just from Gilbert and Sullivan, but also from such novelists as Rhoda Broughton (1840-1920) and Vernon Lee (1856-1935).

In her 1880 book 'Second Thoughts', Broughton said of Wilde that he was 'a long pale poet, flaccid limbed, has an early Byzantine face and wears the hair of his Botticelli head very long'.

Vernon Lee (the pen name of Violet Paget) wrote: 'Oscar Wilde talked a sort of lyrico-sarcastic maudlin cultschah for half an hour. But I think the creature is clever, and that a good half of his absurdities are mere laughing at people. The English don't see that'. They remained wary acquaintances.

He was also attacked by Punch magazine under its editor Francis Burnand.

SIR FRANCIS BURNAND 1836-1917

Together with the artist *George Du Maurier*, Francis Burnand found the Wildean aesthete an irresistible butt. As early as 1877, Punch magazine targeted Oscar after his appearance at the Grosvenor Gallery opening: 'And many a maiden will mutter, When Oscar looms large on her sight, 'He quite too consummately utter, As well as too utterly quite'. Burnand was still mining this comic lode in 1890 with the Punch articles 'From the Log of a Log-Roller'.

Burnand extended his attack to the stage when in 1881 he wrote a successful satire on Wilde called 'The Colonel'. Dismissing this play as 'a dull farce', Oscar brushed off the satirists, lightly ridiculing them in return when writing about his experiences with the Red Indians in the American West. 'There are also among them Burnands and Gilberts – in fact 'Burnand' in a blanket and quite covered with scarlet feathers is now trying through the window to force me to buy a pair of bead slippers and making signs to a ruffianly looking 'Gilbert' who is with him to tomahawk me if I refuse'.

The tone of Burnand's 1890s satires against Wilde became quite bitter. The fact that one of Burnand's own sons had been convicted of 'unnatural offences' may have caused the added spite. (After the case, Burnand gave his son an allowance but only on the condition that he changed his name to Anton Strelitski).

Burnand had attended Eton but, unlike some of his school comrades, had no quarrel with Etonian customs. 'Fagging' was a system where junior boys had to work as servants for the seniors; any incompetence was treated harshly. If, for instance, a fag over-burned the toast ordered by a senior, he would be forced to play 'the Highland dance'. This consisted of spreading his hand on a table, while the senior stabbed the table with the toasting fork between the boy's fingers. If, as often happened, the fork stabbed the fingers and the boy cried out, then he would be 'whacked'.

Burnand wrote later that: 'wholesome fagging is far better, physically and mentally, than effeminate favouritism. Fagging, like love, levels all distinctions'. His conclusion on school life was: 'The moral teaching of all public schools is summed up in the formula – Never tell a lie when the truth will do as well.'

In 1854, he went to Trinity College, Cambridge where he became interested in theatre. He founded the university Amateur Dramatic Society (known as the 'ADC'), and also wrote the farce 'Box and Cox'.

One aspect of Cambridge that intrigued Burnand was that some of the undergraduates were by no means young. A few had gone down and up again several times, ('like drowning men' as he put it). One of them, Digby 'Cracker' Cayley, was in the unique position of being, at one time, the only undergraduate at Downing College, despite the fact that the college was fully staffed with deans, professors, chaplains, etc. They existed chiefly for his benefit and left him in a position of almost total control.

The college servant would arrive with a message from the chaplain asking when, or more likely if, he might desire morning chapel. Burnand wrote that Cracker, having probably not arrived back from a drinking expedition until 3am, 'would curtly but decidedly reply with very brief but emphatic recommendations as to the direction in which the chaplain's emissary was to turn his steps'.

Later, another servant would arrive with a breakfast tray and a polite note from a tutor humbly inquiring at what hour Cracker might like to have a lecture, and, if not, might he suggest another day – or indeed week.

For a short time after graduation, Burnand toyed with the idea of becoming a clergyman. He attended Cuddesdon Theological College under the direction of Bishop Samuel ('Soapy Sam') Wilberforce of Oxford, a major opponent of Charles Darwin's theories.

(Wilberforce gained his soubriquet of 'Soapy' during the building of Cuddesdon. The bishop's initials (S-amuel O-xon) were carved on one pillar of the gateway, while the architect's initials were carved on the other pillar. This led to one pillar reading 'SO' while the other read 'AP'.)

Burnand abandoned a theological career and instead chose the theatre, writing over a hundred burlesques and adaptations, the most popular being 'Black-Eyed Susan' (1866) and 'The Colonel'.

During his editorship of Punch (1880 till 1906) the humorous pun reigned supreme. A typical example was the response to the question: 'Is life worth living?' – 'It depends on the liver'. He had a bluff attitude to most things. His view of the supernatural was that 'it was all down to rats', while his membership of the Freemasons was due partly to the craft's attractive instruction 'From labour to refreshment'.

However, he regarded himself as a gentleman and insisted on removing the bohemian 'boozers' of the previous Punch generation. (After one lengthy Punch lunch, two of these gentlemen had fallen down the stairs, then solemnly picked each other up, shaken hands, and had been ushered through the door by Waller, the Punch servant.)

Burnand's answer to the accusation that: 'Punch was not as good as it used to be' was: "It never was."

Although he was the first Punch writer to be knighted for his efforts, Burnand became something of an absentee editor in the later years. One contributor, RGC Price, said that the first signal anyone had of a rare Burnand foray into work was hearing the sound of two heavy thumps as he threw his boots out of the door of his office. Visiting contributors 'would find him looking rather lost and eating shrimps out of a paper bag'.

One day, at a lunch party, he was discussing the anonymous contributions that arrived at the magazine: "It's extraordinary the number of really funny things I get sent to me at Punch". WS Gilbert, another guest, raised his head: "Really! Why don't you put some of them in?"

In September 1881, after a row with Frank Miles, Wilde moved to stay with his mother at Ovington Sq, London, for a few days.

Later that month he moved to two rooms on the third floor of 9, Charles St, London, (now Carlos Place, off Grosvenor Sq). This remained his base until he married in 1884.

In December, the planned opening of his play 'Vera' was cancelled.

On December 24, 1881 Wilde set sail to undertake a tour of the United States.

PART TWO

CAREER

Louisa May Alcott to
Robert Cunningham-Graham

1882

[In Ireland, the Phoenix Park Murders occurred in Dublin on May 6th. Lord Cavendish and Thomas Burke, Irish Under-Secretary, were stabbed to death in Phoenix Park by a gang of assassins called 'the Invincibles'. The gang were eventually captured and five were hanged.
(Before an unrelated but similar incident, one Viceroy of Ireland, Lord Kimberley, received a letter which stated: 'My Lord. Tomorrow we intend to kill you at the corner of Kildare Street; but we would like you to know that there is nothing personal in it'.)
In Egypt, the Arabi revolt was crushed by the British Army at the Battle of Tel el Kebir.
In the USA, the outlaw Jessie James was murdered by relatives on April 3rd.]

VISITING AMERICA

By the 1880s, it had become almost de rigueur for European literati and artistes to tour what was in those days still largely a pioneer society, particularly in the American West. It was said that his energetic touring of the States had led to the early death of Charles Dickens. He had a possible inkling of this when he was told that the people of Chicago would 'have a fit' if he did not visit them. Dickens replied that he would rather they had a fit than he did.

The rewards of touring could be considerable. The singer Madame Patti made over $50,000 a month. On hearing this, one reporter gasped: "Why, our President has to work a year to get that much!" Patti snapped back: "Well, in that case get your President to sing for you".

One young female acquaintance remarked to Wilde that she thought that he was "very brave to go to a strange land, amongst strange people, to mount a stage dressed as an aesthetic young man and lecture on the subject. It is so brave." Oscar replied: "I am touched by your concern. I admit to a little apprehension, but after all they can't shoot me!" The girl's vinegary aunt rasped: "I would not be too sure about that, Mr Wilde".

The trip across the Atlantic in the 'Arizona' was uneventful. Wilde commented that he was 'disappointed in the Atlantic Ocean'; the Pall Mall Gazette printed a letter shortly afterwards: 'I am disappointed with Oscar Wilde, Signed, The Atlantic Ocean'.

The ship's skipper, Captain Murray, did not like his famous passenger and was overheard to say: "I wish I had that man lashed to the bowsprit on the windward side".

Allegedly having declared nothing but his genius at the Customs House, Wilde arrived in New York on the 2nd of January and stayed at the Grand Hotel. He soon began to deliver judgement on the New World.

A New Yorker told Oscar that Christopher Columbus was a wonderful man for discovering America. Oscar informed him that: "it had often been discovered before but it was always hushed up".

Oscar enjoyed the story of George Washington chopping down the cherry tree. 'They have as a national hero a man who, according to his own confession, was incapable of telling a lie. But the amusing part of the whole thing is that the story of the cherry tree is an absolute myth'.

Wilde concluded that: 'America has never quite forgiven Europe for having been discovered somewhat earlier in history than itself.'

LOUISA MAY ALCOTT 1832-1888

During a tour that was to introduce Wilde to a wide range of American celebrities, his first meeting of note was with the writer Louisa May Alcott. They were joint guests of honour at a reception in New York on January 8th 1882. Alcott was curious about Oscar, despite their almost total lack of mutual interests or experiences.

Alcott was very much a tough-minded practical woman who had fought all the way for her success. One of four daughters, she had been raised mostly in Concord, Massachusetts. The efforts of her idealistic father Bronwell Alcott to establish a utopian community failed continuously. His wife said of him that: 'if I ask Mr Alcott to bring home a quart of milk, he is quite likely to bring home a cow'.

Louisa was fortunate that her Concord neighbours included men of great intellectual calibre, among them Henry Thoreau and Ralph Waldo Emerson. ('Sleepy Hollow', the Concord cemetery, eventually contained so many illustrious New Englanders that it was called the 'Westminster Abbey of America'.)

After her father had helped Thoreau build his cabin at Walden, Thoreau used to row the children out on to the pond and play the flute for them; she enjoyed quoting his maxim: 'Beware of all enterprises that require new clothes'.

Emerson also provided intellectual rigour and a beady eye on theological excess. One day he was stopped in the street by a religious fanatic who shouted: "The world ends tonight!" Emerson drawled back: "OK, I can get along without it".

Louisa soon realised that if her family were to rise above poverty it would have to rely on her efforts. Alcott: 'I was born with a boy's nature and have fought my fight with a boy's spirit under my bib and tucker'. She worked as a domestic servant while writing potboilers that failed to attract attention.

In 1861, the long simmering American Civil War broke out. The Alcott family were devout anti-slavers, who had aided escaped slaves and were friendly with the arch abolitionist John Brown. (After he was executed for rebellion, his daughters, Anne and Sarah, stayed at the Alcott house).

Louisa, shocked by the initial Union defeat at the Battle of Bull Run, trained herself to be a nurse by studying a handbook by Florence Nightingale. She arrived at the front during the Battle of Fredericksburg, and was horrified both by the appalling Union casualty rate and by the discovery that some of her fellow nurses were robbing the wounded of their possessions. One nurse was forcing her patients to make out their wills in her favour.

Alcott soon fell victim to the unsanitary hospital conditions and contracted typhoid. She was sent home where, in 1863, she wrote 'Hospital Sketches' about her experiences. This book won her a measure of respect; one Union army company marched to Concord, paraded outside her house, and saluted in her honour.

When the war finished in 1865, still poor, she travelled around Europe as the companion/nurse to a rich Boston woman. (Wilde mentioned the type in 'The Canterville Ghost': 'Many American ladies on leaving their native land adopt an appearance of chronic ill health, under the impression that it is a form of European refinement'.)

In 1868, Alcott finally achieved her ambitions when her book 'Little Women' was published. It was a sentimentalised account of her early life with her three sisters in which she glossed over the poverty, and mixed fact with fiction. It was a worldwide success. By the 1880s she was rich enough to move her family into an elegant house on Louisburg Square in Boston.

Despite this triumph, Louisa remained levelheaded about herself and often was irritated by her lasting fame. She was once accosted by a gushing female fan. "If you ever come to Scranton your feet will not be allowed to touch the ground! You will be borne in the arms of the people! Will you come?!"

"No".

134

On *9th January, Wilde started the first part of the lecture tour that was to last till the 12th May 1882.*

The first show was at the Chickering Hall in New York City. At the reception afterwards, the band struck up 'God Save the Queen' in his honour – a strange experience for a pro-Home Rule, socialist Irishman.

On January 12th, on the strength of a friendly letter of introduction from Lord Houghton, Wilde met Sam Ward.

SAM WARD 1814-1884

In 1880, the London magazine 'Vanity Fair' wrote: 'Every traveller to the USA whose lot has fallen in pleasant places is sure to have met with Samuel Ward, protector of the English and Uncle of the human race'. As the unofficial guardian of the English in America, Sam Ward immediately offered his services and friendship to Wilde.

Despite the ostentatious self-publicity that Oscar was forced to assume on his arrival, Sam quickly predicted that he would be a success 'as he has a substratum of solid intellectuality'. During 1882, Sam's respect for Oscar grew: 'He is one of the few men who gain the more you know him.'

But even the endlessly amiable Ward was perturbed by the bandwagon that accompanied Oscar's travels. In July, Sam wrote to his sister, *Julia Ward Howe*: 'The Americans are a rude, boisterous and uncivil race, and it irks me much to go about with Wilde as the courier of an elephant; wherever he appears by steam or rail, throngs rush to get a sight. He takes it all very coolly, but it must be terrifying to be treated like a Barnum Jumbo'.

Sam Ward was one of the most sympathetic figures of nineteenth century America. Wilde said of him: "You are a magician, and a master of all things from finance to a dinner, and from lyrics to medicine". As a man of the world and social lubricant, his position in American society bore a strong resemblance to that of *Lord Houghton* in England. He was renowned for his wit, his anecdotes, and for his 'marvellously good dinners'. *Lord Ronald Gower* called him: 'the most delightful and the kindest and the most generous of human beings'.

After growing up in a wealthy but puritanical New York banking family, Sam turned his first visit to Europe into a memorable playboy debauch that lasted for four years. Nominally abroad to study finance, he plunged into the Parisian Latin Quarter, where he immersed himself in 'the study of gastronomy' and then in the appreciation of music.

(He reported that he had met the man who had provided the composer Rossini with the theme of the final act of 'The Barber of Seville': 'which is actually the English air of Polly Put the Kettle On!' He attended Sunday breakfasts with another famed composer, Franz Liszt. Ward: 'The piano was always open but Liszt was never asked to play. Consequently he never failed to do so.')

Sam's numerous entanglements with Parisian girls concerned his friend and fellow American, the poet *Henry Longfellow*, who advised him to marry: 'The phantoms of your brain are beautiful, but they are not holy, and in the silence of the night they visit ladies chambers'.

Sam attempted to continue his studies in Heidelburg, Germany. He wrote later: 'The life of a student in those days was a year of play, a year of repentance, a year of desperate effort to obtain his degree'.

Hounded by creditors and badgered by family demands for his return, Sam finally arrived back in New York in 1836. Ward: 'Passing strange that on the day of my arrival the chapter of the Prodigal Son was read in all the churches'.

Ward's entire career was a roller coaster ride. He admitted that he had been a millionaire three times and a pauper three times. At first forced to work as a clerk in the family firm, he married Emily, the grand daughter of John Jacob Astor, whose personal fortune amounted to

$160 million and who owned 3,300 houses in New York City. (Astor: "A man who has a million dollars is as well off as if he were rich").

(Now a rising young celebrity, Ward related the story of how a French silhouette painter named Monsieur Edouart had drawn Ward's portrait. On his return to France, Edouart was shipwrecked in the Channel Islands. Such was his terror of the sea after this event, Edouart refused to board a boat ever again and, despite being able to see France in the distance, spent the rest of his life in Guernsey.)

Sam's wife Emily died three years after their marriage. His subsequent remarriage to Medora Grymes infuriated John Jacob Astor and Sam was banished from the powerful Astor clan. (Ward: "I might have been absorbed in the Nirvana of that golden essence. I prefer my own individuality".)

The marriage to Medora was a failure and they soon parted. 'The loss of fortune which I have several times experienced never gave me one tenth the sorrow I have felt at having lost a woman's affection'. In 1847, the family bank failed and Sam found himself almost broke.

Nothing daunted, he set off to join the Californian Gold Rush, where he established a trading post, lived with the Red Indians, and learned the Piute language in three weeks. Unusually for an amateur miner, he was lucky in panhandling some gold dust but the money was soon spent.

During the 1850s, Ward was involved in many diplomatic missions to Central America to negotiate over United States mining, railway and revolutionary interests. He acted as a secret agent in attempts to rescue such filibustering adventurers as the French Count Raousset-Boulbon in Mexico and the American William Walker in Nicaragua. In spite of Ward's efforts, both of them were executed.

Sam re-built his fortune but promptly lost it again in the collapse of a silver mine company. This time he was so poor that he was forced to stay at New York's most expensive hotel, the Brevoort, "as no creditor would dream of searching for me there". "I had to go to bed in order to have my shirt washed".

Ward was appalled by the approach of the Civil War in 1861 and used all his diplomatic skills to prevent the conflict. Tolerant of all shades of opinion, he said that: 'for all their violence and vapourings, the South does have vested interests'. He hurried to the Southern capital of Richmond to appeal for common sense: "Gentlemen, you are beaten. You had better know it now. All the wealth and all the power of the North are against you!"

He expressed his feelings in a poem: 'We hoped it was a nightmare, Till the news was brought from town, That the horde of Charleston maniacs, Had torn our banner down.' While deeply opposed to secession, Sam was not an Abolitionist either. He was seen by the North as a 'Copperhead' – a Northerner with Southern sympathies. However, in 1865 he was deeply saddened by the killing of Abraham Lincoln.

After the war ended, Ward came into his own as 'the King of the Lobby' in Washington. The knowledge of cooking that he had gained in his early days in Paris was put to good use; his cuisine became a major weapon in his diplomatic arsenal. "I'm the gastronomic pacificator'.

Although avoiding involvement in the political process itself, Ward was an important part of the government structure. His passport gave him accreditation as US plenipotentiary to almost every foreign government, and he became a useful conduit to the ambassadors in Washington. (He was sympathetically amused when the French Ambassador asked for his own recall home declaring that he: "could not live in a country where there were three hundred religions and only one sauce".)

Food was not Sam's only diplomatic weapon. He also gathered a group of 'the queerest lot of deadbeats ever seen' who acted as his spies and messengers all over the capital. Ward: "This morning I had the usual raft of shipwrecked madmen reporting to my room".

Sam could also pull off a crafty ploy when necessary. On one occasion a client wished to prevent a rival's attendance at a Senate meeting. Sam stole the rival's boots, then sat commiserating with him and feeding him cigars until the meeting was over and the boots could be 'found'.

When Ward's close friend James Garfield became President, Garfield said that the only reason that he had not given Sam a place in his cabinet was that Sam would make him not only forgive his enemies but forget who they were. When Garfield was mortally wounded by an assassin, Sam helped to nurse him during the weeks until his death. Sam's curative recipe was milk laced with 100-year old rum.

Lacking a family of his own, Ward gave all his affection to the offspring of his sister Julia Ward Howe, authoress of 'The Battle Hymn of the Republic' and the grandest of American grande dames.

One of these grandsons, Winthrop Chanler, was one of the Harvard students who ragged Wilde by appearing dressed as aesthetes at his lecture. Sam was concerned over another grandson, Armstrong Chanler, who had been judged of unsound mind by a New York court and confined for several years in Bloomingdale Asylum. Armstrong finally escaped to Virginia where the courts judged him sane. Soon afterwards his brother Robert Chanler made a very unwise marriage to a notorious New York lady. Armstrong sent him a telegram that read: "Who's the loony now?"

By 1882, after accumulating another fortune on Wall Street, Ward was cheated by his partners and, facing huge and rising debts, decided that he had to flee the United States.

When he arrived in England, he was greeted with delight by the social set. Remembering his past generosity to the English, they christened him 'Uncle Sam' and placed him at the heart of society life. The future Prime Minister, *Lord Rosebery*, and his wife Hannah, made him so welcome at their home that Sam sighed that he was 'becoming a wheel in the Rosebery family clock'.

In 1884, he travelled to Italy to join the Roseberys for a holiday but died in the town of Pegli, near Genoa. His gravestone there read: 'And God gave him largeness of heart even as the sands on the seashore'.

Sam Ward used his influence to introduce Wilde to several American notables, the most important of whom was the former Union commander-in-chief and ex-President **ULYSSES S GRANT** (1822-1885). In July, 1882, at Long Beach, Sam wrote: 'The next night we saw General Grant, who discoursed eloquently on the East and gave Wilde, who meditates a voyage to Japan, some good advice.'

Despite his spectacular achievements, Grant had a difficult life. During the Civil War, his rise to overall command had been sure but slow; he never displayed the military flair of such Southern generals as Robert E Lee or 'Stonewall' Jackson. Grant preferred the bludgeon to the rapier; his only real martial quality was that he kept on winning.

During his Presidency of 1869-77, Grant was unfortunate to be at the helm during an era of unprecedented corruption in American life. Although he was not personally involved – he truthfully said that "failures have been errors of judgement, not intent" – his administration became a byword for graft. By 1884, he himself was swindled and he struggled against poverty till his death.

In many ways, Grant was the antithesis of a military man. Although trained at West Point Academy, he disdained the strict observance of regulations, clean uniforms, and formal hierarchies. He dreaded the sight of blood so much that he refused to eat meat unless it had been thoroughly cooked.

Originally christened Hiram Ulysses Grant, he reversed his two forenames when he went to West Point. The registering officer erroneously wrote his name down as 'Ulysses S'; Grant never bothered to change it.

He bothered himself even less over public ceremony. In 1864, the town of Galena formally presented him with a sword of honour. When he was asked to make a reply, he fumbled in his pockets till he finally found a crumpled sheet of paper containing his speech and then wordlessly handed it over to the mayor.

One of his officers described Grant: "He habitually wears an expression as if he had determined to drive his head through a brick wall, and was about to do it".

Frank Harris told a story of Grant in his later years. Harris knew an old drunk who used to hang about the bars of Lawrence, Kansas, sometimes making maudlin boasts that he had known Grant when he was young. One day, it was reported that Grant was visiting Lawrence and the barflies decided to tease the aged wastrel by 'presenting' him to the President.

When Grant's carriage arrived, they pushed the drunk to the front of the crowd where he stood self-deprecatingly holding out his hand and saying: "Ulysses, Ulysses". Grant looked at the shabby old wreck without a glimmer of recognition. The crowd grinned in anticipation of a crushing snub. The drunk pathetically tried again to attract Grant's attention and quavered: "Ulysses, you ain't forgotten Ol' Hap, have you?"

Grant's grim face suddenly changed: "Of course I remember you. It must be twenty years ago. You must come in and dine". When the drunk looked down ashamed at his ragged clothes, Grant added: "No matter. These gentlemen will forgive your dress".

To the amazement of the crowd, Grant ushered the old man ahead of him and, placing him beside the seat of honour, the normally laconic President chatted to the man throughout the meal. Harris: "It struck me that there was something noble in Grant".

He also had one great stroke of luck. Grant's wife Julia and President Lincoln's wife Mary could not stand the sight of each other. It was for this reason that the Grants declined an invitation to share the presidential box at Ford's Theatre on the night of Lincoln's assassination.

Grant's close wartime colleague was General **WILLIAM TECUMSAH SHERMAN** (1820-1891) who during the 1880s was a ubiquitous social figure in New York and Washington. Originator of the phrase 'War is hell', he had during his famous march through Georgia proved the truth of his own maxim.

Although mostly known for his campaigns against the South, Sherman had also been involved for many years in fighting against the Red Indians. He displayed an unusual respect for the tribes, (his father had given Sherman his middle name of 'Tecumsah' in honour of the Indian chief). When he was involved in the enforced ethnic cleansing of the Seminole tribe from Florida, he wrote to a friend: 'You doubtless little sympathise with me in hunting and harassing a poor set of people who have had the heroism to defend their homes against such odds for such a period of time'.

In the euphemism of the period Sherman was reputed to have 'kissed' more girls than any other man in the United States. A story still persists that in 1865 he spared the city of Savannah from a fate similar to the burnings of Atlanta and Columbia, SC., because on his arrival, the four most beautiful girls in Savannah came out to give him 'a night to remember' in exchange for mercy.

Before he became a soldier, Sherman had followed a promising career in banking. During the Panic of 1857, his bank had held on as the others failed. Sherman reported that a Frenchman had been squeezed almost to death as he fought his way to the bank counter. When Sherman handed him his money, the Frenchman did not know what to do with it and spluttered: "If you got the money, I no want him. But, if you no got him, I want it like the devil".

Sherman became disillusioned with the job: 'Of all lives on earth a banker's is the worst, and no wonder they are specially debarred all chances of heaven'.

After the war, Sherman travelled abroad several times, on one trip taking Grant's son Fred with him as aide-de-camp. When they reached Turkey, the Sultan, not understanding the United States Constitution, assumed that Fred was heir to the American throne and accorded him full honours. Sherman found this hilarious but was less amused when he received a hospitality bill for $600. The Sultan had assumed also that Sherman was Treasurer to the Royal Household.

Wilde's tour of the United States was attended by a wave of publicity: "I had two secretaries, one to answer my letters, the other to send locks of hair to my admirers. I have had to let them both go, poor fellows, the one is in hospital with writer's cramp, and the other is quite bald".

The East Coast press was mostly hostile, sometimes savagely so. The New York Tribune called him 'a penny Ruskin and a pretentious fraud'; another paper called him 'a spiritless, namby-pamby nondescript', etc. Wilde: "If you can survive yellow journalism, you need not be afraid of yellow fever".

However the most personal attack came from another of D'Oyley Carte's clients, Archibald Forbes.

ARCHIBALD FORBES 1838-1900

Wilde met the Scottish war correspondent and lecturer, Archibald Forbes, on a train taking them from Philadelphia to Baltimore. Although the press had been against Oscar, his audiences had been good and Forbes apparently grew irritated by the young aesthete's boasts over ticket sales.

In his next lecture, Forbes took his cue from the worst of the American newspapers and attacked Wilde, contrasting his own virile experiences with Oscar's effete life. Forbes, a man of bristling moustache (and nature) who wore all his medals on the lecture platform, sneered: "The wild barren waste of Bulgaria was not congenial to the growth of sunflowers and lilies".

The Irish playwright Dion Boucicault wrote of the affair: 'I cannot help feeling that as long as D'Oyley Carte and Forbes thought Oscar was only a puppet – a butt – as a means of advertising the Opera Comique of 'Patience' – they were charming, but when Oscar's reception and success threw Forbes into the shade, Forbes went into an ecstasy of rage, and went back on Wilde, behaving more like a wild bull than a gentleman.'

However, Oscar's comment on Forbes that he was 'a coward and a fool' was well wide of the mark. Forbes was outspokenly opinionated and made many enemies, but he was also spectacularly brave and second only to his inspiration, William Russell, as a war reporter.

After a spell as a trooper in the Royal Dragoons, Forbes became respected both in the English press and in the British Army for his fearless desire to report the heart of the action. During his career he was present at the Franco-Prussian War, the Paris Commune, the Carlist Wars in Spain, the Russo-Turkish War, the Second Afghan War (where he accompanied the British forces to Jellalabad), and the Zulu War (where he out-rode the official despatch to bring the first news of the Battle of Ulundi).

These exertions broke his health and in 1880 he turned to lecturing and later to writing books on military matters. In 1896 he expressed a view that could have had a crucial influence on future warfare. From his observation of tactics in the Franco-Prussian War, he realised that cavalry and frontal assaults were useless and suicidal – a defence armed with repeating rifles and machine-guns was bound to win. The War Office ignored his advice. It was only later in the horrors of the First World War that he was proved to be correct.

In his memoirs, Forbes recalled one of his less well-known exploits. At the end of the Franco-Prussian War, he found himself in a town in French Lorraine, just after the Germans had evacuated it. The Mayor warned him that, as Forbes had a luxuriant yellow beard, he was in danger of being mistaken for a German and could be in danger from French mobs. He advised that if Forbes shaved and left only side-whiskers, the populace would realise he was British and spare him. Although reluctant to remove a growth that it had taken him years to foster, Forbes agreed.

That night, as French troops re-entered the town, a grand dinner was held in celebration. The Mayor proposed a toast saying: "We have all made sacrifices for La Patrie. I myself have sustained the loss of a wooden outhouse burned in the bombardment. But what can be said of an honourable gentleman who has sacrificed the most distinguishing ornament of his physical aspect without the holy stimulus of patriotism. My English friend has by his self-sacrifice and example helped to save France in her hour of greatest peril'.

Forbes: 'Later that night I overheard the Mayor and the Town Clerk discussing whether they should confer the freedom of the city on me'.

While in Philadelphia Wilde visited a distant cousin named Father Maturin. The cleric invited his kinsman to stay, but having seen the austere interior of the house, Oscar excused himself. (Wilde: 'No one cares about distant relations nowadays. They went out of fashion years ago'.)

He found more congenial hospitality when, on January 18th, he was invited to call on Walt Whitman at his Camdon home, (Camdon was a suburb of Philadelphia).

WALT WHITMAN 1819-1892

Walt Whitman was probably the American whom Wilde most wished to meet. On this first occasion (they met also in May 1882), Whitman plied him with homemade elderberry wine. On leaving the house, Oscar commented: "If it had been vinegar I should have drunk it just the same, for I have an admiration for that man which I can hardly express".

When a reporter asked Oscar if he thought Whitman was eccentric, Oscar replied: 'He is not! You cannot gauge great men by a foot rule." Whitman was equally impressed by his visitor: "Wilde is so frank and outspoken and manly".

One conversational exchange though displayed their philosophical differences. Wilde said that: "I can't listen to anyone unless he attracts me by a charming style, or by beauty of theme", to which Whitman answered: 'Why, Oscar, it always seems to me that the fellow who makes a dead set at beauty by itself is in a bad way. My idea is that beauty is a result, not an abstraction".

Wilde never lost his respect for Whitman, although he later qualified his enthusiasm. 'If poetry has passed Whitman by, philosophy will take note of him'.

Although born into the New England Puritan tradition, Whitman rejected its stern disciplines in favour of enjoying life. Raised in Brooklyn, he became a printer, a country schoolteacher, a journalist, and by 1846 the editor of the Brooklyn Daily Eagle.

Walt's idea of editorship was to arrive at the office around 11am, glance through the daily papers, then stroll down to the Battery where he would spend an hour or two enjoying the sea views, then return to the office at about 3pm. One proprietor said that: "he was the laziest fellow who ever undertook to edit a city paper".

After a trip to New Orleans to edit another paper, Whitman's imagination was stirred by his first glimpse of the immensity of America, an impression that deeply affected him.

He took enormous pride in his health and bodily strength, never smoking and rarely drinking. However, in 1841, a temperance society asked him to write an anti-alcohol tract. Whitman, knowing what they wanted, supplied them with a crudely obvious story called

'Franklin Evans – or The Inebriate'. He later claimed to have written it in a Broadway beer-cellar with the aid of frequent gin cocktails.

In 1847, he began to write 'Leaves of Grass', a book of poetry that he constantly expanded over the next 30 years. Its philosophical background was drawn from many sources but Whitman did create a new style of verse akin to the Biblical prophets; he was described as 'a Hebrew bard translated to the American backwoods'. Whitman endearingly said of 'Leaves of Grass': "It's not so much a mess as it looks".

Although it slowly became an acclaimed work in Britain, in the United States its popularity suffered because of its explicit celebration of sexuality. Whitman: 'I wished to sweep away the fashionable delusion of the inherent nastiness of sex'. This openness did not translate into his own life.

Whitman wished to be seen as a great lover but probably never had full relations with a woman. Whitman: 'I had an instinct against forming ties that would bind me'. This detachment led many to consider him as homosexual. He seemed to imply it in his poem 'Calamus', and Wilde certainly assumed it: "The kiss of Walt Whitman is still on my lips". But it is also probable that Whitman simply had a very low sexual drive.

Despite his dislike of slavery, Whitman, like President Lincoln, was not a fervent abolitionist: 'The Negro was not the chief thing; the chief thing was to stick together'. He stayed aloof from the Civil War until 1862 when he volunteered to help in the over forty Union military hospitals around Washington.

In two years he made over 600 hospital visits to talk and distribute small gifts among the wounded; the nurses said that his presence could cheer an entire ward. In 1864, he witnessed the Battle of Culpepper – the sight of real war sickened him.

When he was forced to retire after catching hospital malaria, Whitman wrote 'Drum Taps', based on his war experiences, and 'Democratic Vistas' on his hopes for America. He never regained the robust health of his youth and in 1873 suffered a paralytic stroke that crippled him for the rest of his life.

He moved to an 'unlovely house on an unlovely street' in Camdon. Despite the problem that his home stank from the smells drifting over from a nearby guano factory, it became something of a literary shrine. Among many visitors making the pilgrimage, *Helena Modjeska* said that Whitman's "expressive, rather large-featured face would have fitted King Lear to perfection", while *Edmund Gosse* said that the poet looked "like a dear old Angora tom".

Frank Harris summed up the feelings of Whitman's admirers when he wrote: 'I would die happy if I could believe that America's influence would be anything like as manly and true and clear-eyed as Whitman's in guiding humanity'.

But Whitman had an ideal of American society that had been formed in pre-Civil War days when the country had been mainly agrarian and when an enterprising man had only to 'Go West' to improve his lot. As a humanitarian democrat, Whitman wished to be the voice of that brave New World.

Within his lifetime America became an industrialised nation, dominated by monopoly capitalism. While he realised that a society motivated purely by profit was dangerous – ('in business the sole object is, by any means, pecuniary gain') – he thought that an intrusive government was more harmful to the health of the country.

He failed to see that the triumphant Northern capitalists had instituted covert economic slavery, (where dissidents were free to starve), in the place of overt Southern slavery. He did not realise that the power of the sturdy independent workmen and craftsmen, whom he so admired and extolled, had been destroyed by the subtle and often vicious manipulation of economic forces over which they had no control.

In short, he did not understand that democracy could be eclipsed by plutocracy.

Given Whitman's early, if ambivalent, efforts to promote teetotalism, his funeral had an ironic touch. *Gertrude Atherton* reported that over 4000 people attended the ceremony and that "practically the entire four thousand were as drunk as lords".

Wilde travelled on to Washington, DC, where he lectured at the Lincoln Hall on January 23rd. Wilde: 'Washington is a curious town. Considering it is the capital, it has no gorgeous ceremonies. I only saw two processions. One was the Fire Brigade preceded by the Police, and the other was the Police preceded by the Fire Brigade'. He was not impressed by the statues: 'Far too many bronze generals. To see all those awful double waistcoats perpetuated in marble adds a new dismay to death'.

During a party at Judge Loring's Washington home, he was introduced to General George McClellan.

GENERAL GEORGE McCLELLAN 1826-1885

At the start of the Civil War, George McClellan had managed to hold the area of West Virginia for the Union and had been acclaimed as 'the Young Napoleon of the West'. The North, shocked by its early defeats, eagerly seized on a new military hero to lead them against the Southern capital of Richmond, Virginia.

Accordingly, by May 1862 McClellan had organised an overwhelmingly strong Union army that stood poised to seize the city. However, nothing happened. In a delaying move, the Confederate generals used such stratagems as displaying fake artillery (made out of logs) at the city's approach roads, and marching the same regiment round and round a hilltop to confuse onlookers as to their numbers. Even the Confederates did not believe that such measures could hold off the enemy for long.

One of them, General Joseph E Johnson, mused: "We're trapped, outnumbered, and outgunned. Why in the name of God does the man not attack?"

The answer lay mostly in McClellan's intelligence chief, the renowned **ALLAN PINKERTON** (1819-1884). The Scottish-born Pinkerton had immigrated to the United States in 1842, where he had become Chicago's first appointed detective, before creating his own private agency. On President Lincoln's orders, he created the original US Secret Service.

McClellan was delighted to accept the famous sleuth as his eyes and ears. Unfortunately Pinkerton had no military training at all, and relied on interrogating bewildered civilians. McClellan accepted unhesitatingly Pinkerton's gloomy verdicts that 'Richmond is an armed camp; rebels have flocked there in such numbers that the city is defended by at least 300,000 men'. The genuine number was closer to 50,000.

The Southern General Lee, unable to believe his luck, finally realised that the only way to bring matters to a conclusion was to go on to the offensive. McClellan, still relying on Pinkerton's predictions of an irresistible onslaught of enemy troops, promptly retreated.

Although he managed to stem the ensuing Southern invasion at the Battle of Antietam, (mostly because a Union soldier discovered Lee's battle plan stuffed in a packet of cigars), McClellan was sacked. Nursing a grievance, he stood against Lincoln in the 1864 Presidential election, but lost. In 1877, he was elected Governor of New Jersey.

Pinkerton abandoned his military career after Antietam and returned to his private detective agency. (A rumour circulated that the outlaws Frank and Jesse James once killed two of his detectives and mailed the bodies cash on delivery to Pinkerton in Chicago).

He enjoyed far more success when the great manufacturing corporations employed his agency to break strikes among their workers. In his book 'Strikers, Communists, and Detectives', Pinkerton noted balefully that he had brought 'the leaders and instigators of the

142

dark deeds to the punishment they so richly deserve. Hundreds have been punished. Hundreds more will be punished.'

> *On January 31, Wilde was in the city of Boston where he lectured at the Music Hall. At the time, Boston regarded itself as the height of cultured sophistication, though one otherwise patriotic citizen conceded that: "Shakespeare was a great man. I don't suppose there are more than ten men, even in Boston, who could have written Shakespeare's works".*
>
> *Non-Bostonians were less complimentary. The American actor Maurice Barrymore called it: "that Malvolio of cities - sick of its own self-conceit"*
>
> *Wilde objected that: "If one wants to realise what English Puritanism is, I do not think one can find much of it in England, but much can be found about Boston and Massachusetts. We have got rid of it. America still preserves it, to be, I hope, a short-lived curiosity'.*

> *On January 29, Wilde dined with Julia Ward Howe at her Beacon Hill home.*

JULIA WARD HOWE 1819-1910

Julia Ward Howe, author of the song 'The Battle Hymn of the Republic', met Wilde several times and they enjoyed each other's company. Oscar told her: "You are one of those rare persons who give one the sense of creating history as they live".

Julia became somewhat alarmed when in July 1882 a gossip column spread the rumour that Oscar was about to marry her daughter Maud. Howe: 'If ever there were two people in the world who had no sympathy in common, they were the two'. Both Oscar and Maud hastened to quash the idea.

Ten years later, Julia visited the Wildes at their London home and saw Oscar's play 'Lady Windermere's Fan' at the St James Theatre.

Julia Ward had met Oscar on the recommendation of her brother, *Sam Ward*, whom she adored, (his affectionate nickname for her was 'Old Bird'). Although they were raised together in the same New York banking family, she displayed a more serious view of life than the affable Sam.

In 1843 she married Dr Samuel Gridley Howe, (known as 'Chevalier' by his friends). After attending Harvard Medical School, Dr Howe left for Europe in 1824 where he became involved with various revolutionary groups. Taking his cue from Lord Byron, he threw in his lot with the Greek rebels in their War of Independence; after six years he became surgeon-in-chief of the Greek forces. (A comrade noted that: "the only fault found with him was that he always would be in the fight, and was only a surgeon when the battle was over."). He also raised funds and supplies in America for the relief of civilian starvation in Greece.

In 1831, after he attempted to transport supplies to aid the Poles in a rising against Prussia. Dr Howe ended up in a Berlin prison. He was released after the intervention of the American Ambassador.

Returning to the United States, he dedicated himself to the education of the blind and became famous for being the first man to teach language to a blind deaf mute, (a girl called Laura Bridgman).

After his marriage to Julia, the newly weds left for a honeymoon in England. They made many friends there, including *Lord Houghton* and Florence Nightingale, (who became godmother to one of their children). Julia became something of an Anglophile: "An English friend is a friend for life".

Julia did not include the poet William Wordsworth in this category. On the honeymoon, after a rain-soaked journey through the Lake District, punctuated by the exploits of runaway carriage horses, (Julia: 'I supposed the miseries of wet garments would soon be cancelled by that of a broken neck'), they arrived at Wordsworth's house.

Wordsworth, (Julia: 'a crabbed old sinner who gave us a very indifferent muffin'), had recently lost a lot of money speculating in United States bonds and was in no mood to humour Americans. He ignored Julia and spent the evening complaining to Dr Howe. Julia: 'Incensed at this unusual neglect, I made several interjections in a low tone – my husband allows me to swear once a week'.

When Mrs Wordsworth also began 'to whine over their losses' and bemoan the fact that the Wordsworths should suffer for the misfortunes of another country, Julia pointed out acerbically: "Why must you needs speculate in foreign stocks? Why did you not keep your money at home?" The Howes left amidst a frosty silence.

In 1844, the couple returned to work at Dr Howe's Blind Institute in South Boston. It was to be a stable marriage, despite some discontent on Julia's part. Julia: 'For men and women to come together is nature – for them to live to together is art – to live well, high art'.

They became friendly with many of the literary set of Massachusetts. Julia was amused by her first meeting with the notoriously shy Nathaniel Hawthorne, (author of 'The Scarlet Letter', etc). When they called at his house, Mrs Hawthorne called out: "Husband! Mr and Mrs Howe are here!" Behind her they spotted the famous novelist sprinting across the hall and out of the back door.

When the Civil War began, Julia heard the tune of 'John Brown's Body' for the first time and said she was 'mesmerised' by it. Soon afterwards, she lay half awake in a hotel one night listening to distant guns. Julia: "While waiting for the dawn, long lines of a poem began twining themselves inside me. I did not write them; they wrote themselves." Fearful of forgetting them, she scribbled the lines on the back of playing cards. The result was the lastingly popular 'Battle Hymn of the Republic'.

She spent the rest of her life revered as the composer of these inspirational lines, but she also worked to promote higher education for women, and to aid the victims of oppression, (particularly the Armenian people during the Turkish pogroms). She almost welcomed old age: "Life is like a cup of tea; all the sugar is at the bottom'.

Despite her worries over Wilde's intentions towards her daughter, Julia had a relatively benign view of courtship. She enjoyed relating the dilemma in which a young Boston acquaintance named Edward Everett had found himself. By accident, Everett had promised to take three different girls out riding in his carriage on the same afternoon and was anxious not to upset any of them.

Julia: "To the first he said, 'the horse is perfectly fresh now; you have him in the best condition'. To the second he said, 'The horse was a little antic at first, so you will have the safer drive'. To the third he said, ' Now, that the other two have had their turn, we need not hasten back. You can have the longest drive". Julia said that the boy deserved to become head of the United States' diplomatic service.

One of the greatest friends of the Ward family was the poet **HENRY WADSWORTH LONGFELLOW** (1807-1882), whom they nicknamed 'Longo'. Sam and Julia's sister Louisa Ward found one aspect of Longfellow irresistibly funny – he wore a wig 'of the most indescribable colour'. At one dinner, Louisa could resist the sight no longer and suddenly burst into uncontrollable laughter.

Longfellow politely joined in her mirth but kept asking: "What is so funny, dear Louisa?" The enquiry simply set off more guffaws. Louisa reported that finally "we both turned very red and ceased".

Wilde was invited to breakfast at Longfellow's home on January 30th 1882. "I arrived in a snowstorm and left in a hurricane – quite the right conditions for a visit to a poet". Oscar liked the man while remaining dubious over his poetry: "A fine old man. He is himself a beautiful poem, more beautiful than anything he ever wrote" – 'He is a great poet for those who never read poetry'. Longfellow said of Oscar: "Mr Wilde has written some good verses, he cannot be an ignorant man".

During his twenty years of teaching European languages at Harvard, Longfellow wrote some of the most popular poetry in America. Such highlights as 'The Wreck of the Hesperus', 'The Village Blacksmith' and 'Paul Revere's Ride' became standard favourites, but 'The Song of Hiawatha' (1855) was the poem that sealed his success, selling over 100,000 copies in two years.

He had little practical knowledge of Red Indian customs and relied on books and information given to him by an Ojibwa Indian called Kah-ge-ga-gah'-bowh. Noticing the similarity of the Red Indian myths and a Finnish epic called 'Kalevala', he based the distinctive rhythm of 'Hiawatha' on the Finnish trochaic metre.

Julia Howe said that one of her acquaintances from the Far West told her that: "if Longfellow had ever seen a Sioux Indian, he would not have written Hiawatha".

Longfellow came to England in 1868 to receive honorary degrees from Oxford and Cambridge. Pressed about his impressions, he said that the thing he most admired about the country was Bass Ale.

When he was introduced to *Queen Victoria* at Windsor Castle, being a republican he shook her hand rather than bow to the monarch. He said modestly that he did not realise that he was so well known in Britain. Victoria replied: "I assure you, Mr Longfellow, you are very well known. All my servants read you". He confessed to Wilde that: "Sometimes I wake up at night and wonder if it was a deliberate slight".

After his death, the British paid him the honour of being the first American to have a memorial bust in Westminster Abbey's Poets Corner. His literary reputation on the other hand slumped immeasurably, one critic writing: 'Longfellow is to poetry what the barrel-organ is to music'.

While in Boston, Wilde met two of the Irish-American community, the journalist John Boyle O'Reilly and the playwright Dion Boucicault. Boucicault, though Irish by birth, had become a naturalised American citizen in 1873.

DION(ysus Lardner) BOUCICAULT 1820-1890

Born in Dublin, (and related by marriage to the Guinness family), Dion Boucicault had known the Wildes well and had dined at their Merrion Square home. He was angered by the American press treatment of Oscar: 'The use to which those managing his American tour are putting him is simply disgraceful. He is a gentleman and a scholar. They are making him a show' – 'Those who have known him as I have since he was a child at my knee know that there is a noble, warm, kind and lovable man'.

He was so outraged that he offered Oscar £2000 to free him from his obligations to D'Oyly Carte. Wilde was grateful but turned it down. Boucicault commented: 'Oscar is helpless because he is not a practical man of business. I do wish I could make him less Sybarite – less Epicurean'.

If Oscar had wanted to be a theatrical impresario, he could not have wished for a better mentor. Boucicault was a prolific author and actor who wrote or translated over 250 plays; he once finished seven plays in eight months, five of which ran in the West End consecutively. He ate opium in order to keep up this work rate – "It makes me more capable of mental labour" – but denied having any De Quincy-esque drug visions.

His main successes, amidst many failures, were 'London Assurance', 'The Corsican Brothers', 'The Coleen Bawn', and 'The Shaughraun'. He pioneered the idea of 'sensation' on stage – burning riverboats, avalanches, heroines tied to railway tracks, etc. In an age that gave dramatists only a flat fee, (while managers could pocket thousands from their work), he forced the theatres to introduce a system of percentage royalties.

In 1844, Boucicault worked as a translator in Paris for the American showman Phineas T Barnum, then touring France with his new attraction the midget General Tom Thumb; he gleaned many business tricks from the experienced Barnum. (In 1882, Barnum attended a Wilde lecture to find out if Oscar's act might fit in with his circus, but decided against it.)

Throughout his life Boucicault was constantly accused (usually correctly) of plagiarism. He brushed off the attacks: "Plays are not written; they are rewritten" and added: "Originality is a quality that never existed. An author cannot exist without progenitors any more than a child can. We are born of each other". A sympathetic critic said of him: "if he steals satin, at least he embroiders it with silk".

In his early days in America, Boucicault suffered a reverse in New Orleans when he produced an extravaganza called 'Azael', set in Memphis in Ancient Egypt. He paid meticulous attention to the stage details and was bewildered when some of the audience complained loudly that he had 'got Memphis all wrong'. The inhabitants of Memphis were very different to his stage characters and there was no temple in the town either. It turned out that they meant Memphis, Tennessee.

He soon realised that he would have to adapt his work to suit the tastes of such audiences. Boucicault: "Shakespeare spells ruin and Byron bankruptcy" – "Whilst true genius starves, bunkum feasts in purple and fine linen".

Accordingly, when one of his plays, 'The Octoroon' (1859), flopped because the audience did not wish to see the heroine die, he changed the ending so that she lived happily ever after. He amended the advertisements to read: 'as composed by the public and edited by the author'.

As this play dealt with the then difficult subject of slavery, the public were shocked and titillated by the news that the heroine, (portrayed as one-eighth black), had received a note threatening her with shooting if she appeared again. (Always alert to publicity, Boucicault had sent the note himself.)

When his play 'Formosa' depicted a prostitute, the press controversy was stoked mostly by Boucicault sending anonymous letters of 'outrage' both for and against the idea.

When he had a major success with his play 'The Poor of New York' and took it on tour to Britain, he hit on the idea of changing the script slightly and renaming it 'The Poor of Liverpool'. This proved so popular that Boucicault continued round the country with a production known successively as 'The Poor of Birmingham', 'The Poor of London', 'The Poor of Southampton', and so on ad infinitum.

Boucicault was honest about the situation: "I can spin out these rough-and-tumble dramas as a hen lays eggs. It's a degrading occupation, but more money has been made out of guano than out of poetry".

Taste finally caught up with him and by the end of his life he was regarded as an outdated relic in a world coming to terms with Ibsen.

His cavalier attitude to theatre extended to other areas of his life. Financially, he repeatedly swung from wealth to bankruptcy and back with effortless ease. Reputed to have made love to dozens of women, he was married three times. He told a friend: "None but the brave deserve the fair, and none but the brave can live with some of them".

His first wife, a French widow named Anne Guiot, died in Switzerland after an illness. Boucicault's reputation was such that gossip spread that he had pushed her off a mountain. One report claimed: "Boucicault went up the Alps with a wife, and came down with a black armband".

A friend said that: "His character is so bad that there is not a crime under the sun of which he is not accused. The most dreadful stories are told of him".

His second wife, Agnes Robertson, provided him with six children and at one stage became such a famous actress in America that she threatened to eclipse Boucicault himself. Throughout their marriage he continued to 'aid young actresses in their careers'.

One such performer was Ida Savory, who created a fierce rivalry for her favours by playing off Boucicault against the rising American star Maurice Barrymore, (scion of the future acting dynasty). Eventually they became drinking friends and agreed to share Ida.

In 1885, Boucicault and Agnes parted company; he philosophised that: 'love ends in matrimony, wine in soda-water'. Aged 65, he married a twenty-one- year-old Australian actress called Louise Thorndyke, claiming that he had never been properly married to Agnes. His children were annoyed at being thus declared illegitimate, but he weathered the storm of public condemnation and settled to a benign old age with Louise.

Despite his adopted American citizenship, he retained his affection for Ireland and was proud that his best plays reflected Irish life. He also supported Irish moves towards independence and corresponded with *D'Israeli* on the subject.

(In 1876, his favourite son Willie was killed in a train accident at Huntingdon in England. A grieving Boucicault was so touched by the sympathy shown to him by the people of Huntingdon that he paid for a new school to be erected in the town. It remained in use until 1939 when it was turned into a museum commemorating Huntingdon's most famous son, Oliver Cromwell. It was an ironic fate for the pro-Irish Boucicault's gift.)

When he died in 1890 his funeral was held at 'the Little Church Around the Corner' in New York. The church had gained this name in 1870. An actor called George Holland had died and his friend, Joseph Jefferson, tried to arrange a funeral at a fashionable church.

The prelate in charge refused burial on the grounds that Holland was an actor but said that: 'there was a little church around the corner that did that sort of thing'. Jefferson said pointedly: 'God bless the little church around the corner, then'. It proudly kept its nickname and retained its connection with the stage.

Wilde was also friendly with his son, **DION BOUCICAULT Junior**, (1859-1929, and known as 'Dot'), who had become an important theatre manager in Australia. Dot returned to London in 1895 to become director of the Duke of York's Theatre; his wife Irene Vanbrugh created one of the roles in the original 'The Importance of Being Earnest'. He directed the first production of 'Peter Pan', in which his sister Nina took the title role.

In 1916, the actor Fred Kerr performed in a comedy under Dot's direction. On the first night, Kerr was confidently expecting a huge success in what he knew to be a very funny role. However, before the curtain rose, Dot strode out before the audience and announced that a German air raid was imminent but that the show would go ahead.

After he had given advice as to the whereabouts of the nearest casualty stations, Dot left the stage and retired to a sort of dugout, leaving the cast to carry on. Kerr: 'After which, every door that banged was a bomb, and no smile of any sort or kind could be extracted from an audience in momentary expectation of being hurled into eternity.'

While in Boston, Wilde also met another old Irish-American friend, the poet and rebel JOHN BOYLE O'REILLY (1844-1890), who had published one of Oscar's early poems in his paper, the Boston Pilot. It was O'Reilly who prompted Oscar's admiring comment that: 'The Celtic intellect has had to cross the Atlantic...What captivity was to the Jews, exile has been to the Irish. America and American influence has educated them'.

The hospitable and lively O'Reilly took Wilde around Boston and accompanied him to the theatre there. Later in the year, he provided even more practical aid when Wilde was fleeced in a New York gambling den by a conman called 'Hungry Joe' Sellick. O'Reilly helped him out of the scrape and lent him money to pay a lawyer and to get home.

O'Reilly had lived an extraordinary life of adventure. As a convinced Irish patriot, he joined the British army in 1866 to train himself for future revolt and to foment dissension within the ranks.

After he had recruited over one hundred fellow troopers of the elite 10th Hussars into the Fenian movement, he was arrested and condemned to death. The commanding officer, Colonel Valentine Baker, was furious: "Hang you, O'Reilly! You have spoiled the best regiment in Ireland!"

Although O'Reilly was reprieved, he received a sentence of life imprisonment and transportation to the harsh coast near Fremantle, Western Australia. Escape was extremely difficult; on land, the snake-infested unmapped bush, by sea, the shark-infested Indian Ocean. He was put to work in the road gangs in temperatures that could reach 120F.

(This may have inspired Wilde's later line in 'Earnest': 'You would have to choose between this world, the next world, and Australia... The accounts I have received of Australia and the next world are not particularly encouraging'.)

After two years, O'Reilly achieved the near impossible by escaping. With the help of a friendly priest who made a deal with an American whaling captain, he fled the prison camp and hid in the bush. Using a tiny leaking boat, he attempted to row the twelve miles to the whaler waiting for him in international waters. Twice he failed to find it; on the third time he succeeded and a year later arrived in the USA.

While building a career as a journalist and writer, he worked to help his fellow convicts back in Australia and raised the money to buy and crew a ship called the 'Catalpa'. This expedition managed to pull off an even more spectacular escape, rescuing six Fenians by sea and then evading pursuit by British ships.

O'Reilly's later efforts to destroy the British Navy by building a wooden submarine called the 'Fenian Ram' came to nothing. But he became an accomplished author and poet, writing an excellent novel called 'Moondyne' based on his experiences. (In 1963, President John F Kennedy quoted an O'Reilly poem during a speech to the Irish National Assembly).

Although there are several suggestions as to the origin of the unseen character called 'Bunbury' in 'The Importance of Being Earnest', it has been noted that the prison settlement where O'Reilly spent much of his Australian captivity was called Bunbury.

On February 7th, Wilde lectured at the Opera House, Rochester, NY. Like his previous talk at Harvard, it was a boisterous occasion where students tried to disrupt the event; police were called to eject some of them. Two nights previously, Wilde had dined with the American writer and journalist Joaquin Miller – (Oscar described him as 'a beautiful poet').

JOAQUIN MILLER 1837-1913

Joaquin Miller, (born Cincinnatus Hiner Miller), was angry over the behaviour of the 'ruffians' at Rochester and wrote a letter of sympathy to Wilde: 'Sir, when I see such things here in the civilised portion of my country and read the coarse comments of the Philistine Press, I feel like thanking God that my home lies three thousand miles farther on, and in what is called the wilderness'.

Miller was very proud of his Western antecedents and constructed his entire career on his experience of the American frontier. Although born in Indiana, his family set out by covered wagon on the Oregon Trail in 1852. They were attacked by Red Indians and were fortunate to survive. Miller's father, a resolute Quaker, refused to fight, while Joaquin himself was armed only with an old flintlock rifle which, in the heat of battle, he discovered to have no flint. Fortunately other members of the wagon train drove off the assailants.

In spite of this incident, Miller was impressed by the Plains tribes. An Indian chief spotted the beautiful daughter of one of the wagon train families and offered to buy her. Her father jokingly replied that he wanted ten magnificent horses in exchange. Next day, his good humour was quashed when the chief returned with the required dowry, plus a large and menacing group of warriors.

Faced with a possible massacre, a majority of the wagon train suggested that they should honour the agreement and hand over the girl. She was horrified at the idea and ran to a nearby cliff, threatening to throw herself over the edge if the deal went ahead. The chief realised the situation and relented. He rode off with his warriors, scornfully rejecting the offer of presents from the by now shame-faced wagon train.

After his family had settled in Oregon, in 1856 Miller set off for the Californian goldfields. While there, he fought in several minor skirmishes against the Modoc Indians. Once, when he had been cheated of his wages, he stole a horse from his employer and fled to the mountains.

This was a serious offence. (Wilde: 'In California murder is regarded as a fine art but a horse thief is universally despised.') Miller was captured and imprisoned in a county jail. With the aid of a fellow prisoner named Jack Marshall, he escaped by sawing through the bars of his cell and headed once more to the mountains where he stayed with Marshall and his gang of desperadoes.

Mistakenly thinking that the fuss had died down, he returned to drink in a saloon, was quickly recognised, and had to back out of the bar while covering the clientele with a revolver. After a gunfight with a pursuing posse, Miller made it back into the woods.

For a while he avoided civilisation and followed the Red Indian lifestyle, living by hunting and fishing, and setting up home with an Indian woman who bore him a daughter named Cali-Shasta. Later, he moved on and became a cook at a mining encampment where he became known as 'Crazy Miller'. Finally he returned to Oregon.

His next venture was to become a partner in a pony express company. This was dangerous work, often beset by the ferocious Chinook winds of the Rockies and with the constant danger of attack by 'road agents' (highwaymen).

On one occasion, he was carrying gold dust down a mountain when his horse shied, then plunged off the track and down the hillside. A moment later a hail of bullets swept over the area they had just left. The horse carried him to safety from the road agents before it collapsed and died from gunshot wounds.

By 1860, Miller was studying law while also editing a small newspaper. In 1866 he was appointed as a judge. Dissatisfied with Oregon, he returned to California determined to break into the newly emerging literary circle of San Francisco, (which included *Ambrose Bierce* and Bret Harte).

When his overtures were rejected he decided to try his luck in England and, in 1870, moved into lodgings at 11, Museum Street, London. Initially, he had no more luck than in San Francisco. He attempted to sell his poetry to the London publisher John Murray whose reply was: "Poetry won't do, don't you know". (Murray was quite the wrong person to deal with; he had informed one aspiring female bard: "You think, ma'am, that the public don't like poetry. You're wrong, ma'am. They hate it").

However, Miller was to prove Murray wrong. He decided correctly that, if he wore the flamboyant costume of the Wild West, automatically he would stand out as a sensation amidst the sober attire of Victorian England. Hence he was never seen without a buckskin jacket, a scarlet sash, a large knife in his belt, and with his hair flowing to his shoulders. He published his poems at his own expense and, (with the aid of the ever-helpful *Lord Houghton* who touted him as 'the Byron of Oregon'), they became popular.

His 1871 volumes, 'Pacific Poems' and 'Songs of the Sierras', were acclaimed in Britain, although his own compatriots regarded them as ludicrously romantic. When the American writers *Mark Twain* and *Ambrose Bierce* arrived in London, they found Miller's caricature of an American intensely embarrassing. At one society dinner, they cringed when Miller lifted up a large fish from a tureen and swallowed it whole. He brushed off their objections: "It helps sell the poems, boys! And it tickles the duchesses".

Miller returned to the United States as a relatively rich man and determined to continue his career as a stage American even on home territory. To this end he constructed a log cabin in Rock Creek Park, Washington, DC, and adorned the walls with wild animal skins, bows and arrows, etc.

In his old age, Miller still indulged his taste for adventure. In 1897, working for the William Randolph Hearst newspapers, he travelled to the Klondyke gold rush in Alaska, where he endured a frightful 300 mile journey through blizzards and the loss of all his food to arrive back in Dawson City more dead than alive. Miller: "I would not be tied up in this lorn, large, desolate, largeness another winter for all the Klondike gold".

In 1900, aged 63 and again reporting for Hearst, he accompanied American troops to the relief of the Legations in Peking during the Boxer Rebellion.

He spent his last years back in California. There he was able to indulge his love of hard liquor – his favourite tipples were 'Bad Eye', 'Hell's Delight', 'Rat Pizen', and 'Howling Modoc'.

Miller's contemporary and occasional rival in writing about the American West was the author **BRET HARTE** (1836-1902), whom Wilde described as 'a lord of romance'. During the 1880s, he was the US Consul in Glasgow, Scotland.

On his return to America, Harte was complimented on the great fame he had achieved in Europe. He smiled but shook his head, explaining that he had once delivered a lecture in England and was introduced by the local mayor. The man gave a lengthy introductory speech praising the great qualities and merit that his guest possessed.

Harte: "He wound up his speech with 'And now let me introduce to you, Mr...er – er.. Mr...' Then he turned to me and asked in a furious whisper 'What the deuce is your name?' "

By February 9th 1882, Wilde reached the Niagara Falls. He did not find the sight satisfactory. Wilde: "I was disappointed with Niagara – most people must be disappointed with Niagara... Every American bride is taken there, and the sight of the stupendous waterfall must be one of the earliest, if not the keenest, disappointments of American married life... It is simply a vast unnecessary amount of water going the wrong way and then falling over unnecessary rocks. The wonder would be if the water did not fall'.

WILDE IN THE WEST

Through February and March, Oscar continued his lecture tour through the States of Ohio, Minnesota, Indiana, Kentucky, Wisconsin, Nebraska, Illinois, and Iowa.

When he reached Chicago, he found that the famous boxer John L Sullivan was in town. Sullivan had just beaten a strong contender, Paddy Ryan, after a nine-round bare-fist fight. The rumour circulated that there was going to be a Wilde v. Sullivan world title bout. In reference to Oscar's earlier comments, Sullivan issued a mischievous statement to the press conspicuously praising the Atlantic Ocean.

While in Illinois, Wilde was asked to lecture on art at Griggsville, named after its founder. Oscar: "They sent me a telegram – 'Will you come and lecture us on beauty?' I sent a reply, also by telegram – 'Begin by changing your name'. This they declined to do".

Towards the end of March, Wilde found himself near Sioux City, Iowa. 'I don't know where I am, but I am among canyons and coyotes – one is a sort of fox, the other a deep ravine: I don't know which is which, but it does not really matter in the West'.

Wilde continued his tour on the six-day Southern Pacific train journey from Omaha to San Francisco, stopping at 230 stations on the way, and passing through Cheyenne, Salt Lake City, Reno, the mining villages of the High Sierras, and Sacramento. It had been only thirteen years since this railway had been completed, and the countryside was endlessly boring. The main diversion for passengers was shooting prairie dogs from the windows of the train. Wilde said that the prairies reminded him of a piece of blotting paper. Oscar: 'The desolate prairie, the alkali plains, which conveyed the impression that Nature had given up the job of decorating the country, so vast its size, in absolute despair'.

Finally he arrived in California. Wilde: 'So infinitesimal did I find the knowledge of Art west of the Rocky Mountains, that an art patron, one who in his time had been a successful gold prospector, actually sued the railway company for damages, because the plaster cast of the Venus de Milo, which he had imported from Paris, had been delivered minus the arms. What is even more surprising still, is that he won the case and the damages'.

For once, Wilde's long flowing hair stood him in good stead. Whereas in Britain and the American East Coast it had been regarded as effeminate, in the West long hair had always been associated with frontier heroes such as Kit Carson, General Custer and Buffalo Bill Cody. It was a point of honour among the scouts that they grew their hair long so as to provide a good scalp-lock if they were killed.

One reporter wrote: 'With his long hair and wide-brimmed hat, he is not unlike a Texas ranger who had struck it rich'. Oscar was seen as part of a great tradition of hairdressing.

AMBROSE BIERCE 1842-1914

As he had no connection at all with the man, Wilde was surprised to be the subject of a particularly vicious press attack in April 1882 by the American writer Ambrose Bierce. After describing Oscar as being 'twin show to the two-headed calf', Bierce wrote that: 'in Mr Wilde's lectures there is nothing to criticise, for there is nothing of his own'.

To the arch-cynic Bierce, Wilde was a representative of much that he disliked – Oscar was Irish, sympathetic to socialism, and a Freemason (a group that Bierce said gloried in 'a blazonry of meaningless mystery'). Wilde saw men such as Bierce as having crabbed intellects: 'A cynic is a man who knows the price of everything and the value of nothing'.

As a young man, Bierce had been an anti-slavery supporter and was one of the first volunteers to join the Union forces. Eventually promoted to brevet major, he fought in many of the battles and was seen by his men as brave, (he once rescued a wounded man while under heavy fire), but also aloof and unfriendly. His military career was effectively ended when he was shot in the head at the Battle of Kenesaw Mountain outside Atlanta in 1864.

On recovery, Bierce joined a survey expedition in the Far West, (at Fort Phil Kearney, he dined with the soldiers who shortly afterwards were slaughtered in the Fetterman Massacre), before arriving in San Francisco. He was enthused by the new Western literary movement that had sprung up in opposition to the traditional Boston school.

Then in 1871, on honeymoon with his new wife Mary Ellen Day, he travelled to England. He enjoyed the country so much that he stayed for three years and became part of the Fleet Street set who drank in the bar of the Ludgate Hill railway station. As a drinker he became known as 'an eminent tankard man'; as a writer, he was known as 'Bitter Bierce'.

(One day the Ludgate Hill crowd were discussing a court case where a man was on trial for homosexuality. Bierce said: "I never heard of such a crime before!" A fellow drinker crowed in reply: "What Bierce means is that he never before heard that it was a crime".)

Bierce supplemented his journalistic income by becoming editor of a pamphlet dedicated to protecting the name of the deposed French *Empress Eugenie*. While in Britain she had been defamed by an ex-Communard pamphleteer called Henri Rochefort. Rochefort ceased publication after an onslaught from Bierce that included such comments as: 'Mr Rochefort, we believe, is suffering from an unhealed wound. It is his mouth'.

Returning to the USA in 1875, Bierce spent the next twenty years in California as 'a kind of West Coast Samuel Johnson', except for a brief and unsuccessful trip to the Dakota Territory to look for gold. In spite of his own involvement, he always derided the attempt by Americans to romanticise the conquest of the West, seeing it simply as a land grab, laced by genocide.

After absorbing the works of Voltaire and Jonathan Swift, he realised that satire was his forte. With his motto of 'Nothing matters', he set about demolishing the mores of his age with a fearless malevolence.

He had a strong dislike of religions and the religious. One parson who unwisely called on the Bierce household was shocked to hear Bierce's eldest son shouting: "Damn God!" Bierce turned and upbraided the child with the words: "I have repeatedly told you not to say Damn God when you mean God Damn".

Although rarely without a mistress, Bierce was generally indifferent to women, preferring alcohol by far. He said that the only women he respected were the Empress Eugenie, George Eliot, and the American writer *Gertrude Atherton*.

His admiration for the latter had started when one day she visited his home. Being an abrasive critic herself, she argued with him over literature and said that he was incapable of writing novels. (Atherton: "We almost spat at each other"). In high dudgeon he led her towards the railway station, then suddenly pushed her to the ground between a saloon and a pigsty and attempted to rape her.

To his surprise she burst out laughing. Shocked at this response, he desisted and burst out: "I never want to see you again. You are the most detestable little vixen I ever met in my life, and I've had a horrible day". She adjusted her bonnet and replied: "Well, sir, I have only been mildly bored". Despite (or because of) this inauspicious beginning, they remained lively and even friendly correspondents.

(Later, Bierce was highly amused when he heard that the great Italian tenor, Enrico Caruso, had been arrested after a similar incident. Caruso was found guilty of 'jostling' a woman in the Central Park Zoo monkey house in New York.)

He became a violent opponent of social reform and trade unions. Bierce declared that the average man was 'an immortal ass' and that dictatorship was the only sensible government.

Once, when watching a throng of people gather at a winter fair, he said to a friend: "Wouldn't it be fun to turn loose a machine gun into that crowd".

However, in spite of his aversion to socialism, Bierce was no more complimentary about predatory capitalism. The 'Gilded Age' of America provided him with endless ammunition. During the fifty years from the end of the Civil War to World War One, the USA was awash with corruption. Such men as Jay Gould and Cornelius Vanderbilt led the capitalist plundering of the economy.

Bierce enthusiastically leapt to attack them and their ilk. When Senator Leland Stanford endowed a university in California, Bierce snarled that this represented: "a restitution by Senator Stanford of the money stolen from the people".

In 1887, Bierce began to work for the newspaper owner, William Randolph Hearst. Such was Bierce's reputation that he was allowed unusual liberty – Bierce was the first and last of Hearst's writers to enjoy freedom of speech in his papers.

[WILLIAM RANDOLPH HEARST (1863-1951) had inherited his newspaper, the San Francisco Examiner, and a fortune from his senator father George, who himself had become immensely rich from mining the famed Comstock Lode. William Randolph increased the family riches by pioneering the idea of sensationalist newspaper reporting.

In 1898, Oscar Wilde sold his poem, 'The Ballad of Reading Gaol', to a Hearst publication: 'I rest my hopes on the New York Journal. They have millions, and like what is calculated to make a stir of some kind, or any kind'. Nonetheless, Wilde was attuned to the political ramifications of such power: 'In America the President reigns for four years, and Journalism governs for ever and ever'.

Gertrude Atherton gave an insight into Hearst and his problems. She said that he prided himself on having the most brilliant editorial staff in the United States but he paid a high price in that every single one of them was a steady drinker. "There was a memorable occasion when all of them were down at Los Gatos taking, or pretending to take, the Keeley cure, and Hearst had to get out the paper himself with the aid of the printers. He used to say that no one had ever suffered more from the drink habit than he, although he never drank himself."]

Although the Hearst Press provided Bierce with a platform, he was not blind to the inherent danger of Hearst's control over the media. He realised the dictatorial power that a single person could wield when all his papers spoke with one voice. Bierce: 'Newspapers are sycophants to the mob, tyrants to the individual'.

At no time was this power more nakedly displayed than during the 1890s when the United States embarked on an overtly imperialist strategy. Hearst and his political allies were keen to mop up the possessions of the decaying Spanish Empire, with a particular eye to acquiring Cuba, Guam, Costa Rica and the Philippines, (Bierce: 'War is God's way of teaching Americans geography').

Hearst unleashed a storm of propaganda detailing imaginary accounts of the 'horrors of Spanish rule'. Such items as the 'burning of priests' and the 'violation of nuns' received special prominence. President William McKinley was not in favour of war, (Teddy Roosevelt described him as 'having a chocolate éclair spine'), but was pressured into it by 'public' opinion. Seeing the press manipulations at close quarters, Bierce was unimpressed by Hearst's arguments and declared the resulting occupation of Cuba to be blatant state piracy.

He reverted to a more robust attitude when, after ousting Spain, the USA conquered the Philippines and, (in a brutal campaign that saw the deaths of at least 100,000 Philippinos and 4,200 Americans), crushed the nationalist resistance. Bierce tended to agree with the concept of 'manifest destiny' as espoused by Senator Beveridge: "We will not renounce our part in the mission of our race, trustees under God, of the civilisation of the world". Bierce regarded this view as the practical reflection of Darwin's theory of the 'survival of the fittest'.

In addition to his journalism, Bierce began to write the works that ensured his niche in literature. As well as his excellent short stories based mostly on his Civil War experiences, between 1881 and 1906 he wrote his well-known 'The Devil's Dictionary', in which he created comic definitions for his betes noir. One example was: 'A lawsuit is a machine which one enters as a pig and emerges as a sausage'.

His domestic life collapsed in tragedy. He left his wife Mary after he mistakenly suspected her of having an affair and bitterly added another definition to his Dictionary: 'Husband – one who, having dined, is charged with the care of the plate'.

His son Leigh became drunk one night, ran off into a snowstorm, and died of the resulting pneumonia. His other son Day Bierce, after falling in love with a girl, shot and killed a rival, then committed suicide. As the coffins of her two lovers left the local station on different trains, the girl murmured philosophically: "Life is sure queer. One goes one way and one goes another, but here I am!"

In 1914, and aged 72, Bierce decided to leave for Mexico: "Why should I remain in a country that is on the eve of prohibition and women's suffrage?" He obtained credentials to join the rebel army of Pancho Villa. He sent a final letter stating that he was on his way to the siege of Ojinaga. After that nothing was ever heard of Bierce again. He vanished completely.

A later report circulated that Pancho Villa had ordered him to be put up against a wall and shot. When asked about the alleged incident, Villa replied that, if he had done so, he certainly had no memory of it.

Bierce's mysterious end seemed to fit with his definition of history: 'An account mostly false, of events mostly unimportant, which are brought about by rulers mostly knaves, and soldiers mostly fools'.

Among the legion of Bierce's enemies was the English publisher and pornographer **JOHN CAMDEN HOTTEN** (1832-1873). He was best known for publishing some of *Algernon Swinburne's* sex fantasies – including one in which Queen Victoria's twin sister became a Haymarket whore, and Victoria herself succumbs to ravishment by a rampantly goatish William Wordsworth.

Bierce knew Hotten well in London and wrote some (non-pornographic) pieces for him. In common with many of his contemporary scribes, Bierce despised publishers: 'Men who drink wine from authors' skulls while authors are busy writing applications for admittance to the Poor House'.

On one occasion, Bierce finally managed to extract a £100 post-dated cheque from Hotten and, being short of cash, went to the publisher's Highgate home to ask for an advance. On arrival, he found that Hotten had suddenly died. Realising that his only hope of acquiring the £100 was to reach the bank before they discovered that Hotten was dead, he hailed a cab and rushed 'furiously bankward'.

Unfortunately, he stopped off at the Ludgate Hill tavern to inform his literary friends of Hotten's demise. Delighted by the news of any publisher's death, they called for rounds of drinks to celebrate, and fell to composing epitaphs for the man. The journalist George Augustus Sala was adjudged the winner for his effort – 'Hotten. Rotten. Forgotten.' However, Bierce celebrated for so long that he missed the bank. His delay had cost him £100.

Hotten's firm was taken over by some new publishers called Chatto and Windus who became notorious for cheating their authors. One morning, a defrauded writer burst into their offices in search of vengeance. Not having met the partners before, he glared at the man in front of him and bellowed: "If you're Chatto, damn Windus, and if you're Windus, damn Chatto!"

Another figure who came under Bierce's lethal gaze was President **THEODORE (Teddy) ROOSEVELT** (1858-1919). Wilde had met the Roosevelt family when he stayed with Teddy's uncle, a sportsman and politician called Robert Barnwell Roosevelt, at his Long Island estate in 1882.

Bierce detested Teddy Roosevelt and described him as 'a timid blusterer'. During the Spanish-American War, Roosevelt allegedly had led a famous cavalry charge by the Rough Riders up San Juan Hill in Cuba. He had been widely honoured for this exploit and it had been a factor in his gaining of the US Presidency.

When Bierce visited the White House, Roosevelt tried to charm him by saying that during the charge he had been inspired by one of Bierce's short stories. However Bierce had checked the facts and questioned witnesses. His conclusion was that the real glory belonged to the Negro Tenth Cavalry and that Roosevelt had scrambled up the San Juan Hill on foot with the rest of the troops. Bierce: 'Both he and I knew that the Roosevelt ride had never taken place'.

MORMONS AND MINERS

Returning circuitously eastwards in April 1882, Wilde arrived in Salt Lake City, Utah. For some reason, the Mormon inhabitants seemed to attract opprobrious comments from most of their visitors. Wilde said: "I never saw such an unintelligent or ugly race…. Mormons have no idea of art". Mark Twain also expressed distaste at the ugliness of Mormon women, while Julia Ward Howe said they were "mostly an ill-looking and ill-smelling crowd". A Utah gallant said that the reason for the ravaged complexions of the Salt Lake City women was the dry air.

Ambrose Bierce, on the other hand, thought the Mormons were "the best class of people after the Chinese and the Jews".

Wilde lectured in a building called the Amelia Palace, which had been built in honour of one of the wives of their leader, Brigham Young. (Mark Twain: 'Having seen the sixty wives and how ugly they are, I realised that Brigham Young was in fact a man of immense charity and generosity').

Wilde: 'When Young died, the next President of the Mormons stood up in the Tabernacle and told the assembled multitude that it had been revealed to him that he was to own the Amelia Palace and that on this particular subject there was to be absolutely no future revelations of any kind whatsoever.'

By April 12, Wilde had moved on to Denver, Colorado. The town had been well primed for his entry. Local prostitutes began to sport giant sunflowers, while the miners had taken to complimenting each other's appearance with the words "too utterly utter".

Oscar seemed to take to frontier habits: "I visited a dancing saloon in Denver where I saw the most rational method of art criticism I have ever come across. On the piano was printed a notice 'Please do not shoot the pianist; he is only doing his best'."

The next day he reached the Rocky Mountain mining town of Leadville, Colorado.

Wilde: 'I received a message that if I went to Leadville as I proposed to do, the tougher spirits there would be sure to shoot me or my travelling manager. I immediately wrote and told them that nothing they could possibly do to my travelling manager could possibly intimidate me, and went.'

Leadville was not known for artistic appreciation. The previous week's main attraction had been a foot race between two naked prostitutes. Also the murder rate was unusually high. Oscar later claimed that Leadville used real criminals to play the part of villains in their theatre. 'In a local production of 'Macbeth', the part of Lady Macbeth was played by a real life murderess, whose name appeared on the posters, followed by the statement – "Ten Years Penal Servitude".

Wilde: 'I spoke to the audience, consisting entirely of taciturn miners, about the early Florentines and they slept as if no crime had ever stained the ravines of their wild mountain home. I described to them the pictures of Botticelli and the name, which seemed to them like a new drink, roused them from their dreams. I read them passages from the autobiography of Benvenuto Cellini and they seemed highly delighted. I was reproved by my listeners for not having brought him with me. I explained that he had been dead for some little time, which elicited the inquiry, "Who shot him?" '

Wilde continued his tour in St. Joseph, Missouri. The outlaw Jesse James had been murdered in the town just two weeks prior to Oscar's arrival. Wilde: 'The Americans are certainly great hero-worshippers, and always take their heroes from the criminal classes'. He noticed a crowd near his hotel: 'They were relic hunters. I discovered that they were selling Mr James's dustbin by public auction. The reserve price on it was about the annual income of an English bishop.'

As he moved on through the Mid-West, even Oscar's spirits sagged occasionally. When in arrived in Topeka, Kansas, he sent a letter to a friend: 'The local poet has just called on me with his masterpiece, a sanguinary lyric of 3000 lines on the Civil War. The impassioned part begins thus: 'Here Mayor Simpson battled bravely with his Fifteenth Kansas Cavalry'. What am I to do?'

Having continued on through Iowa, Ohio, and Pennsylvania, Wilde arrived back in New York in May 1882. Although the tour was ostensibly over, D'Oyley Carte decided to extend it and arranged a further tour of Canada. Oscar waited for instructions and spent some of his time visiting the private houses of friends. In one of them he was introduced to a nine-year-old girl. After careful perusal of Oscar, the child turned to its mother and said: "Ma, I don't think that you should bring the baby in here, it might be scared".

Wilde's Canadian lecture tour began on May 13th and continued till August 26th. He gave one of the first talks at the Queens Hall, Montreal; it was well received despite a few faux pas. The populace were not pleased to hear Oscar describe their revered mountain as 'a hill', and when he praised the wonderful Canadian tea and cigarettes, he was told that they had been imported.

He was greeted in Ottawa by the Canadian Prime Minister, Sir John Macdonald, who gave him dinner, and took Oscar to visit the Canadian House of Commons, where he was allowed to sit beside the Speaker's Chair.

One MP, a Mr Arthur Bunster, was reported to have been: "so wrapt in contemplation of the original Bunthorne that he even forgot for a time the burning wrongs of British Columbia".

THE MARQUESS OF LORNE
and PRINCESS LOUISE 1845-1914 / 1848-1939

Two people whom Oscar expected to meet in Ottawa were the Governor-General of Canada, the Marquess of Lorne, and his wife, Princess Louise, one of *Queen Victoria's* daughters. They had both visited the Salisbury Street house back in London, and Oscar's great friend *Ronald Gower* was Lorne's uncle, (though older by only four days). But, for different reasons, they both missed Wilde's arrival. Louise was abroad, while Lorne was anxious to avoid association with the flamboyantly effeminate Oscar, and had disappeared on a golfing holiday.

Son of the Duke of Argyle, Lorne had been introduced to homosexuality while at Eton, and then confirmed in his tastes by Gower who had been his guide to the London gay underworld. Enough rumours circulated about Lorne in Canada without having Oscar in tow.

Princess Louise's absence was a more predictable event. Raised in a court permanently mourning her father, Prince Albert, she reacted to her miserable upbringing by escaping into the bohemian world of art. When her mother, Queen Victoria, realised that she was probably having an affair with the sculptor, Joseph Boehm, (fourteen years her senior), Victoria immediately set about finding Louise a more suitable husband. The Marquess of Lorne turned out to be the unfortunate solution.

After their marriage in 1871, they realised that they were incompatible and mostly went their own ways. Louise continued her liaison with Boehm, while Lorne remained a promiscuous homosexual. Louise became so alarmed at his activities that she bricked up the door that led from their apartments at Kensington Palace to Hyde Park in an effort to prevent her husband's nightly expeditions in search of compliant guardsmen.

In 1878, *Disraeli* appointed Lorne as Governor-General of Canada. Their arrival in the country was not auspicious, as Lorne and Louise were delayed for several days at sea waiting for heavy storms to abate. The Prime Minister, Sir John Macdonald, who had prepared a state reception for the new dignitaries, was similarly forced to wait on land. Being a devoted drinker, he whiled the time away with a lengthy binge. When the pair finally did land, Macdonald had such an appalling hangover that he had to cancel the reception, claiming 'lumbago problems'.

Their journey to Ottawa was accompanied by torrential rain and Lorne and Louise arrived at their official residence at Rideau Hall thoroughly drenched. At the new official reception there, Macdonald again got drunk and allegedly an incident occurred when he 'took a liberty' with Louise.

Bored stiff by her new home, Louise was delighted when she received a minor injury during a sleigh accident. She ruthlessly used this new excuse to spend most of the next few years 'recuperating' at various European resorts.

A Canadian newspaper caustically greeted the news of one of Louise's rare return visits: 'During her trip the Princess should not fail to make the acquaintance of the Marquess of Lorne. She will find him a very intelligent young man'.

Lorne was more conscientious in his duties and carried out a difficult trip to the Canadian Far West; he described it as 'a mixture of Scotland and Heaven'. He reached as far as Fort Calgary where he met representatives of the Blackfoot tribe who bestowed the Red Indian name of 'The Great Brother-in-Law' on him.

In 1883, he left Canada with two permanent reminders of his sojourn. For many years later, 'Lorne' became a favourite name for male Canadian children. Secondly, Sir John Macdonald accepted Lorne's choice of the name 'Alberta' for the new province, after rejecting Lorne's first choice of 'Louiseland'.

On his return to Britain, Lorne faded into the background. He came to public attention only once when he became something of a public joke after falling off his horse during the 1887 Golden Jubilee procession.

His interests were mostly literary and he attempted to rewrite certain parts of the Bible; later he tried poetry. *Henry Labouchere* said of the latter: 'since Lorne's ghastly experiments with the Psalms, one might have supposed he would have spared the world any more of his adventures in verse'.

Louise became a proficient sculptress, (her statue of Queen Victoria still stands outside Kensington Palace), and continued to mix with the artistic set of *Alma-Tadema, Augustus John,* and inevitably Joseph Boehm. Her association with Boehm had a tragic ending.

In 1890, during a bout of sex, Boehm died in Louise's arms. As he was extremely fat, reputedly a small winch had to be employed to pry his corpse off Louise. She concocted a story with the doctor that Boehm had died while 'moving a heavy statue'. Victoria never discovered the truth of the matter, and Boehm was commemorated with a plaque in the crypt of St Paul's Cathedral. It reads enigmatically: 'Born 1844. Died 1890. At His Work'.

The demise of Boehm did nothing to curb Louise's sexual appetite. Her niece said of her that she 'ran after anything in trousers', including the Kaiser. Amongst her lovers, she had an affair with Prince Henry of Battenburg, the husband of her sister Princess Beatrice. Her demands proved so great that a rumour circulated that Henry had signed up to serve in the 1896 Ashanti Expeditionary Force simply to escape the pressure. If so, it was a fatal decision as he died of fever while in Africa.

She remained the least sentimental of Queen Victoria's daughters. After the death of their mother, the bereaved children would gather annually to pay their respects in the family mausoleum at Frogmore in Windsor. One year, during their prayers, a dove entered the room and flew overhead. One of the children whispered that it must be 'dear Mama's spirit'. Louise sniffed and replied: "I don't think so. Dear Mama's spirit would never have ruined Helena's hat".

WILDE IN DIXIE

Returning from Canada to the USA, Wilde decided to continue his lectures in the South and began his new tour in Memphis, Tennessee.

He asked his new temporary manager, Pete Tracey, to exercise discretion over promoting the show: "Do not advertise to catch coarse people as I care only to speak to audiences that are educated and refined". His instructions were ignored and he found that his Pullman rail car was shrouded with a flowing white canvas emblazoned with his name in four-feet high letters.

At one station, the townsfolk gathered to witness the arrival. As Oscar stepped off the coach, the town band struck up with 'See the Conquering Hero Comes' and the crowd gave three hearty cheers, under the impression that he was Buffalo Bill.

Wilde lectured through Tennessee, Mississippi, and Louisiana before making a detour into Texas. His only real success was in San Antonio, where the audience were appreciative, though they considered that the talk, at one hour's length, was 'too long between drinks'. Oscar visited the Alamo which he thought to be 'a noble building' but that it was 'monstrous that it is not better cared for'.

By June 16th he had reached New Orleans where he 'bathed in the Gulf of Mexico and engaged in voodoo rites with the Negroes'. He was fascinated by the black people he met in the South: 'I am surprised that painters and poets have paid so little attention to the Negro as a subject of art'.

Oscar's maternal uncle, Dr John K Elgee, had immigrated to New Orleans in 1831, where he became a judge. He owned property in Louisiana worth £100,000, became a leading Confederate in Rapide parish, and died in 1864. On being questioned, Oscar denied that he had arrived to claim family lands, but admitted that he 'would rather like to own a grove of magnolia trees'.

On June 27, he stayed overnight at Beauvoir, the home of the former President of the Confederacy, the 74-year-old Jefferson Davis.

JEFFERSON DAVIS 1808-1889

After the collapse of the Confederacy, ex-President Davis had experienced difficult times, having been arrested and imprisoned in manacles for two years. In a wise move, the US government released him to avoid creating a martyr, but Davis had not prospered. When his business ventures failed, a sympathetic friend gave him a home at Beauvoir, near Mobile. Wilde: "He lives in a very beautiful house by the sea amid lovely trees. He impressed me very much as a man of the keenest intellect'.

Wilde had a romantic view of the Confederacy, seeing its struggle for independence as similar to that of the Irish experience. Wilde: 'The head may approve the success of the winner, but the heart is more to be with the fallen'. Although he said that Davis's 1881 book on the Civil War was a 'masterpiece', Oscar added: 'the elaborate detail of military manoeuvre is at times a little burdensome'.

Born of Welsh ancestry, Davis attended West Point and came to some prominence during the Mexican War of 1846-8. He fought against the Mexican Army under President Santa Anna at the Battle of Monterey and then, though wounded in the foot, cleverly defeated a flank attack by the enemy at the Battle of Buena Vista. He came to be seen (incorrectly) as having a good military brain.

(Santa Anna later lost a leg fighting against the French and suffered from 'phantom pain'. To alleviate this condition, he chewed gum laced with Mexican chicle root. When he was finally exiled to New York in the 1860s, his gum chewing habit was noticed by the manufacturer Thomas Adams who developed the product for a mass market. Santa Anna, (already famous as the conqueror of the Alamo), could also claim to have invented chewing gum.)

Davis later entered the world of Washington politics where, as a Southern congressional leader, he worked to extend the Southern sphere of interest into Cuba and Central America. He thought that the South's real interest lay, not in the West, but in the tropics. He owned slaves but was known as a fair, even generous, master. No whipping was allowed on his plantations unless a Negro jury, which sat on all offences, had sanctioned it.

Wilde strongly disagreed with this policy: 'The worst slave-owners were those who were kind to their slaves, and so prevented the horror of the system being realised by those who suffered from it, and understood by those who contemplated it'.

In 1861, the long-threatened Civil War broke out. Although it has been generally assumed that the conflict was fought to end slavery, or to hold the United States together as one entity, it is arguable that the major reason was financial. The North was desperate to protect its fledgling industries and introduced strong federal tariffs to deter foreign competition. The South, dependent on easy foreign trade for its cotton exports, strongly resented this suppression of free trade. Some of the war's origins lay in economic rivalry.

When the South seceded from the Union and the Confederacy was formed, Davis became its first (and last) President. He was inaugurated a month after Abraham Lincoln was inaugurated as President of the United States.

(A song called 'Dixie', written by the 'father of Negro minstrelsy' Dan Emmett in 1859, had become a popular hit across the USA. With new words and under the title of the 'Lincoln Quick Step', it was played to celebrate Lincoln's inauguration. Just thirty days later, with even newer words and now with the title 'The Confederacy March', it was played to celebrate Davis's inauguration.)

Although his task of creating a nation in the midst of war was an immensely difficult one, Davis's lack of judgment was a decisive factor in its failure. Even his martial reputation proved illusory and at the First Battle of Bull Run he had received a humiliating rebuff, despite the Southern victory.

Although the Northern army were soundly beaten, the battle had been a confused affair; at one point, some of the Confederate forces had themselves retreated. Davis, riding out to oversee the battle, had met some of these fugitives and assumed the worst. He determined that at least he could fight and die with his defeated troops and spurred on to the battlefield.

On arrival, he noticed an officer being tended for a slight wound and melodramatically harangued the man to return to his duty and fight to the end. The man in question turned out to be 'Stonewall' Jackson, whose brilliant defence in fact had saved the day already. Frostily, Jackson pointed out that the battle had been won two hours previously. A crestfallen Davis slowly ceased gesticulating with his sword and glumly rode off.

Wilde wrote to *Julia Ward Howe* of his visit to meet Davis: 'How fascinating all failures are'.

While in New Orleans, Wilde also met one of Davis's former colleagues, **GENERAL PIERRE BEAUREGARD** (1818-1893), who took Oscar for a carriage ride around the city and showed him the Catholic Cathedral.

Beauregard was a small but fiery man of French-Creole stock, who in common with many military men harboured a fantasy that he was destined to be the new Napoleon. When the South seceded, President Davis sent Beauregard to take command in Charleston, SC.

During the opening engagement of the war, Beauregard opened fire on the Union controlled Fort Sumter in Charleston harbour. Although the bombardment was heavy, it did remarkably little damage; one officer commented: "All it did was to make the fort look as if it was suffering from smallpox". Miraculously, there were no casualties.

However, after a small fire started, the Union commander, Major Anderson, decided to surrender. As a mark of respect, Beauregard allowed Anderson's request to fire one last salute in honour of 'Old Glory', the US flag. Unfortunately the gun misfired and blew up, accidentally killing a Union private – the first victim of the Civil War.

Beauregard had mixed military success during the succeeding four years. He took a major role in the Battle of Shiloh, commanded the Southern troops at Fort Wagner, (an incident dramatised in the Hollywood film 'Glory'), and skilfully defended the trenches round Richmond, (also the subject of a Hollywood treatment in the film 'Cold Mountain').

He had a more solid success in his private life. After the war, a Union official, sifting through the Confederate military papers, was shocked to find that most of Beauregard's correspondence consisted of love letters from girls. 'Beauregard is the veriest coxcomb, corresponding with scores of Misses.'

His main achievement, though, came during the post-war period. Whereas most Confederate generals ended their lives in poverty, when Beauregard died he left over $150,000. He possessed a genius for money making combined with an airy disregard for dignity.

When the Louisiana State Lottery was suspected of corruption, its owners needed to acquire some speedy respectability. To guarantee honesty, they hired Beauregard and a fellow ex-Confederate general, Jubal Early, to sit on the platform and spin the wheel as the draw was made. Then, both in full uniform, they would stand and solemnly intone the winning numbers. For sixteen years, and at a remuneration of $15,000 a year, Beauregard became the official bingo caller for Louisiana.

Wilde continued east through Alabama and Georgia. He spent the Fourth of July in Atlanta, where he came across an experience of southern racial attitudes. When he purchased a sleeping berth rail ticket for his black valet, WM Traquair, he was told that no blacks were allowed in the berths. Oscar protested that Traquair had accompanied him everywhere with no problem, but received the reply that if he went ahead, he would be physically attacked. Wilde was forced to give in.

On July 7th he lectured in Charleston, SC. He noted that whatever he talked about, the invariable reply was: "Ah, but you should have seen it before the war". That evening in Charleston he turned to one gentleman and remarked how beautiful the moon was. The answer came: "Yes, sir, but you should have seen it before the war".

Moving on through North Carolina and Virginia, Oscar reached Richmond. By now he was desperate to escape the heat of a Southern summer. He wrote to Julia Ward Howe: 'I write to you from the beautiful, passionate, ruined South, the land of magnolias and music, of roses and romance, ... living chiefly on credit, and on the memory of some crushing defeats'.

Arriving back in New York in mid July, he found that his agent had booked him into a short tour of the summer resorts, such as Westchester, Saratoga, and Newport, Rhode Island. He said of the latter: "It is not unpleasant to be in this little island where idleness ranks among the virtues."

On July 29th 1882, he met the Congregational minister, the Rev. Henry Ward Beecher, at Peekskill, near New York.

HENRY WARD BEECHER 1813-1887

Beecher, while being a renowned preacher, was unusual as a nineteenth century American churchman. Credited with being the man who introduced laughter into the pulpit, his pugnacious view of the world contrasted with his calling.

Being the brother of Harriet Beecher Stowe, (the authoress of 'Uncle Tom's Cabin'), Beecher was not surprisingly a committed Abolitionist. During the bloody Kansas skirmishes that preceded the Civil War, he raised the money to send Sharps rifles disguised as books to the anti-slavery groups. The guns became known as 'Beecher's Bibles'.

During the war itself he travelled to England to give lectures in support for the North. At one rowdy meeting, a heckler shouted: "Why didn't you whip the Confederates in sixty days, like you said you would?" Beecher retorted: "Because we found we had Americans to fight instead of Englishmen!"

He continued as a popular religious speaker until 1875, when he was sued for $100,000 by a former protégé, Theodore Tilton. Beecher was accused of adultery with Tilton's attractive young wife Elizabeth, after letters had been discovered describing their 'paroxysmal kisses', etc.

After a trial that lasted six months, the jury failed to agree. The American press were divided, one newspaper calling Beecher 'a dunghill covered with flowers', while another more perceptively suggested that 'the women believed that Beecher was innocent and that Mrs Tilton was guilty'.

Wilde was wide of the mark when he wrote of American scandals: 'So paramount in society is female influence that it is the man who is never forgiven. America is the only society in the world where Don Juan is not appreciated'. Beecher in fact received great support from the churches and the Republican Party, and remained influential till his death.

Wilde continued to lecture in such North East resorts as the Catskill Mountains and Atlantic City, and in October 1882, went on a second short trip to Canada. He returned to New York and remained there for two months, attempting but failing to find a promoter for his play 'Vera' and recovering from a bout of malaria. A proposed tour of Japan fell through.

His discovery of Delmonico's Restaurant was one consolation for these later disappointments. Opened as a primitive café in 1829 by Peter and John Delmonico, and staffed by emigrants from their native village in France, after the 1860s it became the haunt of America's rich. Wilde adored its heavy mahogany doors, its antiques, and its Moorish decoration. Oscar sighed that: 'The two most remarkable bits of scenery in the States are undoubtedly the Yosemite Valley and Delmonico's'.

By the end of his American tour Wilde had covered 15,000 miles, spoken in sixty cities, and cleared over $6,000.

As he left by sea on December 27th 1882, he was in a concessionary mood. "The Atlantic has been greatly misunderstood".

On his arrival back in Britain, Wilde stopped for a fortnight at his lodgings in Charles Street, London. During his absence in America, the poet Dante Gabriel Rossetti had died, (on April 9th 1882). Oscar had revered the great Pre-Raphaelite, although the compliment was not returned.

Rossetti's reaction to Oscar's poems had been: "I saw the wretched Oscar Wilde book and glanced at it enough to see clearly what trash it is. Did Georgie Burne-Jones say that Ned really admired it? If so, he must be gone drivelling".

Rossetti's death had stimulated an unseemly rush of biographers to capitalise on the event, one that Oscar, never fond of the biographical genre, derided. He described 'The Life of Rossetti' by Joseph Knight as: 'just the sort of biography that Guildenstern might have written about Hamlet'.

When this book was followed rapidly by Hall Caine's 'Recollections of Rossetti', Oscar said: "Whenever a great man dies, Hall Caine ... goes in with the undertakers".

SIR (THOMAS HENRY) HALL CAINE 1853-1931

The novelist and playwright Hall Caine was often the butt of Wilde's sallies, but remained noncommittal about Oscar until the later trials. Then he burst out: 'To think of it! That man, that genius as he is, whom you and I have seen feted and flattered! Whose hand we have grasped in friendship! A felon, and come to infamy unspeakable! It haunts me, it is like some foul and horrible stain on our craft and on us all, which nothing can wash out. It is the most awful tragedy in the whole of literature'.

Born into relative poverty, Caine was raised mostly in Liverpool, where he became apprentice to an architect. His literary ambitions were boosted after a meeting with *Lord Houghton* who introduced the intelligent young man to the wider world. When he arrived in London in 1881, Rossetti invited him to stay at 16, Cheyne Walk, (in the same room previously inhabited by *Swinburne*). Caine acted as Rossetti's housekeeper and later nurse till the poet died.

(Caine had to share the house with Rossetti's menagerie that included a kangaroo, an armadillo, a bull, a raccoon, a chameleon, a zebra, a succession of wombats, and an emu, (which once chased Rossetti over the garden wall to the safety of Cheyne Walk). It was with difficulty that Caine dissuaded Rossetti from his plan to buy an elephant and train it to wash the windows.)

Caine moved from Cheyne Walk to new lodgings in Clements Inn, which he shared with a friend called Eric Robertson, an MA. Their peaceful bachelor life was soon shattered. It was their habit to order evening meals from local cafes to be brought to the lodgings. The food was usually delivered by two young girls who quickly befriended the two men.

One evening, the door burst open and the girls' fathers appeared, declaring that their daughters' reputations had been ruined, and demanding that Caine and Roberts make 'honest women' of them.

Horrified to discover that the girls were aged 13, the terrified Roberts swiftly obeyed and married one of them. In the knowledge that nothing untoward had happened, Caine resisted for a time. (Previously, he had actually campaigned to raise the age of consent from 12 years old to 13). However, after being hounded with threats of blackmail and violence, he agreed to accept responsibility for the other girl, Mary Chandler.

After a short period of education away at a Kent school, Mary fell in love with Caine and, after she became pregnant, he married her. The marriage proved to be a happy one for many years and she bore him two sons. (A friend told him not to call the firstborn Abel as it would produce 'too many poor jokes').

Meanwhile, his literary career continued. Earlier he had produced an anthology of sonnets. Anxious about approaching poets over whether they would allow publication of their work, he asked Rossetti for his advice. Rossetti replied that wondering how to approach a poet to see if they wished to be published was rather like a fisherman deliberating over how to approach a shark with an offer of blood.

Although based in London, Caine still worked as a journalist for the Liverpool Mercury. One of his jobs was to write obituaries for the deaths column. He pioneered the idea of preparing them prior to the event, and spent many happy hours working with potential clientele on their own obituaries.

With the publication of 'The Deemster' in 1887, Caine's reputation soared. In his lifetime he sold over ten million copies of his novels and became as popular as Charles Dickens. He converted some of his fifteen novels into plays that were equally successful, and, with the arrival of cinema, several of them were turned into films.

(The director Alfred Hitchcock once arrived in the Isle of Man to shoot exterior shots for his adaptation of Caine's book 'The Manxman', (it was Hitchcock's last silent film). While there, he found Caine's interference so irritating that he moved the entire operation to Polperro in Cornwall. Caine went to see the resulting movie but became so angry over Hitchcock's interpretation that he stormed out of the cinema halfway through the film.)

With fame and wealth, Caine became increasingly egotistical. He moved into Greeba Castle on the Isle of Man, became a member of the Manx Parliament, (the House of Keys), and was known as 'the uncrowned king of the island'.

Robert Hichens recalled watching *Herbert Beerbohm Tree* performing a spoof of Caine at a dinner party. Tree invented an account of King Edward VII being conducted around the Isle of Man by Caine. The King was shown all the beauty spots amidst cheering crowds, as Caine tried to restrain the multitudes by lifting his hand and announcing majestically: "No, no, my dear friends, don't trouble about me today! Give all your attention to His Majesty. The King is among us. Today I take second place!"

Caine was very proud of his strong resemblance to the Stratford bust of Shakespeare. One day, he was shaved by a barber who removed too much of his beard, thereby ruining the likeness. As a result, Caine refused to leave his room for five days until the beard had re-grown.

1883

[In the Dutch East Indies, the explosion of the Krakatoa volcano caused widespread destruction.
In Germany, Nietzsche published his book 'Thus Spake Zarathustra'.
In Britain, the writer Karl Marx died.
The French government pursued a policy of aggressive colonisation with wars in Indo-China, Madagascar, and North Africa.
In the Sudan, an 8000 strong Anglo-Egyptian force under Colonel Billy Hicks was massacred by the Mahdi.]

After a few weeks in London, Wilde left for Paris where he stayed from the end of January 1883 till mid May. At first he lived at the Hotel Continental, then later at the Hotel Voltaire on the Left Bank in rooms overlooking the Seine. When a companion praised the outlook from the window, Oscar replied: "Oh, that is altogether immaterial, except to the innkeeper, who of course charges it in the bill. A gentleman never looks out of the window".

His main task was to write a new play. During 1882, he had sketched out a rough scenario for a work called 'The Cardinal of Avignon'. Abandoning this, he started writing a new play for the American actress Mary Anderson to be called 'The Duchess of Padua'.

MARY ANDERSON 1859-1940

Wilde had seen the Kentucky-born actress Mary Anderson perform in the USA when she played 'the living statue' in *WS Gilbert's* 'Pygmalion and Galatea' and commented on her beauty. He negotiated with her stepfather and manager over the idea of a new play and received £1000 down and a further £4000 if she approved the script.

But when he completed 'The Duchess of Padua' in March 1883, she turned it down. Wilde: 'Oh, Art and Kentucky, how ill your alliance is!' He admitted that Mary was 'sweet and good', but that her manager was 'a padded horror'.

Anderson had been a recognised star since her debut aged 16 in her native Louisville, but her main successes came in Britain. She played Rosalind in 'As You Like It' at the opening production of the Shakespeare Memorial Theatre; this was followed by several seasons in London.

In 1889, she suffered a nervous breakdown and, after marrying Anthony de Navarro, retired from the stage to live in Broadway, Worcestershire. Here she became the focus of an American artistic community. Her fellow actress *Genevieve Ward* said of it: 'As for little Broadway, it is a sort of settlement of souls addicted to poetry, painting and other recreations of the simple life, not unadorned with luxury and ease.' She made a return to the theatre in 1903.

Her theatrical reputation came mostly from her good looks rather than her thespian talent. *Adrian Hope, (Constance Wilde's* relation), wrote after seeing Anderson as 'Juliet' that: 'We were in the second row and I discovered that that peculiar garment which Juliet wears as a night gown is as transparent as the shirts of flannel that I have known some people play tennis in. My companion declared himself to have been much shocked by the young lady's dress or rather want of it'.

The professional critics were unimpressed. *GB Shaw:* 'Mary Anderson, before whom the art of acting fled abashed...'; while Frank Harris said of her: "on the stage she was beautiful, the footlights set her off peculiarly, though she could not act for nuts".

Prior to her marriage, one of Mary Anderson's lovers, (who included the ubiquitous Bertie, Prince of Wales), was the actor-manager **SIR JOHNSON FORBES-ROBERTSON** (1853-1937). Wilde was a friend of the Forbes-Robertson family and knew both Johnson and his brothers Norman and Ian.

Although he became a leading figure of the English stage, Forbes-Robertson's real ambition had been to become a famous painter. He reluctantly stayed in the theatre because of the financial rewards. Forbes-Robertson: "Never at any time have I gone on the stage without longing for the moment when the curtain would come down on the last act".

In 1908, he appeared in what became known as his greatest role – that of 'The Stranger' in Jerome K Jerome's play, 'The Passing of the Third Floor Back'.

(Jerome Klapka Jerome (1859-1927), author of 'Three Men in a Boat', was incidentally one of Wilde's greatest detractors during the 1895 trials, demanding not only the most extreme punishment for Wilde but also for 'the 500 noblemen of the world who shared Oscar Wilde's turpitude and so corrupt youth'. *Gosse* described Jerome as: 'a strange little man... bright red hair, a bullet head, and tight little legs set far apart – looks like a stable-man in Sunday clothes'.)

The public approval of Forbes-Robertson's performance as a Christ-like figure in Jerome's play was so great that he was forced to continue playing the part for years. He grew very weary of the job.

The actress *Mrs Patrick Campbell*, (another of Forbes-Robertson's lovers), wrote that she watched him from the wings one evening before he made yet another entrance. 'I saw him suddenly turn his eyes to the roof and burst out: "Dear God! Will they never let me give up this bloody part?" A moment later he was on stage beatifically blessing one and all with a bright halo round his head.'

During this Paris period, Wilde affected a self-conscious style while writing. He wore a white woollen dressing gown with a cowl, as homage to the similar attire worn by the great French author Balzac, and had his hair styled in the fashion of the Roman Emperor Nero, (who had always sported a faultless coiffure whatever his other lapses). Someone said of Oscar's new haircut: "Curly hair to match his curly teeth".

Wilde made the acquaintance of two young Englishmen while living at the Hotel Voltaire. One was a penurious journalist named Robert Sherard.

ROBERT SHERARD 1862-1943 (First Part)

The 21-year-old Robert Sherard was in many ways an unlikely disciple for Wilde to cultivate. Truculent by nature, on their first meetings Sherard deliberately provoked Oscar by his aggressive philistinism. When Wilde praised the beauty in all things, Sherard ground his cigar butt into the coffee dregs in his saucer and asked if there was any beauty in the resulting mess. Wilde replied: "Oh, yes, it makes quite an effective brown".

Despite himself, Sherard became fascinated by the older man, while Oscar enjoyed shocking his protégé. During the four months Wilde spent in Paris, he saw Sherard almost everyday, and later in September 1883, Sherard stayed at Oscar's lodging in Charles Street, London.

Sherard was a great-grandson of the poet William Wordsworth. His original name was Kennedy and, when he was a child, the family shared a house with *Victor Hugo* on the island of Guernsey. (He remained an acquaintance of the great French writer while in Paris). After being sent down from Oxford in 1881 for non-payment of debt, he changed his name to Sherard and settled in Paris to become a writer. He revered the principles of the French Revolution to such an extent that Oscar nicknamed him 'Citoyan Robert'.

Unusually for Oscar's younger friends, Sherard was entirely heterosexual and encouraged Oscar to indulge in some uncharacteristic exploits. In March 1883, Wilde slept with a Parisian prostitute called Marie Aguetant, (later to become a murder victim). A mortified Oscar said of the incident: "What animals we all are". His revulsion was reflected in his later poem, 'The Harlot's House'.

Sherard himself was rather uncomfortable when he encountered Oscar in 1884 during the latter's honeymoon. Oscar insisted on detailing the delights of sex with his virgin wife.

At one stage, Wilde was able to talk Sherard out of a suicidal depression: 'Suicide is the greatest compliment that one can pay to society'. Sherard said of the episode: "If he had taught me nothing but the great value and happiness of life, I should still owe him an unpayable debt".

While Sherard managed to rake a living from journalism, his serious writing never achieved success. Wilde: "Dear Robert is wonderful, quite the worst writer in the world". Oscar's brother, *Willie Wilde*, was even more derogatory. When Sherard's book of poems, 'Whispers', was published, Willie reviewed it: 'Whispers are what the poems are and what they should have remained'.

Given his choleric nature, it was not surprising that Sherard took full advantage of the French tradition of duelling. Although the military did not involve themselves, journalists, politicians and their ilk certainly did – the practise was not banned in France till after the First World War. Sherard bore several scars from these clashes and Oscar once had to dissuade him from taking on an especially skilful opponent.

Oscar: "Although it is not dangerous, like our English cricket or football is, still it is a tedious game to be always playing" – "Once you start to fight duels in France, you have to be always doing it, and it is a nuisance".

During the 1895 trials, a furious Sherard challenged Oscar's enemy, the *Marquess of Queensberry*, to a duel on French soil. For once, the normally bellicose Marquess backed down. Oscar wrote to Sherard: 'Please don't fight more than six duels a week'.

Sherard also introduced Oscar to an infamous Parisian night haunt called the Chateau Rouge, close to Notre Dame. Originally built by Henri IV, the Chateau Rouge was a doss house for the Parisian underworld. The main room was a long low chamber under the eaves, its grimy walls decorated with frescoes of hunting scenes. It had a dangerous reputation as a refuge for thieves and murderers; the male clientele mostly wore red ties in ironic acknowledgement that they might one day be food for the guillotine.

Its notoriety attracted visits from some surprising 'slummers'. Wearing the thin disguise of a peasant girl, the *Rani of Sarawak* spent an evening there. After a bandit had played guitar for her, she purchased a round of drinks for the house and toasted her companions: "I did enjoy myself that night!" Though not a habitué, Oscar also enjoyed the vicarious thrill of the place: "Myself, I go to all those spots where I might experience emotion. I frequent the Chateau Rouge as much as the English Café".

The painter *William Rothenstein* was not so smitten. In 1891, he accompanied Wilde and Sherard on another visit. Rothenstein: 'The sight of the sinister types lounging about the crowded rooms, or sleeping on benches, made me shudder'. 'Sherard, to add to my discomfort, kept shouting that anyone who meddled with his friend Oscar Wilde would soon be sorry for himself.'

' "My dear Robert, you are defending me at the risk of my life," said Wilde.'

[See Sherard – Second Part – Page 444]

While at the Hotel Voltaire, Wilde also played host to the young English painter Walter Sickert, (at the time apprenticed to Whistler). Sickert had arrived in Paris to deliver Whistler's portrait of his mother to the annual Salon exhibition and Whistler, then still friendly towards Oscar, sent Wilde a note admonishing him: 'Attempt not to palm off wine of an inferior quality upon my ambassador'.

SIR WALTER SICKERT 1860-1942

For some time, Wilde had been a friend of the Sickert family. He had known Walter's parents and was particularly close to their daughter, Helena. She always kept fond memories of his company: "I have never known any grown person who laughed more whole-heartedly and who made such mellow music of it". She said that Wilde always retained a 'big-brotherly attitude' towards her and later helped her writing career by commissioning her first article when she was still an unknown Girton College undergraduate.

When her father, Oswald Sickert, died, her mother Nellie had hidden herself away, stricken with grief. Oscar insisted on talking to her and Helena reported: "my mother laughed when she had thought that she would never laugh again"

Walter Sickert, on the other hand, remained a distant figure in Wilde's life. He shunned Wilde after he left jail and admitted to *Robert Ross* that, "I dislike violently, so far as I can

166

understand it, Oscar's writings. Chiefly because they have always, in spite of an old friendship with him, seemed to me a sort of gratification of nonsense".

Sickert became one of the major English artists of the early twentieth century, expressing what *Andre Gide* called 'his morose and powerful art' in such sets of work as the 'Camden Town' series, and in his drawings of Dieppe in France. He was possibly a unique figure in that he gave Winston Churchill art lessons, while, (in 1937), publishing newspaper letters praising Adolf Hitler's landscape paintings.

He was noticeable for the constant chameleon-like changes that he made in his appearance. He repeatedly switched from long hair to shaven head, and from beard or moustache to no facial hair at all. His friend, the French artist *J-E Blanche* described: 'his genius for camouflage in dress.... he could be as well dressed as a tailor's dummy, or as raggedly as a tramp'.

In 1885, he married Ellen, daughter of Richard Cobden, (famous for repealing the Corn Laws), but by 1899 she refused to live with Sickert any longer and they divorced. Whenever he passed the statue of his father-in-law in Camden High Street, London, he would remove his hat and give the sculpture an ironic bow.

He married twice more but was never particularly sympathetic to women in general. One female acquaintance once gushed to him: "You and I are so much in sympathy that I feel we must have met in some former life'. A bored Sickert replied: "Isn't it bad enough that we know each other now".

The town of Dieppe remained one of the loves of his life, as it did with many of Wilde's friends. The arrival of the railways had opened up the Normandy coast to Parisians, (in a similar way it had opened up Brighton to Londoners), and such towns as Dieppe, Trouville and Deauville became popular resorts. The English artistic world, inhibited by social mores at home, found relief in Dieppe's bohemian atmosphere. *Henry James*: 'Dieppe is a reduced Florence, every type of character for a novelist seems to gather there'.

Sickert also had a perverse attraction to the seediest areas of London, in particular Camden Town. He was interested by lowlife pubs and music halls, which he visited night after night, memorising the songs and sketching the artistes. While working on his Camden Town series, he dressed as a roughneck, with cap and muffler concealing his face, and spent nights prowling the alleyways.

His fascination with crime inspired one painting that he called 'Jack the Ripper's Bedroom' – it was in fact his own room at 6, Mornington Crescent. His life-style and innate morbidity have led some commentators to suspect Sickert of being yet another of the multitudinous candidates for the role of Jack the Ripper himself. (Scotland Yard recorded a total of 140 possible suspects for these famous but ultimately insoluble murders).

His most eccentric obsession was that of secretly renting studio after studio in the most hideous hovels he could find; he called them his 'rat holes'. His friend, *William Rothenstein*, wrote: 'I had known many poor studios, but Walter Sickert's genius for discovering the dreariest house and most forbidding rooms in which to work was a source of wonder and amusement to me'.

One day, Sickert was walking with a friend when, passing a particularly horrible slum, he spotted a notice that read, 'Studio to Let'. The friend gripped Sickert's arm and pushed him onwards with the words, "Be a man, Walter, pass it, pass it!"

One of Sickert's Dieppe acquaintances was the young French artist JACQUES-EMILE BLANCHE (1862-1942), who in 1883 befriended Wilde while he was in Paris. Blanche was helpful in introducing Oscar to the French literary circle and later engineered a meeting between Wilde and *Marcel Proust*. He flattered Wilde by exhibiting a portrait of a young woman reading Oscar's book of poems.

This early enthusiasm was dashed by Wilde's disgrace, and, in 1897, Blanche did not welcome the news of Oscar's impending arrival in Dieppe. Blanche: "One day while Sickert and I were going for a walk, Oscar, who was sitting in the Café Suisse, beckoned to me. I pretended not to see. I know for a fact that he was wounded to the quick by my action, and the recollection of that episode still fills me with remorse".

Blanche was the son of a wealthy bourgeois family, whose Dieppe home, Bas Fort Blanc, became a centre for artists such as *Condor* and *Beardsley*. He was fascinated by society and the art world, and his criticism was often very intelligent. He noted that: 'artists like *Degas*, Renoir and Cezanne looked upon themselves as students'. His own work, however, was second-rate; he was regarded as having 'a failed career but a delightful life'.

At one period, Blanche lived in London in the Kensington slum area that was cleared later to make way for the new shop, Harrods. He rented a studio from an old Cockney couple who viewed his artistic endeavours with suspicion. When he decided to paint two Guards regiment band-boys, the Duke of Connaught helpfully sent a fifer and a drummer in parade uniform to pose for the portrait at Blanche's studio.

Having no idea of the homosexual undertones that attached themselves to guardsmen in London, Blanche was utterly bewildered when his landlord approached him that evening. Winking his eye, the landlord whispered, 'If I may say so, sir, you'd be better off paintin' some of your lydies, sir'.

Intellectually, Wilde was always more at home in Paris than in London. While on this first sojourn in Paris, Wilde was able to meet some of the major figures of the French artistic world; they included the poet Paul Verlaine, the writers Victor Hugo and Edmond Goncourt, the dandy Count Robert de Montesquiou, and the painter Edgar Degas.

(HILAIRE-GERMAIN-) EDGAR DEGAS 1834-1917

By 1883, Degas had become something of a recluse; even old friends found it difficult to gain entry to his studio. After ringing the bell, they would have to wait while Degas peered down from a rooftop turret and decided whether it was worth opening the door. Wilde, accompanied by Whistler, solved the problem by using a ladder to climb to Degas' garret.

Oscar was respectful of Degas but not overwhelmed. He wrote to a friend: 'You asked me about Degas. Well, he loves to be thought young, so I don't think he will tell his age. He disbelieves in art education, so I don't think he will name a Master. He despises what he cannot get, so I am sure he will not give any information about prizes or honours. Why say anything about his person? His pastels are himself'.

Degas, more succinctly, described Oscar as looking "like an actor playing Lord Byron in a suburban theatre".

Degas's spiky nature ensured that their relationship never advanced beyond acquaintance. When Wilde's increasingly flamboyant behaviour began to cause comment in the 1890s, Degas replied to Oscar's remark that Degas was very well known in England, with: "Fortunately, not as well known as you are".

Although surrounded by the new art form, Degas never regarded himself as an Impressionist painter. He acknowledged that much of his art was voyeuristic: "It is as if you looked through a keyhole". Throughout his life he worked on a series of topics – racehorses, musicians, laundresses, café concerts and circus scenes. At one time he became absorbed with painting naked women washing their bodies in household baths, (a relatively new practice due to the improvements in gas heating).

168

Above all else, he adored painting the world of ballet, (the subject of over one third of all his work). In the 1880s, French ballet had sunk to little more than thinly veiled erotic shows, in which the extremely short tutu worn by the girls, (introduced from Italy), provided extra titillation for the patrons. The girls were invariably young, working class, and very badly paid. When one director was asked why he would not increase their wages to a living level, he said that the girls could always find more money by having sex with customers.

One of Degas's best known works, a small statuette called 'The Little Dancer' (1881), was of just such a girl. Named Marie van Goetham, she came from a family of prostitutes; shortly after she posed for Degas, her sister Antoinette robbed a client of 700 francs and Marie was jailed for complicity in the crime.

Although remaining aloof from the Impressionist circles, Degas was friendly with Edouard Manet. However, this amity suffered after Degas painted a work entitled 'Manet Listening to His Wife Play the Piano', in which he represented Manet as looking extremely bored. Manet was so angry that he tore off the right-hand section of the picture.

In 1893, one work by Degas produced a storm of condemnation in the British press. Originally called 'Au Café', when it arrived for exhibition in London the name was changed by the promoter to 'Absinthe'. This was calculated to shock the bourgeoisie, as absinthe was the symbol of bohemian decadence. The newspapers unleashed a predictable tirade of abuse – 'vulgar, loathsome, revolting, ugly, degraded and repulsive' representing the general tone.

Degas was amazed at this reaction. The man portrayed in the picture, far from being a drunken tramp, was a highly respectable Parisian etcher called Desboutin, while the offending 'absinthe' was, in fact, a cup of coffee.

In later years, Degas's work became valuable. Paintings he had sold for a few francs suddenly realised huge sums for their new owners. After watching one such auction, he was asked for his reaction and replied: "I feel as a horse must feel when the beautiful cup is given to the jockey".

Through his French Creole mother, Degas had a strong connection to the USA and, in 1872, visited his maternal relations in Louisiana. A friend said that Degas was excited about the trip: "he has become crazy about learning to pronounce English and has been repeating 'turkey buzzard' for an entire week". Homesickness soon set in and Degas moped: 'everything is beautiful in this world of the people. But one Paris laundry girl, with bare arms, is worth it all for such a pronounced Parisian as I am'.

He also found American morality somewhat trying. One US art gallery refused to buy one of his paintings, 'Interior', because it portrayed a man, a woman, and a bed in the same room. Degas grunted: "I would have sent a marriage licence along with it!"

Degas's own sex life appeared to be virtually non-existent. There was no hint of homosexuality about him, in fact he was aggressively homophobic. One of his rare mistresses suggested that he was impotent. Vincent Van Gogh thought that Degas possibly needed celibacy to heighten his sense of voyeurism: 'Degas lives like some petty lawyer and doesn't like women, knowing very well that if he did like them and bedded them frequently, he'd go to seed and be in no position to paint any longer'.

Degas sometimes went through the motions and professed a liking for 'gamahuching' (fellatio) and 'minetting' (cunnilingus). When an acquaintance condemned these practices, Degas sighed: "What a dreary old age you are making for yourself".

His Parisian friends often teased him about his general lack of interest in sexual matters and he decided to prove that he was capable of a display of gallantry. Learning that one of his ballet models was sailing to America, he booked a passage on the following ship. Once in New York, he remained quietly on board, then returned to France. He silenced his tormentors by declaring that no man could prove his ardour more than by chasing a woman across two continents and an ocean.

As he grew older, he became more cantankerous and drifted into extreme right-wing intolerance and a sentimental nationalism. He grew increasingly anti-Semitic and passionately supported the army case during the Dreyfus Affair. He was furious when *Alfred Dreyfus* was revealed to be innocent. Degas was described as 'a personality gone sour'.

He maintained a profound scepticism about religion all his life. One day, pointing at the picture on his easel, he declared: "I believe in that and in nothing else".

When he realised that he was dying, he instructed his friend Jean-Louis Forain that there should be no funeral oration. "But if there has to be one, Forain, you get up and say 'He greatly loved drawing. So do I'. Then go home".

One offshoot of Degas's American family connection was his peripheral involvement with the Union **GENERAL BEN BUTLER** (1818-1893). When New Orleans was captured during the American Civil War, the Southern civilian population were openly contemptuous of the occupying Union troops. Butler, as commanding officer in the city, issued an order stating that any Southern woman found insulting a Northern soldier would be treated as 'a woman of the town plying her avocation'. This was seen as an open invitation to rape, and Degas's female relations hastily fled from New Orleans to Paris and to his protection.

(It is likely that it was this event that prompted Degas to depict rape and murder in his 'War Scene in the Middle Ages' painting of 1865.)

Butler became the most hated Union figure in the South not only for this action but also for his brutality and his rapacious looting. *Mark Twain* said of him: "When Butler smiles it is like the breaking up of a hard winter".

The English society hostess, *Lady St Helier*, visited Baltimore in the 1870s and reported seeing a man on a street corner who gave exhibitions of trained canaries. Each bird had been given the name of a Union general and, on command, 'Generals Grant, Sherman, and McClellan, etc' would hop out of their cages to perch on the showman's arm. The bird named 'General Butler', though, refused to budge from his cage until his trainer, with a twinkle in his eye, produced a shiny silver spoon from his pocket. 'Then 'General Butler' would happily hop out to sit on the spoon to roars of laughter from the audience'.

PAUL VERLAINE 1844-1896

On the first two occasions that Wilde met the poet Paul Verlaine, (in 1883 and 1891), he was unimpressed by the seedy drunk. Verlaine watched Oscar closely though and whispered to a companion: "This man is a true pagan. He possesses the insouciance which is half of happiness, for he does not know penitence".

By 1893, Wilde realised Verlaine's real worth – 'Verlaine is in the gutter but he writes poetry on the pavement' – and, at a London society party, insisted that the ex-convict recite his verse about his prison experiences aloud to the audience. By 1899, Wilde was identifying himself with the Frenchman: 'The century will have two vagabonds, Paul Verlaine and me'.

Verlaine was one of the most extraordinary figures in literature who, together with his companion and lover Rimbaud, changed the course of French poetry. He was also a violent, bisexual alcoholic of such remarkable ugliness that an early teacher said of him: "his hideous head made one think of a brutalised criminal".

He grew up in a petit bourgeois background and married a conventionally minded girl called Mathilde Maute in 1870. When the Franco-Prussian War broke out in the same year, Verlaine behaved in what was to become a fairly typical fashion.

During the siege of Paris, as a member of the Garde Nationale he was ordered to defend the city. He sent two notes, one to his commanding officer claiming that he had vital work at his copying clerk job, the other to his office claiming he was needed to defend the ramparts. He received two days in prison for this attempted deception.

When the siege ended and the Paris Commune was declared, Verlaine became a minor functionary in the doomed Communard administration. The bombardment by the government forces became so heavy that he lost his nerve and, instead of going himself to rescue his mother, he sent his 18 year-old pregnant wife on the perilous errand. After three days of dodging through the battle, Mathilde arrived home to find that Verlaine had tried to seduce the maid during her absence.

Terrified that he might be arrested for his part in the Commune, Verlaine went to stay with Mathilde's family. Already a heavy drinker, he quickly tired of the enforced respectability of his in-laws' quiet existence. It was at this stage of his life that he met the young poet Rimbaud.

[ARTHUR RIMBAUD (1854-1891), described by *Edmund Goncourt* as 'the pederast assassin' and 'perversity incarnate', was a psychopath who unerringly pursued his philosophy of 'derangement of the senses'. He despised the conventional life: 'Man hopes to spend three quarters of his life suffering in order to spend the last quarter taking his ease. Usually, he dies of poverty without knowing how far along he is with his plan'.

At the start of the Franco-Prussian War, Rimbaud interrupted his brilliant school career and ran away to see the action in Paris. Arrested because he had failed to pay the rail fare, he was thrown into prison. While there, he became the object of sex attacks by both convicts and policemen, but appeared to be unfazed by such incidents and later recalled them quite fondly.

Escaping back through the Prussian lines to his hometown of Charleville, Rimbaud became a feared hooligan, espousing anarchic revolution. He quickly lost his heterosexual virginity to a prostitute, (although he claimed it was with a dog), and opened derided the concept of marriage in favour of untrammelled bi-sexuality. Having read Verlaine's early poetry, he corresponded with someone he saw as of like mind, and in September 1871 was invited to visit Verlaine in Paris.]

Although ten years younger, Rimbaud soon dominated Verlaine's weaker character, and for two years the couple combined a homosexual love affair with a campaign of unbridled alcoholic excess. With good reason, Mathilde Verlaine called Rimbaud 'that doll-faced destroyer of domestic bliss'. Under this influence, Verlaine's already shaky marriage was wrecked after he drunkenly hurled his three-month-old son against a wall and attempted to strangle Mathilde after setting fire to her hair. Her father insisted on drawing up a legal case against Verlaine.

[Rimbaud meanwhile had behaved in such a manner that even bohemian Paris shunned the pair. Having been thrown out of the Maute residence for stealing, Rimbaud rented new lodgings and on the first night there was spotted dancing naked on the rooftop. Having wrecked the place, he sold off the landlord's remaining furniture.

Moving on the terminally seedy Hotel Etrangers on the Boulevard Saint Michelle, Rimbaud took up smoking hashish, while doing bar work and selling key rings to survive. One freezing winter's night, as a joke he used a glasscutter to remove the windowpanes of the hotel pianist, Ernest Cabaner. He then finished off Cabaner's absinthe supplies and left.

He repaid *Degas's* friend Forain's hospitality by defecating in his host's morning milk before departing. Replying to objections about his filthy appearance and lice-ridden hair, Rimbaud excused himself on the grounds that he needed the lice to flick at passing priests.

During one absinthe-drinking bout, a companion returned from the toilet to find to his horror that Rimbaud had laced his drink with sulphuric acid.

In another incident, after an acquaintance described him as 'a little toad', Rimbaud stabbed the man twice with a swordstick. This was a pattern he was to repeat with Verlaine, indulging his sadistic urges by stabbing his friend when life got dull.]

In 1872 Verlaine finally left Mathilde, (who had turned down his offer of living in a ménage a trois with Rimbaud). He accompanied his lover on a wild carouse through Belgium. They spent their rare moments of sobriety composing poems, of which Verlaine said: "We flogged them along the way with lots of other things to pay for absinthe and cigars". He added that they dined 'on public condemnation and countered poverty with courage, joy and potatoes'.

Feeling in Rimbaud's words like 'exiles in our own land', the couple moved on to London where they lived in lodgings at 8, Royal College Street, and mingled with the French expatriates in Soho. They spent their time touring the sights of the city, attending lectures by Karl Marx, and, in Verlaine's case, acquiring syphilis off a prostitute picked up at the Alhambra Theatre.

Their life continued in a confused welter of poetry composition, inebriated debauches, and quarrels. Rimbaud created a duelling game where the two would wrap knives in towels so that only the point protruded (to reduce injuries), and then try to stab each other. When one of them received a serious enough wound, they would stop and retire to the pub.

Eventually the tensions in their relationship escalated to the point of explosion. One day, Verlaine hit Rimbaud in the face with a dead fish and departed to Brussels. A furious Rimbaud sold Verlaine's remaining possessions and used the money to leave London and follow him.

More quarrels broke out in the Belgian capital, and finally Rimbaud decided to leave for good. A very drunken Verlaine produced a revolver and shot him through the left arm. Refusing Verlaine's remorseful request to shoot him in return, Rimbaud dressed his wound and left, only to be pursued through the streets of Brussels by a pistol-waving Verlaine. The police stepped in and arrested the raving poet.

Although Rimbaud refused to press charges, the case went ahead and Verlaine received a two-year prison sentence for attempted murder. After he was released, Verlaine again sought out his old lover who finally ended their affair by knocking him out cold and leaving him by the roadside.

[After finishing his greatest work, 'Une Saison en Enfer', the 19-year-old Rimbaud abandoned poetry forever. Leaving Verlaine behind in prison, he moved back to England where he spent three months teaching in Reading, Berkshire, (in a school quite close to Reading Gaol). He offered his tutoring services in a newspaper advertisement claiming that he had 'Good References'.

Leaving England, he moved on to Italy where he became an itinerant dock labourer, then on to Marseille where he signed up to join the Carlist rebel army for duty in Spain. He deserted the same day and fled, taking the enlistment fee with him.

He next signed up with the Dutch colonial army and trained for jungle combat. In 1876, he sailed with other recruits via Suez and arrived in Java in August 1876. Hearing unpleasant stories about the horrific war being waged in the interior and also fearing the strong possibility of disease, Rimbaud again deserted. He was pursued through the jungle but after a fortnight reached the port of Surabaya, where he signed on under a false name as a sailor on a British

172

ship. By December, he arrived back in Cork, Ireland, and made his way back to Charleville. A friend described Rimbaud's journey as: "a little voyage from Brussels to Cork – via Java".

He then arrived in Hamburg, Germany where, under another false name, he rejoined the Dutch army as a recruitment agent for the army he had just deserted. Deserting it a second time, he moved to Bremen where he was rejected when he tried to enlist in the American navy. He then joined a Swedish circus as a ticket seller, but abandoned them in Stockholm.

By 1878 he reached the new British colony of Cyprus where he found a job as foreman of a stone quarry. When he was asked how he managed this job while knowing nothing about quarrying, he answered: "Easy. I watched them doing what they did, and then I told them what they had to do. And they took me very seriously". However, during an altercation, he threw a stone at a recalcitrant local worker and killed the man. Rimbaud escaped by rowing himself out to a departing ship.

He travelled on down the Red Sea and acquired a job supervising the women in a coffee import factory in Aden: "the most boring place in the world". To alleviate the ennui, he made a series of hazardous treks into the Somalian and Ethiopian hinterlands. He became the first European to cross the region of the Danakil tribe, (twenty Europeans had been murdered attempting the journey within the previous two years).

He stayed on several occasions in the Ethiopian city of Harar, where he acquired a harem of mistresses, took up the local drug habit of chewing qat leaves, and studied the Amharic language.

In 1886, King Menelik of Ethiopia consolidated his unification of the country by capturing Harar, (six thousand testicles were harvested from the losers as spoils of war). Rimbaud responded to the new political situation by running guns to the Emperor, delivering several thousand rifles to the new capital of Addis Ababa. (These new armaments proved to be crucial when, in 1896, the Ethiopians decisively defeated the Italian attempt to conquer their country at the Battle of Adowa).

Now quite rich, Rimbaud settled for a time in Harar where he increased his wealth by trading slaves and coffee. His popularity in the city slumped when it was discovered that Rimbaud, annoyed by local dogs urinating on his coffee bales, had strewn the ground around his house with strychnine pellets. Local protests mounted as the heap of hyena, sheep, vulture, and dog corpses piled up around the residence.

Rimbaud, after studying the Koran, started to supply his own interpretations of the sacred text and, in a new role as an Islamic imam, acquired a personal religious following. This heresy infuriated the local Moslem leaders and he came under attack by stick-brandishing fanatics.

By 1891, Rimbaud was forced to return to France where he died of bone cancer aged 37. During the 1890s, his teenage poetry was recognised as the greatest of his age.]

Meanwhile, Verlaine had found jail to be a godsend: 'a real haven, after all the sufferings of the past'. He responded well to the calm prison regime and was allowed decent food, limited alcohol, and even his own library. Under these conditions, he reverted to Catholicism and wrote some of his most profound poetry.

On release, he went to England to teach French, working in Stickney, near Boston, Lincolnshire, and then in Bournemouth. In 1877, he moved to a French school in Rethel, France, where his abstemiousness was so marked that the headmaster, not realising who the new teacher was, assured Verlaine that a little wine would not harm him.

This state of affairs ended when Verlaine spectacularly fell off the wagon, and invited his pupils to join him for drinks in town. This resulted in half his class ending up in the school sickbay with hangovers, and Verlaine's dismissal.

Despite his return to the bottle, in 1880 Verlaine published a new book of poems called 'Sagasse', a deeply Catholic work. Wilde called him: 'the one Christian poet since Dante'.

The piety of his work was in sharp contrast to his actual life during this period. He became so notorious in the Rethel area for his alcohol fuelled homosexual orgies that local mothers used his name to scare their children. After he threatened his mother with a knife in an effort to extract money, he was arrested and spent another month in prison.

After his release, he left Rethel to live a vagabond life for a time, tramping through the Ardennes and living with tinkers. His only clothes were an increasingly dilapidated fur-lined overcoat and a top hat, survivors of better times.

He moved on to live in Paris with his long-suffering mother. After her death in 1886, he became reliant for aid on a series of friendly prostitutes, and took up residence above a brothel. His most enduring supporter was a woman called Eugenie Krantz, who provided Verlaine with sex and food; she obtained recompense by selling his poetry.

Although he declined into even further squalor, his very degradation became his salvation. The younger generation came to see him as a great anti-hero and during the 1890s turned him into the unchallenged 'king' of the bohemian Latin Quarter. Café waiters would point him out to foreign visitors as one of sights of Paris.

In spite of his decay, Verlaine had an air of grandeur. Wilde said of him: 'His life was nameless and terrible…yet there he would sit in a café on the Boul Mich and everyone who came in would bow to him and call him maitre'. One night at the Chat Noir on the Right Bank, not normally Verlaine's territory, an elegant gathering rose to its feet to salute the filthy tramp who had entered the cafe.

Some observers saw him as a figure of pity. *Robert Sherard* reported that "Verlaine was drunk one night, and, as usual, he was dressed in rags. He had a false nose on his face (for it was carnival time), and he was piping on a little tin whistle. The spectacle had the terrible comedy touch of Aristophanes". But when he recited his poems, he could still create an unforgettable effect on his listeners. One friend said of him: "At the words of this vagabond, quite unconsciously, they rediscovered their souls".

Despite his celebrity, Verlaine remained incorrigibly disreputable. When a friend told him that someone had abused him behind his back, he demanded to know the name of the culprit. The friend, fearing trouble, replied: "Someone you don't know". A furious Verlaine drunkenly weaved to his feet, declaring: "I'm going outside, and the first passer-by I don't know, I'll smash his jaw".

In practical terms, he became immune to normal dangers. One of his prostitute girlfriends had a powerful pimp, Paul Lacan, as her protector. Lacan decided to extend his protection to the poet. Lacan: "Monsieur Verlaine is a great writer. If anyone touches him, they'd have to deal with me. A good many times I've followed him home late at night when he didn't know it. I didn't want anything nasty to happen to him."

At the same time, the Prefect of Police, M.Lepine, gave strict orders to his force that Verlaine should never be arrested, no matter what happened. The criminal world and the police vied with each other to protect him.

During the early 1890s, Verlaine's work became known internationally and he was invited to perform lecture tours in Holland, England, and Belgium, (where he offered to give a talk to lawyers of the junior bar on the Belgian prison system – a topic on which he was eminently qualified to comment).

After a lecture in Ghent, an unsuspecting host, the aristocratic Jean Casier, lent Verlaine the Casier family carriage for his guest's convenience. Casier came to regret his generosity. Next morning the inhabitants of Ghent were highly amused to hear that the Casier carriage, with its very distinctive family insignia, had spent the night parked outside a notorious brothel.

By 1894, Verlaine was suffering from at least ten different illnesses, including gonorrhoea, diabetes, and cirrhosis. This meant that he spent a large amount of time in hospital. His reputation was so high that the doctors waived their usual fees and themselves organised subscriptions to pay for his treatment.

Among the intelligentsia, it became de rigueur to visit the ailing writer, and the hospitals became accustomed to a procession of famous figures bringing orchids and surreptitious bottles of absinthe to cheer the patient. Well-known artists sketched the scene, while society women and Latin Quarter vagrants shared the bedside vigils. In Verlaine's last years, there was intense rivalry between the hospitals for his patronage.

When Verlaine died in 1896, his funeral became one of the grandest events of the 1890s. After the composer Faure had played the organ at the ceremony, 2000 of the leaders of French arts and society marched together down the Boulevard St Michelle to accompany the coffin through a blinding snowstorm – 'a white army of poets'. The writer Maurice Barres wrote: 'Eugenie at the grave bent over and called "Verlaine! All your friends are here!" A magnificent cry. And that was why he loved her.'

Unfortunately, Eugenie discovered that there was a huge market for literary memorabilia of the dead writer, and purchased hundreds of bogus pens and penholders to meet the demand. The resulting income was so lavish that she drank herself to death on the proceeds.

When it was proposed that a statue should be erected in memory of Verlaine, Wilde suggested that, instead of being positioned on some solemn pedestal, it should be placed in one of Verlaine's favourite cafes: 'The hero's statue must be placed on his life's battle-field'.

Verlaine's most faithful adherent during the latter years was an indefinable factotum called **BIBI LA PUREE**. His real name was Andre Salis, the son of a wine dealer from Angouleme, who had cut himself off from his relations to live on the streets of Paris. He was a beggar, thief, poet and police spy, who was said to have: 'a horrible, grinning face, with a mouth slit from ear to ear, who smelt of rotting rat'.

Bibi was described as 'like some grotesque survival from the Middle Ages'. The painter *Augustus John* wrote of him: 'Bat-like, he was only seen to flit at night; a figure from Toulouse Lautrec's sketchbook'. Sherard was horrified to see Oscar Wilde sitting for hours chatting to this pariah.

Bibi was homeless and his only means of income came from working as a street shoeblack and by stealing umbrellas from cafes. He was later to die of tuberculosis, privation, and exposure.

He was devoted to Verlaine and it became a common sight to see the drunken writer being ushered down the street by the cavorting dwarf. Bibi wore an ancient tailcoat with one tail missing. From the remaining tail he would produce his blacking brushes and proceed to polish Verlaine's shoes as an act of homage, before clearing a passage to the poet's favourite café seat.

When the impecunious poet *Ernest Dowson* moved into some new lodgings in Paris, Verlaine kindly sent along his 'secretary' to provide Dowson with some domestic help. This almost ended in catastrophe when Bibi attempted to re-ignite the embers of Dowson's coal fire by pouring on petrol. The resulting explosion left both men shaken and blackened.

Bibi was devastated by Verlaine's death. He was seen at the funeral with tears streaming down his face, but still managing to conduct his usual business of purloining the umbrellas of the illustrious mourners.

VICTOR HUGO 1802-1885

Wilde's only meeting with the great French writer, Victor Hugo, was at an evening reception at Hugo's house engineered by their mutual acquaintance, *Robert Sherard*. Although Oscar was on sparkling form, Hugo fell fast asleep. Oscar's admiration for the old man remained undiminished by this disappointing introduction and he commented: 'Between them, Hugo and Shakespeare have exhausted every subject. Originality is no longer possible, even in sin. So there are no real emotions left, only extraordinary adjectives'.

Hugo was a man of abounding natural energy whose main fear was boredom, a condition he defined as being one where 'life seems entirely logical'. He summed up his attitude to writing as: "Reason is intelligence taking exercise. Imagination is intelligence with an erection".

Although later known for his deeply felt liberal socialism, Hugo's early political stance was rightwing. He was the son of a Napoleonic general, who had been the last officer to flee Madrid before the advance of the Duke of Wellington. The ten-year-old Hugo's most searing memories were those of seeing public garrotting, and severed limbs nailed to crucifixes during the retreat from Spain.

By sixteen, his extraordinary intelligence was recognised and he quickly became a favourite of the restored French monarchy. When he was chosen as the official poet for the coronation of King Charles X, the resulting royal pensions enabled him to marry his youthful bride, Adele, who was to bear him four children.

In 1831, after braving the church towers to research the subject, (he suffered badly from vertigo), Hugo published his book 'Notre Dame de Paris', becoming overnight the most famous living writer in Europe. He thoroughly disliked its translated English title – 'The Hunchback of Notre Dame'.

This success enhanced his position at the royal court and he became a confidante of King Louis-Phillippe. In 1837 he was created Viscount Hugo. Despite these favours though, he gradually became convinced of the case for socialism and rejected his own past allegiances. Hugo: "Not to believe in the people is to be a political atheist".

When the 'middle class monarchy' of Louis-Phillippe was overthrown in 1848, Hugo was persuaded to stand as mayor of his Paris arrondissement. In this new role, Hugo was at the heart of the action, storming barricades, directing troops and taking prisoners.

(Oddly enough, the only time his life was in serious danger was two years later when he attended the funeral of the writer Honore de Balzac. The horses pulling the hearse slipped, and the cart slid back pinning Hugo to a tombstone. Hugo: 'Without a man who clambered on to the tomb and hoisted me up by the shoulders, I should have presented the curious spectacle of Victor Hugo killed by Honore de Balzac'.)

Although Hugo was initially a supporter of Louis Napoleon, when in 1851 Louis carried out a coup d'etat and turned himself into *Emperor Napoleon III*, Hugo was outraged. He described the leaders of the Second Empire as 'senile adolescents' and asked: "Just because we had Napoleon le Grand, do we have to have Napoleon le Petit?"

Napoleon III struck back and arrested Hugo's son Charles. Hugo insisted on defending Charles in court. A critic commented that: "Hugo, by dint of eloquence and genius, has had his son sentenced to six months in jail. With a tenth-rate lawyer, poor old Charles would have got off with two weeks".

Under increasing pressure, Hugo fled from France to the safety of England. He was not impressed by the English attitude to political refugees, (claiming that the policy was 'Let them in and let them starve'), but finally he found a refuge in the Channel Islands where he was to stay in exile for nineteen years.

(Even here he had problems. After three years, he was expelled from Jersey. He was given sanctuary by the Island of Guernsey on the traditional principle that whatever Jersey disliked was approved of by Guernsey.)

He developed some of his main ideas while in exile, becoming a fierce opponent of the Church, and a strong supporter of abolishing executions. He once pointed to a Christian crucifix and declared: "In the presence of that victim of the death penalty, I swear that I shall continue to fight capital punishment with all my might".

After seventeen years work, in 1862 he published 'Les Miserables', a book that has been called 'the Magna Carta of the human race'. When Hugo wanted to find out what his publishers thought of his initial manuscript, he sent them a note reading simply: '?'. They replied with equal brevity: '!'.

This reaction was the first of a stream of praise. Its brilliant dissection of the ills of society caused Hugo to be known as 'the French Dickens' and had a profound effect in France. It was just as popular abroad, becoming a favourite of General Lee's army during the American Civil War. His troops described themselves as 'Lee's Miserables'. The Russian writer Dostoevski said he was glad to have been imprisoned as it gave him the time to re-read 'that great book'.

When Napoleon III fell during the Franco-Prussian War, Hugo was finally allowed back into France, where in 1871 he was elected to the National Assembly. Politically, times had changed though and his influence had waned. As a revered man of letters, however, he stood head and shoulders above anybody else.

His home in Paris became a magnet for admirers, including such luminaries as the fairy-tale writer Hans Christian Andersen. When Andersen asked him for his autograph, a suspicious Hugo became worried that Andersen might misuse his signature to forge an acknowledgement of debt or something of the sort. To prevent such skulduggery, he squeezed the words 'Victor Hugo' into the extreme right-hand top corner of the page so that nothing could be inserted above it. Andersen left the house, still puzzling over his autograph book.

Hugo felt justifiably proud over his life's achievements and brushed off most critics easily. When Leconte de Lisle said of Hugo that he was "as stupid as the Himalayas", Hugo replied: "I do not find the remark unpleasant and I forgive Leconte de Lisle, who seems to me to be just plain stupid". Hugo: "The good thing about pride is that it saves you from envy".

However, on one occasion, he was upset about a comment made by the actress *Helena Modjeska*. He asked her which theatrical roles she enjoyed performing best. Forgetting that Hugo had written some successful plays himself, she immediately answered: "Shakespeare's, of course!" Modjeska: 'In an instant, realisation of my mistake dawned upon me. The great man sank deeper in his armchair and said nothing. It was time to say goodbye'.

Hugo's funeral in 1885 was a major event; over two million people, larger than the entire population of Paris), followed the coffin to its resting place in the Pantheon, (which Hugo always said reminded him of 'a giant sponge cake'). A large carnival had been held the previous night and thousands of mourners had indulged in mass public copulation in the parks of Paris.

This unusual accompaniment to the obsequies may well have been a tribute to Hugo's other great talent – that of sexual athleticism. Although both were virgins when he married Adele, in his own words he went after her on the wedding night 'like an inebriated grape-picker' and coupled with her nine times before dawn.

She became exhausted by his demands and they both settled for other lovers. Adele became the mistress of the critic Charles Sainte-Beuve, (who would visit the Hugo home disguised as a nun), while Hugo acquired an actress and courtesan named Juliette Drouet, (described by Gautier as 'like a snake standing on its tail'). Juliette was to remain his main companion for fifty years.

When Charles Dickens visited Hugo in 1847, he wrote: 'His wife is a handsome woman with flashing black eyes, who looks as if she might poison his breakfast any morning when the humour seized her'.

Hugo had an insatiable desire for sex – 'To love is to act' – and his boast that 'women find me irresistible' was amply borne out. Throughout his adult life hundreds of women offered him their bodies; Juliette made the sour comment that "Hugo was a sucker for trouser-hunters and unsatisfied bitches".

He eagerly accepted this carnal tribute and recorded his sexual career in a secret diary. His numerous encounters with prostitutes also provided him with much of the information about the underbelly of society that he needed for his novels.

On one occasion in 1845, his affaires almost landed him in trouble. Under the direction of her irate husband, the police raided Hugo's apartment, where they discovered him in bed with Leonie Biard. Much to the amusement of Parisians, the pair were charged with having been in 'criminal conversation' (adultery) and 'in uncrumpled attire' (naked). Hugo claimed immunity as a French count, but Leonie spent some weeks in prison for the offence. Hugo went on to bed over two hundred women between 1848 and 1850.

During his Channel Islands exile, Hugo was inexhaustible in his pursuit of the island girls, often making love to two at a time. On his return to Paris during the 1870 siege, he specialised in the young actresses who auditioned for charity shows. After a day of sex with these girls, each night he would return home to find a group of women, street whores mingling with society ladies, waiting for him.

Although his potency was not in doubt, he also derived great pleasure from voyeurism. Watching tableaux vivants, where actresses would recreate famous works of art wearing only transparent body stockings, satisfied his hunger for visual excitement. Even in his private orgies he would often eschew full sex in favour of watching the girls perform lesbian acts on each other.

When Hugo was 81 years old, his small grandson accidentally walked into his grandfather's bedroom to find Hugo making love to a young laundress. Hugo stopped for a moment to proudly exclaim: "Look, little Georges, this is what they call genius!"

COUNT ROBERT DE MONTESQUIOU 1855-1921

For two men who held such similar views on life, it was surprising that Comte Robert de Montesquiou and Oscar Wilde remained distant acquaintances. They met occasionally at the Parisian salons but Montesquiou declared that he found Wilde a repulsive man – "the Antinous of the horrible" – and avoided him as much as possible.

However, Montesquiou was so extraordinary that several writers used him as the original for characters in their novels. Notably, he was the model for 'Baron Charlus' in *Proust's* 'Remembrance of Things Past', and 'Des Esseintes' in *Huysmans'* 'A Rebours'. It is highly likely that Wilde had Montesquiou partly in mind when he created the character of 'Dorian Gray'.

Montesquiou was a member of an ancient French family that was 'allied to the greater part of the European aristocracy'; (he claimed direct descent from Charles de Batz, the original of 'D'Artagnan' in Dumas's 'The Three Musketeers'. Wilde once reviewed a theatre adaptation of this book, claiming that it should have been called 'Athos, Pathos, and Bathos').

Montesquiou's more immediate family carried on a tradition of aristocratic insouciance. One relative, on hearing of the death of his wife while he was preparing to go to a fancy costume ball dressed as a bee, sniffed: "These things get exaggerated", and continued to the party. Montesquiou's aunt once remarked peevishly: "Now that men no longer wear breeches at balls, one can't tell what they are thinking!"

Montesquiou's father, the vice-president of the Jockey Club, viewed his son with distaste: "Children! Those strangers we introduce so imprudently into our lives". When Montesquiou said in his own defence: "You made me what I am", his father replied: "Well, I didn't do it on purpose".

Montesquiou upheld the family trait of polished hauteur. When a bourgeois banker begged to be allowed to join an aristocratic salon, Montesquiou told him: "But don't you understand that your mere presence would rob the salon of the glitter that now attracts you to it".

One acquaintance said of Montesquiou: "There's one good thing about the French Revolution. If it hadn't happened, that man would have had us beating his ponds to keep the frogs quiet."

Montesquiou, who described himself as 'a greyhound in a greatcoat', was a tall, thin man, who looked, in the words of Lucien Daudet, 'varnished for eternity'. Surpassing even Oscar's taste for bizarre dress, he was known to wear a white velvet suit, with a spray of violets at the top of his shirt replacing the usual cravat.

His Paris top-floor apartment was a series of attics each decorated as different tableaux. His friend, W Graham Robertson, said that: "you went up through tunnels of tapestries into an 'exotic Arabian Nights translated into Japanese' ". His 'winter room' was adorned with polar bear rugs, a sleigh, and mica-flake snow, while his bedroom was dominated by a huge black dragon that turned out to be his bed.

Although his family assumed that he was homosexual, Montesquiou did have some heterosexual liaisons as well. All his life he was fascinated by *Napoleon III's* mistress, the Comtesse de Castiglione, and his most valued possession was a plaster cast of her knees. He had sex with the actress, *Sarah Bernhardt*, though afterwards he spent a week of uncontrollable vomiting as a result.

Edmund Goncourt reported that Montesquiou once made love to a female ventriloquist. In the midst of the activity, he was terrified when the woman teasingly imitated the voice of her angry pimp emanating from the wardrobe.

(One of his friends and probable female lovers was Elsie, Baroness (Madeleine) Deslandes. This German-born baroness was one of the Oppenheim family, and had been married previously both to Count Fleury and Prince Robert de Broglie. She told the latter that he would be "the perfection of beauty if it were not for the smallness of that little thing you have between your legs".

Elsie's habit was to receive her guests, lounging on a precious carpet, dressed in a floating tea-gown, and feeding jewels to a pet toad. Wilde visited her house often and persuaded *Burne-Jones* to paint her portrait. Oscar would arrive bearing armfuls of lilies and spent hours relaxing with her on luxurious bearskins. She later proudly proclaimed that he had been her lover.

In later years she attempted to seduce the Italian poet, *D'Annunzio*, who rejected her with the sneer: "Yes, I shall take you – in your coffin". She turned instead to a lesbian affair with the Comtesse D'Orsay.

Eventually she grew very fat and her life-long myopia worsened. On one occasion she agreed to appear in a cage with some lions during a Castilian fete. She was too short sighted to be afraid.)

Montesquiou's most intense homosexual relationship was with his male secretary, the Argentinian born Gabriel Yturri, who remained his faithful servant for twenty years. Yturri finally grew so ill that Montesquiou said that he "could barely summon the strength to take the borzois for a walk".

After Yturri's death, Montesquiou held a memorial poetry reading at his apartment. The uncle of the Tsar, Grand Duke Vladimir attended it but whispered to another guest: 'No, thank you, I won't have a chair. In this house I always feel safer with my back to the wall".

Montesquiou was a devotee of the arts and numbered *Whistler* and *Verlaine* amongst his close friends. He was a minor poet himself and would recite his verse to the salons in a high-pitched grating voice. Although he had inherited great wealth, such was his extravagance that occasionally he would find himself temporarily short of funds. (Montesquiou: "It's bad enough not to have any money, it would be too much if one had to deprive oneself of anything.")

During these financial embarrassments, he would invite groups of people to his house. Yturri would raise a finger to command silence and announce gravely: "Listen to the County! He is about to make speeches for you!" After Montesquiou had finished his squeaky oration, he would leave the room while Yturri would remove the cover from a table stacked with copies of Montesquiou's verse. It was socially impossible not to buy one. A guest said of them: "They milked money wherever they could".

Montesquiou, as befitted a French aristocrat, was involved in several duels. (The practice, involving as it did some very unmilitary civilians, produced some odd duellists. Charles Sainte-Beuve, the lover of *Victor Hugo's* wife, once arrived at a duel carrying a pistol in one hand and an umbrella in the other. He explained that he was prepared to go to his grave 'shot full of holes but not soaking wet as well'.)

One such event had been caused by Montesquiou's review of a book by a writer of mildly erotic novels, Madame Ernesta Stern. One of her chapters was entitled 'How to Choose a Lover'. Montesquiou's review commented: 'This is absurd, because everyone knows she never bothers to choose'. Her son, a noted swordsman, immediately challenged him to defend himself.

This ended in farce, as Montesquiou's method of duelling was to whirl his sword around like an aircraft propeller. After three quarters of an hour, the famed swordsman was at a loss as how to break through this unorthodox defence. Finally, Montesquiou received a wound on his thumb and left the field to recuperate.

Montesquiou was capable of quite extreme refinements of cruelty. One woman found this out to her cost. For many years she had deluded herself that he was in love with her and had sent him dozens of letters. When Montesquiou died, his only bequest was to leave her a casket.

After it had been delivered by a solicitor, she gathered her friends to witness the revelation of Montesquiou's last gift. Opening the casket with a flourish, she found all the letters that she had ever sent him tied up neatly in a bundle. None of them had ever been opened.

EDMOND DE GONCOURT 1822-1896

On April 21, 1883, Wilde had dinner at the home of Edmond Goncourt, the surviving member of the two Goncourt brothers, of whom Oscar said: "What artists! And proud, and arrogant, and jealous of their fame, and rightly so'. Edmond was less enthusiastic, describing Wilde as 'an individual of doubtful gender, with a ham actor's turn of phrase. He told us some tall tales, but gave us an amusing picture of a town in Texas'.

Edmond and his brother Jules (1830-1870) were writers who collaborated so closely with each other that they could be called the Siamese twins of French literature. Their lives and personalities were so welded together that they became effectively one person. For instance, if one brother paused in his conversation, the other would continue the sentence without skipping a beat.

When their mother died in 1848, they inherited enough money to live modest but independent lives, and to follow their own interests. At first they turned to journalism and started their own newspaper. It struggled to survive; a friend visited the editorial office one day and noticed a dejected man sitting in a corner. She asked why the man looked so miserable. Edmond replied: "He's our accountant".

Although they were acquitted when their paper was sued for obscenity, they decided to abandon the publication. Edmond: "I think that men of wit and intelligence pass through journalism and do not remain there; it is for literature like garrison life is for the army".

For twenty-five years their domestic life was reliant upon a seemingly impeccable maid and mother figure called Rosalie Malingre. When she died, the brothers discovered that Rosalie had led an extraordinary double life, and had stolen large sums of money from them to pay men to join her in nocturnal orgies; she had borne several children as a result. The astounded Goncourts eventually wrote a novel, 'Germinie Lacerteux' (1864), based on Rosalie's exploits.

They sublimated their own sexual drives in the Paris brothels, (where Jules caught the syphilis that later was to kill him). But in general they disliked women and reserved their true (though platonic) affections for each other.

In their novels, the Goncourts were mostly known for their devotion to naturalistic writing and their meticulous attention to detail. They applied this same technique of brutally honest recording of fact when they wrote a series of pen portraits of real historical figures called 'Les Portraits Intimes'. They answered their critics by declaring that their real task was to look at the private life, not the public.

In 1870, Edmond was shattered by Jules's death; he became known as 'the widow'. He became an intense elitist and anti-Semite, and expressed his strong dislike of democracy. Edmond: "There are only two main currents in the history of mankind – meanness that makes men conservatives and envy which makes them revolutionaries'.

His dedication to writing total realism, (he recorded the death agonies of his own brother), led to the publication of the Goncourt Brothers' famous 'Journals', a immense work covering every aspect of their lives from 1851 to 1896. Edmond unrelentingly exposed not only his own life, but also that of their wide acquaintanceship. Weathering the appalled reaction of this circle, Edmond replied to the effect that indiscretion was the soul of memory.

As he grew older, Edmond became increasingly jealous of the success of other writers. He was reported as going from bookshop to bookshop 'glowering at the piles of best sellers'. One rival confessed: "More than once I had occasion to meet him in these circumstances and I humbly confess that I'd invent stories of fabulous sales just to drive him up the wall".

Also present at Oscar's meeting with Edmond Goncourt was Edmond's great friend, the novelist **ALPHONSE DAUDET** (1840-1897). Daudet took a distinct dislike to Wilde and wrote of him: 'His voice was at once pallid and fat, the words came tumbling out of his frightful slack mouth and when he had finished he would roar with laughter like a fat, satisfied, gossipy woman, and order an exotic drink'.

Daudet was delighted at Wilde's downfall and rebuked *Robert Sherard's* defence of his friend on the grounds that, as Sherard had no children, he had no right to say anything on the subject. Daudet refused to sign a petition for Oscar's release, proclaiming solemnly, "I have sons". Ironically, one of these sons, Lucien Daudet, turned out to be homosexual.

Daudet's abhorrence of Wilde may have stemmed from a comment Oscar once made: "Rodin's statue of Balzac is an astonishing masterpiece, a gorgeous leonine head, stuck on the top of a cone-shaped dressing-gown. I have suggested that the statue to Alphonse Daudet should consist merely of a dressing-gown without any head at all."

Despite meeting this glittering group of French cognoscenti, Wilde's sojourn in Paris was something of an anticlimax. He wrote a poem 'Helas' and much of another poem 'The Sphinx' but his failure to sell 'The Duchess of Padua' was a real blow. By May 1883, Oscar had no money left from his US tour.

Returning to London, (possibly via a short trip into Switzerland – 'so vulgar with its big ugly mountains'), he stayed with his mother, Speranza, at her home in Park Street.

After borrowing some money from a moneylender called Levy, Oscar now moved back into rooms at 9, Charles Street.

In July, he began a short tour of Britain giving lectures about his American experiences.

Then on August 2 he sailed from Liverpool bound for New York on his second foray into the United States.

An actress named Marie Prescott had agreed finally to produce Oscar's first play 'Vera'. The show opened in New York on the 20th August on a boiling hot night and came under heavy attack from the critics. One of the kindlier reviewers wrote that 'it comes as near failure as an ingenious and able writer can bring it', while Punch exercised its inimitable command of humour with the comment that the play was 'vera bad.' The play closed after seven nights.

Wilde turned down Prescott's offer of touring the show with Oscar himself playing the lead role of 'Prince Paul'.

During August 1883, Wilde was taken to visit the inventor, Thomas Edison at Menlo Park.

THOMAS EDISON 1847-1931

By the 1880s, Thomas Edison's research laboratories at Menlo Park, New Jersey, 25 miles from New York, had become an attraction for visiting celebrities, including *Sarah Bernhardt,* (who described Edison as 'the giver of light'). When Wilde spent an afternoon there he chatted with Edison and told him that, after the failure of 'Vera', in future he was only going to write plays that were 'actor-proof'. Edison laughed: "You're learning!"

Oscar was impressed by the respect accorded to Edison. Wilde: 'In England an inventor is regarded almost as a crazy man, and in too many instances invention ends in disappointment and poverty. In America an inventor is honoured.'

Known as 'the Wizard of Menlo Park', Edison was a key figure in the technological revolution. He was responsible for over one thousand patents, including the phonograph, home electricity, and the moving picture camera. By 1923, the New York Times estimated that his genius was responsible for the employment of one and a half million workers, and the value of his inventions at $15,000,000,000.

Beginning his career as an itinerant Mid-West telegraph operator, in rapid succession Edison invented a stock ticker machine and an automatic copying device that provided enough money to fund future projects. He declared that: "I want none of the rich man's usual toys. I want no horses and yachts – I have no time for them. What I want is a perfect workshop'. In 1876, he created the first laboratory for organised industrial research at Menlo Park.

It was here that he discovered electric waves, developed the light bulb, and, in 1876, invented recorded sound on his new phonograph machine, (the famous first recorded words were 'Mary had a little lamb').

Occasionally, Edison made mistakes. During the practical application of electricity, his company incorrectly backed the system of direct current (DC) against the alternating current system (AC) espoused by his rivals, Westinghouse. In what became known as 'the war of the currents', Edison conceived the idea of discrediting Westinghouse by allowing them to use the AC system to fuel the first execution by electric chair.

He hoped and expected that the prisoner, rather than being carbonised, would become mummified though the evaporation of body water. When the experiment was carried out at

182

Sing Sing Prison, the man chosen, William Kemmler, was declared dead, then found to be breathing and had to be electrocuted all over again. Although Edison was delighted to hear this news, the authorities refused to change the system. AC remained the favoured method, and Edison's company lost the electrocution contract.

Nothing daunted, Edison went on to develop his phonograph machine to record music, thus creating the huge market for home entertainment. (Due to the fact that brass instruments were far easier to record than violins, brass band music became the mainstay of the original record industry).

By 1904, Edison's development of his film camera led to the production of the first commercial motion picture, 'The Great Train Robbery'.

His only major financial failure involved his attempt to extract magnetic iron ore, but he soon recouped his losses and went on to develop cement works, (the basis of the prefab house), and to research methods of creating domestic natural rubber. He became enthusiastic about developing motorcars that were powered by electricity, but was argued out of this idea by Henry Ford who preferred the gasoline option.

By this time Edison had become deaf and had to converse with Ford via an assistant who tapped out Ford's conversation in Morse Code on Edison's knee.

Edison was a profound believer in hard work, famously declaring that: "Genius is one per cent inspiration and ninety-nine per cent perspiration". When he married in 1871, he dropped his bride off at home on the wedding night while he went to his factory to adjust some machinery. When he arrived home after midnight he was bewildered to find his new wife in tears.

When he attended the Paris Exhibition in 1889 he was interviewed by *Robert Sherard* for the London Pall Mall Budget. Edison told Sherard: "What struck me so far chiefly is the absolute laziness of everybody over here. When do these people work?" Wilde differed on this point: 'Hard work is simply the refuge of people who have nothing better to do'.

Oscar also injected a note of caution over the nineteenth century technological explosion: 'People should not mistake the means of civilisation for the end. The steam engine and the telephone depend entirely for their value on the use to which they are put'.

Wilde stayed for a while around Coney Island and Newport, then returned to England in mid September 1883.

He remained at Charles Street, London, for a week before resuming his nationwide lecture tour that was to last, on and off, till September 1884.

His two main talks were entitled 'Personal Impressions of America' and 'The House Beautiful'. Obeying John Ruskin's precept of 'taking culture to the masses', Oscar said that his task was 'to civilise the provinces'. It also provided much needed cash.

He spoke at over 150 venues from Scotland to Penzance.

In November 1883, he reached Dublin where he stayed at the Shelbourne Hotel. During his visit, he became engaged to an Irish girl named Constance Lloyd.

1884

[In Britain, William Morris formed the Socialist League.
The French government continued its colonial expansion across Southeast Asia, while in France itself miners began a nationwide strike.

In the Sudan, an attempt to relieve Khartoum by the Anglo-Egyptian forces was repulsed at the Battle of El Teb. A second force marched south from Egypt under Sir Garnet Wolseley, resulting in the Battle of Abu Klea.]

Wilde's speaking tour of Britain continued until, on May 29, 1884, he married Constance Lloyd at St James Church, Sussex Gardens, Paddington, London.

CONSTANCE WILDE 1858-1898 (First Part)

Oscar's bride, Constance Mary Lloyd, had been raised in Dublin and was the niece of the Solicitor-General of Ireland, Baron Hemphill. Her father died when she was aged 16, and she and her brother Otho became wards of their paternal grandfather, John Horatio Lloyd. Constance lived at his house at 100, Lancaster Gate, London.

Their grandfather was a well-known Queens Counsel, who had gained his reputation and wealth as one of the two leading lawyers during the railway boom of the 1840s, (the other lawyer – and rival – being Henry Hawkins).

Although her life held nothing in comparison to the immense scandal that was destined to overwhelm her as a result of the marriage to Oscar, Constance's family had its full share of eccentrics and disgraces.

Grandfather Lloyd himself had his career curtailed after he had indecently exposed himself in Temple Gardens, London – 'to the great consternation of strolling nursemaids'. There was no prosecution because the Temple Gardens were private property, but he was forced to retire from public life for a period, and the incident probably cost him the post of Solicitor-General of England.

Her maternal uncle Lt. Col. William Hope, (father of Adrian Hope, the future guardian of the Wilde children), became the despair of his rather pompous son with his fixation on inventing a new gun. He spent so much money on this pursuit that Adrian had to forgo university. Adrian's letters give some idea of his growing irritation: 'My father has just given birth to a new Gun. Yet another invention. How I wish he would coin sovereigns instead'. After a trial of the new weapon: 'The Gun burst into a thousand pieces. It is a wonder that the Colonel still lives for he was the centre of a whirlpool of steel'. A month later: 'The Colonel is, I think, raving. He is now inventing a Hair Wash! It makes me sick'.

Constance's brother Otho Holland Lloyd was the centre of a widely publicised and unpleasant court case when he was divorced by his wife in 1886. He was forced to change his name to Otho Holland and live abroad as a result. (*Gertrude Atherton*: 'The law had been altered years before to allow people to change their names – the first to take advantage of this new privilege was a man named James Bugg who became 'Norfolk Howard'.)

[One of Otho's sons, **FABIAN LLOYD** (1887-1918), alias 'Arthur Craven', managed to continue the family misadventures into the 20th century. He became a boxer and said of himself that he was a "hotel thief, muleteer, snake-charmer, chauffeur and poet with the shortest hair in the world".

In 1917, he gave a lecture at the Grand Central Gallery in New York where, after cursing the audience and stripping naked onstage, he was carried off dead drunk and in handcuffs. The artist Marcel Duchamps had egged him on and described the event afterwards as 'an excellent lecture'. Fabian Lloyd was drowned off the coast of Mexico in 1918, after fleeing conscription in the First World War.]

At first, Oscar's marriage to the girl he described as 'quite young, very grave, and mystical, with wonderful eyes, and dark brown coils of hair' was a happy one. While he continued on his lecture tour, he telegraphed daily to his bride and said that the telegraph clerks were becoming quite romantic as a consequence: 'I hand in my messages, however, very sternly, and try to look as if 'love' was a cryptogram for 'Buy Grand Trunks' and 'darling' a cipher for 'sell at par'. I am sure it succeeds'.

However, within a couple of years, his undoubted early infatuation with Constance wore off, though she remained deeply in love with him. While, at first, he had been intrigued by her mystique, ('She scarcely ever speaks. I am always wondering what her thoughts are like'), by 1886, he had concluded that "Women are sphinxes without secrets'. His disillusion deepened: 'Men marry because they are tired; women, because they are curious; both are disappointed'.

Though she concealed the identity of the couple, the writer *Ada Leverson* definitely implied the Wilde household when she wrote: 'I knew a case of a man of remarkable and brilliant gifts who fell in love with and married a simple, sweet little woman, not clever, who worshipped him. He thought this ideal at first, but his point of view gradually changed. She had, alas, no tact – tact is part of cleverness…The result was that, though he was deeply attached to her, and felt for her always a sincere affection, he gradually could not stand her society. It became more and more irksome to him'.

Oscar's comments on marriage reflected his own doubts: 'As for domesticity, it ages one rapidly, and distracts one's mind from higher things'; 'Those tedious tetes-a-tetes that are the dream of engaged couples, and the despair of married men – that eternal duologue about bills and babies'; and 'Women give to men the very gold of their lives but they invariably want it back in such small change'.

The birth of their two sons, *Cyril* and *Vyvyan,* compounded the marital problems. Repulsed by the 'hideousness' of Constance's body after pregnancy – ('Desire is killed by maternity, passion buried in conception') – Oscar gave up having sex with Constance, claiming among other reasons that they could not afford any more children.

(Except for an incident with a prostitute in Dieppe in 1897, this appears to have been Wilde's last heterosexual activity. But it was highly unlikely that Constance realised that Oscar was homosexual until the denouement of 1895).

After 1887, although still under the same roof, they began to lead increasingly separate lives. In this, they were not unusual. Wilde: 'All the married men nowadays live like bachelors, and all the bachelors like married men'.

Constance filled the void by interesting herself in politics. She joined the Chelsea Women's Liberal Association, worked for female suffrage, and edited a magazine devoted to rationalising women's dress. In 1889, she persuaded Oscar to attend a demonstration in Hyde Park in support of the Dock Strike.

She became an enthusiast for spiritual development, firstly as a follower of the savant and mystic *Madame Blavatsky*, then in 1888 as a member of the Order of the Golden Dawn, a group founded on Buddhist and cabbalistic thought. The poet *W.B. Yeats* was another adherent.

The respectability of her matronhood may have grated on Oscar. As he wrote in 'A Woman of No Importance': 'Twenty years of romance make a woman look like a ruin; but twenty years of marriage make her something like a public building'.

Occasionally, Constance displayed her anger at Oscar's absences. Wilde: 'Women defend themselves by attacking, just as they attack by sudden and strange surrenders'. Rather absurdly in hindsight, she suspected that he was having affairs with actresses.

When she tackled him on the subject, she accepted his excuse that he had become addicted to golf. Constance: 'Oscar has become mad about golf and spends two or three hours on the links every day and this is so good for him'. Wilde: 'The one charm of marriage is that it makes a life of deception absolutely necessary for both parties. I never know where my wife is, and my wife never knows what I am doing'.

Robert Ross said of Oscar at this time: "He really did not understand how cruel he was to his wife, but I never expect anyone to believe that".

Constance wrote two books of children's stories and later in January 1895, (just three months before the family downfall, and in what was one of the most unconsciously sad publications in literary history), she arranged and privately published a book of Oscar's aphorisms called 'Oscariana'.

It was this publication that led to her increasing involvement with Arthur Humphries, the manager of Hatchard's bookshop in Piccadilly. In Oscar's absence, it is possible that she may have had an affair with Humphries. Certainly some of her letters to him seem to suggest that this was the case, for example: 'My Darling Arthur, How much I love you, and how dear and delightful you have been to me today. I have been happy, and I do love you, dear Arthur!'

If so, the liaison was brief. In January 1895, Constance fell down the stairs of her home at Tite Street, and damaged her spine. In March, the trials of her husband began.

[See Constance Wilde – Second Part – Page 425]

Despite their intense battles in the courtroom, Constance's grandfather and his rival, **SIR HENRY 'HANGING' HAWKINS** (1817-1907), had great respect for each other. Hawkins, (cousin of the author of 'The Prisoner of Zenda', Anthony Hope Hawkins), said of John Horatio Lloyd: "He was an advocate whom no opponent could treat lightly, and was uniformly kind and agreeable".

Few people were able to say the same about Judge Hawkins, however; the actor *Seymour Hicks* called him 'a hard, terrifying little man'. Some lawyers said that his ferocious reputation as a judge was exaggerated and that he was capable of acts of judicial kindness, but the respected barrister *Sir Edward Clarke* was unequivocal. "Sir Henry Hawkins was the worst Judge I ever knew or heard of. He had no notion whatever of what justice meant, or of the obligations of truth and fairness".

As his nickname of 'Hanging' suggests, Hawkins was a merciless proponent of capital punishment. At one famous trial in Northampton, a witness recalled: "Justice Hawkins sat all Christmas Eve in the case till midnight chimed, then finished, on the stroke of Christmas Day, by sentencing the prisoner to death".

As a young (and more naïve) barrister, he once defended a man on a charge of killing his wife. Hawkins called the defendant's children as witnesses, and the sight of the two little waifs sobbing bitterly at their father's predicament persuaded the jury to an acquittal.

That evening he was approached by an old gentleman who told him that this sympathy might have been misplaced. "Last night I saw the little children who sobbed so violently in court this morning, and to whom you made such pathetic reference, playing on an ash-heap near their cottage. They had a cat with a string round its neck, swinging to and fro, and, as they did so, they sang: 'This is the way old daddy will go – daddy will go – daddy will go!' "

Some victims of the scaffold displayed extraordinary sang froid, a fact that Hawkins acknowledged. His favourite story was of an 1870s murderer who, with the noose around his neck, made his final speech beginning with: "My friends, I am going to die for the murder of Charles …. Charles …. what the devil *was* his name? I forget?"

Hawkins could be cutting in his demolition of lawyers who came before him, but occasionally he was on the receiving end. One day, Hawkins expressed his contempt for an advocate by interrupting him in mid flow. Hawkins rasped: "Your speech is just going in one of my ears and coming out of the other one!" The lawyer replied: "I do not doubt it, my lord. What is there to prevent it?"

Hawkins attempted to enter Parliament and stood for the constituency of Barnstaple in 1865. When he arrived in the town he was gratified to hear a crowd in the street cheering his name. Later that night, he discovered that this approbation was the result of his political agent distributing £500 in small change. Hawkins was shocked and refused to hand out another penny – thereby losing badly. On his departure he delivered a ringing speech denouncing bribery. As he left, one hopeful, taking pity on the defeated candidate, approached Hawkins with the information that he could be MP for Totnes for only £7000.

(The corruption of politics had been even worse in the previous century. When John Wilkes stood as a candidate for a parliamentary seat at Berwick-on-Tweed, the opposing party sent up a cargo of voters from London by sea; the plot failed after Wilkes bribed the captain to land them in Norway.)

In his later years, Hawkins married his cook, a cheerful Cockney woman who became notorious for her malapropisms. During a dinner at the Hawkins's home, one gentleman complimented her on her splendid carpet. She replied innocently: "Oh, thank you! I don't know how many men have copulated me upon that carpet."

Given 'Hanging' Hawkins's harsh record, his supervision of the 1891 case against **HORATIO BOTTOMLEY** (1860-1932) was extraordinary in its laxity. Bottomley was one of the most notorious swindlers of his age, yet somehow he managed to shamelessly flatter Hawkins, 'the toughest judge for 50 years', into becoming almost a character witness for his defence.

Defending himself, Bottomley gave a brilliant speech interweaving charm and humour to win the court over. When questioned about where the sum of £700,000 had gone, Bottomley replied: "In all sincerity and honesty, I have not the remotest idea" – a statement which was greeted by roars of laughter.

During the prosecution's interminable closing speech, Hawkins sent the jury a note. It read: 'Patience Competition. 1st Prize, Henry Hawkins. Honourable Mention, Job.'

When the twelve jurymen acquitted Bottomley, Hawkins congratulated them with the words: "That makes thirteen of us".

After the case, Hawkins took Bottomley to one side and advised him to take up the law as a career. Many years later when Hawkins retired, he presented Bottomley with the wig and gown that he had worn throughout his judicial life.

In spite of an appalling record of financial misdemeanour and a private life festooned with blowsy chorus girls, Bottomley managed to become a Member of Parliament. His past finally caught up with him when he received a seven-year prison sentence for fraud and his name became a byword for corruption.

The journalist *Herbert Vivian* recalled: 'Soon after his sentence, I heard two villainous looking tramps discussing his case on a bus. "Garn!" said one, "you never knew Bottomley". "Wot?" returned the other with a murderous scowl, "me not know Bottomley! Why, I was at Eton wiv 'im".'

Bottomley was only one of several crooks who reached the top of the financial and political world of the 1890s. Other well-known figures were Ernest Terah Hooley and Jabez Balfour, the latter becoming the Liberal MP for Tamworth. (As Wilde suggested: "There is hardly a single person in the House of Commons worth painting; though many of them would be the better for a little white-washing".)

During one parliamentary debate, the silky Jabez Balfour, (later sentenced to hard labour in prison, followed by a job on Lord Northcliffe's Daily Mail), was extolling the virtues of a colleague called Forster. Suddenly an elderly opposition MP, Sir Robert Moncrieffe, angrily burst out: "Forster! Why, he's nothing but a thundering cad!" In dulcet tones, Balfour replied: "Oh, if he has a fault, I admit that it is in that direction".

After the wedding reception at Lancaster Gate, Oscar and Constance Wilde set off on their honeymoon. The New York Times generously reported: 'A happy group of intimates saw them off at Charing Cross and few married couples ever carried better wishes with them'.

They arrived for the first part of their holiday in Paris, where they stayed at the Hotel Wagram on the Rue Rivoli.

While in Paris, the couple had dinner with an American artist, John Singer Sargent (1856-1925), who was later to become their near neighbour in London, and known as 'the Van Dyck of Tite Street'. Sargent, already on his way to becoming the leading portrait painter of the period, drew a sketch of Oscar sitting at the Café Lavenue, near the Gare Montparnasse. The picture has since been lost.

In early June, Wilde visited the French writer J-K Huysmans.

JORIS-KARL HUYSMANS 1848-1907

While on his honeymoon, Wilde had read a new book called 'A Rebours' by J-K Huysmans. He was deeply impressed by the work: 'This last book of Huysmans is one of the best I have ever seen'. Later Oscar was to mention it in 'Dorian Gray' where he described it as 'poisonous' – an approving adjective in the context. In early June 1884, Wilde visited Huysmans to compliment him on the book.

Although he wrote several other novels, 'A Rebours' remained the most memorable as the pivotal work of the French Decadent movement. Although Huysmans never met *Robert de Montesquiou*, the foibles of the eccentric nobleman provided much of the material for the book. However, it was noticeable that the heroes of Huysmans' novels were always thinly disguised versions of Huysmans himself. In 'A Rebours', the hero 'Des Esseintes' was what Huysmans would have liked to have been, given unlimited money.

In contrast, his real life was rather humdrum. The only major excitement occurred in 1870-1, when he, like many other Parisians, was caught up in the events surrounding the siege of Paris. However he managed to avoid any serious involvement and, after history had calmed down a bit, he returned to his job as a clerk at the Ministry of the Interior as if nothing had happened.

The government job, though it bored him, provided him with a modest but adequate income. He slowly ascended the ranks of bureaucracy until, during the period of bomb outrages by the French anarchists in the 1890s, he was made sous-chef de bureau at the Sureté Générale.

The writer Paul Valery visited him in his office one day to find Huysmans complaining that a provincial police chief had informed him that the local 'anarcho' had gone missing. Huysmans: "Whenever this happens, it costs France thirty thousand francs! I have to telegraph a description of the suspect to every police force in the world". Huysmans turned down Valery's suggestion: "Wouldn't it be cheaper just to give ten thousand francs to the anarchist to remain in touch".

Huysmans spent most of his time at the Ministry quietly writing his own books. In common with many young writers of the 1880s, he rebelled against the romanticism of his literary predecessors. He soon found himself equally out of sympathy with the 'naturalistic' school of *Emile Zola* and turned instead to occultism, at the time very popular in France.

After some involvement with the Kabbalistic Order of the Rose Cross, he dabbled with black magic and attended séances and Masses that culminated in sexual orgies. He wrote 'Le Bas', a book based on these experiences, but finally realised that his occult guide, a mystic called 'Abbe' Boullan, was in fact a fraudster, and left the movement.

His embarrassment over this episode was not helped when the publication of 'Le Bas' led to him being regarded as an authority on the occult. Various strange individuals started to arrive at the Ministry, asking him to introduce them to black mass orgies. This was not regarded with favour by his Ministry superiors.

On one occasion a man, wearing cyclist's knickerbockers and a check cap, arrived, claiming to be the Archbishop of Columbo, and offering to consecrate a pile of baguettes to be divided up and used as holy wafers by the black magic practitioners. Thereafter, Huysmans kept two files in his office labelled respectively 'Lunatics' and 'Bores'.

By 1898, Huysmans became interested in the Catholic Church and retired from the Ministry, informing his office that he had 'religious atavisms'. He wrote a book during this later period called 'St Lydwine of Schiedam' – a saint mostly remembered for having suffered every disease known to the Middle Ages, with the exception of leprosy.

Huysmans spent the rest of his life living in a series of monasteries. He was cautious about the idea of becoming a monk, after one abbot had asked him if he was prepared to make the supreme sacrifice: "Give me your pen". Instead Huysmans lived the life of an oblate – one who rejected the world and lived in an enclosed society but did not take the full vows.

When Wilde heard about this, he said approvingly: "It must be delightful to see God through stained glass windows. I may even go to a monastery myself". There is some evidence that Huysmans had occasional doubts. He wrote to a friend that: 'I am with wonderful people who are excellent Christians and moreover I do not have to see too much of them'.

Huysmans's life settled into one of spirituality and pious acts, but once one of his kindly gestures came adrift. Some friends of a struggling writer called Leon Bloy arranged a collection to help launch one of his books. The first person they asked to subscribe was Huysmans, who generously put his name down for fifty francs. The collection was made and presented to Bloy, together with the list of subscribers' names.

After examining the list. Bloy, far from being grateful, exploded with fury. His friends asked what was wrong, telling Bloy: "Huysmans was not only the first to sign, but also the most generous'. Bloy spluttered his reply: "The bastard! He set a maximum!"

After leaving Paris, the Wildes continued their honeymoon with a week in Dieppe where Constance introduced Oscar to two of her friends – Alice, then wife of the Duc de Richelieu, and Margaret, the Rani of Sarawak, who were holidaying in the town.

PRINCESS ALICE OF MONACO 1858-1925

Constance Wilde had become acquainted with Alice, the grandniece of the German poet Heinrich Heine, during her teenage years when she had been taken by her relative and mentor, Lady Georgiana Mount Temple, on holiday to Italy. The friendship blossomed, as Constance enjoyed the company of non-conformist women such as Alice and the third member of the group, the Rani of Sarawak.

Oscar was impressed and a little surprised that his bride had such exalted contacts. On the death of her husband, the Duc de Richelieu, Alice (besides being left over 17 million francs) re-married, this time to Prince Albert of Monaco (1848-1922). In 1891, Wilde dedicated his fairy tale, 'The Fisherman and the Sea', to the new princess. Even after Wilde's downfall, Alice remained friendly with Constance and looked after the interests of Oscar's second child Vyvyan, when he later attended boarding school in Monaco.

Born in New Orleans, Alice left for France when she was still a child but never lost her American accent and her love of Creole cooking, which she helped introduce to Paris. Aged 17, she married Richelieu in 1875, and after his death married Albert in 1889, becoming the first (though not the last) American Princess of Monaco.

The Monaco royal family (the Grimaldis) held a strange position in the principality. While nominally in full feudal control, they actually owed everything to the good will of Francois Blanc, the manager of the wildly profitable casino. Prince Albert resented the power of M. Blanc who, in a highly popular move, had forced him to abolish taxes in Monaco. The income from the casino had proved to be ample, without additional levies.

Blanc also assumed some of the Grimaldi privileges. When the Monaco carabinieri refused to salute Blanc's wife, Blanc stopped their wages until they obeyed. (The English politician, *Sir Charles Dilke*, wrote an amusing novel called 'The Fall of Prince Florestan' based on this situation).

[It was also the Blanc family, not the Grimaldis, who had been at the heart of the famed 'LEGEND OF MONTE CARLO'. When the principality had been destitute, an old monk in a nearby monastery had invented a game with a wheel and numbers. He convinced a local café owner, Camille Blanc, that the game would be popular and would always end in profit to the bank (Blanc). All the monk asked in return was that, once a year, he would return and use his own infallible system to win enough at the tables to keep the monastery in funds for another twelve months. Blanc started the roulette game, the monk's vision proved to be correct, and Blanc, Monaco and the monastery prospered immensely.

When the old monk died he passed on the secret of his winning formula to his successor, Father Ambrose, who took over the duty of annually winning at roulette. One year, he was at the table when he noticed a beautiful woman who had lost everything except her last coin. He leaned over and told her where to place it. She won back all her money.

Ambrose fell in love with the woman and they planned to elope together. He returned to the monastery to deliver the winnings, then set off back down the mountain path to Monte Carlo. Then, overcome by conscience and his breaking of his vow, he staggered to his death over a cliff edge. The secret of Monte Carlo was lost forever.]

The marriage of Alice and Albert was not successful and they gradually became more distant. She was interested in the arts and in recreating in Monaco the intellectual world she had known in Paris. Albert, on the other hand, was obsessed by oceanography (he carried out 26 different research voyages).

Oscar Wilde visited her during this period. She enjoyed his company, although her children were less welcoming. Her daughter, the Comtesse Gabriel de la Rochefoucault recalled: 'My brother and I called him the slug, and we couldn't bear him because each morning he asked us to recite a poem in English and he invariably said to my mother "Alice, your children's accent is atrocious" and our governess punished us.'

Finally, Alice took a new lover, the pianist and composer Isidore de Lara (whom Wilde called 'the poet of the musicians'). Albert remained unaware of the liaison until, returning from a voyage, he saw the graffiti 'Here sleeps de Lara' scrawled in chalk on his palace wall.

The next night, Alice accompanied her husband to the opening night of a new opera. She stopped to have a word with de Lara, whereupon Albert lost control and publicly slapped her face. Alice froze, then majestically walked on to the Royal box; Albert left the building.

Within a few days, their separation was completed. By the divorce settlement, she paid Albert five million francs and agreed never visit Monaco again. Even this did not placate the furious Prince who tried to eradicate all evidence of Alice's memory, excising the Royal archives, destroying all photos and portraits, and even renaming a variety of rose in the palace gardens.

Alice and de Lara retired to London where they lived in two large suites at Claridge's Hotel (originally called Mivarts Hotel – and mentioned by Wilde in 'An Ideal Husband'). Here she created another salon that attracted such figures as Edward Elgar, *Rudyard Kipling*, and *Winston Churchill.*

Prince Albert continued his sea voyages. (In 1913 he visited the USA to go bear hunting with *Buffalo Bill Cody*. Their enjoyment was mildly upset by their hunting camp cook in Wyoming. One night, this cook stamped off in fury after serving the meal. Puzzled, Albert and Cody asked him what was wrong. It transpired that the cook had been deeply insulted by Albert and his French entourage exclaiming 'Merci' when presented with their meals. The cook thought they were mocking him by crying 'Mercy'.)

Albert made one lasting contribution by his examination of oceanic drift. His research proved invaluable during the First World War when it aided the location of German mines in the North Sea, thereby saving many lives.

RANI OF SARAWAK 1849-1934

Constance Wilde's other great friend was the English-born Margaret Brooke, the Rani of Sarawak, to whom Oscar dedicated his story 'The Young King' in 1891. After Wilde's downfall, the Rani remained loyal to Constance and tried to help Oscar by asking the powerful political figure, *Richard Haldane*, to intervene with the prison authorities.

Margaret Brooke, (nee De Windt), owed her exotic title to her marriage to Sir Charles Brooke, son of James Brooke and heir to his father's personal fiefdom of Sarawak in the East Indies.

When they married in 1869, Charles Brooke was in his mid forties and had spent the previous seventeen years in Sarawak; Margaret was twenty and had never been outside Western Europe. He was a frigid man of Spartan habits and few words who, although not consciously cruel, was hopelessly out of touch with English life and incapable of expressing emotion.

He had arrived back in England to find a child bearer, and originally paid court to Margaret's mother. When this was rejected, he proposed to Margaret by handing her a note. Margaret found his total lack of a sense of humour and his bizarre attitude to marriage rather amusing.

Their honeymoon was spent at Burrator in Devon in a small house left to Charles by his uncle. Margaret wrote later: 'Arriving at the station he went to a bookstall and bought the Times and Punch. He sat me in a corner with Punch and himself sat back with the Times and was immersed in it to Exeter'.

At the Exeter hotel that evening, a waiter asked if the couple would like to have dinner. The Rajah grumpily declined saying that it was too expensive, but agreed to allow Margaret some bread and butter.

The next day they drove on by carriage towards Burrator. When they reached Crediton, Margaret shyly mentioned that she was a little hungry. The Rajah turned down the idea of a meal at a pub but, stopping at a baker's shop, walked in, slapped five shillings on the counter, and asked for 'Captain's Biscuits', an almost inedible concoction used mainly as hard tack by the British Navy.

He emerged bearing two-dozen paper bags of biscuits. Although the Rajah doggedly munched his way through them, Margaret found them completely indigestible. Margaret: 'Can anyone now living remember the nastiness of 'Captain's Biscuits?'

On arrival at Burrator, they found that the servants had used their own money to pay for a wedding cake to greet the newly weds. The Rajah scowled at the sight, barking: "Quite unnecessary and very expensive".

If the honeymoon was odd, the marriage was even stranger. Christmas festivities were discouraged and the exchange of gifts prohibited. Margaret was banned from wearing low-cut gowns, and all invitations to local balls were turned down. The Rajah: "I will never allow another man's arm around the waist of my wife".

When her mother-in-law visited the couple, Margaret innocently announced one morning that she was thinking of "saddling my horse for a ride". The mother-in-law sniffed: "*Your* horse! Remember, young lady, that nothing is yours but your wedding ring". Margaret's patience finally snapped. Smiling sweetly, she replied: "If that is the case, I shall appear tonight at dinner with nothing on but my wedding ring". A bleak silence ensued.

The couple finally left Devon bound for Sarawak. For Margaret, the monotony of the journey was broken only by her frequent bouts of extreme seasickness. During one such bout, the Rajah insisted that the best cure was to come up on deck to attend an impromptu ship's concert. As she listened to a large gentleman bellowing a song called 'Ocean! Thou Mighty Monster!', she unavoidably threw up again, and was rushed below.

On arrival in Sarawak, the Rajah took her into the interior to inspect her new kingdom. They were greeted in one village by an orchestra staffed by Dyak headhunters. One dancer was waving what Margaret took to be a coconut but discovered was a human head. When the Rajah explained to her that this was an honour, Margaret replied faintly: "But, Charlie, I have never seen skulls brought out at parties before".

Back in the capital, Kuching, Margaret gradually accustomed herself to tropical life, though occasionally betraying her naivety. After one dinner party, she was sitting on the verandah with her guests discussing the lack of and need for rain in the country. Suddenly she heard the sound of drops of water and leapt to her feet, exclaiming: "The rain is coming, can you not hear it?" She wrote afterwards: 'The silence with which my words were greeted grew into a sea of amused glances and giggles. The sound that I thought was rain, was, in fact, the Rajah relieving himself over the verandah railing'.

Margaret encountered some dangerous moments when she accompanied the Rajah on his military expeditions. On one trip she was left behind at a base camp which itself was at risk of attack. The young British officer left to guard her was beset by nerves and forced her to hide behind a small piano. All night long he divided his duties between patrolling the perimeter, and pushing plates of ham sandwiches under the piano to keep up her morale. Margaret: "I was perfectly calm already".

She again displayed her courage when, in the Rajah's absence, a gang of bandits forced their way into the compound to loot the place. Margaret strode out to confront them and pointed to a cannon on the roof. She told them that, if they did not leave, the compound would be swept by grapeshot. They left quickly, not realising that Margaret was alone and that there was nobody on the roof to fire the (empty) weapon.

She soon found the English community in Sarawak to be rather dreary and wrote that she hated 'the detestable attitude assumed by Westerners towards the Native races'. She learnt Arabic, took to wearing a sarong, and went out of her way to meet the women of Sarawak.

At one Dyak village, she was invited to climb up into one of the 30-feet-high bamboo houses. She was led to a throne at the middle of the room where she invited the whole entourage to sit around her. Unaccustomed to this unusual weight, the floor gave way, leaving Margaret and twelve others wrapped together 'like a bag of plums' in a carpet that luckily had held. Margaret: "It was very undignified to be hauled out of the abyss".

Finding out that the Rajah preferred native women, Margaret returned to England, though still dutifully travelling to Sarawak every couple of years to allow the Rajah to impregnate her. This produced three sons in six years.

Back in Europe, Margaret mingled with the more bohemian artistic circles of London and Paris. Once, the 20-year-old *Rudyard Kipling* rebuked her for her friendship with the notorious French writer *Guy de Maupassant*. Giving Kipling a cool glance, she replied: "My dear little boy, mind your own business."

As Margaret grew older, her amorous ventures became more desperate. Among many others, she had an affair with a bi-sexual writer called Morton Fullerton, (also one of *Lord Ronald Gower's* lovers). When he tried to break off the relationship, she threatened him with exposure of his compromising letters. The author *Henry James* advised Fullerton to ignore the threat: "If she uses them she will be seen as a mad, vindictive and obscene old woman".

Margaret retired partly to Cornwall, (where she spent her days deciphering inscribed ancient stones in Lelant), and partly to St John's Wood, London, (so that she could hear the tropical birds and animals at night in London Zoo).

> The honeymoon over, the Wildes returned to London. They stayed firstly at the Brunswick Hotel, Jermyn St, then a few days at Constance's old home in Lancaster Gate, then at 7, Great College St, in Westminster. Finally they settled back in Oscar's old lodgings at 9, Charles St.
>
> On their marriage, Constance's grandfather had given the couple £5000 to lease and decorate a new house at 16 (now 34), Tite St. Grandfather Lloyd died in July 1884, leaving a fair inheritance to Constance – it was this money that paid for the new house.
>
> The Wildes stayed at Charles St for six months waiting for the builders to finish work. There were numerous delays.
>
> In October, Oscar resumed his lecture tours of Britain, this time with a new theme, 'The Value of Art in Modern Life'.
>
> In December, he crossed over to Ireland and fulfilled 21 engagements.

1885

> [This year saw the discovery of radio waves and the invention of the internal combustion engine. On the 26th January, General Gordon was killed in Khartoum in the Sudan.]
>
> Wilde completed his Irish tour and returned to London, where his new home at Tite St. had finally been completed.
>
> He incorporated many of his own ideas on decoration into the house – a tiled entrance hall, no artificial flowers, chandeliers replaced with side brackets, etc. He painted a large star on the ceiling of his bedroom.
>
> Meanwhile, in the British Parliament, the Criminal Law Amendment Act was passed, a piece of legislation that was to have a massive impact on Oscar's life. The MP who engineered the Bill was Henry Labouchere.

HENRY LABOUCHERE 1831-1912

Wilde had been acquainted with Henry Labouchere, (known to all as 'Labby'), for some years before the passing of Labouchere's famous Act. Wilde liked him and said that Labby was "the best writer in Europe and a remarkable gentleman".

At first, Labby returned the compliment and, before Oscar's American trip, wrote that: 'his aesthetic message might be a useful antidote to US hyper-materialism'. Labby: 'Mr Wilde – say what one may of him – has a distinct individuality and, therefore, I should fancy that his lectures will attract many who will listen – and look.'

His opinion of Oscar as a lecturer dwindled after he heard one of the British talks. He complained that Oscar had used the word 'charming' 17 times, 'beautiful' 26 times, and 'lovely' 43 times.

In 1885, Labby became involved in the efforts to clear up the sexual exploitation of children in Britain. This movement came to fruition with the Criminal Law Amendment Act, which was aimed primarily at raising the age of female consent from 13 to 16, and at criminalizing brothels.

Sodomy, whether practised on males or females, had been an offence since 1553. However, one section of this Act, for the first time, made *all* homosexual acts, public or private, regardless of age or consent, punishable by two years imprisonment. Where previously there had been only social stigma, now there was criminal prosecution. The Act quickly became known as 'the Blackmailer's Charter'.

Labby was indeed deeply antagonistic to homosexuals and was unsympathetic to Wilde during and after the 1895 trials. Labby: 'In view of the mischief that such a man does, the sentence he has received compares but lightly with those almost every day awarded for infinitely less pernicious crimes'.

He was mystified by Wilde's actions – 'He must have known in what a glasshouse he lived when he challenged investigation in a court of justice. After he had done this, he went abroad. Why did he not stay abroad?' – but attributed them to a craving for scandal. Labby: "The possibilities of a prison may not be pleasing to him, but I believe that the notoriety that has overtaken him has such a charm for him that it outweighs everything else'.

Labouchere's sternly moralistic position during the late Victorian period concealed his real character. He was a man of great humour and charm, whose own past was more than a little chequered.

In 1850, he started as an undergraduate at Trinity College, Cambridge, and became an enthusiastic employer of the local prostitutes, a practice frowned on by the college authorities. At the time, under university law, the proctors had the right to lock up a town whore and remove her from Cambridge or Oxford, (*La Terriere* – 'They frequently made abominable mistakes').

One evening, Labby was strolling arm in arm with a prostitute when he was confronted by a proctor and asked to account for his companion. He thought fast and introduced her as his sister. The proctor snorted: "Nonsense, man! She's one of the most notorious whores in Cambridge!" Labby looked disconsolate and nodded: "Yes, I know, sir, and both Mother and myself are very worried about it".

During his years at college, Labby failed to attend a single lecture. The patience of the authorities finally snapped when, during an exam, he was spotted glancing at a sheet of paper beneath the desk. It turned out to be the photo of a music-hall star. Although Labby claimed he needed it to inspire him with her beauty, he was suspected of cheating and sent down in 1852.

His father decided to remove Labby from the temptations of Europe by sending him to the Americas. At the end of 1852, he arrived in Mexico City and gambled away his travel allowance. Falling in love with a circus girl, he applied for and gained a job as an acrobat in her circus, specialising in an act he described as 'standing jumps'. Dressed in pink tights, he was billed as 'The Bounding Buck of Babylon'.

Losing both the girl and the job, he moved on to the USA, where he joined the California Gold Rush; a few months later, he was living with a tribe of Chippewa Indians in Minnesota. Meanwhile, his influential family had been working on his behalf, and in 1854 Labby was surprised to find that he had been appointed as a diplomatic attaché in Washington.

Although untrained, Labby turned out to be an accomplished, if highly unconventional, diplomat. At one point, some treaty negotiations between the USA and British-controlled

Canada were being held up by the intransigence of an ill-tempered American Secretary of State. Labby discovered that the man was addicted to whist but was unable to play, as he had no partners.

Thereafter, Labouchere and his minister played whist with the American every night – and industriously lost every night. The American was ecstatic at 'beating the Limeys at their own game'. Then, each morning, Labby would wheedle a few more concessions on the Treaty, thereby "scoring a few points for Canada".

If the British wished to interfere in Central America, it was customary to arrange a commercial treaty with the state concerned. Labby discovered a bedraggled barfly, known as 'the King of Mosquito', who, in return for a bottle of whisky, would sign any treaty the British wanted. This document then would be solemnly handed to the Americans as a bona fide excuse for intervention.

While in Washington, Labby did not neglect his amorous inclinations. He was interested to note that the American girls spent many daylight hours sitting in darkened rooms in an effort to whiten their skins.

One day, he called on a young lady called Miss Becky and was ushered into a pitch-black parlour where the disembodied voice of his intended lover asked him to sit down. He did so, only to find himself pitched back into the air, and a howl of pain emerging from the chair beneath. Miss Becky's voice called out in alarm: "Why, you've sat on Pa!"

By 1855, after serving at various posts in Spain and Germany, Labby arrived at the British Legation in St Petersburg, Russia. He found out that the husband of his laundress was a compositor at the Russian government printing office and therefore had access to the Cabinet minutes. Seducing the laundress with sex and money, Labby was able to provide information of astounding quality back to the British Foreign Office.

However, when the British Foreign Secretary, Lord John Russell, discovered how the reports were obtained, he ordered Labby to stop immediately. Labby was amazed: "What on earth does Russell imagine diplomacy was invented for?"

On one occasion, a pompous Russian nobleman arrived at the Legation, stating that he wished to see the ambassador immediately. Labby replied: "Please take a seat. His Excellency will be here shortly." The nobleman considered this to be too offhand. He barked: "Young man, do you know who I am?" and recited a list of his titles. Labouchere listened, then replied humbly: "My apologies, my lord, I had not realised your eminence. Would you like two seats?'

In 1862, Labby was appointed to the embassy in Constantinople, Turkey, where his Ambassador was a man called Sir Henry Bulwer. Bulwer was addicted to medical pills that were sent out to him from London at a cost to the Foreign Office of £300 per box. Labby commented: "Well, they're more useful than most things sent out by the FO".

Bulwer himself was rather hard up and, at the embassy dinners, used to provide his guests with a Greek wine that tasted like tar. The butler would pour this hideous brew while gravely intoning: "Chateau Lafitte,'48" or some other superb vintage. As his guests attempted to down the 'wine', Bulwer would pretend to join them while surreptitiously gulping pills to offset any ill effects.

While in Constantinople, Labouchere made himself popular by handing out certificates of nobility to anyone who wanted one: "If a man wants to be a baron, why on earth shouldn't he be one?"

Eventually, Labby received a message appointing him as Legation Secretary in the Republic of Parana. As neither he nor anybody he knew had ever heard of Parana, he ignored the order and went off on holiday to Florence. A year later, another letter arrived from the Foreign Office asking him why he had not taken up his new posting.

He made more enquiries and found out that the Republic of Parana actually had existed once, but had vanished during the convoluted wars of South America. He informed the Foreign Office and, six months later, received a further letter from them, grudgingly admitting that: "Indeed, the Republic seems to have disappeared".

Labby had no intention of being deposited anywhere other than plumb European embassies and ignored instructions to move to an obscure African legation on the grounds that he thought the Under-Secretary to the Foreign Office was joking.

In 1864, he was appointed as second secretary in Buenos Aires, Argentina. He replied that he did not mind accepting the post as long as he could carry out his duties while remaining in the agreeable spa town of Baden-Baden in Germany. When this proposal was turned down, Labby decided to leave the diplomatic service.

This cavalier approach to diplomacy may have been encouraged by the fact that he was due to inherit a huge sum of money from his uncle, Lord Taunton. Taunton was always worried that Labby would gamble away this fortune, but an unbreakable clause in the will forced him to leave his money to a male heir. Despite two marriages and two large families, there was no other male heir than Labouchere.

Taunton's temper was not improved by Labby's arrival, after the birth of yet another ineligible daughter, with a huge grin on his face and with the words: "My dear uncle, this is most gratifying". Lord Taunton died in 1869, surrounded by daughters. Labouchere inherited £250,000.

For a while, Labby dabbled in theatrical ventures and bought the Queen's Theatre on Long Acre, London. As a producer, he was subjected to the usual onslaught of scripts from would-be playwrights. One author asked him to consider a play entitled 'Time and the Hour'. When Labby told him that it was a brilliant title the author looked gratified, until Labby continued: "Yes, it would do for any play whatever that was ever written".

Another playwright sent in a drama that opened with the stage directions: 'The broad Mississippi is seen rolling its turbid flood towards the ocean, and carrying with it the debris of a village. Steamers come and go on its surface. On a frail raft a man and a woman are crossing the river. Enter the Negroes from a plantation monotonously singing'.

In 1868, Labby made an attempt to enter politics and stood for Parliament. He was not immediately successful, mostly due to the fact that the voters of Middlesex discovered that, at the time, he was not married to his actress companion, Henrietta Hodson. He was greeted constantly by electors shouting: " 'Ow's 'Enrietta? " He was forced to open one meeting by walking out on the podium and announcing: "I wish to convey to you all the gratifying intelligence that Henrietta is quite well".

He finally married Henrietta and by 1880 found a safe seat as MP for Northampton, a position that he held till 1905. In the Commons, he became known as 'the Nihilist of English politics'.

In 1870, Labby happened to be in Paris when the Franco-Prussian War broke out. By now interested in journalism, he decided to stay and report on the ensuing siege of the city, assuming that it would only last a month or so.

He was not impressed by the Paris citizen's militia force, known as the National Guard. Labby: 'A battalion of National Guards were drawn up and began cooking their food, when some tin pans fell against each other. Thinking it was a bomb they scattered, and the General was obliged to ride along the line shouting "Courage, courage, it is the soup, my children".'

Labby commented: 'The Parisian is not a coward, but his individuality is so strongly developed that he objects to that individuality being destroyed by some stray shot' – 'Laugh at the French, abuse them as one may, it is impossible to help liking them'.

As the siege intensified, the food shortage became acute and such items as horses and cats became delicacies. Labby left a record of his culinary exploits:

'Cat was something between rabbit and squirrel, with a flavour all its own. It is delicious and the price for a cat has risen to 20 francs'.

'Donkey is now all the fashion'.

'Today, I had rat – it was excellent – something between frog and rabbit – I was curious to see whether the proprietor of the restaurant would boldly call rat 'Rat' on my bill. His heart failed him – it figures as 'Game' '.

'Today I dined on mufflon, an animal which is, I believe, found entirely in Corsica. I can only describe it by saying that it tasted of mufflon, and nothing else but mufflon'.

By December: 'All the animals in the Zoological Gardens have been killed except the monkeys. These are kept alive from a vague Darwinian notion that they are our relatives. Or at least the relatives of some of the members of the government.'

In 1877, Labby became the owner-editor of 'Truth', a magazine that was in some ways the forerunner of such modern day publications as the British 'Private Eye'. He became a convinced radical and, as a man of wealth but little ambition, and with no personal axe to grind, became a genuine champion of the poor. *Wilfred Blunt*: "There must be a few lovers of liberty left in England, but for the moment they have no voice more powerful than Labouchere's".

His targets were mainly the rich and powerful. His weekly attacks on fraudsters and company-promoters were feared by the City of London and he acquired many enemies. He also objected to the creation of 200 new peerages between 1886-1914, many of them being bestowed on luminaries of the alcohol trade. He described them as 'The Beerage'.

He attacked the monarchy as too expensive and characterised the regally-linked commander of the British Army, the Duke of Cambridge, as 'standing at the head of the troops with his drawn salary in his hand'. Queen Victoria responded by calling him 'that horrible lying Labouchere', while Edward VII described him as 'that viper'.

Nothing upset the establishment more than Labby's revelation that the Tory enemies of the Irish leader *Charles Stuart Parnell* had conspired to ruin him by forging letters purporting to show Parnell's support for the Phoenix Park assassinations. The Times newspaper had published these letters after receiving them from a counterfeiter named Richard Pigott.

When the Parnell Commission was formed to enquire into these events, Labby provided the evidence that destroyed Pigott's testimony. After Pigott fled to Madrid and committed suicide, Labby displayed his good nature by providing money to help Pigott's children. Parnell later admitted that Labby was the only Englishman he trusted.

The Tories were furious at Labby's exposure of the Parnell plot and one of them, in a campaign of petty annoyance, ordered a series of goods in Labby's name.

Over a two day period, Labby was the recipient of a representative of a cremation company to arrange disposal of his remains, a wedding cake, a four-poster bed, seventy tons of coal, a billiard table, some expensive carpets, a large consignment of wines and spirits, an umbilical belt for hernia relief, many prescriptions for a variety of diseases from physicians, and news of tickets booked for him to India, Japan and the USA. Also, dozens of invitations in his name were sent to people inviting them to dine with him. Ruefully appreciating the joke, Labby published the list in 'Truth'.

Labby's personal habits at the 'Truth' offices were idiosyncratic. He preferred old clothes to such a degree that the staff said that they could smell his jacket coming up the stairs. Voules, his deputy editor, found Labby's practice of taking out his false teeth and placing them on the desk especially distressing. Voules would leave the room, complaining: "I can't sit there any longer with those confounded teeth grinning at me. They get on my nerves". Labby could never find a decent set and occasionally would set about the existing one with a hammer.

Labby's kindlier side showed itself when Voules, briefly having become editor of 'Truth', had to leave over a private matter. Rather than wound Voules's feelings by appointing a replacement, Labby told him: "My dear Voules, I have now been connected with newspapers for over thirty years and I have never yet discovered what an editor is". So 'Truth' remained without an editor for the next seven years until Voules died.

Labouchere himself retired from Parliament in 1905, something to the relief of his colleagues. The incoming Liberal Prime Minister, Campbell-Bannerman, made him a Privy Counsellor as a leaving present. Labby wrote: 'I have not the slightest notion what a Privy Counsellor is. All I know is that I took half a dozen mumbled oaths before a dignitary – then, with my companion also honoured, we performed a sort of cake-walk backwards'.

The start of 1885 witnessed the conclusion of one of the most confused and embarrassing passage of arms in the history of the British Army.

With the construction of the Suez Canal and its later purchase by Disraeli, Egypt had become an area of vital interest to the British Government. In 1882, at the Battle of Tel-el-Kebir, the British Army had quelled an abortive nationalist rising under Colonel Arabi, and the subsequent occupation gave Britain de facto control of the country and suzerainty over its southern colony, the Sudan.

However, also in 1882, there had been a much more successful rising in the Sudan under the guidance of a religious leader called the Mahdi. In 1883, an Anglo-Egyptian force of 10,000 men, (under Colonel William 'Billy' Hicks), had been sent to restore authority. They were annihilated by the Mahdi's forces.

The British Government decided to abandon the Sudan to the Mahdi. There remained the problem of rescuing the existing Egyptian garrisons from the country, in particular the large community in the capital, Khartoum. The Prime Minister Gladstone sent a renowned war hero, General Gordon, to expedite the evacuation. The resulting impasse was to involve several of Wilde's friends and acquaintances.

FENWICK BULMER DE SALES LA TERRIERE (1856-1925) and THE SUDAN CAMPAIGN

GENERAL CHARLES GEORGE GORDON (1833-1885), while unquestionably heroic, was a disastrous choice to oversee a retreat. He was an ascetic, evangelical Christian, who regarded himself as being above ordinary mortals, (including governments), and acted according to his own beliefs. His attitude to danger was summed up by his comment: "I died long ago, and it will not make any difference to me; I am prepared to follow the unrolling of the scroll".

The empire-builder Cecil Rhodes described him as 'a fanatical enigma', while the British in Cairo thought he was 'weird to the point of dementia'. *Lady St Helier* said of him: "He was a curiously listless-looking, nervous little man, with a sort of furtive look and expression as if he always anticipated something unpleasant'. *Arthur Rimbaud*, who watched the unfolding fiasco from Ethiopia, was more succinct: "Gordon is an idiot".

His career had been dazzling and unconventional. But even in his days as a junior officer, some people had their doubts about him. Garnet Wolseley later told *Frank Harris* of an incident during the Crimean War, when he had shared a shallow trench outside Sebastopol with Gordon and another officer, Gerald Graham.

Every night at six pm, Graham would stand up, put his hands in his pockets and stroll off back to his quarters. The Russians noticed this and started to take pot shots at Graham, which fortunately always missed. This deadly game continued for weeks. Wolseley: "I assure you after ten days or so it was a miracle how he escaped, for some hundreds used to shoot at him and bullets buzzed like bees".

Wolseley decided not to join Graham in this suicidal gauntlet and instead would crawl along the trench till he reached safety. "None of us could make Gordon out at that time. One evening he would crawl after me through the slush and mud and the very next evening he'd get up, bold as brass, link arms with Graham and stroll off with him as if the nearest Russian marksman was a thousand miles away!"

Wolseley concluded that it was a question of how Gordon's daily prayers had fared. "If God had accorded him some sign of approval he'd stroll away with Graham wholly unconcerned; if on the other hand he was left in doubt of the divine guidance, he'd crawl through the mud lower than I thought necessary and longer. Graham was the bravest of the brave but Gordon was a queer fish.'

In 1860, Gordon took part in the Siege of Peking in China and in the subsequent looting of the Summer Palace. Over the next four years, he built his extraordinary reputation, (and gained his nickname of 'Chinese Gordon'), by raising a force known as the Ever Victorious Army and helping to crush the appallingly bloody Taiping Rebellion. (With 30 million dead, this proved to be the most costly conflict in history – surpassed only by the 60 million of the Second World War). His officers regarded his habit of going into battle armed only with a light cane as odd, but acknowledged that he was a great commander.

In 1877, the Egyptian Government appointed him as a governor in the Sudan. On arrival in Khartoum, Gordon surprised the somewhat louche authorities by his reaction to their welcoming banquet. They provided an entertainment consisting of a ballet performed by Egyptian soldiers and naked dancing girls. When both the Austrian and Egyptian consuls flung themselves with enthusiasm into the performance, an enraged Gordon flounced from the room. The authorities had not known that, when he was aged fourteen, Gordon's dearest wish had been to become a eunuch.

However his reputation as a military man was undeniable and it was with this in mind that, in 1884, Gladstone asked Gordon to supervise the withdrawal of the Egyptian forces from the Sudan. The British quasi-viceroy in Cairo, *Lord Cromer*, was more wary but agreed on condition that Gordon understood he was to evacuate the Sudan, not to hold it.

Gordon's stature in British society was now so great that, when he left Charing Cross Station in London on his new mission, the British army commander, the Duke of Cambridge, held the carriage door; the Foreign Secretary, Lord Granville, purchased the ticket for him; and Lord Wolseley carried his bag. As a final gesture, Gordon made them agree to supply a copy of a biblical tome, 'Scriptural Promises', to every member of the Cabinet the following morning.

Accompanied only by his aide-de-camp, Colonel JD Stewart, Gordon arrived back in Khartoum. He then ignored his orders and flatly refused to abandon the city. Instead he fortified it as best he could and awaited the arrival of the overwhelmingly superior army of the Mahdi.

During the siege, a Khartoum official arrived at Gordon's palace to suggest that Gordon douse the bright lighting in the building as it was attracting heavy fire. Gordon angrily called for his guards and ordered them to shoot the man if he moved. Seizing a large lantern and several candles, he set them in front of a window and forced the official to sit with him at the window for an hour. Then he released the man, shouting: "Go, tell the people in Khartoum that Gordon fears nothing, for God created him without fear".

In case of an enemy breakthrough, Gordon had the house packed with gunpowder but refused to fire it in case he was accused of suicide. He reputedly enjoyed the sensation of being trapped as it enhanced his feeling of 'being alone against the world'. Gordon: "Better a ball in the brain than to flicker out unheeded".

(The siege lasted ten months while the flummoxed Government in London debated how to keep control of events. To make matters worse, the rescue of Gordon became a national obsession; Queen Victoria led the demands for action. Finally, a reluctant Gladstone was forced to give away and to authorise a British army to relieve their errant representative.

The first attempt to rescue Gordon came from the east, where the English Colonel Baker led an Egyptian force from the port of Suakin on the Red Sea in an effort to cross the 250 miles of desert to Khartoum.)

COLONEL VALENTINE BAKER (1827-1887) had been a regular soldier in the British Army. He had seen service in the Kaffir War of 1852 and on Lord Raglan's staff in the Crimea. In 1860 he was appointed to command the crack regiment of the 10th Hussars, (in which capacity he arrested Wilde's Fenian friend, *John Boyle O'Reilly*, for treason). He was made a royal equerry and became part of *Bertie, Prince of Wales's* social set.

However, in 1875, his early career ended in disgrace. On a train journey to London, he met a young woman called Miss Kate Dickinson. According to her story, they chatted inconsequentially for a time, before Baker suddenly attempted to insert his hand in her knickers. She screamed and struggled, before breaking free and opening the carriage door. With the train moving at top speed, she swung out still clinging to the door; Baker was forced to hold on to her to prevent her falling. When the train stopped at Esher, a sobbing Kate ran for help and, on arrival at Waterloo Station, Baker was arrested.

At the trial, (in which the later *Judge 'Hanging' Hawkins* acted as his junior counsel), Baker did not testify in his own defence or allow his lawyers to cross-examine Dickinson, as he refused to dishonour a lady by calling her a liar. He was given a 12 months prison sentence and dismissed from the British Army.

(As a result of this case, connecting corridors were introduced on all trains, together with 'Ladies Only' carriages – a practice that only ended in 1975.)

On emerging from jail, Baker left England and took service in the Turkish army. When the Russian-Turkish War broke out in 1877, he distinguished himself by his courage and won particular fame with a brilliant cavalry attack that routed the Russian forces. The war correspondent, *Archibald Forbes*, met a Russian officer after the action who told him that Baker was "the finest light cavalry officer I ever saw. Had he belonged to us do you think we should have lost him to the service he adorned because of a wretched private folly?"

(In 'Vera', Wilde referred to this conflict in a speech by one of his characters: 'I have seen wave after wave of living men sweep up the heights of battle to their death; ay, and snatch perilous conquest from the scales of war when the bloody crescent seemed to shake above our eagles'.)

By 1882, Baker had moved on to Egypt where he was put in command of the Egyptian gendarmerie. When the 1884 Sudan crisis developed, Baker sailed this force to Suakin to try to aid the Sudan evacuation. His luck and his judgement failed when he led his 3,500 gendarmerie against a 200 strong detachment of the Mahdi's men at the first battle of El Teb.

Despite Baker's desperate efforts to stem the panic, the entire Egyptian force ran after the first volley. 2,300 men were killed and all the equipment lost as the survivors were chased back to the sea.

Baker was removed from command and replaced by General Gerald Graham (of Crimean fame), who brought in reliable British regiments to avenge the defeat. Baker accompanied the new army as an intelligence officer and was present at Graham's ultimately successful action against the Arab forces, (also at El Teb).

Baker was wounded during this battle when a shell fragment struck the roof of his mouth just below the eye; he wrapped his head in a towel and continued fighting. Despite the victory, General Graham returned to Suakin and did not venture into the desert again.

(With Gordon still holding out at Khartoum, a second British relief force was assembled near the Egyptian-Sudan border. Its officers included a group of men who, back in England, were part of the Prince of Wales's social set, and who had met or were to meet Oscar Wilde on different social occasions. The general in command was Lord Wolseley; other members included Lord Charles Beresford, Colonel Fred Burnaby, Lord Arthur 'Podge' Somerset, and Fenwick La Terriere.)

FENWICK BULMER DE SALES LA TERRIERE (1856-1925), known as 'The Hatter',

had been an unusual friend for Wilde when they both studied at Magdalen College, Oxford. He had a hearty philistine disrespect for the artistic world but thought that Oscar himself was simply playing a game. La Terriere: "He must have laughed up his sleeve when he started all that aesthetic rubbish. He was really clever in his fooling and he knew it paid".

Perhaps because of this, he liked Oscar and enjoyed lightly teasing him. La Terriere: 'I remember playing a shocking trick on him at Commem one year. Lunch and tea parties in each other's rooms – I arrived first. Oscar had some really beautiful nude drawings by *Frank Miles.* Looking round with an eye to mischief I attached some penny stamps to clothe the pretty ladies'.

When the party arrived later: 'First one looked up, giggled and blushed, and then another, till the whole party was convulsed; but all Oscar said to me was 'It's really too bad of you'; he had to laugh at my inane joke like the rest'.

La Terriere wrote of Oscar: 'There was no trace of that particular madness that wrecked his life later on, at the time he was at Magdalen. He was very cheery and festive and lived exactly the same sort of life – card playing, singing, room-visiting, wine-bibbing – that we all did; and I think everybody liked him'.

Having been at Eton, a school where titles counted for nothing and which La Terriere described as 'the greatest self-contained democracy in the world', he found 1870s Oxford bewilderingly snobbish – 'a narrow and cliquish life'.

His expertise as a boxer and wrestler, (he was strong enough to carry chairs in his teeth), led him to mix mostly with the rowdy hard-drinking set in college. Among the many venues they frequented was Evans Supper Rooms in London: 'It was always a point of honour to have a general hustle and free-fight on the main stairs outside Evans at shutting-up times. We enjoyed it though we sometimes got landed at Vine Street police station'.

Despite these London sprees, he declared that the heaviest drinking scene he had ever come across was at Magdalen itself. After a breakfast of port, it was normal to drink wine and whisky for lunch. Every meal was accompanied by a pint of claret, followed by huge quantities of gin punch in the Common Room. This was followed by parties in the evening.

Given this intake, it was not surprising when La Terriere was rusticated for firing off a keg of gunpowder in the Magdalen Quad and almost killing the Dean. He was allowed back after a term, but left for good in his second year.

In 1877, he joined the Hussars and was pleased to find that his army companions also enjoyed the more boisterous side of life. At his new quarters at Aldershot, his initiation included having to stand on the mess table stark naked and sing 'John Peel'. La Terriere: "It knocked some of the Oxford self-sufficient nonsense out of me".

Sometimes officers who did not fit in with the regiment were given short shrift. La Terriere and his new friend and fellow officer, 'Podge' Somerset, witnessed an occasion when an unpopular newcomer, a captain in the Blues, was stripped naked and paraded wearing only a necklace that he had bought for 'some low class lady of his acquaintance'. The captain had ordered a new piano that had arrived in a packing case. 'This was opened and the keys and innards thrown out to decorate the trees'. The man was then nailed, still naked, into the packing case, labelled for home, and placed outside to await collection.

In 1882, La Terriere arrived at Alexandria, Egypt, to command a squadron of 19th Hussars during the Arabi Rising. One night, he led some troopers on a raid to capture some extra mules from the neighbouring Irish Brigade. Galloping back furiously with the plunder, they knocked down an old gentleman. The man was so overcome with rage and threats of retribution that La Terriere decided to lock him up for the night so that he could get in the first word next day at any inquiry. It turned out that the gentleman was in fact the French Consul. Fortunately, later that day the Battle of Tel-el-Kebir started and the affair was forgotten.

La Terriere stayed on in Alexandria after the victory and became a cavalry major in the Egyptian army. For a time he shared a house in the desert with a captain of sappers called Herbert Kitchener, (later *Lord Kitchener*). They hired an Arab cook: this proved unwise as the cook spent most of the time insensible from smoking hashish. One day, an irritated La Terriere stripped the unconscious man, painted him in red and white stripes, and turned him loose in the desert. The cook was almost shot by British sentries.

His Aldershot friend, Lord Arthur (Podge) Somerset, also arrived to join the growing new army. 'Podge', a superb horseman and one of Bertie's intimates, (his sister married Lord Charles Beresford's elder brother), had been appointed as an equerry to the Prince of Wales, but it was in his role as a major in the Horse Guards that he arrived in Egypt. He was the third son of the Duke of Beaufort, an especially scandal-haunted family, (see *Prince Eddy*). When Podge himself later fell into disgrace, La Terriere commented: "Poor Podge. I certainly thought him one of the nicest men I ever knew".

The commander of the relief force was the Dublin-born GENERAL SIR (later Viscount) **GARNET WOLSELEY** (1833-1913), a man who shared Gordon's fatalistic view of soldiering. In later life he said: "The first business of the young officer who wishes to distinguish himself in his profession is to seek to get himself killed". He certainly lived up to this principle and his military career seemed almost like a roll call of Victorian warfare.

After being wounded in the leg during the 1852 invasion of Burma, and losing his right eye during the Crimean War, he took part in the relief of Lucknow during the Indian Mutiny. At the end of the latter, the young Wolseley was sent to recover the corpse of the district commissioner of Futteepore, a man who had remained at his post asserting incorrectly that his own staff would never attack him. Wolseley found his skull and a few other bones, but the only coffin available was an empty brandy case. Wolseley: "We buried him with full military honours. The sole inscription upon the box that contained his bones was 'Old Cognac'."

Moving briskly on through the 1860 Siege of Peking, Wolseley next arrived in Canada to confront a breakaway rebellion led by Louis Riel, which he crushed during the Red River campaign in Manitoba.

In 1873, he commanded the British forces during the Ashanti War, (in modern day Ghana). In one incident, he created terror in the opposition by strapping a captured Ashanti warrior to the front of a large steamroller, then sending the machine crashing down a hill into the enemy headquarters delivering a grim warning. These methods proved successful and he was able to blow the enemy capital, Kumasi, to pieces.

Although he arrived too late to take part in the defeat of the Zulus at the Battle of Ulundi in 1879, he did capture the Zulu king, Cetewayo, soon afterwards.

In 1882, his victory over the Arabi rising in Egypt set the seal on his reputation and he became a popular British hero. The slang expression for 'all correct' was 'All Sir Garnet', a tribute to his efficiency. When George Grossmith played the part of 'The Modern Major-General' in *Gilbert* and *Sullivan's* 'Pirates of Penzance', he made himself up to resemble Wolseley. Described as 'vivacious', Wolseley enjoyed social occasions and occasionally shared a dinner table with Wilde.

COLONEL FRED BURNABY (1842-1885) was another useful recruit to the Gordon Relief Force. Six feet four inches tall and eighteen stone, he was an immensely strong man who once carried two Icelandic ponies down a flight of stairs, one under each arm. He was a keen balloonist and made nineteen ascents, culminating in crossing the English Channel alone in 1882.

After some initial experience in the Spanish Carlist War of 1874, and having accompanied Gordon on a trip up the Nile almost to the Equator in the same year, Burnaby became a key player in the mock-diplomacy-cum-warfare of 'the Great Game' between Britain and Russia. He worked as a spy mostly along the southern Russian border, and managed a very difficult reconnaissance in horrific winter conditions across three hundred miles of steppe. He recorded these adventures in his 1877 best-selling book, 'The Ride to Khiva'.

During the Russo-Turkish War in the same year, he joined Valentine Baker and fought with the Turkish forces. Shortly afterwards, Burnaby and Baker survived an attempt by a Bulgarian infiltrator to poison them while they were staying at the house of the Greek Bishop of Guxnurdjina.

Burnaby arrived back in London where he continued a friendship with the Prince of Wales, (with whom he met Wilde). This royal favour dissolved when it was alleged that Burnaby had sent an unsigned article to the press stating that another royal crony, General Owen Williams, had been turned down for the post of brigadier of the Household Cavalry. Burnaby categorically denied the charge but his fellow officers sent him to Coventry and refused to attend royal dinners if Burnaby was to be invited.

Burnaby was shattered by this unjust attack on his character and told *Frank Harris*: "I was a personage in society, a colonel in the Guards, received at court – then through no fault of my own, an outlaw, an outcast. Thank God I know how to die".

He left England without leave and volunteered his services to Valentine Baker and the original relief army at Suakin. Despite being wounded at El Teb, he fought heroically, 'clearing out a building alone with his double-barrelled shot-gun'. A Russian general once said of Burnaby: "Quite mad, of course. Always was."

Being a naval officer rather than army, *LORD CHARLES BERESFORD* was an exception in the relief force. Previously, during the 1882 Arabi Rising, Beresford had assisted Wolseley greatly by using his gunboat, the Condor, to bombard the port of Alexandria. Then, arriving ashore, Beresford made himself chief of police and prevented local mobs from burning the city.

(Two weeks later, Beresford's sailors were present at the capture of the Suez Canal. The Frenchman, Ferdinand Du Lesseps, who had built the Canal, met them and angrily declared that the waterway was neutral and that: "No one shall land except over my dead body!" One of Beresford's larger boatswains gently urged him to one side saying: "We don't want any dead bodies about here, sir. All you've got to do is just step back a bit.")

Being a close friend of the Prince of Wales, (and yet another of Wilde's dining companions), Beresford thought he would amuse the Prince by bringing back a memento of this campaign in the form of a dud shell that had passed through the magazine of the Condor without exploding. He sent it to a London factory to be cut in half and polished. While at the factory the 'dud' shell exploded, blowing off a workman's leg. Beresford commented that: "Explanation would have little availed had the shell burst in the smoking room at Sandringham Palace".

In August, 1884, he was appointed to Wolseley's staff, in which capacity he added the Naval Brigade to the relief force. In the autumn of 1884, the assembled army set off to rescue General Gordon.

EVENTS DURING THE SUDAN CAMPAIGN

Wolseley decided that the best way to reach Khartoum was to divide his forces into two groups, the 'Nile Column' following the course of the River Nile, (and bringing the heavier equipment by boat), while the 'Desert Column' attempted a short cut by travelling directly south across the desert, (thus avoiding the wide easterly detour of the river).

On 16th January, 1885, the Desert Column, now including Burnaby, Beresford and the Naval Brigade, reached the wells of Abu Klea, only to find a large Mahdist army between them and the vital water supply. That night they prepared for battle on the following day. Beresford: 'The tom-toms played all night – it haunts those who have heard it to the last day of their lives'.

At dawn, Fred Burnaby and Beresford were waiting for the attack, when Burnaby's horse was shot from under him. Burnaby lit a cigar before muttering to Beresford: "I'm not in luck today, Charlie".

The British army formed a traditional square but, before it could be completed, the Mahdists attacked in strength, leaving the left rear angle of the square still unformed. Beresford: 'They bore down on us with a roar like the roar of the sea'. With other members of the Naval Brigade, he was able to bring their large Gardner gun into play just outside the square and fired into the oncoming enemy ranks. Then the gun jammed.

Beresford: 'The next moment the enemy was on us. The feed plate dropped on my head, knocking me under the gun and across the trail. Simultaneously a spear was thrust through poor Rhodes (the boatswain's mate) who was instantaneously killed at my side. Miller the armourer was speared beside the gun at the same time. I was knocked off the back of the gun by a blow with the handle of an axe, the blade of which missed me. An Arab thrust at me with his spear and I caught the blade, cutting my hand, and before he could recover his weapon a bullet dropped him'.

Beresford was swept back into the army square by the weight of bodies. 'Nobody could use a weapon because we were so squashed. My Arab opponent in front of me could not bring his sword down, while I could not get my pistol out off my belt'.

Then the British rear ranks stood back and, firing into the Arabs, relieved the melee. Beresford found that he had a bullet through his helmet. After desperate hand-to-hand fighting, the British finally drove off the attacking force.

Beresford surveyed the carnage – over 1,100 Arabs had died. On the British side, all of his gun crew were dead. One of his naval officers, Lieutenant de Lisle, had had his whole face sliced off. One large able seaman nicknamed Jumbo had been knocked unconscious early in the fight and each passing Arab had stabbed him. He was found to have suffered seventeen separate wounds from swords and spears, but somehow survived. All the Naval Brigade officers had been killed except Beresford, a sub-lieutenant and a boatswain. In a moment of almost Shakespearian reflection that night, Beresford commented that it would be "hard to die without knowing who had won the Derby".

Fred Burnaby had been correct about his own lack of luck. When the attack started he had been dismounted and outside the square. Seeing the danger that the Arabs could rush the still unformed British ranks, he thrust his powerful frame into the gap and fought the onslaught with his cavalry sabre. As the ranks hastily redeployed behind him, Burnaby, bleeding from a dozen wounds, fought on until he finally went down with a spear gash to his throat.

The Desert Column fought its way on, without sleep and under incessant sniper fire, to fight another battle at the town of Metemmeh, where the column's commander, General Sir Herbert Stewart, was killed. The Column finally reached the Nile after days of constant desert marching and two battles.

When the column, (now commanded by Sir Charles Wilson), embarked on two steamers for the last dash to Khartoum, Beresford was left behind to recover from his Abu Klea wounds and to take charge of the base camp. The second Naval division arrived as reinforcements – Beresford: 'an inexpressible pleasure'.

His mood altered abruptly on hearing the news that, on January 26 1885, Khartoum had fallen to the Mahdi's army and General Gordon, the object of the rescue attempt and of all their efforts, had been killed. Even worse, Sir Charles Wilson's relief boats had been wrecked on the river and the Desert Column itself was hard-pressed and under attack.

Beresford patched together an old steamer called the Safieh and, under attack from both sides of the Nile, sailed south to relieve Wilson. At one point the ship's boiler burst and they were forced to spend twelve hours under heavy fire while it was mended. Beresford: 'Mr Benbow the engineer managed a miracle'. Eventually they found Wilson and, taking his force on board, returned between the murderous hail of fire from the Nile banks to relative safety.

Meanwhile the Nile Column also had been in difficulties and their commander, General Earle, had been killed. Fenwick La Terriere had been sent out to scout the land ahead of the column. On one occasion, he became lost in the desert and went blind in the sun. Tying himself to a camel, he allowed the animal to guide him back, although he was unsure whether he was being led to the river or to the enemy. It turned out to be the former and he was equally fortunate in that his eyes soon recovered.

Rejoining the army as Wolseley ordered the retreat of both columns, La Terriere found that Podge Somerset had been badly wounded and so took over Podge's job as an officer in the depleted Blues regiment.

Charles Beresford sank the steamer Safieh to prevent it falling into enemy hands, then set off north. By now, both columns were in bad shape and the troops marched in bare feet. Beresford arrived back at the Abu Klea wells to find himself part of a rearguard, under the command of Redvers Buller. Already plagued by snipers, the situation worsened when a force of 8000 Arabs arrived; Beresford advised Buller to retreat rapidly. That night, leaving their camp fires burning to fool the enemy, they escaped northwards.

With Wolseley's army scattered over a wide area, La Terriere was given the job of liasing between the various units. Five times he travelled alone through the desert at night with a compass, continuously dodging Mahdist warriors. He said later that this task was so dangerous that his nervous system never recovered.

The position of Wolseley's army by now was desperate. La Terriere commented that only two things saved the force from annihilation – pure luck and the order by his immediate superior, Sir Evelyn Wood, to poison the desert wells so that the Mahdi could not continue the pursuit. An outraged La Terriere retorted that he was certain the Mahdi himself would not have performed such a dishonourable act. Nevertheless the order was carried out and the bedraggled British army finally reached safety in Egypt.

AFTERMATH

The fall of Khartoum had severe political consequences for the British Prime Minister, *William Gladstone*. His nickname of 'GOM' ('Grand Old Man') was reversed to 'MOG'

('Murderer of Gordon'), he was roundly jeered in the streets of London, and, in an atmosphere of thwarted imperialist pride, Gladstone's government fell.

Of the military figures involved, Gordon and his aide, Colonel Stewart, were of course dead. After he had been hacked to death on the steps of his palace in a suitably spectacular finale, Gordon's corpse was carried to the Mahdi's camp. His head was removed and jammed in the fork of a tree where it was used as a macabre Aunt Sally as hundreds took turns to stone it.

Before the final assault, Colonel Stewart had been ordered by Gordon to evacuate the remaining Europeans and had left Khartoum by steamer. The boat was captured at the town of Dongola and Stewart and the others were killed.

(*JEC Bodley* later noted acidly: 'The brother of Colonel Stewart, killed at Dongola, called to see me; he is exploiting his brother's death and grounding a claim upon the Government on it. He is the man who, by chance meeting in Dublin ten years ago, introduced me to Oscar Wilde, then of TCD'.)

La Terriere told an odd story concerning Gordon and Stewart. On his original advance into the Sudan, La Terriere came to the village of Bab-el-Korosko, where the local people demanded payment from travellers in return for good luck. Sham graves were built for those who refused to pay. La Terriere did give them money, but noticed two recently dug graves already in existence. It turned out Gordon and Stewart had passed through the village and had ignored the demand. Neither returned from the desert.

Fred Burnaby's body was buried at Abu Klea and a cairn raised over the grave. *Frank Harris* wrote: 'As I read of his heroic death I cried like a child and then wondered whether his fellow officers were still proud of their idiotic boycott. To me dear Fred Burnaby was the hero of the Sudan, and not Charles Gordon.'

(*Lord Rosebery's* brother, Everard Primrose, also died during the expedition.)

Despite all his efforts on Britain's behalf, in the eyes of Queen Victoria and the British press Valentine Baker remained a pariah. His fellow officers petitioned for his reinstatement in the British army, but a barrage of newspaper editorials on the lines of: 'His presence is an insult to every woman in the nation' and: 'Even the mention of this man's name is a gross indecency' destroyed his chances. He died in Egypt in 1887.

In spite of some censure over his failure in the Sudan, General Wolseley's career was not affected and in 1895 he became the Commander-in-Chief of the British Army. Lady Wolseley complained that one unexpected side effect of her husband's Egyptian adventures was that dozens of influential Cairo officials presented the Wolseleys with ancestral mummies. JEC Bodley suggested that he gave them away as wedding presents.

Podge Somerset recovered from his wounds and returned to London to continue his duties as superintendent of the Prince of Wales's stables. Four years later, he was involved in a debacle of his own making in the Cleveland Street scandal, (see *Prince Eddy*).

Fenwick La Terriere resigned from the army in 1888 after he found that the continuous camel riding during the retreat had permanently injured his spine. He took up market gardening and the restoration of old houses.

A shared interest in the latter hobby led to his meeting with the Russian Prince Yusupov, then 'an innocent at Oxford who loved fancy dress balls' and who, according to Lady Diana Cooper, was 'deeply in love with my sister Marjorie'. Later, Prince Yusupov was to assist in the murder of the monk Rasputin.

La Terriere's subsequently peaceful life was disturbed only by his appointment as an officer in the Yeomen of the Guard during the First World War. He was in charge of a nightly detachment sent to guard Buckingham Palace. Unfortunately, his troops were unarmed and

206

some of them were over eighty years old. When the chilly nights set in during the autumn of 1914, the Palace guard was abandoned as most of the Yeomen were disabled by heavy colds.

LORD CHARLES BERESFORD 1846-1919

('And I have a wooden leg, love, And the title of K.C.B., For bringing Her Majesty's Fleet, love, Over the stormy sea.' – from 'The Little Ship' by Wilde).

The Sudan campaign was only one incident in Beresford's action-packed life. Born in Ireland, he was the second son of the Marquess of Waterford, a family wealthy enough to provide Charles with ample private means.

Deciding on the British Navy as a career, he became a midshipman in 1861. On his first voyage, when he was tested on his navigational skills, he carefully calculated the ship's position and took his results to the captain. The captain informed him that, according to Beresford's reckoning, they were sailing through the Great Hall of Windsor Castle.

In his memoirs, he recorded some of his early experiences of life travelling the world in the 1860s Royal Navy. One of the pastimes on board was cockroach racing. The game consisted of setting two cockroaches on fire and watching them race from one end of the table to the other. One night, an incendiary cockroach escaped and set the ship on fire.

In the Falkland Islands, Beresford accompanied the crew on a walking tour ashore only to find the place covered in pampas grass. This grass was so tall that the expedition spent days trying to find their way out again. The body of one paymaster was not discovered for eight years.

While in New Zealand, Beresford recorded meeting a retired cannibal who told him that the tastiest part of the human body was the flesh from the ball of the thumb. (In Tahiti, the French writer *Pierre Loti* was told that the flesh of white men tasted of ripe bananas).

In the Sandwich Islands, (now Hawaii), a young lady dared Beresford to climb the roof of the United States Consulate and steal the Stars and Stripes from their flagpole. Nothing loath, Beresford accepted the challenge, only to hear later that an angry US government had dispatched two warships to recover the trophy.

Dodging the diplomatic recriminations, in 1866 Beresford was appointed to command the royal yacht 'Osborne' and spent more time in home waters. During one leave in London, he managed the possibly unique feat of riding a pig down Park Lane. Again as the result of a dare, he had seized the animal and got as far as Piccadilly before being punched off by a furious swineherd.

In 1874, while still remaining in the Navy, Beresford decided to run for Parliament. Although he won the Waterford seat and retained it till 1880, he was not well respected in the House of Commons. After he gave one speech, a fellow member commented: "When the Honourable Member rose to make a speech he didn't know what he was going to say, while he was making it he didn't know what he was saying, and when he sat down he didn't know what he had said".

His actions in Egypt and the Sudan won him some renown and he continued his Parliamentary career, eventually taking over the York constituency, (previously held by his 'old friend' Sir Frank Lockwood – a lawyer who had been a major figure in Wilde's trials).

Beresford rose to full admiral within the navy and, to the general public, became the best known sailor of his day. His attention to detail on board his ships was the despair of the junior ranks. One midshipman asked permission to go ashore to have a tooth extracted. Beresford checked the records and, summoning the midshipman to the ship's bridge, barked: "How many teeth have you left? I find that you have had forty six extracted in Scotland alone!"

Having grown up in the wilder days of the 1860s Royal Navy, where 'sobriety was not regarded as a virtue', when in 1905 he was asked to give a lecture on temperance to the ships' companies of the Gibraltar command, he rather missed the point. Instead of denouncing drink, he merely explained the best methods of avoiding a hangover.

He remained a sturdy defender of the interests of the Royal Navy. In 1897, the Dean of St Paul's proposed to remove one of the Cathedral's monuments, an effigy to Captain Richard Burges RN, as he found it distasteful. Beresford sprang to the defence and argued that once future generations started removing monuments on grounds of taste, even the Victorian dignitaries might disappear. Despite the Dean's argument that: "The monument is unsightly. Captain Burges making love to Victory over a gun is not a very suitable image for a church', the statue remained.

Beresford was on easy social terms with Bertie, Prince of Wales – (he once replied to a royal dinner invitation with a telegram reading, 'Very Sorry Can't Come. Lie Follows By Post') – and they shared many mistresses, including Patsy Cornwallis-West. But their mutual involvement with Daisy Brooke, Countess of Warwick, led to a serious breach.

In 1888, Beresford managed to impregnate both Daisy and his own wife, Jeromina, at the same time. Lady Beresford, becoming aware of her rival after reading a compromising letter, instructed *Sir George Lewis*, the supreme legal fixer of his day, to threaten Daisy with exposure of the letter unless she gave up any claim on Beresford.

Daisy appealed to Bertie for help and, when Lewis refused to surrender the letter, Bertie banned Lady Beresford from society. Having been thus introduced to Daisy, Bertie promptly took her to bed himself. (Oscar Wilde commented: "Since the Prince has met Lady Brooke, how do you imagine that Lord Charles Beresford could become First Lord of the Admiralty?")

Beresford returned from naval duty and called on Bertie to complain angrily about the social exclusion of his wife. Receiving an evasive reply, Beresford lost his temper, called Bertie 'a blackguard and a coward', and knocked the Prince backwards over a sofa. It took the combined efforts of *Queen Victoria*, Bertie's wife Alexandra, and the Prime Minister, *Lord Salisbury*, to cover up the scandal.

This incident did nothing to douse Beresford's sexual drive. While staying at the Vyne in Hampshire, he made an assignation to spend the night with a beautiful girl who was one of the fellow guests. Before entering the room, he removed his clothes to expedite matters. He opened the door, tiptoed naked across the darkened bedchamber, slipped into bed, only to find himself being violently repelled by its occupant, the Bishop of Bath and Wells.

His redoubtable wife Jeromina treated Beresford's sexual activities with equanimity. In later years, they used to visit the *Richard Wagner* Festival in Bayreuth – (Lady Beresford said after watching 'Tristan and Isolde': "The love duet! It was time for their golden wedding before they got to the end".)

During one such visit, *EF Benson* reported that one of the Rhine Maidens, 'a large woman with a suitably Wagnerian voice', fell in love with Beresford and arranged for a love letter to be placed on his seat every time he attended a performance. Not understanding German, Beresford would ask Jeromina to translate the epistles: "Don't leave out the warmer passages. She's a well-nourished woman and comes from Palestine, I think. She called me her little partridge yesterday. Spit it out; perhaps I'll be a pheasant today".

In their old age, the Beresfords remained a happily married couple. He became known as an indefatigable anecdotalist, while she was famed for having complete disregard of her clothes and appearance. (Wilde possibly was recalling Jeromina Beresford in 'Dorian Gray' – 'A curious woman, whose dresses always looked as if they had been designed in a rage and put on in a tempest'). Together they were described as 'the Windbag and the Ragbag'.

One of Jeromina's eccentricities was her attempt to compensate for her lack of eyebrows. She would absentmindedly pencil in one eyebrow and affix adhesive fur to the other. On one occasion, bursting in late to greet her guests, she caught sight of herself in a mirror and

208

rushed off again, shouting: "Good God! I've forgotten my left eyebrow! Why didn't you tell me?"

EF Benson said of her piano recitals that: "Her playing of Chopin was a nightmare". Her husband Charles regarded her as 'an entertaining spectacle'.

Beresford's brothers were also figures of some note in society. Lord William Beresford was aide-de-camp to the Viceroy of India, *Lord Lytton*, and also had received the Victoria Cross after the Zulu War of 1879. When closely pursued by the enemy at the Battle of Ulundi, he had stopped to pick up a wounded British soldier. The man had told him to gallop on or they would both be killed. Lord William replied that if the soldier did not climb up on the horse, he would get down and punch his head.

Lord Marcus Beresford was another crony of the Prince of Wales and a well-known clubman. Once, when emerging from the Turf Club, he was accosted by another member who indignantly told him that: "A fellow in the card room has just had the impertinence to offer me £50 to resign from the club! What shall I do, Marcus?" Beresford considered for a moment and replied: "Well, if I were you, I should wait about six weeks, because by then he'll offer you £500".

Marcus also had a taste for practical jokes. Once he was travelling on a train with five companions. One of them, Dudley Milner, fell asleep and, as he snored on, Marcus removed Milner's train ticket from his pocket. When Milner awoke, he realised his ticket was gone and, realising the ticket collector was approaching, begged the others to give him the price of the fare. They all claimed to have left their wallets at home, but sympathetically suggested that he hide under the seat. Milner, faced with no alternative, did so and his companions arranged their legs to cover him.

When the collector arrived, Marcus and the others handed over all the tickets. The puzzled collector asked: "You have got six tickets here and only five gentlemen?" Marcus looked up: "Yes, that's quite correct. The other gentleman is under the seat. He prefers travelling like that."

One of Marcus's club friends was known to suffer from hard-earned delirium tremens. One evening, this friend was sitting in the club when a rat ran across the carpet. Marcus looked across to see his friend's reaction. The man hesitated for a few moments, then beamingly announced: "Ah! You thought I saw a rat. But I didn't!!"

Meanwhile Wilde continued his British lecturing tours, including a talk on the 18th century poet Thomas Chatterton.

He made his last ever visit to Ireland in March 1885, and his last lecture on March 30th.

After a renewed but fruitless attempt to become an inspector of schools, Oscar turned to journalism. Between 1886 and 1888 he published over one hundred book reviews in such publications as the Pall Mall Gazette and the Dramatic Review, stating that: 'Criticism is the highest form of autobiography'. Oscar: 'For a time reviewing interested me a little, but I tired of it very soon'.

In May 1885, his essay, 'The Truth of Masks', was published under the title of 'Shakespeare and Stage Costume'.

On June 5, Oscar and Constance's first son, Cyril was born. His godfather was the explorer Walter Harris.

WALTER HARRIS 1866-1933

Although Walter Harris's parents had known Constance Wilde before her marriage, and Harris had been a frequent guest at the Wilde's Tite Street home, at only eighteen years old, he was a surprising choice of godparent. He was also made a trustee of Oscar's marriage settlement.

After attending Harrow School and then (for a very short period in 1884) Cambridge University, Harris followed his true instincts and, almost penniless, left England and his wealthy family to wander the world. By begging passages on tramp steamers, before he was twenty he had visited Turkey, Egypt, India, South Africa and Archangel in Russia.

Then, in 1886, he arrived in Morocco and settled in Tangier. He was to make further trips elsewhere, (in 1892, he made an dangerous excursion into the Yemen, where he was imprisoned by the Turkish authorities), but Morocco became his real home. He survived financially by becoming the Moroccan correspondent of the London Times.

Harris's marriage to Lady Mary Savile, daughter of the Earl of Mexborough, ended abruptly the day after the honeymoon and was later annulled on the grounds of non-consummation. Walter claimed the reason was that Mary wore her pearls in bed, but the real reason was that, though highly discreet, he was homosexual.

Oscar Wilde said of Morocco in a book review of 1886: 'The Moors are the masters of a beautiful country and of many beautiful arts, but they are paralysed by their fatalism and pillaged by their rulers.... Freedom of thought has been killed by the Koran, freedom of living by bad government'.

Harris may have agreed with him on the latter, but felt an affinity with the people that overrode most of the usual Western prejudices. He was also rare in that, disguised as an Arab, he could fool even the natives as to his origins and visit places where other Europeans would have been killed automatically.

Harris had first hand experience of what Wilde described as Moslem fatalism. The Moroccan soldiers had a habit of burying their wounded alive, to prevent the enemy carrying off their heads as trophies. He heard of one unfortunate who protested that, as he was still alive, he did not want to be buried. One of his companions told him to be quiet: "You were killed at least an hour ago. Don't you realise that you are dead?"

They continued shovelling on earth until the indignant invalid was smothered in the grave below. One of the burying party told Harris: "This man had no confidence in us, his comrades, when we assured him he was dead. I hate ingratitude."

Harris's friendship with the Sultan of Morocco gave him a close perspective on the governance of the country. The Sultan, bored by traditional Arab entertainments, turned eagerly to Europe to provide diversion. The result was a grotesque mixture of East and West. Harris: 'It is no wonder that the tribesmen looked askance on the high palace walls'.

Having been impressed by the mechanism of his French dentist's new operating chair, the Sultan ordered that the royal throne of Morocco should be reconstructed to work on the same mechanical principles.

The Sultan surrounded himself with a coterie of Europeans that included a conjurer, an American portrait-painter, a German lion-tamer, a French soda-water manufacturer, a Kew gardener, a firework expert, and a Scottish bagpiper. Among the duties required of this disparate group was that of having to turn out to play bicycle polo with the Sultan, while the Scots piper fed the palace kangaroos, and the Kew gardener was allotted the task of teaching the macaw parrots to swear.

Having seen photographs of the British royal coaches, the Sultan ordered a similar vehicle at huge expense from London. When the sumptuously embroidered and jewel-inlaid carriage arrived in Morocco, the Sultan encountered a difficult problem in that the country had no roads.

The coach was deposited in a large grass field outside the Palace that normally housed the royal menagerie. The excited Sultan ordered the immediate harnessing of four horses to the vehicle, only to be told that no horse in the Imperial stable had ever been in harness. He then commanded that his soldiers and slaves should replace the horsepower.

With the Sultan and Harris precariously installed inside, the massive carriage slowly started to move, with teams of sweating slaves in front, and with the royal menagerie, led by an emu, following on behind. Then, gradually, as the enormous weight of the equipage began to tell, the wheels sank deeper and deeper into the swampy ground.

Finally it could move no further and the Sultan and Harris alighted. That night it rained and the next day the magnificent carriage stood abandoned in a small lake. It remained there until it rotted.

Harris had an amiable character and was on friendly terms with many of the more exotic Europeans who ended up in Morocco, including the Arabist Bibi Carlton, the explorer *Robert Cunningham-Graham*, and the diplomat Reggie Lister.

SIR REGINALD LISTER (1865-1912), who became British Minister in Tangier, (and died there of malaria aged 47), was another acquaintance of Wilde. Wilfred Blunt wrote of a luncheon given by the Asquiths in 1894: 'The other guests were *Mrs Ettie Grenfell*, Lord Ribblesdale, his brother Reggie Lister and Oscar Wilde, all immensely talkative so that it was almost like a breakfast in France.'

Although he married and produced a son called Charles, Reggie was also homosexual and, at one point, had a relationship with *EF Benson*. Early in his diplomatic career, he was a junior attaché to *Lord Lytton* at the Paris Embassy. The French writer Jean Lorrain alluded to Reggie's strange tastes by describing him, (with a dubious pun on the Treaty of Friendship between France and Britain, L'Entente Cordiale), as 'The Cordial Aunt'.

> *Wilde continued with his journalism throughout 1885.*
>
> *On October 18th he wrote to the new President of Magdalene College, Sir Herbert Warren (1853-1930), to congratulate him on his appointment. In the early 1890s, Oscar was to cause concern when he told Warren that he was thinking of presenting a statue of himself to the College. Warren's relief was visible as Oscar added, with a twinkle in his eye: "Yes, I want it to stand in the middle of the quad. A colossal nude equestrian statue!"*

1886

> *[In Britain, after a short return to power, Gladstone was defeated by the defection of the anti-Irish Home Rule Liberal Unionists under Joseph Chamberlain. The Tory Party under Lord Salisbury came to power for the next six years.*
>
> *In the USA, the French government presented the Statue of Liberty to the American people. It was erected outside New York harbour.*
>
> *In May, the Haymarket Riots broke out in Chicago.]*

> *During this period, Wilde met and befriended three men who were to remain his loyal friends throughout his life. The first two were a homosexual couple, Charles Ricketts (1866-1931) whom Oscar called 'Orchid', and Charles Shannon (1868-1937), dubbed 'Marigold'. They were gifted painters, printers, stage designers and collectors, who shared a house called the Vale just off the Kings Road, Chelsea. They were to design almost all of the frontispieces of Oscar's literary works, except 'Salome', and remained staunch supporters during his downfall.*
>
> *Ricketts said of Oscar: "There were two personalities in him, the exhibitor of well-rehearsed impromptus, of which he had a stock, and the spontaneous and witty critic of Life'.*
>
> *In October 1886, Wilde met the third new acquaintance – Robert Ross.*

ROBERT ROSS 1869-1918 (First Part)
Wilde: "Ah, Robbie, with the face of Puck and the heart of an angel".

As Oscar grew less interested in conjugal relations with his wife, the meeting with Ross was to re-orientate his sexual world. When in early 1887, Ross's mother arranged for Ross to stay at the Wilde's home as a paying guest, the scene was set for homosexual seduction.

However, although only seventeen, Ross was the experienced partner and it appears that he was the initiator of the affair. Oscar later said that Ross was 'the first boy I had'.

The physical side of their relationship did not last long, but Ross soon 'graduated from lover to confidante'. The biographer Rupert Croft-Cooke observed that: "From the first time that Ross met Wilde he had no other serious interest. Wilde, in triumph or prison, alive or dead, was Ross's life". Although not especially talented himself, Ross's true worth lay in his genius for friendship, a trait he displayed all his life. Ross: "Making other people a success is my only real vocation".

Ross provided a responsive sounding board for Oscar's wit; Wilde admitted that many of the lines in 'Intentions' originated in remarks made by Ross. He was also an invaluable amanuensis. Ross: 'I stayed with him in 1887 for two months and used then to write down what he said, but to tell you a great secret which I ought not to do, I gave him my notes and he used a great deal of them for one of his later plays which was written in a great hurry and against time as he wanted money. This is of course is private'.

Ross came from a family of Canadian grandees, being the son of the Canadian Attorney General, and the grandson of the first Premier of Upper Canada. He never lost his North American accent and Oscar occasionally teased him about 'becoming depressed and Canadian'.

As a child, he had lived in Onslow Square in South Kensington, London, where he had been introduced to the critic and historian Thomas Carlyle. The famous Scottish writer and historian had told the young boy that he should always refer to himself as 'Robbie' in true Scots fashion, rather than 'Robert'.

[The Wilde family had also met **THOMAS CARLYLE** (1795-1881) in 1874, when they were on holiday in London, and after Carlyle's death, Oscar purchased his writing desk. Wilde described the writer as a 'Rabelaisian moralist', and Carlyle's most famous work, his history of the French Revolution, as 'one of the most fascinating historical novels ever written, where facts are either kept in their proper subordinate position, or else entirely excluded on the general ground of dullness.']

In October 1888, Ross became an undergrad at King's College, Cambridge where he came under the professorial wing of *Oscar Browning*. (Wilde wrote to Browning recommending his protégé as 'excessively clever and amusing'). Oscar also wrote to Ross: 'I hope you are enjoying yourself at Cambridge – whatever people may say against Cambridge it is certainly the best preparatory school for Oxford that I know.'

Unfortunately, Ross's college career ended suddenly. Writing in the university Granta magazine in March 1889, he criticised the choice of the new Dean, EH Douty. One of Douty's supporters, a junior tutor called AA Tilley, encouraged a gang of students to dump Ross in the college fountain. As a result of his ducking, Ross caught pneumonia and was forced to leave Cambridge. After his recovery, Ross obtained a job writing for the Scots Observer, under its charismatic editor, *WE Henley*.

Notwithstanding his remorse at flouting his then devout Roman Catholic beliefs, Ross continued to practise homosexuality. In 1893, his behaviour almost caused an open scandal when he seduced a sixteen-year-old schoolboy named Philip Dannay. This incident, which involved both Wilde and *Lord Alfred Douglas*, led to Ross's family insisting that he left England for a suitable time. He spent the next two years in Davos, Switzerland. The Dannay affair was a harbinger of the storm yet to come.

[See Robert Ross – Second Part – Page 489]

On November 5th 1886, Oscar and Constance's second child, Vyvyan Oscar Beresford Wilde, was born.

1886 was an especially ripe year for scandals in British society, in which divorce cases provided a wealth of salacious material for the newspapers, and public ruin for the participants.

Wilde disapproved of what he saw as little more than a vicious display of hypocrisy by the public. In 'Dorian Gray' he wrote: 'The masses feel that drunkenness, stupidity, and immorality should be their own special property, and if any one of us makes an ass of himself he is poaching on their preserves. When poor Southwark got into the Divorce Court, their indignation was quite magnificent. And yet I don't suppose that ten per cent of the proletariat live correctly'.

In 1894, he followed the same theme in 'An Ideal Husband': 'Nowadays, with our modern mania for morality, everyone has to pose as a paragon of purity, incorruptibility, and the other seven deadly virtues – and what is the result? You all go over like ninepins – one after the other. Not a year passes in England without somebody disappearing. Scandals used to lend charm, or at least interest, to a man – now they crush him'.

The two main 1886 cases that fascinated the public were those concerning Sir Charles Dilke and Lady Colin Campbell. Enough time elapsed between the two scandals for them both to be savoured to the full. Wilde in 'Dorian Gary': 'They have only been talking about it for six weeks and the British public are really not equal to the mental strain of having more than one topic every three months'.

SIR CHARLES DILKE 1843-1911

Wilde had met Charles Dilke on several occasions and, with one proviso, had liked him. Wilde: "I've only one fault to find with Dilke; he knows too much about everything. It is hard to have a good story interrupted by a fact. I admit accuracy up to a certain point, but Dilke's accuracy is almost a vice."

First elected to Parliament as a Liberal in 1868, Dilke was a staunch radical. Together with his then close ally, *Joseph Chamberlain*, he became one of the 'terrible' twin advocates of whatever 'showed red or even pink upon the political horizon'. He was also a republican who infuriated the notoriously penny-pinching *Queen Victoria* with his demands that she and the rest of the Royal Family should pay income tax. He had a wide knowledge of foreign affairs and was such an ardent supporter of the Greeks that a street in Athens was named after him.

During the Franco-Prussian War of 1870, Dilke visited both armies as an observer. While touring the German lines at Wissembourg, he met and talked with the town commandant. Dilke was amused to discover that the man was in fact an English escaped lunatic who had assumed the role under no authority but his own. He remained town commandant for several months until discovered.

When he reached Paris, Dilke witnessed the collapse of *Napoleon III's* Imperial government and the birth pangs of the new Third Republic. After several days of heated discussion, the new French leaders emerged and chalked up the names of the emerging provisional government on a city wall. Dilke reported: "I drew the moral that, on the day of revolution, always have a bit of chalk handy".

During *Gladstone's* next period in office in 1880, Dilke was made under-secretary at the Foreign Office. Part of his job was to oversee the appointment of the new French Ambassador.

The French had proposed a Marquis de Noailles for the job. Dilke had to veto the man because: "Queen Victoria has been told that Madame De Noailles before her marriage used to have four lovers, one for each season of the year, and that the Marquis de Noailles was only the summer one'.

By 1885, Dilke seemed set for a high-flying political career, despite the enmity of the Queen who saw him as an impertinent troublemaker, and the covert envy of Chamberlain who saw him as a dangerous rival.

After the early death of his first wife in 1874, Dilke met Mrs Emilia Pattison, the wife of Mark Pattison, the Rector of Lincoln College, Oxford.

[The Pattison marriage was not a happy one. George Eliot, who knew them both, reputedly based her 'Middlemarch' characters, 'Edward Casaubon' and 'Dorothea Brooke', on the couple.

Although **MARK PATTISON** (1813-1884) had shown some livelier tendencies in his younger days – (his colleague, *Walter Pater*, sniffed in disapproval that 'Pattison likes nothing better than romping with great girls round gooseberry bushes') – marriage had dampened his fire and he had become a bibliomaniac with far more interest in his library.

Emilia, on the other hand, was a novelist and a sprightly leader of female Oxford society, who delighted in surrounding herself with young men. One day, a worried Pattison told a friend: "My wife tells me that she thinks she's pregnant". The friend gasped: "Good God! Whom do you suspect?"

In 1884, Pattison died. To the end, his main thought was for his library: "Ah! I am to leave my books. They have been more to me than my friends". He asked for one of them, then another, and another, until the bed was covered with volumes. He died beneath this literary cairn.]

With the death of her husband, Emilia married Dilke in October 1885, (Chamberlain was the best man at the wedding). Dilke's reputation for sexual misbehaviour caused comment among observers as to Emilia's wisdom in this marriage. *Frank Harris's* friend, Lord Folkestone stonily remarked: "Dilke was known as a loose fish". Constance Wilde's cousin, *Adrian Hope*, wrote: 'I wonder if Lady Dilke has extracted any guarantee of faithfulness from her too amorous spouse. Or is she too much of a blue stocking to care?'

In February 1886, a divorce case began in London that was to confirm their misgivings and would destroy Dilke's career. Donald Crawford, the MP for Lanark, suspected his young wife of adultery and one night asked her point blank: "Virginia, is it true that you have defiled my bed?" She broke down and confessed that she and Dilke had been lovers for over two years and that Dilke "taught me every French vice. He used to say that I knew more than most women of thirty!" She had made love also to a Captain Forster.

Crawford filed for divorce and, during the case, Virginia Crawford admitted to the court that Dilke had introduced her to his maid Fanny.

Virginia: "He told me she was very nice and quite young; he said that she was about my age. He said that he wanted to see us together, and one day when I was at his house we went upstairs, and after I had been in the bedroom for a little, he brought Fanny in from the next room. Fanny came to the bedroom naked and joined us in bed. To please him I let her stop longer – when Dilke left she helped me dress'. One observer, *Frank Harris*, was highly amused by the additional testimony of a chambermaid that often three pillows were wanted for Dilke's bed.

Dilke was not called to give evidence and the case against him as co-respondent was dismissed. However, Crawford obtained his divorce solely on the grounds of his wife's confessions. This produced the odd judicial result that Virginia was guilty of adultery with Dilke, but that Dilke was innocent of adultery with Virginia.

WT Stead, the moralistic editor of the Pall Mall Gazette, seized on this absurdity and mobilised a campaign of public opinion against Dilke, demanding his resignation as an MP. When the case was re-opened, despite much confusion, the conclusion amounted to a verdict against Dilke.

Wilde commented: "Regarding poor Dilke, monstrous as it may appear, you can take it from me that not only will he be hounded from Society, but he will be cut by every lady in London and also by most of the men" – a prediction that turned out to be true.

Dilke always protested his innocence and, over the next ten years, much evidence came to light that appeared to support his claims. Previously, the main assumption had been that a genteel young girl like Virginia would have been very unlikely to have invented such details as 'threesome' sex.

Later, however, it emerged that she and her two sisters, Mrs Harrison and Mrs Ashton Dilke, (to complicate matters further, the wife of Dilke's brother), had been involved in similar activities with other men, prior to the divorce case.

It had long been the practice of the sisters to visit a brothel at 9, Hill Street, London, for assignations with men. Captain Forster, Virginia's other admitted lover, far from seducing her, had been introduced to the brothel by Virginia herself. He had indulged in sex with all three sisters, claiming that Virginia was much better in bed than Mrs Harrison. Also, Dilke's detectives discovered letters from a Dr Freddy Warner implying that the sisters were well known for their affairs with various medical students at St George's Hospital.

The women had indulged in threesomes on many occasions, where one sister would first seduce a man, then another would join them in bed. Warner claimed that Virginia thoroughly enjoyed these romps.

Soon it was suspected in political circles that the case had been a plot to bring about Dilke's downfall. His secretary, *JEC Bodley*, thought, (without much evidence), that the instigators were *Lord Rosebery* and his wife Hannah. A more likely culprit was Dilke's best friend, Joseph Chamberlain.

As they were both rivals for the leadership of the Liberal Party, the elimination of Dilke was much to Chamberlain's advantage. He certainly had no compunction over destroying another rival, *Charles Parnell*, in similar fashion. Two days before her confession of adultery to her husband, Virginia Crawford had visited Chamberlain – a fact that he covered up from Dilke.

During the case, an excited Chamberlain buttonholed *Henry Labouchere* in the lobby of the House of Commons and asked: "What are people saying?" The disconcertingly honest Labouchere replied: "They are all saying that they wish it was you instead".

By 1900, *Gertrude Atherton* reported that it was generally believed that Dilke had been the victim of a conspiracy. He later became a locally popular MP for the Forest of Dean, but his effective political career was over.

LADY COLIN CAMPBELL 1857-1911

The other sensational divorce case of the year involved the British aristocracy and one of its prettiest ornaments. Lady Colin Campbell, (born Gertrude Blood), was a slim brunette who was described by the American writer *Gertrude Atherton* as: "one of the most beautiful women I have ever seen, quite six feet tall but perfectly made – she reminded one of a spirited clean-limbed racehorse".

She was described also as 'a glamorous nymphomaniac', and by her husband as possessing: "the unbridled lust of Messalina and the indelicate readiness of a common harlot".

To the disapproval of his family, Lord Colin Campbell had married Gertrude in July 1881. Colin was the son of the Duke of Argyle, the brother of the *Marquess of Lorne*, and the nephew of *Lord Ronald Gower*. The homosexual Lorne was horrified by the match: "Miss Blood is a penniless and groat-less grenadier of a girl, who can offer only flesh and stature!'

The Duke of Argyll attempted to discourage the match by informing Gertrude's mother that: "My son is no man for a decent girl to marry. I spend my nights pulling him out of the maidservants' beds, and he is steeped in vice of every kind".

The Duke's warning seemed to be borne out during the Campbells' honeymoon, when Gertrude had to practise 'compulsory virginity' as her new husband was suffering from a bout of syphilis.

The pair had little in common and each followed their own interests during their short married life. Gertrude became friendly with her sister-in-law, Lady Archibald Campbell, (born Janey Callendar, who had married Colin's elder brother in 1869), and together the two ladies became patrons of the arts.

(Lady Archie was a cultivated amateur actress who promoted open-air theatre at Coombe Park, near Kingston. Oscar Wilde enjoyed her mercurial nature and, in reviewing her production of 'As You Like It', wrote that 'Lady Archie was more charming than Rosalind'.)

The two women fell under the artistic spell of *James McNeill Whistler*, who painted them both. Lady Archie's portrait was rejected by the Campbell family on the grounds that 'it seemed to represent a street walker encouraging a shy fellow with a backward glance'.

Whistler's portrait of Lady Colin, (whom he called his 'lovely leopard'), had even less luck. She had posed nude for the painting, 'Harmony in White and Ivory', an act that seems to have aroused the ire of Mrs Whistler. The women quarrelled so violently that Whistler was forced to order both sitter and wife out of the house until they had cooled down. Trixie Whistler was rumoured to have destroyed the painting.

Gertrude's marriage had been in trouble for some time and her behaviour became increasingly reckless. By 1886, she had committed the cardinal sin of being found out, and a legal tempest broke loose in a welter of claim and counter-claim over each spouse's infidelities.

Backed by her great friend, Lady Frances Miles, (who roped in her relative *Frank Miles* as a witness), Gertrude claimed that Lord Colin had seduced his young and startlingly good-looking housemaid, Amelia Watson. Lady Miles stated on oath that she had seen Lord Colin kissing the girl in his bedroom and that she herself had told Lord Colin to sack the girl because she was 'much too pretty to be a housemaid'. Amelia denied the accusation and, when a medical examination proved she was a virgin, Gertrude's case collapsed.

(Given the trial outcome, Lady Miles and Gertrude had been guilty of a genuine moral crime. At the time, the seduction of servant girls was an everyday sport but one where, if caught, it was the girl who was punished, not the seducer. Without proof of her innocence, Amelia's only option would have been to work in a brothel.)

The details of Lord Colin's case against his wife were a gift to the London press. As Wilde commented: 'In centuries before ours the public nailed the ears of journalists to the pump. That was quite hideous. In this century journalists have nailed their own ears to the keyhole. That is much worse.'

Among the lovers that Lord Colin claimed that Gertrude had slept with was the Duke of Marlborough, (Winston Churchill's uncle). A housemaid named Rosa stated in court that she and other servants had watched the Duke having sex with Gertrude.

Also on the list were Dr Thomas Bird, a society physician, and General William Butler, an eminent soldier (and colleague of *Fenwick La Terriere* on the Sudan campaign).

216

The fourth named lover was the redoubtable chief of the London Fire Brigade, Captain Shaw (1830-1908). Tall, robust and handsome, with a degree from Trinity College, Dublin, Shaw was a popular public figure and the object of considerable female attention.

Gertrude had attended the opening night of *Gilbert* and *Sullivan's* 'Iolanthe', in the company of Shaw and could not have failed to notice Gilbert's lyrics in the Act II song: 'O Captain Shaw, Type of true love kept under, Could thy brigade, With cold cascade, Quench thy great love, I wonder'.

During the trial, a servant called O'Neill testified that, while employed at Cadogan Place, (the home of the Campbells), he had peeped through a keyhole and had seen a bare-breasted Gertrude lying on a carpet while Captain Shaw climbed over her. He went on to describe various details that even the press reported as 'unfit for publication'.

Gertrude's counsel produced her brother, the splendidly named Colonel Neptune Blood, who refuted O'Neill's testimony by saying that there was a brass fingerplate that fell into place over the keyhole when the key was removed. Therefore, O'Neill could not have witnessed what he said he had seen.

Much to the disgruntlement of the judge, (who also lived in Cadogan Place), the jury insisted on visiting the house in question. While there, they found that the fingerplate was too stiff to move and hence did not fall over the keyhole.

In spite of this evidence, Gertrude was acquitted, mostly on the grounds that the jury considered that no noblewoman could have acted as it was claimed she had done. Thus both defendants were found to be innocent.

The scandal, however, took its toll. Lord Colin resigned as an MP and left to practise law in India, where he died of pneumonia aged 42. Gertrude was abandoned by society, but showed her resilience by becoming a journalist. When *Bernard Shaw* left 'The World' magazine, Gertrude took over his job as art critic.

She also took up charitable work, serving soup in a workhouse in Stepney, and earning the disapproval of Oscar Wilde. He loathed the concept of charity.

Oscar said that the poor regarded charity as 'a sentimental dole, usually accompanied by some impertinent attempt on the part of the sentimentalist to tyrannise over their private lives. Why should they be grateful for the crumbs that fall from the rich man's table? They should be seated at the board, and are beginning to know it'.

When Gertrude published her novel 'Darrell Blake, a Study' in 1889, Oscar gave the book a barbed review: 'It seems that Lady Colin has exhausted all her powers of imagination in the witness box'. Thereafter she referred to him as 'the Great White Slug'.

1887

[Britain celebrated Queen Victoria's Golden Jubilee.

On 13, Nov 1887, the authorities broke up a protest rally against unemployment by socialists and trade unionists in Trafalgar Sq, London – an event that became known as 'Bloody Sunday'. Police and military were involved; one person was killed and many injured. It probably acted as a spur to development of the trade unions.

A bad fire occurred at the Theatre Royal in Exeter, where 186 people died.

French imperial operations spread to Tunisia, Cambodia, Cochin China, Annam, Tonkin, Madagascar, and the Upper Niger.

In France itself, Sidi Carnot became President, despite a failed rightist military coup by General Boulanger.

(The flamboyant General Georges Boulanger, concocted a plot to end the Third Republic and replace it with his own presidential regime. Having won various elections in Paris, he delayed at the vital moment and

failed to bring down the government. Threatened with arrest, he fled to Brussels and in 1890 shot himself on his mistress's grave. The novelist Emile Zola dismissed Boulanger as 'a hat on a stick'.

Wilde referred to the incident in his short story 'Lord Arthur Savile's Crime': 'Francois used to make excellent soup once, but he is so agitated about politics at present, that I never feel quite certain about him. I do wish General Boulanger would keep quiet'.)]

Wilde spent most of the year writing for various journals. Between 1887 and 1891, he wrote nearly 100 anonymous reviews for the Pall Mall Gazette. The editor of this paper was WT Stead.

WILLIAM T STEAD 1849-1912

Born and raised a Tynesider, Stead had been made editor of the Northern Echo at the very early age of 22. Moving south to London, his talent led him to become first a major contributor to, and then by 1888, editor of the Pall Mall Gazette. He radically altered the style of this paper from staid journalism to yellow press sensationalism by concentrating on exposing corruption.

He was unpopular in many quarters, the artist *Sir William Rothenstein* calling him 'an obnoxious kill-joy Puritan', and *Bernard Shaw* describing him as 'a complete ignoramus, who had the gift of being able to articulate the dumb paranoia of the masses'.

Grant Richards, (later a well-known publisher), spent seven years working for Stead at his Mowbray House offices in London. He viewed his employer with an amused but wary eye. Richards: 'Stead had an idea for boiling down the great novels of the world so that they might fit into, say, sixty four pages instead of six hundred, and so become in a sense easily available to the penny public. I myself treated 'Jane Eyre' for the series. It was not an idea that did any credit to any one of us at Mowbray House'.

Richards said that the only thing that got him out of bed in the morning was the thought of opening the letters at the office. 'Lots of madmen wrote to Stead. And they would go on writing to him week after week, year after year'.

Each week would see the steady arrival of yet more confessions to being Jack the Ripper. Richards: 'There was one man who told in detail how he had seen nothing for it but to get rid of the temptation of sex once and for all, and then proceeded to narrate how he had done so with a shilling penknife'.

One visitor to the office was Louise Michel (1830-1905). She had been a famous French revolutionary known as the 'Red Virgin of the Commune', (despite being yet another of *Victor Hugo's* bed partners). She claimed to have set fire to the Tuileries in 1871, and had been transported to New Caledonia for espousing communism.

Now elderly and poor but with a steely dignity, she arrived one day at Stead's office accompanied by an aged gentleman with an equally incendiary background. Already nervous of their guests, Stead and his staff scattered in panic when, at the prompting of the 'Red Virgin', the man reached into his coat pocket and produced what appeared to be a bomb. It turned out to be a new contrivance for keeping water hot, (an early version of the thermos flask).

Richards was also fascinated by his employer's attitude to sex. He said that one lady, Mrs Lynn Linton, told him that, while: "allowing Stead absolute probity in respect of sexual matters, he exudes semen through the skin". *Frank Harris* wrote that another woman, Mrs Julia Frankau, had jokingly flirted with Stead: 'till one day he fell on his knees before her and put his arms round her, and she said to herself 'At last' – when he suddenly told her that he was going to pray that she might always be faithful to her husband. I laughed till I cried'.

Concluding that Stead was a repressed puritan obsessed by sex, Richards commented that: 'I say, with experience, that most workers for purity are over-sexed – and they all seemed to arrive at Mowbray House'.

Whatever Stead's personal motivation, the conditions prevalent in London in the 1880s provided much material for his moral campaigns. In a population of two and a quarter million, the city had over 100,000 prostitutes, (with another 300,000 people connected to the profession). The police were regarded as 'the brothel-keeper's best friend', kept quiescent through bribery and regular free use of the girls.

The French newspaper Le Figaro reported that: 'Every evening towards midnight more than 500 girls in ages between 12 and 15 years parade between Piccadilly Circus and Waterloo Place – a stretch of ground no more than 300 yards long'. Various London locations provided specialities. The Haymarket was the place for streetwalkers, Mayfair for high class whores, Leicester Square for ordinary brothels, and Spitalfields for child brothels. Girls of eight or nine were easily available, as there was a widespread belief that intercourse with a virgin could cure venereal disease.

Stead determined to tackle at least some of the problems, and started a campaign to bring in a law that would raise the age of consent from 12 to 16 and to make it more difficult to abduct young girls for prostitution. In 1885, to force attention to the situation, he purchased a 13-year-old girl, Eliza Armstrong, from her mother for £5, and published the story under the title, 'The Maiden Tribute of Modern Babylon'.

The middle-class public was more shocked by Stead's exposure of the trade than by its existence. On the grounds that he had not gained the permission of Eliza's father when purchasing her, Stead himself was arrested, and jailed for two months on a charge of criminal abduction.

There was a backlash of protest against the 'Maiden Tribute' articles, (Lewis Carroll wrote a letter of complaint against it), and a pro-brothel lobby was organised in Parliament by one Cavendish Bentinck. However, Stead found enough political allies, (including *Labouchere*), to force the introduction of a Criminal Law Bill to raise the age of consent.

When the Bill came under attack in the House of Lords and was in danger of being defeated, a supporter, Lord Oranmore and Brown, (with a hint of blackmail in his demeanour), pointed out that 'there are very few of your lordships who have not at some point in your lives not had intercourse with a partner under the age of sixteen'. The Bill was passed rapidly.

Encouraged by this success, Stead and his adherents founded the National Vigilance Association, the aims of which included the introduction of greater censorship within the artistic world. Stead aimed his attacks mostly at the drama, despite never having been inside a theatre until he was fifty-five years old – with the exception of one visit to a Passion Play at Oberammergau. (His daughter became an actress).

The Vigilance Association were especially keen on banning the novels of the French writer *Emile Zola*, and brought successful prosecutions against his English publisher, Henry Vizetelly. (The 70-year-old Vizetelly spent some time in prison as a result). Although the idea was dropped, they also considered prosecuting Wilde over his novel, 'The Picture of Dorian Gray'.

Oscar hit back at Stead's polemical press attacks: 'It was a fatal day when the public discovered that the pen is mightier than the paving-stone. They at once sought for the journalist, found him, developed him, and made him their industrious and well-paid servant...But what is there behind the leading article but prejudice, stupidity, cant and twaddle? And when these four are joined together they make a terrible force, and constitute the new authority.'

Later, in 1905, a forgiving Stead wrote to *Robert Ross* after the publication of part of Oscar's famous prison letter. 'I think De Profundis will live long after all that the rest of us have written will be forgotten'. He mentioned that he had met Wilde in Paris shortly before

Oscar's death and had 'greeted him like an old friend'. 'I am glad to remember that he always knew that I, at least, had never joined the herd of his assailants'.

After he left the Pall Mall Gazette, Stead became an influential freelance writer interested in the promotion of world peace and, as such, managed to obtain the first press interview ever given by a reigning Russian Tsar. Nicholas II and his wife Alexandra had been crowned in 1896 and, in an early flush of idealism, had become enthusiastic over the concept of disarmament.

The interview itself was unusual in that, having questioned Nicholas as to his views, Stead brought about the conclusion of the conversation by jumping up and declaring that he had 'kept the Tsar too long from his many duties'. Nicholas was unused to being so abruptly dismissed.

In spite of this infringement of protocol, the unlikely pair managed to convene a genuine peace conference at The Hague in 1899. The gathering, which included important delegates from Germany, Britain, the USA, China, Persia, France, Italy and Spain, had the aim of stemming the growth of armaments and outlawing aggressive conflicts.

Unfortunately, a dispute between the British *Lord Salisbury* and the American Dick Olney encapsulated the problem that was to dog world politics to this day. What could the delegates do to enforce peace if the conference condemned a war and an individual, powerful nation was to ignore that decision? (This same dilemma was to ruin the League of Nations when Nazi Germany and Fascist Italy behaved in just such a fashion, and later still it was to plague the United Nations).

Perhaps the problem was best pinpointed by the American writer *Mark Twain* when Stead wrote to ask his opinion. Twain replied: 'Dear Mr Stead, The Tsar is ready to disarm. I am ready to disarm. Collect the others; it should not be too much of a task now'.

Towards the end of his life, Stead became interested in the psychic world and predicted his own death: "My end is near." With this in mind, he did not bother to buy a return ticket when he sailed to America in April 1912. This was financially foresighted, as the ship he sailed on was the Titanic.

According to witnesses, he made no effort to escape the disaster and instead concentrated on assisting women and children on to the lifeboats. The socialite Lady Dorothy Nevill reported: 'By all accounts, by the irony of fate he met his death clinging to a piece of wreckage in company with an American millionaire'.

After the publication in March 1887 of his short story, 'The Canterville Ghost' in the Court and Society Review, Wilde ceased to write poetry, (with one exception in 1897).

In a letter dated April 13ᵗʰ 1887, Oscar mentioned his great American contemporary humorist, Mark Twain.

MARK TWAIN 1835-1910

Although there was no record of the two men meeting, (and in spite of the wide differences between their comic styles), Twain and Wilde appreciated each other's work so much that there is evidence of intellectual crossover. Twain borrowed and adapted Oscar's quip: 'I never put off till tomorrow what I can possibly do the day after', while in his 1887 letter, Wilde proposed to write an article called 'The Child Philosopher'.

This would have been based on Twain's collection of definitions provided by American children, which Oscar called: 'amazing and amusing'. These included such lines as: 'Republican – a sinner mentioned in the Bible; Democrat – a vessel usually filled with beer', etc.

Praised by WD Howell as 'the Lincoln of our literature', 'Mark Twain' was the pseudonym of Samuel Langhorne Clemens. He had been born in Missouri, USA, and raised on the banks of the Mississippi, where, as a young man, he spent four years as a river boat pilot: "the most carefree years of my life".

In 1861, the Civil War brought an abrupt end to river traffic and Twain joined the Confederate militia as a second lieutenant, ('we didn't have a first lieutenant'). He was a lukewarm supporter of the Southern cause and later blamed the war on the Scottish novelist Sir Walter Scott. Scott, he claimed, had done so much to create the image of the Southern white aristocrat that he was to a great extent responsible for the chivalric bone-headedness that perpetuated the conflict.

Twain's military career was short-lived. "I was a soldier two weeks and was hunted like a rat the whole time". After a fortnight of rain and boredom, his unit disbanded. "I learned more about retreating than the man who invented retreating. There was but one honourable course for me to pursue and I pursued it. I withdrew to private life and gave the Union cause a chance".

He spent the rest of the war mostly in Nevada, dabbling in mining and journalism, and concentrating on drinking. He fondly recalled those days: "when bohemianism was respectable – ah, more than respectable, heroic".

On occasional trips to San Francisco, he mingled with other Western writers such as Bret Harte and *Joaquin Miller*, living a chequered life, dining in chic restaurants one day, in jail for drunkenness the next.

His lifestyle changed after he was commissioned to write articles about foreign travel. He started with a successful account of life in Hawaii, then followed it with a superb travelogue, 'The Innocents Abroad', about a tour of Europe and the Middle East in 1867. The trip took five months, during which he observed his fellow passengers, ('a funeral excursion without the corpse'), and his experiences in such areas as France, Italy, and the Holy Land. When his party was charged an exorbitant price after they had hired a boat to sail on the Sea of Galilee, Twain commented: "Well, now do you wonder that Christ walked?"

The book sold 100,000 copies, began his career as a public speaker, and turned Twain into 'the People's Author'. It also gave him the financial security to start a family. Having married Olivia Langdon in 1870, he settled in Connecticut and raised three daughters.

Despite having strict moral views on sexual propriety, he was still able to give earthy advice on the subject. He discouraged masturbation, not on the usual Victorian grounds of causing blindness, but because: 'of all the various kinds of sexual intercourse this has least to recommend it. As an amusement it is too fleeting. As an occupation it is too wearing. As a public exhibition, there is no money in it'.

Between 1876 and 1884, Twain published the books which were to seal his success as a great American writer. 'The Adventures of Tom Sawyer' (1876), 'Life on the Mississippi' (1883), and 'The Adventures of Huckleberry Finn' (1884) took, not just America, but the whole literary world by storm.

The only opposition came from the Boston area where 'Huck Finn' was banned by the Concord library. *Louisa May Alcott* wrote: 'If Mr Clemens cannot think of something better to tell our pure-minded lads and lasses he had best stop writing for them'. Twain said he was delighted because this embargo would increase sales by at least 30,000 copies.

He continued his lucrative lecture tours, becoming a particular favourite in England, where he met his most avid fan, Charles Darwin. Twain was equally impressed by Britain, an Anglomania aided, in part, by his increasing disillusion with his native country.

Twain, in company with *Walt Whitman* and WD Howells, felt that true American democracy had died in the Civil War, and had been replaced by a cynical plutocracy and self-interested political leadership: 'My kind of loyalty is loyalty to one's country, not to its office-holders'. For the rest of his life, he increasingly became the scourge of capitalist profiteering and warmongering. He saw the unions as the only possible resistance: 'In the Unions is the working man's only present hope of standing up like a man against money and the power of it'.

Previously, in 1873, he had published a savage satire called 'The Gilded Age' on the greed and corruption surrounding *Ulysses S Grant's* presidency. By 1884, Grant himself had been ruined financially by a Wall Street swindler. Twain came to his rescue by agreeing to publish Grant's autobiography, thereby saving the ex-president from destitution.

However, soon it was Twain himself who needed financial salvation. He indulged his fascination with new inventions by investing money in a series of disastrous ideas. He said later that almost the only impoverished inventor that he did not back was a young man called Alexander Graham Bell, who asked him to support his new-fangled machine called a 'telephone'. Twain: "I declined. I said I didn't want anything more to do with wildcat speculation".

(Twain once considered buying a hotel in Downieville, California. He said that one of the house rules read: 'None but the brave deserves the fare'.)

In 1894, during a general financial collapse in the USA, (five hundred banks failed, and two and a half million people were unemployed), Twain had to file for bankruptcy. He was $100,000 in debt and aged sixty.

Pledging his creditors that he would pay them off in full, Twain set off on a worldwide lecture tour and spent the next six years earning the money. In 1900, he settled for a time in the suburb of Dollis Hill, London, claiming that: "Dollis Hill comes nearer to being a paradise than any other home I ever occupied". In 1901, he returned to the USA solvent again.

He continued to write and to enjoy his restored wealth, scorning the more puritanical restrictions of old age. Twain: "The only way to keep your health is to eat what you don't want, drink what you don't like, and do what you'd rather not".

During Mark Twain's wilder days in the West, he befriended another American humorist named Charles Farrar Browne, who used the pen name of **ARTEMUS WARD** (1834-1867). On Christmas Eve, 1863, Twain, Ward, and two friends were involved in a major drinking bout. As they sprawled at the table, Ward made a fuddled proposal that they have 'a shtanning toasht'. After a failed attempt to rise to his feet, Ward slumped back in his seat and said: "Well, consider it shtanning".

During a more formal evening, Ward was just capable enough to get to his feet and offer another toast: "I give you Upper Canada!" The gathering rose and dutifully drank the toast. Then a puzzled Twain asked: "But why did you give us Upper Canada?" Ward replied: "Well, I don't want it".

In May 1887, Wilde's short stories, 'The Sphinx Without a Secret' and 'Lord Arthur Savile's Crime' were published in, respectively, The World and The Court and Society Review.

He was also a member of the audience for a performance by the American showman, 'Buffalo Bill' Cody.

'BUFFALO BILL' CODY 1846-1917

'May, 1887, Tite St. Dear Colonel Cody, We hope so much that you will be able to come and have tea with us on Wednesday, as we would be much disappointed not to see you, Yours sincerely, Constance Wilde'.

As part of Queen Victoria's 1887 Golden Jubilee celebrations, Cody's Wild West Show had arrived in London prior to a tour of Britain. *Lord Ronald Gower,* the official director, greeted

Cody personally before the opening at Earls Court, (the last performance being at Hull football ground). Wilde attended the show and Vanity Fair magazine teased him by reporting that: 'during the attack on the Deadwood Stage, Mr Oscar Wilde was greatly alarmed for the safety of his scalp'.

It was not the first time the two had been linked. In the USA, in 1882, when Cody had been creating his show, he had a Sioux chief with him who gave a speech in his own language before the footlights. Reporters said that it translated as meaning: "a desire to be left alone in a forest for a few minutes with Oscar Wilde".

Before Cody's first tour of Britain in 1883, Oscar had written: 'Buffalo Bill... is certain to draw; for English people are far more interested in American barbarism than they are in American civilisation.'

The biographer Evan Connell described William Frederick Cody as 'a curious mixture of thespian and assassin'. Before he had reached the age of thirty Cody had taken part in many of the pivotal events in the history of the American West.

As the son of a prominent anti-slavery man, the nine-year-old Cody was almost murdered during the savage fighting that broke out during the free-state versus slave-state debate in Kansas in the 1850s. When attacked by slavers, he managed to save himself through his astonishing horse-riding skills.

Aged thirteen, he used this same talent when he went to work as a mounted messenger for the short-lived Pony Express. The dangers of this job were acknowledged by the company itself. Its advertisement read: 'Wiry young fellows needed – willing to risk death daily. Orphans preferred'. During one trip, after his relief rider had been killed, Cody covered the most dangerous stretch of the journey – a distance of 320 miles across Utah – in only 22 hours.

When the new telegraph rendered the Pony Express obsolete, Cody joined a punitive expedition to avenge the 1857 'Mountain Meadows' massacre of an emigrant wagon train by the Mormon militia, (known as the Danites). The expedition itself failed when its members were captured by the Mormons and made to walk back to Kansas.

During the Civil War, Cody joined a band of Union irregulars called the Red Legged Scouts, and became engaged in guerrilla warfare against William Quantrill's Confederate raiders, (who included the future outlaws, the James and Younger Brothers). In 1863, he was in the regular Union forces that drove off the Southern General Nathan Bedford Forrest at the Battle of Tupelo, Mississippi.

After the war, Cody became a renowned buffalo hunter attached to the railroad companies. The relentless diet that he provided for the rail workers led to his nickname. It was not entirely complimentary, being a contraction of "More goddamn buffalo from Bill".

As an army scout, he knew many of the military leaders on the frontier, working for General Custer, (known as 'Iron Butt' by his men), guiding General Sherman at the Council Springs Indian conference, and, (after a heroic 24 mile ride through a Great Plains blizzard), being made chief scout for the Fifth Cavalry by General Sheridan. Cody was involved in over a dozen battles with the Indian tribes, personally killing Chief Tall Bull at the Battle of Summit Springs.

During the early 1870s, as the frontier became pacified, Cody settled in Nebraska (his home for the next forty years), and became the guide of choice for the exclusive hunting parties arranged for rich Easterners and foreign dignitaries, amongst them Tsar Alexander II's son, the Grand Duke Alexis of Russia.

Cody had become a figure of some importance in the West and in 1871 was made a Justice of the Peace. In this guise, he once presided over a marriage ceremony. Being unable to remember the correct words, he recited as much as he could and ended with: "Whomsoever God and Buffalo Bill hath joined together, let no man put asunder".

In 1876 Cody was involved in his last real fighting when, as retribution for the death of General Custer, he intercepted a Cheyenne warrior band and killed their leader Yellow Hair in single combat. Cody scalped his fallen enemy, thereby claiming 'the first scalp for Custer'.

He was magnanimous in victory and said later that: "The defeat of Custer was not a massacre. The Indians were being pursued by skilled fighters with orders to kill. For centuries they had been hounded from the Atlantic to the Pacific and back again. They had their wives and little ones to protect and they were fighting for their existence".

As a result of their meeting during a hunting party trip, Cody was invited to visit New York by the influential Leonard Jerome, (grandfather of Winston Churchill). While in the city he met Ned Buntline, an impresario, who had already started weaving a mythology around Cody's exploits in his melodrama, 'Buffalo Bill, the King of the Border Men', and in various dime novels.

Buntline managed to persuade Cody to play himself on stage in their first collaboration called 'Scouts of the Prairie'. Buntline wrote this play in four hours in a Chicago hotel room. One critic wrote that: 'Everything is so wonderfully bad it is almost good'. Another reviewer asked, that if it had taken Buntline four hours to write it, what on earth he had been doing the rest of the time.

Despite this critical reaction, the audiences responded with huge enthusiasm, and Cody blossomed as an outrageously ham but very popular stage performer. When the language of Buntline's plays and books was criticised for lack of authenticity, one old frontiersman commented: "Well, maybe we didn't talk that way before, but we sure all talked that way after the books were published".

By 1882, Cody graduated to creating his own spectacular Wild West Show, which included a twenty-piece band, a group of Pawnee Indians, a replica of the Deadwood stagecoach, an exhibition shooting match, a 'buffalo chase', and a reconstruction of Custer's Last Stand, (at the end of which Cody would ride onstage on a white horse, while a printed banner behind him read 'Too Late!'). The show, in various forms, ran for decades, creating its own stars, and touring the USA and Europe with unprecedented success.

Cody refused to abandon his own hard-living lifestyle. On one occasion, his business partner, during a show season, insisted that Cody cut down on his usual alcoholic intake. Cody agreed to limit himself to one drink a day, but circumvented the ban by finding an enormous jug that allowed him to continue drinking all day without breaking the agreement.

In 1866 he had married Louisa Frederici, (a union that produced four children, two of whom died young). They spent long periods apart and Louisa came to bitterly resent Cody's mistresses. She once arrived unexpectedly at a Chicago hotel and was sent up by the desk clerk to 'Mr and Mrs Cody's suite'. In a fury, she proceeded to wreck the bedroom.

Eventually, Cody filed for divorce: "It has been nag, nag, nag; it has worn me out and I want to get away from it". Louisa counter-charged on the grounds of Cody's infidelity and drunkenness; (she accused him of having sex with, among others, Queen Victoria, and the Prince of Wales's wife Alexandra).

Cody claimed that Louisa had tried to poison him by putting a substance called Dragon's Blood in his coffee, after which he had collapsed. This was substantially true. However she had inserted the Dragon's Blood, (a love potion obtained from a passing gypsy), not in an attempt to kill Cody but to revive his flagging sexual interest in her. Cody lost his suit and they remained married.

Although he had made a fortune through his shows, his natural profligacy, combined with some dreadful investments, brought him into debt. After borrowing money from a Denver profiteer named Tammen on the strength of his name and services, Cody was reduced to what in effect was forced labour. Aged 67, he had to work on a series of 'farewell' tours in order to pay off the debt to Tammen. Cody performed his last show in November 1916.

Just two months later, Cody asked his doctor how long he had left to live. The doctor replied: "Thirty six hours". Cody nodded then said: "OK, let's forget about it and play some cards". In a generous obituary the New York Times wrote: 'He delighted millions and became better known than the equator.'

The Wild West Show introduced several Western folk heroes to a wider audience. Among them was **WILD BILL HICKOK** (1837-1876), who joined Cody's entourage after his own show had failed. While on tour in Niagara Falls, one of Hickok's trained mountain bears had broken loose and attacked a baked sausage stand. Hickok, never a good manager, abandoned the idea.

Hickok's drinking eclipsed even Cody's and, after an incident when he fired on a group of show extras, Buffalo Bill had to sack him. Hickok was killed soon afterwards when he was shot in the back during a poker game in Deadwood, South Dakota. The cards he was holding at the time, aces and eights, are still known in some quarters as a 'dead man's hand'.

Another Wild West Show star was **ANNIE OAKLEY** (1860-1926, real name Phoebe Moses) who said of Cody that: "he was the kindest, simplest, most loyal man I ever knew. He was the staunchest friend". Oakley herself was regarded by the company as a tightwad, who only drank lemonade unless somebody else bought her a small beer.

On the other hand, she was also a great markswoman. In an 1885 competition she broke 4,772 out of 5,000 glass balls at fifteen yards distance within nine hours, while loading her own shotguns. After being seriously injured in a train crash, Oakley retired from professional shooting aged 41.

One of her most famous tricks was to invite an audience member to stand on stage while she shot the ash off his cigar. To avoid trouble, the 'audience member' was always her husband, Frank Butler.

However, during one show in Europe, she was horrified to see Crown Prince Wilhelm of Germany bounding up on stage before Butler could make a move. When Wilhelm waved away his guards, Oakley was left with no choice but to go ahead. Wilhelm's ash was duly despatched to his great admiration. When the USA eventually joined the First World War in 1917, Oakley wrote to Wilhelm, now the German Kaiser, offering to repeat the trick. She did not receive a reply.

The most exotic member of Cody's show, although only recruited for the 1885 season, was the Sioux Indian chief, **SITTING BULL** (1831-1890, real name Jumping Badger). As the most noticeable representative of the defeated tribes, often his appearances on stage were booed by audiences.

Bearing in mind the Sioux saying: 'The white man made us many promises but only kept one; they promised to take our land and they took it', Sitting Bull would stare down his detractors with iron dignity. When he was attacked by a man whose brother had been killed with Custer, Sitting Bull, in self-defence, smashed the assailant's face with a sledge hammer.

He soon left Cody's show and returned to his reservation in South Dakota. When the US Congress, realising that the Sioux were no longer dangerous, cut the tribe's beef ration by half, Sitting Bull became a supporter of a religious Sioux group called the Ghost Dancers. Despite the non-violence of their protests, the authorities saw them as a threat and sent police to arrest the old chief.

In the melee that took place as a result, fourteen people, including Sitting Bull, were killed. When the firing began, his horse, thinking that it was the cue for the Wild West Show, went into the practised routine of resting back on his haunches and raising his front hoof aloft. The terror-stricken police scattered, believing that Sitting Bull's spirit had entered the horse.

By May 1887, Wilde was looking for a more permanent job than freelance journalism. He applied to become the secretary of the newly opened People's Palace in Mile End Road, London: 'I am very anxious to be connected officially with the People's Palace, as I have devoted myself entirely to the spreading of art-culture among the people'.

His application was unsuccessful. The People's Palace later became part of Queen Mary's College.

In June 1887, Wilde's story 'The Model Millionaire' was published in The World.

Still in need of work, Wilde applied for and gained the job of editor of 'Lady's World', the name of which he quickly changed to 'Women's World'. He enthusiastically set about recruiting help from the leading London society women. Lady St Helier was his most valuable catch.

LADY SUSAN ST HELIER 1849-1931

Susan St Helier, (born Susan Stewart-Mackenzie, became Mrs Stanley by her first husband, then Mrs Jeune by her second, finally Lady St Helier by her husband's ennoblement), was one of the great society hostesses of the period, and Wilde was determined to gain her support. Oscar: 'No man has any real success in this world unless he has got women to back him, and women rule Society. If you have not got women on your side you are quite over.'

Fortunately, she not only provided two articles for the Women's World, but also offered to encourage her female friends to help as well. Oscar in May 1887: 'Yesterday I spent the whole afternoon with Mrs Jeune, who was very delighted with the idea of our project, and I drew up with her our list of names'.

During the 1880s, Wilde had come into his own as a dinner party guest and thereby became a peripheral member of the English ruling classes. Oscar: 'A man who can dominate a London dinner-table can dominate the world'. He began to disapprove of disrespectful jibes against Society: 'Only people who can't get into it do that'.

British Society was still dominated by the roughly ten thousand members of the land-owning aristocracy. Lady Dorothy Nevill wrote: 'When I first knew London Society in the 1880s, it was more like a large family than anything else. It was impossible for a stranger to obtain a place until credentials had been carefully examined and discussed. Mere wealth was no passport'.

However, this 'family' knew that the secret of its continuation was its elastic ability to absorb new faces and forces into its ranks and, among others, Wilde became a beneficiary of this enlightened if self-interested attitude.

Susan St Helier was one of the hostesses who used her social network to become a prime mover in the liberalising process. Her evening receptions were renowned for the extraordinary mixture, and sheer numbers, of guests who would cram into her home; (Oscar: 'There are three inevitables – death, quarter days, and Lady Jeune's parties').

St Helier: "I heard a guest say that she felt rather like a herring packed in a barrel, and some of her friends pleasantly described my parties as being like the Day of Judgment". Before one gathering, so many MPs were invited that they held an early count on a House of Commons debate, so that they could arrive on time.

In this potentially awkward miscellany of disparate guests, Susan went to great pains to avoid social embarrassment. Once, before introducing one gentleman to a female arrival, she hissed: "Don't allude to railway accidents! Her aunt was cut to ribbons on the underground!"

Wilde was amused at the lack of discrimination in Susan's choice of partygoers; their only qualification appeared to be that they were celebrated. He invented a story in which an explorer in Africa was captured by a tribe of cannibals. Just as the explorer was about to be boiled in the pot, the cannibal chief appeared and hurriedly released him, saying: "My humblest apologies, sir. Surely we met at Lady St Helier's?"

Wilde: 'I love London Society. It is entirely composed now of beautiful idiots and brilliant lunatics. Just what Society should be.'

Susan Stewart-Mackenzie was the daughter of an ancient but impoverished Scottish Highland family. She was brought up mostly by her grandmother, a redoubtable but gout-stricken old lady whose main enjoyment in life was to battle with the local Free Church minister. One Christmas, she decided to make peace with the man and, in an effort to induce fellow feeling, asked him: "My dear fellow, did you ever suffer from the gout?". The minister sniffed censoriously and replied: "Nae, nae. I was never rich enough". War resumed.

As a girl, Susan used to visit relatives in Dublin and near Lough Erne, ('I loved the rackety, reckless life which one associates with Ireland'). One family friend, Tom Connolly, adored parties and often insisted that his guests remain for days. When one lady was called away because of severe family illness, Connolly refused to let her go and locked all the doors and windows. After the ball that night, she was obliged to clamber down from an upstairs window at 5am and walk to the nearest town.

Susan's uncle, Lord Ely, adored telling stories about Ireland and embroidering them with wild embellishments. However, he was also under the thumb of his valet, Woodruffe, a stern believer in truthfulness. If Lord Ely had a story that he wanted to exaggerate, he would send Woodruffe off on an errand and try to complete the tale before Woodruffe's return. This usually failed and the valet would loom back into earshot. Susan: 'I have constantly seen Lord Ely stopped by a warning cough when he had exceeded the bounds of veracity and when Woodruffe's scruples would not allow him any longer to stand quietly by without correcting his master'.

In 1871, Susan married Lt. Col. The Hon. John Stanley (1837-1878), an army veteran of the Crimea and India and, more recently, a witness to the horrors attending the suppression of the Paris Commune. He had narrowly escaped becoming a victim himself, after being arrested first by the Communards on suspicion of being a government spy, then by the Government on suspicion of being a Communard. On both occasions he was rescued by the British Embassy.

THE PARIS COMMUNE

[After the collapse of Napoleon III's Empire at the Battle of Sedan, and the humiliating surrender of Paris to the Germans in 1871, the city had been taken over by a populist left-wing movement. President Thiers, the new leader of the official Versailles government, recaptured Paris after a savage battle with the populace, (Bismarck assisted Thiers by releasing thousands of French prisoners of war to rejoin the Versailles army). Thiers decided to eliminate French socialism by teaching the workers a lesson they would not forget. Twenty thousand Communards were killed in battle or executed on the spot, while forty thousand were either deported or executed later.

One English witness reported: 'I saw an old couple who could not walk the great distance. The woman was a cripple. She said 'Shoot me. I cannot walk any further'. The husband stood by her. They were shot down after thirty shots of revolvers'.

A Versailles general, the Marquis de Galliffet, had 115 men shot dead because they had white hair and therefore were old enough to have been able to fight in the 1848 Revolution.

Stanley said that the German troops had been remarkable in their moderation towards French women. The British ambassador, Lord Lyons, responded: "Yes, but I believe the French thought the Germans were great muffs for showing that consideration". The government troops certainly had no such scruples. Susan: 'The story of how the women of Paris suffered at the hands of the Versailles soldiery has never been written'.

Stanley had an ambivalent attitude to the Communards: "Though I despise them, I have got into a strong, unreasonable sort of sympathy with the best of the Reds. All these agitations against the clergy, violent and vulgar as they are, have a basis of truth'.

Wilde shared this feeling. Although he was repulsed by anarchy and the unthinking violence that surrounded it, he wrote in 'Sonnet to Liberty': 'And I remain unmoved — and yet, and yet, These Christs that die upon the barricades, God knows it I am with them, in some things'. When Oscar saw the Tuilleries Palace ruins, destroyed by the Communards, he commented: "There is not there one little blackened stone which is not to me a chapter in the bible of democracy'.]

Susan and John Stanley, mostly for business reasons, travelled around the USA, where Susan was bewildered by the American habit of providing everyone with a military rank. Susan: 'There was an old mining engineer from Bradford on board who, when we started from Liverpool, was plain Mr Snowden. By the time we got to New York he was Captain Snowden, and when we met him a fortnight later in Utah he had become Colonel Snowden.'

In England she once asked a visiting American General which branch of the army he had served in. He answered: "Well, ma'am, in my country I am Receiver-General, but when I come to England I drop the Receiver".

She was not the only person to comment on this phenomenon. *Sam Ward* said that in Virginia a man was promoted to the rank of Colonel if he killed a rattlesnake. Wilde wrote: 'When I went to Texas I was called 'Captain'; when I got to the centre of the country I was addressed as 'Colonel'; and, on arriving at the borders of Mexico, as 'General'. I didn't mind that but I was much distressed at being called 'Professor'.

After John Stanley died, in 1881 Susan married Francis Jeune (1843-1905), later to become Lord St Helier, and the only bearded judge on the English judiciary. Jeune had been a successful barrister who, in 1869, had been closely involved in the infamous Tichbourne Claimant case.

In 1866, a butcher known as Castro, working in Wagga Wagga, Australia, contacted a bereaved mother, Lady Tichbourne, in England, claiming to be her son, Sir Roger, who had been lost, presumed drowned, at sea in 1854. As such, he was entitled to be the heir to the Hampshire estates and the baronetcy. Lady Tichbourne met him and was convinced by his story. The rest of the family were not.

Francis Jeune was sent to Wagga Wagga where he discovered that 'Castro' was in fact Arthur Orton (1834-1898), who was wanted in Australia for horse theft. Nothing daunted, Orton arrived in England to stake his claim in court.

During the trial, it transpired that 'Sir Roger' did not know his mother's maiden name, did not have the correct tattoos, and did not know the school Roger had attended. While Roger had been slim and spoke French, Orton was 21 stone and did not speak a word of the language. Also, Roger had an abnormally small penis, while Orton was relatively well endowed. Orton's case collapsed. In 1873 he was tried for perjury and received fourteen years hard labour in prison.

[Orton was released in 1884 and became a music hall act, explaining his case. His memory was perpetuated by a genuine music hall star called Harry Relph. When he was a baby, Relph looked a lot like Orton and thus became known as 'LITTLE TICH' (1867-1928). Relph himself was a remarkable figure – only four feet tall, he had an extra finger on each hand, and performed a routine called the 'big-boot dance' in which he would balance on the tips of a pair of boots almost as tall as himself. He died in 1925 after being hit on the head by a mop during his act.)

Francis Jeune, after his involvement in the Orton case, eventually became President of the Divorce Court. One day, when he was out riding with a notorious rake named Hugh Drummond, he decided to remonstrate with his companion over his disreputable behaviour. "My dear Drummond, why on earth don't you marry and settle down?" Drummond snorted back: "Oh, for Heaven's sake, Judge, don't talk shop!"

His position in the Divorce Court gave St Helier forewarning of future trials and scandals. According to *Gertrude Atherton*, on one occasion he was examining some papers for a forthcoming divorce suit that threatened to become a cause célébre. To his horror, he found evidence that implicated his own son.

St Helier immediately hurried the young man out of England to join a regiment in India. Atherton: 'The family honour was saved but the son had barely reached Calcutta when he was stricken with fever and died. The news killed his father.'

Among other things, Lady St Helier was known for her relentless pursuit of famous people whom she could present at her parties, (Atherton: 'Unkind persons called her Mrs Leo Hunter over her celebrity hunting'). Her most notable catch was the writer **THOMAS HARDY** (1840-1928).

Hardy had an air of unsophisticated gravitas that attracted comic remarks especially by his Irish acquaintances. Wilde wrote: 'Thomas Hardy has just found out that women have legs underneath their dresses and this discovery has almost wrecked his life'. *Bernard Shaw* added: 'As we grow older, we become serious and concerned for the opinion of posterity. Thomas Hardy had a portrait destroyed because it depicted him laughing'.

According to his contemporaries, much of Hardy's gloom stemmed from his marriage in 1874 to Emma Gifford. Reporting on his appearance at another St Helier party, Atherton wrote: 'Hardy drifted in. In his wake was an excessively plain, dowdy, high-stomached woman with her hair drawn back in a tight little knot, and a severe cast of countenance. "Mrs Hardy" said TP O'Connor, "Now you may understand the pessimistic nature of the poor devil's work". No doubt Hardy went out so constantly to be rid of her'.

Violet Hunt noted: 'His wife takes the words out of his words all the time. She is a lady much 'superior' to him. The daughter of a consumptive parson, and he the son of a stone mason.' *J-E Blanche* supported this impression: 'Mrs Hardy has an air of saying, 'They are of less social standing than I am'. Manifestly, Hardy was Jude the Obscure. Mrs Hardy told me: "Thomas is very vain and selfish, and the smart people he meets in London encourage his bad habits. They are poison to his system, and I'm the antidote".'

Whatever his marital problems, Hardy always resented the charge of pessimism in his work. He claimed that if he had told the truth about village life, no one would have believed him. According to Lady Dorothy Nevill, this was an accurate view of the countryside.

She described some of the village customs that were still in use almost till the twentieth century. For instance, it was seen as vital to inform a beehive of the death of its owner, or else the hive would dwindle and die. This etiquette required taking the key of the house and knocking it three times against the hive, while shouting to the inmates that their master or mistress was dead.

She also reported that, as late as 1892, under the old belief that food should be provided for a corpse, a Nottinghamshire labourer was buried with a tin of salmon and an opener in his coffin.

Hardy's exposure of some of the seamier sides of rural life provoked critical attack, until the brutally hostile reviews of 'Jude the Obscure' in 1895 convinced him to abandon novel writing.

He was so upset by the reaction that at one London luncheon, when his host showed him a travel memento, (Sitting Bull's war club), Hardy picked up the weapon and muttered: "How much I should like to have that in my hand when I encounter the critic who calls my 'Jude the Obscure', 'Jude the Obscene'!" He did not realise that the actual culprit was sitting next to him.

He could not even find peace in his favourite London club, the Athenaeum. 'While I was sitting there reading quietly, I became aware of the menacing figure of a Bishop striding towards me. I thought I was for it now – but the Bishop passed on by'. Despite this escape, Hardy never wrote another novel and turned instead to poetry.

[Although never a member, Wilde mentioned Hardy's club in 'Dorian Gray': 'I am due at the **ATHENAEUM**. It is the hour when we sleep there. Forty of us, in forty armchairs. We are practising for an English Academy of Letters'.

Frank Harris once told a story about the famously polite Athenaeum porter called Courtney. Courtney could identify any hat, umbrella or walking stick belonging to a member and was never known to make a mistake. One day, a dignified Bishop was handed his belongings as he left the building but complained that the umbrella did not belong to him. Courtney replied with deepest respect: "Possibly not, my Lord, but it is the one you brought into the club."]

Among other contributors whom Wilde gathered for his new magazine, the Woman's World, were three redoubtable female novelists – 'Violet Fane', Edith Nesbit, and 'Ouida'.

LADY MARY CURRIE ('Violet Fane') 1843-1905

Lady Currie, (under her pen name of 'Violet Fane', borrowed from a character in a *Disraeli* novel), provided a poem for the first edition, and an article on the Stuarts the following year.

Born Mary Lamb, in 1864 she married Henry Singleton and was known as Mrs Minnie Singleton. By the 1880s, she was a society hostess, a novelist, and a writer of *Swinburne*-esque poetry, considered improper at the time.

Her statement that: "I am quite unused to good things, as I think I have the nature of a student or the anchorite and that I was intended only to live on roots and nuts in some sort of hole or cave in the rocks', was somewhat at odds with the fact that she lived in a large house in Grosvenor Place, London.

In 1880, Mary became the lover of the adventurer, *WS Blunt*. They acquired a love nest near Victoria Station, and indulged in what Blunt called a 'wholly pagan' affair. Blunt soon found that he was sharing her favours with his own cousin, Philip Currie (1834-1906). In later years, Blunt said of the situation: 'I have always maintained that it is a great bond between men to have loved the same woman – have loved, in the past tense'.

When her husband Henry died in 1893, within the year Mary married the newly knighted Philip, thus becoming Lady Currie. When he became a British Ambassador, she accompanied him firstly to Constantinople, Turkey, (a post he held till 1898), and then to the Rome Embassy until his retirement in 1903.

The future ambassador *Rennell Rodd* said of Mary: "I cannot honestly say that nature had designed her to play the part of Ambassadress. She was essentially bohemian – it requires a certain discipline in early years to merge the bohemian in the diplomatist".

It was while he was in Constantinople in 1893 that Philip Currie, (now created Baron Currie), offered the job of honorary attaché to Wilde's youthful lover, *Lord Alfred Douglas*. However, warned by *Rennell Rodd* of Douglas's suspect reputation, and further annoyed by Douglas's flippant decision to go for a holiday in Paris before turning up for work, Currie rescinded the offer.

Douglas was predictably furious about 'this middle-class fussiness', and snapped: "Had he been a little more grande seignoir he would not have made such a ridiculous fuss – he was only a newly created peer anyway".

Currie made himself equally unpopular in Constantinople; his brusqueness appalled the Sultan, while travelling Britons were infuriated by his arrogance. One snubbed visitor shouted: "You do not seem to be aware of who I am!" Currie sneered back: "No, who the devil are you?" "I am a bloody British tax-payer, one of the people who pay your damn salary!"

When Currie was replaced as British Ambassador in 1898, the miserliness of his successor, Nicholas O'Connor, proved to be even less attractive. The journalist *Herbert Vivian* reported that one visitor to the embassy found O'Connor seated at the immense ambassadorial desk carefully counting the contents of a matchbox he had bought in the streets and complaining: "What cheats these Turks are! This box is supposed to contain 100 matches and I can only find 97!'

Another contributor to Wilde's 'Women's World' was the novelist **EDITH NESBIT** (1858-1924). Described by Noel Coward as 'the most genuine Bohemian I have ever seen', Edith was a founder member of the socialist Fabian Society and the author of the perennial children's book favourite, 'The Railway Children' (1898).

Edith was a firm believer in the 'free love' theories that were emerging at the time. She was supported enthusiastically in these views by her husband, Hubert Bland, whom she had married in 1880, when seven months pregnant. She not only ignored his many affairs but also befriended his girlfriends. When their companion-help, Alice Hoatson, became pregnant by Hubert, the three lived together in a relatively harmonious ménage a trois.

Edith enjoyed several extra-marital affairs of her own, most notably with another of Wilde's ex-lovers, *Richard Le Gallienne*. He was attracted by her 'boyish, bird-like charm', but their planned elopement came to nothing. Even as late as 1905 Edith contemplated another elopement, this time with the Egyptologist Dr Wallis Budge, but he backed out, claiming that it might jeopardise his position at the British Museum.

Her most frustrating experience as a femme fatale came when she tried to seduce *Bernard Shaw*. Although he considered her to be 'a very clever woman' and indulged in a mild flirtation, he turned down the opportunity to sleep with her. Shaw: 'I remember her saying to me, when I refused to let her commit adultery with me, 'You had no right to write the preface if you were not going to write the book'.'

Shaw later explained: 'What nobody realised was that I was raised in Ireland and they did not understand that my natural flirtatiousness was misunderstood by English women. If you pay an Irishwoman a gallant compliment, she grins and says, "Arra, g'long with you." An Englishwoman turns deathly pale and says in a strangled voice, "I hope you meant what you just said". And it's devilish difficult to explain that you didn't.'

By 1910, Edith had lost her popularity as a writer and, in 1914, Hubert Bland died. Edith ended her days married to Tom 'Skipper' Tucker, the captain of the Woolwich ferry, London.

Although born in Bury St Edmunds, Suffolk, Marie de la Ramee, better known by her pen name of OUIDA (1839-1908), spent most of her life living in Florence, Italy. She published 44 works of fiction, and also supplied four articles for Women's World. Oscar called her 'the last of the lionesses'.

Contemporaries portrayed her as cynical and petulant, with a rapier-like repartee that she delivered in a voice 'like a carving knife'. She was noted for her indefatigable efforts to bed young guardsmen at a variety of exclusive hotels. In particular, she pursued the ex-Viceroy of India, *Lord Lytton.* Wilde wrote: 'Ouida loved Lord Lytton with a love that made his life a burden.'

Her taste for grand extravagance, although ameliorated at first by the substantial income from her book sales, led to severe financial difficulties, and she became known for leaving a trail of unpaid hotel bills in her wake. By 1894, as her literary profits declined, she came close to destitution. Wilde, hearing of her troubles, gave her money to cover a return fare to Florence and to pay her rent while there. After a decade of desperate poverty, in 1906 she was granted a civil list pension by the British government.

One quality she never lost was a robustly high opinion of her own talents. She always considered that her flair for painting was superior even to that of her writing, and constantly presented her friends with gifts of her sketches.

One Italian art critic, a Signor Fenzi, visited her apartment and was taken on a tour of what he described as the 'terrible daubs' that hung on her walls. Aghast, he asked who her master was. Ouida snorted: "Master! I never had a master. I would not take a master on any account".

Ouida once remarked that only two people had ever been able to write real English – herself and Lord Byron.

Although Wilde was very successful in his pursuit of 'literary lionesses', he failed to obtain the services of his main quarry, the British Prime Minister's wife, Lady Georgina Salisbury, (born Alderson 1827-1899). She read 'Women's World', but refused to submit an article.

LORD SALISBURY 1830-1903

It was unfortunate that Georgina Salisbury did not write for the magazine, as an insight into her husband's private life would have made rich copy. Robert Gascoyne-Cecil, 3rd Marquess of Salisbury, was descended from one of the leading aristocratic families of England, whose influence stretched back to the sixteenth century. (In 1895, there were suspicions that Wilde's play was satirising the Cecil's family motto: 'Late but in Earnest'.)

Lord Salisbury upheld the family tradition of political service, becoming successively Secretary of State for India, Foreign Secretary, (who played an important role at the Congress of Berlin), and three times Conservative Prime Minister, (1885-86, 1886-92, 1895-1902). However, he was never fully convinced of the legitimacy of the democratic principle: "a dangerous and irrational creed by which two day-labourers shall outvote Baron Rothschild".

Salisbury had an aristocratic contempt for ambition and ostentation. He was such a scruffy dresser that in 1886 he was refused entrance to the Monte Carlo Casino as they thought he was a tramp, and he was once arrested in his own grounds on suspicion of being a poacher. When reproved by the meticulous Prince of Wales for arriving at a function dressed in the coat of one uniform and the trousers of another, he replied airily: "My apologies but my mind must have been occupied by some subject of less importance".

He also suffered from bad eyesight and, at a court ceremony, complained that some young man kept on grinning at him. He was informed that the young man was actually his eldest son.

On one occasion, Salisbury entertained a friend in the library of his home, Hatfield House in Hertfordshire. He had instructed that some decorative alterations be carried out, included fitting a door in the library in such a way that it dovetailed perfectly with the shelves of books and gave the impression of visual continuity. The work had been done so well that Salisbury and his friend spent an hour trying to find the exit, before having to ring for a servant to release them.

Another of Salisbury's foibles was a distrust of experts. Salisbury: 'No lesson seems to be so deeply inculcated by the experience of life as that you should never trust experts. If you believe the doctors, nothing is wholesome; if you believe the theologians, nothing is innocent; if you believe the soldiers, nothing is safe'.

He spent much of his life involved in foreign affairs, and, in 1896, succeeded in preventing war between the United States and Britain over the Venezuela Crisis. A dispute had broken out over the boundary between Venezuela and British Guyana – the Monroe Doctrine clashed with the rights of the British Empire. After months of serious contemplation of war, Salisbury secured a satisfactory arbitration.

Despite such Foreign Office triumphs, according to various reports, Salisbury appeared to have little grasp of the actual terrain. *Frank Harris:* 'Salisbury was blissfully ignorant of geography and gasped with astonishment when told once that Zanzibar was an island.'

Sir Richard Burton: 'He was so ignorant; he didn't know where Mombasa was, and the idea that I had brought back treaties handing over the whole of Central Africa to Britain merely filled him with dismay. He kept repeating 'dreadful responsibility – dreadful'. He was in reality, I believe, a very nice old lady'.

[Wilde did obtain magazine articles from BLANCHE ROOSEVELT MACCHETTA *(1853-1898 – born Tucker), a young American from Ohio, who had married an Italian nobleman. She was an extremely pretty redhead, who had enjoyed a brief singing career at Covent Garden, (which included creating the role of 'Mabel' in Gilbert and Sullivan's 'Pirates of Penzance'), before publishing a novel called 'The Copper Queen'.*

The composer Liszt adored her, while the palmist Cheiro said that 'everyone loved her and everyone called her Blanche, for no title seemed to adorn her more than her own simple Christian name.' (In 1893, it was at a party at Blanche's house at 69, Oakley Street, London, that Cheiro predicted that Wilde's life was due for tragedy). In 1898, Blanche died after receiving fatal injuries in a horse carriage accident in Monte Carlo.]

Blanche provided Oscar with an article on her occasional lover, Guy de Maupassant, a man who she admitted gave her 'the maximum of sensual pleasure'.

GUY DE MAUPASSANT 1850-1893

While grateful for Blanche Macchetta's essay, during the 1880s Wilde was not particularly fond of Maupassant's books. He wrote: 'M. Guy de Maupassant, with his keen mordant irony and his hard vivid style, strips life of the few poor rags that still cover her, and shows us foul sore and festering wound. He writes lurid little tragedies in which everybody is ridiculous; bitter comedies at which one cannot laugh for very tears.' (But by 1899 he had revised this opinion: "I now find much tenderness in him – a great pity for life'.)

In 1889, Oscar circulated a story that he declared to be true. He claimed that Maupassant, on his only visit to London, had gone to an Earls Court restaurant with Blanche and the writer *Henry James*. During the meal, Maupassant asked Henry James to approach a woman at a neighbouring table and tell her that Maupassant wanted to have sex with her.

A horrified James declined at once. Then Maupassant asked him to try the same thing with another woman; an open-mouthed James speechlessly shook his head. When Maupassant tried with yet a third woman, Henry James rose and fled from the restaurant.

Frank Harris described Maupassant as 'a typical Frenchman, in many ways, kindly, good-humoured and fair-minded'. Brought up in Normandy, Maupassant became a civil service clerk in Paris, but soon began to lead a bohemian life, partying at the Seine riverside haunts immortalised by the French Impressionist artists. He was a muscular, physically fit young man who could row a boat fifty miles in a single day.

As well as rowing, he flung himself into the orgiastic atmosphere of drinking and sex that flourished on the riverbanks. He probably contracted syphilis from these encounters, although neither he nor his doctors suspected it until far too late. Maupassant: 'Beware of the embraces of girls you find on the wayside'.

Encouraged by his friendship with the great French writer Gustave Flaubert, (who was rumoured to be his father), Maupassant began to write. Known as 'Guy the Obscene', nearly all his early work was pornographic; his 1880 poem 'Au Bord de l'Eau' landed him before the magistrates on a charge of 'outraging decency and public morality'. Flaubert only just managed to extract him from the scrape.

Under the new influence of *Emile Zola*, Maupassant published a short story called 'Boule de Suif', based on a real incident during the Franco-Prussian War, when a Rouen prostitute called Adrienne Legay had been forced to sleep with a Prussian officer. The story was acclaimed as a masterpiece, and Maupassant was seen as a new and important proponent of 'realism' – 'Life is never so good nor so bad as you think'.

He followed this success with a series of brilliant novels and stories, among them, 'La Maison Tellier' (1881), 'M. Fifi' (1882), 'Une Vie' (1883), and 'Bel Ami' (1885). The wealth that his books provided led him to abandon his civil service career with relief, and immerse himself in the life of a rich man, with a villa at the Cap d'Antibes and a yacht named 'Bel Ami'. (He never lost a certain realistic streak though: 'The rich always fear the poor, and they have good reason for their instinctive dread.')

However, Maupassant was much prouder of his sexual exploits than any of his books: 'I prefer in reality a pretty girl to all the arts. I would put a good dinner – a really good one – almost on the same level as a pretty girl. There's my creed'. Even in the promiscuous world of nineteenth century Paris, Maupassant's sexual tally of literally thousands of young women was seen as exceptional: 'I love the flesh of women with the same love as I have for the grass, the river, and the sea'.

The secret of his success lay in his phenomenal sexual endurance; he could perform again and again without resting. When his mentor Flaubert doubted his boasts, Maupassant, accompanied by an accountant as a witness, went to a Parisian brothel and 'had six girls in an hour'. A visiting Russian writer testified that he had watched Maupassant have six consecutive bouts with a Folies Bergere dancer and, after finishing with her, went to another room and had sex four more times with a young prostitute.

Some of his partners were extraordinary women in their own right. The bisexual Giselle d'Estoc, who wore men's clothes and had short-cropped hair, attracted his attention after she had stabbed her trapeze-artist lover, Emma Bouer, in a fight. Giselle was especially useful to Maupasssant as, in addition to supplying him with hashish, she would bring her lesbian girlfriends to share the bed.

Another mistress was the hugely wealthy Countess Emmanuela Potocka, an Italian princess who had married a Polish count. She was famous for holding what she called her 'Maccabee dinners' – orgiastic parties attended by all the men who had declared that they would die for her love.

As well as some 'honorary lovers' such as *Count de Montesquiou* and *Lord Lytton*, the guests included a young man who was so captivated by the scene that he walked home nude, and Missy, (the lesbian daughter of the Duc de Morny and lover of the novelist *Colette*), who performed a trapeze act above the dining table.

A philosopher called Caro was banned from the dinners and was reputed to have died from chagrin, while another thwarted lover threatened to shoot himself if she did not return to him. She replied tartly: "You have been promising me you would do it for so long now'. When the painter *J-E Blanche* also offered to kill himself, Potocka laughed him off and instead forced him, at the point of a revolver, to paint her portrait.

There may have been another motive as well as lust behind all this attention. So many people borrowed money from Potocka that her Paris house became known as 'the Polish Bank'.

Maupassant's fame led to Baron Ferdinand de Rothschild inviting him to visit England. Maupassant response to the country was lukewarm: "Too many tooth-brushes and not enough bidets". When he stayed at Rothschild's Waddesdon Manor home near Aylesbury, he was introduced to many local notables, including the future King George V, *Lord Salisbury*, and the Archbishop of Canterbury, *Edward Benson*. Inspecting the gathering for his usual quarry, Maupassant was underwhelmed: 'Not many women here. The wife of the Archbishop does not give me any desire to make the eminent churchman a cuckold'.

Maupassant once told *Frank Harris* ('with a certain exaltation') that: "The only woman I really love is the Unknown who haunts my imagination".

By 1890, he had succumbed gradually to the syphilis that had haunted him since his Seine riverbank days. Tormented by hallucinations, he tried to commit suicide. His attempt to shoot himself failed, (as his valet had removed the bullets from the pistol), as did a bungled effort to stab himself with a paper knife. His attempt to throw himself from an upper window was also frustrated as he was unable to open the shutters.

Finally his servants held him down until he could be removed to an asylum. Once there he went fully insane, (*Edmond Goncourt*: 'Maupassant begins to turn into an animal'), and died aged 43.

It was from his office at Belle Sauvage Yard on Ludgate Hill, London, that in November 1887 Wilde issued the first edition of the magazine, 'Women's World'. It was his only full-time job and lasted from May 1887 till October 1889, when he received notice of termination from the parent company, Cassells.

His sub-editor, Arthur Fish, said: "True it only incurred his attendance at La Belle Sauvage twice a week – on the mornings of Tuesday and Thursday – but the very fact that regularity in any form became a factor in his life seemed an incongruity".

A further hindrance to work was Cassell's insistence on a no smoking rule at the office and Oscar's stay was limited by how long he could stay there without having a cigarette.

Much of the magazine was concerned with fashion. Oscar claimed to have seen in a French journal the instruction: 'With this style the mouth is worn slightly open' – a statement he was to echo in 'The Importance of Being Earnest': 'Style largely depends on the way the chin is worn. They are worn very high, just at present'.

In essence he mistrusted the very idea of fashionable modernity: 'Nothing is so dangerous as being too modern. One is apt to grow old-fashioned quite suddenly', and eventually dismissed the whole concept: 'Fashion is what one wears oneself. What is unfashionable is what other people wear'.

The year previously, the Haymarket Riots had broken out in Chicago, after an unknown attacker had thrown a bomb at policemen engaged in breaking up a union demonstration. Several police were killed and their companions fired on the crowd in retaliation. Several union leaders were condemned to death as a result, prompting an international outcry.

In Britain, among the supporters of a campaign to reprieve the men were the anarchist Prince Kropotkin, the socialist Robert Cunningham-Graham, and the writer Bernard Shaw.

Possibly feeling a desire for more serious involvement, Wilde agreed to sign a clemency petition arranged by Shaw. It was to no avail and the union men were hanged on November 11, 1887.

BERNARD SHAW 1856-1950

Bernard Shaw said of the petition: "The only name I got was that of Oscar Wilde. It was really a very handsome thing of him to do, because all the associations of the thing were vulgar and squalid, and Oscar was a snob to the marrow of his bones, having been brought up in Merrion Square, Dublin".

The relationship between these two great Irish playwrights, (just two years apart in age and born less than a mile from each other), remained one of wary respect. They met fewer than a dozen times, firstly in 1879 at one of Oscar's mother's receptions, where Shaw reported that: 'We put each other out frightfully; and this odd difficulty persisted between us to the very last'.

Shaw: 'You must always remember that we were Irishmen, resenting strongly the English practice of making pets of Irishmen'. 'The press treated both of us as jokes; he was Oscar the comic, I was GBS the clown. The result was that we treated one another with elaborate courtesy… and our relationship was really unendurable for both of us'.

They did meet once for an afternoon in 1886 in the unlikely surroundings of a naval exhibition in Chelsea and reputedly reduced each other to tears of laughter. Shaw: 'It was my sole experience of Oscar's wonderful gift as a raconteur'.

Shaw was less pleased when he heard of another Wildean quip, but said: "I did not dislike Wilde; and I don't think he disliked me, though he did say of me – 'An excellent man: he has no enemies; and none of his friends like him'. And that's quite true; they don't like me; but they are my friends, and some of them love me."

When Oscar expressed interest in Socialism, he accompanied Shaw, *Kropotkin*, and *Stepniak* to a lecture by the leftwing journalist, Henry Quelch, (Oscar: "A splendid name for a bourgeois Marat"), and was inspired by one of Shaw's own lectures to write the 1891 essay called 'The Soul of Man Under Socialism'. Shaw wrote of this work: 'It was very witty and entertaining, but had nothing whatever to do with socialism'.

Shaw was much more complimentary about Wilde's first three popular plays, reviewing them with the aside that: 'As far as I can ascertain, I am the only person in London who cannot sit down and write an Oscar Wilde play at will. The fact that his plays, though apparently lucrative, remain unique under these circumstances says much for the self-denial of our scribes'. But he decried 'The Importance of Being Earnest' as 'a soulless farce'.

Almost by chance, Shaw happened to be at the Café Royal lunch in April 1895 when *Frank Harris* implored Wilde not to launch his doomed legal action against the Marquess of Queensberry and instead retreat to Paris. Shaw agreed with Harris, but the idea was quashed by the intervention of Wilde's lover, *'Bosie' Douglas* – in Shaw's words, 'a wretched little brat'. (Shaw and Douglas, however, did have an extended correspondence thirty years later).

Shaw remained a principled supporter of Wilde during his trials and imprisonment, and organised an abortive petition for Oscar's early release. He argued with typical Shavian practicality that if Wilde's health broke down in prison he would not be able to earn his living on his release. When Oscar's sentence ended, the two writers, although they did not meet, politely exchanged copies of their newly published works.

Shaw described Oscar as 'a citizen of all civilised capitals', but 'at root a very Irish Irishman, and as such a foreigner everywhere but in Ireland'. On reading the 1905 version of Wilde's letter, 'De Profundis', Shaw wrote: 'The unquenchable spirit of the man is magnificent', but refused to sentimentalise him: 'Please let us hear no more of the tragedy of Oscar Wilde. Oscar was no tragedian. He was the supreme comedian of his century, one to whom misfortune, disgrace, imprisonment were external and traumatic. His gaiety of soul was invulnerable. Even on his deathbed he played it for laughs'.

Wilde was tolerant of Shaw but had reservations: 'A man of real ability but with a bleak mind. Humour gleams as of wintry sunlight on a bare, harsh landscape', a view endorsed by *Max Beerbohm*: 'The best brain in England but no beauty except that of an engine'.

Born into a genteel but impoverished Dublin family, Shaw described Ireland as 'an island entirely surrounded by footlights'. After working as a junior clerk in an estate agency, in 1876 he moved to London. Shaw: 'I showed my appreciation of my native land in the usual Irish way, by getting out of it as soon as I possibly could'. 'It is only the Irishman whose enthusiasm for his birthplace increases the further away from it he is'.

For nine discouraging years, Shaw's career stalled. He wrote five novels between 1879 and 1883, none of which found a publisher.

(Later he was to describe what happened when he became famous, when 'publishers fell over themselves in the rush to print anything that bore my name'. 'Suddenly, these youthful horrors were resurrected for public consumption. But the buffoons started printing them in the wrong order; starting at the last one and working back to the first'. After his fifth novel came out to reasonable sales, they then published the fourth one – 'in the criticising of which, the more thoughtful reviewers, unaware that the publisher was working backwards, pointed out 'the marked advance in Shaw's style', 'the surer grip', 'the clearer form', 'the more mature view of the world', and so forth'.)

In 1883, Shaw became a convert to Socialism and joined the Fabian Society, (Vladimir Lenin was later to say that: "Shaw was a good man fallen among Fabians".) He became successively an art critic, a music critic (under the pen name of 'Corno di Bassetto'), and a drama critic, (a post he finally relinquished in 1898).

In 1892, strongly influenced by Ibsen, he wrote the first of several plays, none of which received a proper public performance at the time. However as he remarked: "Man is a creature of habit. You cannot write three plays and then stop". His first real success came in the USA, where an American actor called Richard Mansfield produced 'The Devil's Disciple' to some acclaim. Mansfield's wife said that her husband went down on his knees every night and thanked God for 'The Devil's Disciple' and always finished his prayer with: "But, O God, why did it have to be by Shaw?"

Having remained a virgin until the age of 29, Shaw succumbed to the advances of Mrs Jenny Patterson, (a lady who appears to have cut a swathe through the younger men in London, including Wilde's associate *Rennell Rodd*).

Shaw then entered a period of mostly sexless 'philandering', but always with an eye to the avoidance of marriage. Shaw: 'Real married life is too often the story of the youth and the maiden who pluck a flower from the mountainside and bring down an avalanche on their shoulders'.

He said of women that 'their great art is to lie low, and let the imagination of the male endow them with depths', (a very similar view to Wilde's: 'Women are sphinxes without secrets'). Shaw also revealed a distinctly human side with his comment: 'The fickleness of the women I have loved is only equalled by the infernal constancy of the women who have loved me'.

However in 1899, he met and married Charlotte Payne-Townshend – 'my green-eyed Irish millionairess' – and by 1905 they moved into the house at Ayot St Lawrence, Hertfordshire that remained their lifelong home. According to Shaw, despite sharing a harmonious domesticity, they never actually made love.

Through the early twentieth century, Shaw's plays became world famous, and he was known and feared for his scathingly accurate and iconoclastic criticisms. He described all the professions as being "conspiracies against the laity". In the spirit of Wilde's view on fox-hunting, ('the unspeakable in full pursuit of the uneatable'), Shaw was once asked by a bluff country gentleman: "I suppose you're one of those chappies who are against killing for pleasure, eh?" Shaw genially shook his head: "Oh, no, no, not at all. It depends on who you kill".

As a young man, Shaw had become a staunch vegetarian after reading the poet Percy Shelley. In spite of this belief, though, he once refused to attend a gala dinner in his honour because the bill of fare was vegetarian. He explained that: "the thought of two thousand people all crunching celery at the same time was too much even for me".

(Oscar Wilde was did not share Shaw's culinary tastes. Wilde: 'The most violent republicans I know are all vegetarians: Brussels sprouts seem to make people bloodthirsty, and those who live on lentils and artichokes are always calling for the severed heads of kings'.)

In 1913, in his only, (probably unconsummated), extra-marital intrigue, Shaw became blindly infatuated with the actress, *Mrs Patrick Campbell*. She said that, although he was the greatest writer she knew, he was hopeless with love letters. She quoted one of them to prove his incapacity as a romantic: 'Oh, my love, if it were not for my work on Sir Horace Plunkett's agricultural co-operative scheme, I would fly to you'.

At the start of the First World War, Shaw's popularity plummeted when he fiercely attacked the warmongers in a pamphlet called 'Common Sense About the War'. Shaw: 'Any person who has persuaded himself that…. of two custom-houses a few hundred yards apart, one is full of murderers and villains and the other of angels and heroes, clearly ought to be in Broadmoor Asylum and not editing a newspaper'.

He commented on the outcome: 'I was attacked as being pro-German; a pro-German being any person who kept his head amid the prevailing lunacy. *Henry Arthur Jones* said that England was his mother and I had kicked her on her deathbed; ever since he has treated me as a diabolical criminal anarch. I was excommunicated from every tennis club, every golf club, and amazingly from the County Wexford Bee-Keepers Association, an organisation that I had not the faintest memory of ever joining'.

After 1918, much of general opinion began to swing behind Shaw's views and he returned to favour. In 1925, he was awarded the Nobel Prize for Literature. Shaw: 'Heaven knows why they chose 1925. It must have been to reward me because it was the one year that I hadn't written anything'.

By now he had created such classic plays as 'Pygmalion', (later to become adapted as the musical 'My Fair Lady'), 'Man and Superman', and 'Saint Joan'. He claimed that he had wished to write about a historical character but Joan of Arc was not his first choice.

He had considered a Protestant play about the Dutch leader, William the Silent: 'but the idea of William being Silent at the top of his voice for four hours in a Shaw play was too bizarre even for me'. He even considered Mahomet as a topic but was worried 'that some Arab fanatic

238

might decide to assassinate me for blasphemy – assassination being the sincerest form of censorship'.

Although he was often criticised for intellectual ostentation, in fact Shaw always retained the disarming Irish habit of self-mockery: 'I possess a small secret. Every time I see a Chekhov play, I want to go home and burn one of mine'.

In 1931, Shaw visited Soviet Russia; he approved generally of communism and defended it against what he saw as the twin evils of capitalism and fascism. Shaw: 'I never met Marx personally. He was not an infallible man, but what he did do was to impress upon the world that the economic constitution of society was at the bottom of practically everything in society'. He met the Soviet leader, Josef Stalin, who said of Shaw that 'he was an awful man' – something of a backhanded accolade.

Shaw was not enthusiastic over his 1933 trip to the USA, and in particular its politics: 'I have become accustomed to regard the usual American President as a statesman whose mouth is the most efficient part of his head.'

He was especially critical of capitalism disguising itself as fake democracy: 'They hark back to the principles of 1776 with ludicrous reverence. The America of George Washington is as dead as Queen Anne. Admittedly, America has no Star Chamber and no feudal barons. But it has Trusts and it has millionaires whose factories, fenced in by live electric wires and defended by Pinkerton retainers with magazine rifles, would have made a radical of George the Third. Would Washington or Benjamin Franklin have lifted a finger in the cause of American independence, if they could have seen its reality?'

Generally though Shaw preferred to remain at home and only travelled to please his wife. In Sweden he had an awkward meeting with the playwright August Strindberg: 'After a few words of greeting and some further conversation consisting mainly of embarrassed silence, a pale smile or two from Strindberg, and floods of energetic eloquence in a fearful lingo, half French, half German, from myself, Strindberg took out his watch and said in German, "At two o'clock, I am going to be sick".'

Shaw's fame continued to expand when Hollywood took up his plays as material for films. He regarded their efforts with amused toleration: "The film director, Gabriel Pascal, rang me to say that, in box office terms, I am now bigger than Greta Garbo. I suppose this is meant to cheer me up. The Hollywood people suggested Garbo to play St. Joan. I am convinced that, if the play was about the Blessed Virgin Mary, they would suggest Mae West".

The distinctively obese film director Alfred Hitchcock visited Shaw at Ayot St Lawrence. After glancing at Shaw's tall, bony frame, Hitchcock laughed and said: "One look at you, Mr Shaw, and I know there is a famine in the land!" Shaw, without missing a beat, retorted: "And one look at you, Mr Hitchcock, and I know who caused it!"

By the end of his life, Shaw had become a feted international figure, but always kept his mischievous streak. One of the guests at his 90th birthday party was the Scotland Yard detective, Inspector Fabian. At the detective's suggestion, Shaw agreed to have his fingerprints taken for posterity. To their surprise, the fingerprints were so faint that no impression could be taken. Shaw looked at Fabian and muttered: "Well, if I had known this sooner I should certainly have chosen another profession".

While pruning an apple tree at Ayot, he fell and died aged 94. In an atmosphere of world loss, Broadway dimmed its lights and the Indian government, under his friend Pandit Nehru, adjourned a Cabinet meeting in honour of his memory.

Another prominent member of the campaign to stop the Chicago hangings was Prince Kropotkin.

PRINCE PETER KROPOTKIN 1842-1921

Wilde: 'A map of the world that does not include Utopia is not worth even glancing at'.

When they met at William Morris's house in 1888, Kropotkin made a profound impression on Wilde. Oscar wrote that the Prince was 'a man with the soul of that beautiful white Christ that seems to be coming out of Russia'.

Kropotkin even seemed to steer him away from doctrinaire Socialism towards a more anarchic view. Wilde: 'The form of government that is most suitable to the artist is no government at all'. "I think I am rather more than a Socialist. I am something of an Anarchist, I believe; but, of course, the dynamite policy is very absurd indeed'.

Kropotkin himself was ambivalent about the use of violence in pursuit of political ends. His creed was independence of thought, compassion to the unfortunate and rebellion to authority, and he was known for his gentleness, modesty, and sincerity. Not even his enemies ever denied his admirable character. But he felt that he could not condemn the anarchists for the occasional outrage, when such events as the State massacre of thousands during the Paris Commune were ignored.

Born into an aristocratic Russian family, (whose forbears had once ruled the Principality of Kiev), the young Kropotkin had caught the eye of Tsar Nicholas I and he was ordered to join the select military academy of the Corps of Pages. Kropotkin was quickly disillusioned with life at court and in the military, especially after his elder brother was killed during the Crimean War.

He felt more kinship with the Russian serfs than with his fellows. He enjoyed the then current story about one large estate owner who, during a time of agrarian unrest, had gathered his serfs together and reminded them that he had always treated them well. Therefore, there was no reason for them to attack him.

His peasants assured him that they had no intention of committing any such act. They went on to explain: "We have made an arrangement with the serfs on the estate of your neighbour. We shall attack him, and his serfs will attack you".

In 1862, Kropotkin made a surprise transferral to the Mounted Cossacks of the Amur, an unfashionable regiment in Siberia. Even the Tsar was puzzled as to why he was ending his life as a courtier.

Kropotkin made five journeys of exploration in the Far East, including a rescue mission to save a starving colony of convicts, (which involved a return journey of 10,000 miles during a Siberian winter), charting an unknown area of northern Siberia, and using disguise to travel on a dangerous spying mission into China.

His shock at witnessing the brutal Tsarist suppression of a rebellion of Polish convicts at a Siberian salt mine determined his decision to leave the army. 'I lost in Siberia whatever faith in State discipline I had cherished before. I was prepared to become an anarchist'.

After four years of writing about the geography of Asia, he decided that he could no longer stay aloof from politics. He wrote that he wished to follow 'the path of the narodnik, the man who seeks out the people'.

In 1872, he visited Switzerland where he became caught up in the divisions between Karl Marx and Mikhail Bakunin. Kropotkin rejected Marx's belief in State socialism, based on authority, because: 'although a new government would consist of former workers, as soon as they become rulers, they would cease to be workers, and would begin to look down upon the manual workers from the heights of the State'. He preferred Bakunin's anarchic ideas on the abolition of the State and its replacement by a federal society based on free communes.

Returning to Russia, he met *Sergei Stepniak* and they colluded on producing revolutionary pamphlets. Kropotkin's identity was eventually betrayed to the police and he was thrown into a squalid cell in the prison fortress of Peter-and-Paul, St Petersburg.

In 1876, after two years incarceration, an elaborate plot, partly hatched by Stepniak, succeeded in breaking Kropotkin out of prison. During an exercise hour, Kropotkin made a run for the prison gate. Just as he was about to be bayoneted by a guard, a coach hurtled up and snatched him away. Quickly acquiring a disguise, Kropotkin accompanied his rescuers to a smart restaurant while the hue and cry raged across the city – nobody in the Tsarist secret police thought of looking for him in such a place. He was smuggled out of the country to Finland, and then landed in Hull, England.

After some years in Europe, during which he married a young Russian girl, Sophie Ananiev, dodged Tsarist assassins, and spent three years in a French prison on a charge of belonging to the Internationale, Kropotkin finally settled in England in 1886. He lived a frugal and stable life in Harrow, London, practising carpentry and gardening, and making a living through journalism and lecture tours.

He was perplexed by English attitudes. At one Royal Geographical Society dinner, he stayed true to his principles and sternly remained seated as the company rose to toast 'The Queen'. Expecting to be rebuked at the very least, Kropotkin wrote: 'I was thunderstruck when immediately afterwards the same chairman cried: "Long Live Prince Kropotkin" – and everybody without exception rose again'.

He made several lecture tours of the USA, once having afternoon tea with the black educator (and ex-slave), Booker T Washington, and the widow of the former Confederate leader, *Jefferson Davis* – an unlikely trio. However, in 1901, a young Pole, claiming to be an anarchist, assassinated President McKinley. From then on anarchists, including Kropotkin, became persona non grata in the USA.

William Morris wrote that Kropotkin once told him a story that shone an interestingly Russian view on the development of North America.

'There was a little colony of Russians in the far west of America right among the Redskins; one day the Redskins fell on them and burnt their fields and lifted their cattle: now if they had been Yankees they would have shouldered their rifles and gone after the Redskins, and shot as many as they could; and so have established a regular deadly feud between them.

'But the Russians bided their time and, watching an opportunity, kidnapped all the women of the tribe and brought them home to their own blockhouse, where they kept them fast but treated them well.

'Then the Redskins came to them, and demanded their return. The Russians said that they would do so but only after the Redskins did something for them first. 'You must till our land again that you burned.' 'We don't know how.' 'Never mind, we'll teach you.'

'So the Redskins turned to and, as they worked between the plough-stilts and otherwise, the Russians stood by and encouraged them. Then the work done, the Redskins got their women again and they had a feast together, and were very good friends ever after'.

When the revolution overthrew the Tsarist regime in 1917, Kropotkin returned home in triumph, hoping to establish a republican government similar to the USA. This hope died with the swift move to power of the Bolsheviks, whom Kropotkin called 'the Jesuits of Socialism'. Although the Bolsheviks began a persecution of the anarchists, they left Kropotkin alone. He held a position similar to that of Tolstoy under the Tsars – the authorities did not wish to create a high profile martyr.

Through the savage civil war that attended the birth of Soviet Russia, (and claimed 12 million lives), Kropotkin lived in a small village called Dmitrov near Moscow. For all his dislike of the Bolsheviks, he was even more opposed to the reactionary White Russians, backed by the Western blockade and the armed incursions by capitalist troops. He saw them as 'unleashing seas of blood'.

He met the Bolshevik leader, Vladimir Lenin, several times and accused him of creating 'a typical unsuccessful revolution'. Kropotkin eventually despaired of the future, coming to a Tolstoyan conclusion that groups or individuals could not hope to control things; they could only ride the crest of events and hope to turn them to their own advantage. (Wilde had hinted at this: 'Those who try to lead the people can only do so by following the mob'.)

When he died in 1921, the Bolshevik offer of a state funeral was turned down as an insult to the old anarchist. The Red Army did attend the ceremony, but came unarmed as a mark of respect. Thousands of others also attended and, in probably the last demonstration against Bolshevism for seventy years, carried banners declaring Kropotkin's theme – 'Where there is authority there is no freedom'.

Two days after the Chicago hangings, on November 13, 1887, police broke up a protest march in Trafalgar Square, London, in an incident known as Bloody Sunday. One protestor was killed and dozens injured. Wilde and Shaw were involved on the peripheries of the fight, while Kropotkin and Robert Cunningham-Graham were on the march itself.

ROBERT CUNNINGHAM-GRAHAM 1852-1936

Even in an age of unusual adventurers, Robert Cunningham-Graham led a remarkable life. Described by the Times as 'the aristocratic Socialist and cowboy dandy', as a character he was incorrigible, as a politician he was incorruptible. A future Prime Minister, Ramsay Macdonald, said of him: "Graham's socialism was based on romantic ideas of freedom and his profound feeling for the bottom dog. He was a very typical Scot."

Wilde met him in the 1880s and wrote to Graham's wife: 'Give my love to your delightful and dangerous husband'. Graham himself recorded meeting Oscar during his 1895 trials and committing 'a gaffe I will regret to my dying day'.

Graham had met Oscar while the latter was sitting on a bench in Rotten Row, Hyde Park. Oscar explained the appalling situation he was in, and asked for Graham's advice. Without thinking, Graham raised his arm and, pointing at his temple with the first finger, imitated a pistol shot. Wilde burst into tears and sobbed: "I know it's the only way out, but I haven't the courage". Graham admitted that he had shocked himself by his own insensitivity.

In 1897, when Wilde sent out copies of his 'Ballad of Reading Gaol' to friends, he said that the only person to respond for some time had been Graham, with 'a charming letter'. After Wilde's death, Graham read 'De Profundis', Oscar's famous letter from prison, and commented: "I am glad he never repented. How one hates penitents".

Graham was born into a family of minor Scottish nobility and attended Harrow School for a short time. Then in 1869, aged seventeen, he went off to the Argentine in search of profit. He was given a rapid introduction to South American life by being recruited into a rebel army at the point of a dagger, and reluctantly joining his new colleagues in a campaign of pillage across the pampas.

While spending his time escaping battles, typhus, and prisons, Graham became a superb horseman. He was accepted by the gauchos as one of their own and was given the nickname of 'Don Roberto'.

His next exploit was to attempt to drive horses north through Paraguay, still in the throes of its own horrific civil war, up to Brazil. On the journey, all his men deserted, and Graham, unable to break his way through the Brazilian jungle and facing attack from blowpipe-wielding tribesmen, had to escape with his one remaining horse by floating down river on a raft.

Ending up in Montevideo, he reported that all his friends were dead: 'drink, shot, or married'.

Back in the Argentine, he survived an Indian attack that left hundreds of others dead along the frontier, and rode bareback through the night to reach a settlement on the River Plate, where his pursuers were driven off by cannon fire.

Flat broke, he worked in a Buenas Aires road gang till he raised the fare to sail back to England. On the returning ship, the crew got drunk and mutinied. They were overcome by passengers and locked below deck, leaving Graham to steer the ship home.

While perfecting his skill as a sword fencer in Paris, he met, eloped with, and married the 18-year-old Gabrielle de la Balmondiere, ostensibly a Chilean aristocrat. (In the 1970s, research by Lady Polwarth discovered her genuine name was Caroline Horsfall, daughter of a Yorkshire doctor, who had run away from home to become an actress).

In 1878, the couple, again in search of a fortune, arrived in New Orleans, but departed soon afterwards, as Graham had duelled with 'a certain gentleman who came out second best'. They moved on to Texas, a state that Graham despised; he said it was a place where murder was as common as cactus and where there were about ten different churches all hating each other for the glory of God: "The churches in Texas seem to be based on spite."

The Grahams decided that their best financial prospect was to export cotton into Mexico. Having fought off Indian and bandit attacks on their way south from the Texan border, they arrived in Mexico City to find that the bottom had fallen out of the cotton market. Thwarted and almost penniless again, Graham renamed himself 'Professor Bontini' and opened a fencing academy in the city, while Gabrielle gave guitar lessons.

Returning to Texas, Graham lost his remaining cash when his new cattle ranch was destroyed by another Indian attack. Gabrielle left for New Orleans to give language lessons, while Graham became an interpreter for *Buffalo Bill Cody's* hunting expeditions. They cleared enough money for the return home.

Once back in England, Graham became interested in socialist politics and befriended such like-minded men as *Bernard Shaw*, Keir Hardie, John Burns, and the Irish republican, James Connolly, (later executed during the 1916 Easter Rising.)

(Graham was present at the founding of the Independent Labour Party in 1889 – this was at a time when his brother Charles Cunningham-Graham was commanding Queen Victoria's royal yacht, the Osborne.)

In 1886, Graham was elected to Parliament for a Scottish constituency and arrived in London for his maiden speech, an event, then as now, meant to be jovial and non-controversial. Graham, a tall, strikingly handsome man with long flowing hair, rode down to the House of Commons on his favourite Argentinian horse Pampa.

Ignoring the polite conventions, Graham's speech began by describing the Liberal members as 'crutch-and-toothpick gentlemen'. Turning to the subject of House of Lords bishops, he continued: "I need not remind the House that when the debates for abolition of slavery took place in the Lords, almost every bishop voted for its retention. Therefore I am not inclined to attach much importance to the testimony of bishops".

On the subject of Empire, he said that the only real pillar of British civilisation was the Hotchkiss machine-gun, while he described the Conservative domestic policies as: "A society in which capital and luxury makes a Heaven for thirty thousand and a Hell for thirty million. A society which has placed the mainspring of human action, and the absolute power to pay labour and to reward honour, in the greasy pocket of the capitalist."

The Radical members were told that they: "are all Tories in disguise, trying to get their snouts into the State swill. They are men of straw. The bottle-washers of capitalism."

Leaving the Commons aghast, he strode out of the chamber into the Palace Yard, leapt on his huge black stallion, and galloped off up Whitehall.

Graham heartily despised his party leader, *William Gladstone*. Once, after Graham had delivered another fiery and politically embarrassing speech, Gladstone decided to give him a moral lecture. The Prime Minister's usual method of intimidation was to keep his victim standing in silence for some moments, then Gladstone would rise and stare at him while tapping the table with his finger. Usually it worked, but Graham simply stared back bringing his face closer and closer to Gladstone's, until the latter was forced to drop his gaze.

Partly as a response to the imprisonment of William O'Brien and *Wilfred Blunt* for agitating over Irish Home Rule, a protest meeting was called in Trafalgar Square, London, on November 13, 1887. The authorities were determined to block it and the Metropolitan Police chief, Sir Charles Warren, put 4000 police in position in the square, with 300 Grenadier Guards and 400 Life Guards in reserve.

The event turned into what became known as 'Bloody Sunday'; the police smashed up many of the protest processions before they even reached the square, while those protesters who did arrive were attacked by mounted police with batons. Many people were injured and one was killed.

(The conductor of a bus from Charing Cross, en route to the West End, decided instead to offer circular sight-seeing trips of the square at two pence a head and did a roaring trade. One man stayed on for six trips and remained unscathed through the thickest of the fighting.)

Cunningham-Graham and John Burns, marching with the protestors, arrived at the square, where Graham used his equine skills to calm the police horses and slip through their ranks before anyone noticed. Unfortunately they were soon spotted and beaten up so badly by police that Graham's skull was cracked open. John Burns, an excellent boxer, stood over him in defence.

They were arrested and beaten with rifle butts as they were frogmarched through the ranks of the Grenadier Guards who were drawn up on the steps of the National Gallery. Burns said later that: "We had the satisfaction of having had what was probably the biggest police escort in English history".

They spent the night in a cell where Graham, who had been badly hurt, tried to stem the blood flow from his head. Burns tried to cheer him up by singing bits of 'The Mikado'.

Next morning in court, despite the presence of such friends as the future Home Secretary *Richard Haldane*, the future Prime Minister *HH Asquith*, the future suffragette Mrs Pankhurst, and Oscar Wilde, Cunningham-Graham was found guilty of 'unlawful assembly and assault on the police' and received a six week sentence in Pentonville prison.

After he left the Commons in 1892, Graham resumed his travels, this time arriving in Morocco where he befriended *Walter Harris*, (Cyril Wilde's godfather). *Bernard Shaw* was to base his play, 'Captain Brassbound's Conversion', on Graham's adventures in North Africa.

In 1897, Graham was captured in the Atlas Mountains by a notoriously brutal local chieftain. One of the man's specialities was to imprison his slaves and prisoners at night by lowering them down by rope into a deep well and rolling a boulder over the top. Graham was subjected to this treatment, but found a way to smuggle out two letters.

One went to the British consul asking for aid. The other one went to *Frank Harris*, the editor of the Saturday Review. It read: 'I fear it will be impossible for me to review the book you sent as I have spent the last four days as a prisoner down a well in the Atlas Mountains'.

On another occasion, while riding in the Moroccan desert, Graham was waylaid by a gang of fanatical Moslems. Brandishing rifles and knives, they demanded: "Are you a Christian?" Graham roared back: "No! I'm a United Presbyterian!" This so puzzled the gang that they let him go.

In 1914, when war broke out, Graham volunteered immediately for the Rough Rider Corps but was rejected as being, at 62, too old. Instead he was given the rank of colonel and sent to the Argentine to bring back horses for the cavalry. The gauchos were amazed that care should be taken to provide only the best horses, as they would all be dead within a few months.

Graham: 'When the last animal had passed and the gate swung to, a young gaucho rode to my side and looking at the herd said, "The dead salute you. This is the last time they will feed in Bopicua".' (8,000,000 horses died in WWI.)

On the return trip, the ship was torpedoed in the English Channel but the captain managed to run the vessel on to a sandy beach where all the passengers and horses were safely landed.

Graham hurried to London to give a verbal report about what had happened. The War Office official began the interview by rebuking Graham for not wearing a uniform. An initially amused Graham told the general that he had never bothered to buy one, but that he had brought the horses safe home. When the now furious general spluttered: "Indeed! And why the devil did you beach the ship?", Graham's blood boiled over and he roared back: "For fun!"

He had some more dealings with British politics later in his life. In one election he was persuaded to stand as an Independent Liberal, but upset the party by urging the electorate to vote for the Socialists; not surprisingly he lost.

He became President of the Scottish Nationalists on the principle that 'at least the Scots would have the satisfaction of knowing that their taxes were being wasted in Edinburgh instead of London'.

At one dinner party, a guest sitting next to Graham was very impressed by Graham's aristocratic lineage. She asked him whether it was true that there was royal blood in his family. "Madam", replied Cunningham-Graham, "if I had my rights, I should be the King of England. And what a two weeks *that* would be!"

Cunningham-Graham went back to the Argentine to see the pampas one last time and died there aged 84. Before his body was returned to Scotland, the Buenas Aires Herald wrote: 'On the procession down to the ship, the streets were lined with people, while two horses with empty saddles were led by gauchos behind the coffin. Thus Argentina bade farewell to one of the greatest friends she ever had, an ambassador of the heart'.

Graham's pugilistic defender in Trafalgar Square, **JOHN BURNS** (1858-1943), having led the 1889 London Dock Strike, became a Liberal MP and the first working-man to achieve Cabinet office. (He left the government in protest at the outbreak of the First World War.)

In 1898, after Wilde had sent letters to the press protesting against British prison conditions, he wrote: 'I think that, aided by some splendid personalities like John Burns, I have been able to deal a heavy and fatal blow at the monstrous prison system of English justice'.

Both Graham and Burns received anonymous commemoration in Parliament when the artist Solomon J Solomon was commissioned to work on some historical paintings for the House of Commons. He chose Graham to be the model for 'Sir Walter Raleigh' while Burns posed as another Elizabethan grandee.

When Burns saw the completed set of figures, he burst out laughing: "Here we are posing as courtiers at the throne of England, and the last time we were together we were had up before the beak for creating a disturbance in Trafalgar Square".

Cunningham-Graham was also a friend of another renowned left-wing politician, **JAMES KEIR HARDIE** (1865-1915), a former coalminer and trade unionist who stood for Parliament in 1892. Graham decided to help Hardie with his election campaign.

At one public meeting in a tough Glasgow slum, pandemonium broke out when a gang of thugs entered the hall intent on disruption. Graham slipped away from the platform, told the attendants to bolt all the doors, and, picking up a toy revolver left behind by a theatre group, strode back on stage.

Pointing the gun at the audience, he bellowed for silence and told the startled assembly that the doors had been locked, and that, if anyone moved from his seat, or interrupted a speaker, he would blow his brains out.

He announced: "I am going to introduce my friend, Keir Hardie, and until he has finished his address, not a man will interrupt him, or try to move, unless he wishes to be carried out of this room as a corpse!"

For a moment there was awed silence, but then the audience caught the joke and a storm of laughter erupted which soon turned to applause. When Keir Hardie appeared, immediate silence reigned.

Hardie won the election and, on his first day at the House of Commons, arrived wearing his working clothes of tweed cap and boots. The gate policeman took one look at him and asked suspiciously: "Are you working here?" "Yes". "On the roof?" "No. On the floor."

Cunningham-Graham also wrote about his travels, (books that were greatly appreciated by the US President 'Teddy' Roosevelt), and it was in this capacity that the then struggling writer **JOSEPH CONRAD** (1857-1924) asked for his help. Conrad had despaired of ever achieving recognition as an author and asked Graham to help him obtain a maritime job on a good ship. Instead Graham contacted all his friends in the shipping lines and asked them to ensure that, on no account, should Conrad be offered a job of any sort at all.

Conrad, bewildered by the solid wall of rejection that he met everywhere, was forced to return to writing. Which, of course, was what Cunningham-Graham had planned all along.

The policeman who had overseen the arrest of Cunningham-Graham and John Burns at Trafalgar Square was unfortunate in his later career. **GENERAL SIR CHARLES WARREN** (1840-1927), who Graham described as 'a psalm-singing, sanctimonious swashbuckler', was evidently an arrogant man who delighted in wearing over-elaborate uniforms.

In 1888, he was placed in charge of the hunt for the serial murderer, Jack the Ripper, and decided to make the use of bloodhounds his main instrument in the chase. He invited the press and the public to witness an experiment in Hyde Park to test the capabilities of his hounds.

Unwisely deciding to use himself as the quarry, he unleashed the dogs who promptly vanished in pursuit of anything they fancied. The public display of the Metropolitan Police Commissioner running around Hyde Park and losing his bloodhounds in the process caused endless official embarrassment. When all his efforts were crowned by the news of yet another Ripper murder, Warren bowed to the inevitable and resigned.

He later moved to the British army where, during the Boer War, he proved to be an outstandingly inept general.

PART THREE

TRIUMPH

Madame Blavatsky to Baron Corvo

<u>**1888**</u>

[The bicycle was invented, and George Eastman introduced his Kodak portable camera over most of Europe.

In Britain, an attempt was made to discredit the Irish Home Rule leader, Charles Parnell. This led to the setting up of the Parnell Commission.

The Jack the Ripper murders were committed between August and November.]

WILDE AND SUPERSTITION

[Despite the material prosperity of England, it was felt that the country was spiritually adrift. The Church of England had been dealt a hammer blow by the publication of Charles Darwin's 'Origin of Species' – religion in general was under attack from scientific discovery and rationalism.

Faced with this problem, there was an intellectual revulsion against Darwin's bleak revelations. Bernard Shaw articulated this trend: 'Darwin's natural selection produced the only result possible in the ethical sphere and that was the banishment of conscience from human nature; or, as Samuel Butler put it, of mind from the universe. What damns Natural Selection as a creed is that it takes hope out of evolution, and substitutes a paralysing fatalism. It might be better to cling to the hoariest of the savage old creator-idols, however diabolically vindictive, than to abandon all hope in a world of 'angry apes'.'

A desire for spiritual re-affirmation led in part to the Anglo-Catholic revival, but it also led to the spread of belief in a variety of phenomena such as table-rapping, séances, clairvoyance, astrology, and palmistry. It tended to prove the view that 'when men cease to believe in God, they will believe in anything'.

Oscar Wilde was not immune to these influences. Both of his parents had written books on the subject of Irish rural superstitions and he was certainly sensitive to magical thinking: 'Superstitions are the opponents of common sense. Common sense is the enemy of romance'.

In his adult life he continually relied on fortune- tellers like Cheiro and Mrs Robinson, who he called 'the Sybil of Mortimer Street'. The latter proved especially disastrous as she encouraged him to believe that his 1895 legal actions would prove successful: "She prophesied complete triumph and was most wonderful". Later he asked sadly: "Why did the Sybil say fair things?"

Oscar was often plagued by strange beliefs, including a refusal to ride in a hansom cab drawn by a white horse. When a warder accidentally trod on a spider in his prison cell, Oscar was horrified, prophesying ill luck. That night he claimed to have heard the cry of the Banshee, and the following morning received the news that his mother, Speranza, was dead.

Later, in Naples, his friend, Vincent O'Sullivan reported that Oscar was highly agitated by the presence of an old woman whom he thought to be a witch. Oddly he hired the same woman to clear his house of rats.

Wilde: 'The gods mark out a path for us which we must follow to its conclusion'.]

His wife Constance also became caught up in the world of the paranormal and in 1888 met the mystic, Madame Blavatsky.

MADAME HELENA BLAVATSKY 1831-1891

During 1888, Constance Wilde, in common with many other members of English society, became an adherent of the teachings of the famous Russian mystic. The actress *Elizabeth Robins* was less enthusiastic.

Constance told Robins that Madame Blavatsky had been killed in her youth while riding as a circus performer, but a Mahatma sitting in the Himalayas had projected his earthly being into her dead body and she revived. Since the incident, Blavatsky had worn a wig to cover the hole in her head where the spirit had entered. Robins asked: "Do you really believe that?" Constance replied: "Well, they say its true".

In spite of his own superstitions, Oscar Wilde had little time for his wife's guru. Oscar: 'I must confess that most modern mysticism seems to me to be simply a method of imparting useless knowledge in a form that no one can understand'. He teased the mystic, claiming that: "three youths at Trinity, Cambridge, nearly poisoned themselves with hashish in an attempt to project their astral bodies – they were only saved by a tutor armed with a stomach pump".

Oscar was not alone in his scepticism. The shrewd socialite, *Margot Asquith*, invited Blavatsky and some of her supporters to visit the Asquith home. As they sat in the living room, Blavatsky gave a theatrical shudder and hissed that a murderer had just passed by in the street outside. The company was suitably shocked, except for Margot who had been standing near the window. Margot: "I was the only one who could see outside and nobody had passed at all. Blavatsky was an audacious fraud".

Whatever the truth about her insights, Blavatsky was an extraordinary personality in 1880s London. Now in her fifties, she had become obese; Elizabeth Robins described her as 'a huge bulk'... "Her hands were enormous but seemed to be boneless. What an actress she would have made. A marvellous personality but I would not trust her".

She was conspicuous for her penetrating gaze, her 'swarthy, Tartar aspect', her chain-smoking of her hand rolled cigarettes, and her own description of her manners as resembling those of 'a Prussian grenadier on furlough'.

Born Helena von Hahn at Ekaterinoslav near the Black Sea, as a teenager she was noted as being a brilliant horsewoman, with a gift for languages and for the piano that she played 'in bursts of savage improvisation'.

In 1849, aged 17, she married the 40-year-old Nikifor Blavatsky, a Russian provincial vice-governor. She had no feelings whatever for her husband, seeing the marriage simply as a way out of a stifling family life. She insisted on remaining a virgin.

Bored by the frustrated Nikifor's attempts on her purity, Helena absconded on a ship bound for Turkey. On arrival at Constantinople, she survived by winning the prize money in a steeplechase, riding a horse that already had killed two grooms.

Drifting across Egypt and Europe, she arrived in London in 1851, where she met an Indian prince in Hyde Park who told her that she had a great spiritual quest ahead of her, and that her secret lay in Tibet.

Despite this rather obvious clue, Madame Blavatsky set out on her journey of mystical discovery in the opposite direction, living with the Canadian Red Indians, then travelling to meet the Mormons in Illinois, (but arriving after they already had left for Utah), investigating voodoo in New Orleans, then moving on through Texas and Mexico to Peru.

In 1852, she left the West Indies and sailed round the Cape of Good Hope, firstly to Ceylon (Sri Lanka), then to Bombay and southern India. She returned, via Singapore and Java, to England in 1853, where she played piano with the London Philharmonic Society. She continued her travels to Japan where she met the Yamabushi Brotherhood, before finally reaching Tibet.

In 1858, after four years in the Himalayas, she came home to Russia where her family and the local peasants said that she was 'a haunted woman', a medium whose mere presence provoked mysterious rapping and supernatural whispering. She dismissed these new powers as a nuisance and something of an embarrassment.

At the same time, she did consider that she was developing an astral 'other self'. Some local boatmen claimed to have seen this spectral figure rise and float across a river while Blavatsky was asleep on their boat.

By 1867, Blavatsky had travelled on to Italy where she volunteered to fight as a soldier in Garibaldi's army. She was wounded at the Battle of Mentana – her arm was broken by a sabre stroke and she received musket shots in her shoulder and one leg. She was left for dead but later recovered.

Moving on again, she lived firstly with the Whirling Dervishes, then with the Druze tribe of Mount Lebanon, then with Bedouin Arabs, then with the Marabouts of Damascus. Returning to Shigatze, Tibet in 1869, she studied with an Adept and gained entrance to the lama monasteries.

By 1870, the USA was as shaken by Darwin's theories as Britain had been, and the quasi-scientific methods of Spiritualism seemed to provide an antidote. (The need for belief in an afterlife had been reinforced by the heavy death toll of the recent Civil War. The First World War carnage produced a similar surge of interest in the occult.)

In 1875, while she was in New York, Blavatsky was well placed to start her Theosophical Society, based on linking spiritualism with the Kabbala and Eastern religions. She was helped by Colonel Henry Olcott (1830-1907), a well-respected man who previously had been one of the officers investigating the assassination of President Lincoln. His new enthusiasm found little favour with his puritanical wife, (whom Blavatsky nicknamed 'Kali'), and they divorced. *Thomas Edison* also became a prominent member.

The original US Spiritualists were wary of Blavatsky. She said that the spirits that they were raising were not their own lost kin but just odd astral figures; (this was in spite of having her own spectral familiar on call, who claimed to be the pirate Sir Henry Morgan).

Her American enemies struck back, claiming that she was a thoroughly debauched woman who had enjoyed sex with the Pope and with Otto von Bismarck. Which would have been news to her new husband, a New York Russian whom she had married under the impression that her first husband Nikifor was dead and this second one was wealthy.

Both parties were disappointed, as the Russian was penniless, and Helena still stoutly refused to consummate any marriage. They parted after four months.

With the formation of the British branch of the Theosophical Society in 1878, Blavatsky and Olcott arrived in London, (where Wilde referred to them as 'the Brompton Buddhists'). It became an immediate success and attracted interest from figures such as *Robert Browning, Matthew Arnold, WT Stead*, and *WB Yeats*. Yeats, in particular, was drawn to Blavatsky and said of her that: "She calls herself a Russian savage. To me she's still an interrogation mark, but wonderful in every way". The young Mahatma Gandhi also was influenced by the new philosopher.

In Britain, Blavatsky found herself suffering from what she saw as a grave social embarrassment. She had been taught English as a child by an English governess called Miss Jeffers. Miss Jeffers came from Yorkshire and had passed on her strong accent to the child. Blavatsky became very irritated when she saw her listeners struggling with suppressed laughter at the sound of her most sacred occult visions being delivered with a broad Leeds intonation. She found a guru who taught her upper class English by telepathy.

In 1884, the movement suffered a schism and Blavatsky allowed the formation of a sister sect called the Hermetic Lodge. Constance Wilde became a member.

When the Theosophist movement gained ground in India, Blavatsky and Olcott arrived there on a lecture tour and bought an estate in Madras as a permanent headquarters. However, this was a time of uneasy relations between Britain and Russia, (known as 'The Great Game'), and Blavatsky, as a Russian, was suspected of espionage. A British Secret Service spy, noticeable by his red face and drooping moustache, followed them on a tour north to Rajputana.

Olcott and Blavatsky were highly amused by the spy's attempts to remain inconspicuous. During one lecture, Olcott spotted the man at the rear of the audience – on this occasion he had shaved off the moustache to aid his disguise. Afterwards, they crossed over to him and congratulated him on his props and wardrobe.

A far more dangerous enemy appeared in the form of Mr Richard Hodgson of the British Society for Psychical Research, who came to India to investigate the Blavatsky phenomenon. In 1886, (Blavatsky's 'black year'), he published a report claiming that her miracles were fraudulent, she was 'one of the most accomplished, ingenious and interesting impostors in history', and a Russian spy as well. News also arrived from Russia, that Nikifor Blavatsky was not dead after all, and therefore Helena was a (virgin) bigamist.

In failing health, she left India for good and settled back in London at the St John's Wood home of an admirer, Annie Besant, where she died of bronchitis in 1891.

In 1867, **ANNIE BESANT** (1847-1933), Madame Blavatsky's protector in her last years, had married Frank Besant, (later the Vicar of Sibsey, Lincs, and the younger brother of the novelist Sir Walter Besant). Annie lost her religious faith, and, in 1873, left her husband and two children, having obtained a legal separation.

Bernard Shaw reported: 'Annie Besant was the most frightful romantic. She found that she could not be the bride of heaven, and therefore became the bride of Mr. Frank Besant, who was hardly an adequate substitute. She followed this by becoming infatuated with me, who was an even worse one.'

Annie joined the National Secular Society, collaborated with Charles Bradlaugh on a book describing the methods of birth control, (for which she received a suspended six month prison sentence), participated in the 'Bloody Sunday' march, and helped to organise and unionise the 1888 Match Girl's Strike.

Her life took another dramatic shift when, also in 1888, she converted to theosophy. The editor *WT Stead* took her to meet Blavatsky, who said to her, 'with a yearning throb in her voice': "Oh, my dear Mrs Besant, if only you would come among us". Annie said that she felt 'an overwhelming desire to kiss Blavatsky but resisted'.

Not for long, it appears, as an observer who visited their home reported seeing Blavatsky playing her favourite game of 'Patience' while on the floor beside her: 'was a little woman who pressed one of the card dealer's hands close to her cheek, who only inclined her head at the introduction, who did not speak. All the evening she held the hand'.

After Blavatsky's death, Annie Besant carried on her work and, from 1895, made India her new base. She became involved in Indian nationalism and helped to found the Hindu University. In 1916 her efforts to start a Home Rule for India League led to her internment by the British authorities. Her distaste for violent resistance led to her ousting from her position as President of the Indian Congress by more extreme elements, although Mahatma Gandhi held her in high regard.

For many years she promoted a claim that her adopted son, a Madras boy called Krishnamurti, was Christ reincarnated in an Indian body, and a following grew up around him called 'The Cult of the Silver Star'. In 1932, Krishnamurti repudiated Annie's claims of supreme holiness on his behalf. The writer *Robert Hichens* wrote: 'The last I heard of him was that he had become very fond of lawn-tennis and ballroom dancing.'

By 1888, Wilde had reached a position in London society where he had enough influence to be able to assist other, younger, talents. Among them was the American actress, Elizabeth Robins.

ELIZABETH ROBINS 1862-1952

Robins was an ambitious, beautiful, chestnut-haired young woman who had been raised mostly in Ohio and Colorado, and had been a medical student at Vassar College before going on the stage. In 1885, she had married a fellow actor called George Parkes.

It had been a childless and unhappy relationship, as Elizabeth made it clear that she had no intention of giving up her career to make a home for George. Two years later, George donned full theatrical armour, jumped in the Charles River at Boston, and drowned himself.

Hoping to make her breakthrough, Robins arrived alone in London in 1888. Wilde, who had met her cousin in St Louis while on his American tour, went out of his way to help her and to introduce her to the theatrical manager, *Herbert Beerbohm Tree*, (with whom she fell in love).

At first, Robins, who had suffered some humiliating sexual propositions from London theatrical managers, was cautious about Oscar: "He appeared in public as though he would bleed absinthe and clotted truffles". Soon she was entirely won over: "He had possibilities of disinterested forbearance few would have credited. A blessed man is Oscar Wilde".

Influenced by the widow of the famous Norwegian violin virtuoso, Ole Bull, whom she had met on her passage from the USA, Robins travelled to Norway. While there she became captivated by the plays of Hendrik Ibsen; she said that being involved with his works was 'like being a blind swimmer who had been picked up by a battleship'.

In 1891, she produced and starred in the first English speaking production of 'Hedda Gabler' in London. It was a controversial but distinct success. Although Wilde admired the production, ('I felt pity and terror, as though the play had been Greek'), he could not help adding, (in a letter to *Lady Ettie Desborough*): 'I went there on Thursday night and the house was dreary – the pit full of sad vegetarians, and the stalls occupied by men in mackintoshes and women in knitted shawls of red wool. So at least it seemed to me'.

After several years of promoting Ibsen and achieving an acknowledged position in English theatre, Robins retired from the stage in 1897 and turned her attention to writing. Amongst her fifteen novels, one book 'The Magnetic North', was a bestseller, and was based on her own experiences while travelling through the Yukon to the Arctic Circle during the Klondyke Gold Rush. She also deeply involved with the suffragette movement in Britain.

Robins never remarried but had many admirers, including the future Poet Laureate, John Masefield. When *Bernard Shaw*, (during his 'philandering' stage), made a pass at her, she reputedly drew a revolver on him. During her last forty years she lived with her close companion, Dr Octavia Wilberforce, in their Sussex home at Backsettown.

As well as being the posthumous inspiration for Robins's encounter with Ibsen, the violinist **OLE BULL** (1810-1880) had been the man who gave Ibsen his first chance. When the future playwright, then a raw youngster, had been out of work, Bull employed him for seven years and encouraged his interest in drama.

Although he spent much of his life in the USA, Bull was a resolute Norwegian patriot who had resisted the encroachment of Sweden in his country's politics and Danish influence in its culture. Most Norwegian homes possessed a bust of him as a symbol of the soul of Norway. The American *Sam Ward* once heard Bull extolling the beauty of his native fjords and asked him: "Do you play to them, Ole?" Bull replied: "No, I listen to them".

Bull was known for his brilliant improvisations, but sometimes these could be misinterpreted. In New Orleans, the composer Henry Russell heard him play 'The Carnival of

Venice – with Variations'. There were so many variations that the original melody appeared to become lost in the pyrotechnics. Russell heard one listener grunt: "He may be a great player but he's a damned long time tuning. When is he going to play?"

Bernard Shaw, in his role of music critic, once attended a Bull concert in London. Shaw: 'I was under the impression that Ole Bull was a Mississippi blues singer.'

In May 1888, 'The Happy Prince and other Tales', Wilde's book of fairy stories, was published. He was ambivalent about their use as stories for children: "I had about as much intention of pleasing the British child as I had of pleasing the British public".

The book had immediate success with both though, and the 'Athenaeum' compared Wilde to the famed Danish fairy-tale writer, Hans Christian Andersen (1805-1875).

(Edmund Gosse amused Wilde when he told him that Hans Christian Andersen refused to tell his stories to children unless there was an admiring circle of adults present.)

After his introduction to active homosexuality with Robert Ross, over the next four years Wilde indulged in several affairs, usually with young lower-middle class men with literary interests.

In June, Wilde met the English poet, Richard Le Gallienne.

RICHARD LE GALLIENNE 1866-1947

Aged 17, Le Gallienne had attended a Wilde lecture in his hometown of Birkenhead and had been very impressed. His father was also there and told Le Gallienne: "Don't make any mistake. That man is no fool".

In June 1888, Le Gallienne, now aged 22, came to London and stayed at Tite Street with the Wildes. Initially, Le Gallienne had reservations about his host: 'there is a certain fat effeminacy about him, suggesting a sort of caricature Dionysius, disguised as a rather heavy dandy of the Regency period'.

His attitude changed and he noted that Wilde was 'incapable of selfishness'. They soon became lovers, (Wilde wrote to him: 'I hope the laurels are not too thick across your brow for me to kiss your eyelids'). Much later, he was to write with perception about Oscar. Le Gallienne: 'From the beginning to the end he was a great actor – of himself. There was in him a great simplicity. His poses were self-dramatisations of which he expected others to see the fun as he himself saw it'.

Their physical intimacy soon cooled as, more slowly, did their friendship. Once, when Oscar rebuked Le Gallienne over a set of reviews, Le Gallienne retorted that he hadn't even mentioned Oscar in them. Oscar nodded: "Ah, Richard. That was just it".

During the 1890s, Le Gallienne made a direct attack on Oscar in his poem 'The Decadent Poet to His Soul'. Oscar was wounded by it but philosophised: "It has always seemed to me that the finest feature of a fine nature is treachery. The burden of gratitude must be overwhelming to a sensitive nature, therefore the debtor must betray his benefactor".

Le Gallienne had intended to enter chartered accountancy, but became bored with the life, failed his exams, and turned to writing. The publisher *John Lane* was impressed by Le Gallienne's early poetry and, having encouraged the young man to leave Liverpool and come to London, published his work in 1889.

In the same year, Le Gallienne travelled to Norway to meet the playwright Hendrik Ibsen. He accompanied Ibsen to a local café and was greatly impressed when the whole company stood up as a mark of respect to the famous writer. Le Gallienne noted the contrast to what would have happened if, say, Tennyson had entered a London café, where, at best, the company would have ignored him. Le Gallienne: 'Certainly it is worth while to be a great man in a little country'.

As Ibsen did not speak English, a mutual friend had taught Le Gallienne the Norwegian sentence: 'All English women adore Mr Ibsen'. Le Gallienne gingerly delivered this statement and was amazed to see a beam of gratified vanity spread across the playwright's face.

(Le Gallienne rather ruined this good impression by going to visit Ibsen's hated enemy, another Norwegian writer named Bjornstjerne Bjornson – who in 1903 became Norway's first Nobel Prize for Literature winner in preference to Ibsen. Bjornson snapped to Le Gallienne: "Ibsen is not a man, he is only a pen". Later, to the utter fury of both fathers, Ibsen's son married Bjornson's daughter.)

Le Gallienne returned to London and obtained regular work reviewing books for the Star, publishing more poetry, and, in 1896, writing a successful romantic novel called 'The Quest of the Golden Girl'. He was also an original member of the Rhymer's Club, and helped produce the Yellow Book. In 1901, he settled in the USA, then later in France, where he died in Mentone in 1947.

Le Gallienne was well known for his good looks – Edith Nesbit, (with whom he had an affair), described him as 'tall and slim, with a long pale face, dark eyes, and black glossy hair in curls around his head', while the journalist *TWH Crosland* said: "he really did look as Narcissus may have looked". *Swinburne* said that he was 'Shelley with a chin'.

In spite of his affair with Wilde, Le Gallienne was interested in women and married three times. His friends believed that domesticity ruined him as a poet. *WB Yeats* said of Le Gallienne: 'I have known, certainly, more men destroyed by the desire to have wife and child and to keep them in comfort than I have seen destroyed by harlots and drink'.

The death, after only three years of marriage, of his first wife, (a Liverpool café waitress, whom Wilde called 'a poem') left him devastated; his second marriage failed badly and was dissolved; only his third, in 1911, to an American woman, Irma Perry, survived. Two of his daughters became notable in their own right – Eva as an actress, and Gwen as a painter.

Although TWH Crosland, usually the scourge of aesthetes, called Le Gallienne 'the delicate high priest of a little school of hot pressed poetry and vapid prose', he found the poet to be good company.

On one occasion, they were at dinner in a restaurant, when Le Gallienne presented a cheque for ten dollars, (drawn on a small American bank), as payment for the meal. When it was refused, Le Gallienne, somewhat the worse for drink, got into an altercation that ended with a policeman being upended into the gutter. Their continued attempts to pass the cheque were to no avail, and the note became increasing crumpled and bedraggled. Finally they hit on the idea of taking it to a laundry and then, after it had been carefully ironed, they managed to 'sell' the cheque for ten shillings.

HUBERT CRACKENTHORPE (1870-1896) was a fellow writer and friend of Le Gallienne's during the early 1890s. He wrote short realistic stories in the style of *Guy de Maupassant* and edited the magazine 'The Albemarle' in 1892. Although regarded as immoral and decadent, Crackenthorpe was actually rather timid and would have preferred a humdrum life. However, his association with the genuine decadents kept landing him in undignified and ultimately tragic situations.

For instance, once when he accompanied a group including *Walter Sickert*, to Dieppe, the party met up with an English travelling circus. Hearing that the circus owner was hampered by not knowing French, Crackenthorpe offered to translate for him in the next town. The following morning, Crackenthorpe's companions were reduced to hysterical laughter by the sight of him being led off down the road perched on top of an elephant.

His wife Leila firmly believed in the concept of free love. To this end, she had an affair with a French artist called Comte d'Artaux, and encouraged Crackenthorpe to follow her example by having sex with Le Gallienne's sister, Sissie Welch. All four of them lived together at a house in the Avenue Kleber in Paris.

This arrangement came to grief when Comte d'Artaux discovered he had a sexual disease and accused Leila of infecting him. She in turn accused Crackenthorpe of infecting her and demanded a divorce. Sissie left the ménage and returned to her husband, the actor James Welch.

The unfortunate sequel to this domestic farce came when Crackenthorpe, aged 26, drowned himself in the River Seine. After going missing for two months, his unrecognisable corpse was discovered on Christmas Eve, 1896. It was identified by his brothers through his cufflinks.

Wilde was asked once if he would try to stop an attempted suicide: "I should consider it an act of gross impertinence to do so. His suicide would be a perfectly thought-out act, the definite result of scientific process, with which I should have no right whatever to interfere'.

In spite of this rationalism, Oscar did not adhere to it in practice. One night, he was walking along the banks of the Seine, when he saw a shabbily dressed man staring down into the depths of the river. Concerned, he shouted across to him: "My poor man, are you desperate?" The stranger looked up and shouted back: "No sir, I'm a hairdresser'.

During this period Wilde became friendly with the editor of another Cassells magazine, WE Henley, who invited him to lunch at the Savile Club. Oscar said that he felt ' like a lion that has rashly intruded into a den of Daniels'.

Although he regarded Henley's suggestion of proposing him for membership as 'a merry jest', Oscar did accept nomination by another member, Rev. William Loftie, (supported by the writers Henry James and Rider Haggard). However, the proposal was blocked by an opponent, and his membership was postponed indefinitely.

He visited the club on another occasion and, glancing around, commented: "True democrats. Not a sovereign between them". (A contemporary verse ran: 'I do not like the Savile Club – The wine is bad, and worse the grub'.)

WILLIAM ERNEST HENLEY 1849-1903

A witness, Lewis Hind, described one of the first meetings between the two London editors. Hind wrote that: 'There were at least twenty other men present, all voluble talkers...But all were content to stand back and let two hold the stage, a duel, a combat of giants – broadsword and rapier. These two were Henley and Oscar Wilde'.

Initially, Oscar expressed high regard for his rival: 'There is something wholesome, virile, and sane about the man's soul. Anybody can be reasonable, but to be sane is not common'.

As they both worked for Cassells, Henley once tried to compare notes on their working habits and asked Oscar how often he visited his office. Wilde replied: "Three times a week for an hour a day. But I have since struck off one of the days". An astonished Henley replied: "My God. I went five times a week for five hours a day and when I wanted a day off they had a special committee meeting".

Oscar added: "Furthermore, I never answered their letters. I have known men come to London full of bright prospects and seen them complete wrecks in a few months through a habit of answering letters".

Frank Harris wrote that Henley was 'a big man with broad shoulders and an immense leonine head...but his legs were all twisted and standing he looked a quite short man'. This physical deformity was the result of Henley contracting tubercular arthritis at the age of twelve.

256

In 1873, as the disease worsened, one foot was amputated; the other one was only saved through the skill of the surgeon Sir Joseph Lister.

Henley spent many months as a convalescent in Edinburgh and during this time became a close friend of the writer Robert Louis Stevenson, (they collaborated on four unsuccessful plays, among them 'Deacon Brodie'). Stevenson described his friend as 'boisterous and piratie' – he later acknowledged that Henley was the inspiration behind his 'Treasure Island' character, 'Long John Silver'.

In 1875, Henley made his reputation with a poetry collection called 'Hospital Verses'. He moved to London in 1877 to edit several magazines before becoming editor of the Scots Observer in Edinburgh, (which by 1891, was renamed the National Observer and relocated to London).

Frank Harris disapproved of his editorial methods: 'Henley edited everything sent to his magazine with the result that the whole paper seemed as if it had been written by one man.'

In fact, at the National Observer, Henley's flamboyant personality inspired a sparkling entourage of young contributors, who included such names as Thomas Hardy, *Rudyard Kipling*, James Barrie, RL Stevenson, HG Wells, and *WB Yeats*. This group established themselves at the Solferino Restaurant in Rupert Street, Soho, where *Max Beerbohm* nicknamed them 'the Henley Regatta'.

Yeats said of Henley that 'he was a great actor with a bad part', but was impressed by his 'unanalysable gift of keeping all men near him at the stretch, of sending all away wearied out with the prolonged giving of their best'.

The less robust found it difficult to cope with such a powerful persona. The artist Aubrey Beardsley once went to Henley's office looking for work. 'As I climbed the stairs, I heard a terrible voice raised in anger and saw through an open door a large red man haranguing a youth. Realising that the man was Henley, I turned and fled and did not return'.

Herbert Beerbohm Tree was more capable of dealing with the mercurial editor. Tree: 'I have always liked Henley in spite of his bludgeonesque manners. One day I met him in the street in Edinburgh. He asked me: "Why did you not come to see me?" To which I replied: "My dear Henley, I forgot for the moment whether we were on speaking terms or not".

Henley used his papers as vehicles for an anti-Gladstonian, drum-beating imperialism and, together with *Rudyard Kipling*, provided a bombastic counterweight to the aesthetes of the 1890s. In common with Kipling, (and perhaps stemming from both men's physical incapacities), Henley idolised wholesome muscular strength and the deeds of men of action.

His attack on the decadents found an obvious target when Wilde published 'Dorian Gray'. A review appeared in the National Observer labelling Oscar as a writer fit only for 'outlawed noblemen and perverted telegraph boys', (a reference to the recent Cleveland St scandal – see *Prince Eddy*). Back-peddling from his previous assessment of Henley as 'sane', Oscar now described him as 'my last pet lunatic'.

In spite of this new enmity, Wilde was deeply sympathetic when Henley's only child, a five-year-old daughter named Margaret, died in 1894. (Henley's grief was exacerbated by the knowledge that she probably had died of inherited syphilis). Oscar urged Henley to bury himself in work as a consolation: 'That is what remains for natures like ours. Work never seems to me a reality, but a way of getting rid of reality'.

Oscar's magnanimity had little effect on Henley's attitude when the 1895 scandal broke. Although he asked Yeats: "Why did he do it? I told my lads to attack him and yet we might have fought under his banner", Henley was unrelenting in his onslaught. He wrote: 'Wilde has made of infamy a new Thermopylae', and advised suicide. Even after Oscar left jail, Henley kept up the attack, branding the 'Ballad of Reading Gaol' as having 'the trail of the Minor Poet all over it'.

In 1898, Oscar made the still applicable observation: 'Have you noticed that if a man has once been an editor he can always be an editor? The fact that a paper has a way of dying when he is on it is of the smallest importance. He is in demand before the corpse is buried. Here is Henley. He kills the Scots Observer. Hey presto! He is made editor of the New Review. Then the New Review dies.'

Oscar had one final grouch about his old Cassells colleague: "Henley owes me seven-and-six. The other day I read a review of his praising a novel by somebody called Mary Cholmondeley. I bought the book, and before I had read very far I came on this sentence: 'The birds were singing on every twig and on every little twiglet.' Now, you know, when an artist comes on a sentence like that in a book it is impossible for him to go on reading it. So I consider that Henley owes me seven-and-six.'

Wilde was still interested in the tangled affairs of his native land: 'I am not English. I am Irish which is quite another thing'.

During the 1880s, Irish political agitation for Home Rule reached a crescendo, both in Parliament and in Ireland itself. Oscar: 'If in the 18th century England tried to govern Ireland with an insolence that was intensified by race hatred and religious prejudice, she has sought to rule her in the 19th century with a stupidity that is aggravated by good intentions.'

(In 1891, he was at a House of Commons dinner attended by Scots and Welsh MPs. He suggested that they inaugurated a 'Celtic' Dinner to "assert ourselves, and show these tedious Angles or Teutons what a race we are, and how proud we are to belong to that race".)

However he disliked overt nationalism – 'Patriotism is the virtue of the vicious' – and had little to do with any Home Rule political activity.

The one event that did attract his attention was the libel trial between Charles Parnell and the Times newspaper and the subsequent Parnell Commission. Encouraged by his brother Willie's interest, he attended many of the sessions and openly supported Parnell. The libel trial opened on October 22 1888.

CHARLES STUART PARNELL 1846-1891

Charles Parnell was a Protestant Irish nationalist who entered Parliament in 1875 and became leader of the Home Rule Party in 1880. He advocated a series of parliamentary and extra-parliamentary campaigns, including filibustering in the House and boycotting and unrest in Ireland that, in 1881, led to his arrest and the highly publicised 'martyrdom' of six months imprisonment in Kilmainham Jail.

These tactics proved so successful that the Prime Minister *Gladstone* agreed to the so-called 1882 Kilmainham Treaty whereby the British Government, in return for an end to violence, offered to assist the plight of Irish tenants ruined by agricultural depression.

In a wave of popularity, Parnell was acclaimed as 'the uncrowned King of Ireland', although he himself was dubious about any lasting reform. When a labourer cheered him as he passed by, Parnell told the man: "Ireland shall get her freedom and you will still break stones".

Then in 1882, two English dignitaries were assassinated in the Phoenix Park Murders. Although Parnell immediately denounced the crime – "He who commits a crime gives strength to the enemy" – much of what he had gained was lost in the wave of revulsion.

For two years Irish patriots carried on a campaign of terrorism in England, including an attempt to blow up the Houses of Parliament and the Tower of London in 1885.

In 1887, the 'Times' newspaper published a letter purporting to have been written by Parnell in extenuation of the Phoenix Park murders. Parnell indignantly dismissed the letter as a forgery and sued the Times for libel.

During the libel trial, with the aid of the MP *Henry Labouchere*, Parnell's lawyers broke down the main prosecution witness, one Richard Pigott, who was forced to confess that he had forged the letter. A few days later he fled to Madrid where he committed suicide in a hotel bedroom. The Times case collapsed.

Meanwhile, after fifteen months, the Special Commission that had been established by the government to examine the case exonerated Parnell.

The Tories and Unionists had been closely associated with the 'Times' plot and were thoroughly discomforted by its failure. Having been thus foiled, Joseph Chamberlain and his allies turned to another target of attack, where Parnell was genuinely vulnerable.

For ten years he had been the lover of Kitty O'Shea, (the wife of another MP), who had borne him three children. Her husband, Captain O'Shea, had acquiesced complaisantly in the situation, hoping for political advancement and part of his wife's inheritance, neither of which materialised.

In 1890, amidst the shambles of the Times case, Chamberlain eagerly encouraged O'Shea to sue for divorce, citing Parnell as co-respondent. O'Shea won the case easily and Parnell was ruined.

Gladstone made it clear to Parnell that he had to resign, much to Kitty's disgust. Kitty: 'For ten years Gladstone had known of the relations between Parnell and myself. But this was private knowledge. Now it was public knowledge and an English statesman must always appear on the side of the angels'. Parnell's attempt to remain leader of the Irish Home Rule Party only split his support.

The Times, in belated revenge, described the divorce as 'a story of dull and ignoble infidelity …comparable only to the dreary monotony of French middle-class vice'.

Having been deserted by the Liberals and the Irish, Parnell married Kitty in a ceremony denounced by the Irish Bishop of Raphoe as 'the climax of brazened horrors'. Worn out by his political battles, he died a few months later. Kitty's daughter said that her mother never ceased to mourn Parnell.

Through his last years, several witnesses commented on Parnell's strange behaviour. *Frank Harris* said: "I always felt there was an insane streak in Parnell. He was very superstitious and the number 13 terrified him".

Harris once walked with him to a dinner party. On reaching the door, Parnell stopped and refused to go in. Asking Harris to accompany him, he then strolled around the house till he felt satisfied. He explained: "I hate four and eight but when my last step brings me to the count of nine, I'm happy; seven even will do, but nine's a symbol of real good luck and I can go inside rejoicing!"

Harris added that Parnell was obsessed with disguises: 'Sometimes he would appear in the House of Commons with a full beard; a week later it was shaved off; now he wore his hair down on his shoulders; next week it was cropped close; and again the top of his head was clean-shaven, as if he had been playing priest.'

Labouchere also thought Parnell was suffering from 'cerebral excitement', verging on paranoia. Parnell insisted on carrying a revolver and constantly changed his abode at a time when there was no fear of assassination.

One night he called on Labouchere wearing a slouch hat shading his face and, refusing to come inside, slunk off into the shadows. Labouchere returned to his dinner guests and announced: "I do believe that I've just parted from Jack the Ripper. Parnell is the only man who fits the description".

During the period of the Parnell Commission, Oscar was in close contact with his brother, Willie Wilde, who was also fascinated by the case. Willie acquired a brief fame for his journalistic coverage of the Commission – 'the best in England'.

However, an animosity had begun to grow between the two men. Oscar was to write in 'An Ideal Husband': 'Extraordinary thing about the lower classes in England. They are always losing their relations.' – 'Yes, my lord. They are extremely fortunate in that respect'.

WILLIE WILDE 1852-1899 (First Part)

Given their fraternal similarities, it was probably inevitable that the two Wilde brothers would fall out. *Max Beerbohm* said of Willie: "Quel monstre! Dark. Oily, suspect, yet awfully like Oscar – he has Oscar's coy, carnal smile and fatuous giggle and not a little of Oscar's esprit. But he is awful – a veritable tragedy of family likeness'.

Despite being close during their younger days, increasingly Oscar became irritated by having what he saw as a gross caricature of himself constantly on parade around London. Oscar had carefully constructed his own public persona, and Willie's presence was a permanent reminder of the reality of his background. One observer noted: "Scratch Oscar and you will find Willie".

In 'Dorian Gray', one of Oscar's characters was given the line: 'I can't help detesting my relations. I suppose it comes from the fact that none of us can stand other people having the same faults as ourselves'. Willie possibly realised the problem. He had a heavy beard and joked that Oscar paid him to wear it so that people would differentiate between them.

Compared to Oscar, Willie was a nondescript but he had a breezy cordiality and an engaging wit of his own. The impresario *Jimmy Glover* said of him: "The personification of good nature and irresponsibility, Willie with ten thousand a year would have been magnificent".

His full name was William Robert Kingsbury Wills Wilde, and, being two years older than Oscar, he had led the way through Portora School and Trinity College Dublin. His initial intention to follow a career in law soon dissolved in drinking sprees. When asked what he was working at, he replied: "At intervals". Oscar admitted that his brother enjoyed taking 'the occasional alcoholiday'.

Willie dabbled in writing and had two plays printed in Dublin, (in 1878 he wrote a poem on 'Salome'). When the family moved to London after the death of Sir William, Willie stayed with his mother *Speranza*. He became a journalist and had working stints as drama critic for Punch and leader writer for the Daily Telegraph.

Despite having many girlfriends and making several marriage proposals, including one to the composer *Ethel Smyth*, Willie remained single. Speranza began to despair: 'Poor Willie – will he ever find the right woman? But just now he has no other means of salvation but through a good marriage'.

Then, in October 1891 Willie, now aged 39, married Mrs Frank (Florence) Leslie, a rich American aged 55. She was a powerful feminist, (the rumoured part-descendant of black slaves), who had inherited a newspaper empire from a previous marriage – Willie was her fourth husband.

During the reception at Delmonico's and the honeymoon at Niagara Falls, Willie got drunk and decided to stay that way. In an attempt to 'create a leisure class in America', he refused to work and instead spent his time at the Lotus Club in New York drinking steadily and becoming 'the laziest man who ever wore shoe leather'.

A tight-lipped Mrs Leslie paid his way for a period then stopped. In due course Willie was expelled from the Lotus Club for cadging drinks from members and not paying his dues. Early in 1892 she deposited Willie back in London, declaring: "He was of no use to me, either by day or by night". The London newspaper placards gleefully proclaimed: 'Tired Of Willie!'

After only eight months of marriage, Willie returned to stay with Speranza at her Chelsea home in Oakley Street, and worked again sporadically at the Daily Telegraph.

Oscar was not amused to hear reports that Willie had been performing parodies of Oscar's 'fat, potato-choked voice' at the Lotus Club and also gossiping about Oscar's private life. Neither had he enjoyed Willie's drama review of his 'Lady Windermere's Fan': 'The author peoples his play with male and female editions of himself ....The play is a bad one, but it will succeed'. For his part, Willie was hurt that Oscar had left him out of his social circle.

Back in London, Willie was reported as being 'drunk at all hours of day or night'. Max Beerbohm wrote to a friend: 'It was Willie, by the way, who was found by his host in the smoking room filling his pockets with handfuls of cigars – wasn't it dreadful?'

The always impending split widened into animosity. In July 1893 while staying at Goring-on-Thames, Oscar made a last gesture and invited Willie to join him at the Henley Regatta. Willie failed to arrive.

[See Willie Wilde – Second Part – Page 411]

THE PELICAN CLUB

[Willie Wilde was a well-known figure around various London hostelries but his favourite was the PELICAN CLUB in Soho. (The actor *Seymour Hicks*: 'Willie was the butt of the Pelican Club'). The clientele of the Pelican was a mixture of millionaires and bohemians and was especially popular among the sporting peers such as Lord Lonsdale and Lord Marcus Beresford. (The 20th century writer PG Wodehouse often referred to the club in his 'Blanding Castle' books as being the old haunt of 'Galahad Threepwood').

It had an unusually boisterous reputation and some outrageous members. Jimmy Glover described one of them, Hugh Drummond, as 'entering the Club and clearing its long bar counter of three dozen glasses, smashing them on the floor, and calling for a whisky and soda'. One uproarious night, Drummond was accused of throwing a moose's head that had knocked a peer of the realm unconscious. He indignantly denied the charge, claiming: "I've not thrown anything except trifle all night".

Some evenings, another member, the *Marquess of Queensberry*, having discovered music, could be heard pounding out tunes on the club piano with one finger and bellowing the words to the latest music hall songs.

Another member, the Marquess of Aylesbury, (alias 'Sporting Joe'), took a gang of racecourse touts down to his house in Savernake Forest. Too drunk to go out on a shoot, he ordered his gamekeepers to drive dozens of deer, rabbits, and other game past his dining room windows so that his company could take pot shots at them.

Another Pelican member treated his city clerk to a day at his country estate. He sent the man off for an afternoon's shooting with a gun and a pair of retrievers. An hour later the clerk returned and said excitedly: "I really enjoyed that. Have you got any more dogs?"

One member, known as 'The Shifter', was revered for his alcoholic intake even in the Pelican. His main problem was that his redoubtable wife subjected him to lengthy vituperation because he kept waking her up when he arrived home drunk every night. A friend advised him that, if he just took off his boots and clothes on the stairs, he could creep into bed without disturbing her. The Shifter gratefully accepted the advice. A week later, his friend asked him how he had got on. The Shifter rumbled uneasily and replied: "Well, I did exactly what you told me. I took off my boots at the bottom of the staircase. I took off all my clothes when I was half way up. I listened as you advised me to, and crawled quietly to the top of the stairs. And found myself on the platform at Waterloo Station".

Owing to the amount of champagne bottles that had been hurled from its windows onto the street below, the Pelican Club became the object of frequent police raids. It was finally closed in 1892, after a scandalous prizefight on its premises.]

DAME ETHEL SMYTH 1858-1944

One of Willie Wilde's more unlikely amorous episodes involved the composer Ethel Smyth, then a girl of seventeen. They met in 1878 when returning by sea from a trip to Dublin. Oscar was also on board and Ethel recalled seeing 'a tall figure clad in dark blue, leaning over the bulwarks and gazing seaward', who Willie introduced as 'my brother the poet'.

After Willie had attempted to cure her seasickness with brandy, (a remedy that induced violent vomiting), Ethel recovered enough to meet him on board the train at Holyhead. Her chaperone having vanished to recuperate from her own encounter with the Irish Sea, the couple settled in a deserted horse box, Willie 'sitting on a Huntley and Palmer's biscuit tin at my feet'.

Willie lost little time. Ethel: 'He seized my hand and began an impassioned declaration, in the middle of which the biscuit-tin collapsed. This mishap he passed over with some remark I have forgotten and resumed his tale of passion; and before the train steamed into Euston I was engaged to a man I was no more in love with than I was with the engine-driver.' Within three weeks, Ethel decided to break off the engagement, 'probably to Willie's secret relief'.

(Oscar may have had this incident in mind when, in 'An Ideal Husband', he wrote the lines: 'Did you know her well?' – 'So little that I got engaged to be married to her once. The affair lasted for three days – nearly'.)

The daughter of an ex-Indian Army Major-General, Ethel Smyth as a child had been a perceptive but mischievous tomboy. During the Franco-Prussian War, she had been in the charge of a German governess. Each morning the nine-year-old Ethel would rush to the governess's room with news of some appalling German defeat. The governess, being a bit dim, swallowed it every time.

Ethel's sister Nina Smyth was an eccentric influence. Blessed with unusual strength, Nina had 'at Frimley Fair, after watching the failure of several brawny youths to 'ring the bell at the top,' picked up the hammer and did it without effort.'

When she later married and produced children, Nina's eldest son became ill and was put into solitary confinement in his nursery. In an effort to relieve her son's boredom, Nina laid a trail of gunpowder opposite his window and blew up a flower-bed full of geraniums.

Although married, Nina preferred women and began an affair with a champion lady golfer. Her husband accepted the situation, despite his fury on finding that, when a large Ascot Week party had assembled at his house for dinner, Nina had forgotten all about it and had gone off to spend the night with her golfer.

Nina eventually settled down to live with another woman, Lady Helena Gleichen. During the First World War, the couple raised a mobile ambulance unit and were decorated for valour on the Italian front.

Ethel's other sister Mary, (later Mrs Charles Hunter), was a society beauty who modelled for such painters as John Singer Sargent and *Auguste Rodin*. The latter insisted on sculpting Mary's bust. During one session, Rodin told her: "Your skin has the whiteness of turbot that one sees lying on the marble slabs of your amazing English fishmongers; it looks as if it were bathed in milk. Ah, madame!" 'Then', Mary reported, 'he kissed my hand a little too greedily. Mr Sargent is less lascivious. We discuss music together'.

Even as a child, Ethel Smyth admitted she had 'wild passions' for girls and women, (she later claimed to have had over 100 female lovers, whom she described as 'cultes'). While at her school in Putney, 'passions raged all the time'.

[LESBIANISM had long flourished in high society where it was known as 'a game of flats', and several lesbian clubs could be found in London. The sexologist Havelock Ellis wrote that, in general, the middle class and lower class girls were too hidebound by convention, (except among actresses and prostitutes), but that such practices were rife among upper class girls, particularly in the boarding schools.

Another commentator, Huttner, observed: 'These inexperienced young creatures, full of sensuality, are left together without any supervision whatever, especially when they are in bed, and they spend their time reading obscene novels or in even more shameful amusements that are unmentionable'.)

As she grew up, Ethel became absorbed with an ambition to compose music. Her dyspeptic father was vehemently opposed to the idea; (Wilde described a similar military man in his short story, 'A Model Millionaire': 'A retired Colonel who had lost his temper and his digestion in India, and had never found either of them again'.) In the teeth of family rows, Ethel finally got her way and in 1877 went off to study at the Leipzig Conservatorium in Germany.

During her five years in Leipzig, she became part of the circle dominated by the composer Johannes Brahms with whom she became well acquainted. Brahms thought that everyone resembled an instrument in an orchestra and declared that Ethel was 'the oboe'.

She was scathing about Brahms's attitude to women: 'If they did not appeal to him he was incredibly awkward and ungracious; if they were pretty he had an unpleasant way of leaning back in his chair, pouting out his lips, stroking his moustache, and staring at them as a greedy boy stares at jam tartlets'.

Ethel acquired a dog in Germany, (and was never again without a dog throughout her life). He was a huge half St Bernard called Marco who terrorised her friends. At one of Brahms's rehearsals Marco, angered by being left outside, burst in through the door and charged into the room scattering the rehearsing quintet, upsetting the music stands, and barging into Brahms.

The Russian composer Peter Ilich Tchaikovsky, (who disliked Brahms's music), also fell foul of Marco, having been terrified by the slavering hound during a visit to Leipzig. Ethel was amused to read in Tchaikovsky's memoirs that he had bracketed Brahms and Marco together as 'the eccentricities of Ethel Smyth'.

Ethel did receive some male attention in Leipzig. The Anglo-American writer Henry Brewster fell in love with her then, discovering she was having an affair with his sister-in-law, went off to Africa to shoot lions to overcome his infatuation. He returned home cured. He declared that he found male homosexuality 'indefensibly ugly' but said philosophically that he had a tolerant sympathy for sex between two women: "Woman is a caressing animal".

Ethel certainly did a fair share of caressing, including amongst her lovers Lili Wach (Mendelssohn's youngest daughter), the Princess de Polignac (formerly Wineretta Singer, the sewing machine heiress), Vernon Lee, (the authoress who enjoyed dressing her girlfriends as Botticelli pages), and Baroness von Meyendorff. Ethel: "'I confess to having worshipped at many shrines in my life but never I think with more wholesale devotion than at the Baroness's". Von Mayendorff had been also a lover of another composer, Frans Liszt. Ethel: 'She was one of the many ladies in whose arms Liszt is said to have died'.

The longest and possibly the happiest affair of Ethel's life was with Lady Mary Ponsonby, the wife of *Queen Victoria's* private secretary, Sir Henry Ponsonby. Under Mary's patronage, Ethel was able to visit the royal residence of Balmoral. She soon found life tedious at the Highland retreat and suggested building a nine-hole golf course. Sir Henry helped out by providing nine jam jars and the idea proved to be an immense gift to the bored Balmoral courtiers.

The affair between Lady Ponsonby and Ethel Smyth was punctuated by titanic rows, as Ponsonby's daughter Maggie testified. Once when Maggie was out for the evening with their neighbour, the *Rani of Sarawak*, an argument broke out at home. Replying to a taunt by Ethel, Lady Ponsonby snarled: "Would you kindly shut that door unless you wish every word you say to be overheard by the servants you are so fond of imitating". Ethel leapt to her feet, marched out of the house, slammed the door, and peddled off furiously on her bicycle. Maggie said that when she arrived back half an hour later, 'the house was still rocking'.

Ethel also had affairs with both the wife and the daughter of the Dean of Windsor, (later Archbishop of Canterbury), Edward Benson. She became friendly with most of the numerous Benson family. (One of the Benson children's games was called 'Bedding Out'. The idea was to select any two public figures and try to picture them together in a four-poster bed. Someone 'bedded out' Mrs Benson with *William Gladstone.*)

However, the one family member who could not stand Ethel was the Archbishop himself. As Mrs Benson put it: "We all realise that you and the Head of the Church are not two dewdrops destined to roll into one." Ethel admitted that her presence was 'a red rag to a bull', and often she had to be smuggled up the back stairs in case Benson was distracted from his work by the sight of her.

Much to the Archbishop's displeasure, Ethel sometimes attended family meals. Ethel: 'At dinner one night the conversation had turned to printers' errors and I had got as far as saying I had recently read about a printer's error that had caused amusement merely by the omission of a final 'd'.

'Here I stopped, overcome with misgiving. But there was no disobeying His Grace's acid-affable: 'Pray let us hear the case in question,' and I told them how a local newspaper had stated in connection with a recent visit from General Booth of the Salvation Army, that 'after his train had left the station, a large crow remained on the platform for half an hour singing 'Rock of Ages.'

There was silence all round, then Mrs. Benson quickly asked the Archbishop whether the Dean of Rochester had spoken well at the Meeting that morning.'

Only once did the ice break. In 1893, Benson's son, Fred, published a satirical novel, 'Dodo', in which Ethel was recognisable as the character of 'Edith Staines' – 'a young lady who ate bacon and eggs on the lid of her piano while composing'. At their next meeting, Ethel was amazed to find the Archbishop almost fawning on her. Mrs Benson later explained that he thought Ethel might have been offended by his son's book.

Ethel finally achieved some recognition for her compositions and in 1889 her work was performed in London by the conductor Sir Auguste Manns. (When Manns was knighted, *Bernard Shaw* mused in print: 'A Manns a Man for a' that'.)

When her major opera, 'The Wreckers', was produced, *Edward VII* was brought to the first night. His private secretary reported that the King's only comment occurred when he opened his eyes towards the end of the performance and grunted: "That's the fourth time that infernal noise has woken me up!"

Although she was perceived as perhaps the first genuine English female composer, Ethel never reached the front ranks of music. Her friend Henry Brewster consoled her: "What does it matter if your work never achieves anything at all. If you have laboured well enough you have already received your wages". Ethel accepted that as she grew older she began to agree with Brewster's theory.

In 1911, she became a passionate supporter of the suffragette movement, (as well as enjoying an affair with its leader, Emmeline Pankhurst), and composed a musical piece entitled 'March of the Women'. When she received a two month prison sentence for activism, she conducted the singing of the 'March' by her fellow prisoners with a toothbrush from the window of her cell at Holloway Jail.

Shortly after leaving prison in 1913, Ethel went off on a trip to Egypt, where her comment that 'One's own strange proclivities lead to strange human contacts' came startlingly true. While travelling in the desert, she came across a beautiful woman who turned out to be a hermaphrodite. Ethel invited her to a tent so that Ethel could photograph her naked. On examination, the woman proved to possess both male and female genitalia.

The hermaphrodite explained that she paid young girls to kiss her but refused to allow men to touch her. Ethel admitted that she was carried away by 'the most ridiculous action of my life' and embraced the hermaphrodite, afterwards paying her several sovereigns. A friend told Ethel later that, after such generosity, the next time they came into the desert the place would be teeming with hermaphrodites.

Old age did nothing to decrease Ethel's libido. In the 1920s, she became infatuated with the writer Virginia Woolf and publicly pursued her prey. When invited to a dinner party at the Woolf's home, Ethel made the journey on her bicycle. En route, she decided that her clothes were not becoming enough and stopped at a village shop to buy a corset. As there were none available, she bought a large birdcage instead.

Half an hour later, Virginia walked out into her garden to look for her guest, only to find Dame Ethel in the shrubbery in a state of undress. She was struggling with the birdcage and trying to wrench it into the shape of a corset to force under her tweeds.

While in Germany, Ethel Smyth became friendly with **COUNT PHILIP VON EULENBERG** (1847-1921), the great favourite of Kaiser Wilhelm II. At one point, he had been the German Ambassador to Vienna, appointed because he was 'an unequalled organizer of fancy balls and theatrical entertainments and an all-round slave of the Arts.'

Eulenberg and his great friend General von Moltke, (they called each other 'Phili' and 'Tutu'), represented the moderate party at the German court. In 1906, they were accused by a bellicose right-wing journalist, Maximilian Harden, of being homosexuals. In an echo of the Wilde case, Eulenberg lost the libel suit he had instigated against Harden, and was brought to trial himself. (As a married man in his sixties and having fathered eight children, Eulenberg expected to win, but his case was undermined by the testimony of a milkman with whom he had had sex in the 1880s.)

Eulenberg was never convicted, as he kept on fainting at crucial moments of the trial, but his political position was destroyed. Others of his circle, including the Commandant of Berlin, the Master of Ceremonies, and three Imperial Aide-de-Camps, were all relieved of their posts. In the furore surrounding the cull, King Edward VII commented that: "Not even the Hohenzollerns have behaved as stupidly as this before".

Forgetting that Eulenberg had been a strong counterweight in their favour, the French found the affair hilarious. 'Do you speak German' became a favourite graffiti in public latrines, while Berlin became known as 'Sodom-on-Spree'.

The Kaiser abandoned Eulenberg's group and instead surrounded himself with right-wing militarists, (one probable cause of the approaching First World War). Rennell Rodd: 'His faith in his own judgment was shaken. From then on, he had to follow in the path of public opinion. The hand of the war party was strengthened and the Emperor identified himself with the aggressive Junkerism'.

> *In December 1888, Wilde published his story 'The Young King' in the Lady's Pictorial magazine. It was regarded as very sympathetic to socialism.*
>
> *The young poet WB Yeats had attended Wilde's lecture in Dublin in November 1883, then met him at WE Henley's home in 1888. In December, Wilde, thinking that Yeats might be lonely, invited him to have Christmas lunch at Tite Street.*

WILLIAM BUTLER YEATS 1863-1939

The youthful Yeats found himself intimidated by Wilde's savoir faire – 'his hard brilliance and dominating self-possession' – when contrasted with Yeats's own gaucheness. During the meal, Oscar told Yeats: "We Irish are too poetical to be poets; we are a nation of brilliant failures, but we are the greatest talkers since the Greeks", (not the most accurate of Oscar's observations, considering his guest's future career). Yeats recalled: 'I remember thinking that the perfect harmony of his life, with his beautiful wife and his two young children, suggested some deliberate composition'.

Yeats did not particularly admire Oscar's writings but saw him instead as a man of action. 'It was the man I admired, who was to show so much courage and who was so loyal to the intellect'. He regarded Wilde as 'one of our eighteenth century duellists born in the wrong century. He would be a good leader in a cavalry charge'.

Oscar told Yeats that he 'had turned down a safe seat in Parliament'. Yeats thought that, if he had taken this course, his career might well have followed that of *D'Israeli*, 'whose early style resembles his, being meant for crowds, for excitement, for hurried decisions, for immediate triumphs'.

(Oscar, however, wrote in 'An Ideal Husband' that: 'Only people who look dull ever get into the House of Commons, and only people who are dull ever succeed there'.)

Yeats was asked once if he thought that Oscar was a snob and replied: "No, I would not say that. England is a strange country to the Irish. To Wilde the aristocrats of England were like the nobles of Baghdad'. However, Yeats said that Oscar 'hated Bohemia' and was vastly happier when staying in the homes of the rich.

During Wilde's trials, Yeats, at his father's prompting, visited Oscar and delivered some letters of support from various Irish literati. He also attended court, but thereafter did not see Oscar again. Yeats wrote that the fall of Wilde endangered many of his friends – he himself had to take care on the streets to avoid being beaten up. Yeats: 'The rage of the mob against Wilde was really the rage of the British against art and artists'.

Yeats noted that the end of the Decadents coincided with Wilde's death and the turn of the century: 'In 1900 everybody got down off his stilts: henceforth nobody drank absinthe with his black coffee: nobody went mad: nobody committed suicide: nobody joined the Catholic Church; or if they did I have forgotten'.

His father, John Butler Yeats, had been a friend of the Wilde family and had dined at Merrion Square in the 1860s. Having trained as a barrister, he abandoned the law, and became a distinguished portrait painter. Oscar once recounted to a friend how one morning John Yeats had come down to breakfast and announced: "Children, I am tired of the law, and shall become a painter". The friend asked Oscar: "Did he know how to paint?" 'Not in the least, that was the beauty of it'.

WB Yeats spent his early years mostly in Dublin and London but was drawn to the West of Ireland and in particular Co. Sligo. He later explained that the inspiration for his most famous poem had sprung from his nostalgia for this elective heartland: "I was going along the

Strand and, passing a shop window where there was a little ball kept dancing by a jet of water, I remembered waters about Sligo and was moved to a sudden emotion that shaped itself into 'The Lake Isle of Innisfree'.".

In 1889, he published his first poems, a volume called 'The Wanderings of Oisin and other Poems'. Soon afterwards he met the woman who was to be both his muse and his heartbreak. He fell in unrequited love with the Irish nationalist Maud Gonne and as a result became embroiled in political activity. He said he marched beside her 'like one in a dream'.

Maud became the central motif for many of Yeats's love poems, an effusion with which Wilde had little sympathy: 'Poets know how useful passion is for publication. Nowadays a broken heart will run to many editions.' In 1903, Maud married another man, John McBride.

In 1896, Yeats, now aged 33, finally lost his virginity to a novelist, Mrs Olivia Shakespear, (the cousin of the poet, *Lionel Johnson*). In order to provide a suitable love nest for the event, he rented an unfurnished room. Realising the need to provide some furniture, Yeats went shopping. 'Olivia came with me to make every purchase and I remember an embarrassed conversation in the presence of some Tottenham Court Road shop man upon the width of the bed. Every inch increased the expense'.

Having met *Madame Blavatsky*, Yeats became interested in the occult and in 1890 joined *Constance Wilde* as a member of the Hermetic Students of the Golden Dawn. His poetry reflected his new obsession.

The actress *Mrs Patrick Campbell's* daughter-in-law Helen reported: 'The only time I found Yeats worth listening to was when he could be coaxed out of his bee-loud glades and induced to talk about spirits and levitation. He solemnly swore that he'd seen a full-sized billiard table lifted six feet in the air and rooted there so firmly that it had to be chopped to pieces to get it down'.

On a more mundane level, Yeats became a founder member of the Rhymer's Club, a literary group that established itself at the Cheshire Cheese pub, off Fleet Street in London. Wilde occasionally attended their meetings, (Oscar: 'I have always had grave suspicions that the basis of all literary cliques is a morbid love of meat teas').

In 1898, Yeats was invited to stay at Coole Park, the Co. Galway home of Lady Gregory, (he was to spend his summers there for the next thirty years).

[LADY AUGUSTA GREGORY (1852-1932) became his closest ally in the development of the Irish National Theatre. She was the wife of the ex-Governor of Ceylon, Sir William Gregory, (and had also had an affair with the sexually ubiquitous *Wilfred Blunt*). She had met Wilde but turned down his requests for contributions to the Women's World.

Although the painter *Augustus John* described her as looking 'like Queen Victoria, only uglier', she was still capable, aged 60, of an affair with the American lawyer and art patron John Quinn.

Yeats was also friendly with her only son, Robert Gregory, and her nephew, Sir Hugh Lane. Accordingly to *George Moore*, Lane was a transvestite who used to try on his aunt's dresses – he was nicknamed 'Petticoat Lane'.]

With the backing of his new patroness, Yeats was able to start work on creating a specifically Irish theatre, a battle that he had to fight in the teeth of opposition for over thirty years. Almost every major new development in Irish drama that he supported produced a literal riot.

In 1899, 'The Countess Cathleen', co-written by Yeats and Lady Gregory, was attacked by reactionary Catholic elements. The performance was not aided by the arrival of a number of anti-clerics, sent by the future revolutionary leader Arthur Griffiths, with orders to: "Applaud everything that sounds as if it might be disagreeable to the clergy". Police finally restored order and the play proceeded.

In 1903, the pair formed the Abbey Theatre in Dublin. It soon became the scene of another riot when JM Synge's play, 'The Playboy of the Western World', (which questioned Irish rural morality), was produced. Lady Gregory dismissed their opponents, saying that the battle was 'between those who use a toothbrush and those who don't'.

One of Yeats's supporters, a young doctor, was infuriated by the hypocrisy of the audience: 'It was all I could do to keep myself from jumping up on a seat and pointing out among the howling men in the pit those whom I was treating for venereal diseases'.

When Sean O'Casey's play, 'The Plough and the Stars', opened in 1926, it was greeted with yet another riot. Yeats strode onstage in a fury and bellowed at his detractors: "You have disgraced yourselves yet again".

Given the regularity of disorder at his theatre, Yeats developed a foolproof method of quelling the mob. He would stand silently at the front of the stage, then in measured tones boom out the words: "Charles....Stuart....Parnell!" This inevitably produced a patriotic hush in the house. Then Yeats would proceed with a speech that bore absolutely no reference to Parnell whatsoever.

Yeats was in England when the 1916 Easter Rising broke out in Dublin. Major John Mcbride, his rival for the hand of Maud Gonne, was executed for his part in the rebellion, leaving Yeats free to propose again. Maud once more turned him down, (as did her daughter Iseult when he proposed to her a few months afterwards.)

Finally abandoning his hopes of wedlock with the Gonne family, he married Georgina Hyde-Lees in 1917, and gradually settled into a position of a world-respected laureate, a Senator in the new Irish Parliament, and a 'smiling public man'.

He occasionally ruffled his companions when he forgot his immediate surroundings in the pursuit of a concept. The Oxonian scholar John Sparrow was with him one morning in the Mitre Tavern, Oxford, when the lounge full of newspaper readers was startled to hear Yeats's high voice ringing round the room with the words: "The tragedy of sexual intercourse is the perpetual virginity of the soul".

At a party, George Moore cornered Yeats and jokingly recited a scurrilous new limerick: 'There was a young man from St Johns, Who wanted to roger the swans, 'Oh no' said the porter, 'Oblige with my daughter, But the swans are reserved for the dons'.

Yeats gravely considered the verse but questioned the last line, unsure whether the mot juste should be 'swans' or 'birds'. He retired into the conservatory for half an hour and could be seen (and heard) comparing the two versions by chanting the lines and rhythmically moving his hand up and down as he did so. Finally he burst back into the room to announce authoritatively to the company and to the now embarrassed Moore: "Birds, Moore, birds!"

Yeats, although a courteous man, had a chilly lack of humour and an exaggerated sense of his own dignity that turned him into a comic butt, especially for his Irish contemporaries. The writer Oliver St John Gogarty said that: "Yeats became so aristocratic that he started evicting imaginary tenants", while George Moore wrote that Yeats's habitual costume of flowing cape and wide hat made him 'resemble a huge umbrella left behind at a picnic'. Moore: 'Yeats would order a mutton chop off a waiter in a voice that suggested he was seeking the Holy Grail'.

Yeats cultivated an air of remoteness from the minutiae of everyday life. Gogarty was convulsed with laughter when he heard that Yeats, when attending to business that involved signing many cheques, absent-mindedly had signed them all: 'Yours sincerely, WB Yeats'.

When Yeats was awarded the Nobel Prize for Literature in 1923, Gogarty could not resist spreading an apocryphal story around Dublin. He claimed that Yeats had received the news in a telephone call from an old friend called 'Smiler'.

"Senator Yeats" said Smiler, "Through you and to you a great honour has been paid to our country and to yourself. I have just received a cable from Stockholm telling me that you have won the Nobel Prize for Literature. This is a remarkable day for the Irish nation and for the Hibernian diaspora in many a farflung land. It is as if the harp of Blind Rafferty had been restrung to herald a....."

Yeats interrupted: "For Jaysus sake, Smiler, pull yourself together. How much?"

Yeats became part of the folklore of the people of Dublin. They nicknamed him 'Willy the Spooks'. The 20th century playwright Brendan Behan recorded a story that he had heard in his youth. One day, Yeats was sharing a bench with an old man when the bells of St Patrick's Cathedral burst into loud peals above them. Yeats was enthralled by the sound.

He turned to the old man and said: "Wonderful, wonderful, don't you think, to hear those chimes that once rang on Dean Swift's own ear. That Robert Emmet listened to. That Thomas Moore in his old father's house heard?"

The old man bent his head over to Yeats and cupped his hand to his ear: "What's that you're saying, mister?"

Yeats spoke louder: "I was just commenting how strange it is about time, or should I say the concept of time, that Wolfe Tone and Lord Edward Fitzgerald would have heard those same..."

The old man interrupted him: "To tell you the truth, mister, I can't hear a word you're saying for the noise o' them fuckin' bells".

1889

[In Paris, France, the Exposition Universelle, (World Fair), opened and exhibited such inventions as the telephone and the incandescent bulb. Also the Eiffel Tower was completed.

In Britain, 'The Doll's House', the first production of an Ibsen play, opened in London.

When the Dock Strike succeeded in gaining 'the dockers' tanner', raising their pay to sixpence per hour, it led to an increase of trade union activity.

The match girls of Bryant and May's factory went on strike for higher wages and against their dangerous working conditions. They were being slowly poisoned by the phosphorus in the matches. Reformers used to exhibit this by turning the lights out to show the girls' jaws glowing in the dark. The match girls' strike was partially successful.

In October, the Cleveland Street scandal involved senior members of London society.)

In January, Wilde published his dialogue 'The Decay of Lying' in 'The Nineteenth Century' magazine. He named the two characters after his sons, Cyril and Vyvyan.

Also in January, he published 'Pen, Pencil, and Poison' in 'The Fortnightly Review'. Oscar had long been fascinated by the psychology of criminals, seeing them in some ways as being allied to artists. He was particularly interested in the forger Thomas Chatterton (1752-1770) and the murderer Wainewright.

[THOMAS WAINEWRIGHT (1801-1859) was a painter and aesthete who, having defrauded the Bank of England of £2000, successively poisoned his uncle, his sister-in-law, and his mother-in-law, mostly it appears for the insurance money. When yet another acquaintance died after Wainewright had insured his life for £3000, the insurance company became suspicious and he was

arrested. Found guilty of his original fraud, Wainewright was transported for life to Tasmania. On his deathbed, he admitted that he had murdered his mother-in-law because he disliked 'her thick ankles'.

In a haunting hint of his own fate, Oscar wrote of Wainewright's imprisonment: 'The sentence now passed on Wainewright was to a man of his culture a form of death'.]

In March, Wilde published 'The Birthday of the Infanta' in 'Paris Illustré'.
In May he met the young poet, John Gray.

JOHN GRAY 1866-1934

Described at the time by Shaw as 'one of the more abject of Wilde's disciples', the very handsome John Gray became Wilde's lover during 1889. Oscar used his surname as the fictional hero for his new novel, 'The Picture of Dorian Gray' and, at first, John Gray was happy to live up to the image, signing himself 'Dorian'. In 1892, Oscar helped pay the publishing costs for Gray's book of poems, 'Silverpoints'.

Gray was an unusual figure for the nineteenth century, being a man who had risen from very humble beginnings simply on his own ability. Being from the first generation to have profited by the new State schools, he helped set a pattern that was followed increasingly in the decades to come.

He was a carpenter's son, born in the poverty-stricken area of Bethnal Green, London, and, as a youth, had worked as a metal-turner at Woolwich Arsenal. However, aged 16, he passed a Civil Service exam and in 1888 matriculated from London University. He became one of the very rare Foreign Office clerks who had a Cockney accent.

Prior to the establishment of competitive examinations, entry into the Civil Service had been predominantly the preserve of young men of good family. The entry qualifications were something of a farce. One applicant reported that he was sent to be examined by a chief clerk with a reputation as a brilliant, if brusque, mathematician. He nervously entered the office and waited for the interrogation. The chief clerk looked up from his papers and barked: "Well, sir, add up two and two?" The applicant stuttered out: "Four, sir". The examiner bellowed back at him: "Quite right, sir. You'll do, sir, you'll do!" and walked out of the room.

In 'Dorian Gray', Wilde alluded to the new system when a character was given the line: 'When I was in the Diplomatic, things were much better. But I hear they let them in now by examination. Examinations, sir, are pure humbug from beginning to end. If a man is a gentleman, he knows quite enough, and if he is not a gentleman, whatever he knows is bad for him'.

Once established as a civil servant, Gray found himself attracted to the London literary world where he mingled with the Rhymer's Club and Wilde's Café Royal set. He soon realised that his career might be in jeopardy if he became too associated with the character of 'Dorian' – he might be regarded as a security risk. When the Star newspaper claimed that he was the original of 'Dorian', Gray sued them for libel and won his case.

In 1892, Wilde became infatuated with his new lover, *'Bosie' Douglas*, and the jilted Gray contemplated suicide. He left the Wilde circle, (one of them, the poet Theodore Wratislaw, said that: "He is an artist with a promising career behind him"). But, in November 1892, Gray met another poet, Raffalovich.

MARC-ANDRE RAFFALOVICH (1865-1934) was a wealthy young man from a Russian-Jewish banking family whose mother held a regular salon for Parisian high society. It was rumoured that she considered him to be so ugly that in 1883 she had sent him to London to avoid looking at him. Accompanied by his Scottish nanny/housekeeper, Miss Florence Gribbell, he set up home in England.

Although on first acquaintance they had some rapport, Raffalovich soon became wary of Wilde whom he regarded as dangerously indiscreet. Oscar also angered him by mocking his poetry book, 'Tuberose and Meadowsweet'.

When Raffalovich attempted to copy his mother by opening a salon in London, Wilde was openly contemptuous: "Andre came to London with the intention of opening a salon and has succeeded in opening a saloon".

On one occasion, Wilde arrived for dinner at Raffalovich's house in South Audley Street with five other guests. When the butler opened the door, Wilde announced: "We want a table for six, please". Raffalovich overheard the joke and did not forgive the joker.

Meeting John Gray on the rebound from his affair with Oscar, Raffalovich fell in love with him and became his patron/partner. Their combination of pique and rejected love soon congealed into an active hatred of Wilde and they became two of his most bitter enemies. During Oscar's trials, a worried Gray hired a lawyer to keep an eye on events in case his name was mentioned during the evidence; luckily for him, it did not arise. After Oscar's conviction in 1895, Raffalovich attacked him savagely in a book called 'L'Affaire Oscar Wilde'.

However, Wilde's fall seemed to have a salutary effect on the pair. Having set off for a Mediterranean cruise in Raffalovich's black-painted yacht, (named 'Iniquity'), for what was intended to be a relaxed debauch, they underwent a Damascene conversion and returned to shore converted to piety and Catholicism.

Gray tried to buy up all the copies of his own poetry book, (which he now called "the odious 'Silverpoints' "), to destroy any reminder of his decadent past. Then in 1898 he resigned from the Civil Service to study for the priesthood at the Scots College in Rome.

Ordained in 1901, he was sent as assistant curate to a poor district of Edinburgh. He was not a great orator in the pulpit, (admitting in a letter that 'I'm told that the monotony of my voice drives them to drink'), but proved his worth to his parishioners by his ability to mend electrical fuses.

Raffalovich, accompanied by his ever-faithful nanny, Miss Gribbell, also came to live in Edinburgh. Although he never tried for the priesthood, Raffalovich was admitted to the third order of Dominicans, and took the name of Brother Sebastian, (Sebastian being a favourite name among homosexuals). They remained lifelong friends.

Gray graduated to parish priest in the city and was made a canon in 1930. In an echo of his past, Gray's church was possibly unique in Scotland for its habit of saying an annual mass for the soul of Paul Verlaine. He was one of the founders of Edinburgh Zoo, and also became a keen golfer, describing the course at St Andrews as being 'the only competition to Jerusalem as a place I would choose to end my days'.

Marie Corelli was another contributor to Wilde's 'Women's World and provided an article in June 1889.

DAME MARIE CORELLI 1864-1924

Marie Corelli, (real name Mary Mackay), was an aspiring novelist who had achieved some fame with her 1887 novel 'Thelma'. In the 1890s, she was to become the most popular novelist in Britain, with astonishing sales of her main books on quasi-religious themes, 'Barabbas' (1893) and 'The Sorrows of Satan' (1895). The journalist *Herbert Vivian* said of her that: 'I should not credit her with vast intelligence, but she evidently possesses the gift of assimilating simple ideas in a way that makes them appeal to the lower-middle class'.

Although she had obvious public appeal, the literary critics were unanimous in deriding her books. *Ambrose Bierce* reviewed one of them: 'The covers of this book are too far apart'. An immensely vain woman, Corelli dismissed such criticism as blasphemous carping, and eventually refused to submit her novels for review.

Not surprisingly, her work became a favourite butt of the Wilde circle. When Oscar was in Reading Gaol in 1896, a warder asked him for his opinion on Corelli. He replied: "Now don't think I have anything against her moral character, but from the way she writes she ought to be here". He later chided the artist *William Rothenstein* for spreading this story but added: "I don't mind so much, as long as it gets to her ears".

In 1901, Corelli settled in Stratford-on-Avon where she spent the rest of her life. She left the world one lasting legacy when she helped prevent the 'modernisation' of the town in the early 20th century, an act of foresight that earned her the enmity of the town council.

She became a well-known figure in Stratford, particularly when she bought her own gondola and hired a Venetian gondolier to pole her up and down the River Avon. When she reached middle age, she altered her publicity photographs so that she still appeared as a waif-like teenager. Very self-conscious about her shortness, she would greet guests while standing on a small stool hidden beneath her long dresses.

Her constant companion, a Belgian woman called Bertha Vyver, provided Corelli with dogged devotion but received little respect for her efforts. The writer *Robert Hichens* reported visiting the pair in Stratford: 'When Miss Corelli and I were preparing to go to her carriage Miss Vyver appeared dressed for going out. As soon as Miss Corelli saw her she said, "Oh no, Bertha! You're not coming! Mr. Hichens and I prefer to go alone." "Oh – I see, Marie! Oh, of course, darling Marie!" ' Bertha then scuttled off upstairs shamed by her own presumption.

Corelli's popularity plummeted as her public grew more sophisticated, but she continued to publish increasingly less successful novels. During the First World War, she became a fervent propagandist for the British cause. This did not prevent her enemies on Stratford town council from taking revenge when she was accused of hoarding sugar. Despite her protestations that the sugar was intended for the making of jam, (to be later sold for public consumption), she was convicted of the offence.

Queen Victoria was a great admirer of Corelli in the 1890s and once argued with her daughter over the novelist's merits. They summoned a gentleman-in-waiting to ask his opinion. Not having heard the previous conversation, he declared that: "The secret of Miss Corelli's success is that her writing appeals to the semi-educated". His opinion was received in icy silence.

Towards the end of his stint working for Cassells, Wilde seemed to have grown weary with the ephemera associated with the job. In 'Dorian Gray', he was to write: 'Yet in his inmost heart he desired to be something more than a mere leader of fashion, to be consulted on the wearing of a jewel, or the knotting of a necktie, or the conduct of a cane'.

Later still, in 'An Ideal Husband', he inserted a stage direction that seemed to reflect his own position: 'Lord Goring, pulling himself together for a great effort, and showing the philosopher that underlies the dandy'.

Bored after editing 20 issues of Women's World, he drifted away from the magazine in July 1889, (receiving a termination notice in October).

During July and August 1889, Oscar went to Germany and travelled by steamer from Cologne to Kreuznach to meet a theatrical producer, Lawrence Barratt. They discussed the possible presentation of Oscar's play, 'The Duchess of Padua' – though, this time, the title would be changed to 'Guido Ferranti'. He returned to London via Wiesbaden and Ostend.

Oscar: 'The Rhine is of course tedious, the vineyards are formal and dull and, as far as I can judge, the inhabitants of Germany are American'.

In September 1889, Wilde had dinner at Langham's Hotel, London, with the American publisher, Joseph Stoddart, and the writer Arthur Conan Doyle.

SIR ARTHUR CONAN-DOYLE 1859-1930

Over the dinner at Langham's, the two authors discussed their new projects with the publisher and, on the strength of their synopses, Stoddart agreed to publish Oscar's book, 'The Picture of Dorian Gray', and Conan Doyle's book, 'The Sign of Four'. The latter was to be the second outing for Conan Doyle's fictional detective, Sherlock Holmes, (originally to have been called 'Sherrinford Holmes), the first having been 'A Study in Scarlet' (1886).

Conan Doyle later wrote of the meeting: 'It was a golden evening for me – Wilde's talk left an indelible impression on my mind. He towered above us all and yet had the art of seeming to be interested in all that was said. He took as well as he gave, but what he gave was unique'.

Although the two men were never close, Conan Doyle did not join the attack on Wilde during the 1895 scandal. Conan Doyle: 'I thought at the time, and still think, that the monstrous development which ruined him was pathological, and that a hospital rather than a police court was the place for its consideration'. Given his early medical training, it was perhaps not surprising that Conan Doyle took this view.

After studying medicine at Edinburgh and gaining his MB degree in 1881, he went into private practice as a doctor. He set up his first surgery in Plymouth, sharing it with an eccentric friend called Budd. It was not a success, mostly due to his partner's behaviour. Budd insisted that all his patients took an oath not to drink tea. Whenever the pair did make some money, Budd would grab the takings and stride through the streets of Plymouth waving the money in the faces of rival doctors. Conan Doyle soon quarrelled with Budd, marched out of the surgery and, being a man of considerable strength, pulled his brass plate off the door with one wrench.

Moving on to Southsea, his next practice proved to be even more disappointing. During his first year, he lived on less than one shilling a day and was left with a net profit of £2. He returned his income tax form after entering 'no taxable income'. The tax inspector returned the form with a scribbled comment in the margin: 'Most unsatisfactory'. Conan Doyle sent back a note: 'I entirely agree'.

He tried London next, setting up his new surgery in Devonshire Place: 'Every morning I walked from the lodgings, reached my consulting rooms at ten and sat there until three or four, with never a ring to disturb my serenity'.

When he decided to commit himself entirely to writing, the enormous (and lasting) popularity of his 'Sherlock Holmes' stories turned him into a famous name. He also wrote historical novels, such as 'The White Company', and regarded them as greatly superior to his detective fiction. Rather in the way that *Gilbert* and *Sullivan* underestimated the longevity of their light operas, so Conan Doyle underestimated 'Holmes'.

Having 'killed off' his hero in 'The Final Problem' (1891), public pressure forced him to resurrect him in 'The Hound of the Baskervilles' (1902). He also turned to the drama and a production called 'Sherlock Holmes' appeared at the Lyceum Theatre.

During the rehearsal for one of his plays, a young and impecunious actor joked with the (by now Sir) Arthur Conan Doyle that the two should pool their incomes and share out their lifetime incomes half and half. Although amused by the young lad's impudence, Sir Arthur turned him down. The actor later became well known as Charlie Chaplin. (Famously, Chaplin once entered a 'Charlie Chaplin' look-alike competition anonymously. He came thirteenth.)

Conan Doyle became so identified with 'Holmes' that many people asked him to aid them in their campaigns for justice. He helped several individuals, and, on the wider political spectrum, supported *WT Stead* in his 1899 Peace Campaign, attacked the holocaust in the Belgian Congo, and in 1916 attempted unsuccessfully to save the life of the Irish rebel Roger Casement.

He travelled to various war fronts, serving in a medical capacity in the Boer War, and advocated mercy for the defeated Boer leaders, ('The making of political martyrs is the last insanity of statesmanship'.)

During the First World War, he advocated inflatable lifeboats on warships, was among the first to realise the implications of the tank, and, even before the war, predicted the possible risks from submarine attack. In 1915, the German Naval Secretary announced: "The German people can thank the British Admiralty for disregarding the warning on U-boat warfare given by Sir Arthur Conan Doyle".

After the war, he became a convinced spiritualist and spent much of the rest of his life touring the world giving lectures on the subject of communication with the dead. Once when he said that he would visit a seriously ill friend the next day, he was told that the friend might not survive the night. Conan Doyle replied: "In that case, I'll have a word with him next week."

Wilde's ex-lover, *Lord Alfred Douglas*, by now a fervent Catholic, attacked him over his rejection of Catholic belief. With typical Douglas melodrama, Bosie sent a message: 'You are a disgusting beast who ought to be horse whipped'. Conan Doyle replied: 'I am relieved to get your letter. It is only your approval that in any way could annoy me.'

Conan Doyle claimed that Oscar Wilde himself had been in touch from beyond the grave. Via a medium called Mrs Hester Smith, Oscar had grumbled about the publication of James Joyce's 'Ulysses', remarking that: "It is a singular matter that a countryman of mine should have produced this bulk of filth".

In 1923, Oscar contacted Conan Doyle through automatic writing. This time he complained indignantly about conditions in the afterlife: "Being dead is the most boring experience in life, that is, if one excepts being married or dining with a schoolmaster".

Wilde's next essay, 'The Portrait of Mr W.H.', appeared in Blackwood's Magazine.

News of the first major homosexual scandal since the passing the Labouchere Act four years earlier broke in the British press on November 16, 1889. It involved an important member of the Royal Family.

PRINCE EDDY 1864-1892

Although he was always known as 'Eddy', the *Prince of Wale's* eldest son had been christened Prince Albert Victor after his grandparents. He was Heir Presumptive to the British Throne and the future King-Emperor and therefore, in the words of Queen Victoria, heir to 'the greatest position there is'.

Aged 13, he and his younger brother George were placed in the British Navy, firstly on the training ship Britannia at Dartmouth for two years, then for three years on a ship of the line cruising the world. Although carefully guarded by the captain, the two boys became well aware of the Navy world of 'rum, bum, and baccy'. (Buggery was common on Navy ships and was known as 'a feed'.)

Even at this early age, Eddy was seen to be unusually stupid, although his captain couched it more euphemistically as 'the abnormally dormant condition of his mental powers'.

When, on leaving the Navy in 1883, he was sent to Trinity College, Cambridge, his academic performance was predictably awful. However, under the obsequious tutelage of *Oscar*

Browning and given the fact that he did not have to sit exams, he survived the ordeal. Punch magazine picked up on college gossip about Eddy and mildly hinted at his 'delicate side'.

Moving on to the British Army, he joined the 10th Hussars at Aldershot where he proved to be an even worse soldier than he had been a scholar. The Army commander, the Duke of Cambridge, was astounded at just how obtuse the Prince was. The Duke, an old veteran, once questioned Eddy about the Crimean War at a dinner. He discovered that Eddy had never heard of it.

If society was unimpressed by Eddy, Eddy was even less impressed by his position and birthright. He told a friend: "I would chuck it all up for five thousand a year". *Jimmy Glover* reported that Eddy's main amusement appeared to be repeatedly shouting out a favourite song, 'Two Lovely Black Eyes'.

If his intellect was suspect, his morals caused even more concern. He was reported as 'indulging in every form of vice and dissipation'. He twice had to be extracted from compromising entanglements with extremely unsuitable young women by the legal guardian angel of society, *Sir George Lewis*. At the transvestite club, the 'Hundred Guineas' in Portland Place, Eddy's nickname was 'Victoria'. He was even suspected of being yet another 'Jack the Ripper' candidate, (though in this case he had a watertight alibi – during the evening of one of the murders he was dining with Queen Victoria).

The Prince of Wales finally decided that Eddy should leave the country on an extended Royal Tour of anywhere sufficiently remote. Given Bertie's own spectacular sexual antics, and the fact that Eddy's brother George was known to keep two mistresses, (while rumoured to be married to a woman in Malta), Eddy's depravities must have been phenomenal to warrant such a drastic reaction.

> [One major reason for Eddy's removal was the growing scandal concerning an old friend of the Prince of Wales, **LORD ARTHUR 'PODGE' SOMERSET** (1852-1926), (the army companion of *Fenwick La Terriere* – see *Sudan Campaign*). Now aged 37 and fully recovered from his wounds, Podge was the Superintendent of the Royal Stables.
>
> Podge's family had already had its share of notoriety. His father, the 8th Duke of Beaufort, (of Badminton House in Gloucestershire), was known for his penchant for what he called 'unripe fruit' – prepubescent girls mostly supplied by a notorious procuress named Mrs Mary Jeffries.
>
> Podge's elder brother, Lord Henry Somerset (1849-1932), had been found by his wife Lady Isabella in the arms of a footman. She had brought a divorce case against Henry and showed no reticence in proclaiming him to be a sodomite. Although he was ruined, she also brought down the wrath of the aristocracy on her own shoulders by ignoring their code of silence over such matters. She was banished from society no less than her husband. (Wilde: 'To be in Society is a bore. But to out of it is a tragedy.')
>
> Henry retreated to Florence, Italy, where he wrote a book of poems called 'Songs of Adieu', (Wilde reviewed it with: 'He has nothing to say, and he says it'). Henry turned to song writing, his most famous composition being 'All Through The Night'. In 1893, Wilde and his lover Bosie stayed with Henry in Florence.
>
> The previous escapades of the Somerset family, however, paled before the storm that was about to break over Arthur Somerset.]

In July 1889 a telegraph boy at the main General Post Office in the City was found in possession of an unusually large amount of money. Suspected of theft, he confessed that he had earned it at a homosexual brothel in Cleveland Street, off the Tottenham Court Road, London.

The police were called in and arrested a further four telegraph boys, including one called Henry Newlove. Newlove made a statement implicating Lord Arthur Somerset and the Earl of Euston, saying that they were frequent visitors to the brothel.

The police kept a close watch on the building and observed many male visitors, including Podge together with a Life Guards corporal. In spite of ample proof, the police authorities were dissuaded from issuing any immediate warrants.

At first, the Prince of Wales refused to accept the police report on Podge: "I won't believe it, any more than I should if they accused the Archbishop of Canterbury". Even more surprising was the involvement of Henry Fitzroy, the Earl of Euston (1848-1912). Generally regarded as a persistent 'stage door Johnny', Euston had married a chorus girl, (before discovering that she was already married and divorcing her within months). But even more disastrously, it appeared that Prince Eddy also frequented Cleveland Street.

In a welter of cover-up, mostly orchestrated by the Prime Minister, Lord Salisbury, the warrants were delayed until Eddy had been sent to India and Arthur Somerset had resigned his commission and fled to France. Salisbury then allowed a warrant to be issued accusing Podge of 'committing acts of gross indecency and procurement'.

In September 1889, almost three months later, Newlove and an accomplice were tried in virtual secrecy; the case was over in thirty minutes and took place at the end of the day when the spectators had left believing the sitting was over. They received the incredibly light prison sentence of a couple of months, (previously a Hackney clergyman on similar charges had received life imprisonment).

Then, on 16 November 1889, the North London Press broke the story mentioning Podge and Lord Euston and hinting that 'a far more distinguished and highly placed personage' was 'inculpated in these disgusting crimes'.

As a result, in January 1890, Euston brought proceedings for criminal libel against the offending editor, Ernest Parke. The case was heard before *Judge 'Hanging' Hawkins*.

Euston claimed that the only reason he had ever been to Cleveland Street was because he thought it was a female striptease club. On finding it wasn't, he had left indignantly. (*Francis Burnand* of 'Punch' explained: 'He thought the game was going to be poker, but when he found it was baccarat he came away'.)

Despite a mass of evidence in favour of the defendant from rent-boys, Judge Hawkins summed up bluntly: "Would you believe a peer of the realm or self-confessed male prostitutes?" The jury chose the Earl of Euston and Hawkins gave the editor Parke twelve months in prison.

In truth, Euston had been a very well known figure in the homosexual underworld. Robert Clibborn, who was later to blackmail Oscar Wilde, also blackmailed Euston. (Oscar later claimed that Clibborn deserved the Victoria Cross for the pure nerve he displayed while fleecing the Earl.)

Euston survived the furore to become an aide-de-camp to King Edward VII in 1901.

(When *WE Henley* attacked Wilde in 1890 for writing 'Dorian Gray', he wrote in direct reference to the Cleveland Street scandal: 'If Wilde can write for none but outlawed noblemen and perverted telegraph boys, the sooner he takes to tailoring the better'.)

[On his departure from England, Arthur Somerset took the Orient Express to Constantinople, where he presumed that the Sultan, (who rejoiced in the daunting title of 'Abdul the Damned), would have no moral objection to his residence. But learning that the British Government had an obscure right of jurisdiction over British subjects in Turkey, Podge made a further retreat to Vienna.

The Austrian police unfortunately had heard of his case and, assuming that all homosexuals were also paedophiles, decided to try to entrap him by sending a group of attractive street boys to follow him. Just in case Podge's tastes might have altered during the previous month, they hedged their bets by dressing up one of the boys as a girl. Podge left for France.

When a royal courtier begged him to tell the truth and clear Prince Eddy's name, Podge replied that Eddy was precisely the reason why he was staying silent: "If I went into Court and told all I knew, no one who called himself a man would ever speak to me again. Hence my infernal position."

Unable ever to return to England, he remained in France until he died in Hyeres in 1926.]

Meanwhile, Prince Eddy, at least publicly, weathered the storm and in May 1890 was created Duke of Clarence. He was provided with a new 'best friend', the respected scholar and sportsman Dr Alfred Fripp, in an effort to keep him on the straight and narrow.

(Fripp later recounted a story in which he and Eddy had visited the immensely rich but immensely mean Duke of Fife. When Eddy saw the Duke's larders were stuffed with venison, (the result of endless deer shoots), he suggested that, as there was far more meat than the household could ever consume, it would be an appropriate gesture if the Duke sent some haunches as a gift to the nurses at Fripp's hospital, Guy's, in London.

The Duke grimly asked how many Fripp needed. Fripp glanced around the eighty haunches on display and answered six. Fripp: 'As the servant left the room, I overheard the Duke mutter: "Three will do, John". As the servant was closing the door, the Duke whispered again: "Oh, John, one will do".'

Two days later, Fripp received a note from the matron of the hospital: 'Venison returned as carriage costs were not paid'.)

It was decided that the best way of coping with Eddy was to marry him off. The first two choices fell through – Princess Alix of Hesse turned him down and went on to marry Tsar Nicholas II of Russia (and to die in front of a revolutionary firing squad); while the wildly unsuitable Catholic Princess Helene d'Orleans married the Italian Duke of Aosta and became a fanatical Mussolini supporter.

The third possibility, Princess May of Teck, did not know Eddy but had no particular objection to marrying him. A very speedy engagement was planned in case she did get to know him. However, before the nuptials could take place, Eddy died from a cocktail of illnesses including flu, gonorrhoea and syphilis.

As several contemporaries commented, Eddy's greatest contribution to the British Imperial Crown was to die. Most of the documentation on his life vanished – the Royal Archives announced later that 'unfortunately his file has not survived'.

His younger brother **GEORGE** (1865-1936) succeeded not only to Eddy's inheritance but also to his intended bride, May of Teck. They were married just eighteen months after Eddy's death; (Wilde travelled up from Goring-on-Thames in July 1893 to watch the celebrations at St James's Palace). On the death of his father, Edward VII, the couple became King George the Fifth and Queen Mary.

Possibly as a reaction to his brother's lifestyle, King George was decidedly homophobic. On hearing that the homosexual King of Siam had connived with a courtier to impregnate the

Queen of Siam, George spluttered in disgust: "How could any decent person talk to him again?" George considered it the duty of an unmasked homosexual to shoot himself.

(During the First World War, with anti-German feeling at its height, George V found himself – and the Royal Family – in the embarrassing position of bearing a German name, that of Saxe-Coburg-Gotha. To defuse resentment, he changed it to the very British name of 'Windsor'. The German Kaiser, (his cousin and enemy), observed that he was very much looking forward to his next visit to the theatre: "where presumably there will be a performance of Shakespeare's 'The Merry Wives of Saxe-Coburg-Gotha'.")

During November 1889, Wilde was angered when an article appeared in the press written by the journalist and travel writer, Herbert Vivian.

HERBERT VIVIAN 1865-1940

On the strength of a introductory meeting in 1888, Herbert Vivian published a (slightly) mocking article about Oscar's domestic life, including a story about his children, and his advice to them: ' "I plaster the walls of their rooms," Oscar said, "with texts about early rising and sluggards, and so forth, and I tell them that, when they grow up, they must take their father as a warning and occasionally have breakfast earlier than two in the afternoon." '

Oscar was uncharacteristically furious over what he regarded as an intrusion into his private life and responded: 'Meeting you socially, I, in a moment which I greatly regret, happened to tell you a story about my little boy. Without asking my permission you publish this in a vulgar newspaper'.

He went on to attack Vivian's precocious 1889 effort at autobiography, (he was aged 24): 'Believe me, your style is quite impossible, and vulgarity is the worst debut a man can make in life'.

Vivian was stung by Oscar's rebukes and counter-attacked: 'It is too much to say that Mr Oscar Wilde is only a clever assimilator of other people's conceptions, but he certainly has a marvellous memory'.

Vivian's clash with Oscar attracted the attention and approval of Wilde's other enemies, including *Charles Brookfield* and *James Whistler.* Vivian: 'My acquaintance with Whistler arose through a press criticism of Oscar Wilde from my pen, and soon ripened into a long intimacy.'

Vivian remained not only Oscar's lifelong enemy, but also continued the feud beyond the grave. Vivian: 'I do not share any of the posthumous admiration which Wilde seems to attract on the Continent'. Wilde's son, *Vyvyan Holland,* reported that the only man who ever refused to shake hands with him because of his father was Herbert Vivian.

Educated at Harrow and Trinity, Cambridge, Vivian began his career as a secretary to the adventurer *Wilfred Blunt.* He turned to journalism, working for *WE Henley* at the National Observer and for Pearson's Weekly, and specialising as a foreign correspondent. Although he reported from many countries, including Russia, Turkey, and Ethiopia, he became an expert on Balkan affairs.

He regarded Balkan politics with a jaundiced if amused eye. Vivian: 'An interesting but little-known fact about the Serbo-Bulgarian war of 1885, was the simultaneous flight of the two sovereigns, Prince Alexander of Battenburg galloping back headlong to Sofia, and King Milan towards Belgrade, each under the impression that his army had been routed'.

He became friendly with the next Bulgarian monarch, Prince Ferdinand, and witnessed a supreme diplomatic faux pas when Ferdinand first met the new bride of the British ambassador. Never having left London before, she was bewildered by the capital Sofia, then 'a mixture of Oriental barbarism and new German buildings'.

Ferdinand began with his usual question to visitors: "What do you think of my capital?" The bride innocently replied: "Well, it was a bit of a shock at first, but I am growing used to it. After all, now that the railway has reached here it won't be so bad. One will always be able to run over to Vienna." Fortunately, Ferdinand had a sense of humour.

Vivian became acquainted with another English girl, a Miss Durham. She had fallen in love with Albania and became a fierce defender of its political rights. In time, the Albanians came to see her as a kind of uncrowned queen. Very occasionally Miss Durham would leave her wild life in the Albanian mountains and return to argue their case in London.

At one dinner party in Kensington, Miss Durham became bored with the company and decided to liven things up a bit. The man seated opposite her was an exceptionally dreary professor. Miss Durham took off her shoes and placed them on her lap with the toes showing over the top of the table. Then, with a blast of mock indignation, she shouted: "Dr. Mackintosh! Will you oblige me by taking your feet off my lap?"

During the First World War, Vivian became a YMCA (Young Men's Christian Association) lecturer, and in this capacity was sent to preach to the British troops based at Salonika.

He reported back that the Tommies and the enemy Bulgarian soldiers, although battling along a murderous front line, actually got along quite well with each other. Vivian: 'They had a similar sense of humour, and the Bulgarians had good memories of Gladstone. During a nocturnal bombardment they often made their guns play mischievous tunes while ours replied with counter-tunes'.

1890

[In Germany, Kaiser Wilhelm II dismissed Otto von Bismarck, the man who had guided Germany's fortunes since the 1860s.

The relationship between France and Britain deteriorated to such an extent that war became a serious possibility.

During the winter of 1890, London was hit by a very bad influenza epidemic.

The Prince of Wales became involved in the scandal known as the Tranby Croft affair.]

In mid February 1890, Wilde visited Oxford to see a performance of Robert Browning's play, 'Strafford'. While there he called on his old tutor, Walter Pater, who recommended a visit to the rooms of a protégé – the young Oxford undergraduate and poet, Lionel Johnson.

LIONEL JOHNSON 1867-1902

When Wilde arrived at Lionel Johnson's rooms at New College, Oxford, although it was lunchtime he found the poet still asleep in bed, (a habit that was soon to become a lifetime practice). Johnson was delighted by his guest: 'He discussed, with infinite flippancy, everyone: laughed at Pater: and consumed all my cigarettes. I am in love with him'.

This meeting led to a strong friendship and probably to a sexual relationship, (Johnson himself being homosexual). However later in his life he abandoned all attachments and, according to *WB Yeats*, 'hated all thoughts of sex'.

In 1891, Johnson initiated the crucial relationship of Wilde's life when he introduced Oscar to his cousin, *Bosie*, (*Lord Alfred Douglas*). Johnson later recognised the fatal nature of what he had unwittingly engineered. After the contretemps of 1895, a friend reported seeing Johnson drunkenly gazing at the portraits of Oscar and Bosie, and moaning: "Mon Dieu! Mon Dieu!"

He later fell out with Wilde over what he considered to be Oscar's harsh treatment of Bosie and wrote a poem beginning: 'I hate you with a necessary hate'.

On leaving Oxford in 1890, his private means enabled him to start a literary career in London. Acquiring lodgings in Fitzroy Street, he became a member of the Rhymers' Club, converted to the Catholic Church, (although previously declaring himself a Buddhist while a pupil at Winchester School), and began a friendship with his fellow poet WB Yeats.

Described as 'a sort of young old man' by *Frank Harris*, Johnson never physically developed past the age of 16 and, at 5ft 3ins, was always mistaken for a boy. Wilde commented: "Every morning at 11 o'clock you can see him come out very drunk from the Café Royal and hail the first passing perambulator".

After a visit to Ireland in 1893, Johnson became fascinated by the country and its culture. He began to claim Irish descent after his discovery of a vaguely Hibernian ancestor and at one stage assumed a brogue and addressed everyone as 'me dearr'.

The habit of staying in bed till lunchtime that Wilde had noted at Oxford, now extended to teatime. One day Yeats called on Johnson at 5pm to be informed by a servant that Johnson was not yet awake. Yeats wrote: 'The man then said with an accent of slight emotion as though the feat touched him to admiration: "But he is always up for dinner at seven" '.

As his alcoholism increased, Johnson was ejected from his Fitzroy Street lodgings. His landlord was understandably anxious about Johnson's nocturnal practice of wobbling around the house with a lighted candle.

He then lived in a series of rooms around the Fleet Street area, occasionally venturing out to the local bars. *Richard Le Gallienne* once accompanied Johnson back to his lodgings and was invited in for a drink. Le Gallienne expected tea, until his host told him: "I hope you drink absinthe, Le Gallienne, for I have nothing else to offer you".

Johnson finally retreated into total seclusion, fortified by two pints of whisky a night, (according to the testimony of his laundress).

Reports of his death differed. Either he was knocked down by a hansom cab in Fleet Street while weaving his way across the road, or he had been perched on a bar stool in the Green Dragon and fallen off in a drunken stupor. Whatever the truth, he died two days later in St Bartholomew's Hospital, aged 35. Yeats: "Johnson had refused rather than failed to live".

> *During the spring of 1890, Wilde made the acquaintance of a young actor called Seymour Hicks.*

SIR SEYMOUR HICKS 1871-1949

The friendship between Wilde and Hicks was originally fortuitous. Hicks: 'I lived at Earl's Court, and more than once, on leaving an evening party, dropped him at his house in Tite Street, Chelsea, which was on my way home.' But Hicks soon became intrigued by his late night passenger.

He later wrote at length on Oscar's appearance and manner, noting that: 'His teeth were not good, and he had a habit of talking with his hand before his mouth'; and that: 'In company he conveyed gentleness and distinction, and there was nothing in the slightest degree effeminate about him either in his action or speech'.

Hicks remained an admiring observer during Wilde's trials: 'I went to the Old Bailey to see the last day of this great genius's trial. I knew that he was doomed, and I thought to myself, if by chance he should catch sight of me he would see at least one sympathetic and sorrowing friend'.

After Oscar's sojourn in prison, Hicks agreed to take money from the impresario Charles Frohman to Wilde in Paris, on the pretext that Frohman needed a new play, (all three realised that no play would be forthcoming). Hicks: 'I made it my business to find Wilde, and ran him to earth one evening at a small restaurant in Montmartre... I delivered the message and hastily bade him goodbye, for he had as his companions two creatures of the kind who had been his ruin. I was sick and disquieted'.

Seymour Hicks's long and distinguished career in the English theatre lasted from 1887 till his knighthood in 1935. His first job was with the husband and wife team called the Kendalls, who worked from the Court Theatre in Sloane Square, London, (formerly a dissenting chapel). Mrs Kendall gave him what he said was the best piece of theatrical advice he ever received: 'Never pause on the stage unless it is necessary; but if you do pause, pause for an hour if you want to'.

Hicks wrote that his initial entry into the theatre world had its problems. His first critical review was from Clement Scott: 'And the Prompter, although seen at rare intervals, soon became a favourite with the audience'. Soon after his debut, Hicks was gratified when *Sir Henry Irving* said that Hicks reminded him of the great actor Charles Mathews. Then Irving added: "Yes. You wear the same sort of collars".

To bring in extra money, Hicks often found himself performing in plays starring wealthy amateurs who could hire theatres and casts for matinees to display their own talents, or lack of them. One such man cast himself as 'Othello'. He had an atrocious memory and towards the end of the play forgot the lines completely. In desperation, he placed one hand on Desdemona's head and, pointing to Heaven with the other, announced: 'More I cannot tell you, child! But there is One above who knows all. Ring down the curtain!'

As Hicks's career progressed he was often pestered to find jobs for new actors. One acquaintance kept badgering him on behalf of a young gentleman who, the acquaintance added, "comes from a very good family. In fact one of his ancestors was killed at Waterloo!" Hicks replied coolly: "On which platform?"

The acquaintance was annoyed by this offhand reaction and later grumbled to his girlfriend: "Don't you call that rude, asking me what platform he was killed on?" "Yes," replied the girl, "As if it mattered."

Hicks also had a very successful career as an author, particularly with his volumes of reminiscences, 'Vintage Years' being a good example. He reported a story by a medical friend concerning an ancient Scottish doctor who always refused to tell anyone his age. When he died, his friends thought that they would finally discover the truth from the inscription on the coffin lid. They had reckoned without the parsimony of the old man's son. He had simply removed his father's surgery doorplate and fixed it on the coffin. It read: 'John McPherson. Office hours – 10am till 4pm'.

One of Hicks's anecdotes summed up his affection for his own profession. He wrote of two old actors, weary and footsore, trudging along a muddy road with their possessions on their backs, en route to their next engagement. Hicks: 'A magnificent car passed them with a gentleman and lady sitting proud as peacocks in the back seat. One actor turned to the other and said, "Here, Bill, don't you wish we were them?" The other shook his head, "No, not for a minute, lad. You see, they can't act!"

In 1893, Hicks married Ellaline Terriss, the daughter of one of Henry Irving's star actors, **WILLIAM TERRISS** (1847-1897), of whom Wilde had written an approving review in 1885, ('Mr Terriss's Squire Thornhill was an admirable picture of a fascinating young rake').

Terriss's real name was William Lewin, but he was known throughout the profession as 'Breezy Bill', (*Bernard Shaw*: "Terriss was a play in himself"). Hicks described his father-in-law as 'a transparently honest man, incapable of intrigue'.

This character assessment seems to have been borne out during a rehearsal with Irving. After Terriss had given a recitation, Irving suddenly asked him what the speech meant. Terriss mumbled vaguely, then confessed: "So help me, guv'nor, I'm blowed if I know what it means".

In 1897, Terriss was performing at the Adelphi Theatre in London. One of the extras in the cast was a deranged young man from Dundee called Prince. He had no talent for acting, but his fellow extras teased him into believing that he had huge potential and that only Terriss stood between himself and his destiny. Terriss barely knew of Prince's existence.

One night Prince positioned himself in Maiden Lane and, when Terriss passed, leapt out and fatally stabbed the actor with a butcher's knife. His son-in-law Seymour Hicks was one of the first to attend the dying man. Prince was sentenced to life in Broadmoor Asylum.

Ellen Terry commented: "Poor dear Terriss. I do hope he lived long enough to realise that he had been murdered. How he would have enjoyed it".

THE PICTURE OF DORIAN GRAY

Despite writing in 1888: 'I wish that I could write a novel, but I can't', in June 1890 Oscar published his only novel, 'The Picture of Dorian Gray' in Lippincott's magazine.

The book was inspired by *Huysmans's* 'A Rebours' and *Pater's* 'Studies in the History of the Renaissance', and bore a resemblance to RL Stevenson's 'Doctor Jekyll and Mr Hyde'. The South Kensington Museum helped by providing the lists of jewellery, etc, that appear in the book.

Oscar said of the main characters in the novel: 'Basil Hallward is what I think I am; Lord Henry what the world thinks me; Dorian what I would like to be – in other ages, perhaps'.

'Dorian Gray' came under immediate attack for its 'immorality'. Jerome K Jerome called it corrupt and advised its suppression, while the WH Smith's bookstores banned it as 'filthy'. Wilde was bewildered by this reaction and wrote to *Arthur Conan-Doyle* that: 'I cannot understand how they can treat Dorian Gray as immoral…. It still seems to me that the moral is too obvious'. He had actually added a comic preface to make it less censorious.

Oscar resignedly observed that: 'The English public, as a mass, takes no interest in a work of art until it is told that the work in question is immoral'. His wife Constance said: "Since Oscar wrote Dorian Gray no one will speak to us".

When the novel was published as a book in April 1891, Wilde revised the script to avoid any further accusations of immorality.

Between July and September 1890, Wilde published his 'The Critic as Artist' article in two parts in the Nineteenth Century magazine.

In August 1890, Wilde visited Bamff, Alyth, in Perthshire, Scotland. He wrote: 'I am far away from the Athenaeum in the midst of purple heather and silver mist – such a relief to me, Celt as I am, from the wearisome green of England.'

He was ambivalent about the Scots in general. In 1899, he wrote to Lawrence Houseman, (brother of the poet, AE Houseman): 'Your Scotsman believes only in success. How can a man, who regards success as the goal of life, be a true artist? God saved the genius of Robert Burns to poetry by driving him through drink to failure. Think what an appalling figure in literature a successful Burns would have been'.

Oscar returned to London in early September.

1891

[In France, the Panama Canal Scandal made headlines, while the French government agreed an Entente Cordiale with Russia to offset the threat of the Triple Alliance between Germany, Austria, and Italy. In Norway, Hendrik Ibsen published 'Hedda Gabler'.]

Having re-written his play 'The Duchess of Padua', (originally 'The Duchess of Florence'), and renamed it 'Guido Ferranti', Oscar gave the script to the American actor Lawrence Barratt, who opened the show to respectful reviews on January 26, 1891, at the Broadway Theatre, New York. It lasted till February 14, when Barratt was taken ill and died shortly afterwards.

Oscar was dissatisfied with the play and never revived it: 'The Duchess is unfit for publication – the only one of my works that comes under that category'.

Although he had turned down 'The Duchess', another actor-manager, George Alexander, showed Wilde the way forward by suggesting that he write a modern play.

On February 1st 1891, Wilde attended a meeting of the Rhymer's Club at the Cheshire Cheese tavern in Fleet St, London. The tavern had a prestigious literary history, hosting, (at different periods obviously), Ben Jonson, Herrick, Oliver Goldsmith, and Dr Johnson. It was also famous for its rump-steak puddings.

The Rhymer's Club was formed to help establish a London equivalent of the Parisian Latin Quarter. It had a large proportion of Irish Protestants in its ranks and lasted three years.

Ernest Dowson, Herbert Horne and Arthur Symons were leading members of the Rhymers.

ERNEST DOWSON 1867-1900

Dowson had previously met Wilde at *Herbert Horne's* house in 1890. *Robert Sherard:* 'Ernest Dowson was not at all the kind of man with whom Wilde would ever have cared to associate ... for he was untidy, even dirty in his dress. ... He was usually drunk and, at most times, when so, noisy and boisterous. Yet Oscar Wilde, because he admired his genius, was at all times glad to see him.'

In fact, Oscar dismissed the attacks on Dowson, saying: "If he didn't drink, he would be somebody else. You must accept a person for what he is. It is not regrettable that a poet is drunk, but that drunks aren't always poets".

Dowson remained a friend throughout Oscar's imprisonment and later sometimes stayed with him in France. On one visit to Dieppe in June 1897, he attempted to expand Wilde's horizons by inviting him to the local brothel. Oscar agreed and was accompanied to the door by Dowson and a cheering crowd who waited until Oscar emerged. The experience did not alter Oscar's tastes: "It has been the first time for ten years and it will be the last. It was like cold mutton. But do spread the story all over England. It should entirely restore my reputation'.

TS Eliot said of Dowson that he was 'the most gifted and technically perfect poet of his age'. When DH Lawrence read Dowson's poem 'Non Sum Qualis Eram', which contains the famous line – 'I have been faithful to thee, Cynara, in my fashion', he commented: "Cynara inclines me to weep". Dowson's poetry also provided Hollywood with two of its most famous film titles – 'Days of Wine and Roses' and 'Gone With The Wind'.

Despite his brilliance as a poet, his life was one of almost unmitigated disaster. Having left Queens College, Oxford, in 1888 without a degree, at first he helped to manage his family docking business in the East End of London. He soon drifted into the more congenial company of the Rhymers and the Decadent movement, later contributing to such publications as the 'Yellow Book' and 'The Savoy'.

Whereas for most members of the Rhymers their image as 'tipplers and whoremongers' was to some extent a pose, Dowson flung himself wholeheartedly into the role. *John Gray* said that only Dowson really carried on the tradition of Christopher Marlowe. After Dowson lost his job as a critic in 1890, he relied for the rest of his life on translation work and the miniscule income from his writing.

Already attracted to young girls – ('What a charming world it would be if women did not exist – or rather if they never grew into their teens') – he encompassed his own ruin when in 1891 he fell deeply and permanently in love with a 12-year-old girl called Adelaide Foltinowicz, known as 'Missie'. He met her when she served him in her parents' restaurant, 'The Poland' in Sherwood St, Soho. As a result, he committed himself to years of dining every evening in this shabby café simply to observe Missie. Despite his obsession, Dowson realised the absurdity of his position – 'the veal cutlet and the dingy green walls of my Eden'.

[Dowson was certainly not alone in his adoration of pre-pubescent girls. Edgar Jephson: 'There was at Oxford in the eighties a cult of little girls, the daughters of dons and residents: men used to have them to tea and take them on the river and write verses to them'. This practice was regarded as charming rather than as perverted; it merely attracted light ridicule. In 1894, Punch produced a spoof poem entitled 'To Dorothy, My Four-Year-Old Sweetheart'.

The most famous relationship of this type was between the **REV. CHARLES DODGSON** (1832-1898), and Alice Liddell, the inspiration for his 1865 book 'Alice in Wonderland', (written under Dodgson's pen name of 'Lewis Carroll'). Although he was teaching at Oxford during Wilde's student days, his subject of mathematics was not calculated to attract Oscar's interest. *Mark Twain* said of Dodgson: "He was the shyest full-grown man, except Uncle Remus, I ever met".

When the 31-year-old Dodgson proposed marriage to the 11-year-old Alice, a rift developed with the Liddell family. *Lord Salisbury* commented: "Dodgson went half out of his mind in consequence of having been refused by the real Alice".

Perhaps as consolation, Dodgson turned his affections to the child actress *Ellen Terry*, 'a beautiful little creature'. He visited her to take photographs and said that: "I can imagine no more delightful occupation than brushing Ellen Terry's hair".

Outside of genteel Oxford, the general population also took a more relaxed attitude to sex at an early age. In England, between 1851 and 1881, children under 15 outnumbered adults, and, given the high rate of infant mortality, girls were encouraged to marry young in the hope of raising as many offspring as possible. (Until 1890, the age of consent in most American states was ten. In some states it was seven).]

Dowson, although severely tempted, never took sexual advantage of his young waitress. Partly he was frightened by the new 'Labouchere' Act that had raised the age of consent from 13 to 16, but also he had moral reservations: 'I swear there never was a man more fanatically opposed to the corruption of innocence – even where women are concerned – than I am'.

But while the innocent might be safe, he had little compunction about the more experienced. *WB Yeats*: 'Dowson sober would not look at a woman; did he not belong to the restaurant-keeper's daughter? But, drunk, any woman, dirty or clean, served his purpose'.

John Gray said the Dowson would pick up a different woman virtually every night, but occasionally had lengthier relationships. One of them was with a girl called Dulcie who was known as 'a lively companion with a girlish sense of humour'.

On one occasion, she was present with Dowson at a gathering at *Charles Conder's* rooms in London. Bored by the literary conversation, and especially by a verbose translator called

Robert Steele, Dulcie vanished into a bedroom only to reappear stark naked except for shoes. Perching herself on Conder's knee, she gazed up innocently at the astounded Steele. Ignoring the latter's indignant expostulations, Conder 'smiled indulgently and stroked her bare flesh'.

WB Yeats recalled meeting another of Dowson's girlfriends, when Dowson arrived in the company of a woman called 'Penny Plain and Tuppence Coloured'. She was a prostitute who charged different rates depending upon whether she was wearing make-up or not. Again, the company consisted of literary gentlemen, and again, as with Dulcie, 'Penny' stripped naked.

She regaled the company with tales of her clients, in particular an old gentleman who derived sexual satisfaction from watching her wring the necks of two pigeons, which he supplied from a basket. Throughout the evening, she made visits to a bedroom with various guests.

Another Rhymer, *Arthur Symons,* said that the alcoholic *Lionel Johnson* had made a hilariously inept attempt to wean Dowson off his addiction to prostitutes. As the pair staggered along Oxford Street, Dowson announced: "I'm going to the East End to have a ten-penny whore". Johnson, filled with the urge to restrain his friend, had tried to prevent his departure: "No, no, Ernest! Have some more absinthe!"

In fact, Johnson would have had little trouble in convincing Dowson to drink as, (particularly after the suicide of both of his parents in 1894 and the loss of their dry dock business), Dowson hurled himself into alcoholic bouts that surpassed Johnson's own addiction.

He spent his nights mostly in the East End drinking, chasing prostitutes, and brawling with all-comers. The usually tolerant *Frank Harris* complained after sharing a night in Limehouse: 'I still remember Dowson hopelessly drunk at the end screaming with rage and vomiting insults – a wretched experience'. Dowson often appeared the next morning with a cauliflower ear, and once with stab wounds in his forehead. He took to carrying a small revolver that he had won in a card game.

For a time he ate his meals in cabmen's shelters, until he was expelled by the cabmen for being too disreputable. Arthur Symons: 'Without a certain sordidness in his surroundings, Dowson was never quite comfortable, never quite himself'. Sometimes, as a diversion, he took to playing 'Blind Chivvy' – a game that consisted of navigating one's way around London using only the back alleys.

After his conversion to Roman Catholicism, Dowson acquired the habit of dipping a small crucifix into his wine before drinking. It had no visible effect on his decline. WB Yeats reported seeing him 'pouring out a glass of whisky for himself in an empty corner of my room and murmuring over and over in what seemed an automatic apology, "the first today, the first today".'

John Gray said that Dowson had been arrested so often for 'drunk and disorderly conduct' that the magistrate used to greet him in the dock with: "What, you here again, Mr Dowson?"

By the mid 1890s, Dowson had lost his family, any semblance of regular income, and all his teeth, while gaining tuberculosis and a skin disease. In 1897, he went to stay in the village of Pont-Aven in Brittany, France, hoping to live a frugal peasant life. Within two months, things went badly wrong.

One night, after a heavy bout, Dowson smashed in the window of the local baker's house, climbed in, and drunkenly demanded sex with the baker's wife. He was hauled off to prison where he stayed for two weeks.

On his release, the American writer *Gertrude Atherton,* who was also staying in Pont-Aven, made a short-lived attempt to reform the hapless poet, but soon abandoned the job. The penniless Dowson managed to make his way back to England by winning a game of cards with the ferryboat captain.

In London, Dowson discovered that his beloved Missie had married a tailor called August Noelte. The news destroyed him. Frank Harris: 'When she chucked him for a tailor, the wound served, and Dowson died of it'. Harris added: 'Dowson had the gift of making himself loved by every one, save that once when love meant everything to him'.

Diseased, impoverished, and heartbroken, Dowson buried himself in rented lodgings on the Euston Road, until the journalist *Robert Sherard*, finding his friend unable to pay the rent, rescued him and took Dowson to the Sherard's family home in Catford. There, the Sherards nursed him until, in February 1900, Dowson died of tuberculosis. Wilde replied to the news: "It is all so sad. Ernest was a child doomed to darkness" … "But he knew what love was".

(Missie cheated on her new husband with a German lodger and became pregnant by her lover. She had an abortion but died of blood poisoning as a result, aged 25. The abortionist was sentenced to seven years in prison.)

WB Yeats said of Dowson: "I cannot imagine the world in which he would have succeeded".

HERBERT HORNE 1864-1916

The central figure of the Rhymer's Club, at least in the social sense, was the architect, poet, critic, and art collector Herbert Horne. Wilde had met Horne in 1886 when they collaborated over a memorial to the memory of the 18th century poet Thomas Chatterton. It was to have been erected at Chatterton's birthplace at Pyle St School in Bristol. Oscar had advised Horne to be cautious: 'Perhaps after all, cleaning, repairing, and a tablet would be enough'.

In his early career, Horne concentrated on architecture and, with his senior partner AH Mackmurdo, designed the new Savoy Hotel. Nearly all of Horne's London buildings were destroyed by bombs during World War Two. He also became editor of an artistic magazine, 'The Hobby Horse', until 1894.

In 1896, Horne roused the enmity of a fellow Rhymer, *Arthur Symons*. Symons: 'Horne was a man you could never trust … His manner was cold, restrained, with a mingling of insolence and diffidence. He never mentioned love except to jest at it.' Symons became incensed especially by Horne's treatment of their shared lover, Muriel Broadbent.

Muriel had been the daughter of a doctor but, after the death of both her parents, was forced to work in a laundry. Although a shy, nervous girl, she decided to try to improve her luck by becoming a prostitute in London. The day after her arrival, Symons met her at the notorious pick-up promenade of the Alhambra Theatre and soon made her his mistress.

Symons later introduced her to Horne and the two men began to share her favours. They quarrelled when Muriel complained of sadistic treatment by Horne; (while under Horne's 'protection', she also had been subjected to a drunken attempt at rape by the artist *Aubrey Beardsley*). The quarrel caused a permanent split in the ranks of the former Rhymers.

Horne moved to Florence, used his wealth to buy and restore a 15th century house called the Palazzo de Fossi, and filled it with his artistic collections. (When Horne died, he bequeathed the house to the city of Florence where, under its new title of Musee 'Orne, it became a popular sight).

Seeking to restore the ideal of medieval life in his Palazzo, Horne stripped out all the modern improvements, including the electric lighting. However, as Wilde's friend *Reggie Turner* observed: "Even Homer nods. He did put in a bath and – alas – an appliance for heating".

Horne's latter years were spent writing a biography of the artist Botticelli. He was painstaking over his intensive research into every possible detail of the painter's life. Reggie Turner: "Dear Herbert Horne! Poring over Botticelli's washing bills – and always a shirt missing!"

Horne's associate and fellow Rhymer, **JOHN DAVIDSON** (1857-1909), previously had been a Scottish schoolmaster who had tired of the grind and had arrived in London in 1890 to further his literary career. He soon wearied of the Rhymers also, saying that they lacked 'blood and guts'. Davidson: "If a man must be a connoisseur, let him be a connoisseur in women".

Davidson wrote plays and vaguely Nietzschean philosophical works, but was best known for poetry, particularly his 1896 'Fleet Street Eclogues'. He had a naturally truculent character that was exacerbated by a raging inferiority complex.

Davidson's life was tormented by the lack of recognition for his talents and by lack of money. By 1908, *Frank Harris*, realising just how desperately poor Davidson had become, cornered the then Prime Minister, *HH Asquith*, in the Savoy. He suggested that Davidson should given a pension from the Royal Literary Fund. Asquith had never heard of the poet, so Harris sent him a copy of Davidson's verse. As a result, Asquith provided an allowance of £100 a year.

Unfortunately, the arrival of this money actually inflamed Davidson's persecution complex and the aggrieved poet left London to live in Penzance, Cornwall. Overwhelmed by depression, he drowned himself in 1909; six months later, fishermen discovered his decomposing body in the sea near Mousehole.

JOHN BARLAS (1860-1914) was another Scots poet who attended meetings of the Rhymers and who had as difficult a life as Davidson's.

In 1883, Barlas had visited Wilde's Charles St home at the invitation of *Robert Sherard*. The fiery young anarchist was accompanied by his girlfriend, (a lady who expressed her political opinions by habitually wearing blood-red flannel underwear). Barlas, searching for a reason to take offence at what he perceived to be the bourgeois Oscar, decided that his girlfriend had not been offered enough respect and, after delivering a tirade against middle class snobbery, stormed off back to Lambeth in a fury.

As a devoted follower of *William Morris*, Barlas joined the 'Bloody Sunday' march to Trafalgar Square in 1887, where he received a blow on the head from a policeman's truncheon that permanently affected his reason. Probably as a result of this, in 1891, he lost control and fired a revolver shot at the House of Commons.

At his trial, he was judged to be of unsound mind and bound over for the sum of £200. Wilde, forgiving Barlas's previous behaviour, immediately went bail for him, later writing: 'I am so glad you are feeling better. I now know nerves myself, what they are, and what rest can do for them'. A grateful Barlas inscribed one of his books to 'King Oscar'.

Barlas finally succumbed to insanity in 1898, lingering on in a Glasgow asylum till his death in 1914.

ARTHUR SYMONS 1865-1945

Although Arthur Symons knew Wilde from meetings at the Rhymers Club and the Crown tavern, and had contributed two articles to 'Woman's World', they were never close friends. When Oscar's 'Ballad of Reading Gaol' was published in 1897, Symons reviewed it enthusiastically and promised to aid any future literary efforts. But, in his mentally troubled later years, Symons attacked Wilde's memory bitterly, comparing him unfavourably to the Roman emperors Nero and Tiberius.

Symons was a key figure of the Decadent movement who hosted *Verlaine's* memorably drunken visit to London, shared a flat with *WB Yeats* and shared Muriel Broadbent with *Herbert Horne*, took hashish and mescal with *Ernest Dowson*, and wrote for the magazines, the Yellow Book and the Savoy.

In spite of these impressive credentials his contemporaries saw him as somewhat colourless. Wilde called him 'an egoist without an ego', while *Max Beerbohm* said that: 'He was perfectly agreeable but perfectly uninteresting – like one of those white flannels that nurses give children to wipe their faces on.'

Symons reacted to his upbringing as a West Country Methodist minister's son by moving to London to become a poet and critic, and to embrace notoriety. His book of verse, 'London Nights', published in June 1895, certainly provided the latter. The Pall Mall Gazette reviewed the volume as the work of 'a dirty-minded man whose mind is reflected in the puddle of his bad verses'. A later book provoked *TWH Crosland* to characterise Symons's poetry as: 'tumbled skirts, cigarette ash, and empty eau de Cologne bottles'.

Considering sex to be the source of his inspiration, Symons became a rather self-conscious debauchee. Yeats: 'Symons has always had a longing to commit a great sin, but he has never been able to get beyond ballet girls'.

He made a point of recounting these numerous adventures to Yeats, describing the tactful way in which one lover had left him. "She has such nice feeling. You know she must have somebody. She knew I would be jealous of a man, so she chose a woman!' Yeats: 'I have heard him say after a visit to some theatre of varieties, "Oh Yeats, I was never in love with a serpent charmer before".'

After his marriage in 1901 to Rhoda Bowser, he settled into a career as a highly respected critic and editor until, in 1908, while travelling in Italy he went suddenly insane. Extracting Symons with difficulty from a medieval jail in Ferrara where the local authorities had locked him in manacles for safe keeping, Rhoda brought him back to a mental home in England.

The asylum doctors predicted that Symons had only a few months to live. Touched by his plight, his friend, the painter *Augustus John*, decided to make Symons's dying days as pleasurable as possible. He gained permission to take the patient out of the asylum for a few hours of healthy exercise, accompanied by a keeper.

They managed to lose the keeper within minutes, and repaired instead to the Café Royal for an afternoon of high living. Unfortunately, they both became extremely drunk and ended up having a fistfight with some beggars. They were forced to escape from the fracas by fleeing in a hansom cab.

Augustus John's altruistic impulses became strained when he slowly realised that the medical estimate of Symons's lifespan was seriously awry. Symons not only failed to die on time but also went on to live for another 37 years.

As he gradually recovered from his breakdown, Symons also recovered much of his libido. John found himself bombarded by poetry that 'grew more and more lurid'. After receiving a Symons effusion entitled 'Prologue to a Modern Painter', John complained that it was 'all about bones and muscles and blatant nakedness. I ask myself what have I done to merit this?'

Symons wrote a new translation of Casanova's memoirs in 1922, and attempted the amorous pursuit of Iris Tree, the actress daughter of *Sir Herbert*. A friend warned him off: "There is a quarter of a century between you and Miss Tree – she is still hungry for sensation but you cannot keep up her pace".

He lingered on into the 1940s as a ghostly reminder of the Victorian decadents. The Laureate John Betjeman mentioned him in his poem 'On Seeing an Old Poet in the Café Royal': 'I saw him in the Café Royal, Very old and very grand, Modernistic shone the lamplight, There in London's fairyland'.

Symons was a devotee of the London music halls and became the Star newspaper's critic on the subject. Wilde shared this interest, though *Seymour Hicks* said his attitude was more one of 'good-humoured tolerance'. At one show Hicks and Wilde watched the performance of a mediocre mimic. Oscar whispered to Hicks: "I do think it so kind of him to tell us who he is imitating. It avoids discussion, doesn't it?"

By the 1890s there were over 200 music halls in London, chief of which were the Alhambra in Leicester Square, and Gatti's under the Charing Cross station arches. Although at first little more than entertainment backdrops for drinking and prostitution, they developed into a showcase for genuine talent and popular international acts.

Among the great names who made music hall respectable were Dan Leno and Harry Lauder; (the latter was knighted for his charitable efforts during World War One). Oscar Wilde's particular favourites were Albert Chevalier and Marie Lloyd, (*Sarah Bernhardt* called Lloyd 'a theatrical genius').

Perhaps in a nod of respect to her admirer, on her 1907 tour of the USA, **MARIE LLOYD** (1870-1922), echoed Oscar's most famous quip. She replied to the usual questioning at the New York customs house with: "I have nothing to declare except a cough".

Although she won the affection of the British and performed with Harry Lauder at the Lord Mayor's dinner in 1909, Marie was always seen as too risqué to become entirely respectable. She was once brought before the Licensing Committee of the London County Council to be questioned over the content of her act.

Marie replied by singing one of her most salacious songs, 'She'd Never Had Her Ticket Punched Before', with an air of virginal purity. She followed this by singing 'Home, Sweet Home' with all the obscene innuendo in her considerable armoury. The Committee acknowledged her point that prurience lay in the mind of the audience.

Not all music hall acts were as accomplished as Lauder and Marie Lloyd. Seymour Hicks reported that one comedienne, a Miss Jennie Macpherson, gave a very poor performance one evening. Later on, the chairman (compere) of the music hall rapped his gavel to announce that: "Miss Jennie Macpherson will now appear again". A man interrupted from the audience: "But she's awful!" The chairman turned to the heckler and replied smoothly: "Nevertheless, she will appear again".

In February 1891, Wilde travelled to Paris and mingled with more of the intellectual groups around in the city. He enjoyed the company of 'les flaneurs' – young men who protested against the tyrannous speeding up of modern life by indulging in public dawdling. The more extreme flaneurs took tortoises with walks along the boulevards.

He attended some of the celebrated 'Mardis', (Tuesdays) – parties held each week by the leading Symbolist poet, Stephane Mallarme (1842-1898) where, in his tiny flat, Mallarme held court among his disciples. Mallarme approved of Oscar's writing and praised 'Dorian Gray' and 'Salome'. Oscar liked the French poet, but said of his poetry that he preferred it when Mallarme wrote in French rather than in English: "because, at least in French Mallarmé is incomprehensible, whereas in English, unfortunately, one can understand him".

Oscar also met the American Symbolist poet Stuart Merrill (1863-1915). Although born in the USA, Merrill had been raised in Paris and now resided there. He described Wilde at their first meeting as: "gigantic, smooth-shaven and rosy, like a great priest of the moon in the time of Heliogabalus". In 1895 Merrill started a Parisian petition for clemency during Oscar's imprisonment, and was instrumental in producing 'Salome' in Paris in 1896.

Merrill introduced Oscar to the Paris-based Greek poet Jean Moréas, (1856-1910 – born Iannis Papadiamantopoulos); previously Moréas had been an enthusiastic Symbolist but was now calling for a return to French Classical poetry. His first café meeting with Wilde was not a success. Moréas commented succinctly: "This Englishman is a shit".

Wilde also met the writers Anatole France and Marcel Proust, and the English artist Will Rothenstein.

ANATOLE FRANCE 1844-1924

Wilde had met Anatole France, (the pseudonym of Jacques-Anatole-Francois Thibault), previously in 1883 and, though never close, the two men enjoyed each other's company. France was a novelist of sparkling irony who held cynically humanist views on life.

Only rarely did he step out of his role of detached observer, though he did defend Alfred Dreyfus during the infamous Affaire, (which reached its climax in 1898). As he grew older he became attracted to communism; in 1921 he was awarded the Nobel Prize for Literature.

France himself was a striking figure with a long beard and twinkling eyes, who favoured wearing flowered dressing gowns and skullcaps. Friends described him as having a Rabelaisian look. He summed up his attitude to life with: "A man's gaiety is the measure of his genius".

He was also capable of quick thinking. One day, a lunatic arrived at France's home waving a self-penned manuscript for a new Constitution in one hand and a revolver in the other. France soothed him slightly by reading the document and bursting out in admiration: "I have been waiting for you, my friend! You have written what I dared not write. Now I can die in peace. This must be published for humanity!"

The madman blinked with surprise and nodded furiously. France seized a pen and rapidly scribbled and sealed a note. Handing it to the man he continued: "Take a cab and before the rabble know you are here, go to my publisher. I would offer to go with you but I am too well known. Give him my letter. He will publish your book. Adieu, philosopher! Speed and prudence!"

The man took the note and charged off, still flourishing his Constitution and his revolver. France sank back in his chair with relief. Hearing the story at lunch that day, a friend asked France what he had written in the note. France replied: "I wrote – 'Here is a total maniac. Telephone the nearest asylum and keep him amused till they bring the strait-jacket'."

Both France and Wilde had a deep aversion to those afflicted by illness. Oscar wrote in 'The Importance of Being Earnest': 'I do not approve of the modern sympathy with invalids. I consider it morbid. Illness of any kind is hardly a thing to be encouraged in others'. He had a special horror of the maimed. France agreed with him: 'People say that suffering ennobles. There is a whole literature about it. Suffering disfigures, my friend, and we should flee from it'.

But they disagreed over sexuality, France being decidedly heterosexual: 'For me, love is a woman: that is a point on which I am not Greek'. He had no objection to the aberrations of others though, describing them as being merely 'spelling mistakes'. The only sexual taste that angered him was chastity.

France: "The heyday of a man's life is the time of desire and of pleasure, and the wise man does all he can to prolong it. People laugh at an old man in love. Could anything be crueller or more stupid? For myself, I parody the formula of Descartes, and say 'I love, therefore I am'."

In pursuance of this philosophy, France once retired to the Bois de Boulogne in Paris accompanied by a girl. They were indulging in sexual foreplay when a park attendant arrived bellowing imprecations against 'old satyrs'. France handed him a card displaying his credentials as a member of the Academie Francaise. The park keeper's manner changed completely and, with a servile forelock tug, whispered that he was not bothered himself, but that children might spot the couple. He explained: "The unfortunate thing is that your good lady has a red petticoat that can be seen from as far off as if it were a flag. If the lady will excuse the suggestion, black would be much better".

France was not attracted to all women. He was particularly harsh on the English female. Talking of one London girl newly arrived in Paris, France groaned: "How did I recognize her nationality? Everything proclaimed it! Her mannish figure, her strangely coloured hair, her vinous complexion, and her teeth like the keyboard of a piano – her whole chapter of blemishes! When an Englishwoman starts out to be ugly, she doesn't stop halfway, you know".

His first marriage in 1877 to Marie-Valerie Guerin de Sauville ended in divorce in 1893. Although she had been a gorgeous blonde on her wedding day, Marie soon put on a great deal of weight, lost her teeth, and became formidably dominant. France became terrified of her ferocious temper. She was also short sighted but claimed to have good vision. France used to gain a temporary revenge by showing her paintings upside down.

In June 1892, she marched into his study and subjected him to a tirade of abuse. Ten minutes later, France was observed beating a retreat from his front door, wearing his dressing gown, skullcap and slippers, and carrying his pen, inkwell, and unfinished manuscript on a tray.

He later married his housekeeper, Emma Laprevotte, who treated him like a little boy, insisting on tying his shoelaces herself, and once when he had gone out to a literary lunch, dragging him home to change out of his nightshirt. A friend reported her shouting at him: "The idea of it, to be off like that to lunch with swells in a flannel shirt!" – 'Anatole France says nothing but lifts his eyes to heaven as he is led back to be re-dressed'.

To the end of his life, France remained deeply anti-religious: 'There is no clearer proof of the non-existence of God than life'.

His friend *Joris-Karl Huysmans*, shocked by France's atheism and fired by the fervour of his own recent conversion, once sent a message to France urging him to throw himself on the mercy of Christ. France sent a return message suggesting that Huysmans had his urine analysed.

SIR WILLIAM ROTHENSTEIN 1872-1945

One of Wilde's new acquaintances in Paris was the young painter Will Rothenstein. After studying at the Slade School in London, Rothenstein had moved to Paris where he shared apartments with the artists *Charles Condor* and Phil May. He said of this period of his life: 'Like the rest, I was bewitched by that fascinating, overpowering siren, Paris!'

After Oscar had sat for a portrait by Rothenstein, the painter said of his sitter: 'Wilde talked as others painted or wrote; talking was his art. I have certainly never heard his equal... Oscar talked what he should have written.'

He remained loyal to Wilde during the trials. (When Oscar's possessions were auctioned off in 1895, Rothenstein attended the sale at Tite St, bought some of the paintings, and passed on the cash to Oscar in prison).

He met Wilde several times later in France. On one occasion Rothenstein and his wife Alice took Oscar to a Paris restaurant but became irritated when they noticed Oscar trying to seduce the waiter. Next day, they determined to avoid him but, seeing his dejection at their behaviour, relented. Rothenstein: 'He was never a great poet... but, in his deliciously humorous acceptance of any situation in which he found himself, he showed his genius'.

In some ways, Rothenstein was an unusual companion for Wilde and his set. *J-E Blanche*: "Rothenstein had sometimes the severe manner of an Anglican clergyman'. As alcohol gave him jaundice, he was unable to join in the more spectacular binges that surrounded him.

After Wilde had teased him about being 'too sensible', Rothenstein admitted: 'But sensible at bottom I was. So I used to say that half my friends disapproved of me because I sat with wine bibbers, and the other half because I did not drink'.

Rothenstein: 'I didn't care for the poets' cafés – they were too crowded and noisy; and though I could, on occasion, sit up most of the night, I was not a night owl. Wilde said of me that I was like those dreadful public-houses in London – punctually at midnight all the lights went out of my face'.

When he returned to London in 1893, Rothenstein was commissioned to paint a series of Oxford characters. His skill at this work led to national recognition and to meetings and commissions from dozens of British notables; (Rothenstein: 'Vain men make the best sitters').

He became a (lemonade-sipping) habitué of the Crown pub on Charing Cross Road. It was a haunt of the artistic Decadents who shared the saloon bar with prostitutes, cabmen, and ballet girls from the nearby music halls. From 11pm till 12.30am the bar would be crowded with what Edgar Jephson described as 'the spirit of Nineties London in its fullest and freest expression'.

Grant Richards: 'Looking back, it seems to me that one of the oddest things about the Crown was that in spite of the cheapness of the liquor there dispensed no one in the gathering – except, perhaps, Ernest Dowson – ever became drunk'. Wilde occasionally joined the Crown throng but, on the whole, avoided pubs or anywhere else where he had to stand up to drink.

In 1899, Rothenstein married Alice Kingsley, a young actress from *Beerbohm Tree's* company, and gradually he abandoned the bohemian world to become a pillar of respectability. He moved to a house in Church Row, Hampstead, where drink was not served to guests. His friend and fellow artist, *Augustus John*, (who, rather than being seen as a pillar of respectability, was regarded as more of a mineshaft), was forced to drink at various hostelries in Hampstead before arriving at the Rothenstein table.

In 1920, Rothenstein became the Principal of the Royal College of Art and remained there for fifteen years. In 1935, his policy at the College was challenged because Rothenstein wished to train artists rather than just produce designers for industry.

Rothenstein: 'What an outcry there would be, and rightly, if I went to the British Museum and smashed a Grecian marble; but no one is scandalised when the spirit of promising artists is broken, and the nobler gifts become dependent on the caprice and diminishing chances of private patronage'. As a result, he was forced to resign his position.

After travelling to and painting in India in 1910, Rothenstein became a friend of the Bengali poet Rabindranath Tagore, and one evening back in Hampstead held a dinner in Tagore's honour.

Rothenstein reported: 'After dinner we asked Tagore to sing 'Bande Mataram', the Indian nationalist song. He hummed the tune but after the first words broke down; he could not remember the rest. Then WB Yeats began the Irish national anthem – and his memory, again, was at fault. Ernest Rhys could not for the life of him recollect the words of the Welsh national anthem. "What a crew!" I said – then I too forgot the words to 'God Save The King'.'

In 1931, Rothenstein was given a knighthood by his friend, the British Labour Prime Minister Ramsay Macdonald. Rothenstein recounted a story that again involved a social mishap concerning National Anthems.

At the end of a political visit to Rome, Ramsay Macdonald was accompanied to the train station by the Fascist dictator Benito Mussolini. Rothenstein: 'As Ramsay was climbing up to his compartment, the band struck up the British National Anthem. He had to remain, with one foot on the platform and the other on the running board, while the band played 'God Save The King' three times in succession, until Mussolini furiously signalled them to stop'.

MARCEL PROUST 1871-1922

Perhaps Wilde's oddest encounter during this 1891 Paris trip was with the young boulevardier Marcel Proust. Having been introduced by friends, Proust invited Oscar to visit him at his parents' home on Boulevard Haussmann. Proust arrived late for the meeting only to be told that Oscar had locked himself in the lavatory.

Proust asked gingerly at the lavatory door if Oscar was ill and received the reply: "No, I am not in the least ill. I thought that I was to have the pleasure of dining with you alone but I looked in the drawing room and saw your parents and my courage failed me. Goodbye, Monsieur Proust, goodbye". Proust's parents then told him that Oscar had peered into the room and said: "How ugly your house is". A bewildered Proust said: "I don't think Monsieur Wilde has been well brought up".

Proust himself had been born into a wealthy middle-class half-Jewish family where, as an asthma sufferer, he had been raised as an invalid. In his late teens, his friend *Robert Montesquiou* introduced him into Parisian high society, where Proust spent his time studying the foibles of the great salons.

Aged 17, he had fallen in love with a fellow schoolboy, the son of the composer Georges Bizet, (of 'Carmen' fame). When the young Bizet rejected him, Proust transferred his affections to Bizet's mother, Genevieve.

[After her husband's early death aged only 36, **GENEVIEVE BIZET**, (1846-1926), married a barrister named Emile STRAUSS and created one of the most interesting salons in Paris. She was a great friend of *Robert Montesquiou, Princess Alice* of Monaco, and the British Ambassador *Lord Lytton,*. Later her salon was a centre for the pro-Dreyfus faction.

Even after his passion for Genevieve faded, Proust remained a close friend, and she provided the model for his character 'the Duchess of Guermantes' in his renowned novel, 'A La Recherche du Temps Perdu'.

Wilde visited her salon in 1894 and wrote: 'Madame Strauss was quite charming to me'. It was at one of Genevieve's dinners that Oscar re-met Proust where the two men 'eyed each other with a complex curiosity'.

Genevieve Strausss had a mildly risqué reputation, leading the diarist *Edmond Goncourt* to write of her: 'she was idly ensconced in a deep armchair, with her soft black velvet eyes darting about feverishly and each ailing pose a coquettish invitation.' She once remarked about one admirer: 'Poor Achille, it would be so much less trouble to make him happy than it is to make him unhappy'.

She once convulsed Paris with laughter after she had arrived at an 'intellectual' dinner given by another hostess, Madame Aubernon. The topic to be discussed that night was 'Adultery'. Genevieve suddenly blurted out: "Oh dear, I'm so sorry! I've prepared 'Incest' by mistake!"]

Proust was able to find many such outré characters among the Parisian haut monde, not least Madame Aubernon herself. One of the rules at her dinners was that she would ring a little bell to signify which guest was allowed to speak without interruption at any given time. A man called Labiche, attending one such dinner for the first time, was heard to mutter something during another guest's allotted time and was sternly rebuked by the formidable Madame Aubernon: "Monsieur Labiche, you will have your turn in a moment!"

After the speech was over, Aubernon turned and announced: "Now you may speak, Monsieur Labiche". An embarrassed Labiche replied: "Well, I just wanted to ask for another helping of peas".

Proust's doctor, Dr Robin, provided some eccentric remedies for his patients, although he advised Proust not to cure his asthma as it acted as a protective against other diseases. His proscription for one old lady was: 'You must take off all your clothes, and then hop round a table at least six feet in circumference, eating an artichoke one leaf at a time'.

The death of Proust's mother in 1905, although traumatic for him, actually transformed him from being regarded as a lightweight dandy into being one of the greatest writers of the 20th century. It also provided him with an inheritance worth about £4 million in today's currency.

Proust's sexuality was always an uncertain area. Homosexuality in France had been decriminalised during the 1789 French Revolution, (though penalties were briefly reinstated during the Nazi occupation of the 1940s). However, while lesbianism was regarded merely as titillating, male homosexuality was not openly accepted, even if most Parisians saw it as a subject for humour rather than for outrage.

Proust had male lovers, most notably a young chauffeur called Alfred Agostinelli, who was killed in a flying accident. The novelist *Colette* noted archly that Proust was 'graceful and a whisperer, who left in step with his young male companion'.

One of Proust's sexual foibles was to watch rats being tortured with hatpins. He explained to a friend: "I have a desire to conjoin the most disparate sensations and emotions for the purpose of orgasm".

All his life, Proust made a point of frequenting both hetero and homosexual brothels. But these visits had something of a social air about them. In one brothel, rather than sex, the girls spent an evening providing extra blankets and hot water bottles after Proust complained about the cold.

He became acquainted with the notorious American lesbian *Natalie Barney* in 1921. (She complained that she thought Proust's literary treatment of lesbians was 'not so much charming as improbable'). When she invited him to attend a lesbian party at 'The Temple of Love' at her home, he turned down the offer, saying that 'The Temple' might be too draughty for him.

Proust retreated to his cork-lined, permanently curtained, six-room apartment in Paris. Engrossed in his monumental work, 'A La Recherche du Temps Perdu', for years he rarely emerged into the world outside.

As he had with Genevieve Strauss, Proust used many of his acquaintances as models for his characters. They included the Countess Greffulhe who described her husband's mistresses as 'those little ladies who make such good mattresses'; the outrageous snob Comte de la Rochefoucauld, who said of another family: "They were mere nobodies in the year 1000"; and Dr Pozzi who excused his infidelities to his wife with: "I don't deceive you, my dear, I supplement you". (Pozzi was a surgeon and immensely proud of his own good looks. Alphonse Daudet said of him: "I wouldn't trust him to cut my hair if there was a mirror in the room".)

Very occasionally, Proust would interrupt his secluded life in his Boulevard Haussmann apartment for relaxation. One night, he arrived at 1am in a taxi at the home of the leader of a string quartet, the Quatuor Poulet. Waking him up, Proust demanded that the quartet came back to Proust's flat to perform for him. The bleary-eyed leader eventually agreed and the pair circulated Paris to collect the remaining three members. Proust quietened their protests by feeding them mashed potato in the back of the taxicab.

Once back in Boulevard Haussmann, Proust reclined on his bed as the quartet sat around the room performing the works of Cesar Franck. At 3am, Proust insisted that they repeat the show and plied them with champagne until they consented. Finally, as dawn broke at 6am, he allowed them to go, having paid them in fifty-franc notes from an overflowing Chinese casket.

He later returned to the life of a socialite, living at home but dining out every night, (and becoming known as 'Proust of the Ritz'). At one party, he encountered the famous Irish novelist, James Joyce. Neither had read the other's works, and the meeting was not a success.

When they shared a taxicab home Joyce lit a cigarette, much to the chesty hypochondriac Proust's horror. Joyce grumbled about his eyesight, while Proust grumbled about his stomach. Proust asked Joyce if he liked truffles; Joyce replied that he did not. The two giants of the twentieth-century novel spent the remainder of the journey in silence.

During one dinner at the Ritz, Proust was flattered to find himself seated next to the English aristocrat Lord Derby. The perennially cold-obsessed Proust insisted on wearing his greatcoat during the meal.

Two years later, Proust was even more flattered to hear that Lord Derby had told a mutual friend: "Of all the impressions my wife and I took home with us from Paris, Monsieur Proust was the most indelible". However, he was not so pleased to hear that Lord Derby had continued: "He was the first chap we'd ever seen dining in a fur coat".

Proust's great work, 'A La Recherche du Temps Perdu', was finally published in 1927, five years after his death. It did not meet universal approval. *Anatole France*, commenting on its enormous length, said: "Life is too short and Proust is too long".

The French writer Jean Cocteau, though, visited Proust on his deathbed. He spotted the twenty volumes of Proust's book stacked up on the mantelpiece, "continuing to live" he said, "like the ticking watch on the wrist of a dead soldier".

Meanwhile back in England in February 1891, Wilde's essay, 'The Soul of Man under Socialism' had been published in 'The Fortnightly Review'.

THE SOUL OF MAN UNDER SOCIALISM

The piece encapsulated Oscar's highly individual views on politics. Having seen the effect on nineteenth century Britain, his instincts were always anti-capitalist and he was in favour of 'substituting cooperation for competition'. He despised the Victorian concept of solving society's ills through private charity and individual whim. Charity balls in particular attracted his mockery – the absurdity of trying to eliminate poverty through conspicuous consumption.

Among other things, he pointed out that mass communication was just as likely to lead to mass indoctrination as to enlightened improvement.

However, he also pointed out some of the problems that socialism could produce: 'It is to be regretted that a portion of our community should be practically in slavery, but to propose to solve the problem by enslaving the whole community is childish'.

He warned against authoritarianism, whether socialist or capitalist: 'If there are Governments armed with economic power as they are now with political power; if, in a word, we are to have Industrial Tyrannies, the last state of man will be worse than the first'. He concluded: 'To make men Socialists is nothing, but to make Socialism human is a great thing'.

The Marxists did not take the essay seriously; it appealed more to the followers of Mikhail Bakunin. But in Russia Wilde became known as a revolutionary writer. When Robbie Ross visited the country in 1911, he found that 'Soul of Man' was a bestseller that had been reprinted dozens of times.

Leaving Paris in April 1891, Oscar returned to England and to the social round. By now, Oscar's fame as a conversationalist had led to many invitations to mingle with the aristocracy and with such politically powerful groups as 'the Souls', although he was treated as a guest rather than as an insider.

> Wilde: ' 'The Peerage' is the one book a young man about town should know thoroughly, and it
> is the best thing in fiction the English have ever done'.
> At the end of April he visited the Willie Grenfells, (later Lord and Lady Desborough), at
> Taplow Court, their country house overlooking the Thames near Maidenhead.

WILLIE GRENFELL 1855-1945

William Grenfell had known Wilde at Oxford and had been initiated into the Apollo Masonic Lodge on the same evening.

He was a massively strong man renowned for his athletic prowess, and also as a Master of Hounds, a war correspondent, an explorer, and a big game hunter in India and Africa. He had rowed an eight across the English Channel, and had swum Niagara twice. *Margot Asquith*: "He's so tough that when he dies they'll turn him into Bovril".

As a Member of Parliament, Willie switched his political allegiance from the Liberals to the Conservatives after breaking with *Gladstone* over the issue of Irish Home Rule, and later supported *Sir Edward Carson's* defence of Ulster to the point of advising civil war if necessary. He was created Lord Desborough in 1905.

His main enthusiasm was for bi-metallism. It was a topic on which he could and did expound at interminable length after dinner at Taplow to his long-suffering guests. It was probably Grenfell's obsession that tempted Wilde into making bi-metallism a subject of fun in at least two of his plays. ('Fortunately I don't know what bimetallism means. And I don't believe anybody else does either' – 'A Woman of No Importance').

Grenfell's wife, Ettie (born Ethel Fane), who he married in 1887, was thought to be the most beautiful and the cleverest of the women who made up 'the Souls'. Through her wide network of friends she became a woman of considerable importance. As the most celebrated hostess of the age, the names of her weekend guests would be printed in the Times on the following Monday mornings.

Ettie indulged in numerous romantic friendships that occasionally developed into full sexual affairs. When Willie was being considered for the post as Governor-General of Canada, the gossip among Ettie's women friends centred on how Ettie would cope with the situation. Lady Mary Elcho: 'Margot Asquith is most anxious to know whether she will drop her lovers or take them with her!'

As a result of his 1891 visit, Oscar Wilde dedicated his story, 'The Birthday of the Infanta', to Ettie – 'as a slight return for that entrancing day at Taplow'.

(While there, Oscar met the two Grenfell sons, William and Julian. During the First World War, the latter wrote poetry, and became known for his poem 'Into Battle'. As a young man, Julian had been a jaded critic of the social world into which he had been born. The war came as something of a relief. He wrote home: 'I adore war. It is like a big picnic'.)

In 1908, Willie, now Lord Desborough, had an unfortunate experience that threatened his reputation as the greatest sportsman of his day. While fishing in the Thames in the company of a young lady called Miss Fisher, he accidentally fell in the river.

Desborough was mortified by this collapse of dignity, but Ettie rescued the situation by spreading the story that Miss Fisher had pushed him. As a result, Miss Fisher was ostracised by society and gained the reputation in London as 'the girl who ducked old Desborough'.

> *Despite Wilde's acceptance by and of the country house world, privately he acknowledged that the strain of appearing brilliant at all times was wearisome. Wilde: "I have known what it is to come back from a weekend – one of those ordeals by tattle which the stately homes of England provide for the passing guest – almost literally at death's door, from which nothing but hermetic seclusion, until the*

following week-end, enabled me to escape. One of my doctors called it heart-strain, the other brain-fag. It was really both".

After one such visit and having missed the early Monday morning train to London, Oscar was forced to return 'for four hours to the bosom of the ducal family when its exhibition hours were over'. He described it as 'a charnel-house' where 'time remained motionless'. An indignant host claimed that it was Oscar who was 'the extinct volcano with all the fire gone out of him. He could no longer talk, he was played out; his powers of performance were over'.

In 'An Ideal Husband', Wilde wrote: 'Oh, I can't stand your English house parties. In England people actually try to be brilliant at breakfast. That is dreadful of them. Only dull people are brilliant at breakfast'.

Also in April 1891, 'The Picture of Dorian Gray' was published in book form, with an additional preface. In May, this was followed by the publication of 'Intentions' – a book collection of essays including 'The Truth of Masks', 'The Critic as Artist', 'Pen, Pencil, Poison', and 'The Decay of Lying'.

'Intentions' was published by the firm of Osgood, McIlvane and Co., a business that made a point of advertising that they 'published simultaneously in London and New York'.

One day Richard Le Gallienne met Wilde in the street and told him that one partner, Osgood, had died suddenly. Oscar paused and said: "Poor Osgood. He is a great loss to us all. However, I suppose they will bury him simultaneously in London and New York'.

In late June 1891, Lionel Johnson introduced Wilde to his cousin, the 21-year-old third son of the Marquess of Queensberry, Lord Alfred Douglas, (known by his childhood nickname of 'Bosie'). They met at Tite Street.

LORD ALFRED 'BOSIE' DOUGLAS 1870-1944 (First Part)

In some ways, Bosie Douglas was the ideal homosexual lover for Wilde – extremely good-looking, aristocratic, and possessing a minor poetic talent of his own. In other ways, Bosie's character and family connections were to become lethally dangerous.

Max Beerbohm: 'Bosie is for one thing obviously mad, (like all his family I believe)'. The more circumspect *William Rothenstein* thought Bosie was 'an erratic but most attractive person, defiant of public opinion, generous, irresponsible and extravagant'. (Much later in their relationship, Oscar himself said of Bosie: 'He really had no motives in his life at all. He had passions merely'.)

Bosie's nephew considered that: 'Bosie would have been far more at home with Raleigh and Essex in the 1590's.' His mother, Sybil Douglas, stated that: 'Bosie was the one of my children who has inherited the fatal Douglas temperament', and warned of 'his inherited fits of almost epileptic rage', expressing itself in 'brutal invective'.

Ignoring all such advice, Oscar fell in love.

Despite the difference in their ages, (Oscar was now 36), any idea that he was the prime mover in debauching Bosie was comical. Bosie had been at Winchester School during the 1880s.

While at school, Bosie proved himself to be a fine runner, and edited the school magazine, (the only one of his papers that ever made a profit). In most other respects, Winchester was a disaster.

Bosie: 'Religion simply did not exist in my day at Winchester… For example, there was a picture of The Last Supper hanging above the High Table in the dining room of my House. There being no master present, a prefect made a practice of hurling a piece of bread at this picture every time he came in to tea, his object being to hit the figure of Christ'.

But blasphemy was a minor problem for the formerly sensitive 14-year-old. He later wrote: 'Winchester, truth to tell, was a sink of iniquity. My first eighteen months there were pretty much of a nightmare' – 'Winchester was a carnival of unbridled lust…thriving on bigotry and buggery'.

However, he continued: 'After that, I got used to the conditions, adapted myself to the standard of morality, (or rather immorality), and enjoyed the whole thing tremendously'. One old boy, *Sir Edmund Backhouse*, claimed to have had 'carnal intimacy with at least thirty boys, ascendant and descendant' – including Bosie.

Bosie: 'I left Winchester neither better nor worse than my contemporaries – that is to say, a finished young blackguard, ripe for any kind of wickedness'.

Leaving on a Grand Tour of Europe, Bosie was accompanied by a tutor/chaperone called Gerald Campbell. When they arrived at the Hotel de Paris in Monte Carlo, Bosie met an older but still celebrated beauty called Lady Desart, who proceeded to expand his experience.

(In 1876, Wilde had met Lady Desart – formerly Minnie Preston – shortly before her husband the Earl of Desart divorced her for adultery. Oscar said of her: "The most lovely and dangerous woman in London. She is very fascinating indeed.")

One evening at the hotel, Gerald Campbell realised what was happening. He immediately marched to Lady Desart's bedroom to hammer on the door and demand the return of "the innocent lamb!" After much scuffling, punctuated by the enraged yapping of Lady Desart's Pomeranian lapdog, Bosie emerged from the bedroom dressed in one of her ladyship's fluffy nightdresses and bellowing at Campbell: "I am *NOT* innocent! Good God, I've just spent four years at *Winchester!*"

Bosie returned to England in family disgrace and was packed off to Oxford University. Here, he became well known for his passion for both sexes, although he claimed that, among both undergraduates and dons, he was far from alone. Bosie: 'Ninety per cent of my contemporaries at Winchester and Oxford indulged in homosexual pursuits'.

(One of Bosie's friends at Oxford was the organist of Magdalen College, John Varley Roberts. Roberts was known as something of a musical martinet. Once, when he was practising in the organ loft, a visitor attempted to join in a hymn. Roberts stopped playing and bellowed down at the visitor: "You're mistaken, sir! This isn't the House of God. It's Magdalen College Chapel!")
[See Bosie Douglas – Second Part – Page 379]

As well as overlooking Bosie Douglas's heedless bisexual promiscuity, Oscar Wilde, flattered by his new proximity to an ancient lineage, failed to realise the implications of involvement with the Douglas family. In particular, he ignored the initially quiescent, (but later baleful), presence of Bosie's father, John Sholto Douglas. Oscar: 'A man cannot be too careful in the choice of his enemies.'

If his son might have been better suited to the life of an Elizabethan courtier, then John Sholto Douglas, **MARQUESS OF QUEENSBERRY** (1844-1900), was really a throwback to an 18th century hell-raiser.

Aged 14, he had succeeded to his title, and inherited £780,000, 30,000 acres of property, and the family home of Kinmount Castle, near Dumfries, Scotland. After some boisterous years in the Royal Navy and then at Cambridge University, which he left without a degree, Queensberry spent much of his life hunting foxes.

He also became a celebrated pugilist; (in 1866, he won the Amateur Lightweight Boxing Championship of England). While visiting California with his friend, the Duke of Manchester, the two men dropped into a local saloon. A huge (and Anglophobic) cowboy sneered at the seemingly effete couple and spat on Queensberry's elegant boots. In the ensuing fight, the cowboy was knocked cold within two minutes.

The Duke of Manchester: 'When the air cleared, Queensberry was to be seen leaning nonchalantly against the bar counter, immaculate as on his first entrance, minus even a scratch. His opponent was stretched out at his feet. The onlookers were very much impressed, but Queensberry treated the incident as too trivial to trouble about'.

Queensberry was genuinely interested in the science of boxing and was instrumental in creating the code of conduct known as 'the Queensberry Rules', although they were actually drawn up by his colleague John Chambers. (The Rules had become necessary – previously the only real prohibition had been 'No Biting', while in 1870 one fight had lasted for 136 rounds.)

Queensberry became a convinced supporter of the agnostic Charles Bradlaugh, believing that Christianity was just 'tomfoolery'. When in 1882 the Poet Laureate, *Lord Tennyson*, wrote a play called 'The Promise of May' in which an agnostic was portrayed as the unattractive villain of the piece, Queensberry was outraged. He interrupted the performance, hurled a bouquet of vegetables at the stage, and was carried out of the theatre by ushers. (It was a tactic that he was to attempt again in 1895).

His refusal to take an oath of allegiance on anti-religious grounds led to the Scottish members of the House of Lords rejecting his re-election as one of the 16 Scottish representative peers. Furious, he moved to London, and never returned to Scotland.

Perhaps his greatest disappointment was his failure to win the Grand National horserace, in which he competed several times. He suffered several broken collarbones, four broken limbs, and concussion in the process. He became an enthusiastic cyclist – (in 1890, he rode from the Star and Garter pub in Richmond to his flat in St James in under forty minutes) – but after numerous accidents took to riding a tricycle instead.

His 1866 marriage to **SIBYL MONTGOMERY** (1845-1935) produced four sons and a daughter. However his irascible nature and his deliberate flaunting of his mistresses eventually broke the union. An observer once reported on Queensberry's seduction technique: "Often he'd got them into the bedroom before the second course of dinner was served".

In 1886, Sibyl and the children were staying in a rented house near Ascot called the 'Hut', when Queensberry arrived with a mistress and a gang of friends intent on enjoying Race Week. Annoyed at finding his family in residence, he summarily turned them out.

In 1887 Sibyl, taunted by this continuous public humiliation and Queensberry's suggestion that his mistress join them in a ménage a trois, sued for divorce on grounds of cruelty and adultery, (with a woman called Mabel from Camden Town). Sibyl's children, who hated their father, enthusiastically supported her action.

Queensberry took revenge by endlessly delaying alimony and by disparaging his own offspring. Queensberry: 'The only consolation I have in such children is further proof positive, if I required any, of how right I was to break with a woman who was bringing such children into the world with me'. He also claimed that he had not fathered her children at all.

[Sybil's father, **ALFRED MONTGOMERY** (1814-1896) provided a further domestic irritant to the choleric Queensberry. Montgomery's character was in stark contrast to the pugnacious Douglas clan, as he was a good-looking, foppish wit, friendly with the Prince of Wales's set, and a Commissioner of the Inland Revenue.

There was a strong suspicion that Alfred was the illegitimate son of the Duke of Wellington's elder brother, the Marquess of Wellesley. When Alfred was aged 16, Wellesley appointed him as his private secretary and was said to dote on the boy. They bore a strong physical resemblance.

(In 'A Woman of No Importance', Wilde appeared to allude to this situation when 'Lord Illingworth' hired his son 'Gerald' as secretary. Illingworth: 'The world will know him merely as my private secretary, but to me he will be something very near, and very dear.')

Alfred married Fanny Wyndham, thereby relating himself to the aristocratic families of the Wyndhams and the Bourkes. Although the union produced three children, the couple eventually separated and Fanny left England to settle in Naples. After this family breakdown, Alfred became very fond of his grandchildren, and Bosie later said that the various disasters that overtook them hastened his death. In particular, the 1895 Wilde trials provided 'the finishing blow to him'.

In 1892, while on holiday at Homburg, Bosie introduced Oscar to his grandfather, who was also taking the waters at the German spa. Alfred took a strong dislike to Wilde, particularly after Wilde adopted one of Alfred's best witticisms – 'I can resist everything except temptation' – and claimed it as his own.

Another probable reason for Alfred's aversion to Wilde was that Alfred himself was suspected of homosexuality; (certainly, Queensberry believed this, and lost no opportunity to attack his father-in-law on the subject). Alfred, being terrified of scandal, wished to distance himself from the obvious and flamboyant Oscar.]

In 1893, Queensberry married a respectable lower-middle class girl called Ethel Weedon, whom he had met on the promenade at Eastbourne. Although she claimed to be 17, Ethel was actually underage and, according to Bosie, Queensberry departed the day after the wedding. The 'marriage' was soon annulled on account of the bridegroom's 'frigidity and impotence' and the 'malfunction of the parts of generation'. Having just been divorced for adultery, Queensberry was livid over the accusation of impotence and unsuccessfully contested the case.

By the time Oscar Wilde appeared on his horizon, the Marquess of Queensberry was already a smoking bomb.

Queensberry's nature perhaps became more understandable when one took his ancestral background into consideration. As Bosie once observed: "We are such a theatrical family".

The Douglas family achieved prominence in the 1320s, after Sir James, 'the Black Douglas', became the right hand man of King Robert the Bruce of Scotland. His descendents continued to influence Scottish life until they reached their nadir in 1707 with the 3rd Marquess, otherwise known as '**THE CANNIBAL**'.

This unfortunate man had gone insane and was confined at Holyrood Palace, Edinburgh. One day he escaped his guards and arrived in the Palace kitchens. Finding a lone sous-chef, he killed the boy before proceeding to spit and roast him over the kitchen fire.

It was not until the 1790s that another Douglas managed to match the reputation generated by 'the Cannibal'. Then the fourth Duke, known as '**OLD Q**', achieved the considerable feat of being banned for misconduct by the notorious Hell Fire Club. During one of their Black Mass orgies at Medmenham, Berkshire, he unleashed a chimpanzee dressed as Satan amongst them. The terrified members, thinking that they had indeed conjured up Beelzebub, scattered into the night. On recovery from the shock, they did not forgive Old Q.

But his major claim to fame was his extraordinary sex life, during which he bedded possibly thousands of women. From the window of his home at 138, Piccadilly, he would watch until a suitable beauty passed, then he would send out his grooms to bring the girl inside. He enjoyed holding nude beauty contests in his bedroom, his preference being for slim girls aged about 15.

He once inveigled the three most beautiful women in London to parade before him dressed, (or rather undressed), as the Three Graces while he paraded as a Greek god. Amazingly he avoided syphilis and died of over-eating aged 86.

Queensberry's father, **ARCHIBALD DOUGLAS**, the 7th MARQUESS (1818-1858), became an MP and occasionally dabbled in politics, but preferred 'fox hunting, steeple-chasing, wenching and the Turf'. Like his son, he enjoyed pugilism and once went two rounds against the famous boxer Jemmy Mace. His love of gambling caused his downfall. Aged 40, after a devastating loss at the Goodwood Races, he was found shot dead by his own gun and was assumed to have committed suicide.

His wife, and Queensberry's mother, was **CAROLINE CLAYTON** (1821-1904). In 1840, she romantically eloped with Archibald and was married in the blacksmith's forge at Gretna; she afterwards enjoyed being known as 'the Gretna Green Marchioness'. After bearing six children, her interest in her marriage waned and she lived mostly at her father's house on the Thames at Harleyford, Bucks.

In 1861, much to the anger of the Presbyterian Douglas family, Caroline converted to the Roman Catholic Church. When her mother-in-law tried to seize the youngest three children to prevent further conversions, Caroline escaped with them to France. She was given protection and even some guards by a former lover, *Emperor Napoleon III.*

During the 1860s, she outraged English public opinion by becoming an open supporter of the Irish revolutionary Fenian movement. After a bomb attack in Manchester and the subsequent execution of three Fenians, Caroline sent £100 as aid to their families. She remained a staunch defender of Home Rule, dying with the words 'God save Ireland' on her lips. (When a memorial to the Fenians was erected in Cork, one of its inscriptions read: 'Catherine (sic), Marchioness of Queensberry. Friend of the Manchester Martyrs'.

The careers of Queensberry's siblings also provided substantial fodder for the nation's press. He had three brothers, (Archie, Francis, and James), and two sisters, (Gertude and Florence).

In total contrast to Queensberry's aggressive agnosticism, his brother **ARCHIE DOUGLAS** (1850-1938) became a Catholic priest and was placed in charge of the St Vincent's Home for Boys in Paddington, London. He hit on the idea of partially maintaining the institution by starting a bakery on the premises.

His sister **GERTRUDE DOUGLAS** (1842-1893) also became a Catholic and, after an unsuccessful engagement, (broken due to religious differences), became a nun. In 1874, she gave up her vocation and joined Archie in running the Boys' Home.

While there, she began to write three-volume novels such as 'Brown As A Berry'; although published, they lacked merit. (Wilde: 'Anybody can write a three-volumed novel. It merely requires a complete ignorance of both life and literature'.)

Archie decided that the best future that could be offered to his charges was to resettle them in Western Canada and set off with the first batch of forty boys, leaving Gertrude to preside over the Home.

While he was away, Gertrude fell for the charms of Thomas Stock, a boy who had risen through the bakery ranks to become the chief bun seller at the Home. Much to the horror of her family and the salivation of the popular Press, Gertude, aged 40, married Thomas, aged 16.

Haughtily dismissing the protests, Gertrude announced to the newspapers that: "My husband and I have now opened a bakery business in Hammersmith". When the bakery failed, the pair retreated to Scotland to take up market gardening and for Gertrude to write more laborious novels. In 1891, Thomas ran away to join the Bechuanaland Police Force.

Archie continued to run the Home and to transport boys to Canada. On one occasion, the party was shipwrecked and were left clinging to a rock for hours before their eventual rescue.

Gertrude resumed her religious vocation and retired to a convent in Hendon, London, while Archie became a chaplain to retired nuns and spent a quiet old age in Dover.

Queensberry's second brother was **FRANCIS DOUGLAS** (1847-1865). Regarded as the most intelligent member of the family, Francis was also a brilliant athlete who, aged 14, had scaled the walls of Edinburgh Castle and, two years later, had swum the Hellespont. When he was 18 he was accepted as an officer in the Black Watch Regiment but, before joining the Army, he determined on a mountaineering adventure in the Alps.

In 1865, he joined Edward Whymper's expedition to the Matterhorn in Switzerland and was part of the victorious team that first conquered the summit. Unfortunately, during the descent, the rope connecting the party snapped, sending Francis and three others to their deaths on the rocks below. The incident caused consternation back in England, *Queen Victoria* herself proposing that mountaineering should be banned as a result. Although the corpses of his fellow victims were reclaimed, the body of Francis Douglas was never found.

The youngest of Queensberry's brothers was **JAMES DOUGLAS** (1855-1891), a manic-depressive whose main interest was alcohol. In his earlier years he travelled to South America and South Africa in the company of his dynamic sister Florence, and also wrote three lacklustre novels; (one commentator said that the writing of awful books seemed to have been a family trait).

However, in 1888, he married Martha Hennessy, a rich Catholic widow and a member of the Cognac family. In tribute to his new in-laws' business interests, James added three bottles of brandy to his daily intake of champagne and claret.

Not surprisingly, his behaviour began to deteriorate and he was arrested for attempting to abduct an underage Ward of Court. The girl's parents did not press charges and the matter was kept from public knowledge, (although James was subjected to unmerciful teasing on the subject by his sister Florence).

His next clash with the law came in 1891 when he was one of only two Londoners summonsed for misinforming the National Census. In his form he described his wife as 'a crossing sweep and lunatic' and his stepson as 'a shoeblack born in darkest Africa'. Martha rescued him from the magistrates. (Wilde might have sympathised with James's irritation over the census. Oscar: 'When I had to fill in a census paper, I gave my age as 19, my profession as genius, my infirmity as talent'.)

By this time, Florence had become worried over the increasingly violent and irrational outbursts from her drink-sodden brother. When she asked Queensberry for help, he suggested that James took a holiday in Ireland. As a result of accepting this advice, James completely flipped over the edge. A police inspector had to be detailed to return the raving drunkard from Dublin.

On arrival back at Euston Station, James booked himself into a hotel, retired to a bedroom, and slit his throat from ear to ear.

James's twin sister, **FLORENCE DOUGLAS** (1855-1905), was the most forceful of Queensberry's family. Known as a boisterous tomboy as a child, aged 17 she insisted on marrying a feckless but amiable baronet who rejoiced in the name of Sir Alexander Beaumont Churchill Dixie. Almost his only joke, (one that he continually repeated), was to refer to himself as 'Sir ABCD'. Together, they were known as 'Florrie and Beau'.

Although she had two children by Beau, Florrie soon grew bored with them. In 1878, she dragooned a party, (consisting of Beau, her brother James, and *Herbert Beerbohm Tree's* brother, Julius Beerbohm), into accompanying her on an expedition to Argentina.

Queensberry himself joined the group, but he got into a fight with an American in Rio de Janeiro, and they lost him somewhere in Monte Video. They continued to Cape Horn and set out across the barren and then little known wastes of Patagonia.

Although Florrie's main objective was the hunting and shooting of new and exotic animals, the party also took a large amount of whisky with them, and the expedition turned into an extended drinking spree. Florrie, Beau and brother James became inseparable through these experiences. Having survived earthquakes and near starvation, the party straggled back to Cape Horn when the whisky ran out.

(On their return voyage, they stopped in Brazil long enough for Florrie to buy a jaguar that she named 'Affums'. She later paraded Affums around her home near Windsor on a leash, until it escaped one night and ate Queen Victoria's deer herd in Windsor Great Park.

Under the weight of Royal displeasure, Affums was banished to London Zoo. Florrie and James sometimes visited their erring jaguar, and shocked other sightseers by climbing into the cage to groom and pet Affums.)

Having written a bestseller called 'Across Patagonia', Florrie looked around for further adventures. She found the USA rather boring, except for some grizzly bear killing in the Rockies. But when the First Boer War broke out in 1880, Florrie saw a new role for herself as the first female war correspondent.

This ambition was frustrated when she arrived in South Africa to discover that the war had just ended with the British defeat at Majuba Hill. The British general, Sir Evelyn Wood, allowed her to accompany the army on their journey to the peace talks in Pretoria.

Although Florrie adapted easily to army camp life, Beau, (who had been hounded into accompanying her), found the going harder. Florrie generally woke before dawn and could only rouse her usually hung-over husband by releasing the guy ropes until the tent collapsed on top of him. His mood was not improved to find that the rest of the army were still asleep.

When they arrived in Pretoria, Florrie was invited to stay at Government House where the main conference was being held. This arrangement provided her with an ideal opportunity to overhear the negotiations and scoop her press rivals.

Each morning as the talks commenced, Florrie would take a seat on the veranda outside the open windows. Unable to insult a lady by asking her to leave, the negotiators would shut the windows, until the oppressive heat of the veldt summer forced them to reopen them. The talks would then continue as much as possible in whispers, while Florrie gazed innocently at the landscape and jotted the occasional note.

On their return to England, Florrie and Beau rented a house called the Fishery near Windsor. There, together with brother James, they lived in an alcoholic haze, becoming known as 'Sir Always and Lady Sometimes Tipsy'. A neighbour reported that one afternoon: "I saw Lady Dixie sprawling on the lawn with a jaguar. Sir Beaumont was dressed as a harlequin reading a newspaper. The gong sounded for dinner and he started up like a gazelle and leapt off to the house".

After James committed suicide, his body was taken to be buried at the family home of Kinmount Castle. On the day of the funeral, Florrie decided that Beau was too drunk to attend and hid his clothes to prevent his arrival. Beau woke up in time to borrow a pair of trousers off a waiter, and reached the ceremony in time. Flinging himself down by the graveside, he bawled: "My God! How I loved that man! We were like a pair of apes!"

Florrie's most newsworthy exploit was also the murkiest. In 1883, she claimed that she had been out for a walk along the Thames towpath with her St Bernard dog, Hubert. Suddenly she was attacked by two men dressed as women. One had held her down while the other lunged at her with a knife. She had avoided injury only because Hubert had bounded to the rescue and chased off her assailants.

Assuming that Irish rebels were responsible, the press seized on the account and the story received national attention. As a near neighbour at Windsor Castle, Queen Victoria, (having forgiven the loss of her deer herd), was especially sympathetic. She sent her trusted servant John Brown to make inquiries and to request a photograph of the heroic Hubert.

Having examined the scene of the alleged assault and finding no evidence, John Brown grew suspicious. He left, sniffing meaningfully: "There's nae trace o' a brawl here, lassie".

Unfortunately for Brown, the weather that day was bitterly cold and he returned frozen to Windsor Castle. That night, erysipelas set in and, to the horror of Queen Victoria, Brown died within a few days. The queen's grief was not assuaged by the receipt of a photograph of the dog Hubert, signed by Florrie herself.

Although Parliamentary questions were asked, (with Irish members claiming that *Gladstone* had masterminded the affair to discredit *Charles Parnell*, while the Fenian leadership in the USA declared angrily that they knew nothing about it), the incident was allowed to fizzle out. Florrie was furious that the Government had dismissed her claims and equally annoyed when the newspapers blamed her for the death of John Brown. Hubert later appeared as a star exhibit in local dog shows.

(Afterwards, when Bosie told Wilde in secrecy that the whole affair had been dreamt up by his alcohol-befuddled aunt, Oscar roared with laughter: "Too wonderful!")

Like Queensberry, Florrie was an avowed agnostic and later became a socialist. Although she had been a superb shot, as she grew older she turned violently against blood sports and led a crusade against them. Later she turned her vitriol on vivisection, then on the wearing of skins and fur, finally on using feathers in women's hats.

She became a strident supporter of women's rights, declaring that women were 'the bond servants of their husbands' and that: "Women submit in the slavery, body and soul, of being the property of others". A cowering Beau nodded his agreement.

After Florrie's death in 1905, Beau married a middle-aged widow and retired to Scarborough. Whilst there, he undertook a muddled and ultimately embarrassing attempt at charity work by 'providing free beer for the inmates of the workhouse at Christmas'.

> *Wilde's book 'Lord Arthur Savile's Crime and Other Stories', (including 'The Sphinx without a Secret', 'The Canterville Ghost', and 'The Model Millionaire'), was published in July 1891.*
>
> *On July 4th, Oscar accepted an invitation to attend a weekend with the 'Crabbet Club' at the ancestral Sussex home of the poet and explorer Wilfrid Blunt. The other guests included George Curzon, George Wyndham, and Harry Cust.*

WILFRID SCAWEN BLUNT 1840-1922

To be invited to mingle with the Crabbet Club was a sign of considerable favour in 1890s England. It consisted of no more than 21 members of the social elite chosen to 'discourage serious views of life' and to celebrate conviviality; (any member who became a Cabinet Minister or an Archbishop was forced to resign). One of its leading figures, the politician *George Wyndham* said that: 'the party was not literary but lawn-tennisy'.

Although flattered to be amongst such company, Wilde did not enjoy the hearty atmosphere of the weekend festivities. He was subjected to an embarrassing speech by George Curzon that made overt reference to Oscar's effeminacy, while Blunt's daughter Judith described his attempts at tennis as: 'a great wobbly blancmange trying to serve underhand'.

Oscar wrote of the occasion: 'We all trooped out to see the dawn, and some of the young ones stripped off their clothes and rushed down to the lake and began swimming and diving about like a lot of schoolboys. When they came out they began playing lawn tennis, just as they were, stark naked – the future rulers of England.... Blunt changed into some fantastic pyjamas and perched himself, cross-legged, on the balcony, looking down at the mad game of lawn tennis, for all the world like a sort of pink and green Buddha'. Oscar never went back to Crabbet Park.

Initially, Blunt admired Wilde: 'He was without exception the most brilliant talker I have ever come across.... Nobody could pretend to outshine him, or even shine at all in his company'. However, when Wilde began his association with Blunt's distant cousin, Bosie Douglas, Blunt was shocked: 'It was difficult to realise that there could be passion felt for one so physically repulsive as Wilde was. Yet the fat sensual man had already thoroughly debauched the boy, as a girl is debauched, mind and body'. In 1897, he wrote: 'If Wilde had then begun a decent life, people would have forgotten him, but he returned to Paris and to his dog's vomit'.

Blunt's defence of the family honour did not prevent a major row breaking out between himself and Bosie in later years. After being refused a loan by Blunt, Bosie snarled: "To be known as your friend or associate has always been something in the nature of a social handicap". In political and sexual terms, Bosie may well have had a point.

Blunt was one of the most extraordinary men of the Victorian age – Byronic in appearance, politics, and sexual appetite. In addition to being a remarkably handsome and swash-buckling explorer, horseman, and marksman, he was also a poet and a quixotic politician, who was 'related to about half the English peerage'.

He was unusual in being aggressively anti-imperialist at a time when such writers as *Rudyard Kipling* and *WE Henley* were extolling the virtues of the British Empire at the height of its power. Blunt treated them with contempt: 'Their poets who write big of the White Burden. Trash! – The White Man's Burden, Lord, is the burden of his cash'.

He might be described as the romantic knight-errant of the Victorian leftwing in the same way that *Sir Richard Burton* was the eccentric champion of the right – however, their similarities far outweighed their differences.

In 1858, Blunt entered the Diplomatic Service, where he spent a lackadaisical ten years pottering around various embassies, including Madrid, (where he considered taking up bull-fighting as a profession), and Buenos Aires, (where he indulged in week-long drinking binges with Burton).

After marrying and succeeding to the ownership of Crabbet Park, Sussex, in 1869, he left the Service and, accompanied by his wife Anne, travelled to Arabia. He became fascinated by the desert Bedouin: 'I felt that these wild people were wiser than ourselves. They had solved the riddle of life by refusing to consider it, or even considering that there was a riddle'.... 'They are a people whose public life was based, not in word only but in fact, on those three principles, Liberty, Equality and Brotherhood'.

In 1878, the Blunts set off on an expedition into the Arabian heartland, being the first Europeans to penetrate the desert without disguise. Ignoring the Turkish authorities, living mostly off Blunt's shooting skills, and allowing themselves only one drink a day, they managed to cross the terrifying Nafud desert, a 100 mile trek across bare rock, being constantly plagued by locust swarms.

After meeting up with and joining a Muslim pilgrimage (Haj), they managed to reach Baghdad, and continued on into Persia, each night sleeping with their guns for fear of attack. Finally they reached Bushehr on the Persian Gulf, where Blunt made his first purchases of the Arab horses that were the foundation of his famous Crabbet Stud.

Moving on to India, the Blunts stayed with Wilfrid's lifelong friend, the Viceroy *Lord Lytton*, at Simla. Blunt disliked what he saw of the Raj: 'The natives are a race of slaves, frightened, unhappy and terribly thin. My faith in British institutions and the blessings of British rule have received a severe blow'. As a fluent speaker of Arabic, he gained considerable respect from the Muslim community, especially when he later engineered the creation of the Muslim university at Hyderabad.

In 1882, Blunt publicly supported the Egyptian nationalist leader Colonel Ahmed Arabi (1841-1911), after his defeat and capture at the Battle of Tel-el-Kebir. (Lord Granville: "Blunt is acting almost as an agent for Arabi'). At his own expense, he hired a Queen's Counsel on behalf of the defence, although Arabi subsequently pleaded guilty and was sentenced to death, (later commuted to life banishment in Ceylon).

(Wilde was on his USA tour during these events in Egypt. He commented: "Now that we have caught Arabi we do not know what to do with him.".....How much better it would be if countries went to war over who had the most beautiful women, rather than the senseless disputes about getting Egypt and possessing Arabi".

During his exile, Arabi met the Irish tea merchant Thomas Lipton who managed to persuade Arabi to endorse his new coffee and chicory essence – the advert read: 'I have never tasted better'. Lipton later used his influence to secure Arabi's release in 1903.)

Despite the unpopularity that he had gained over his support for Egyptian nationalism, when the crisis over the Mahdi's conquest of the Sudan came to a head in 1884, there were calls for Blunt to be sent to Khartoum instead of General Gordon. *WT Stead* in the Pall Mall Gazette: "Mr Blunt is no less brave than General Gordon and he could be sacrificed at least as safely'.

In 1886, Blunt became deeply involved in the troubles in Ireland. He witnessed a brutal eviction in Co. Roscommon, in which armed men were brought in to drive half-starved women and children from their homes. Even the local police were disgusted at the sight and raised £5 between them to help the destitute families. Blunt: "No one can understand what the Irish land question is till he has seen an eviction".

His outspoken attacks angered the landed gentry who came to regard Blunt as a class traitor. Defying a ban on public meetings, Blunt was arrested after making a speech in 1887, and was sentenced to two months imprisonment in Kilmainham Gaol, Dublin. (During this imprisonment Blunt wrote some sonnets called 'In Vinculis'; Wilde wrote a very supportive review: 'an unjust imprisonment for a noble cause strengthens as well as deepens the nature'.)

Blunt made one foray into parliamentary politics when he was chosen as a Tory candidate for Camberwell North. He turned his 'Tory Democracy' campaign into a platform for rampant socialism. To the bewilderment of the voters, (whom he described as 'the miserable Camberwell rabble'), he delivered speeches in Arabic and then came out in full support of Parnell and Irish Home Rule. After several meetings had ended in fistfights, he lost the election.

He spent many years living in and exploring Egypt. On one occasion, he visited a Coptic monastery at Wadi Natrun and asked the monks if they still feared Arab attacks. One elderly monk nodded, quoting 'the Beni Hallal attack'. Blunt found that the Beni Hallal attack had occurred in the 10th century AD.

In 1897, he was attacked himself by tribesmen in the Western Desert and escaped back to Cairo barely alive and only after forced marches across the desert. During his last desert journey to Damascus in 1904 he caught malarial fever and permanently damaged his spine.

He returned to live in Sussex where he maintained his attacks on European imperialism. His reaction to the Fashoda colonial confrontation of 1898 was that: 'there was no more difference between England and France than between two card-sharpers'. During the Boer

War, he condemned both the British and the Boers, reserving his sympathies for the black population caught up in the conflict.

He christened the First World War, 'The White Man's Suicide', while supporting the 1916 Easter Rising in Ireland and sending over £1000 to aid the defence of the Irish rebel Sir Roger Casement. Before his execution, Casement's last letter contained the sentiment: 'Give my love to Wilfrid Blunt'.

In spite of their deep political differences, Blunt remained a close friend and drinking companion of Winston Churchill. He also knew Lawrence of Arabia, (who called Blunt 'a Prophet'), and *Robert Cunningham-Graham*, who said of him: "Blunt was a greater patriot than any of the speechifying and flag-waving politicians and sheep-like citizens who strain their vocal chords singing 'Rule Britannia'."

Blunt would have been an unusual man simply because of the political journey he took from Tory squire to anti-racist radical. What marked him out even more from the Victorian image was his bewilderingly complicated sex life.

The major female figure through much of Blunt's life was undoubtedly Anne, (Lady Annabella King-Noel), whom he married in 1869. She was the grand daughter of the poet Lord Byron.

(Although Byron was the epitome of the English romantic hero, *Lord Houghton*, while in Greece was amused to learn that Byron always carried a contraceptive in his waistcoat pocket. Byron also had a pragmatic streak: "My mother-in-law has been dangerously ill; she is now dangerously well".)

The Blunts' married life was marred by a succession of miscarriages and only their daughter Judith survived to adulthood. (In the 1890s, Blunt suggested that Judith would make a good bride for *Bosie Douglas*).

In later years, sexual relations between the Blunts dwindled as Anne became more eccentric. *Herbert Vivian* said of her: 'Lady Anne was a shrivelled and austere little woman with a bulldog chin and a pertinacity that would have dominated any husband but Blunt, who defended himself by simply not listening'.

The coup de grace for Blunt's desires came when Anne insisted on wearing a fishing hat and mackintosh to bed instead of a nightgown. Her son-in-law Neville Lytton commented: "She dressed for bed as though for a south- westerly gale in the English Channel".

Given Blunt's libido, it was fortunate that Anne rarely became jealous of her husband's extra-marital affairs; they remained on generally good terms throughout their lives.

As an adolescent, Blunt had enjoyed fumbling semi-platonic affairs with Queensberry's later wife, Sibyl Montgomery, and with the grandniece of the Duke of Wellington, Lady Feodore Wellesley. But in Madrid he learnt the full techniques of lovemaking from a 23-year-old abandoned wife called Lola, and began his real sexual career.

In 1863, he fell in love with the famous courtesan, *Catherine 'Skittles' Walters*. At the time she was the paramour of *Emperor Napoleon III* and, although very fond of Blunt, she sent him away. He was devastated by her rejection and resolved never to become so infatuated ever again.

To recover from Skittles, Blunt went to Paris and had affairs with another well-known courtesan, Cora Pearl; with Zizi Arcos, the wife of a Brazilian official; with a blonde who had previously been one of Victor Hugo's lovers; with a Polish aristocrat; with the wife of an English diplomat; and with an English lady he met in Lausanne called Mrs Ella Baird.

To complete his sexual education he devoured various works of pornography recommended to him by the disgraced English politician *Sir Charles Dilke*.

Back in England, Blunt plunged into affairs with a cousin, Madeline Wyndham, (the wife of Percy Wyndham and an acknowledged beauty who modelled for GF Watt's sculpture of

'The Three Graces'); Mrs John 'Minnie' Pollen; and another cousin, Georgina Sumner, (who bore him a son called Berkeley in 1873). In time, Blunt was also to have sex with Madeline Wyndham's daughter Mary, and with Minnie's daughter Pansy (a then 16-year-old who later became a nun).

After a complicated affair with the intended bride of Lord Zouche, the Honourable Dorothea Frazer, (see Algernon Bourke), Blunt spent a short time in South America being comforted by an Anglo-Indian mistress named Anita.

Moving on to Spain for a holiday with Lady Anne, Blunt became involved, 'more by accident than by romance', with the 22-year-old wife of a British Army officer, a Mrs Thurloe, They were caught in flagrante delicto in Seville Cathedral; Blunt explained to an outraged priest that Mrs Thurloe 'was my fiancee'.

Blunt once explained his feelings: 'Friendship plain and simple with a woman is to me an impossibility. It is not that in theory I should not delight in such a friendship, I have often wished for one but in practice and in spite of all goodwill I find it freezes me. If I do not make love, I don't know what to do or say and she is bored and I am bored and insensibly the friendship and all else withers away'.

Due to his remarkable good looks and virility, he also found himself the target of machinations devised by the ladies themselves. Lady Kenmare told Minnie Pollen that she herself fancied Blunt and when he visited her home at Killarney she had had to station her chaplain in the bedroom next to her own to ward off temptation.

His next major affair was with Mrs Mary Singleton, a liaison he called 'wholly pagan' and which was conducted in a room near Victoria Station, London. As well as the problem of her husband Henry, Blunt also had to compete for her favours with his own cousin, the diplomat Philip Currie. After her husband's death, she married Philip and became *Lady Mary Currie*.

Blunt moved swiftly on to Mrs Batten, the wife of the private secretary of *Lord Lytton*. Blunt: 'I found her door ajar about 12 o'clock and stayed with her till daylight'. Mabel Batten's descendent, Lady Cara Harris, said of her forbear: "she was surely the only woman to have slept with Edward VII, Radclyffe Hall and Wilfred Blunt – though they all seem to have had Wilfred Blunt".

Next was Lady Augusta Gregory, wife of the former Governor of Ceylon and *WB Yeats's* patron and muse. Blunt: 'a quiet little woman of perhaps 25. We found comfort in each other's arms. It was a consummation neither of us, I think, foresaw, and was quite a new experience in her quiet life'.

Lady Gregory was succeeded by Blanche Hozier, (Winston Churchill's future mother-in-law), a lady of some appetite. Blunt: 'She is just as passionately inclined as ever'. He ended the affair when another of her lovers, the Tory MP Sir Ellis Bartlett, threatened to reveal all to Blanche's husband and to commit suicide unless Blanche took him back. Blunt: 'Fond as I was of her I could not accept the position of a furtive lover playing at hide and seek with a personage who had not even the right of being her husband'.

His next encounter was with Janey Morris, wife of the socialist poet William Morris, (and ex-lover and Pre-Raphaelite model of Dante Rossetti). Blunt stayed at their home: 'Kelmscott Manor was extraordinarily uncomfortable. Mrs Morris slept alone at the end of a short passage. The hall was uncarpeted, with floors that creaked. To me such midnight perils have always been attractive'.

He found Janey so weirdly silent that they never even used their Christian names: 'We could not become intimate except through the physical senses'. After Morris's death, Janey visited Blunt in Egypt, together with her daughter May Morris. After inspection, Blunt found May even more uncommunicative than her mother: Blunt: 'she is a most obstinately silent woman'…. 'I cannot make love to either of them, and what else is there to be done?'

He found Mrs Margaret Talbot, the wife of the Military Secretary at the Paris Embassy, much more to his taste. After a visit to the Paris Zoo, Margaret was inspired by the sight of a giant python. There followed what Blunt called: 'two of the most passionate hours of my life. When it was over she rushed to the looking glass and surveyed herself – "What a bacchanalian figure! And to think that it is me!" '

After she confessed to her husband, Blunt beat a retreat to Cairo, but soon returned for an affair with Margaret's sister, Caroline Grosvenor, ('She is one I could be in love with if I had time'), but failed in his attempt on Margaret's bosom friend, Mary, Lady Edmund Talbot, (Blunt: 'She went to Paris for her bonnets, but on to Lourdes for her soul'.)

Blunt: 'I have now got to the age when I like to be amused without giving myself much trouble, and there are several women who amuse me. I don't care which of them it is, but I must have someone'.

However, Blunt flirted with real danger when he became involved with Sibell, the wife of his cousin and close friend, George Wyndham. Blunt: 'This must go no further. I cannot run risks with George. Heaven knows I have not sought it…and yet it tempts me, like looking down a precipice'. He became obsessed by thoughts of Sibell's green stockings.

After more entanglements with Dora Chamberlain, ("So here is another woman in my life!'), and Lady Helena Carnegie, ('an unmarried girl, inquisitive, unbelieving, sad, but with a wild love of life – and of love'), Blunt met Mary, Lady Galloway. She was the daughter of the Prime Minister *Lord Salisbury*, and the wife of Lord Galloway, (a man reported by Judith Blunt as 'weird, bent double, and always wearing cotton gloves – and with a taste for underage girls'). After sex with Blunt, Lady Galloway wrote threatening to leave her husband. Blunt : 'I trust she will do nothing of the kind'.

Hastily moving on, Blunt had a romantic attachment with Princess Helene of Orleans, one of *Prince Eddy's* potential brides, (and therefore a possible Queen of England). This probably remained unconsummated, as Blunt next ended up with Lady Wenlock. Although she was only 30, Lady Wenlock was partially deaf and Blunt grew weary of shouting his poetry into her affected ear. An attempt to bed the redoubtable novelist *Mrs Alice Meynell* came to nothing.

More successfully, Blunt managed to seduce Margot Tennant, the future wife of the twentieth century Prime Minister *HH Asquith.* Margot said of Blunt that 'he was one of the four most beautiful men I have ever seen'. Blunt: 'Her bed is a little iron one, plainly virginal. Margot is no great beauty, but she has a sweet little body'… 'I think she never really loved me at all — spent that night with me perhaps through weariness of her virginity — and is now ashamed at what she has done'.

One of Blunt's long-term affairs was with Lady Mary Elcho, (who once expressed an desire to play a walk-on part in Wilde's 'Lady Windermere's Fan' until Blunt dissuaded her). Her husband, Lord Hugh, (later Earl of Wemyss), was more interested in the Duchess of Leinster, by whom he had an illegitimate child. In his frequent absences, Mary had pledged her heart to the future Prime Minister, the languid *Arthur Balfour.* (OW – 'There's nothing in the world like the devotion of a married woman. It is a thing no married man knows anything about'.)

Although Mary and Balfour indulged in a long romance, it seems that they may have never actually consummated this passion. Balfour became uncharacteristically annoyed when she admitted that Blunt had slept with her in Cairo. Blunt: 'I do not think she intended quite all that happened'.

When Mary Elcho became pregnant she surprised both Balfour and Blunt by declaring that the father was her own husband. After seeing the child, Blunt agreed: 'The new baby is the most hideous little monster imaginable, ignoble, pale, with wandering weak blue eyes and an idiotic stare – palpably legitimate'.

Another of Blunt's affairs created a curious lovers' triangle. When he made advances to Emily Lytton, ('a pretty, provoking child' – and the daughter of his great friend, Lord Lytton), he found that his main rival was his own daughter Judith, who had lesbian intentions towards Emily. When Emily confessed that she hoped to elope with Blunt, a jealous Judith informed her that recently she had seen Mary Elcho in Blunt's bed. Emily was shocked by the news and broke with Blunt. Judith: 'Father told me I was a fool to interfere... because it would have done Emily a world of good'. Emily went on to marry Sir Edwin Lutyens, the architect of New Delhi.

Blunt considered that 16 and 32 were the best ages for women, the former were trying to escape girlhood, and the latter evading age. Hence his next two lovers were the 32-year-old Gay Windsor, ('the exact age for romance'), and the 16-year old Lady Margaret Sackville, daughter of Lady De La Warr. (Blunt at 60 found Margaret wearisomely keen on poetry: 'Literature without love is tiresome in a woman'.)

Another autumnal affair was with Lady Adeline Russell, the wife of the Lord Chief Justice, (and mother of *Queensberry's* solicitor in the 1895 trials). They indulged in 'afternoons of love' that sent her back to her husband with a renewed interest in sex. Blunt: 'her domestic peace is signed and sealed.... What wonder men are cynics who have made a study of the human heart'.

He finally settled into a form of domestic peace with Dorothy Carleton, (31 – 'and very rosy and pretty'). Dorothy was the niece of a former lover Madeline Wyndham and the intended bride of Lady's Gregory's son, Major Robert Gregory. Mary Elcho still sometimes dropped in for the occasional fling.

In 1913, his first and great love, 'Skittles' Walters, suggested that he might be interested in her niece. Blunt: 'I laughed and said it was too late and I was no longer capable'.

The poet *Alfred Austin* once asked Blunt what was his idea of Heaven. Blunt: "To be laid out to sleep in a garden, with running water near, and so to sleep for a hundred thousand years, then to be woken by a bird singing, and to call out to the person one loved best 'Are you there?' and for her to answer 'Yes, are you?' and so turn round and go to sleep again for another hundred thousand years."

His last years were dogged by illness and quarrels with his difficult and objectionable daughter Judith, who attempted to sell off his beloved Crabbet Park. In an effort to forestall her plans, Blunt was about to give the property to the National Trust. Then, one day, he was introduced to the founder of the Trust, Miss Octavia Hill, and two of her supporters. Blunt recoiled: "They were three old women like the witches in Macbeth. If such are to be its guardians it would be desecration!"

Deciding eventually that 'the less religion in the world perhaps, after all, the better', when Blunt died he was buried without ceremony, wrapped in his oriental carpet, in a glade in the Sussex woods.

The Indian Minister, Dr Syed Mahmud, wrote many years later that Blunt was a 'true interpreter of the deepest and wisest instincts of the Anglo-Saxon race...England's greatness will hereafter be remembered through Blunt's ideas and work, and not through Balfour, Curzon and suchlike'.

The **HON. ALGERNON BOURKE** (1854-1922) was another of Bosie Douglas's cousins and also a member of the Crabbet Club.

In 1875, his elder brother Alec Bourke had been involved in a farcical incident with Wilfrid Blunt. When Blunt was asked to assess the suitability of the 18-year-old Hon. Dorothea Frazer for marriage to Lord Zouche, he upset the arrangements by falling for her himself.

Dorothea, (known as 'Doll'), was a dazzlingly pretty 'wild child' who consented to an affair with alacrity. But she was also sleeping with Alec Bourke.

The intended marriage with Lord Zouche went ahead but, when Zouche discovered that Doll was still involved with her lovers, he pursued his errant wife to a hotel in Albemarle St, London. Hearing his arrival in the foyer, Doll was forced to push Blunt out of one bedroom door, while concealing Alec Bourke in a cupboard, and then greeting her fuming husband at another door.

Given that he might have been cited as co-respondent in the following divorce case, Blunt was highly relieved when Doll eloped with Alec Bourke.

Avoiding the amorous adventures of his brother, Algernon Bourke instead became embroiled in the even more tortuous affairs of the Douglas family and in particular with the battle between the Marquess of Queensberry and his son Bosie.

As a neutral cousin, Algernon acted as go-between with the pair both before and after the 1895 denouement. When he learnt that Queensberry was intending to disrupt the first night of 'The Importance of Being Ernest', he informed Wilde, thus frustrating the Marquess's plan. He also attempted but failed to repair the family rift.

Nicknamed 'Button' and describing himself as 'a sort of sub-sub-sub-editor of the Times', Algernon was a wealthy member of the London Stock Exchange, and the younger son of Viscount Mayo. (Mayo had been the Viceroy of India, but in 1872 was stabbed to death by a prisoner while inspecting the Port Blair Jail in the Andaman Islands).

In his time, Algernon was possibly the most influential member of the famous St James London club, White's. After Bertie, Prince of Wales, (having been banned from smoking in some of the rooms), cold-shouldered the establishment, White's had become unfashionable and was on the point of closing until Algernon restored its old glory by decorating and extending the premises.

Bosie became a member of White's and took Wilde to lunch there in 1892. Oscar mentioned the club several times in his writings. In 'De Profundis', he wrote to Bosie: 'There is no harm in your seriously considering that the most perfect way of passing an evening was to have a champagne dinner at the Savoy, a box at the Music-Hall to follow, and a champagne supper at Willis's for the end. Heaps of delightful young men in London are of the same opinion. It is not even an eccentricity. It is a qualification for becoming a member of White's'.

Later, when Bosie Douglas was made bankrupt he automatically ceased to be a member of the club although, (as there was no suggestion of dishonesty), technically he could have been re-admitted. When Algernon made no effort to do so, Bosie huffed: 'I will never ask my relatives in White's Club to put into force the spirit of the rules which govern their select establishment."

White's always prided itself on its relaxed atmosphere. A very new member once asked the barman if the bar was still open. "Bless my soul, sir, it has not been closed since the reign of Charles II".

Among the women who festooned Wilfrid Blunt's life, **CATHERINE 'SKITTLES' WALTERS** (1839-1920) stood out as not only his greatest love, but also as one of his greatest friends. In his 1892 poem 'Esther', he described her thus: 'Her brow was pale, but it was lit with light, And mirth flashed out of it, it seemed in rays. A childish face, but wise with woman's wit, And something too, pathetic in its gaze.'

Blunt was not her only admirer. *Henry Labouchere* said of Catherine: "She had the most capacious heart I know and must be the only whore in history to retain her heart intact". In 'Dorian Gray', Wilde was probably referring to her in his line: 'There are only five women in London worth talking to, and two of these can't be admitted into decent society'.

Born in a slum in Toxteth, Liverpool, she became known as 'Skittles' due to her childhood skill in setting up the pins in pub bowling alleys. She was a highly intelligent girl who soon realised that, in this world of beer-brothels, (where a pint and a girl cost one shilling), her only real way out lay in constructive fornication. Aged 16, she moved to London to join the, at the most conservative estimate, 120,000 prostitutes plying their trade in the city.

What marked Skittles as exceptional was her earthy enjoyment of sex combined with an air of angelic innocence. She was also lucky in that she was a born horsewoman in a society that revered equestrian skills.

At this time, Rotten Row in Hyde Park had become a social meeting point where eligible young women (of all classes) could display themselves on horseback for the perusal of potential partners. It was known as 'the human Tattersalls'. Wilde referred to its risqué reputation in 'An Ideal Husband': 'Then he proposed to me in broad daylight this morning, in front of that dreadful statue of Achilles. Really the things that go on in front of that work of art are quite appalling. The police should interfere'.

(The Row was used occasionally for other purposes. Some young blades rode there early in the day to recover from hangovers – they were known as 'the Liver Brigade'.)

Spotting her opportunity, Skittles met a livery-stable owner and traded sex in return for the use of his best horse. He also supplied a beautiful dress that was so close-fitting that she had to strip naked to get into it. Thus armed, Skittles joined the Rotten Row parade; her beauty and riding abilities immediately attracted a stream of customers.

Although initially she relied on servicing army officers on the early morning milk train back to Aldershot, she came to popular notice when the respected artist Sir Edwin Landseer painted her in his Royal Academy offering, 'The Taming of the Shrew', in 1861. An embarrassed Landseer vehemently denied that the young woman depicted was Skittles, though the likeness was unmistakeable.

Her real breakthrough arrived when she became the mistress of Spencer Cavendish, Marquess of Hartington, (nicknamed 'Harty-Tarty'), brother of Lord Frederick Cavendish, (assassinated in the Phoenix Park murders), and son and heir to the Duke of Devonshire.

[The **MARQUESS OF HARTINGTON** (1833-1908) was also a prominent Liberal politician although not regarded as one of the brightest luminaries of the House of Commons. *Gladstone* despaired of improving his colleague's cultural hinterland: "Hartington won't read anything – not even 'Treasure Island'". Hartingdon admitted ponderously that: "The proudest moment of my life was when my pig won the prize at Skipton Fair".

He claimed that he had suffered an awful nightmare once in which he dreamt that he had been making a speech to the House of Lords and, when he woke up, he found that he was.

Hartington was keen on shooting but was notorious for being an appallingly bad shot. His probably unique feat was, with a single bullet, to have hit a pheasant, the retriever chasing it, the retriever's owner, and the chef who had arrived bearing a tray of sandwiches.]

When he finally ended his affair with Skittles, Hartington provided her with a house in Mayfair and a lifetime annuity of £2000 a year. Again, Wilde may have had Skittles in mind when he wrote of a character in 'Lady Windermere's Fan': 'I have been told that this woman has got a great deal of money out of somebody, for it seems that she came to London six months ago without anything at all to speak of, and now she has this charming house in Mayfair and drives her ponies in the Park every afternoon'.

In spite of her new riches, Skittles continued her career of high-powered seduction, adding *Emperor Napoleon III, Bertie, Prince of Wales*, and the poet *Algernon Swinburne* to her extensive list of lovers, (although Swinburne was usually too drunk to achieve anything). She rode with the prestigious Quorn Hunt; three novels were written about her life; and she managed to create what amounted to a London salon at her home in South St.

Both General Kitchener and the Prime Minister William Gladstone treated her as a trusted friend, although Gladstone used to proclaim on arrival at South St that he had 'not come to talk about politics'. Instead, he would congratulate her on her diminutive waist and test its size 'by manual measurement'.

Her least pleasant lover was Lord Hubert de Burgh, (later Earl of Clanricarde), whom she met at the Paris Embassy during the 1860s. As the owner of extensive estates in Galway, Ireland, it was his especially brutal policy of evictions that later so enraged Wilfrid Blunt.

De Burgh had the unpleasant habit of sneaking about outside Skittles's house at night to spy on her activities. One evening the Prince of Wales noticed De Burgh in the garden below and emptied a chamber pot over his head.

[Although worth over £2,000,000, **HUBERT DE BURGH** (1832-1916) lived a miserly existence, habitually eating his lunch out of a paper bag in Hyde Park. In an effort to soften the old skinflint, his nephew, Lord Dungarvan, although himself impoverished, sent De Burgh a portrait of one of their ancestors worth £100.

A few days later Dungarvan received a note of thanks but a request for Dungarvan to pay the seven shillings carriage charge on the delivery. When Dungarvan ignored the letter, he received two more, then a demand for payment. An astounded Dungarvan wrote back telling De Burgh precisely what he could do with the demand. As a result, De Burgh cut him out of his will and left the huge fortune elsewhere.]

GEORGE, VISCOUNT CURZON 1859-1925

Among the three young men seen in 1891 as 'the future', (George Curzon, *George Wyndham* and Harry Cust), Curzon was the only one who had been relatively close to Wilde. As a fellow undergraduate at Oxford, according to Oscar, they had spent many afternoons 'talking and thinking in Greek'.

When, in 1881, Oscar's book of poems, a copy of which having been requested by the Oxford Union, was turned down by vote, an indignant Curzon stoutly defended his friend. Wilde wrote to him: 'You are a brick. Our sweet city with its dreaming towers must not be given entirely over to the Philistines'.

During the weekend of Oscar's visit to the Crabbet Club, Curzon was given the task of acting as devil's advocate to oppose his election. In fact he did too good a job, dwelling at length on Oscar's homosexual reputation. *Blunt* said that 'poor Oscar sat helplessly smiling, a fat mass, in his chair', although he later made a more than adequate speech in his own defence, (using almost the same argument that he later employed in court, that of 'the Love that dare not speak its name').

In his maturity, Curzon seemed to epitomise English aristocratic grandeur at the height of the Empire; he moved as if 'accompanied by elephants'. One sardonic verse haunted him throughout his life: 'My name is George Nathaniel Curzon, I am a most superior person, My cheek is pink, my hair is sleek, I dine at Blenheim once a week.' *Margot Asquith* commented on his 'expression of enamelled self-assurance', while *Max Beerbohm* called him 'Britannia's butler'.

He had been raised at the ancestral family home at Kedleston, Derbyshire, where he became an unquestioning feudal Tory with a deep belief in the imperial mission. After Eton and Oxford, he graduated seamlessly into the heartland of governance, being seen as the 'Captain of the Souls', (the dominant political and social group in London).

Occasionally a dissident voice was raised against him. When Curzon was given a dinner by his admirers to congratulate him on his first government appointment, he gave a flowery speech during which he told the company that his success was due entirely to his personal decision only to associate with his intellectual superiors. As these 'superiors' were duly preening themselves on the compliment, a slightly drunk *Lord Houghton* sat up and growled: "Good God! That wouldn't be difficult!"

As part of his plan to train himself firstly to become Foreign Secretary, then Prime Minister, Curzon travelled widely. He was fascinated by the Japanese sumo wrestlers and described the East as 'a university in which the scholar never takes a degree'.

He acquired a lifelong loathing for missionaries after he was forced to accompany some American clerics at sea: 'They contributed about as much excitement to the voyage as would a company of tortoises'. (Wilde's view was more supportive: "Missionaries! Don't you realize that missionaries are the divinely provided food for destitute and under-fed cannibals? Whenever they are on the brink of starvation, Heaven, in its infinite mercy, sends them a nice plump missionary".)

After a trip to Persia, Curzon wrote a book in which he described the Shah's wife as 'looking like a melon who wandered around in a ballet tutu with naked legs'. The Prime Minister, *Lord Salisbury,* advised him to delete the passage as it might harm Anglo-Persian relations: "It would not be safe to handle the Shah with the truth and freedom which is permissible and salutary in the case of Mr Gladstone".

Given Curzon's stately demeanour, his friends were surprised by the 'earthy vitality bordering on coarseness' with which he pursued his love affairs. In addition to such ladies as Sibell Wyndham, (George's wife), Charty Tennant (Margot Asquith's sister), and Pearl Craigie, (*George Moore's* girlfriend), Curzon was involved in dozens of reckless incidents with young actresses and street girls, at least one of whom attempted to blackmail him.

When he travelled on the Northwest Frontier, he found himself so bereft of female company that he said he 'could feel desire for a telegraph pole surrounded by a petticoat'. In 1895, he settled into a happy marriage with a graceful American girl called Mary Leitner.

In 1899, Curzon achieved his real pinnacle when he was appointed Viceroy of India; it was also where his reputation for ludicrous pomp became established. Rumours circulated that, when Curzon retired to bed, two aide-de-camps had orders to precede him, carrying silver candlesticks and walking backwards. When his wife Mary awoke in the morning, she had to curtsey to him.

(However true these stories were, it was certain that when prospective footmen were interviewed for the job – which would include holding out plates at dinner – their wrists were inspected for elegance.)

In fact, as Viceroy, Curzon was noted for his honesty, (he returned from India poorer than he arrived), and his fairness: "I have never wavered in a strict and inflexible justice between the two races. It is the sole justification and the only stable foundation for our rule." He had little time for any pretence at nascent democracy: "the government of India consists of a confidential correspondence between the Secretary of State in London and the Viceroy in India". He also coined the phrase 'masterly inactivity'.

After a bitter row with his military commander, *Lord Kitchener,* Curzon was manoeuvred into resignation as Viceroy in 1905 and returned to virtual unemployment in Britain.

To his great sadness, his wife Mary died in 1906. Curzon consoled himself with a long affair with the romantic novelist, Elinor Glyn, (the unwilling subject of the music-hall song, 'To sin with Elinor Glyn on a tiger skin'), and eventually married another American, Grace Duggan.

His love of ritualistic pomp created a lasting British memorial. At the end of World War One, he arranged for the installation of the Tomb of the Unknown Soldier in Westminster Abbey, and the Cenotaph in Whitehall. He also created the Remembrance Day service, including the two minutes silence and the Last Post. For a nation stunned by grief, the event proved so popular that the public insisted on its annual repetition.

When he became Chancellor of Oxford University in 1907, he found to his chagrin that the inaugural ceremony consisted simply of a deputation of dons turning up at his house. Curzon unearthed a 17th century document that permitted a procession through Oxford and various attendant pageants. With the additional invention of an oath and speeches in Latin, (written by the ever obsequious President of Magdalen, Sir Herbert Warren), Curzon was then installed in the manner to which he had become accustomed. This essentially bogus event still continues to this day.

He remained as majestic as ever; after he bought a house on Carleton Terrace, he seriously attempted to silence the chimes of Big Ben, complaining that they kept him awake at night. One MP saw him at the Madame Tussaud's exhibition: "gazing with concentrated attention but a trace of disappointment at his own effigy in wax".

In 1919 he achieved at least one of his ambitions and took control at the Foreign Office. His imperious manner still raised hackles. On one occasion, several fellow ministers were waiting for Curzon's arrival, when a servant arrived carrying his footstool. Lord Derby rose and bowed to the stool, commenting: "Lord Curzon has not yet arrived but we see premonitory symptoms".

When King Amanullah of Afghanistan made a state visit to Britain, Curzon tried to interest him in English ways. This was to prove unfortunate as, on his return home, the King attempted to pass a law requiring all Afghan men to wear bowler hats. Rejecting this sartorial dictat, the Afghans promptly deposed him.

Occasionally a beam of wit shone through Curzon's formal exterior. When he received one Foreign Office document, he noticed a misprint – 'Even the monks of Mount Athos were violating their cows'. Curzon quipped: "Better send them a Papal Bull".

As Foreign Secretary, he played an important role in aiding the creation of the modern Turkish state and in sorting out the chaos of post-war Europe. At one Lausanne Conference, he was accompanied by his faithful valet, a man called Tivendale. Curzon overlooked Tivendale's habitual drunkenness until one night the valet was spotted reeling wildly round the dance floor with the conference delegates and had to be sent home.

Puzzled as to how Tivendale had obtained so much alcohol, Curzon learnt that he had convinced the hotel management that Curzon, frightened of being poisoned, had ordered him to taste every bottle in the establishment before serving it.

Curzon was wary of the rise of Fascism. When one of his daughters married the British Fascist leader, Sir Oswald Mosley, Curzon described him as 'my sinister son-in-law'. When he called Mussolini 'a thoroughly unscrupulous and dangerous demagogue', the Rothermere Press was angered by this lack of respect for the Italian dictator and launched an attack on Curzon.

His refusal to follow the pro-fascist rightwing mainstream, combined with doubts over his capacity to delegate, meant that when the opportunity to become Prime Minister arose, Curzon was passed over. In the end, he was the grandest of grandees, but a rather honourable failure.

Perhaps the story that most summed up Curzon concerned an occasion when his friends teased him about being out of touch with ordinary life, saying that he had probably never even been on a London bus. He admitted that this was true, and decided to board the first one he came across. When the conductor asked him: "Where to, Guv'ner?", Curzon replied: "137A, Eaton Square, if you please".

Wilde also met another member of the Crabbet Club during his weekend visit, the politician, journalist and man-about-town, **HARRY CUST** (1861-1917) – one of the nude tennis-players. Cust was a close friend of the *Prince of Wales*, a member of the Marlborough Club set, and a successor to *WT Stead* as editor of the Pall Mall Gazette.

He was also a prodigious womaniser, (although possibly not in *Wilfrid Blunt's* league), and came under the lash of Crabbet Club teasing as being 'of great abilities but given up, so his friends say, to vice, the vice of women'.

In 1902, Cust gave a dinner party where the guests included the politicians *FE Smith*, Winston Churchill, and *Arthur Balfour*, and the novelist HG Wells. Halfway through the meal, a servant arrived to announce that the house was on fire. Cust dismissed the man, telling him: "We have not finished dinner. Bring in the next course, and then ring up the fire brigade."

As the flames licked the windows, and the spray of the firemen's hoses doused the room, the party continued unabated. HG Wells was later to use this incident as a scene in his novel, 'The New Machiavelli'.

> *At first, Wilde's relationship with Bosie Douglas was fairly low-key. Concentrating on work, Oscar decided to follow the actor-manager George Alexander's suggestion that he write a modern play, and spent the summer of 1891 in the Lake District working on the script that became known as 'Lady Windermere's Fan', named after the local lake.*

SIR GEORGE ALEXANDER 1858-1918

George Alexander, (born George Alexander Samson), was to produce and perform in two of Wilde's great dramatic triumphs, 'Lady Windermere's Fan' and 'The Importance of Being Earnest'. Although their collaboration proved to be very valuable, Wilde and Alexander constantly bickered over both scripts and interpretations. Oscar claimed that the stress of argument often made him ill.

For instance, Alexander (wisely) insisted that Wilde cut the original four acts of 'Earnest' down to three. After the first night, Wilde congratulated Alexander: "My dear Aleck, it was charming, quite charming. And, do you know, from time to time, I was reminded of a play I once wrote myself, called The Importance of Being Earnest".

When Wilde's world collapsed in 1895, Alexander was criticised, (by Oscar's friends), for his unsympathetic reaction, in particular for removing Oscar's name from the play advertisements outside his theatre. However, there was a strong possibility that Alexander took this decision because he realised the play might run for a longer period without its association with Wilde, and that this would increase Oscar's income at a time when he needed it most.

Less defensible was Alexander's behaviour when he accidentally came across Wilde on the French Rivera in 1899, after Oscar's release. Oscar: 'He gave me a crooked, sickly smile and hurried on without stopping. How absurd and mean of him.'

Alexander appears to have suffered a guilty conscience over his behaviour, because when he next encountered Oscar in Paris, he made a point of alighting from his cab to speak to him. Having bought the rights to Wilde's plays at the 1895 bankruptcy sale, in later years Alexander was to revive 'Earnest' several times. He insisted paying royalties to Wilde's sons, and on his own death left them the rights in his will.

In November 1895, Alexander had his own brush with the law when he was arrested in Chelsea for 'intercourse with a prostitute in the ordinary pursuit of her trade'. Shaw published a letter in the Daily Chronicle in his defence: 'the circumstances as described by Mr Alexander (of being accosted by a woman of the streets, and moved by her plight, of offering her charity) up to the point of the intervention of the policeman have occurred to me more than once'. Alexander managed to clear himself.

Alexander was one of the major figures of the Victorian stage. After an acting apprenticeship with *Henry Irving*, he took over the management of the St James Theatre in 1890 and ran it successfully for the next 27 years. He was knighted for his achievement in 1911.

Handsome but humourless, Alexander was a devout believer in promoting the integrity of the theatre and the social status of the acting profession. It was not an entirely popular stance even with actors. *Mrs Patrick Campbell* complained that: "What stops most really fine acting in this country is that actors and actresses want to be thought ladies and gentlemen". Even the sympathetic Irving was forced to advise him during a rehearsal: "Now, Alexander, not quite so much Piccadilly'.

GB Shaw once reviewed his portrayal of a drunkard with: 'he played the part like a seasoned teetotaller' and, out of pure devilment, offered him the part of the Dustman in 'Pygmalion'. Mrs Pat: "But Alexander would never have seen the joke".

Although he had one of his greatest successes acting opposite Mrs Pat in Arthur Pinero's 'The Second Mrs Tanqueray', their relationship was a fraught one. Mrs Pat: "We simply could not get on with each other".

During the run of one play set in ancient Egypt, Mrs Pat explained: 'I had to sit through an endless scene with Alexander prancing around as a Savile Row Pharaoh. Well, you know how things happen when you are bored – I started flicking chocolates at the backcloth. Every few moments, Alexander's immortal speech was interrupted by a plonk as a chocolate hit what appeared to be a star-spangled sky and then dropped with a dull thud into what was supposed to be the River Nile'.

When an enraged Alexander stormed at her during the interval, she replied: ' "Your wife would not like me to speak with you when you are angry. She says it upsets your digestion". 'Then I walked speedily to my dressing room and locked the door. He refused to speak to me after that, which made things very difficult on stage'.

Alexander said that he was prepared to "go to the workhouse rather than go through another London run with Mrs Pat".

When Alexander asked Wilde how long 'Lady Windermere' would take to write, Oscar mused: "I wonder can I do it in a week, or will it take three? It ought not to take long to beat the Pineros and the Joneses". Although he was a reluctant writer, ("I hate writing: the mere act of writing a thing down is troublesome to me"), once he became enthused he wrote very quickly indeed. He always composed his plays on holidays, and they were usually finished within three to four weeks.

Frank Harris claimed that Oscar wrote his play simply because he was irritated by the praise bestowed on **ARTHUR WING PINERO** (1855-1934). Oscar: 'Pinero can't write at all: he can make plots and scenes and nothing else. His characters are made of dough'.

Born into an affluent London family of Portuguese Jews, Pinero was a tall, thickset man with large black eyebrows below a completely bald dome of a head. *Max Beerbohm* said of the eyebrows that they looked like 'the skins of some small mammal just not large enough to be used as mats'.

After an undistinguished few years acting with Irving, ('Mr Pinero's 'Claudius' is the worst Birmingham has ever seen'), and influenced by Ibsen, he switched to writing drama. In 55 years he wrote 54 plays, including his greatest hit in 1893, 'The Second Mrs Tanqueray', (with its famous line: 'I believe the future is only the past again, entered through another gate').

Although he was later to be eclipsed by Shaw, at one time Pinero's reputation was so great so he was able to dictate his demands. No manager possessed the courage to reject him.

Gerald du Maurier told Mrs Pat that his life was made miserable by the fear of a new Pinero manuscript arriving on his desk.

Asked for his views after watching a Pinero play, Wilde replied: "It is the best play I ever slept through".

After Wilde had finished the manuscript of 'Lady Windermere's Fan', he returned from the Lake District to London in October 1891. He offered the play to the American theatre impresario Augustin Daly in the hope that Daly would produce the show with his star actress Ada Rehan in the leading role of 'Mrs Erlynne'. Daly rejected the script.

AUGUSTIN DALY 1838-1899

By 1897, Augustin Daly, annoyed over his initial failure of judgement on Wilde's talent, was keen to acquire any new scripts that Oscar might produce. Oscar, knowing in his heart that further plays were unlikely, hesitated over Daly's offer: 'I don't feel really at liberty to take his money, though I would like it. I have never done that sort of thing, and I can't begin. It is merely the weakness of the criminal classes that makes me refuse'. He did eventually accept an advance, but no new work emerged.

Daly, although born in the south of the USA, was raised in New York City where he acquired a boyhood love of the theatre and a particular reverence for the acting skills of the Booth family – father Junius, and his sons Edwin and John Wilkes.

[JUNIUS BOOTH (1796-1852) was a popular example of a type of actor known at the time as the 'talented drunkard'. His standard of performance was dependent on the amount of alcohol taken and, indeed, the outcome of the play was sometimes excitingly doubtful.

During one performance as Shakespeare's 'Richard III', Junius was so carried away that in the final scene he chased 'Richmond' off the stage and out into the street, thus reversing the tide of history. 'Richmond' survived only by hiding behind some dustbins in an alley.

Edwin Booth was a more reliable performer but as *Genevieve Ward* said: "The great tragedy of his life was his brother John Wilkes's murder of President Lincoln. Edwin retired from the stage for over a year, and was with difficulty persuaded to resume his career; but all America stood by him in these trying circumstances'.]

Inspired by the Booths, Daly nursed his ambitions to become a theatre impresario but, unable to make a breakthrough, for ten years he remained a reporter and drama critic for the New York newspapers. In this capacity he was fortunate to survive an incident during the Civil War Draft Riots in the city.

In 1863, a pro-Confederate New York anti-draft mob mistook Daly for a reporter on the unsympathetic Tribune paper. He was about to be lynched when some firemen rescued him by pulling him inside their station. When the mob attacked the fire station itself, Daly decided to slip outside through a side door. Daly: 'The door slammed behind me and I tried to run. My coat however had been caught in the door and I turned to hammer on the door to get it open. The mob spotted this and assumed that I was one of them. I got away in the confusion'.

A year later, Daly got his break when he was asked to arrange a theatre tour of captured Confederate towns. He overcame his inexperience and travelled with his troupe down the Mississippi, in the teeth of gunfire from guerrillas and a narrow escape from capture by the Confederate raider Nathan Bedford Forrest.

By 1869, Daly finally gained control of a New York theatre, and by dint of extremely hard work and involving himself in every aspect of the business, turned it into a success, producing 21 plays in six months. By 1891, he had opened a theatre in London. Daly: 'If you pause to consider the chances of failure, you will never accomplish anything'.

In 1879 Daly was joined by Ada Rehan (1860-1916), an Irish comedienne who had emigrated to the USA, and who remained his leading lady for many years. (Heavily dependent on his direction, she failed as an actress after his death, and became the companion to the American poet Amy Lowell.)

Daly was known as a strange, autocratic man who was as insistent on decorum in the American theatre as *Sir George Alexander* was in the English theatre. *Shaw*: 'He ordered his company never to speak to him or claim his acquaintance outside of the theatre premises'. But he was also good at his job – Shaw again: 'He was very largely right; that is why it was impossible to convince him when he was partly wrong'.

By chance in June 1899, Daly, his wife Mary, and Ada Rehan were dining in the same Paris restaurant as Wilde and avoided an embarrassing moment by inviting him to join them. Oscar delighted Ada by accusing her of dyeing her hair white. Ada: 'We had a lovely evening'.

A few days later, Daly collapsed and died. With his widow prostrate with grief, the difficult arrangements were left in Ada's hands. Ada: 'And then Oscar Wilde came to me and was more good and helpful than I can tell you – just like a very kind brother. I shall always think of him as he was to me through those few dreadful days'.

THEATRE FIRES

[In 1873, Daly's Fifth Avenue Theatre burnt down; he was uninsured and lost a huge amount of money. Theatre fires were a common problem in the 19th century. In 1882, the Park Theatre was destroyed; then in 1883, the Standard Theatre; and in 1891, the Fifth Avenue Theatre was burned again.

The worst fire was at the Brooklyn Theatre in 1876. It started on stage and the theatre staff and the stalls audience all escaped unharmed. But the upper circle exit was jammed shut by people falling against the door. When the police saw that no one was coming downstairs, they assumed that the circle had been cleared already and closed the doors without checking further. Over 300 died. For years afterwards ticket buyers preferred to chose seats, not near the stage, but near the exits.

Wilde once told *EF Benson* a story that he said would form part of a series of 'Great Thoughts' and be entitled 'The Value of Presence of Mind'. "It would be designed as a token of ill will at Christmas, and carry a message of sorrow into many otherwise hilarious homes".

Oscar described how one evening a fire broke out in a theatre, causing the panicking audience to fight their way to the exits. The leading actor, seeing the chaos, immediately called for silence and ordered the audience back into their seats, telling them that the fire was now under control and that their lives depended upon their self-discipline.

'Feeling thoroughly ashamed of themselves, the audience did as they were bidden. When the exits were clear and the seats occupied once more, the actor leapt lightly over the footlights into the stalls and vanished through the first convenient doorway. Then the auditorium filled with smoke, the flames raced in from every side and not another soul left the place alive.']

At the end of October 1891, Wilde went to stay in Paris for two months, lodging for some of the time in the Boulevard des Capucines. On this occasion, his visit was described by L'Echo de Paris as the literary event of the season. In November he met the French writers Pierre Louys and Andre Gide.

PIERRE LOUYS 1870-1925

The young Louys, (born Pierre-Felix Louis), was fascinated by Wilde, addressing him as 'Cher maitre', and guiding him to the best salons. They remained friends for three years and, after Louys had corrected Oscar's French grammar in 'Salome', Oscar dedicated this play – 'A mon ami Pierre Louys'.

Although prominently heterosexual himself, Louys enjoyed Oscar's homosexual milieu: "they know how to envelop everything in poetry". But this attitude began to change by 1894.

On one occasion, he called on Oscar at the Savoy Hotel and found *Bosie Douglas* in the bedroom. As they talked, *Constance Wilde* also arrived and begged Oscar to return home. Although Oscar made light of the situation by pretending that he had forgotten the address, Louys was touched by the sight of Constance's tears.

He decided that, unless Oscar abandoned Bosie, they could no longer remain friends. Wilde was saddened by this decision, writing: 'Farewell, Pierre Louys. I wanted to have a friend; in future I shall just have lovers'. They parted for good, although when Oscar died Louys did attend the funeral.

During the 1890s, Louys became well known for his erotic novels, which focussed mostly on lesbianism. *Ernest Dowson* proclaimed Louys to be: "the greatest authority in Europe on Lesbianism except myself", (perhaps forgetting the lesbian community itself).

Having inherited 100,000 francs in 1891, Louys indulged in a boisterous sex life among the Parisian prostitutes, often accompanied by *Robert Sherard*. He also befriended the youthful *Andre Gide* and encouraged the shy young writer to explore heterosexuality. One morning, Gide opened his front door to be confronted by a naked girl and the sight of Louys and friends roaring with laughter across the street.

However, Louys teased Gide one step too far when he insisted that Gide accompany him to a sordid brothel in Algiers. Gide was persuaded to bed the prettiest girl in the house but afterwards told Louys of his fears about possible syphilis. Louys's reply was not helpful.

He explained that, as Gide's bed-partner had been the most attractive girl in the brothel, it stood to reason that she had slept with the most clients, thereby increasing her chances of disease. When Louys told him to cheer up because most of France's greatest writers had been syphilitic, Gide was annoyed at the flippancy. A rift opened between them that did not heal.

Louys visited North Africa six times between 1894 and 1901, finding that it fired his imagination. On his first trip to Biskra, he met and slept with a 16-year-old Algerian girl called Meriem ben Atala. His infatuation with her inspired the writing of his first successful erotic book, the 1895 'Les Chansons de Bilitis'. It was partly dedicated to her.

Louys pretended that 'Bilitis' was the translation of a hitherto unknown Ancient Greek poetess and lesbian friend of Sappho. In fact it was a brilliantly written pastiche that fooled many people and charmed even those who saw through the hoax. The work was so successful that in 1900, the composer Claude Debussy set the poems to music. A later performance, (involving ten naked girls miming actions to the score), caused some offence in conservative circles, notably from a self-appointed moral censor, Senator Rene Berenger, (nicknamed 'Pere-la-Pudeur').

In 1896, Louys published his most successful book, 'Aphrodite', which sold 50,000 copies within the year. The Italian composer Puccini considered it as the subject for an opera, (but chose 'Madame Butterfly' instead). Wilde was unstinting in his praise: "Nothing is as beautiful as that book".

However, Louys could not repeat these triumphs in his subsequent work, and he gradually sank into mental lethargy and financial ruin. His marriage to Louise de Heredia ended when she tired of the poverty and of Louys's pursuit of other women.

He moved to Bordeaux, where his sexual exploits earned him the nickname of 'Tom-Cat'. Here, he became addicted to morphine, cocaine and alcohol, and died of tertiary syphilis in 1925.

Some of his works survived his death. One of them, 'The Woman and the Puppet', provided the material for a 1935 film starring Marlene Dietrich, and a 1958 film starring Brigitte Bardot, while a soft-core porno film named 'Bilitis' appeared in the 1970s.

As befitted his obsession with Sapphic activity, he became friends with the lesbian writer, the American *Natalie Barney*. She once presided over a performance of a piece by Louys, in which the leading roles were taken by the young French actress *Colette* and an American girl called Eva Palmer.

Both girls were nervous of acting before their peers and the great Pierre Louys himself, and their accents suffered accordingly. Eva reverted to American, while Colette fell back into her native Burgundian, (which sounded very much like Russian).

After the show, Colette asked Louys what he thought. Louys replied: "I have experienced one of the greatest emotions of my life – the unforgettable hallucination of hearing my words spoken by Mark Twain and Count Leo Tolstoy".

ANDRE GIDE 1869-1951

Although when they first met in Paris, the 22-year-old Andre Gide was mesmerised by Wilde, ('he emitted rays'), he considered Oscar to be potentially corrupt. Gide: 'Wilde was always trying to insinuate inside you the authorisation of evil'. Oscar himself seemed to take a perverse pleasure in shocking the young writer. Wilde: "The trouble is that Andre is a French Protestant – the worst kind, except of course for the Irish Protestant'.

They met again, firstly in Florence in 1894, then by accident in Blidah in Algeria in 1895, (Algeria being a centre for sex tourism, particularly for English homosexuals). Oscar and *Bosie Douglas* took the shy repressed young man out for the evening and encouraged him into bed with a young male musician. Amazed to find that he was capable of six orgasms in one night, Gide was forced to reassess his own tortuous sexuality.

Gide was able to repay the pair by introducing them to hashish. He had acquired a liking for this drug when his doctor suggested that Gide cured his breathlessness by smoking cigarettes laced with cannabis. Gide: "It gave me great relief". Wilde was also impressed: "It is quite exquisite: three puffs of smoke and then peace and love".

Although Gide met Wilde occasionally on the latter's release from prison, he found Oscar to be 'portly and seedy' and with teeth 'in a shocking state'. After the spring of 1898, (as Gide was flirting with respectability and, indeed, had been elected Mayor of La Roque), they did not meet again.

Through the first decades of the 20th century, Gide became one of the foremost explorers of the intellect. He had been born into both position and wealth, but his early years had been blighted by his dominating mother and his own timidity. After the liberating experience of his mother's death, the publication of such works as 'L'Immoraliste', (his memories of the 1890s), 'Corydon', (a robust defence of homosexuality in 1911), 'The Coiners', (1919-25), and his 'Journals', (1939), turned him into a world-famous figure.

Following the tradition of political involvement by French intellectuals, Gide became a committed supporter of Dreyfus during the infamous Affaire, and an opponent of capitalist exploitation in Africa, the conditions of which he observed at first hand. Gide: 'What demon brought me to Africa? I was at peace: and now I know, and I must speak'.

By the 1930s, he sided with communism: 'I feel a brother only to those who have come to communism through love. What leads me to communism is not Marx but the Gospels'. However, after a visit to Russia, he became disillusioned with what he saw as the betrayal of the revolution. The Stalinists dismissed him as 'a bourgeois individualist'.

Gide had a curious sex life that began, inopportunely, with his expulsion from school for masturbation when he was aged 8. At 13, he fell in love with his 15-year-old cousin, Madelaine Rondeaux. He acknowledged his homosexuality after his adventures with Wilde, but nonetheless married Madelaine in 1895, in what proved to be an unconsummated 'mariage blanc'.

While he admitted that his true desires were for pre-pubescent children, (what in a later era would be called paedophilia), in practice he directed his sexual drives towards young men in their late teens. Then, aged 46, he had an uncharacteristic heterosexual affair with Elizabeth van Rysselberghe that produced a daughter called Catherine.

Gide spent the early part of the Second World War as an 'interior émigré' living in Nice in Vichy France. In 1942, feeling under threat, he sailed to North Africa, where he was lucky to survive the Allied bombing of German-occupied Tunis.

In the post-war years, Gide was awarded the Nobel Prize for Literature and also a doctorate from Oxford University. When he visited the city to receive his degree, he expressed a desire to be taken to see Wilde's old quarters at Magdalen College. His hosts took him to the rooms where, by chance, a cricket team were having a party. The cricketers watched in silence as the famous old writer wandered around reverently stroking the walls.

Gide had little time for religion and publicly rejected an attempt by the Catholic poet Paul Claudel to convert him. Shortly after Gide's death, a telegram was found pinned to the notice board of the Sorbonne University in Paris. It read: 'Hell doesn't exist. Better notify Claudel. Signed A. Gide'.

While in Paris, Wilde also stayed with a rather exalted friend, Lord Lytton, the British Ambassador to France, at the Embassy in the Faubourg Saint-Honore.

LORD LYTTON 1831-1891

Although Robert Lytton thoroughly liked Wilde and enjoyed his writing, his daughters were more cautious. In 1891, one of them, Lady Emily, (afterwards married to the architect Lutyens), wrote about Oscar's presence at an embassy lunch: 'We all thought him very amusing and not so odious as we expected though he is evidently fearfully conceited'.

Lytton, (who succeeded to his title in 1873 on the death of his father, the popular novelist Lord Edward Bulwer Lytton), was raised at the family home of Knebworth, and married one of GF Watts's pre-Raphaelite models, Edith Villiers. His friend *Benjamin Disraeli* commented: "She rules her husband, but that I suppose is always the case where marriages are what is called happy".

In 1876, during Disraeli's premiership, Lytton was made Viceroy of India, where he became involved in the complex manoeuvring between Britain and Russia known as the 'Great Game'. After the massacre of the British legation (led by Sir Louis Cavagnari) in Kabul, Afghanistan, Lytton instigated the Second Afghan War and the capture of Kabul by British forces under General Fred Roberts in 1880. Realising the value of a buffer state, he created the still-existing strip of north-eastern Afghan territory between Russia and India known as 'the scientific frontier'.

His tenure of office in India came under attack as he was regarded as too unconventional and insouciant for the post of Viceroy. His refusal to attend Sunday church services and his incessant cigarette smoking during meals caused particular offence. As befitted

322

a friend of *Wilfred Blunt*, he indulged in clandestine affairs, although his attempt to seduce one of Blunt's old flames, Mrs Batten, was constantly frustrated by the tight security enforced on Viceroys following the assassination of a predecessor, (Algernon Bourke's father, Viscount Mayo).

Lytton memorably described his administration of India as: 'a despotism of office-boxes tempered by the occasional loss of keys'.

In 1880, with the collapse of Disraeli's government, Lytton resigned his post and resumed a literary career of writing mostly poetry under the pseudonym of 'Owen Meredith'.

In 1887, he was appointed as British Ambassador to Paris. In 'Dorian Gray', Wilde made mention of the qualifications for this post: '...the Embassy at Paris, a post to which he considered that he was fully entitled by reason of his birth, his indolence, the good English of his despatches, and his inordinate passion for pleasure'.

Lytton certainly found the job highly congenial, and his bohemian nature fitted in perfectly with Parisian high society. When he turned the Embassy into a centre of culture, his popularity soared and he received invitations to such events as Countess Potocka's orgiastic dinner parties. Lytton puzzled: "I devoted my life to India and everybody abused me. I come here, do nothing, and am praised to the skies".

On 24th November 1891, he died suddenly at the embassy. During his last few days, Wilde was almost the only person whom Lytton wished to see, and Oscar comforted him on his deathbed. Wilde wrote: 'Lytton's death has been a source of great grief to me', and dedicated the published script of 'Lady Windermere's Fan': 'To the dear memory of Robert, Earl of Lytton, in affection and admiration.'

The Times obituary was less affectionate: 'Lytton frequented French literary and artistic society of the semi-bohemian type.... The conventions of polite society were as incomprehensible to him as to a child of some savage race...His clothes were like nobody else's – certainly not English'.

During Wilde's absence in Paris his short story collection, 'A House of Pomegranates', was published. It included 'The Young King', 'The Birthday of the Infanta', 'The Fisherman and His Soul' and 'The Star Child'.

In addition to polishing 'Lady Windermere's Fan', and working on a new play, 'Salome', Oscar enjoyed a hectic social life, breakfasting with Lord Curzon and Wilfred Blunt, drinking with Verlaine and Aristide Bruant, and dining with Marcel Schwob and Andre Gide. He also met up with his old Oxford friend, JEC Bodley, and his brother-in-law, Otho Lloyd.

With 'Salome' almost finished, on December 22, 1891, he returned to London, where he spent Christmas at Tite St with his family.

1892

[In Britain, after winning a fresh election, WE Gladstone became the Prime Minister of Britain for the fourth time.

In France, there was civil unrest during a series of strikes and riots by the working class. Paris itself was hit by a wave of terrorist bombings carried out by anarchists.

In India, the rupee collapsed in value. (As 'Miss Prism' said to 'Cecily' in 'The Importance of Being Earnest': 'The chapter on the fall of the Rupee you may omit. It is somewhat too sensational for a young girl'.)]

Wilde spent most of January in Torquay, Devon, finishing his two new plays, then came back to London to oversee the rehearsals for 'Lady Windermere's Fan'.

The Wilde family was scattered during February. As Oscar explained in a letter: 'I have been very ill, and the drains at Tite Street have gone wrong, so we are all separated and Vyvyan, who is ill, to Lady Mount-Temple's, Cyril to Mrs Napier's, myself to a quiet room here'.

'Here' was the Albemarle Hotel in the West End of London where, after the triumphant first night of 'Lady Windermere's Fan', Oscar took advantage of Constance's absence to sleep with a young publishing clerk called Edward Shelley.

LADY WINDERMERE'S FAN

Probably due to the failure of his early plays back in the early 1880s, Wilde was tentative about the new show. *William Rothenstein* said: "In Paris he had been rather apologetic about his play; as though to write a comedy were rather beneath a poet"; and when Vincent O'Sullivan suggested that his reason for writing plays was his fondness for applause, Oscar agreed: "Yes, the immediate applause!" He called 'Lady Windermere's Fan', (originally titled 'A Good Woman'): "one of those modern drawing room plays with pink lamp shades".

He was quite open about what he perceived as his own weaknesses of technique, telling *Ada Leverson* that he felt unable to create character: "My people just sit in chairs and chatter".

When *Frank Harris* told him that the play was admirably constructed: 'Wilde confessed to me quite frankly that he had gone away by himself for a fortnight, and studied the construction of half a dozen of the best French and English plays, and from that study had gained the craft'. Indeed, his favourite characters of the dandy, the woman with a past, and the idealistic young lady, were all stock theatrical figures that Oscar adapted for his own purposes.

At times, Wilde was unsure even on basic English grammar, asking one friend: "Will you also look after my 'wills' and 'shalls'. I am Celtic in my use of these words, not English". *Bosie Douglas* commented that Oscar used a lot of split infinitives: 'but he always winced when they were pointed out'.

Frank Harris also claimed that he had heard many of the play's witticisms before while listening to Oscar's conversation – (one such line: 'Experience, the name men give to their mistakes' made almost ubiquitous appearances in Wilde's plays) – though made the point that 'the effect on the stage to those who had never heard them was really overpowering'.

But, beyond his own insecurities and the sniping of critics, Wilde had managed to create the first English language play of genuine worth since the days of Sheridan almost 100 years previously. He had turned the accusation of 'lack of dramatic action' into a virtue; he had re-discovered the Shakespearean secret: "Never be afraid that by raising a laugh you destroy tragedy. On the contrary, you intensify it"; and, through his own mastery of conversational timing, created a style of brilliant dialogue.

'Lady Windermere's Fan' opened at the St James Theatre on February 20th 1891, (and ran till the 29th of July, toured in Britain, then returned on 31st October).

Oscar's curtain call speech after the first night's performance was daringly unconventional. Wilde told the audience: "I congratulate you on the great success of your performance, which persuades me that you think almost as highly of the play as I do myself".

Part of that audience failed to appreciate his humour and went on to attack both Oscar and his play. The author Henry James was among his chief detractors.

HENRY JAMES 1843-1916

The two men had already had a bruising encounter during Wilde's 1882 tour of America, when Oscar had accidentally snubbed Henry James by airily dismissing the latter's stated nostalgia for London, and announcing his own belief that 'the world is my home'. The proudly internationalist James was piqued by this presumption and dismissed Wilde as 'a fatuous fool and a tenth-rate cad'.

Although Wilde was unaware of the depth of the hostility that he had aroused in the American novelist, James himself became increasingly malicious in his remarks about Oscar. Referring to Wilde as 'the unspeakable one', he described 'Lady Windermere's Fan' as 'infantine', 'A Woman of No Importance' as 'a piece of helpless puerility', and 'An Ideal Husband' as 'clumsy, feeble and vulgar'.

It was unfortunate that James's major humiliation coincided with Oscar's greatest success. In January 1895, James's play, 'Guy Domville', was produced at the St James Theatre by *George Alexander*. James, nervous about its chances, decided not to attend the first night and instead went to see Wilde's 'An Ideal Husband' at the Haymarket Theatre. Emerging from the cheers for his hated rival, he returned to the St James Theatre in time for the curtain call.

Unbeknownst to James, his own play had had a disastrous first performance. During the third act, when Alexander had delivered the line, 'I am the last of the Domvilles', a loud voice had echoed from the gallery, "Well, thank Gawd for that!"

James arrived in the theatre wings and mistook the howls of derision for applause. When he went out on stage to receive the plaudits as author, he was greeted by increased booing. Transfixed with horror, he stayed shaking and white-faced to endure the catcalls. One audience member, *Violet Hunt*, said that: "it was like prodding a soft, large animal in the zoo".

To make matters even worse, after what James called 'the horridest four weeks of my life', 'Guy Domville' was taken off, only to be replaced by Oscar's new triumph, 'The Importance of Being Earnest'.

Although in truth Wilde thought highly of James as a novelist, he also had irritated the American with such comments as: "Henry James writes novels as if they were a painful duty", and describing his literary style as: "like an elephant picking up a pin".

When Oscar's career was destroyed in 1895, James reacted with ill- concealed glee, calling the trials: 'hideously, atrociously dramatic, and really interesting'. Refusing to sign any clemency pleas, he said that maybe the sentence of hard labour was too severe – it would have been better simply to isolate Wilde, (not realising that Oscar underwent both punishments).

James's animosity was driven perhaps by the fact that, though he was a life-long celibate who would have rejected the description, he was latently homosexual. The repressed James was appalled by Wilde's open flamboyance. In the furtive world of Victorian homosexuality, Oscar's outspokenness represented a threat to many such men, (including *Walter Pater* and *Bosie's* grandfather Alfred Montgomery).

Henry James was undoubtedly one of the major novelists of the English language, creating between 1876 and 1904 such masterpieces as 'The Ambassadors', 'The Wings of a Dove', and 'The Turn of the Screw'. Born in New York City, but raised mostly in the Boston area, he was not always appreciated in his native land. *Ambrose Bierce* wrote of James and his contemporary, WD Howells, as: 'two eminent triflers and cameo-cutters-in-chief to Her Littleness the Bostonese small virgin'. *Mark Twain* remarked of one of James's novels: "Once you put it down, you simply can't pick it up".

In 1868, James left the USA to travel in Europe, eventually settling in England where his literary eminence soon gave him entry to the respectable social world he so enjoyed. His rather ponderous personality was lightened by his occasional capacity to land himself in absurd situations.

Once, after a woman friend had committed suicide in Venice, James travelled to the city to pay his respects. He decided that he would gather her many voluminous black dresses, row himself out in a gondola, and throw them beneath the waters of the lagoon. Unfortunately, after he had reverently cast them away, the dresses remained filled with air and floated back up to the surface. James was left snared in mid-lagoon, surrounded by enormous black bubbles.

James spent most of his life living tranquilly at his home Lamb House in Rye, Sussex, and at the Reform Club in London. He had a large circle of English friends, including *George du Maurier* and *Edmund Gosse*, who were constantly entertained by James's weighty judgements on everyday life. *JE Blanche* said that: "When Henry James laboured to reply to someone it took him some time to start. He was like a heavy aeroplane taking off".

At one of Gosse's literary parties, James was subjected to watching a puppet show. Asked for his opinion of the performance, he yawned: "An interesting example of economy. Economy of means and…. economy of effect".

After a group of actresses had been invited to tea at his Rye home, Gosse asked him whether they had been pretty. Gosse: "Henry replied, 'Pretty? Good Heavens!' and then, with the air of one who must be scrupulously fair, he added, 'One of the poor wantons had a certain cadaverous grace'.

The outbreak of the First World War in 1914 placed James in a difficult moral position. Although still a US citizen, he regarded the American President Woodrow Wilson's neutral stance as cowardly and self-seeking. As a gesture of solidarity with his adopted homeland, he applied for British citizenship.

(On his application form, James needed sponsors to confirm that he was literate in the English language. Highly amused, the Prime Minister, *HH Asquith*, agreed to be one of the signatories.)

The British press were unanimous in their praise for James's action, but in the USA he was reviled. The New York Times: 'His desertion is good riddance'.

[After Henry James's death, the USA did eventually join forces with Britain, but one of the reasons for the alliance might not have appealed to him.

In April 1916, with money for the war effort fast running out, a representative of the British government, Lord Reading, went to Washington to negotiate a loan of £1,000 million. The recent suppression of the Easter Rising in Ireland had generated a strong anti-British popular feeling in the USA, and the American government, suspecting that a German victory was likely, refused Reading's request.

Instead, he turned to the American private banks. At the time, as they were forbidden by law to have branches, there were 25,000 different banks and no overall strategy. On the promise that the loans would favour US trade, Reading managed to raise the money from dozens of different financial groups.

It was only then that realisation dawned that with so much money owing to American institutions, the USA had to ensure a British victory simply to recover the cash and avoid mass bankruptcies in America. The financiers, now desperately worried, forced President Wilson to declare war.

By Armistice Day in 1918, Britain owed £850,000,000 to the US banks.]

CLEMENT SCOTT (1841-1904) was another reviewer who took exception to Oscar's first night speech, declaring it to be 'insolent effrontery'. As the theatre critic of the Daily Telegraph for almost thirty years, Scott was feared for his acidic pen; (he reviewed one actor's performance as 'the King' in 'Hamlet' with: 'This gentleman played the King as if he expected that at any moment someone would play the Ace').

When commenting on some of Scott's own minor verses in 1886, Wilde had gently ridiculed one of the poems, (an effusion on Ireland): "I think you might correct the one very Irish oversight, or slip – Erin can do most things, but she can't, bless her, 'remember the days to come'."

Scott was an effective athlete in his youth and in 1874 took part in one of the first ever games of lawn tennis at Hans Place, London. He was married to *George Du Maurier's* sister, Isabel, but was known to be a considerable lecher.

This did not prevent him from adopting a highly moralistic pose in his newspaper columns and, when the Wilde scandal erupted, he thundered his approval of the guilty verdict in an editorial blast: 'Open the windows! Let in the fresh air!'

It was possible that he was still smarting from Oscar's comment in 'Dorian Gray': 'All drama critics can be bought. But, judging from their appearance, most of them cannot be at all expensive'.

After his triumph with 'Lady Windermere's Fan', Wilde worked through the spring of 1892 preparing for the production of his play 'Salome'.

At the same time his affair with Bosie Douglas intensified. Wilde visited Oxford and successfully dealt with an attempt to blackmail Bosie over his homosexuality. They spent much of the following summer together.

During June 1892, the rehearsals for 'Salome', starring the French actress Sarah Bernhardt, were nearing completion when it was realised that Oscar had forgotten to apply for a theatre licence. When he did so, the Lord Chamberlain, Edward Smyth-Pigott, (according to Bernard Shaw: 'a walking compendium of vulgar insular prejudice'), banned the show on the grounds that it depicted Biblical figures on the stage.

An outraged Oscar threatened to leave Britain and become a French citizen: "I will not consent to call myself a citizen of a country that shows such narrowness in artistic judgment".

He abandoned the idea when it was pointed out that if he became a naturalised Frenchman he would become liable for compulsory service in the French Army. The New York Times reported: 'All London is laughing at Oscar Wilde's threat to become a Frenchman'.

The abandonment of 'Salome' was a genuine blow to Wilde. Ada Leverson said: "In truth Oscar cared little for any of his plays excepting only Salome"; and it was the only one of his works quoted on his tomb at Pere Lachaise.

SALOME

'Salome' finally received its first performance in 1896 in Paris and became popular in Europe; in 1905, the composer Richard Strauss created his opera based on Wilde's work.

In Ireland, the play was not performed until 1928, when the theatrical partnership of Michael Macliammoir and Hilton Edwards produced it at the Gate Theatre in Dublin. The production was under-funded and some of the smaller parts were acted by local amateurs. When the 'First Soldier's' line, 'The Tetrach has a sombre look', was delivered in a strong Dublin accent, the audience dissolved in laughter.

The play was given its first British public production in 1931 at the Savoy Theatre, London. It was not well received. The Daily Mail headline was: 'Wilde's Play Sadly Dull', while another critic described it as: 'like sitting on a tombstone in the moonlight eating a box of caramel chocolates.'

William Archer was one respected critic who was angered by the banning of 'Salome', which he called 'an Oriental Hedda Gabler'.

WILLIAM ARCHER 1856-1924

Archer was a staunch advocate of the new intellectual drama of Hendrik Ibsen, and indeed translated some of his plays into English. As such, he maintained that 'there is no real substance in Wilde's work'. However, he realised that Oscar was a genuine playwright and not simply another propagator of the stock Victorian melodrama.

In 1895, he was unstinting in his support for 'The Importance of Being Earnest', reviewing the play thus: 'the artist's fingers ran with crisp irresponsibility up and down the keyboard of life'.... 'It is delightful to see, it sends wave after wave of laughter curling and foaming round the theatre'.... 'farce' is far too gross and commonplace a word to apply to such an iridescent filament of fantasy'.

Bernard Shaw, a lifelong friend who was very fond of the tall Scots critic, found him also to be 'a constant source of amusement'. Shaw: "Archer had a habit of wearing a winged collar, which gave his head the appearance of being wedged in a jam pot".

When Shaw first attempted to write drama he was discouraged by the fact that when he read his first draft aloud to his friend, Archer fell fast asleep. Shaw: 'It convinced me that I did not have the makings of a playwright'. Shaw later discovered that Archer's somnambulism was habitual and that 'any play by any author invariably sent him to sleep as surely as any drug'.

This problem once led Archer into the most embarrassing incident of his life. At the first night of one play he had, as usual, nodded off during the second act. As the play continued, the action demanded that a thunderous pistol shot sounded on stage.

Archer, suddenly aroused from slumber, started wildly to his feet with a thin scream and automatically buried his clenched hands in the hair of the lady in front of him. To Archer's horror, the lady's hair came off, and Archer was left standing there, holding the wig in his hands.

Sarah Bernhardt, who had thoroughly committed herself to performing 'Salome', was furious at the cancellation but eventually forgave Wilde and they resumed their usual harmonious relationship.

SARAH BERNHARDT 1844-1923

Oscar Wilde had been an admirer of 'the Divine Sarah' Bernhardt ever since 1879 when he had greeted the arrival of the famous actress at Folkestone by strewing an armful of lilies at her feet. Charmed by his flamboyant gesture and by his sonnet, 'To Sarah Bernhardt', she visited his home at Salisbury Street where she signed her name on the ceiling and demonstrated her agility by displaying how far up the wall she could kick.

Bernhardt, well aware of the usual motive behind male attentions, appreciated Wilde's more altruistic esteem: 'Oscar was a devoted attendant, and did much to make things pleasant and easy for me in London, but he never appeared to play court'.

In 1888, she was happy to supply an article entitled 'The History of My Tea-Gown' for Wilde's 'Women's World'. Oscar then suggested that she wrote a second article, this time on 'America'.

He suggested that, as most Americans claimed that they visited France in order to complete their education, her piece should begin with: 'The French have to tolerate people who are so fascinatingly unreasonable as to attempt to finish in a foreign country what they could never begin in their own'. As she was due to start a tour of the USA, Sarah declined.

In 1893, Oscar took his lover, *Bosie Douglas*, to meet Bernhardt in Paris. Sarah greeted Bosie by calling him 'mon cher enfant', presented him with a box of chocolates, and told him to sit in the corner while she talked to Wilde. Bosie, (who was at least 23), was flabbergasted at being treated like a schoolboy. Oscar, on the other hand, thought that the scene was hilarious.

In spite of Bernhardt's failure to supply financial support by buying the rights to 'Salome' during Wilde's trials, (as suggested to her by *Robert Sherard*), when they met again in 1898 during her run playing 'La Tosca' in Cannes, in Oscar's words: 'She threw her arms around me and wept and I wept and the whole evening was wonderful'.

Although it is often claimed that Wilde was the inventor of self-promotion through judicious manipulation of the press, he was actually only copying what Sarah had been doing already for at least ten years. *Henry James* said: "She has in the supreme degree 'the advertising genius'; she may, indeed, be called the muse of the newspaper'. It was Bernhardt, not Oscar, who created the concept of the modern 'celebrity'.

Her most widely reported eccentricity was the fact that she travelled with her own silk-lined coffin. She was photographed in it, occasionally slept in it, and reputedly made love in it.

Her fondness for exotic pets also excited comment. Several of her dinner parties were enlivened by her habit of allowing her snarling tiger cub to stroll about on top of the table.

When she took up residence in Chester Square, London, her neighbours were horrified to see a leopard, six chameleons, three mastiffs, and a monkey inhabiting her back garden. (The leopard inevitably attacked the dogs, whereupon Bernhardt pushed the famous French painter Gustave Dore out into the garden where he nervously attempted to halt the frenzied battle.)

Although her use of cocaine would have caused comment in the modern press, in the 1880s it was of little account, (it being a habit she shared with *Queen Victoria,* President Grant, *Thomas Edison,* and Pope Leo XIII).

However her fame depended, not on her foibles, but on her extraordinary abilities as an actress. She received international acclaim, including from such varied sources as the Austrian psychologist Sigmund Freud, who wrote: 'After the first words of her vibrant, lovely voice, I felt I had known her for years'; and from the English writer DH Lawrence: 'She represents the primeval passion of woman and she is fascinating to an extraordinary degree'.

Her audiences reacted even more ecstatically. After one triumphant evening, two one-armed men in the front stalls were so enthused that they were seen to be clapping their remaining hands together.

As well as her remarkable voice and mesmerising stage presence, Bernhardt also displayed a total lack of inhibition in her performances. She revelled in risqué roles, and her sensual portrayal of Cleopatra in a London theatre prompted one elderly audience member to utter the immortal line: "How unlike, how very unlike, the home life of our own dear Queen".

Bernhardt was the illegitimate daughter of a Parisian courtesan, one of whose clients was *Napoleon III's* half-brother, the Duc du Morny; (his daughter, Missy, became the lesbian lover of the writer *Colette*). Morny saw that Sarah had talent and, dismissing her adolescent desire to become a nun, arranged for her entry into the Comedie Francais.

She rose swiftly to the heights of French theatre playing the leading roles in *Victor Hugo's* 'Ruy Blas', Racine's 'Phaedre', and the younger Dumas's 'La Dame aux Camilias'.

In addition to her mercurial personality, Sarah was physically striking, her wild blonde curly hair framing her attractive face, above her famously slim body. She kept this 'nicely polished skeleton' of a figure all her life; (it was rumoured that she hated eating because, as a child, she had been forced to perform fellatio).

Proclaiming herself 'one of the great lovers of my century', Sarah was reputed to have had hundreds of affairs, including the seduction of every European head of state, including the Pope. However unlikely this might have been, she certainly never stinted herself sexually.

Sometimes her sense of humour took over, as when, after one admirer had paid a huge sum for a night of passion, he found her waiting in bed made up as an aged and toothless crone.

Others questioned where the actress ended and the woman began. In his book 'La Faustin', *Edmond Goncourt* portrayed one character that he based on Bernhardt. In one scene, the character, an actress, is alone with her dying lover. The lover awakens from unconsciousness to see the actress practising in the mirror the deathbed facial agonies she has just observed on his own face. However, Goncourt was not the kindest of critics.

Although Sarah indulged in only the occasional lesbian affair, she had a virile edge that many women found sexually attractive; (she was famous for performing male roles, including 'Hamlet'). *Robert de Montesquiou* saw her as the arch representative of the bisexual nineties.

To confound stereotyping even further, she became a very happily unmarried mother when she gave birth to her son Maurice in 1864. The father was probably the Prince de Ligne, (though there was an outside chance that it was *Prince Eddy*). Ligne rejected the honour, informing Sarah: "When you sit on a bunch of thorns, it's hard to know which is the one that pricked you".

In 1882, she married an exceptionally good-looking Greek playboy called Jacques Damala. The marriage failed and Damala ran away firstly to join the French Foreign Legion, then to sink into a terminal morphine addiction. (*Bram Stoker* met him at this time and was struck by Damala's ravaged appearance. Stoker wrote that: 'The idea that he was dead was strong on me', and, with Damala's image freshly in mind, soon afterwards began his famous work 'Dracula').

With Sarah's phenomenal good looks and appetite still intact in her sixties, Marshal Canrobert once said to her at a party: "I've thought of your epitaph. All you'll need on your tomb is, 'Resting at last'." Sarah shook her head and, indicating a group of lovers, replied: "Not exactly, Marshal. It would be better to inscribe, 'They can rest at last'."

[It was Sarah's habit to sleep with her leading men, at least for the length of the theatrical run. One such lover was **BENOIT COQUELIN** (1841-1909), a famous actor in his own right who enjoyed great success playing 'Cyrano de Bergerac'.

Coquelin once invited Wilde to visit him, saying: "I am always at home about nine o'clock in the morning". Oscar looked at him in astonishment and answered: "I am much more middle class than you, I am always in bed by four or five. I could never stay awake as late as that. Really, you are a remarkable man".]

Bernhardt became probably the most widely travelled of all the theatre stars, notching up successes across the USA, Australia, Russia and even in Manaos on the Amazon, (where she played in Fitzcarraldo's Opera House).

At first, the American clergy attacked her as 'The Whore of Babylon'. She replied by letter to one of them, who had called her 'an imp of darkness': 'My dear confrere, why attack me so violently? Actors ought not to be so hard on one another, Love, Sarah Bernhardt'.

When the Episcopalian Bishop of Chicago also launched a virulent attack on her character, he received another note with $200 enclosed: 'Your Excellency, I am accustomed, when I bring an attraction to your town, to spend $400 on advertising. As you have done half the advertising for me, I herewith enclose $200 for your parish'.

She took subtle revenge on her less discriminating audiences. As her performances were given in French, the vast majority had no idea what was being said. In Youngstown, Ohio, her curtain call speech was greeted with tumultuous applause, in spite of the fact that she had just told them, with the sweetest of smiles, that they were morons.

After her fame was assured, she made numerous tours by train across the States, becoming known as 'the Muse of the Railroads'. On one journey, the train driver refused to cross the bridge at St Louis as it was threatened by floodwater. Impatient as usual, Sarah bribed him $500 to keep going. They managed to reach the other bank, but the bridge collapsed behind them as they did so. The rest of her company was not amused.

Even in her old age she managed to keep up the punishing pace of touring. Aged 73, to raise funds during the First World War, she played in almost one hundred different US towns between August 1917 and October 1918. When she reached Los Angeles, she took part in a parade to promote Liberty Bonds.

One official, remembering Sarah's marriage to the Greek Jacques Damala, provided her carriage with an escort dressed in what he fondly imagined were Greek army uniforms. Unfortunately they were Turkish army uniforms; (even more embarrassingly, Turkey was at war with the Allies).

During the early 20th century, Bernhardt's star began to wane. The new playwrights were interested more in the workings of the human mind and preferred the introspective style of the rising Italian actress, *Eleanour Duse*. Sarah was dismissive of this trend: 'If you identify yourself with your part to the point of asking yourself, as you look at the audience – 'What are those people doing here?' – you have ceased to be an actor: you are a madman'.

Although still looking uncannily youthful, Sarah's health began to fail after she was forced to have a leg amputated in 1915. When she died in 1923, her funeral in Paris was the largest since that of Victor Hugo in 1885. She was buried in Pere Lachaise cemetery.

After her leg had been amputated, an impresario offered her $100,000 for permission to exhibit it. Sarah sent a telegram in reply: 'Which leg?'

The costume designer for 'Salome' was the painter and writer, **W. GRAHAM ROBERTSON** (1866–1948). When he tentatively inquired how Bernhardt was going to perform the striptease 'Dance of the Seven Veils', she winked at him and smiled: "Never you mind".

Robertson never used his first name, ('Willard'), and, when they met in 1888, Wilde teased him by asking: "What do you allow your friends to call you? W or Graham?"

The same year, Oscar spent a few days at Robertson's home in the country village of Sandhills, Surrey. Robertson: 'He was like a fish out of water'.

Oscar certainly did not take to country life: 'They get up so early because they have so much to do, and go to bed so early because they have so little to think about. There has not been a scandal in the neighbourhood since the time of Queen Elizabeth, and consequently they all fall asleep after dinner'.

One of Sarah Bernhardt's closest friends, Pierre Loti, also expressed his appreciation for 'Salome'. (Wilde had published an article on Loti in 'Women's World' in 1889).

PIERRE LOTI 1850-1923

When 'Salome' appeared in print form in 1893, Wilde sent a copy to the French novelist. Loti replied by letter: 'Thank you, sir, for having introduced me to your Salome – it is fine and sombre like a chapter of the Apocalypse – I admire it deeply'.

Even in the extravagant gallery of 19th century French literary figures, Loti was regarded as bizarre. *Edmond Goncourt* commented that Loti's life 'was one long carnival', in which he interwove a career as a libidinous bi-sexual writer of exotic romantic fiction with a dual role as a French naval officer.

His first meeting with *Sarah Bernhardt* in 1875 was typical of his unabashed élan. Desperate to sleep with her, he had himself delivered to her house wrapped up in an expensive carpet. Once unrolled, he charmed the actress into bed, and then into a lifelong friendship.

He possessed a strong sexual magnetism; one lady described his 'special way of kissing one's hand, as if he wished to draw out one's very soul'. Despite this ability, he was not a physically confident man. He was overly conscious of his lack of height and once ruefully admitted: "I was not my type".

He compensated by joining a school of physical education and in time became a first rate athlete. To provide extra height, he wore shoes with elevated heels that meant that he always walked on tiptoe. Later in life he resorted to further cosmetic aids. *Frank Harris* sniffed: 'Loti certainly wore stays, if indeed, he didn't rouge as well'.

Born in Rochefort, France, (under his real name of Jean Viaud), Loti joined the French navy and went to sea in 1869. Although involved in a homosexual relationship with a fellow junior officer, Joseph Bernard, Loti lost little time in exploring the heterosexual freedoms of the South Seas. Employing his natural gift for empathy, he was soon a favourite with the girls of Easter Island and Tahiti. One Tahitian mistress, Rarahu, while teaching him to treat sex as an art, also urged him to lose his name of 'Viaud' and instead baptised him 'Loti', after a marine flower.

(Many Europeans were intrigued by the South Seas. According to Lady Dorothy Nevill, the French aristocrat Princess Clementine begged her brother to bring back a Tahitian costume for her to wear at a costume ball. When he handed her a string of red beads, she admired them, then asked for the rest of the outfit. On being told that there was no more, she fell into a thoughtful silence.)

Loti's next naval assignment was in Senegal, West Africa, where he became involved with the wife of a rich merchant. To recover from the torrid lovemaking, Loti relaxed by playing piano. (One evening, while he was playing a particular tune, a huge snake slid into the room. He became fascinated by the fact that every time he played the same tune the snake would reappear.)

Moving on to Constantinople in 1876, Loti noted that 'in Turkey women are for the rich, who can have many; for the poor, there are boys'. He became involved in a love affair with Aziyade, the harem wife of a Turkish official. This was extremely dangerous for both of them, as harem women were expressly forbidden to fraternise with other men. Loti learnt enough Turkish to pass as an Albanian, and purchased a small house for their secret trysts. The next year, Loti was recalled to patrol in northern waters and was forced to leave Aziyade behind.

(In 1888 he returned to Constantinople to find her and was told that Aziyade's husband had discovered their affair. She had been locked in a separate room in the family home where she soon sickened and died. Loti was taken to see her gravestone by a sympathetic slave girl.)

By this time Loti had become an accomplished gymnast. The French navy turned a blind eye when he employed his skills at the Etruscan Circus in Toulon, where he performed backward somersaults while standing on horseback. When questioned whether this might be an odd occupation for a second lieutenant, one admiral explained: "As he succeeded, I knew nothing of the whole business – but if he had failed I should have bloody well clapped him in irons".

The real reason for the navy's indulgence was that, by this time, Loti had become a hugely popular author with books based on his erotic experiences while with the fleet. Such works as 'Le Mariage de Loti', (based on Tahiti), 'Le Roman d'un Spahi', (on Senegal), and 'Aziyade', (on Turkey – and dedicated to Bernhardt), proved to be superb recruiting propaganda.

In 1877, Loti tested this extraordinary freedom from naval discipline when, depressed by his enforced separation from Aziyade, he entered a Trappist monastery. Fortunately for

French marine recruitment, he quickly grew bored with monastic life and spent most of his time drinking cider at the local village inn.

By the 1880s, Loti was both famous and wealthy, but the sea remained his most potent drug. He said of his navy life: 'I could not live, were I to be deprived of that'.

It also provided him with some amazing stories. On a voyage to the Far East, a sailor on Loti's ship was washed overboard during a storm. As there was no hope of rescuing him, a chaplain was summoned to perform burial rites over the man while he still clung to his lifebelt in the sea below. Having watched his own funeral, the sailor drifted away on the waves.

In 1883, Loti risked his career by indignantly exposing to the press the systematic massacres being carried out by French colonial forces in Vietnam. Although he was ordered back to home waters, such was his reputation that even this affront to military discretion was excused.

He used his time back in France to produce two books that were to be reckoned his finest, 'Pecheur d'Islande' and 'Mon Frere Yves'. The latter was based on Loti's new homosexual lover, a navy deckhand. His description of Yves so excited Sarah Bernhardt that she insisted Loti drew a picture for her of the sailor in the nude.

In 1884, Loti enjoyed a chaotic social life back in France, one evening dining with duchesses, the next brawling in bars with his tough crewmates.

After a further trip to the Far East, Loti wrote a novel called 'Madame Chrysantheme', based on his affair with a Japanese girl in Nagasaki. Later the story was turned into an opera by Puccini under the title of 'Madame Butterfly'. (In 1950 the Japanese erected a statue in Nagasaki in Loti's memory – 'to the author of Madame Chrysantheme'.)

By 1886, feeling an itch for paternity, Loti absent-mindedly married a French woman called Blanche de Ferriere, who did provide him with a son. But the seeds of disunity were evident even during the marriage ceremony, as Loti was infatuated with his own niece Ninette. Ninette reciprocated his interest: 'I would have liked you for my bridegroom, ton-ton, but Mama would not hear of it'. A disconsolate Loti wrote: 'It seems I am taking part in someone else's wedding'.

He had recovered his poise by 1887, when he visited Queen Elizabeth of Romania at Castel Pelesh in the Carpathians. Under the pen name of 'Carmen Silva', the queen wrote poetry and Romanian fairytales, (and had contributed an article on Carpathian folklore to Wilde's 'Women's World'). Known for her flowing white robes and vaporous languor, her subjects regarded her as an insufferable poseur. She and Loti got on splendidly. The King of Romania, who was not so impressed by the Frenchman, asked him to leave.

In 1891, 'Carmen Silva' was also banished by the king. She retired to Venice where *Herbert Vivian* reported: 'the poet-queen was living in seclusion and taking no interest in anything but her large family of dolls, over which she wept most of the time'. Loti joined her in Venice and they enjoyed a few weeks of 'moping about in gondolas' before he was ordered to leave by the Romanian embassy. As usual he turned the doomed affair into a romantic novel, called 'L'Exile'.

He also enjoyed royal sexual favours from the immensely rich *Princess Alice of Monaco* who remained a staunch friend. Loti: 'And to think I could have married her'.

Back in his birthplace of Rochefort, Loti enlarged his house to include a Japanese salon, a Louis XVI drawing room, a Chinese pagoda (with a well-frequented opium den attached), and an entire Islamic mosque, (which he had had dismantled in Damascus and secretly brought to France). He held large fancy dress parties in the resulting architectural menagerie.

In the early 1890s Loti was promoted to the rank of naval lieutenant commander with responsibility for the Basque region of France. He came to revere the Basque way of life and joined in many aspects of their social life, including giving gymnastic performances for the local circus.

Although he was meant to be an authority figure, he thoroughly enjoyed accompanying the local smugglers on their many nocturnal trips across the Spanish border. During this sojourn he acquired a Basque mistress, who was to produce three more sons after he brought her back to Rochefort. Also during this period he was made a member of the prestigious French Academy.

Still attracted to adventure, he visited India and Persia, and was a member of the force that relieved the Peking Legations during the 1900 Chinese Boxer Rebellion, (incidentally becoming involved in the second looting of the Summer Palace).

But the country that attracted his permanent affection was Turkey. He was appointed as a naval attaché in Constantinople and as an unofficial ambassador for France. Overlooking Loti's seduction of a harem girl, the Sultan declared him persona grata in the country and their relationship blossomed.

When Sarah Bernhardt arrived to see Loti, he took her to see the famous Whirling Dervishes. Such was the popular enthusiasm for the pair that Sarah had to slash her way through the fans with her parasol.

In 1911 Italy seized Tripoli and Libya, (part of the Turkish Empire). Loti leapt to the public defence of Turkey with ferocious denunciations of the Italian action in the press. On his return to Turkey in 1913, he was met by a vast cheering crowd and a personal invitation to stay at the Sultan's Seraglio. To his great regret, (and his personal attempts to forestall it by secret negotiations), two years later France and Turkey became enemies during the First World War.

Although he had left the navy in 1910 after 42 years service (on and off), Loti insisted on joining the army on the Western Front and received a commendation for gallantry under enemy fire. Finally, aged 67 and sick with fever, he was sent home in November 1917.

He spent his last few years back in Rochefort, complaining about old age and infirmity. Loti: 'Only youth and the sun are worth having'. Sarah Bernhardt visited him but, as she had lost a leg, she could not get her wheelchair upstairs and he could only stagger to the front door. The old lovers were forced to spend their last meeting sitting out in the street and reminiscing.

When Loti died, the French government paid him the honour of dispatching three warships to escort the coffin to his grave on the offshore island of Oleron. In a gesture that he perhaps would have appreciated even more, the flags of Constantinople flew at half-mast.

Wilde withdrew his threat to become a Frenchman after the banning of 'Salome. Instead, on July 3rd 1892, he left for a holiday in Bad Homburg with Bosie Douglas. While in this German spa town, he attempted the 'cure' – taking the waters, eating a strict diet, stopping smoking, and being obliged to wake at 7.30am and sleep at 10.30pm. He was unenthusiastic about this regimen, but Constance Wilde thought the idea was hilarious.

He returned to England and spent August and September in Norfolk, at Grove Farm, Felbrigg, near Cromer. While there, he wrote his new play, 'A Woman of No Importance', which he finished by October 14.

In October, leaving Norfolk, he visited the Reading home of Walter and Jean Palmer, (of the well known biscuit manufacturers, Huntley and Palmer). Jean Palmer, who Wilde knew well and had christened 'Moonbeam', had invited him to one of her literary weekends. During the weekend Wilde read his new play aloud to the company.

[One of his fellow guests was the novelist and poet, GEORGE MEREDITH (1828-1909), visiting Reading from his usual lair at Box Hill, Surrey. Oscar respected the older writer,

describing him as 'incomparable' and his style as 'chaos illumined by brilliant flashes of lightning'. Meredith, on the other hand, had little truck with Wilde, later refusing point blank to sign a clemency petition during Oscar's captivity.

The bane of Meredith's existence was that he suffered from extreme flatulence. It also made life for his immediate circle very difficult.

It was a condition that he shared with the Lord Mayor of London, Sir Robert Fowler, (1828-1891). Frank Harris described a dinner that he attended with the Lord Mayor: 'He sat intent on cutting and swallowing huge gobbets of meat while beads of sweat poured down his great red face. Suddenly there came a loud unmistakable noise and then an overpowering odour. Fowler remained unconscious of the event. The atmosphere got worse and worse, the smells stronger and stronger, till I rejoiced every time a servant opened a door. Another unmistakable explosion and I could not but look at my hostess. She was as pale as death and her eyes met mine in despairing appeal. We got up quietly and left the room'.

Fowler was also a Member of Parliament. During one of his orations in the House of Commons, (accompanied by the usual noises off), he ended by announcing that he did not wish to end his speech with a proposal. A fellow member, holding a handkerchief to his nose, stood up and suggested that it might be best to end such a speech with a motion. This quip circulated London society, much to Fowler's indignation.]

Late in October 1892, Oscar and Constance Wilde were invited to stay with Lady Sibyl Douglas at Bracknell in Berkshire, where, at Sibyl's request, 'in the yellowing woods at Bracknell' they discussed her son Bosie's deepening academic problems at Oxford.

Although now deeply involved with each other, Bosie had begun to introduce Wilde into the world of homosexual rent boys, a milieu that Oscar had avoided previously. (As Wilde had written prophetically three years earlier in 'Dorian Gray': 'from time to time strange rumours about his mode of life crept through London and became the chatter of the clubs'.)

To facilitate these encounters, Oscar now started to spend less time at home in Tite St, and instead frequented London hotels such as the Albemarle and the Savoy. According to the trial evidence, Oscar spent a night at the latter with one youth, Sidney Mavor, in October 1892.

SAVOY HOTEL and KETTNER'S RESTAURANT

The SAVOY HOTEL, opened in 1889, was one of the best in London, having 520 bedrooms (most possessing telephones), 70 bathrooms, and the first lift in a London hotel. The general manager was the famous Swiss hotelier, Cesar Ritz, and the chef, Auguste Escoffier, had previously worked for *Napoleon III.*

To the embarrassment of the management, Wilde openly brought his boys to stay at the hotel, while Bosie Douglas insisted that he and Oscar paraded through the foyer arm-in-arm. They became the soul of indiscretion.

Cesari, the headwaiter of the Savoy, once whispered to Frank Harris: "I do wish that Mr Wilde and Lord Alfred wouldn't come here; it does us a lot of harm".

KETTNER'S Restaurant, opened in 1867 by another of Napoleon III's chefs, Auguste Kettner, was another of Oscar and Bosie's favourite haunts. Its name was mentioned during the 1895 trial; Wilde: "Kettner's is not so gorgeous as some restaurants, but it was Kettner at his best." It possessed private dining rooms that offered seclusion. During October 1892, he dined there with Mavor, and two new acquaintances, Alfred Taylor and Freddie Atkins.

In November, according to the trial evidence, he visited Paris for sexual purposes in the company of Atkins and another youth, Maurice Schwabe.

1893

[During 1893, the French government instigated trial proceedings over the Panama Canal scandal. Domestic trouble sparked in Paris when a terrorist bomb exploded in the Chamber of Deputies, and students rioted in the Latin Quarter.

Britain underwent a coalminer's strike that lasted for thirteen weeks.

In East Africa, British military units carried out the Witu Campaign against slavers in Kenya.]

Now at the age of 39, Wilde's appearance had coarsened considerably, and people commented on his increased flabbiness. One acquaintance greeted him with the words: "Oscar, you are getting fatter and fatter", and received the reply: "And you are getting ruder and ruder".

His indulgence in rent boys continued unabated – taking another one, Alfred Wood, to the Albemarle Hotel, and, in February, taking Sidney Mavor to Paris.

After dining with Wood at the Café Royal, Oscar took him home to Tite St during one of Constance's absences.

CAFÉ ROYAL

The Café Royal was, at the time, the best restaurant in London, where the owner, M. Nichol, provided his customers with the unaccustomed taste of perfect French cooking. By 1895, after 25 years of judicious purchases, M Nichol also had the finest vintage wine cellar 'ever seen on earth'. When asked about the small profit that he made on his meals, M. Nichol shrugged: "They eat me poor but they drink me rich". He died a very wealthy man.

On his first visit, *Max Beerbohm* was very impressed: 'There in that exuberant vista of gilding and crimson velvet set amidst all those opposing mirrors and upholding caryatids, with fumes of tobacco ever rising to the painted and pagan ceiling... I drew a deep breath. This indeed, said I to myself, is life.'

Wilde excused his frequent and riotously expensive visits to the Café Royal as 'the duty we owe to the dignity of letters'. *Herbert Tree* was less in awe: "If you want to see English people at their most English, go to the Café Royal, where they are trying their hardest to be French".

Its reputation was long lasting. In 1922, when *TWH Crosland* was told that the Café Royal was being pulled down and rebuilt, he burst out: "'They might as well have told us that the British Empire is to be pulled down and redecorated'.

During the spring of 1893 Wilde made two trips to Babbacombe, near Torquay in Devon. 'I have been idling by the sea and driving through Devonshire lanes'. On his second visit, in March, he was accompanied by Bosie Douglas and, (in an effort to coach Bosie), his Oxford tutor, Campbell Dodgson.

It seems that not much work was done. Wilde invented a spoof list of school rules that suggested, among other things, breakfast at 10.30am, compulsory hide and seek, and brandy and soda for tea, ('not to exceed seven').

[The confused tutor, CAMPBELL DODGSON (1867-1948), later said of Oscar: "I think him perfectly delightful with the firmest conviction that his morals are detestable".

Dodgson himself became an art historian and keeper of the British Museum department of prints and drawings. With the exception of a spell in Military Intelligence during the First World War, he remained at this post till he retired in 1932. In 1913, Dodgson married the daughter of Oscar's old Oxford tutor, the Reverend William Spooner.]

On his return to London in March, Oscar took rooms at the Savoy where he continued 'the terrible pleasure of a double life', entertaining more male prostitutes, including a man called Herbert Tankard.

During this whole period, Wilde had been working on the publication of his play 'Salome'. His illustrator was the young artist, Aubrey Beardsley.

AUBREY BEARDSLEY 1872-1898

Wilde once described Beardsley as having 'a face like a silver hatchet and grass green hair'. After their first meeting in 1891, Oscar had befriended Beardsley but soon came to be uneasy in the presence of the derisive young iconoclast. Beardsley refused to be patronised by Wilde – or anybody else – and maintained an air of mockery towards the now famous playwright. Oscar found this disconcerting and *Frank Harris* suspected that he was slightly afraid of Beardsley.

This discomfort found expression in unusually biting comments on the artist: "Dear Aubrey's designs are like the naughty scribbles a precocious schoolboy makes on the margins of his copybook". Wilde: "Dear Aubrey is almost too Parisian; he cannot forget that he has been to Dieppe – once".

When the publisher *John Lane* commissioned Beardsley to draw the illustrations for the English version of 'Salome', (finally published in February 1894), Oscar was annoyed to find that he had been caricatured in one of the pictures as 'the moon' – 'a mad drunken woman seeking everywhere for lovers'.

Beardsley revelled in teasing his publishers by concealing libellous obscenities in his work. (Lane had already had a taste of this when Beardsley presented him with a painting, based on *Degas's* 'L'Absinthe', showing a fat prostitute waiting for clients in a café. To his horror, Lane found out that the face of the woman looked remarkably like *James Whistler's* wife, Trixie, and hastily withdrew it.)

'Salome' provided ample scope for Beardsley's sense of humour, and Lane, almost paranoid over the possibility of concealed obscenities, took to examining every drawing with a magnifying glass. While worrying over the obvious nude in 'Enter Herodias', he failed to spot the phallic candlesticks. He censored 'Salome on the Settle' as he was suspicious over what Salome intended to do with her candle.

(When Beardsley later suggested that he would like to illustrate the Book of Leviticus with particular reference to 'Neither shall any woman stand before a beast to lie down thereto', it was rumoured that Lane choked over a cup of tea.)

Oscar found Beardsley's drawings unsympathetic to his play and was annoyed by the obscenities: "Aubrey's art, like absinthe, gets on one's nerves and is cruel". Although they remained on speaking terms, a coldness grew between them, Beardsley eventually commenting that Oscar and Bosie were 'really dreadful people'.

When in 1897 after his release, Oscar invited Beardsley to dinner in Dieppe, Beardsley refused. Wilde, who claimed that he had 'made' the young artist, thought his action 'lache' (cowardly).

While described by *WB Yeats* as 'the first satirist of the soul English art has produced', many observers shared Oscar's uneasiness about Beardsley. *Sir William Rothenstein*: 'For Aubrey, perversities were largely an attitude he adopted pour épater les bourgeois... He had something harsh, too sharply defined in his nature. He had the eager, feverish brilliance of the consumptive'.

Gertrude Atherton said bluntly: "He looked as if he might die at any moment", while *Arthur Symons* wrote that: 'He was the thinnest young man I have ever seen – rather unpleasant and affected'. Someone added: "even his lungs were affected". He had suffered as a child from tuberculosis and, from 1889 till his early death, he was prone to haemoptysis – a sudden rush of blood from his mouth.

During service in the British Raj, his maternal grandfather, Surgeon-Major William Pitt, had married an Indian woman, therefore making Aubrey Beardsley one eighth Bengali. (Major Pitt had been involved in the defence of the Lucknow Residency during the Indian Mutiny. *Sir Frank Benson* noticed how the Major, like many of his fellow survivors, had a quirk of knitting gloves and socks while they talked in company. This habit had been acquired by the army officers as a way of calming their nerves during the horrors of the lengthy siege.)

Born in Brighton, Aubrey had accompanied the Beardsley family when they moved to lodge in London at the home of Henry Russell, a retired music hall star and composer of the song 'A Life on the Ocean Wave'.

Helped initially in his artistic career by *Robert Ross*, (a man for whom Beardsley always had the highest respect), he became influenced by Japanese art and by 18th century European pornography.

He realised that the camera was forcing artists to create portraits that had little to do with simple representation. Beardsley: 'In the old days before photography came, a sitter had a perfect right to say to the artist 'Paint me just as I am'. Now if he wishes absolute fidelity he can go to the photographer and get it'.

His insistence on painting his subjects as he saw them rather than as they saw themselves inevitably led to dissatisfaction. The only portrait that was generally accepted was that of the French actress Madame Rejane. However, as the critic *William Archer* pointed out, this was because: 'Madame Rejane is the only woman in the world who actually looks like a Beardsley drawing'.

In 1894, again under the control of the publisher John Lane, and with Henry Harland as editor, Beardsley became the chief illustrator of a new magazine called 'The Yellow Book'. Although it largely represented the viewpoint of the Decadent movement, Beardsley, fearing that Wilde's personality would monopolise the operation, insisted that Oscar should have nothing whatever to do with it.

In spite of this caution, Wilde's downfall in 1895 backfired spectacularly on Beardsley's career. When Wilde was arrested at the Cadogan Hotel, he was carrying a book bound in a yellow cover. Although the book was actually a copy of *Pierre Louys's* 'Aphrodite', the press reported him not as carrying 'a yellow book', but as carrying 'the Yellow Book'.

This mistake, combined with Beardsley's role as illustrator of 'Salome', was enough to link him quite unfairly with all of Oscar's misdemeanours, while never having indulged in any. He once said: "Yes, I look like a sodomite. But no, I am not one".

This was not enough to save him and the thoroughly frightened John Lane sacked him from the magazine. (His departure was said to have turned the Yellow Book grey overnight.) Beardsley: "The Wilde scandal killed the Yellow Book and it nearly killed me".

(Curiously, soon after the debacle, he moved into the Geneux Private Hotel at 10/11 St James Place, London. This was exactly the same establishment where Wilde had lived in 1893 to compose 'An Ideal Husband' and to entertain male lovers. Whether Beardsley knew of the connection or whether he acted out of devilment was, and is, debateable.)

338

Beardsley's career was rescued temporarily when the publisher *Leonard Smithers* asked him to illustrate another new magazine called 'The Savoy'. Fellow contributors included *GB Shaw*, WB Yeats and *George Moore*. Even at this late date, Beardsley could not restrain his compulsive love of mischief.

One day, a horrified George Moore noticed that Beardsley's cover drawing of the figure of 'John Bull' had a tiny but still noticeable erection. A hastily formed committee of contributors elected Bernard Shaw to complain to Smithers and demand that he withdraw the edition. As all 80,000 copies had already been distributed, the devious Smithers agreed immediately.

Another ironic result of the Wilde affair was that for the first time Beardsley appeared to hurl himself into the pursuit of women. He had always been obsessed by sex but had restricted himself mostly to masturbation. He described himself as 'the solitaire'.

Suddenly, in May 1895, as if he wished to disassociate himself publicly from Wilde's sexual disgrace, Beardsley took to frequenting the dives and brothels around London's West End. Although his aforementioned attempt to rape *Herbert Horne's* mistress, Muriel Broadbent, was embarrassingly foiled by Muriel herself, his efforts were rewarded by the more welcoming female members of a supper club called the Thalia, (nicknamed 'The Failure'). After a fling in Paris with Smithers and a girl from the Thalia, he continued to Brussels to enjoy 'Flemish lewdness and Belgian lubricity'.

In Brussels, however, he was struck down by ill health and retreated firstly to Bournemouth in England, then to Dieppe, finally to Menton on the French Riviera. In financial trouble, he appealed to *John Gray's* wealthy friend, Andre Raffalovich, for aid. Raffalovich supported him for the last two years of his life and persuaded him to convert to the Catholic religion.

Beardsley continued to work to the end: 'How can man die better than by doing just what he wants to do most?' When he died aged 26 in 1898, he was buried in the hilltop cemetery in Menton. Wilde wrote of him: 'There is something macabre and tragic in the fact that one who added another terror to life should have died at the age of a flower'.

Although Aubrey Beardsley's Art Nouveau style died quickly, his work again became popular in the mid twentieth century. In an action that might have raised a ghostly chuckle from the Menton cemetery, a collection of Beardsley prints was confiscated during a 1960s police raid for obscenity.

Although there was no real evidence to back the claim, there was a strong rumour that, at one point, Aubrey had an incestuous affair with his attractive actress sister **MABEL BEARDSLEY** (1871-1916). Aubrey made little effort to dispel the gossip.

He told Frank Harris, in Mabel's presence, that: "It's usually a fellow's sister who first tells him about sex. I know it was Mabel here who first taught me." Ignoring Mabel's blushes, he continued: "Mabel was my first model, weren't you, Mabs? Her breasts were so high and firm and round that I took her as my ideal." Mabel burst out laughing and replied: "Your figures, Aubrey, are not exactly ideal!"

Wilde said of the Beardsleys: "What a contrast the two are, Mabel a daisy, Aubrey the most monstrous of orchids". As a joke, Mabel once impersonated a youth and joined Oscar's entourage; she attracted his immediate interest until, to his disappointment, her true gender was revealed.

Mabel certainly had no qualms about joining in the high jinks of her brother's circle. In the spring of 1893, she accompanied Aubrey and his English friends on a boisterous trip to Versailles that included nude bathing and temporary arrest by the Versailles stationmaster for overloud singing on the platform. Mabel: 'Some extraordinary things happened. Some can't even be told now'.

Before Aubrey Beardsley died, in a fit of remorse he asked Smithers to destroy his most obscene drawings. Smithers agreed but, knowing their value, did not carry out his instructions. At first, Mabel was annoyed at Smithers's dereliction but, realising later that he had acted for the best, she acquired a set of them for her own interest.

Eventually she had become so blasé about their subject matter that, when an innocent young actress asked to borrow some amusing reading material, Mabel absent-mindedly handed over a folder full of Aubrey's wildest sexual fantasies.

The youthful Beardsley's landlord in London, **HENRY RUSSELL** (1812-1900), was the singer and composer of over eight hundred songs, (including 'The Ivy Green' with lyrics by Charles Dickens).

In his teens, Russell had studied music in Italy under Rossini's tutelage. While in Parma he became involved in a boxing bout with another young Englishman, with whom he exchanged bloody noses. His opponent later became famous as Captain Lou Nolan, (who died in the Crimea during the Charge of the Light Brigade).

During the 1830s Russell found success performing one-man concerts across North America. Although his real circuit was in Canada and the American eastern seaboard, he once travelled to the (then very) Wild West to listen to Red Indian music. After a horrible journey through the trackless prairie, ('the tall rank grass grew to nine feet high – a great yellow sea'), Russell met the Indians. He was unimpressed by their musical skills: 'Their yelling was truly fearful. It was just hideous noise'. When he eventually staggered back to St Louis, he reported that it had been: 'a hellish trip just to hear a few men howling'.

(On a similar visit to the prairie in 1833, one night a Scottish friend of Russell's found his party surrounded by wolves. The terrified group huddled around the fire and tried to keep the wolves at bay by throwing out cheese and pickle sandwiches. As their supplies ran out, the party gave themselves up for lost. Then the Scotsman had an idea. As he told Russell; "I picked up ma bagpipes and started to give the wolves a bit of a fantasia. Och, mon, ye should have seen the beasties flee".)

Returning to England in 1841, Russell used his popularity and the content of his songs to raise awareness and funds for such causes as the Anti-Slavery Movement and the Relief of the Irish Famine, (for which he raised £7000).

After the lyricist Epps Sargent had been inspired by watching ships in New York harbour, he offered the words of 'Life on the Ocean Wave' to Russell. The pair went immediately into a Broadway music store where Russell, sitting at a display piano, picked out 'the melody that seemed to be floating in my brain'. The song became an immediate hit. Russell dedicated it to another friend, the American novelist Fenimore Cooper.

In 1889, the British Admiralty authorised the use of 'Life on the Ocean Wave' as the regimental march of the Royal Marines.

On April 19th, 1893, Wilde's next play, 'A Woman of No Importance', (originally called 'Mrs Arbuthnot'), produced by and starring Sir Herbert Beerbohm Tree, opened at the Haymarket Theatre in London.

A WOMAN OF NO IMPORTANCE

Regarded as the weakest of his four big plays, there did seem to be an element of the slapdash in the script. Many of the epigrams were recycled from 'Dorian Gray', while Oscar also allowed the risibly melodramatic line – 'Child of my shame, be still the child of my shame' – to slip under his artistic radar.

When he was congratulated on the plot of this play, Oscar stated that he had borrowed it from a newspaper called The Family Herald. Wilde: 'Plots are tedious. Anyone can invent them. Life is full of them. Indeed one has to elbow one's way through them as they crowd across one's path'.

Some critics have claimed that Wilde's reliance on uncertain parentage in his plays, (especially this one), was due to his experience of having three illegitimate siblings in his own family. But in fact, Victorian literature was riddled with such plot devices, (*Gilbert and Sullivan*, and Dickens, most obviously). It would be just as viable to suggest that Wilde was merely satirising the convention.

SIR HERBERT BEERBOHM TREE 1852-1917

The rehearsals for 'A Woman of No Importance' had difficult moments for both playwright and leading actor. When asked whether he was producing the play with Oscar Wilde, Tree groaned: "With the interference of Oscar Wilde!"

Generally speaking though, Tree liked Oscar immensely. Tree: 'Wilde did not mind having suggestions made about his work. He was too big for that'. When Tree said that he could not afford the expenses involved with one of Wilde's ideas, Oscar exclaimed: "But that is exactly why you should do it. Extravagance is the luxury of the poor; penury the luxury of the rich!" Tree was so impressed by the epigram that he inserted the line into the play.

Already having had the experience of imitating Wilde in a spoof called 'Where's the Cat' in 1880, Tree employed the same mannerisms when he came to play the part of 'Lord Illingworth'. He became enamoured of Wilde's style – "Oscar turned his words into gems and flung them to the moon" – and began to copy it in his everyday speech. Wilde: "Every day dear Herbert becomes de plus en plus Oscarise; it is a wonderful case of Nature imitating Art". Not surprisingly Tree's performance as 'Illingworth' was excellent.

They always remained on good terms. In 1894, Oscar took his two small sons to see Tree in a play for children called 'Once Upon A Time'. The younger son, *Vyvyan Holland*, wrote that afterwards Wilde took them backstage to meet Tree, whom he described as 'having an impenetrable vagueness'. At a total loss for conversation, Tree gravely asked the small boys whether they had been to see 'A Woman of No Importance'.

Tree even forgave Oscar's comment about his performance in 'Once Upon A Time': "Since the appearance of Mr Beerbohm Tree in pyjamas there has been the greatest sympathy for Mrs Tree".

During Oscar's troubles, Tree stayed sympathetic. When earlier, in April 1893, a male prostitute (Alfred Woods) attempted to blackmail Oscar by showing a compromising letter to Tree, the actor ignored him and alerted Wilde to the danger.

After Wilde's disgrace, Tree was one of the very few people who sent him money. He did so with an accompanying letter in which he wrote: 'No one did such distinguished work as you; I do most sincerely hope that your splendid talents may shine forth again. I have a lively remembrance of your many acts of kindness and courtesy, and was one of those who devoutly hoped that misfortune would not submerge you.'

With the exception of *Henry Irving*, Beerbohm Tree, (who added 'Tree' to his name for theatrical reasons), was the most famous actor-manager of the late Victorian and Edwardian ages, celebrated for creating the roles of 'Svengali' in *Du Maurier's* 'Trilby' and 'Professor Higgins' in *GB Shaw's* 'Pygmalion', and for his lasting legacy – the establishment of the Royal Academy of Dramatic Art, (RADA).

His contemporaries viewed him as essentially a brilliant but light-hearted amateur, and opinions on his acting varied. The playwright *HA Jones* admired him: 'The difference between Irving and Tree as actors was that Irving made a character come to him, whereas Tree went to the character'.

On the other hand, *WS Gilbert*, despite his friendship with Tree, was no admirer of his thespian skills: "Do you know how they are going to settle the Shakespeare-Bacon dispute? They are going to dig up Shakespeare and dig up Bacon and let Tree recite Hamlet to them. And the one who turns over on his grave will be the author".

Tree's main acting weakness stemmed from his conviction that he was best in tragic roles when in fact he was a born comedian. Maybe his worst performance was that of 'Hamlet' in 1892.

He always suffered terribly from nerves before a first night. As he said himself: 'Why do we choose a calling that causes us such unutterable agony?'

Before 'Hamlet', his nerves were so bad that his dresser found him in the dressing room chewing a stick of greasepaint while applying make-up with a mutton cutlet.

The performance itself failed badly. WS Gilbert described it as being 'funny without being vulgar'. At the end of the show, amidst a storm of catcalls, Tree walked out to the footlights and, holding up his hands for silence, announced: "Thank you, ladies and gentlemen. I still have a few pearls to cast".

Back in the dressing room, a friend came to visit him. Tree asked: "Um...What did you think of my Hamlet, dear chap?" The friend hesitated then admitted "Well, frankly, Herbert, I didn't much care for it". "Um...no...But it's a good part though, isn't it?"

Even his devoted staff didn't help matters. The ancient stage doorman always took a paternal pride in Tree's activities. As Tree left the theatre, the doorman called him over and, glistening with approval, said confidentially: "You've had a great success tonight, sir. I overheard one gentleman say as how he couldn't think of more than, oh, ten or twelve actors in the whole of London who could have played it better".

As Tree said, "It's so difficult to live up to one's posters'.

Tree considered his great achievement to be his 1897 reconstruction of Her Majesty's Theatre in the Haymarket. He was inordinately proud of everything to do with the building, even the 'House Full' boards. Once he boasted about them to the stage manager of the Haymarket Theatre opposite who pointed out that there were 'House Full' boards outside the Haymarket as well. "Ah, yes", breathed Tree "but not so many boards".

During a rehearsal for 'Macbeth', Tree was interrupted by an unexpected clap of thunder. He bellowed up to the stage manager: "When I need the assistance of sound effects, you may be sure that I will ask for them". The man called back: "I think you will find, sir, that the sound was real thunder". Tree thought for a moment, then said: "Ah, yes. I thought it wasn't as good as ours".

The 'Her Majesty's' project could not have worked without the backing of his enthusiastic backstage team. Chief amongst them was his business manager, Henry Dana, whose practicality managed to counterbalance Tree's wilder enthusiasms.

Dana was crucial to the success of the operation because Tree thought of money as something to spend on comfort or on work. When he was told that the bank would not increase his overdraft, Tree boomed majestically: "Tell them we will transfer the account to another bank!"

His generosity was legendary but also threatened to bankrupt the company accounts. One day he saw a ragged ex-actor reciting to a theatre queue and taking his hat round for donations. The man received so little that Tree drew him aside, asked him if he wanted a walk-on part on the show inside, and placed him on the salary list.

On another occasion, one of the stage crew stole some money to pay gambling debts and, as the rest of the company knew what had happened, he had to be prosecuted. However, secretly, Tree arranged for the culprit's escape and for some financial support, while privately very amused at the fact that he was also paying detectives to track down the missing man.

Much to Tree's discomfort, Dana tried to stem the haemorrhage of funds. One day, Dana finally trapped him in his office and insisted that he make some cuts. Tree sat listlessly turning the pages of the ledger, bemused by Dana's explanations. Occasionally he would put his finger on some huge expenditure and murmur: "Um…That's a big one, isn't it".

Finally he spotted what he considered to be a reasonable saving and suggested that in future the theatre green room should be supplied with the Daily Telegraph rather than the Times – a saving of one shilling a week.

Dana replied that Tree should perhaps cut down on his own expenses by not lunching every day at the Carlton. In response, Tree led Dana across the road to a confectioner's shop, ordered a bun and a glass of milk, and abandoned him there. Tree: "Thrift is a virtue it is easy to urge on others".

Dana eventually won through and a reluctant Tree was forced into prudence. Discussing the scenery with a new designer, he enthused: "Now, don't forget. The keynote of the play is to be joy – Joy – JOY!!" Then Tree's face fell as he added disconsolately: "With economy".

Tree was also famous as a theatre director. The designer, W. Graham Robertson, wrote of him 'He liked to cast himself as a man of mystery, dignified, yet full of eccentricities. There was nothing at all mysterious about Tree. He would have been horrified to discover how perfectly he was understood in the theatre. And perhaps a little surprised to find how much he was liked'.

Tree directed one rehearsal of a play in which he felt that the actresses had not quite caught the nuances of their roles. He stopped them with the words: "Ladies, ladies, just a little more virginity, if you don't mind".

His performers treasured his rehearsal advice. He told one actor: "You should suggest…um…well, you know, don't you?… um… a cross between a whitebait and a marmoset".

One plummy-voiced actress kept speaking about the 'glorious *skay*'. Tree stopped her: "Oh, my God, no. It's called the *sky*. Remember you're in Egypt. The *skay* is only seen in Kensington".

His methods of hiring and firing were unusual to say the least. He was frankly terrified of interviewing applicants for his company. One young actress entered his office equally frightened by the occasion. Tree was sitting slumped behind his desk so that only his head and shoulders could be seen. When he saw her, he slid even further down in his seat so that only his eyes and the top of his head were visible. The actress gave a scream and ran out of the room. Tree was completely bewildered by her behaviour.

When Tree played Cardinal Wolsey in Shakespeare's 'King Henry VIII', one matinee the 'King' came offstage cursing heartily about a member of the audience who was reading a newspaper: "Herbert, we are all being insulted". "Um… leave it to me" said Tree.

He strode on stage, a towering figure in long, flowing Tudor robes, dignified and massively imposing. Spotting the offending spectator in the front row, he swept down to the footlights. The man still did not notice. So Tree knelt down and leant over, gazing straight at the reader. The man sensed something was wrong, looked up and found himself staring directly at Cardinal Wolsey. Tree peered back. "Tell me, my man, which horse won the two thirty?"

Despite his many affairs, his marriage to Maud Holt was mainly a happy one. Lady Maud was known for her impeccable poise. Once when she was being driven in a coach along Sloane Street in London, the horses took fright and bolted as hard as they could go towards

Knightsbridge. Clutching her hat and leaning out of the window, she drawled up to the coachman: "I say, Tom, this is a little trying. Might I suggest that you crash into something cheap?"

His eldest daughter, Viola, even as an infant, displayed considerable intelligence. When their family friend, WS Gilbert, visited their house, he made a fuss of Viola and, as he was about to leave, Tree encouraged her to kiss Gilbert goodbye. She pouted and refused. Tree pressed her further: "Oh, kiss Gillie, darling. Daddy loves Gillie". With irrefutable logic, the three-year-old replied: "Then Daddy kiss Gillie".

When she was aged five, her father rebuked her for breaking a window. Tree announced gravely: "This, child, is wickedness!" She shook her head: "No, father, this is heredity".

The actress *Elizabeth Robins* said that Tree's vagueness was 'a kind of physical mannerism'. His disconnection from the everyday world occasionally approached the surreal. On one occasion Tree went into a post office. After pondering for a few minutes over why he was there, he approached the counter. "I hear that you sell stamps?" "We do, sir" "May I see some?" "You may, sir". Tree surveyed the sheet of stamps, then pointed to one right in the centre and said: "Um...I'll take that one".

Tree often boasted to his friends that his sister possessed an amazing parrot that was capable of detecting both the vintages and years of wine. When Vyvyan Holland mentioned this to Tree's niece many years later, she burst out laughing: "That's so like Uncle Herbert. He had the story all wrong. My mother had a wonderful *palette*, not parrot!"

Tree enjoyed practical jokes. At one of his dinners, a guest found himself seated next to a Madame Brieux. As the lady was stone deaf and did not speak English, the guest found that he could only communicate by shouting into a box device at her side. Tiring of the effort, he turned to his other neighbour, a Mrs Hecht, and tried to start a conversation. She lifted up an ear trumpet.

For the rest of the meal, the guest was forced to bawl his remarks in French into Madame Brieux's hearing box and in English into Mrs Hecht's ear trumpet. It was not until he spotted Tree's shoulders heaving with suppressed laughter that he realised that his host had planned this situation all along.

Sometimes Tree was on the receiving end. He once attended a select party in London that continued till 4am. Tree told a friend later: "Um... On my way out I saw Hilaire Belloc and... um... H.G. Wells poaching eggs in somebody's hat over a spirit lamp. I thought this to be intensely humorous until I discovered that it was my hat. Then I thought it was very vulgar".

It was sometimes difficult to know whether some of his most famous statements were intentional or not. He once strode into Waterloo Station, in top hat and cane, and followed by a retinue of theatrical flunkies. He marched up to the ticket office and boomed: "I wish to purchase a ticket". "Oh, yes, sir. What station do you want?" "What stations have you got?"

One of Herbert Beerbohm Tree's less wise decisions was to turn down the offer to produce the children's play 'Peter Pan' in 1904. After the Scottish playwright and novelist **SIR JAMES BARRIE** (1860-1937) read him the first two acts, Tree begged him to stop. "I thought Barrie had gone mad". When later asked why he had rejected the play, Tree replied: "God knows, and I have promised to tell no one else".

Barrie was a prolific playwright and involved himself in various aspects of production. At one rehearsal, he became irritated by the impossible subtleties demanded of the actors by an inexperienced director. Barrie interrupted the action with an innocent suggestion to one actor: "Mr Smith, I want you to cross the stage from left to right silently conveying to the audience that you have an aunt who lives in Chiswick".

When one particularly arrogant actor insisted that his name be given star billing on the posters by adding 'AND' before his name, Barrie advised the producer to alter it to 'BUT'.

Barrie gathered both fame and fortune through his plays, though he was slightly flummoxed by the latter. When his friend and partner, the American Charles Frohman, sent him an enormous cheque for royalties from one USA production, Barrie grumbled to his wife: "Look at this, Mary! What on earth are we to do with this?"

Known as 'the Napoleon of the Drama', **CHARLES FROHMAN** (1860-1915) produced several of Wilde's plays in America, including 'The Importance of Being Earnest'. Opening on April 22 1895, the production was ruined by the scandal surrounding its author and closed within a week.

Seymour Hicks reported that in 1898 Frohman gave him a cheque for £200 payable to Oscar Wilde to take to Paris. Frohman told Hicks: "Give him this if you can find him and say it is on account of a new play I want him to write for me. Of course I know he'll never send me anything, but – well, he was a great man, and I expect he's in a pretty bad way and that's all there is to it."

In 1915, although warned of danger in an anonymous letter, Frohman sailed from the USA to England on the Lusitania. Just off the Irish coast, the ship was torpedoed by a German submarine and, in company with many other passengers and crew, Frohman drowned. It was said that his last words were a quote from 'Peter Pan': "To die will be an awfully big adventure".

> *It was during the rehearsals for 'A Woman of No Importance' that Wilde became friendly with Beerbohm's Tree's younger half brother, Max Beerbohm.*

SIR MAX BEERBOHM 1872-1956

While he enjoyed the Wilde set immensely, (and always remained a close friend of *Reggie Turner*), Max Beerbohm kept his distance from the wilder excesses of the group, being neither homosexual nor particularly at odds with the conventional world.

He regarded Oscar with affectionate mockery, seeing him as 'an enormous dowager – or schoolboy', and noting down some of Oscar's characteristics as being: 'effeminate, but the vitality of twenty men – magnetism – authority – deeper than repute or wit – hypnotic'.

As the leading satirical cartoonist of his day he caricatured Wilde unmercifully. Wilde felt the sting of the lampoons but never expressed any resentment towards his genial tormentor.

Max disliked what he saw as Oscar's growing arrogance but offered his moral support during the 1895 trials. After attending the second trial, Max reported: "I have been all day at the Old Bailey – Oscar has been quite superb. His speech about the Love that dares not tell its name was simply wonderful".

Afterwards, Max again remained distant but sympathetic and, commenting on Oscar's death, wrote: 'If he had lived to be an old man he would have become unhappy. Those whom the gods, etc. And the gods did love Oscar, with all his faults.'

Max had an unquenchable appetite for comic teasing. In Oscar's case, as well as his cruel but hilarious cartoons, Max constructed a fantasy, (in an essay called 'A Peep into the Past'), that Oscar was an earnest and laborious mid-Victorian writer who had achieved minor notability due to 'unremitting effort and Northern grit'.

Among many other targets, Max also burlesqued the Oxford professor *Walter Pater*. Max invented some quotes to accompany this timid aesthete's delicately written book on the Renaissance. The Spectator's review, according to Max, recorded that the volume displayed 'something of raucousness but much of virility', while the Manchester Guardian was meant to have called Pater's book: 'Thor's hammer on Vulcan's anvil'.

Sometimes Max's sense of mischief slipped out into everyday life. When he attended ***George Meredith's*** funeral in 1909, a young woman in the crowd mistook Max for the very Scottish ***James Barrie*** and begged him to write something in her autograph book. Max: "I know it is in poor taste; I said nothing, but when I took her volume my pen ran away with me, and I wrote 'Och, ay, Lassie! It's a sad day the noo. J. M. Barrie'."

With a large rounded head and protuberant eyes, Max had the appearance of a prim little dandy. He projected an air of world-weary irony even as a schoolboy. Oscar commented: 'The gods have bestowed on Max the gift of perpetual old age'. The writer Gerald Cumberland explained that: 'serenity is Max's secret', while Virginia Woolf called him 'the Cheshire cat'.

He attended Merton College, Oxford but left in 1893 without a degree to become secretary to his half-brother Herbert Beerbohm Tree on the latter's theatrical tour of the USA. This tour proved to be an eye-opener for the fastidious Max.

He wrote that: 'in Chicago, we visited certain houses where black women danced naked to the sound of the piano – and one where French women gambolled with one another in a room cushioned with blue silk. I did not get to bed till six'.

Max described his relationship with Tree as 'terrified love', but in reality Tree adored the whimsical outbursts of his younger brother. He spent days roaring with laughter over Max's suggestion that, in a historical play they were considering, the hero's last line should be: 'Farewell, my love! I'm off to the Thirty Years War'.

Returning to London, Max lived with his widowed mother and sisters and developed his outstanding abilities as a cartoonist. When the first collection was published in 1896, one man purchased his own portrait off Max just so that he could destroy it. Max was essentially a conservative but enjoyed riling both sides of the political spectrum. In turn, he was attacked as being both reactionary and iconoclastic.

In 1898 (till 1910), he became the drama critic for the Saturday Review in succession to ***Bernard Shaw***, who hailed him as 'the incomparable Max!'

Although too demure and aloof to involve himself in many sexual forays, he was engaged twice before his marriage. His first fiancée was a young actress from Tree's company officially called Grace Conover, but unofficially known as 'Kilseen' from her ability to 'kill any scene she appeared in'.

When this half-hearted arrangement ended, Max became engaged to another actress, Constance Collier. This ended after Max learnt that the carefree and promiscuous Constance had indulged in an affair while on tour. (Collier: "Well, you know what it's like on tour"). ***Robert Ross*** said of this second engagement: "Max has jilted Scylla in order to get engaged to Charybdis'.

After a brief fling with another woman, Kathleen Bruce, (who later married Captain Robert Scott, destined to die in the Antarctic), in 1910 Max finally married a young American actress named Florence Kahn. The marriage, although lifelong, was probably never consummated.

Max settled happily into this new domesticity and, in spite of his fame as a critic and artist, always enjoyed being idle. Max: 'I never had any ambitions – only modest wishes – to make good use of such little talent as I had, to lead a pleasant life, to pass muster' – 'The ant sets an example to us all; but not a good one'.

His friends noted that in spite of his coolly superior views, Max had a curious shyness when it came to coping with the lower classes. He became very nervous if forced into asking hotel servants to perform errands. On one occasion, after the fire brigade had been called to his home to extinguish a small fire, Max was in a quandary over how to treat them. When he tentatively pressed a pound into one fireman's hand, the man replied that they were not allowed to accept tips. Covered in confusion, Max quavered: "Oh, please treat it as a loan".

He had little time for his countrymen's obsession with sport. When he was asked to send a donation to a fund for the famous cricketer WG Grace, Max obliged but added a note. 'I send you this shilling not because I am a great admirer of cricket, but as an earnest protest against golf'.

In 1910, tired of the pressures of London life and in reduced financial circumstances, Max and Florence left England to live in Rapallo, Italy. They resided quietly there for almost all of the remaining 45 years of his life, occasionally emerging for a new exhibition of cartoons and for the 1911 publication of his comic novel about Oxford called 'Zuleika Dobson'.

As the years wore on, Max mellowed in his Italian retreat. 'I lost my zest for cartooning. It is a young man's hobby – you get kinder as you get older'.

His benevolence suffered a rebuff when he met the tramp-poet WH Davies at a dinner party once. Davies had something of an inferiority complex and was consequently prone to be over-defensive. By chance, during the meal, Davies mentioned that, in his early years, he had been helped by Bernard Shaw.

Max nodded understandingly and added that Shaw liked helping lame dogs over stiles. The meal curdled into silence as Davies glared at Max. It so happened that the poet had a wooden leg, (he had lost a foot when trying to catch a train in the Klondyke), and he immediately leapt to the conclusion that Max was being cruelly humorous as his expense. When later informed of his gaffe, Max was horrified.

The only interruption to Max's life in Italy came with the Second World War. He had long ignored Mussolini, considering him to look like 'a larger and darker Horatio Bottomley', but, as Florence was Jewish, he viewed the rise of the Nazis with concern. They spent the war years staying with friends in England, but returned to Rapallo in 1945.

He still retained an exile's fondness for some aspects of English life; in particular, the songs of Noel Coward. He never lost his enjoyment of Coward's 'Don't Put Your Daughter on the Stage, Mrs Worthington', playing it over and over on his gramophone.

(Despite his own life as a homosexual wit, Noel Coward had a surprisingly vituperative distaste for Oscar Wilde. In his diaries he wrote: 'Am reading more of Wilde. What a tiresome affected sod.' – 'I have read the Oscar Wilde letters and have come to the reluctant conclusion that he was one of the silliest, most conceited and unattractive characters that ever existed'.)

Max had a late blossoming in his career when the BBC asked him to broadcast talks on the radio. He agreed as long as he could appear as 'a character from an older age' – 'It is only when they try to be young that the old seem old'.

Although he had been recognised with a knighthood in 1939, now aged 63, these broadcasts made him a nationally known figure. The artist Graham Sutherland proposed to paint his portrait but Max turned down the offer. He told a friend that he had seen Sutherland's portrait of Somerset Maugham. "Maugham looked as if he had died under torture".

Other members of the Beerbohm family included their father, Julius, a successful corn-seller who celebrated his seventieth birthday by starting the study of the Anglo-Saxon language. At one boring party in London, one of his daughters-in-law spotted Julius peering uneasily round the room. When she asked him: "Are you looking for something?", Julius nodded: "Yes. The door."

Of Herbert and Max's other two brothers, Ernest Beerbohm emigrated to South Africa where he married a Xhosa girl and became a sheep farmer in Cape Colony.

JULIUS BEERBOHM (jun) (1853-1906) attempted to become a poet and a financier. Although much appreciated by his friends, Julius's poetry was far too risqué for publication. After an exotic but drunken tour of Patagonia with some of the Douglas family, (see Florrie Douglas), Julius involved himself in the opening of a luxury hotel in Marienbad, (present-day Czech Republic).

Leaving Marienbad for a tour of European casinos, he forgot all about the venture until forcibly reminded of it by creditors. His efforts to found a company to drag the River Nile looking for Ancient Egyptian jewels also came to nothing.

Herbert Vivian reported that Julius once spent three hours at a café drinking absinthe and trying to persuade Vivian to become a Jesuit. Vivian: 'He explained that part of their training is to make novices fish with long rods for hours and hours in footbaths containing nothing but water. What an epitome of most of our lives!'

Like Max, Julius, despite his ramshackle finances, remained a dandy to the end. When Herbert Beerbohm Tree visited him on his deathbed in 1906, Julius took one look at the colour of Herbert's suit, groaned the word "Ginger!" and turned his face to the wall.

During his years at Merton College, Oxford, Max Beerbohm became acquainted with a fellow undergraduate named **SIR EDWARD (TRELAWNEY) BACKHOUSE** (1873-1944). Although from a highly respectable background – (his father was a director of Barclay's Bank, his brother Roger became Admiral of the Fleet, and he was educated at Winchester College) – Backhouse was always regarded as 'a queer fish'.

At one point, he claimed to have known Wilde well 'in the days of his fame' while knowing nothing of 'his perverted tastes'. Later on he changed this story and claimed to have had sex with Wilde, Bosie, and an actor named Harry Stanford while in Paris. During Wilde's trials, Max Beerbohm reported that 'Trelawney Backhouse is raising money for the conduct of the case'.

The shadowy Backhouse appeared to vanish after 1895 only to reappear in Peking in 1899 as one of the defenders of the Legation during the Boxer Rising. A relative commented that: "I doubt whether he was much help to anyone as I heard that he had managed to shoot his own sergeant-major by mistake".

He returned to Oxford to present 17,000 volumes of ancient Chinese scripts to the Bodleian Library and was hailed as one of its greatest benefactors. It transpired that he had looted the collection during the turmoil following the rout of the Boxer rebels.

Backhouse moved on to a career of spectacular if ultimately incompetent frauds involving, among others, the British War Office (and *Lord Kitchener*), the American Bank Note Company of New York, and the shipbuilding firm of John Brown, all of whom made the mistake of relying on Backhouse as their agent in China.

Backhouse persuaded one agent of the American Bank Company, George Hall (a dubious character himself), to provide a revolver and $50,000 to aid in a plan to steal the Empress Dowager of China's pearl jacket. When Backhouse failed to deliver the jacket or return the money, Hall determined to unmask him.

In a chase that continued via Yokohama to Seattle, Hall lost touch with his quarry after being informed that Backhouse had acquired a job as Director of Coolies on the Western Front. Hall baulked at the idea of pursuing his man into the First World War trenches, despite his fury at discovering the Empress's pearl jacket did not even exist. In fact, Backhouse was lying low over the Canadian border in Victoria.

After he slipped back into China in 1918, Backhouse succeeded to his baronetcy on the death of his father. Unfortunately he did not receive any accompanying legacy and was forced to rely on a small allowance from his family. It seems that one of the conditions of this allowance was that he remained in China.

He now dressed only in Chinese clothes, rejected the Western world entirely, and supplemented his income by forging ancient Chinese documents.

When the Second World War broke out, Backhouse sympathised with the Japanese and, after he had moved into the Peking Austro-Hungarian Embassy, (a forgotten but still functioning outpost of a country that no longer existed), was left alone by the invaders.

In the final three years of his life, Backhouse wrote what he claimed were his memoirs – a scandalously obscene and probably fictional list of sexual encounters with *Paul Verlaine, Walter Pater* (finding Pater's genitals 'undersize'), *Henry James* ('a passive voyeur'), *Ellen Terry*, the Prime Minister *Lord Rosebery, Lord Kitchener, Sarah Bernhardt*, Andre Raffalovich, *Bosie Douglas* (at Winchester School), and the 70-year-old Dowager Empress of China.

> *After the first night of 'A Woman of No Importance', Wilde attended a gala dinner given by Guy de Maupassant's mistress, Blanche Roosevelt Macchetta, at her house in Oakley St, Chelsea. It was at this party that he met the society palmist, Cheiro.*

CHEIRO 1866-1936

Sir George Alexander once asked Wilde if he believed in palmists; Oscar replied: "Always – when they prophesy nice things". The prophecy that he received at Blanche Roosevelt's party was anything but 'nice'. Concealing themselves behind a curtain so that Cheiro could not tell who they were, the guests thrust out their hands for analysis.

When it came to Oscar's turn, he was given the news that: "Your left hand is the hand of a king, but the right hand that of a king who will send himself into exile", and that this banishment would occur within two years. The superstitious Wilde was shocked and abruptly left the party.

Although the truth of this account, (reported by Cheiro himself), has been questioned, there was no doubt about Wilde's interest in palmistry. It provided the basis of his short story, 'Lord Arthur Savile's Crime', in which the hero's attempts to avoid a palmist's prediction that he would become a murderer ends in his murder of the palmist.

Palmistry reinforced Oscar's belief in the inevitability of destiny; as he remarked to Cheiro: "Fate does not keep road-menders on her highways". In 1900, after the prophecy had proved to be true, Cheiro encountered Wilde at the Paris Exhibition. Unlike many others, he greeted the exile warmly. Oscar: "How good of you, my dear friend, everyone cuts me now".

Cheiro's origins, like much else in his life, were debateable. Probably born in Bray, Ireland, his original name was either Lewis Warner or Count Louis Hamon. After studying in India with a mystical sect, he arrived in London and began to make a living by palm reading.

This practice was regarded by many people as bordering on the satanic, and his first landlady in the West End only allowed him to rent his rooms on condition that she daily sprinkled the carpet with holy water. When he left, she charged him extra for the moisture damage done to the carpet.

Later he based himself in Bond Street where he became exceptionally successful, building a fortune not only out of palmistry but by trading in champagne and Irish peat moss. He became a Freemason and a Rosicrucian, (and possibly a secret agent).

After he had deeply impressed *Arthur Balfour*, (the future Prime Minister and President of the Society of Psychical Research), his client list expanded to include many leading figures. On a visit to the USA, he met President Cleveland at the White House, and also Mark Twain who said of Cheiro: "He has exposed my character to me with humiliating accuracy".

In Britain, his numerous clients included *King Edward VII, Lord Kitchener,* and the explorer Sir Ernest Shackleton, (the date and manner of whose deaths he predicted with total accuracy). Many clergymen, including the Bishop of Birmingham, were drawn to visit him.

One of Cheiro's main interests was the promotion of world peace. In 1895, he started a magazine called 'Entente Cordiale – A Journal in the Interest of International Peace'. Unfortunately, his editorial staff included a xenophobic Englishman, a resentful Frenchman, and an Irishman with a strong partiality for alcohol.

On the night before the first edition was due, Cheiro arrived at the offices to the sound of smashing glass and the sight of the Frenchman falling through the plate glass front door. Inside the office, the Englishman had a violent nosebleed, while the Irishman lay prone amidst the shattered remnants of the furniture.

He restored order long enough to publish the first few editions until the Peace Journal became bankrupt. Cheiro: 'The superb ideal of international peace is a dream only to be indulged in by the very rich or the very foolish'.

About 1898, Cheiro predicted that the 20th century would see a terrible war, then a false peace, followed by an even worse war. This warning was one of the reasons why *WT Stead* and Tsar Nicholas II of Russia convened the 1899 Hague Peace Conference. On a trip to Russia in 1905, Cheiro met the Tsar and gave him the disconcerting news that he and his family would all die violently in 1917.

While in Russia, Cheiro also met Rasputin and forewarned the influential monk that his death would include poison, knives, bullets, and drowning. Cheiro realised the power of Rasputin's hypnotic stare, but avoided being dominated by it. He concentrated his own gaze at a point just above Rasputin's nose, thus avoiding the all-absorbing eyes.

Cheiro had great success with women, one of his conquests being the spy Mata Hari. When she was executed by the French, even the firing squad were impressed by her courage. One officer said: "Mata Hari was our enemy, but I honour her for a brave woman. She died magnificently". Cheiro claimed that, to allow her the illusion of safety, he had told her that the execution would be faked and that the bullets were blank. Thus reassured she went to her death with equanimity.

Suffering from stab wounds inflicted by a jealous husband in New York, Cheiro moved to Hollywood, California, in 1930. It was, he said, 'the one place in the world where the vibrations and climactic conditions would restore my health'.

When he died in 1936, (a date he had predicted), despite his request for simplicity he was given a Hollywood funeral, lying on a bed of roses, while film stars sang his favourite melodies.

(One of his clients was a Captain Lionel Bowles, who told Cheiro privately of the curious way he had won the Victoria Cross. During the Boer War, he had been trapped by withering rifle fire at the Battle of the Modder River. As his comrades were shot down around him, Bowles had become terrified and decided to run away. Picking up a corpse and holding it over his back as protection from the bullets, he managed to regain the safety of the British lines. Once there, he realised that the 'corpse' was actually still alive and was indeed a high-ranking officer. Bowles received the acclaim of the British Army and the highest attainable medal for bravery.)

Another of Cheiro's clients was **KING LEOPOLD II** of Belgium (1835-1909), the nephew of *Queen Victoria*. Although he was involved in many sex scandals, the most potentially embarrassing was his taste for pre-pubescent girls. His main supplier was the procuress Mary Jeffries, who ran three London brothels and had a hand in the lucrative white slave traffic to Belgium; (the girls were aged 12 to 14 and were known as 'English parcels').

When *WT Stead* launched his campaign to end this traffic in 1885, he forced the Government's hand by threatening to reveal King Leopold, among other Royal figures, as a major patron.

Leopold's main contribution to history lay in his involvement in the development of the Congo. The explorer HM Stanley secured this rubber-rich colony for the Belgian King in 1885. At first, it was not an especially important asset but, with the invention of the rubber tyre for cars and bicycles, suddenly Leopold had a monopoly on a vital raw material. His exploitation of the rubber sources was described as 'a masterpiece of high finance'.

However, the conditions under which his company extracted the rubber soon became a cause of concern involving, as it did, the effective enslavement of the Congolese people. Resistance was crushed by a savage policy of village burnings and death camps. Any worker who failed to supply the required quota of daily rubber had his or her hands cut off. (The company troops were ordered to collect a hand for every cartridge issued.) Women were not only systematically raped, but any woman who complained about her treatment was killed.

Reports of these atrocities eventually began to emerge and international pressure, led by the subsequent Irish rebel Sir Roger Casement, *Sir Arthur Conan Doyle*, and the writer Joseph Conrad, forced Leopold to hand over control of the company to the Belgian Government. Leopold was given 50 million francs in compensation for his loss.

With ten million Congolese either worked to death or murdered by Leopold's private company, between 1880 and 1920 the population of the Congo halved. It was numerically one of the worst holocausts of the twentieth century.

On one of his visits to Cheiro, Leopold was given a meal of Irish stew and enthusiastically begged for the recipe. When Cheiro attended him again in Brussels, the King insisted on personally cooking an Irish stew for his visitor and sat watching fondly as Cheiro ate the royal offering.

With 'A Woman of No Importance' starting its successful run in London, Wilde spent much of May 1893 visiting Bosie Douglas in Oxford. At the end of the month, he made a short trip to Paris where he stayed in the Hotel des Deux-Mondes in Avenue de l'Opera.

In early June he returned to Oxford, where Bosie was in the process of being sent down from the university.

Wilde rented the 'Cottage', a house in Goring-on-Thames, now known as the 'Ferry House'. (Much later, it became the home of Sir Arthur 'Bomber' Harris, the strategist behind 'saturation' bombing during the Second World War, especially of the city of Dresden).

While staying in Goring, Oscar corresponded with Lady Jennie Churchill, the wife of the politician Lord Randolph Churchill, and later the wife of the socialite George Cornwallis-West.

LADY JENNIE CHURCHILL 1854-1921

In June 1893, Jennie Churchill wrote to Oscar to clear up a bet she had made concerning one of his epigrams. He replied confirming that she was correct over his line: 'The only difference between the saint and the sinner is that every saint has a past and that every sinner has a future'. Jennie said of Wilde: "a more brilliant talker did not exist".

Jenny (Jerome) was born in New York City, where her father had made a fortune on the stock exchange. In 1874, she married Lord Randolph Churchill, the second son of the Duke of Marlborough. Both her sisters were to follow her example of marrying into the British aristocracy. Wilde: 'American women adore titles and are a permanent blow to Republican principles.'

In her new role as a political wife, she encountered the international diplomatic set. At a dinner party she was seated next to the Japanese Ambassador and they began to discuss the proverbs of their different countries. She asked the Ambassador if there was a Japanese equivalent of the English saying, 'Penny wise and pound foolish'. He flushed and replied: "In my country, the equivalent would be: 'The man who goes to bed early to save candles gets twins'."

Having fulfilled her conjugal duty by producing two sons, Jack and Winston, Jennie at 27 was considered to be a ripe recruit for the sexual merry-go-round of aristocratic Victorian Britain. Her husband, nicknamed 'Randy Pandy', was a sexual predator of some note who observed: "I don't like ladies at all. I like rough women who dance and sing and drink – the rougher the better".

Jennie was not only attractive, but also, as Wilde pointed out, 'she behaves as if she was beautiful. Most American women do. It is the secret of their charm'. In 1881, she had an affair with Count Charles Kinsky, the attaché at the Austro-Hungarian Embassy, (and in 1883 the first amateur to win the Grand National horse race). There was also a strong probability that she became yet another of the Prince of Wales's bedfellows, (in fact her son Jack was likely to have been fathered by Bertie). Following Randolph's early death in 1895, she met and married *George Cornwallis-West*, (who at 26 was the same age as her son Winston).

In 1900, during the Boer War, together with fellow expatriate Americans, Jennie equipped a hospital ship called the Maine to travel to South Africa. She arrived with the Maine in Durban in time to tend the casualties from the Siege of Ladysmith (and, incidentally to meet her son Winston who had just escaped from a Boer prisoner-of-war camp). One of her jobs was to compose letters home for the illiterate soldiers. One of her most severely wounded charges amused her by sending the message: 'Dear Mum and Dad, I hope this finds you as well as it leaves me'.

On return to Britain Jennie's marriage to *Cornwallis-West* began to falter. She attempted to write plays, one of which, 'His Borrowed Plumes', was produced with *Mrs Patrick Campbell* in the lead. Mrs Pat: 'It was a rather awful play. Some of the actors started calling it 'Sorrowing Blooms'. When you are rehearsing, the worst possible of all signs is when the actors start congratulating each other on having a sense of humour'.

An even worse side effect of this doomed production was that Mrs Pat and George Cornwallis-West met and became lovers. After George's swift divorce from Jennie, he married Mrs Pat.

Jennie gamely struggled on and, in 1918 aged 64 married a Mr Montagu Porch, (aged 37). In an echo of her correspondence with Wilde, she said of the match: "He has a future and I have a past so we should be all right". They remained happily together till Jennie's death three years later.

Jenny's first husband, **LORD RANDOLPH CHURCHILL** (1849-1895), through birth and talent, had the prospect of a brilliant political and social career, but was ruined by his own impulsive nature.

He was wrecked socially because of his involvement with the sexual affairs of his brother, George, Marquess of Blandford (1849-1892), who succeeded to the title of 8th Duke of Marlborough in 1883. Blandford was an unapologetic lecher, (later to be exposed as one of *Lady Colin Campbell's* lovers in the celebrated court case).

Frank Harris said of Blandford that: "He liked a good dinner and noble wine...but above all he loved women. After a dinner at the Café Royal one night he discoursed to me for an hour on the typical beauties of a dozen different races, not excluding the yellow or the black".

The main trouble occurred when Blandford moved in with the wife of Lord 'Sporting Joe' Aylesford. Aylesford, not quite such a sport as to tolerate this situation, sued for divorce and challenged Blandford to a duel. Hoping to diffuse the crisis, Randolph Churchill appealed on behalf of his brother to Bertie, the *Prince of Wales*, to calm down Sporting Joe.

When Bertie ignored his request, a furious Randolph threatened to release letters that proved Bertie had himself had an affair with Lady Aylesford. He also informed Bertie's wife, Princess Alexandra, of her husband's dalliance. Bertie, now equally furious, was on the point of challenging Randolph to a duel on his own account.

However, in a cooler mood and fearful of the publicity, Bertie persuaded all the protagonists to withdraw their accusations. Although Randolph's blackmail had worked, it was ten years before he was readmitted to Court society.

For some time though it seemed that the political seam of his life would be spectacular. Elected as an MP in 1874, Randolph was the stormy petrel of the House of Commons for twelve years.

An incident related by *Herbert Vivian* gave some indication of Randolph's style. 'Churchill told me of an incident with Sir William Harcourt in the House of Commons: 'I had shouted some interruption across the floor and Harcourt cried 'Little ass!' in a loud stage whisper. I retorted with 'Damned fool'. I shall never forget his expression of amazement and indignation when I said it. He got up two and three times to call the Speaker's attention to the expression, but each time his heart misgave him as he remembered his own share in the controversy. The Speaker told me afterwards that it was the most succinct debate he had ever heard'.

Together with a fellow Conservative, *Arthur Balfour*, Randolph formed a group known as the 'Fourth Party' to promote the concept of 'Tory Democracy'. When asked what Tory Democracy was, Randolph confessed: "To tell the truth I don't know myself. But I believe it is principally opportunism".

A fierce opponent of Irish Home Rule, he became notorious for his catch phrase of 'Ulster will fight and Ulster will be right'.

With *Lord Salisbury's* new Tory government elected in 1886, Randolph became Chancellor of the Exchequer and Leader of the House of Commons. He was recognised as the main contender for the next Tory Premiership.

His character remained a major obstacle however, as he constantly enraged his colleagues. Salisbury himself complained that Randolph had a 'wayward and headstrong disposition'. Randolph was trapped once into a boring conversation at his club by a dreary but influential party member. He gave a despairing glance around, then summoned a waiter and said: "Will you please hear the rest of this story for me? I haven't time", and abruptly left the club.

In December 1886, Randolph finally overplayed his hand. When he threatened to resign if the defence spending cuts in his budget were not agreed, to his utter surprise Salisbury accepted his resignation. He was replaced as Chancellor by a colleague called George Goschen. (Goschen was not a success in the post. One colleague said of him: "Goschen always looks like a man who is wearing a kilt for the first time".)

Randolph, who perennially lived on his nerves, went into a rapid mental and physical decline, becoming in *Lord Rosebery's* famous line "the chief mourner at his own protracted funeral'. His death at the age of 46 was probably the result of syphilis.

Randolph's aloofness towards his children left an indelible mark on his younger son, **WINSTON CHURCHILL** (1874-1965). Winston said later: "He wouldn't listen to me or consider anything I said".

In spite of this distance between them, many observers saw the youthful Winston as a similar type. *Max Beerbohm* said that he was a 'clumsy edition of his father' who possessed the 'hereditary bad manners, being courteous and brutal alternately'. The writer *Alice Meynell* wrote that the three things Winston most resembled were 'a seraph, a rat, and a rat-catcher'. *Wilfred Blunt* was much more sympathetic saying that Winston had three great qualities: 'great ability, honesty in politics, and a good heart'.

In November 1894, it appears that Winston added demagoguery to this list of attributes. After a campaign by the moralist National Vigilance Committee, led by the redoubtable Mrs Laura Ormiston Chant, the promenade section of the Empire Theatre was surrounded by partitions and closed down. It had been the preserve of prostitutes, 180 of whom had been counted in one night proffering their wares to the music hall enthusiasts.

One week later, Winston stood up in the Empire and, after delivering a fiery oration denouncing the Vigilance Committee, led an attack that tore down the partitions. Comparing his speech to the storming of the Bastille, Winston wrote excitedly to his brother Jack: "Did you see the papers about the riot at the Empire last Saturday? It was I who led the rioters and made a speech to the crowd!'

When Winston joined the British army, he was not popular with many of his fellow officers. *Fenwick La Terriere* complained that Winston was fond of 'airing his views to his elders'. He suggested that if Winston had been thrown into a horse trough 'he might have become a less arrogant and dangerous personality in later life'.

Winston's career was threatened in 1896 when the father of an officer in the Fourth Hussars accused him of homosexual practices. After Winston sued for libel, the case was settled out of court and he won £400 in damages. The officer in question refused to let the matter drop and, when he left the regiment, brought further charges against the whole mess. Winston was advised to remain with the regiment himself as his departure might have been construed as avoidance of investigation. The scandal was kept quiet and allowed to die when the Hussars left for India in September 1896.

In 1898, Winston accompanied *Lord Kitchener's* army when it invaded the Sudan. *Dame Ethel Smyth's* brother Bob met him the night before the Battle of Omdurman, when Winston taught him 'a new game called Bridge'. Winston told Bob Smyth that he did not intend to remain in the Army as he 'did not wish to spend his life in the company of intelligent animals'.

After the Boer War, Winston left the military as promised and went on to a career of some note in politics.

In the 1950s, Winston was asked which figure from the past he would most like to have as a dinner guest. He replied without hesitation: "Oscar Wilde".

In 1908, Winston married Clementine Hozier; after his honeymoon he told a friend: "I find love-making a serious and delightful occupation". His mother-in-law would probably have agreed whole-heartedly with this sentiment.

Clementine's mother, **BLANCHE HOZIER** (1852-1925), was married to Sir Henry Hozier, a member of Lloyds. After she met Wilde she reported: "Oscar Wilde came into Bruton Street while I was there – an affected unpleasant creature – but he says amusing things in an amusing way".

In 1891, Hozier divorced Blanche after finding Sir Ellis Bartlett in her bedroom. During the case, nine other men, including *Wilfred Blunt*, were named as Blanche's lovers.

The most significant of these liaisons was with the famous huntsman, Bay Middleton, Master of the Quorn Hunt in the days when 'a master of hounds preceded a master of arts'. Before his death from a broken neck in 1892, (when his horse put a foot in a rabbit hole), Middleton appears to have sired at least two of Blanche's children, her daughters Kitty and Clementine.

Wilfred Blunt thoroughly approved of this arrangement: 'It is much wiser for a woman who has an inferior husband, to choose a suitable sire for her children and both these girls were delightful, refined and superior in every way'.

Bay Middleton also became the lover of another member of the Quorn Hunt, the Empress Elizabeth of Austria, (nicknamed 'Sissi'). 'Sissi' was assassinated by an anti-royalist fanatic at Geneva in 1898.

Her son, Crown Prince Rudolph of Austria, (whom *Lily Langtry* described as a sex pest), fell in love with a commoner, Marie Vetsera, but was refused permission to marry her. Rather than separate, in 1889 the couple committed suicide in a famous incident known as the Mayerling tragedy. Wilde said of Rudolph that he was one of only two 'interesting Royal personages'.

The Emperor Franz-Josef of Austria was unfortunate in his relations. His great-aunt had been the guillotined Queen Marie-Antonette of France, his wife Sissi was stabbed to death, his son Rudolph committed suicide, his younger brother Maximilian was executed in Mexico, and his nephew Ferdinand's murder in Sarajevo in 1914 precipitated all Europe into the First World War.

GEORGE CORNWALLIS-WEST 1874-1951

In 'An Ideal Husband', Wilde wrote a speech in which one of his characters was accused of laziness. The rebuttal went as follows: 'How can you say such a thing? Why, he rides in the Row at ten o'clock in the morning, goes to the Opera three times a week, changes his clothes at least five times a day, and dines out every night of the season. You don't call that leading an idle life, do you?' This defence could have applied equally to *Jennie Churchill's* second husband, George Cornwallis-West.

His mother was *Patsy Cornwallis-West* and his father was nominally Colonel William Cornwallis-West of Ruthin Castle, Wales. However his real father was most likely to have been the ubiquitously fertile Bertie, *Prince of Wales*, who agreed to stand in as godfather.

As a child, George often travelled to Ireland to visit his maternal family and was staying in Dublin when his uncle Pat was presented at short notice to the Grand Duchess Cyril of Russia. Uncle Pat only realised at the last moment that those being presented had to wear their decorations. Too late to collect his own medals, he grabbed a handful of old Racing Club badges and pinned them to his chest.

Unfortunately, Duchess Cyril became intrigued by the unusual designs and asked Uncle Pat what they represented. Improvising madly, he pointed to the Leopardstown Racing Club badge and announced that it was the Order of the Leopard, to be worn only by those who could claim direct descent of the last King of Ireland.

In 1891, as part of his education, George toured Germany. He was fascinated by the sword duelling tradition among German students, in which the most horrendous wounds, (and thus the famous scars), were inflicted upon each other's faces. One of the rules was that no dogs were allowed into the room during the duels in case a man had his nose cut off.

He reported that one of his compatriots, a dyspeptic old British general, had been taken to see the ancestral home of the Bluchers in Germany. When his hostess proudly showed him the portrait of the renowned Field Marshal, the general grunted dismissively: "Oh yes! I remember, that's the old blighter who turned up late for the Battle of Waterloo".

George later became best known for his marriages to famous and much older women. Aged 26, in the teeth of social opposition he married the 46-year-old *Jennie Churchill.* (A curious offshoot of this union was that George, very probably the son of the Prince of Wales, became stepfather to Jack Churchill, also very probably the son of the Prince of Wales).

Jennie sued for divorce after George met the actress *Mrs Patrick Campbell*, nine years his senior. This new relationship, (and marriage), foundered after Mrs Pat discovered George's continuing infidelities but, as she refused to grant him a divorce, they stayed technically married till her death. George gained the nickname of 'The Old Wives Tale'.

George recounted a story that shed some light on the sexual mores of the Edwardian period. When a member invited a well-known prostitute to have lunch at his London club, another member complained to the secretary. As a result, the secretary pinned up a notice reading: 'Members are requested not to bring their mistresses into the Club, unless they happen to be the wives of other members'.

George's various business ventures failed and he spent much of his time fending off bankruptcy. Described as 'a bit short of brains', he channelled his energies into fishing, shooting and general sports. He enjoyed cricket and was fond of recalling his favourite story of the game.

It appeared that at one match the game was excitingly poised with the home team having to make only ten runs to win, but with only one wicket left. Unfortunately, the last batsman was not only inexperienced but three parts drunk as well. His captain gave him stern advice before he went out to the crease: "All you have to do is to put your bat in front of the wicket".

The batsman blearily peered around and replied: "I know about that, ole boy, but what if I see two balls?". The captain tried to reassure him: "In that case, just aim at the inside one".

The man nodded and reeled out to the pitch. Two minutes later, he returned, having been bowled first ball. His furious captain shouted: "You bloody fool! I told you to aim at the inside ball!" The batsman nodded unhappily and slurred: "I did, ole man, I shware I did. But I hit it with the outside bat".

George made a languid attempt to carve a career in the army, but retired from the Boer War after suffering sunstroke. At the commencement of the First World War, he rejoined the colours and was involved in the defence of Antwerp in 1914.

His battalion, which included the poet Rupert Brooke, spent a frightful night in confused retreat from the Germans, marching 50 kilometres from six in the evening till seven the next morning. Half the battalion accidentally marched into Holland where they were interned for the rest of the war. The other half returned to England, where George caught bronchitis and retired to the USA to convalesce.

On his return in 1915, he was appointed Assistant Provost-Marshall for Surrey and Middlesex, acting in effect as a military policeman responsible for chasing draft-dodgers.

He was called upon to exercise these duties on Armistice Night in 1918, when he was present at the Savoy Hotel during the riotous celebrations. The hotel manager asked him to help clear the restaurant when the damage level grew too much. One very drunk Highland officer obstinately refused to leave and sat grimly clutching a tablecloth over his lap. When George suggested that it was time to leave, the officer growled at him: "Mon, I canna move. Some bastard's stolen ma kilt".

George spent the rest of his life hunting, shooting and dabbling in writing, but subject to long periods of ennui. He once asked his valet how the servants passed their spare time. The valet replied: "Well, sir, one of the favourite amusements is piecing together the letters found in the wastepaper baskets in the morning. Better than any jig-saw puzzle, I can assure you, and much more entertaining".

In 1951, suffering from depression, George went back to bed one morning and shot himself dead with a hunting rifle.

Wilde settled for the summer of 1893 at the cottage in Goring-on-Thames, 'a most unhealthy and delightful place', and began to write his next play 'An Ideal Husband'. Even in the country he continued his social life and, during the Henley Regatta, had to hire extra servants to cope with the overflow of guests.

One of the Yellow Book poets, Theodore Wratislaw (1871–1933), was an acquaintance of Wilde's and visited him at Goring. One morning when Oscar was rowing his son Cyril and Wratislaw in a canoe on the Thames, he told his passengers that: "Life in meadow and stream is far more complex than life in streets and salons".

One reason for this observation may have been his deteriorating relationship with Bosie Douglas. Although the attraction between the two men was still strong, Bosie's volatile temperament led to incessant rows.

A serious incident took place during this summer that endangered the whole Wilde set. Robert Ross had seduced a 16-year-old schoolboy called Philip Dannay, whom Max Beerbohm facetiously described as 'a schoolboy Helen…with wonderful eyes'. On meeting Dannay, Bosie had also fallen for the boy and, stealing him from Ross, installed him in the Albemarle Hotel, London. When the pair visited Goring, Wilde also went to bed with Dannay.

When Dannay's outraged father discovered what had happened, he contacted his solicitors and a major scandal threatened to break out. Luckily, the affair was placed in the hands of the arch fixer, Sir George Lewis, who advised Dannay's father that if the prosecution went ahead his own son could end up in prison. With an ill grace, Dannay's father dropped the case.

However, the effect upon the Wilde set was salutary. Robert Ross retreated to Davos, Switzerland, and did not return to England for two years. At the end of August, Oscar left for Dinard in France, returning in late September when he thought the coast was clear, and taking care to stay well clear of Bosie.

He moved into a hotel at 10/11, St James Place, London, and over the winter continued to write 'An Ideal Husband'. In November, leaving a false address for Bosie, he made a trip to Paris, where he spent some time drinking with Paul Verlaine.

Worried about the Dannay affair, and in an effort to shake off Bosie, Oscar wrote to Bosie's mother Sibyl Douglas, explaining that her son's health was suffering from his habits: 'His life seems to me aimless, unhappy and absurd'. He suggested that Bosie would benefit from a few months holiday in Egypt in 'new surroundings, proper friends, and a different atmosphere'.

Sybil Douglas, (who may have been aware of the Dannay affair herself), was equally willing to remove her son from what she saw as Oscar's evil influence.

She contacted her old school friend, Ethel Baring, (wife of the British Consul-General in Egypt, Sir Evelyn Baring), who agreed to offer hospitality to Bosie in Cairo – at the time a fashionable holiday resort for the British.

[Bosie's host, Sir Evelyn Baring (later LORD CROMER 1841-1917), was the de facto ruler of Egypt from 1883 till 1907. Although admired by Lord Rosebery as 'a good man to go tiger-shooting with', Baring's brusque manner led to his nickname of 'Over-Baring'.

Even Bertie, Prince of Wales, suffered from Baring's directness. When dining as the honoured royal guest at the British Residency in Cairo, the Prince asked for a third helping of prawn curry. Baring snapped: "You had much better not. It is rich enough as it is, and you have already had two ample helpings". Bertie later said of Baring: "An able man but no manners".]

Bosie arrived in Cairo in December 1893, and was reported as flouncing round the Residency wearing shantung suits and 'making eyes' at the British general, Lord Kitchener; (whether the flirtation was reciprocated was debateable).

Although Baring would not give Bosie a job in Egypt, he did arrange for Bosie's appointment as honorary attaché to the British Embassy in Turkey, where Lord Currie was now ambassador.

In the meantime, Bosie grew bored of life in Cairo and set off on a boat trip up the Nile in the company of three young Englishmen – EF Benson, Reggie Turner, and Turner's half-brother, Frank Lawson.

EDWARD F. BENSON 1867-1940

EF Benson, (known as 'Fred'), had been introduced to Wilde at Cambridge in 1889 by *Robert Ross.* He was intrigued by the Wilde phenomenon and had been one of those who had worn the aesthetic symbol of the green carnation at the first night of 'Lady Windermere's Fan'.

After 1895, he reversed his attitude and later attacked Wilde's memory with unusual ferocity. Accusing Oscar of being 'the victim of a monstrous megalomania', Fred suggested that Oscar's fame was due to his notoriety rather than to his talent. In a comment on Wilde's plays, Fred wrote in the 1930s: 'They have aged rapidly and become out of date, their wit to us seems tight-roped and acrobatic, and now no one in England will listen to them'.

After being educated at Marlborough College, (where he was a school friend of Wilde's later co-defendant, Alfred Taylor), and at Kings College, Cambridge, Fred went to Greece and spent much of the 1890s as an archaeologist based in Athens.

During the Greek-Turkish War of 1897, after the Greek army had been comprehensively beaten, Fred went to the ravaged region of Thessaly to administer a Red Cross relief fund. He coped well amidst the chaotic aftermath of battle.

(Fred reported one embarrassing incident that occurred during the Greek defeat. The first new Olympic Games had taken place in Athens in the previous year of 1896. The main event, the Marathon, had been won by a Greek runner called Loues. Loues received the plaudits of the nation for his achievement, one of his rewards being the promise of a free dinner every night for the rest of his life.

When the Greek army collapsed during the 1897 war, the troops scattered in terror and fled. Having outrun the rest of the army, the first man to arrive back in Athens was Loues. It was the end of the free dinners.)

Having achieved an early literary success in 1892 with his satirical novel, 'Dodo', Fred returned to England and became a prolific writer. Between 1921 and 1939, he published the lastingly popular 'Mapp and Lucia' series of novels.

During his later years, he lived in Lamb House in Rye, Sussex, (*Henry James's* old residence), and in 1933 was elected 645th Mayor of Rye. He became very friendly with his Rye neighbours, the lesbian couple, Radclyffe Hall and her girlfriend Una Troubridge, (sister-in-law of Adrian Hope, the future guardian of Wilde's children); *Dame Ethel Smyth* was also a frequent visitor.

Fred was the third son of a highly talented family; his father being **EDWARD BENSON** (1829-1896), the Archbishop of Canterbury from 1882 till 1896, (and sometimes known as 'God's head waiter').

Given his aesthetic attraction to the Roman Catholic Church, Wilde was rarely sympathetic to the Church of England. He said that: 'The Catholic Church is for saints and sinners alone. For respectable people, the Anglican Church will do'. He teased the Anglican bishops with his comment in 'Dorian Gray' on the detrimental effects of thought upon personal beauty: 'But in the Church they don't think. A bishop keeps on saying at the age of eighty what he was told to say when he was a boy of eighteen and as a natural consequence he always looks absolutely delightful'.

In spite of this backhanded compliment, Oscar claimed that he had received a letter from Archbishop Benson expressing approval and support of 'Dorian Gray' during its rocky publication period.

Born into a poverty stricken background in Birmingham, Edward Benson's obvious leadership qualities were spotted at an early age. By 1852, he had become a master at Rugby School and was known to be such a ruthless disciplinarian that his thrashing of miscreants almost provoked a rebellion.

One of Benson's ex-pupils said that during a period of his school life he had four different colours of bruises on his body – purple, blue, green, and yellow – as a result of Benson's attentions. (This brutal behaviour was by no means a rarity; at St George's School in Ascot, the headmaster flogged a boy so violently that the master died of a heart attack).

Far from such savagery damaging his career, it enhanced Benson's prospects. In 1859, he was chosen by Prince Albert to become headmaster of the newly created Wellington College, which he turned into one of the great public schools of England.

Turning his focus from education to the church, Benson became Canon of Lincoln Cathedral, and then in 1876 Bishop of Truro, where he presided over the construction of the first new cathedral to be built in England since the Reformation.

His authoritarian inclinations received a setback when he clashed with the more laidback attitudes of the 1870s Cornish Anglican clergy. (The Rev. Robert Hawker of Morwenstow, composer of the rousing song 'And Shall Trelawney Die?', had a habit of swimming out to a sea rock with a comb and a long wig and pretending to be a mermaid).

One vicar especially irritated Benson, as the man had never set foot in the parish church, let alone held a service in it. The cleric preferred to carry out his duties by occasionally wandering down to the garden gate of the vicarage, 'clad in a flowered dressing gown and smoking a hookah', and chatting amiably to any parishioner who happened to pass by.

To Benson's intense annoyance he found that he had no ecclesiastical power to remove the man.

In 1882, Benson fulfilled his ambitions by becoming Archbishop of Canterbury. Much of his time at Lambeth Palace was spent determining ecclesiastical legalities but he also invented the Christmas service of Nine Lessons and Carols.

Benson enjoyed ghost stories and in 1895 suggested the plot of a new book to the novelist *Henry James*. James liked the story and published it a year later under the title, 'The Turn of the Screw'. It was later filmed as 'The Innocents'.

When he was aged 23, the future Archbishop proposed to **MINNIE SIDGWICK** (1841-1918). As she was only 11 years old at the time, they delayed the wedding for seven years until 1859. Between 1860 and 1871, Minnie gave birth to six children, (the eldest boy, Martin, died aged 17).

After this relentless grind of maternity, she became interested in other women, chief of whom was Lucy Tait, whose family were also involved in the church hierarchy. (Lucy's father Archibald had preceded Edward Benson as Archbishop of Canterbury from 1868 till 1882, while her brother-in-law, Frederick Temple, succeeded Benson as Archbishop of Canterbury from 1896 till 1902 – his son, William Temple, became Archbishop of Canterbury in 1942).

Minnie and Lucy enjoyed sexual relations in the early days of their relationship and always shared the same bed. After Edward Benson's death in 1896, Minnie renamed herself 'Ben' and regarded Lucy as a second husband. But, in spite of all evidence to the contrary,

Minnie refused to accept the implication that she was a lesbian. It was less easy to deny an earlier episode when she had had an affair with the notorious Dame Ethel Smyth.

Having seduced the mother, Ethel Smyth turned her attentions to Minnie's elder daughter, **NELLIE BENSON** (1863-1890). Although she had been involved in lesbian affairs previously at Lady Margaret Hall, Oxford, Nellie's main love affair, before her early death aged 27, was with Smyth.

Moving on to Minnie's other daughter, **MAGGIE BENSON** (1865-1916), Smyth swiftly seduced the girl. It was Maggie, though, who left Ethel behind in favour of a new love named Nettie Gourlay, whom she had met during her archaeological activities in Egypt. Later, Maggie became homicidally insane and ended her days in a mental institution.

Given the proclivities of the distaff side of the family, it was not surprising that a later commentator, Rupert Croft-Cooke, was able to describe Fred Benson as 'one of the three queer sons of the Archbishop of Canterbury'.

Notwithstanding his attacks on Wilde's 'unbridled gratification of animal appetites', Fred's main relationships were with other men. In particular he was closely involved with *Walter Harris's* friend, the diplomat Reggie Lister, (aka 'the Cordial Aunt'), firstly in Athens, and later in Paris.

Fred's elder brother **ARTHUR BENSON** (1862-1925), was known for his aversion to women and it is likely that he remained a lifelong virgin. In 1903 he resigned as a master at Eton. An ex-pupil said of him: "He was an unconventional teacher: one of his odd practices had been to go round the dormitories every night and tickle the boys in their beds."

Arthur became the Master of Magdalene College, Cambridge, an acknowledged essayist and critic, the editor of *Queen Victoria's* letters, and writer of the lyrics to Edward Elgar's 'Land of Hope and Glory'.

As a critic, he had a distaste for the decadent. When told that one of Charles Baudelaire's poems had been written in a Turkish bath, he snorted: "I am not surprised that the poem should have been written in a Turkish bath by a man whose whole work seemed to have been written in a Turkish bath".

The youngest member of the family was **HUGH BENSON** (1871-1914), who also shunned female company. As befitted the son of an Archbishop of Canterbury, he became an Anglican priest, but soon afterwards became involved in a furious row with the next Archbishop, Frederick Temple, (Lucy Tait's brother-in-law), when they both lost their tempers.

Hugh shocked his circle by converting to Roman Catholicism, and becoming ordained in the Catholic Church in 1904. He was granted an audience with Pope Leo XIII in the Vatican. (This meeting caused some embarrassment, not on doctrinal grounds, but because both men dropped their skullcaps at the same time and, bending to retrieve them, Hugh and the Pope painfully cracked their heads together.)

In 1905, Hugh became a priest at Cambridge, where he befriended Wilde's younger son, *Vyvyan Holland*. He also wrote several popular novels and attempted to co-write a book with the notorious *Frederick Rolfe* (Baron Corvo). After being warned of Rolfe's dubious reputation, Hugh backed off and became the recipient of abusive postcards from the angry Rolfe for the rest of his life.

Despite his spiritual vocation, Hugh had a decidedly earthbound view of his fellow man, as his brother Fred testified. Once, when they were playing croquet, Hugh suddenly realised he was late for prayers and dashed off. Fred overheard a gabble of orisons coming from an upstairs room, which were cut short by Hugh's breathless reappearance on the croquet green. Glaring around the hoops, Hugh accused Fred of altering the position of the balls: "I'm sure that ball wasn't there! Fred, do you promise you haven't moved it?"

It was ironic that, although a man of the sternest Victorian moral values himself, the Archbishop of Canterbury had acquired a family in which all five surviving children were either actively or latently homosexual, and a wife involved in a lesbian relationship with the daughter of the previous Archbishop of Canterbury.

REGGIE TURNER 1869-1938 (First Part)

The young trainee barrister Reggie Turner had met Wilde in 1892, but only grew closer to the Wilde circle in 1894. He was an eager and obliging young man, who slipped easily into a subordinate role with Wilde, affecting some of Oscar's mannerisms and performing small errands for his hero.

Oscar liked Reggie but could not help patronising him. The editor Henry Harland told a story that one evening at Harland's house, Oscar had made an expansive gesture and accidentally knocked a glass of whisky over Reggie, who had been sitting in an armchair beneath him. After Reggie had been towelled dry, Oscar continued with his speech. Ten minutes later the same thing happened and the whisky flew all over the chair again. Oscar affected an air of disappointment and drawled: "Oh, what a waste! I had forgotten that Reggie was not sitting there anymore".

Turner was a physically unattractive man, with a large nose on a small head, and constantly blinking eyelids. At Merton College, Oxford, where he arrived to read Modern History in 1888, he acquired the reputation as a phenomenally late riser, who emerged from his bed only in order to read the Daily Telegraph, (as opposed to Modern History). As his family owned the newspaper, a copy was sent up to Oxford each day from London by train.

Perhaps the only lasting advantage that Reggie gained at Oxford was his lifelong friendship with his fellow student *Max Beerbohm* who, (having 'the gift of perpetual old age'), kept a fatherly eye on him.

On leaving Oxford, Reggie entered Clements Inn, London, and began to study law occasionally, although he became much better known among his friends for his ability at menu-selection. *Ada Leverson* said of him that: "Reggie Turner had the appearance always of having very recently been taken out of a bandbox".

Reggie's trip to Egypt was funded by his half-brother, Frank Lawson, who also provided the sumptuous barge for the voyage up the Nile. As the legitimate son of the Lawson family, Frank had inherited a large fortune and, being a kindly man, never stinted Reggie during the latter's financially precarious life. Frank also enjoyed Reggie's quick wit and, particularly on this trip, his invention of new Arab greetings such as: 'May Allah ease your urine'.

Reggie's illegitimacy was a factor that always rankled in his life – and the fact that he never discovered the identity of his mother. His father was a member of the rich Levy-Lawson family, owners of the Daily Telegraph. Reggie once wrote a line that seemed to stem from his own experience: 'He was born with a silver spoon in his mouth – but there was someone else's crest on it'.

[See Reggie Turner – Second Part – Page 494]

The Daily Telegraph was started in the 1850s by a Colonel Sleigh, but by 1855 it had been acquired by his printers, the brothers Joseph and Lionel Levy, in settlement of a debt. The paper, overcoming its nickname of 'The Delirium Tremens' bestowed upon it by *Benjamin Disraeli*, did well under the clever direction of Lionel Levy, (who changed his name to Lawson).

It was originally written with a pro-Liberal slant, but when in 1878 Gladstone launched his campaign against the Turkish government over the Bulgarian atrocities, Lionel changed the editorial policy to attack Gladstone. The reason behind this shift was that Lionel did not wish to damage his many business interests in Turkey.

Then Lionel died in 1879, his nephew (and Reggie Turner's father), **EDWARD LAWSON** (1833-1916), succeeded him. The editor of the 'Truth' paper, *Henry Labouchere*, angered by what he saw as Lionel's dishonest use of newspaper editorials to further his own business interests, wrote a less than flattering obituary.

As Labouchere was leaving the Beefsteak Club one day, he was amazed to receive a violent blow from behind. Turning, he realised his assailant was Edward Lawson. A duel was arranged between the two men, but Edward developed cold feet over the idea and instead decided to use the courts to sue Labouchere for libel.

When a friend suggested to Labouchere that he apply to a police magistrate against further physical attacks from Lawson, Labouchere grunted: "I should as soon think of applying to a magistrate to protect me from an irate jelly-fish". Referring to the Telegraph as 'The Daily Levy', Labouchere added: 'Every morning my dog goes to the station to fetch my newspapers. Ever since the trial started he has refused to bring home the Daily Telegraph".

The case opened in 1881 but after the jury disagreed, Lawson decided to drop the suit. The Telegraph went on to flourish with such coups as the co-backing, (with Gordon Bennett of the New York Herald), of HM Stanley's expedition to Africa. Lawson became a friend of *King Edward VII* and was made Baron Burnham in 1903.

One of the star journalists who helped the Levy-Lawsons build the reputation of the Daily Telegraph was the semi-blind **GEORGE AUGUSTUS SALA** (1828-1896); he was said to have 'revolutionised the daily paper'. Wilde was not an admirer: "You can always tell what Sala writes. No other human being can write such intolerable English".

The writer Vernon Lee was even less flattering: "Sala was a red, bloated, bottle-nosed creature, who poured out anecdotes in a stentorian voice. He used to be an awful drunkard, but was converted by marrying a bar-maid, who being versed in such things, pointed out the adulteration in liquors so effectively that he took to teetotalism'.

Among Sala's other literary endeavours was the 1882 novel, 'The Mysteries of Verbena House; or, Miss Bellasis Birched for Thieving'.

Wilde had an uneasy relationship with the press. The various magazines and newspapers provided much of his income during the 1880s, and both his rise and fall gave pecuniary solace to 'many an ink-stained life'. But his main attitude was one of contempt.

Wilde: 'In the old days men had the rack. Now they have the Press'. In 'The Soul of Man Under Socialism', he wrote: 'Somebody – was it Burke? – called Journalism the fourth estate. That was true at the time, no doubt. But at the present moment it really is the only estate. It has eaten up the other three. The Lords Temporal say nothing, the Lords Spiritual have nothing to say, and the House of Commons has nothing to say and says it. We are dominated by Journalism.'

This distaste did not prevent him writing to Edward Lawson suggesting that the Telegraph print some of Oscar's articles on modern dress, as 'of course yours is the paper that is in quickest touch with the public'.

When Bosie's party arrived at Luxor on the Nile, they stayed at the main hotel there, where they met Lord Charles Beresford and his wife, and also befriended a young English journalist named Robert Hichens.

ROBERT HICHENS 1864-1950

During 1893, Robert Hichens had been seriously ill with peritonitis, and was advised to travel to Egypt to improve his health. His encounter with the exuberant company of Benson, Turner and Bosie enlivened him. In particular, he became fascinated by their endless chatter about Oscar Wilde.

With the recent success of EF Benson's satire 'Dodo' in his mind, Hichens decided that the adventures of Oscar and Bosie would make an equally amusing novel and collected notes on Oscar from his companions. The resulting book, 'The Green Carnation', was written within four weeks and published with huge success in September 1894. Wilde, Bosie, *Ada Leverson, Lady St Helier, George Moore*, and *George Alexander* all featured among its very recognisable caricatures.

As the book had been published anonymously, speculation raged as to its author. The poet *Alfred Austin, Marie Corelli*, and even Oscar himself were suspected, until Bosie finally exposed Hichens as the true author.

Wilde regarded the spoof with equanimity, allowing his character 'Lady Bracknell' to refer to it in his 1895 play, 'The Importance of Being Earnest': 'This treatise, 'The Green Carnation', as I see it is called, seems to be a book about the culture of exotics.... It seems a morbid and middle-class affair'.

Hichens and Wilde only met on a few occasions; Hichens said that Oscar looked like 'a very superior, amiable and successful conjuror', but added that 'he was, I should say, an eminently likeable man'.

When Wilde was arrested, Hichens, (himself homosexual), was mortified that his satire might have been a contributory factor in causing the anti-Wilde ferment, and decided to withdraw 'The Green Carnation' from circulation. He refused to reprint it until 1950, years after the deaths of both Oscar and Bosie.

Hichens was perhaps too hesitant and gentle to be a true satirist. Ada Leverson said that he was: 'a novelist who spends half his time being afraid people should think his work is lurid, and the rest in being simply terrified that people should think it's not'.

Having begun his career as a song lyricist, Hichens became a journalist, and followed *GB Shaw* as music critic of 'The World'. After the popular reception of 'The Green Carnation', he went on to write at least a dozen other novels and plays that were well received, especially in the USA. In 1904, inspired by a trip to the Sahara, he wrote 'The Garden of Allah', a play later filmed with Marlene Dietrich in the lead.

He became something of an opulent nomad roaming North Africa and living mainly in Switzerland or the French Riviera. Someone said of Hichens that he was 'a slave of his own freedom'.

He met many famous personages in Egypt including the archaeologist Howard Carter, ('an extremely rude man' according to Hichens), and was present when King Edward VIII, (later Duke of Windsor) hit a golf ball from the top of the Great Pyramid.

He also witnessed an incident involving the deposed King Alfonso of Spain, soon after he arrived to spend some of his exile in Rome. One evening, the King invited two American ladies to dine with him at the finest restaurant in the city. After an enormous meal, the party continued by car to see the sights of Rome by moonlight.

Unfortunately the meal proved too rich for King Alfonso. At one point, he was suddenly overcome by nausea and, leaning out of the car window, threw up into the Trevi Fountain.

At that very moment, a Spanish tourist rounded the corner and suddenly spotted his lost monarch before him. Instantly sweeping his hat from his head, the man bowed and reverently exclaimed: "Your Majesty!"

Alfonso was forced to attempt the difficult job of simultaneously waving a regal acknowledgement while also vomiting into one of Rome's architectural glories.

1894

[In Britain, William Gladstone resigned as Prime Minister for the last time and was succeeded by the Liberal Lord Rosebery.

There was continuing unrest in France, consisting mostly of the bombings of Parisian restaurants and reprisal executions. After a young anarchist named Emile Henry was guillotined for throwing a bomb into the Chamber of Deputies, President Sidi Carnot was assassinated in Lyons in a revenge attack by an Italian anarchist.

Also in France, a Jewish army captain, Alfred Dreyfus, was arrested and court-martialled, accused of spying for the Germans.]

During Bosie Douglas's absence of almost three months, Wilde had been staying at the St James Place hotel in London. He used the time to complete his new play, 'An Ideal Husband', and to work on two new plays, 'A Florentine Tragedy' and 'La Sainte Courtisane'.

'La Sainte Courtisane', (or 'The Woman Covered in Jewels'), was partly completed when Wilde was imprisoned in 1895. He left the manuscript with Ada Leverson, who guarded it safely till his release. Wilde himself then lost it when he left it behind by accident in a Paris taxicab.

Wilde finished most of 'The Florentine Tragedy' but failed to write the opening act. Robbie Ross: "It was characteristic of Wilde to finish what he never began". The composer Puccini expressed an interest in turning the remaining section into an opera, but the idea fizzled out. In the 1900s, the critic T Sturge Moore constructed a first act for the play and it was performed as a double bill with 'Salome'.

In February 1894, the English script of 'Salome', illustrated by Aubrey Beardsley, was published in London. Wilde disliked Beardsley's contribution – Ada Leverson explained that Oscar wanted everything in 'purple and gold', while Beardsley wanted everything in 'black and white'. Leverson: "Beardsley had the gift of line, but he didn't always know where to draw it".

Meanwhile, in Egypt, Bosie Douglas's attempt to become a diplomatic attaché in Constantinople had been rejected by the British Ambassador, Lord Currie. (It is possible that Currie's aide, Rennell Rodd, knowing what Bosie was like, had warned his superior.)

In March, Wilde, with some reluctance, agreed to Bosie Douglas's pleas for a meeting. Bosie, now returned from Egypt, met him in Paris and on March 31st the pair returned together to London.

On April 16, the first edition of 'The Yellow Book' was published, with Henry Harland as editor, Aubrey Beardsley as art editor, and John Lane as publisher. That night, a gala celebratory dinner was held at the Hotel L'Italie in Old Compton Street, Soho, attended by over fifty contributors.

JOHN LANE 1854-1925

Although John Lane became Wilde's main publisher in the early 1890s, producing among other works 'Lady Windermere's Fan' in 1891 and 'Salome' in 1893, the two men did not like each other. Oscar disdained what he saw as Lane's timidity, in particular when Lane became dubious over the covert homosexual implications of Oscar's story, 'The Portrait of Mr W.H.'

When Oscar came to write 'The Importance of Being Earnest' in 1895, he deliberately named the two butlers in the play 'Lane' and 'Matthews' – (Elkin Matthews being Lane's business partner at the time). Realising that this was a little too obvious, he changed 'Matthews' to 'Merriman' in the finished script, but still retained 'Lane' as the name of the first servant.

For his part, Lane was annoyed when Wilde seduced Edward Shelley, one of the clerks at Lane's publishing firm, the Bodley Head. Shelley complained that he had had to leave the firm after his fellow clerks started calling him 'Miss Oscar'.

Born in Devon, a county for which he held a lifelong affection, John Lane had little formal education. He arrived in London aged 14 and for the next eighteen years worked as a railway clerk. In 1887, he persuaded Elkin Matthews, an Exeter-based book-dealer, to go into partnership firstly in a London bookshop and then in 1889 as publishers. (According to *Arthur Symons*, Matthews was 'the slowest of people' and, although useful to Lane in the early years, was elbowed out of the partnership in 1894.)

Naming his firm the 'Bodley Head', Lane built a reputation for producing books of artistic merit and nurturing excellent new writers. The firm's premises soon became a social centre for poets, with an atmosphere so informal that several of Lane's authors used the floor as impromptu lodgings on impecunious nights. When one poet needed his dress trousers to attend some function, it was Lane who redeemed them from the pawnshop.

As a businessman, Lane was tough to the point of meanness, but retained an element of idealism. He once retorted to a New York reporter: "Do I not sell dreams and live on poetry?" Always well groomed, Lane was known for his pursuit of girls, thereby gaining the nickname of 'Petticoat Lane'.

He had an instinctive eye for spotting artistic talent in others but suffered from his own lack of sophistication on the subject. *Max Beerbohm* claimed that Lane had once enthused over a *Beardsley* drawing: "Look at the technique! What workmanship! Look, he never goes over the edges!"

The concept behind The Yellow Book, though, was a conscious decision to create a magazine that would be a work of art in its own right and, to this end, Lane agreed to ban adverts from its pages. The list of contributors was almost a roll call of 1890s talent – among many other writers, *Ernest Dowson, Sir Edmund Gosse, Henry James, Anatole France, George Moore, Max Beerbohm, Arthur Symons* and Arthur Benson all provided material. The artists included Lord Leighton, *William Rothenstein*, John Singer Sargent, *Walter Sickert*, and, of course, Aubrey Beardsley.

In fact, one of the very few notables missing was Oscar Wilde himself. Lane had agreed with Beardsley that Oscar's presence would overbalance the magazine and the editorial team ignored any possible contribution he might have made.

A decidedly miffed Oscar speculated on the probable 'Yellow Book' frontispiece that Beardsley would produce: "Oh you can imagine the sort of thing. A terrible naked harlot smiling through a mask – and with Elkin Mathews on one breast and John Lane on the other'.

Although the Yellow Book itself, apart from Beardsley's exotic input, was actually quite mild, its critics worked themselves into a frenzy of outrage. As well as repeated attacks from Punch, the Times inexplicably called it: 'a mixture of English rowdyism and French lubricity'.

In April 1895, John Lane was in New York when he spotted a newspaper placard reading: 'Oscar Wilde Arrested: Yellow Book Under His Arm'. To his horror, he realised that the magazine had been linked mistakenly with Wilde's conduct and was tarred irredeemably with the same brush. More worryingly, it dawned on Lane that it might be thought that he had knowingly supplied Wilde with the sexual services of the Bodley Head clerk Shelley.

Matters grew worse when the news arrived that an angry mob had stoned the windows of the Bodley Head offices in London. Then Lane received a telegram from six of his most important authors threatening that, unless he removed Wilde's name from the Bodley Head list and sacked Beardsley from the Yellow Book, they would all withdraw their books from his firm.

Lane made the expedient but un-heroic decision to bow to their demands. It saved the publishing house but brought a lot of criticism, especially over the dismissal of Beardsley. Sir William Rothenstein wrote: 'My scant respect for Lane was still further diminished', while the rival publisher, Grant Richards, said: "Lane was not a man of great courage – he would trim his sails".

Without Beardsley, the Yellow Book struggled on for a couple of years but closed in April 1897.

Having been once bitten, Lane now became obsessively suspicious over any hint of obscenity or deviation – a friend said that Lane 'saw a pervert behind every tree'. The Bodley Head, though, went from strength to strength, publishing the collected works of Anatole France in English, HG Wells, GK Chesterton, Rupert Brooke, and Stephen Leacock. In particular he nurtured the young British comic writer Hector Hugh Munro, known as 'Saki'.

For all his shortcomings, John Lane had an endearing respect for the superiority of the artist. One day he was subjected to a tirade of furious abuse by an agitated poet, which ended with the man hurling an ornamental table against the wall and striding out of the office. Lane, trying to piece together the broken remnants of his table, was heard to murmur: "This is one of the sacrifices that mediocrity must needs make to genius".

Lane's editor at the Yellow Book, **HENRY HARLAND** (1861 – 1905), was a cosmopolitan character of American nationality, born in Russia and partly raised in Rome, who studied at the Universities of Paris and Harvard.

Under the pen name of 'Sidney Luska', he enjoyed some success with sensationalist novels about poverty-stricken Jewish life in America. He married an American girl called Aline Meriam in 1884, and in 1889 came to London to work for the Bodley Head Press.

After the demise of the Yellow Book, Harland continued to write, and his novel, 'The Cardinal's Snuff Box', in 1900 was well received. Vincent O'Sullivan called him 'a sort of lemonade Henry James'.

In spite of his Connecticut background, Harland never tired of hinting that he was the offspring of mysterious but elevated European parentage – Emperor Franz-Joseph of Austria being the usual paternal candidate.

The poet *Richard Le Gallienne* said that Harland was: "One of those Americans in love with Paris, who seem more French than the French, a slim, gesticulating, goateed, snub-nosed lovable figure".

Wilde had dinner with Henry and Aline Harland at a Parisian café in 1898 and said that 'they were both very nice'. He may well have appreciated Harland's full-blooded embrace of Parisian life as described in a letter Harland sent to Le Gallienne: 'Come to Paris! We will spend laborious days and tavern nights…we'll sup with dear old *Verlaine*, and breakfast with the Muses. We'll walk in the Bois de Boulogne, loaf in the Boulevards, and listen to the band in the Luxembourg…'

FREDERICK ROLFE ('BARON CORVO' 1860-1913) was one of the oddest of the Yellow Book contributors. He was an exceptionally hard working teetotaller who somehow managed to ruin almost every opportunity that presented itself.

He was born into a respectable London family and began adult life as a schoolteacher. Then in 1886 he converted to Roman Catholicism and decided to enter the priesthood. Wilde's friend Vincent O'Sullivan, who knew him during this period, said that Rolfe was 'a man with only the very vaguest sense of realities'.

Having been ejected from the St Marie's College of Oscott for spending more time on his hobby of painting than on study, he was next expelled from the Scots College in Rome, owing partly to his lack of a vocation, and partly to numerous outstanding bills. After a fiery interview with the Rector, Rolfe departed snarling about 'the pestilent, pretentious, bestial insanity' of the Scots College.

The one positive result of his Italian sojourn was his friendship with the very elderly Duchess Carolina Sforza, who gave him an allowance and permitted him to use the honorary (but virtually meaningless) title of 'Baron Corvo'. In 1891, he moved to Christchurch in Hampshire, but mounting debts to local tradesmen and the disappearance of the Duchess's allowance forced him to leave.

Having failed to build a career in photography in London, he moved on to Aberdeen, where he was sacked from his new job as tutor to the Laird of Seaton. 'Baron Corvo' was now in dire financial straits.

The landlord of his lodgings in Aberdeen, faced with several weeks of unpaid rent, resolved to remove him from the house. Rolfe was equally determined to stay and refused to leave his room, or even move from his bed, in case he was ejected by surprise.

At length, the landlord secured the services of two burly workmen who arrived in Rolfe's bedroom. Rolfe grabbed the iron bedstead and clung on grimly. His fingers were prised open and he was dragged out to the staircase. The banisters provided a further hold and the struggle resumed. Superior strength won the day and Rolfe was hurled, still in his pyjamas, out into the street, as his possessions cascaded around him from the bedroom window.

Rolfe next appeared, calling himself 'Father Austin', at Holywell, near Flint in North Wales. He secured the commission to paint a series of religious banners for the custodian of the miraculous well of Saint Winefride, the Rev. Father Sidney de Vere Beauclerk. For a short time this arrangement seemed to work, despite 'Father Austin's' occasional trips to Rhyll to hire prostitutes.

On completion of the banners, Rolfe demanded £100 payment, which the shocked Rev. Beauclerk rejected. Rolfe promptly raised his price to £1000. When Rev. Beauclerk offered him only £50, Rolfe accused the Church of defrauding him and began a campaign of vilification against the Reverend.

He rented a first floor room on the main street so that he could shout abuse at Beauclerk as the priest passed by below him on religious processions to St Winefride's miraculous well. Rolfe followed this by starving himself for three days so that he could dramatically collapse from hunger in the street, adding to Beauclerk's embarrassment.

When Rolfe made sure that wide publicity was given to his entry into the workhouse, the scandal forced the Church authorities to remove Beauclerk from his position.

This victory may have satisfied Rolfe's pride, but it did not help his pocket. During 1894/5 he barely survived in London, but in 1896, turning to writing, his 'Stories Toto Told Me' were accepted by Henry Harland for the Yellow Book.

Rolfe was not the most salubrious of literary gentlemen and, after he had been to one of Harland's Saturday afternoon soirees at Harland's home in the Cromwell Road, Harland had to have the furniture sprayed with insecticide to rid the house of Rolfe's fleas.

Under his new assumed name of 'The Reverend FW Rolfe, Late Professor of English Literature and History at St. Marie's College of Oscott', Rolfe was delighted to accept a commission from the publisher Grant Richards to write a book on the Borgias.

He plunged himself unreservedly into the work and after years of research produced a vast genealogical family tree of the notorious Borgia family. Rolfe expressed disappointment on discovery that the last Borgia had been a Methodist. The book appeared in 1901 but was a financial failure, for which Rolfe blamed Grant Richard personally.

In 1903, Rolfe produced a new translation of 'The Rubaiyat of Omar Khayyam'. (The more famous version by Edward Fitzgerald had been attacked by Non-Conformist clergymen for its praise of the salacious. One of them riposted with his own variation of the Rubaiyat: 'Abstain from chambering and wantonness, The lewd lascivious couch forbear to press', etc., while another criticised Fitzgerald's apparent taste for 'wallowing with houris'. In fact, Fitzgerald was homosexual and lived with a huge Norfolk fisherman.)

Rolfe now decided to drop his 'Baron Corvo' persona in favour of 'Fr. Rolfe'. (The 'Fr.' referred to his forename of 'Frederick' rather than for 'Father', but Rolfe was not quick to correct those who assumed the latter). In 1904, he wrote what was undoubtedly his best book, 'Hadrian VII' – a work that was successfully dramatised in 1967 by the playwright Peter Luke.

Rolfe's life was still dogged by poverty, and he hit on the idea of co-writing books with well-connected hopefuls. One of these was *Bosie Douglas's* younger brother, Lord Sholto Douglas, who soon backed off. Another was *EF Benson's* brother, Father Hugh Benson.

Hugh, having described Rolfe as 'a quiet gentle man of great intellectual attainments who has spent most of his life in obscure study at Oxford', agreed to collaborate on a book about St Thomas a Beckett.

Then he heard Grant Richards's account of seeing Rolfe at Oxford: 'He was sitting under the Parson's Pleasure willows on a decrepit chair, rolling cigarette after cigarette in his nicotine-stained fingers, and surveying the flesh tints of youth with unbecoming satisfaction. That was at the time he was acting as secretary to the Principal of Jesus College'. Hugh Benson withdrew from the St Thomas a Beckett project.

While in Wales, Rolfe met an archaeologist, one Professor Dawkins, who was persuaded to take Rolfe on a holiday to Venice with a view to another book collaboration. When Dawkins discovered the extent of Rolfe's extravagance with Dawkins's money, the professor hastily left the city, leaving Rolfe behind.

Nothing loath to remain in Venice, which he adored, Rolfe spent most of his time writing abusive letters to the many people he considered to have let him down. Hugh Benson in particular received insulting bulletins almost daily. In one letter, Rolfe announced his intention of committing suicide 'as slowly and as publicly and as annoyingly' as he could, to embarrass the defaulters. In the event, he didn't.

By 1909, Rolfe was reduced to applying for a job as assistant gondolier. When even this failed, he survived by becoming a homosexual pimp. In spite of his adventures with the prostitutes of Rhyll, Rolfe preferred homosexuality.

He acquired new lodgings through a stroke of luck. One day, he fell overboard from a gondola while smoking a pipe. The Venetian onlookers watched as Rolfe returned to the surface, still with the pipe clenched between his teeth, and climbed back on board. He then refilled and relit the pipe and solemnly resumed his journey.

Such Anglo-Saxon sang froid made a deep impression and he was offered membership of the Bucintoro Boat Club as a result. He accepted with alacrity as this offered him the opportunity to use the club boats as sleeping accommodation.

Eventually living rough in an open boat and constantly bitten by rats destroyed his health and he died in 1913. His last letter ended with the words: 'For God's sake, send me five pounds'.

On April 1ˢᵗ 1894, two weeks before the 'Yellow Book' first edition party, Wilde and Bosie Douglas had been having lunch at the Café Royal. During the meal, Bosie's father, the Marquess of Queensberry, came to sit with them.

Wilde and the Marquess had not met before, and Queensberry rather enjoyed Oscar's company. They left on good terms.

Later that day, the Marquess of Queensberry began to have second thoughts.

PART FOUR

EXILE

Lord Rosebery to Reggie Turner

Wilde travelled to Paris on 27 April 1894; then on 6 May 1894 joined Bosie Douglas in Florence, Italy, where they met up with Andre Gide again.

Returning to London in June, they discovered that the Marquess of Queensberry, having recovered from his lapse into toleration at the Café Royal, had begun a campaign of vilification by letter against Bosie's association with Wilde. Wilde consulted a solicitor, Charles Humphries, over the situation, but took no further action.

On June 11th, Wilde's poem, 'The Sphinx', (originally written in the 1880s), was published. Oscar said: "My first idea was to print three copies – one for myself, one for the British Museum, and one for Heaven. I had some doubts about the British Museum".

On June 30th Queensberry arrived at Wilde's house in Tite Street intending to force Wilde to end his friendship with Bosie; the details of the encounter differed. Although Queensberry failed to in this attempt, Wilde was becoming decidedly edgy about his tantrum-plagued affair with the tempestuous Bosie.

In July 1894, Wilde's 'Poems in Prose' was published in the Fortnightly Review – they included 'The Artist', 'The Doer of Good' and 'The Master'.

Oscar's social life continued at full pelt. On July 17th he lunched with Wilfred Blunt and the rising political star, HH Asquith, and gave, according to Blunt, 'a brilliant verbal display'.

He spent many evenings at the fashionable Willis's Rooms in King St, off St James St. Known for its yellow-shaded candles and scarlet leather seats, it was run by a famous restaurateur called Jules. Wilde mentioned the establishment in 'The Importance of Being Earnest'. (Later it became an auctioneer's saleroom and was destroyed by bombs in 1941.)

In spite of the money that he had earned through his first two plays, Wilde's expenditure was cripplingly large.

When a friend mentioned that money was tight, Oscar replied: "Ah yes, and of a tightness that has been felt even in Tite Street. Believe me, I passed the forenoon at the British Museum looking at a gold-piece in a case".

He wrote to another friend: 'As I have no play going on this season I have no money at all, and indeed am at my wits' end trying to raise some for household expenses and such tedious things.'

Wilde: 'Those who pay their bills are soon forgotten. It is only by not paying one's bills that one can hope to live in the memory of the commercial classes.'

By August 1894, noticing that he now owed £40 to his bank, he determined to try to economise. Instead of spending a summer holiday at one of the more fashionable resorts, he chose to take his family to Worthing in Sussex, (owing to a typhoid outbreak in the previous year, Worthing hotels were very cheap in 1894).

He was to stay on the South Coast from August to October, engaged mostly in writing a new play, 'The Importance of Being Earnest'.

On 12 August, Oscar had a narrow escape from drowning when he and two local boys, one of them named Alphonso Conway, sailed along the coast to Littlehampton. They were caught for five hours in a bad gale, only reaching the pier at Worthing at 11pm.

Oscar reported that it was 'quite a dangerous adventure', but seemed more upset by the fact that, as their return was after 10pm on a Sunday, the hotel proprietor was not allowed to serve them restorative brandy – 'What laws! Both Alphonso and Stephen are now anarchists, I need hardly say!'

According to later trial evidence, Wilde had sex with Alphonso during this period.

Meanwhile, back in London, on the same night as Oscar's maritime escapade, the police raided a house in Fitzroy St, Bloomsbury, and arrested several men on suspicion of having committed *homosexual acts. The raid gained some publicity although, owing to lack of evidence, all were discharged or bound over.*

However one of the accused was an acquaintance of Wilde called Alfred Taylor, who had been arrested wearing a yellow taffeta gown and layered petticoats. Taylor was the son of a wealthy cocoa manufacturer who had inherited £45,000, but who had become bankrupt by 1893. (Later, he was Wilde's co-defendant at the trials and was also to suffer imprisonment before disappearing from England. In 1901, Bosie Douglas stayed in Boston and was amazed to find that Taylor was a waiter at his hotel.)

The law was getting uncomfortably close to the Wilde circle, and when 'The Green Carnation', Robert Hichen's book satirising Oscar's effeminacy, was published in September 1894, it did not help matters.

In October, having been absent for a while, Bosie Douglas arrived in Worthing. Not liking the town, he persuaded Oscar to move to Brighton, firstly staying at the expensive Grand Hotel, then in lodgings. It was a period marked by titanic quarrels between the pair, ending when Oscar fell ill and Bosie abandoned him to return to London.

By 14th October 1894, Oscar had reached a decision that he genuinely wished to break with the difficult and potentially ruinous Bosie.

Then on the 18th October, he heard the news that Bosie's elder brother, Viscount Drumlanrig, was dead.

DRUMLANRIG – FRANCIS DOUGLAS, VISCOUNT 1867 – 1894

As the eldest son and heir of the Marquess of Queensberry, Francis Douglas, (named after his uncle who had died on the Matterhorn), automatically received the honorary title of Viscount Drumlanrig. Educated at Harrow, he was commissioned as a lieutenant in the Coldstream Guards.

Under the influence of his maternal grandfather, Alfred Montgomery, he rejected his father's Tory politics and became a Liberal. Montgomery introduced him to the important politician, Lord Rosebery, who offered Drumlanrig a post as one of his private secretaries. Resigning his commission, he joined the Liberal peer when, with the re-election of *Gladstone* in 1892, Rosebery became British Foreign Secretary.

With Rosebery's help, Drumlanrig was given a place in the House of Lords so that, if necessary, he could represent the Government in the Upper House. Queensberry, who since 1881 had not been allowed to take his place as a representative peer in the Lords, was angered by his son's elevation and political bent, and never spoke to him again.

In 1894, Rosebery became Prime Minister, and his protégé Drumlanrig became engaged to a general's daughter called Alix Ellis. Just before their marriage, on October 18th 1894, while staying at Quantock Lodge, near Bridgewater, Somerset, Drumlanrig was found dead of gunshot wounds. Although the inquest was told that he had been shot upwards through the mouth, (a highly unlikely accident), the coroner's conclusion was 'accidental death'.

Wilde, who had not known Drumlanrig well but was complimentary about him, was immediately sympathetic over Bosie's loss of his eldest brother. Oscar: 'It is a great blow to Bosie; the first noble sorrow of his boyish life... I am perforce the sharer of his pain.' Against his better judgement, he rejoined Bosie, thus setting the stage for the denouement of their doomed affair.

Behind the bare bones of Drumlanrig's life, however, lay a much more complicated situation. His suspicious death gave impetus to the many rumours circulating about his true relationship with Lord Rosebery. Although handsome and hardworking, Drumlanrig was not especially intelligent and showed little aptitude for high-level politics. He had been an unlikely

372

choice to be a close aide to a Prime Minister. As Wilde wrote in 'De Profundis' in 1897, their association was 'stained with a darker suggestion'.

The implication was that Drumlanrig was in fact Rosebery's boyfriend, a possibility that Queensberry certainly believed. Another top Liberal, Lewis Harcourt, (the homosexual son of Sir William Harcourt, nicknamed 'LouLou' – and rumoured to have committed suicide himself to avoid a paedophile scandal in 1921), was also convinced that this was the truth. When he heard of Drumlanrig's engagement, 'LouLou' gasped: "Drumlanrig is going to marry General Ellis's daughter? It makes the institution of marriage ridiculous!"

Later, (and separately), both Drumlanrig's nephew, the 11th Marquess of Queensberry, and Bosie Douglas said that they were convinced that Drumlanrig had committed suicide 'in the shadow of a suppressed scandal'.

ROSEBERY – ARCHIBALD PRIMROSE, LORD 1847 - 1929

Rumours about homosexuality had dogged Lord Rosebery from his Eton schooldays when he was the pet boy of the notorious schoolmaster William Johnson, (later Cory). After they holidayed in Italy together in 1864, it was said that the friendship 'could hardly have been wholesome'.

In his memoirs, Sir Edmund Backhouse claimed to have had 'a slow and protracted copulation' with Rosebery in September 1893. (Although Backhouse's accounts of his sexual adventures were completely unreliable, his choice of famous 'partners' was such as convince his readers that he was telling the truth. Therefore his accounts of sex with known homosexuals like Wilde or *Verlaine* or with a renowned voluptuary such as the Empress of China were intended to make Backhouse's claims more believable. By choosing Rosebery to be one of these 'lovers', the implication was that the public would have little difficulty in believing the allegation.)

When 'LouLou' Harcourt, (admittedly a political enemy), was told that Rosebery, although Prime Minister, still insisted on opening all his own letters and parcels, Harcourt said that he was not surprised, 'considering some of the things which, to my knowledge, some of them must contain'. (Rosebery was a collector of pornography, mostly supplied by Harry Nichols, the partner of the publisher *Leonard Smithers*.)

Whatever the truth, the Marquess of Queensberry certainly believed that the Foreign Secretary had seduced his eldest son, and launched into a campaign of abuse. Having complained to *Queen Victoria* about Rosebery's 'bad influence' over Drumlanrig, in 1893 Queensberry pursued his quarry to the resort of Bad Homburg in Germany. Arriving at Rosebery's hotel armed with a dog whip, he was only dissuaded from thrashing Rosebery by the intervention of the *Prince of Wales*, who was also at the hotel. The Prince of Wales then induced the Homburg Chief of Police to run Queensberry out of town 'by the 7am train to Paris'.

Rosebery tried to dismiss the incident – 'being pursued by a pugilist of unsound mind' was one of the disadvantages of high office. Queensberry continued his attacks by letter, some of his choicer comments on Rosebery being: 'damned cur and coward', 'snob queer', and 'Jew fiend liar'.

Some of these letters emerged at the committal stage of Wilde's prosecution of Queensberry in 1895. Although the presiding magistrate forbade their open disclosure, by chance the jury happened to contain a French journalist who gleefully relayed the information to the Paris press that the British Prime Minister was involved in the already infamous case. During the libel trial against Queensberry and the first trial of Oscar Wilde, (the latter ending in a hung jury), the British press was muzzled and Rosebery's name did not emerge.

There was some puzzlement when the authorities insisted on going ahead with Wilde's second trial; it seemed to many to be unnecessarily vindictive. *Sir Edward Carson*, who as Queensberry's counsel had destroyed Wilde's testimony during the first encounter, was one of the people who questioned it.

He asked the Solicitor-General, Sir Frank Lockwood, (Wilde's next prosecutor): "Cannot you let up on the fellow now? He has suffered a great deal". Lockwood replied: "We cannot, we dare not. It would be said at once that owing to the names mentioned in Queensberry's letters we were forced to abandon it" The Irish nationalist leader at Westminster, Tim Healy, also asked Lockwood to drop the case; Lockwood told him: "I would do so but for the abominable rumours against Rosebery". Additionally, there was a strong possibility that Queensberry had threatened to reveal everything unless Wilde was prosecuted with full rigour.

Rosebery himself asked his Home Secretary, *HH Asquith*, if they could do anything to help Wilde. Asquith replied grimly: "If you do, you will lose the election." During part of the period of Wilde's trials, (from 13th to 20th May), Rosebery, although still Prime Minister, disappeared on a sea voyage for health reasons.

Their paths crossed again when Rosebery bought the Villa Delahante at Posillipo, near Naples, Italy. The area, which included Capri, was a notoriously homosexual resort at the time; (Italy had legalised sex between men in 1891). When Wilde, recently released from prison, rented a villa in the same town in December 1897, the British Consul, E. Neville-Rolfe, sent a letter to Rosebery warning him of the embarrassing new arrival but suggesting that Oscar did not seem likely to produce any new scandal: 'He looks thoroughly abashed, much like a whipped hound…I really cannot think he will be any trouble to you, and after all the poor devil must live somewhere.'

Unsubstantiated gossip about Rosebery's own activities in Posillipo continued to circulate for many years afterwards.

Almost everyone who met Rosebery commented on his unfathomable and contradictory nature. Politically he was almost a Radical, yet described democracy contemptuously as 'the Tom, Dick, and Harry business'. He was a convinced reforming Liberal but also an ardent imperialist. He was an accomplished wit and epigrammatist, ('Vanity is a centipede with corns on every foot'), yet was known for his off-putting silences. He was an aloof aristocrat who as a member of the London Council was nicknamed 'Citizen Rosebery'.

Gladstone called him 'an incalculable man – one of the most incalculable I have ever known', while the Liberal politician John Morley said that Rosebery was 'a dark horse in a loose box'. Rosebery: 'I must plough my furrow alone'.

As a youth Rosebery memorably announced his intention was to win the Derby, to become Prime Minister, and to marry an heiress. He achieved all three ambitions.

He was a keen sportsman whose refusal to give up his stud of steeple-chasers while at Oxford caused the authorities to send him down without a degree. (One of Rosebery's favourite stories involved a fellow undergraduate who, after losing £7000 at the Goodwood Races, sent a telegram to his father asking him to pay the debt. 'Dear Dad, please do cough it up by Monday. Unfortunately I cannot meet you in town as I am now going on to the Lewes Races'.)

Rosebery's other sporting passions were yachting and shooting. Even as an elderly man he was reputed to have killed 651 rabbits in three hours; (he once accidentally shot Margot Asquith's father, Sir Charles Tennant, in the testicles).

In 1873, he travelled to North America where he met *Sam Ward* and paid a visit to the Canadian Parliament, where he was amazed at the length of the speeches. 'I was in the House five days and five nights; in the course of which I heard one speech of five hours, one of four, several of three, the rest of the sitting was filled up by speechlets of two hours.'

When he told one Canadian MP that at Westminster a four hour parliamentary speech was almost unknown, the man replied: "Ah, but in England you have no speakers to whom you could listen for four hours."

After a further trip to Australia, Rosebery returned to Britain convinced of the imperial ideal, despite the prospect of unfettered verbosity.

In 1878, he accomplished his first ambition by marrying Hannah de Rothschild, the hugely opulent daughter of Baron Nathan Meyer de Rothschild. She produced four children before her early death from typhoid fever in 1890.

After the Liberal victory of 1892, Rosebery was appointed Foreign Secretary. Then, after Gladstone's resignation in 1894, Rosebery achieved his second ambition of becoming Prime Minister, albeit reluctantly. He himself doubted his fitness for office, admitting that 'long loneliness and sleeplessness' was blurring his judgement.

His sixteen months as PM were unsuccessful mostly because, as he said himself, 'I never did have power'. His government was forced to survive on a majority of eight votes, while the Tory House of Lords blocked nearly all his initiatives. Even worse, he was faced with deep hostility within his own party.

Sir William Harcourt, Home Secretary and then Chancellor of the Exchequer, loathed Rosebery. Their mutual dislike was rumoured to have begun when Harcourt, (a rotund gentleman), passed Rosebery's desk and spotted a caricature of himself as 'Jumbo', a famous London Zoo elephant. The offended Harcourt retaliated by calling Rosebery 'Pretty Fanny'.

Harcourt had expected to become Prime Minister before being pipped at the post by *Queen Victoria's* preference for 'Pretty Fanny', and made no attempt to hide his annoyance. When Rosebery insisted on making Uganda a British colony, the anti-imperialist Harcourt rasped: "Is there no pie in the world out of which we can manage to keep our fingers?"

Rosebery's fulfilment of his third ambition, that of his horse winning the Derby, became something of a millstone when puritanical elements in the Liberal party objected to a Prime Minister, already seen as an epicurean lightweight, indulging in triviality. Rosebery: 'Although without guilt or offence I might perpetually run seconds and thirds, or even run last, it became a matter of torture to many consciences if I won'.

By the spring of 1895, Rosebery had had enough. When in June, beset by the strains of his job and an attack of influenza, he lost a minor vote in the Commons, he seized the opportunity to dissolve Parliament. (That fact that the Wilde scandal had culminated in a guilty verdict one month earlier may have had some bearing on his decision.)

Rosebery and the Liberals lost the new election, ushering in an eleven-year period of Tory rule. When in 1898, he also lost the leadership of the Liberal party, his state of mind could be judged by his diary entry after his last speech: 'Home to supper. What a relief!'

Although he occasionally dabbled in British politics over the next 30 years, Rosebery seemed more than happy to remain at his Naples villa where, in his own words, he settled into becoming 'a male dowager'. He eventually gave his Italian villa to the British Government in 1909.

Rosebery's marriage to Hannah had given him an entry into the then most powerful clan in the world. Through financial manipulation, the **ROTHSCHILD FAMILY** had become a crucial ally to the governments of several European nations, including Britain and France.

Hannah's father, Baron Mayer Amschel de Rothschild, had died in 1874, leaving her the heiress to £9 million and a stately home called Mentmore, near Aylesbury, Buckinghamshire. (*Lord Ronald Gower* visited the house but dismissed it as 'too gaudy'. He complained about the dangers of a 'great door of glass, twenty feet high by ten wide. No wonder Admiral Rous walked bang up into it'.)

Hannah's relative, Lionel de Rothschild, was the financier who lent the money that enabled the British Prime Minister *Benjamin Disraeli* to purchase the crucial shares in the Suez Canal deal of 1875. *Frank Harris* claimed that Rothschild had backed the arrangement because he wanted repayment of a loan he had made to the Khedive of Egypt. When the British made the purchase, Rothschild was able to reclaim the debt as well as adding his commission.

Harris: "I thought of a drama on the subject and told it to Wilde who used the story in a play'.

The work in question was 'An Ideal Husband'. One speech touched on the influence on the hero, 'Sir Robert Chiltern', of an unseen character called 'Baron Arnheim' during the Suez Canal negotiations. Whether Wilde intended 'Arnheim' to be an oblique reference to the Rothschilds is arguable:

'He made me wonder at the strange loveliness of the luxury in which he lived; and then told me that luxury was nothing but a background, a painted scene in a play, and that power, power over other men, power over the world, was the one thing worth having, the one supreme pleasure worth knowing, the one joy one never tired of, and that in our century only the rich possessed it'.

Frank Harris was fascinated by the obsessive caution displayed by the immensely wealthy Rothschilds, recounting how the family always kept £1 million in gold sovereigns in a strong room. The founder of the dynasty had dictated the rule that they should always hold it to one side 'to give a sense of security'.

Harris expressed surprise when Rothschild told him that he had turned down a transaction that had netted their rival Baring's over £1 million in a day. Lord Rothschild explained that: "When I say 'No' to every scheme and enterprise submitted to me, I return home at night carefree and contented. But when I agree to any proposal, I am immediately filled with anxiety. To say 'Yes' is like putting your finger in a machine – the whirring wheels may drag your whole body in after the finger".

The Rothschilds' prudence did not prevent the family living in great state. The politician *HH Asquith* reported visiting Lord Rothschild's home at Waddesdon Manor, Buckinghamshire. The butler enquired whether Asquith would like: "Tea, coffee, or sherry, sir?" Asquith replied: "Tea, please". The butler continued: "China, Indian, or Ceylon, sir?" "China, please." "Lemon, milk, or cream, sir?" "Milk, please." "Jersey, Hereford, or Shorthorn, sir?"

Unfortunately, even the Rothschilds could not evade the ravages of age. *George Cornwallis-West* was once invited to dinner at Waddesdon Manor. Although the guests included some of the most illustrious names of the business world, the young and relatively undistinguished George found himself seated at Lord Rothschild's right hand.

He discovered why he had been given this honour when Rothschild sat throughout the meal with only a plate of biscuits and a glass of milk in front of him. As each mouth-watering dish was served up by the world famous chef, Rothschild insisted that George describe the sensation of every taste. He realised that Rothschild had been condemned to a strict diet and George, being the junior member of the company, had been given the job of feeding Rothschild's imagination. "He was eating by proxy, and I was his taster!"

On October 19 1894, Wilde returned to London and reconciled with Bosie Douglas.

In November, 'A Few Maxims for the Instruction of the Over-Educated' was published in The Saturday Review, followed in December by the publication of 'Phrases and Philosophies for the Use of the Young' in The Chameleon.

>*Also in December rehearsals started on Oscar's new play, 'An Ideal Husband'. They continued even on Christmas Day.*

1895

>*[The X-ray was discovered.*
>*In France, Captain Alfred Dreyfus was transported to Devil's Island.*
>*In Britain, the Liberal Government was defeated and in June Lord Salisbury began his third premiership. With the knighthood of Henry Irving, the British theatre reached the apotheosis of gentrification.*
>*A woman was burned as a witch at Cloneen, Co. Tipperary, Ireland, and the London School of Economics was founded in London.*
>*In December, Dr Jameson led a raid into the Boer Republics in South Africa, but was swiftly defeated and captured.]*

>*On January 3 1895, Wilde's 'An Ideal Husband' (originally entitled 'Mrs Cheveley'), opened at the Haymarket Theatre.*

AN IDEAL HUSBAND

EF Benson criticised the play, claiming that Wilde's dramatic skills were merely a continuation of RB Sheridan's 18th century style. Wilde: 'I do not rate Sheridan very high. I consider Congreve far beyond him'.

Punch also attacked claiming that 'An Ideal Husband' had 'the plot of a shilling shocker – much diluted'.

Oscar's habit of giving a flippant speech to the audience at the curtain call came under fire as well. *GB Shaw* said that the criticism was too hard on Wilde: "His 'I have enjoyed myself very much' was an Irishman's way of giving all the credit to the actors and effacing his own claims as author".

The play itself rose above its detractors and was an immediate success. The producer and leading actor was Lewis Waller.

LEWIS WALLER 1860-1915

The actor-manager Lewis Waller, (real name William Waller Lewis), had been involved with a Wilde production before when, in conjunction with his co-producer, HH Morell, he had toured Britain with 'A Woman of No Importance' in 1893.

In 'An Ideal Husband', while his wife Florence West played the character of 'Mrs Cheveley', Waller played the central character of 'Sir Robert Chiltern'. Wilde said of Waller's performance as 'Chiltern' that: "he would make a good D'Artagnan".

Waller was a handsome, dashing actor with a superb voice. He had a fanatical band of female admirers who called themselves the K.O.W. Brigade, ('Keen On Waller'), whose attentions he appears to have reciprocated. As a result, his wife Florence separated from him in 1899.

He matched his popular appeal as an actor with a producer's tenacious grasp of the essentials. One night in 1901, during Waller's successful run as 'Henry V', *Queen Victoria's* death was announced. Waller entered the dressing room of a fellow actor with tears streaming down his face, announcing: "She's dead, Bill, she's dead!" Bill tried to comfort his boss: "Well, yes, it's dreadful, I know, but she was a very old lady". Waller shook his head and sobbed: "No, it's not that. It's the box office receipts. The takings are bound to drop!"

Waller always hoped to be taken as a serious actor, but never had the intelligence to be more than a matinee idol. In 1911, he appeared in a production of *Robert Hichens's* 'The Garden of Allah' in New York. Hichens wrote that: 'He had a lack of understanding of the inner meaning of his part'. When Waller took his script to the actress *Mary Anderson* for advice, she said that he had not fully realised the spirituality of his role. Waller was bewildered by this, replying: "Spirituality? Spirituality? What do you mean?   Ghosts?"

> *'An Ideal Husband' continued to do excellent business at the Haymarket, but the owner of the premises, Sir Herbert Beerbohm Tree, who was then in the USA, needed the theatre for a new show of his own.*
>
> *Lewis Waller arranged for a transfer to the Criterion Theatre, then under the control of another actor-manager, Charles Wyndham.*

SIR CHARLES WYNDHAM 1837-1919

Wilde had met Charles Wyndham, (real name Charles Culverwell), in New York in 1882 when they had lunch together at the Lotus Club. He amused Wilde by his efforts, (in perfecting a costume for a new show), to get arrested in order to discover what clothes a prisoner would wear on a 14-day sentence.

In January 1895, Wyndham was contracted to start production on Wilde's 'Importance of Being Earnest', but *George Alexander*, in trouble with the failure of *Henry James's* 'Guy Domville', begged to have it instead.

When the Wilde scandal broke in April 1895, George Alexander ordered that Oscar's name on the St James Theatre posters should be removed. *Lewis Waller* was about to do likewise with 'An Ideal Husband' at the Haymarket, until Wyndham heard about the idea.

Indignant that a man on trial should be treated with such disrespect, he refused to allow Waller to move the show to the Criterion unless Oscar's name remained on the posters. Waller was forced to accept the decision and the Haymarket posters remained unchanged.

After Oscar's release, Wyndham visited him in Berneval in 1897 and commissioned him to write or adapt a new play. Acting more out of kindness than commerce, Wyndham knew the chances of Oscar finishing a show were remote and he was proved correct. Wilde: 'I have no heart to write clever comedy'.

Considering that both Wilde and *GB Shaw* regarded him as the best actor of modern comedy of his age, Wyndham had an unusual stage-apprenticeship. He became a qualified doctor in 1858, before travelling to the USA in 1862 and joining the Union forces as an army surgeon.

He saw action in many of the Civil War battles while, during the slacker winter periods, performing on stage in New York. In one theatre company, he shared the stage with John Wilkes Booth, (later to assassinate President Lincoln).

On his return to Britain in 1865, he abandoned medicine to become a full time actor. As *Lady St Helier* said: "There are many doctors, but only one Sir Charles Wyndham".

In 1886, he appeared in what many thought was his greatest role, playing 'David Garrick', (the renowned 18th century actor). However, praise was not unanimous. One day in the Green Room Club, an admirer exclaimed: "You get more like Garrick every day, Wyndham". A non-admirer named Henry Hamilton retorted: "And less like him every night".

In 1899, Wyndham built and opened a new theatre bearing his name in the Charing Cross Road, London, ('Wyndham's' is still flourishing); and in 1902 he received a knighthood.

One advantage of being in management was that Wyndham could choose the plays and also his own roles, however inappropriate. After she met him, the actress *Elizabeth Robins* commented: "He was an actor I thought too old and ravaged and rasping to play lovers, but secure in his own theatre he was going to go on and on and on."

When *Henry Irving*, who was roughly the same age, heard that Wyndham intended to play the part of 'Young Marlowe', he drawled: "What a wonderful fellow you are, Wyndham. Why don't you do Little Lord Fauntleroy next?"

With 'An Ideal Husband' running in the West End, Wilde and Bosie left Britain on January 17th 1895 to take a holiday in Algeria. They met Andre Gide in the town of Blidah. Wilde left in early February, returning via Paris to London, while Bosie stayed on in Algeria.

Wilde moved into rooms at the Avondale Hotel in Piccadilly, and superintended the final rehearsals for his new play, 'The Importance of Being Earnest'. London was suffering an outbreak of influenza through most of 1895, and the epidemic affected the cast quite severely. Oscar: 'The rehearsals were dreary. The uncultured had caught colds'.

On February 14th 'The Importance of Being Earnest' opened at the St James Theatre, produced by George Alexander. The first night audience had to battle through the worst snowstorm in a decade to reach the theatre but once inside, as Ada Leverson recalled, the atmosphere had 'a glittering warmth'.

THE IMPORTANCE OF BEING EARNEST

The play's first title was 'Lady Lancing', (there is a vestigial inkling of this in the script – the name of an unseen character is 'Lady Lancing').

Wilde said that originally he had intended that the play should be set in the 18th century world of Sheridan and to have had a more complex plot involving extra dual identities. On Alexander's advice, he abandoned the entire fourth act.

When *Ada Leverson* suggested that the direction of the play should be 'like a piece of mosaic', Oscar shook his head: "No. It must go like a pistol shot". He added that: "It is written by a butterfly for butterflies". (Later, the poet WH Auden called it 'pure verbal opera').

As so often with his other plays, Wilde enjoyed playing subtle word games with his audience. Notoriously, the word 'earnest' was Victorian slang for homosexuality, while 'Cecily', (the name of one of the characters), was a nickname for rent-boys.

As much of the play was written at Worthing, the leading character became 'John Worthing', while the practice of avoiding unwanted social events by sloping off to visit expiring friends in the country was called 'Bunburying'. Wilde had known a Henry Shirley Bunbury at Trinity, Dublin, and in 1895 Bunbury lived in Gloucestershire. There was the additional link in that Oscar's Fenian friend, John Boyle O'Reilly, had been incarcerated in an Australian prison camp called Bunbury.

What probably raised 'Earnest' to its position as the greatest of all Oscar's plays was that he now felt able to abandon the purple prose melodramatics that occasionally had slowed his earlier work. For the first time, he refused to allow anything to get in the way of his helter-skelter farce. The world of 'Earnest' is of the 1890s and yet is also a timeless surreal summer of the comic imagination.

In general, the contemporary critics acknowledged the genius of the play. AB Walkley wrote: 'I declare Mr Oscar Wilde to have found himself, at last, as an artist in sheer nonsense', while the New York Times hailed the production with: 'Oscar Wilde may be said to have at last, and by a single stroke, put his enemies under his feet'.

The New York Times, unfortunately, was premature in this assessment. After the first night of the new play, Bosie's father, the Marquess of Queensberry, having been refused entry to the St James Theatre, left a card addressed to Wilde at the Albemarle Club. It read: 'For Oscar Wilde posing as somdomite'. On 28th February, Wilde discovered the note. Despite Queensberry's inability to spell correctly, the message was clear.

On March 1st, Wilde took out a warrant for the arrest of Queensberry on a charge of criminal libel. He was later to write: 'The one disgraceful, unpardonable and to all time contemptible action of my life was my allowing myself to be forced into appealing to Society for help and protection'.

BOSIE AND THE DOUGLAS FAMILY

(Second Part – from page 297)

Since their meeting in 1891, the love affair between Wilde and Lord Alfred Douglas had been through some turbulent episodes. At first the relationship appeared to be almost paternal on Oscar's side, with Douglas in the role of an admiring, if erratic, Ganymede.

Bosie had been notorious at Oxford University for his open bisexuality and when an attempt to blackmail him was made in the spring of 1892, Wilde helped to extract him from the imbroglio. In June 1893, Bosie was sent down, not because of his sexual exploits, but because of his appalling exam results.

Now convinced of his future as a poet, Bosie was unconcerned: "I don't care two pence about having a degree" and wrote to the President of Magdalene College, Sir Herbert Warren, declaring that one day it would be Magdalene's proudest boast that it had once housed him within its walls.

Bosie said that his sexual relationship with Wilde began nine months after they met, when Oscar seduced him at Tite Street during one of Constance's absences. Wilde was besotted by the handsome young aristocrat: 'He is quite like a narcissus – so white and gold…. He lies like a hyacinth on the sofa, and I worship him'.

Bosie, while enamoured of Oscar's mind, was not so inspired by his body. He later revealed that their sexual activities were similar to those he had already experienced at Winchester School and Oxford, 'the usual public schoolboy business', and that Oscar had treated him 'as an older boy treats a younger boy at school'. He claimed that they practiced fellatio and mutual masturbation but that: 'sodomy never took place between us, nor was it attempted or dreamt of'.

It appears that Bosie found Oscar rather unappetising physically and the 'the familiarities were rare but they did occur spasmodically'. He later wrote that that even this degree of sexual activity had ended by October 1894, 'and were never resumed after Wilde came out of prison'.

Wilde, on the other hand, was in love with Bosie to the point of defying his own judgement. But even this commitment did not prevent him from occasional boredom with a younger man who was his intellectual inferior. Also Bosie's constant need for entertainment was a hindrance to Wilde's work and, although Oscar was now earning £3000 a year, a drain on his pocket. (Between late 1892 and May 1895, OW spent over £5000 on Bosie.)

By the autumn of 1892, in the search for sensation, Bosie introduced Oscar to the practice of hiring rent-boys for additional sexual gratification.

RENTBOYS

[During the 1890s, London had a large population of young male prostitutes, servicing what the police estimated as over 20,000 known homosexual men in the city. There was no difficulty therefore in becoming involved in what was a recognised, if illegal, trade.

It was this very illegality that Wilde found appealing: 'It was like feasting with panthers. The danger was half the excitement'. Although he often referred to them as 'boys', there was no suggestion of paedophilia in Wilde's behaviour. None of his pick-ups were under 16, his preferred age being 17.

His actual encounters with the 'panthers' occasionally bordered on the bizarre. As he said himself: 'I am like the great Sappho with urchins who have the eyes of lesbians'. According to evidence later given during Oscar's trials, one young man claimed that, while in a secluded corner of Kettner's Restaurant: "My brother accepted a preserved cherry from Wilde's own mouth three or four times. Wilde fed him off his own fork". Another said that: "I used to sit on his knees and he used to play with my privates as a man might amuse himself with a girl".

Aubrey Beardsley reported that Oscar once had five messenger boys in one night. He told Beardsley that: "I kissed each of them in every part of their bodies, they were all dirty and appealed to me just for that reason".

As in his dealings with Bosie, Wilde appears to have restricted himself to the practices of fellatio and masturbation. It was significant that at his trials even the prosecution did not suggest that Oscar was guilty of sodomy; if there had been evidence, then they would surely have made the most of it. (It was actually Bosie who was the practising 'somdomite').

(It is possible that after 1887 Wilde rarely, if ever, indulged in penetrative sex again. His heterosexual activities ceased – with the exception of one bout with a prostitute in Dieppe in 1897 – while his homosexuality does not seem to have involved penetration. Whether his belief that he was a possible carrier of syphilis had any bearing on this is arguable. Syphilis was to the Victorian age what AIDS became one hundred years later.)

He also seemed to have suffered pangs of conscience over his involvement with rent-boys. Oscar: 'I used to be utterly reckless of young lives: I used to take up a boy, love him passionately, and then grow bored with him…That is what I regret in my past life'.

In fact, his behaviour towards them appears to have both benevolent and generous – even his blackmailers liked him.]

One of the problems that dogged the relationship between Oscar and Bosie was that Bosie had little to do other than distract Oscar from his work. In 1893, Oscar suggested that Bosie should translate 'Salome' from French into English but the results of Bosie's struggles with the French language proved to be un-publishable.

As early as 1893 Oscar was suggesting separation: 'We are spoiling each other's lives. You are absolutely ruining mine and evidently I am not making you really happy. An irrevocable parting, a complete separation is the one wise philosophic thing to do.'

Bosie's dangerous involvement with the schoolboy Philip Dannay in late 1893 led to his departure for Egypt and the possibility of a diplomatic job in Constantinople. While in Cairo he may have had a brief fling with the future *Lord Kitchener*, but definitely availed himself of the Cairo street boys, before holidaying on the Nile with *Reggie Turner* and *EF Benson*.

His nonchalant attitude towards the job as honorary attaché in Turkey led to the offer being withdrawn by the irritated British Ambassador, *Lord Currie*. Instead Bosie went to stay in Athens with EF Benson.

Throughout this period he wrote almost daily letters to Wilde. Oscar, keen to break the involvement, destroyed them, until finally he received an eleven-page telegram from Bosie threatening suicide if Oscar did not meet him. Given the grim history of the Douglas family, Wilde could not take the chance. They were reconciled eventually in Florence.

In April 1894, Bosie's father, the Marquess of Queensberry, began his attempts to break the relationship with a campaign of virulent correspondence and physical harassment. But even this external attack did nothing to still the fluctuating discord between Oscar and Bosie.

In September 1894, while in Brighton, they quarrelled again after Bosie, having passed on his influenza bug to Oscar, refused to nurse the invalid. When rebuked, he screamed: "When you are not on your pedestal you are not interesting". After charging his hotel bill to Oscar's account, he left for Oxford.

Wilde, deeply hurt at this desertion, again determined to break with his petulant lover. Then came the news of the death of Bosie's elder brother, Viscount Drumlanrig. Deeply sympathetic to Bosie's grief, Oscar once more forgave his behaviour. Wilde: 'Desire, at the end, was a malady, or a madness, or both...I ceased to be Lord over myself. I was no longer the Captain of my Soul'.

In January 1895, the pair left for a holiday in Algeria, where they coincidentally met the French writer, *Andre Gide*. Oscar soon returned to London to oversee the production of his new play, leaving Bosie to enjoy himself in the stews of Blidah. Gide admitted that he found Bosie rather horrifying: 'the most compromising company in the world'. One day Bosie told Gide that he was attracted to Oscar's small sons, especially the elder boy *Cyril*, gloating: "He will be for me".

In the midst of his Algerian orgy, Bosie suddenly received a telegram from his brother, Percy Douglas, informing him that their father was causing trouble in London and had attempted to disrupt the first night of 'The Importance of Being Earnest'. Thirsting for battle, Bosie immediately left for England.

Taunting Wilde with cowardice for not having counter-attacked before, Bosie urged Oscar to apply for a warrant for Queensberry's arrest. He added that the whole Queensberry family would be delighted if the Marquess were committed to a lunatic asylum.

A hesitant Oscar agreed, remarking that if they won the libel case they would have to be received into the Catholic Church. Bosie replied that if they lost the case they wouldn't be received anywhere else.

Meanwhile the attitude of their opponent, the **MARQUESS OF QUEENSBERRY**, had curdled into a state of spectacular malevolence. Wilde nicknamed him 'the screaming scarlet marquess' and described him as 'that ape-like spectre with its bestial, half-witted grin, its stableman's gait and its twitching hands'.

By 1895, Queensberry's own life was in tatters. His aggressive atheism had led him to subscribe to a secular belief, partly of his own creation, in the perfectibility of the human body and mind. When the inevitable aging process wrecked this theory, he had little philosophy left on which to rely.

Moreover, his one major ambition, that of winning the Grand National horse race, had been rewarded with nothing more than the fracture of two collar bones, all four limbs, and repeated concussion.

Publicly exposed as a brutal adulterer during his divorce from his first wife Sibyl, he had then been exposed as impotent during his divorce from his second wife Ethel.

His eldest son, Drumlanrig, had joined Queensberry's political and social enemies and accepted a position in the House of Lords, the same institution from which Queensberry had been dislodged. His second son, Percy, had defied his express command and caused a permanent rift by marrying the daughter of a Christian clergyman of limited means. His fourth son, Sholto, after a series of shady escapades, had exiled himself in California.

Drumlanrig died of shotgun wounds in 1894, the result of what Queensberry firmly believed to have been a homosexual scandal involving the British Foreign Secretary, an outcome he was powerless to avenge. Then his third son, Bosie, had begun a homosexual affair with Oscar Wilde.

When Queensberry's own choleric nature was added to this brew of misfortune, the stage was set for a volcanic reaction. His first broadside took the form of a letter to Bosie denouncing his friendship with Wilde: 'With my own eyes I saw you both in the most loathsome and disgusting relationship as expressed by your manner and expression. Never have I seen such a sight as in your horrible features.... Signed, your disgusted so-called father'. To which, Bosie replied with a less than conciliatory telegram: 'What a funny little man you are'.

On 30th June 1894, Queensberry arrived at Wilde's home at Tite Street, accompanied by a prize-fighter. According to Oscar, when the marquess threatened him with a thrashing, he had replied: "I do not know what the Queensberry rules are but the Oscar Wilde rule is to shoot at sight". He then ordered the intruders from his house and announced to his butler: "This is the Marquess of Queensberry, the most infamous brute in London. You are never to allow him to enter my house again".

According to Queensberry, however, Oscar had caved in and agreed to end the affair. 'He plainly showed the white feather the other day when I tackled him – damned cur and coward of the Rosebery type.'

(On balance, Queensberry's account seems more believable. He was spoiling for a fight and, although 51, was easily capable of indulging in one, (as he later proved in combat with his son Percy). Moreover, he had a professional boxer with him, and Oscar was woefully out of shape by this time.)

By July, the war of words was taking an increasingly violent turn. Queensberry declared that: 'Wilde is a monster who I would be justified in shooting in the street', while Bosie responded: 'If I shoot you, or Wilde shoots you we should be completely justified, as we should be acting in self-defence against a violent and dangerous rough'.

Queensberry began to visit various restaurants leaving messages of what would happen if he were to discover the pair together. Bosie retaliated by leaving more messages informing his father of the dates and times they could be found dining.

Queensberry, in Bosie's words 'posing as a moralist', took to carrying a horsewhip as he patrolled the smarter West End restaurants. Bosie acquired a revolver, (it went off accidentally while he was having dinner at the Berkeley Hotel, leaving a bullet hole in the ceiling), and presented Oscar with a swordstick with which to fend off assault.

Queensberry continued sending letters to Bosie, containing such paternal sentiments as: 'You reptile, you are no son of mine and I never thought you were', 'You miserable creature, I think you are demented', and: 'Wishing you my curse and a speedy death and eternal damnation'.

By August, Queensberry had broadened his attack to include his ex-wife, **SIBYL DOUGLAS**. Too frightened of Bosie's temper to approach him directly, Sibyl had several times asked for Oscar's aid in guiding Bosie's career, and had accepted his advice to send Bosie to Egypt.

Despite her later belief that Oscar was corrupting her son and that she 'would like to murder him' because of it, Sibyl welcomed Oscar's assistance in the fight against her husband. Wilde later said that in the ensuing disaster Sibyl's 'unfortunate weakness of will' had been as much a factor as Queensberry's violence.

Queensberry unsurprisingly resented her intervention and wrote to her father, Alfred Montgomery, that: 'Your daughter appears now to be encouraging them, although she can hardly intend this'.

By 1894, yet another member of the family had joined the fray in the person of Queensberry's second son, **PERCY DOUGLAS** (1868-1920). Described by his brother Bosie as 'recklessly generous, confiding, and extravagant', and by Wilde as 'a really good fellow', Percy had left the Royal Navy after an incident involving 'bawdy houses, drink and debts', and attempted life as a cowboy in Canada. He became the manager of a roadside bar in Manitoba for several months.

Back in England in 1893, strongly against the militantly atheist wishes of his father, he married Anna ('Minnie') Walters, the daughter of an Anglican clergyman from Launceston in Cornwall. After Queensberry realised that not only was Minnie a Christian but also had no fortune behind her, he expressed his feelings in a letter to her father protesting about: 'your stuck-up, pauper, impertinent daughter forcing herself into my family'.

The marriage was actually a happy one, and the couple travelled widely, first attempting tea planting in Ceylon, then joining the gold rush to Coolgardie in Australia where Percy gained, (and spent), £20,000. Moving on to Canada, Percy prospected for gold and discovered nickel deposits near Lake Huron. As there was then no market for nickel, they abandoned their claims and returned to Britain. (Later the nickel was profitably extracted and provided the basis for the Alfred Mond fortune).

With the death of Drumlanrig in 1894, Percy became the heir to the titles and property of the Douglas family. A meeting in Carlisle intended to reconcile father and son failed, but Queensberry tried to influence Percy by letter against his errant brother. The notes were written in Queensberry's usual blunt manner: 'This man Wilde is a cocksucker' while 'Alfred, (Bosie), needs the shit kicked out of him'.

When Percy, believing Wilde and Bosie to be innocent of such slurs, decided to support his brother, the quarrel worsened. In a series of letters and telegrams mostly addressed to Percy's wife, Queensberry described his heir as: 'your good-for-nothing, white-livered husband', 'a kicked-out, run-away, turn-up', and 'this squirming skunk Percy'. As Percy's full title was 'Lord Douglas of Hawick and Tibbers', Queensberry renamed him 'Douglas of Hawick and Shitters'.

When Wilde issued his warrant against Queensberry in 1895, Percy gave his full support and volunteered to pay half the costs of the case. Queensberry received the news in characteristic fashion: 'I will meet Percy anywhere, fists or single sticks, to fight to the finish, and try to give him the licking he deserves'.

By February 1895, Queensberry had tired of written threats and moved on to direct action. His first intention had been to repeat his own behaviour of 1882 when he had hurled vegetables and heckled *Alfred, Lord Tennyson's* anti-atheist play.

Warned by Bosie's relative, *Algernon Bourke*, the manager of the St James Theatre *Sir George Alexander* prevented a similar attack on 'The Importance of Being Earnest' by employing twenty police to guard the doors. Refused admission, Queensberry, in Oscar's words, 'prowled about for three hours, then left chattering like a monstrous ape'.

The thwarted Marquess then left his famous card, 'For Oscar Wilde posing as somdomite' at Wilde's club. As Queensberry's handwriting was almost as bad as his spelling, Oscar was in some doubt as to whether the words were 'ponce and somdomite'. Whatever the phrasing, the insult was enough to initiate the legal landslide.

Queensberry was arrested for criminal libel on March 2nd 1895 and released on bail of £500. Although most of the Douglas family supported Wilde, Queensberry's mother, (the dowager marchioness Caroline), his brother Lord Archie, and his sister Lady Florence backed the Marquess. Their support did not extend to actually helping him in any way.

384

However, Queensberry was to receive support from another source. Oscar's enemies in the theatre and in the London clubs saw the opportunity of destroying him forever. One club was later to send a message to Queensberry: 'Every man in the City is with you. Kill the bugger'.

[See Bosie and the Douglas Family – Third Part – Page 414]

Among the people who decided to back Queensberry in his attack on Wilde were two men closely associated with the theatre, Charles Brookfield and Sir Charles Hawtrey.

CHARLES BROOKFIELD 1857-1913

Brookfield had long nurtured a dislike of Wilde, ever since their first meeting in the USA in 1882, when Oscar had snubbed him over his wearing of gloves at a tea party. In 1891, Brookfield joined forces with *Hawtrey* and a musical arranger called Jimmy Glover to write a parody of Wilde's 'Lady Windermere's Fan' called 'The Poet and the Puppets'.

Oscar, according to Bosie Douglas, disapproved of ridicule of his own work and appealed to the theatre censor, Sir Edward Pigott. Pigott ordered that the authors should read their script to Wilde in person. In the event, Oscar heard them out with good humour and allowed the play to go ahead, declaring that he felt 'delightfully spoofed'.

In 1894, in the first production of Wilde's 'An Ideal Husband', Charles Hawtrey took the leading role of 'Lord Goring', while Brookfield played the part of 'Phipps', 'Goring's' valet. Brookfield claimed that he only accepted this small role so that he did not have to learn much of Wilde's script.

Brookfield reported one incident that occurred during the run. One night a small fire broke out backstage. As the Haymarket Theatre fireman was temporarily absent in a nearby pub, a few of the actors quickly stamped it out. When the fireman returned, he was furious that his job had been usurped and stumped off back to the pub, growling "It's a bloody funny thing people can't mind their own business. 'Ow would they like it, I wonder, if I was to go on to the stage and play their bloomin' parts for 'em?"

Brookfield's resentment of Wilde found an outlet when he heard that the Marquess of Queensberry was searching for evidence against the playwright, and eagerly joined the investigation. The writer Vincent O'Sullivan, who otherwise quite liked Brookfield, ('In some respects I liked him better than I did Wilde'), said that: 'With him, alas, Wilde became a monomania'.

Brookfield persuaded the commissionaire of the Haymarket Theatre to supply the information that led private detectives to the house of Alfred Taylor, later to be Wilde's co-defendant. When Oscar heard of Brookfield's involvement with his enemies, he said merely: "How absurd of him".

The son of one of *Queen Victoria's* curates, Brookfield's early life had been spent in court circles, where it was rumoured that his real father was the novelist WM Thackeray.

Sir Seymour Hicks left an unflattering portrait of the adult Brookfield: 'When he smiled he showed a set of teeth which looked like Stonehenge' and 'his tongue was the model from which the first lancet was made'. Hicks added that: 'He was a queer creature and would have dug up his grandmother to get a laugh'.

This propensity showed itself early on when, as a 14-year-old schoolboy, he had returned from a holiday in France on the ferry from Calais. During the rough voyage, Brookfield was thrown against a gangway and cut his head. His fellow passengers, who happened to include the Archbishop of Canterbury Archibald Tait, staunched the wound and generally fussed the boy.

When the ferry arrived in Dover, the Archbishop insisted on carrying the invalid's suitcase. Embarrassingly, Brookfield had stuffed the case with illicit pornographic French novels. Brookfield: 'The amiable prelate, not knowing what he did, carried the contraband past the Customs house officials, who piously saluted England's supreme ecclesiastic and waved him through'.

His schooldays were further enlivened due to an incident involving his headmaster at Westminster School, who invariably wore a flowing full-sleeved black academic robe. After one school function, the headmaster's arm was grasped by a shortsighted earl who steered him out of the room with the words: "Come, my dear, our carriage has arrived".

Brookfield's spent his life as a jobbing actor, an occasional journalist, and as the writer or producer of over forty plays. The painter *James Whistler* befriended him mostly because on one occasion Brookfield had quarrelled with one of Whistler's enemies, Augustus Moore, and knocked him unconscious.

Brookfield had a curious fascination with criminality and policing. He spent many hours hanging around disreputable clubs and bars in London, studying the underworld and its modus operandi. This morbid interest was not restricted to Britain. Armed with letters of introduction, he was able to accompany the Surete in Paris and Pinkerton agents in New York on their investigations.

In 1908, Brookfield adapted a play called 'Dear Old Charlie', which was produced by Charles Hawtrey. The play was a cynical comedy of sexual infidelity that proved so risqué that Hawtrey was forced to close it.

Whether his interest in law enforcement prompted the government to its decision is unknown, but in 1911 Brookfield was appointed as Joint-Examiner of Plays, (the theatre censor). It produced a howl of protest from every quarter. *William Archer* commented: 'That the adaptor of 'Dear Old Charlie' should be selected as the guardian of public morals is a stroke of exquisite humour, quite the most delicious in the history of an office always prolific of absurdities'.

Immediately, the mischievous Hawtrey re-staged 'Dear Old Charlie' on the grounds that the Joint-Examiner could hardly censor his own show.

In the 1870s, Brookfield was acquainted with **ROBERT BADEN-POWELL** (1857-1941), the future Boer War defender of Mafeking and the creator of the Boy Scout movement. (When *Gertrude Atherton* met Baden-Powell he told her that he was descended from the 17th century Red Indian princess Pocahontas: 'He seemed prouder of this fact than all his medals'.)

Brookfield used to recount a story about the youthful Baden-Powell when he was a young army officer. One evening at a music hall, Baden-Powell approached the manager and, claiming to be a conjuror, offered his services. As it was a quiet night, the manager agreed.

Baden-Powell stepped out on stage and announced that his first trick would involve only objects borrowed from the audience. Collecting a silk top hat, a pocket-knife, and a ladies shawl, he proceeded to cut the brim from the hat with the knife and then covered the mutilated headwear with the shawl.

Baden-Powell turned to the audience and announced: "Now, you observe, ladies and gentlemen, there's no deception, no mirrors and no apparatus. I think that everyone will agree that the brim of the hat has been removed, yes?" There was a rumble of assent.

He then asked for a volunteer to time him: "I shall now leave the stage and in two minutes precisely by this gentleman's watch, you shall see what you shall see!" The orchestra struck the tune of 'The Blue Danube' as Baden-Powell strolled off the stage, walked to the stage door, hailed a hansom cab, and drove off to supper at the Café Royal.

Brookfield was a familiar figure in the London club world, becoming a member of the Savile in 1875 at the age of 18. He also frequented the Oriental Club, (known to cab drivers as 'the 'Orizontal'), and the Savage Club.

Wilde was uninterested in club life, ("I am due at the club. It is the hour when we sleep there"), preferring to spend his time in restaurants such as Willis's. In particular, he disliked the Savage Club: "I never enter the Savage Club. It tires me so. It used to be gentlemanly Bohemian, but ever since the Prince of Wales became a member and sometimes dines there, it is nothing but savagely snobbish".

Because of this refusal, Oscar failed to meet the most exceptional member of the Savage, one who most definitely could not be described as 'snobbish'. E.J ODELL (1828?-1928), was an almost permanently out-of-work actor, with shoulder-length straggly hair and white beard, who habitually wore a shabby sombrero and a threadbare frockcoat that had turned green with age.

Seymour Hicks wrote of him: 'The chief thing about Odell was that he was old... He worked at becoming old very hard and with great success.' Brookfield's theory was that: 'I do not believe that Odell was ever born ... I believe that when the Savage Club was started they found him there'.

Each evening he would install himself at the bar where he consumed all the Irish whiskey and cigars he could freeload from the other members, despite being 'abominably rude' to all and sundry. He had the knack of demanding a loan with the air of conferring an honour on the hesitant creditor. When one member reminded Odell of a £5 loan owing for months, Odell rasped: "You want it back? Well, I haven't finished with it yet".

In spite of his behaviour, Odell was adopted as the venomous mascot of the Savage Club. Curious about where he lived, some members secretly followed him one night, only to find that Odell doubled back to the club itself where the servants allowed him to sleep on a sofa.

When, after some social outrage, the Savage Club committee expelled him from the premises, sympathisers parked a hired carriage in the street outside, where Odell lived, his feelings assuaged by gifts of food hampers and whiskey, until his reinstatement.

On one of his rare sorties into employment, Odell became a member of the cast at the Haymarket Theatre in the 1880s. As a professed despiser of the upper classes, he found himself at odds with the refined and well-groomed set of younger performers around him. The leading lady, the rather haughty Miss Linda Dietz, had a particular aversion to the decrepit old curmudgeon and refused to talk to him socially.

One night, just before the Easter break, some of the company were in the green room discussing where they were to spend the holiday. One cast member announced that he was going to Badminton to stay with the Duke of Beaufort, another said that he had been invited to hunt with the Quorn, while a third admitted that "the dear Duchess would be most distressed" if he did not pop up to Chatsworth House.

Another actor turned to Linda Dietz: "And where are you going for your holiday, Miss Dietz". Before she could reply, Odell, with the most lascivious leer in his repertoire, broke in: "Oh, we're not goin' to tell anyone where we're goin', are we, sweetie?"

This appears to have been his last theatrical engagement, as he spent his remaining forty years propping up the club bar. Feeling sympathetic to the old man's lack of a home, *King Edward VII*, also a Savage Club member, arranged that Odell should be provided with a room at the Charterhouse.

Unfortunately, the rules of this institution required that all its inhabitants should be indoors by 10pm. Odell, a committed night owl, totally ignored this instruction. When he received a courteous reminder of the rule from the Master of the Charterhouse, Odell exploded with rage: "The insolent young puppy!" The 'young puppy' in question was a retired general aged 82.

Age did not mellow Odell, nor the years soften. One night, King George V dined as the Guest of Honour at the Savage Club. After the meal, he sat in the most comfortable chair in the smoking room. Unluckily it happened to be Odell's favourite perch. Arriving late at the club, Odell, now in his 90s, spotted the intruder and marched across, yelling furiously: "Out of my chair, sir! Get out, d'ye hear! *AT ONCE!*" The king apologised and beat a hasty retreat to the bar.

When Odell died in 1928, aged at least 100, his fellow Savage members affixed a brass plate to this chair, inscribed 'Here Odell Sat'.

At the time of his death, he was thin to the point of being almost skeletal. Seymour Hicks wondered whether Odell's last grim joke was to leave his body to the College of Surgeons.

SIR CHARLES HAWTREY 1858-1923

The actor Charles Hawtrey also provided information about Wilde to Queensberry's private detectives and earlier had collaborated with *Brookfield* on writing the 1892 parody of Oscar's 'Lady Windermere's Fan' called 'The Poet and the Puppets'.

The co-authors had some difficulty raising the money to stage their spoof, and eventually Hawtrey was driven to approach a notorious moneylender called Mister'arris. (Owing to his permanently drooping eyelids, Mister'arris had never been known to look anyone straight in the face. Also, he was never known by any other name than Mister'arris – even by his wife and sons.)

Having initially agreed to back the production, Mister'arris suddenly pulled out, leaving the show stranded. Hawtrey, with his back to the wall, decided to place the last of his money on a horse. When it won, netting him £1,800, Hawtrey called it 'the most marvellous sensation of my life', and 'The Poet and the Puppets' went ahead.

Hawtrey was an unusual actor in that his real interest lay in horse racing and he acted only out of necessity. This passion sometimes spilt over into his private life. Hawtrey once provided an excellent tip that netted a fellow actor £1000; the thankful recipient gave Hawtrey a ring with the name of the winning horse, 'Mida', inscribed upon it. Later, Hawtrey was harangued by an irate girlfriend demanding to know 'which brazen hussy called Mida' had supplanted her in his affections.

Hawtrey was one of the greatest light comedians of his day, and at one time or another managed sixteen London theatres and produced over 100 plays. One downside of this powerful position was that he was bombarded constantly by unsolicited scripts. He once groaned that these would-be playwrights were: "like the raw country youth who, when asked if he could play the violin, answered 'I don't know – I've never tried'."

One day, he received one dreadful nine-hour-long play script but, by the same post, another that showed promise. His replies, one of rejection and the other an offer to visit his office, were inadvertently placed in the wrong envelopes.

Two days later, a wild-eyed but beaming gentleman arrived to discuss his nine-hour epic. When Hawtrey stammered out that there might have been a mistake, the playwright's mood changed to one of fury. Producing a huge knife known as a 'deeerslayer', he began slashing the air and hissing curses until Hawtrey hastily agreed to reconsider his decision. He later found out, to his intense relief, that the playwright had been committed to an asylum.

Hawtrey had been born into a once important family, (who had owned the country house of Chequers before it was donated to the nation). His father had been a housemaster at

Eton, and Charles attended the school himself. Somerset Maugham said of him that: 'Hawtrey adhered all his life to the aims, ideals and ambitions of the public school boy'.

The fact that his father had been reduced to the relatively humble occupation of schoolmaster made Hawtrey sympathetic to other members of 'the newly poor'. He delighted in the story of one such girl who had been forced to take a position as governess to a nouveau riche family. Soon after accepting the job, her employer reprimanded her for 'getting above her station' with the words: "For Heavens sake, do you consider yourself on a par with *my* children?" The girl snorted imperiously and replied: "Most certainly not!", and promptly handed in her notice.

Benefiting from the newly acquired social status of the acting profession, Hawtrey was welcomed back into the highest echelons of society and became particularly friendly with *Lord* and *Lady Desborough*. He visited their home at Taplow Court and often organised charades for their two boys, Julian and Billy.

Another of his aristocratic contacts invited him to stay at Penrhyn Castle, near Bangor, North Wales. Hawtrey descended to breakfast one Sunday morning to find the house in a state of gloom. His host's forbidding grandfather, Lord Penrhyn, was absent, and Hawtrey overheard a maid saying in hushed tones that: "His Lordship is bearing up and I think it is wonderful the way he has taken it".

Not wishing to intrude on grief, Hawtrey remained in the dark over what had been the nature of the tragedy. At church, the congregation spoke in such hushed whispers that he still could not find out what was going on. Finally he found the castle butler and asked for an explanation. The butler's expression saddened as he gulped: "The Eighteenth Duchess of Richmond has died in the night. She was His Lordship's prize heifer".

Like many of his fellow actor-managers, Hawtrey made several theatrical tours of the United States. On one such trip, he was asked by a local reporter what he thought of New York. He replied that the city was so full of Americans it reminded him of Paris.

In 1912, Hawtrey was performing in a light farce in New York when the news of the sinking of the Titanic arrived. The resulting solemnity meant that the audience drained away from the theatres, and especially from farces.

One evening, Hawtrey performed to a practically empty auditorium. At one point, another actor had to walk on stage and deliver the conspiratorial line: "Are we alone?" Hawtrey gave a glance round the thin sprinkling of heads in the stalls and sighed: "Almost".

The next day they packed up and returned to England.

The third collaborator on 'The Poet and the Puppets' was an Irish-born pianist and musical director called **JIMMY GLOVER** (1861-1924), whose path had already crossed Wilde's during their youth in Dublin.

In 1879, a decision was made to celebrate the centenary of the birth of the Irish poet Thomas Moore. Glover's grandfather, John Glover, as the composer and editor of 'Moore's Irish Melodies', was asked to be the musical advisor to the ceremonies.

After the inaugural meeting, John Glover returned home in a fury complaining about the interference of 'two whipper-snappers' called Willie and Oscar Wilde, who had complained that Glover's specially written 'Celebration Ode' was 'not worthy of Ireland'. Glover: 'This, I think, was the occasion also of the first real public appearance of the Wilde brothers'.

Jimmy Glover's own career in Ireland had been complicated by his father's involvement in the revolutionary Fenian movement. At a very early age, Jimmy had accompanied his father on a successful bid to break the Fenian leader, James Stephens, out of prison by means of a rope ladder over the wall. Jimmy's father was imprisoned himself in Mountjoy Jail in 1868.

Having had a musical education physically thrashed into him by his irascible grandfather, Jimmy left Ireland and became a jobbing pianist who attached himself to various outlandish music hall acts including a sword-swallower and a 'man-fish'.

In 1885, Glover met the greatest theatre manager of his day, Sir Augustus Harris, and became an associate musical director at the Palace Theatre and then Master of Music at Drury Lane. During his many years as a theatrical fixture in London, Glover became a well known man about town who mixed with the bohemian set that included *George Moore*, William Terriss and EJ Odell. In 1905 he received the unlikely honour of becoming the Mayor of Bexhill in Sussex.

One production with which Glover was associated was Gounod's 'Faust', in which, in the last act, the character of Mephistopheles descends through fire into the depths of Hell. When the tour reached Belfast, one night the descending stage trap door became stuck, leaving the very overweight Mephistopheles helplessly wedged at waist level. A voice echoed from the gallery: "Jaysus, would yez look at that, lads! Hell's full up."

Although bolstered by the support of most of the Queensberrys, Wilde was worried by the turn events had taken. At one point he considered flight to France, but was unable to leave the Avondale Hotel as they had impounded his luggage in lieu of an unpaid bill of £140.

In a display of unity, Oscar, Constance and Bosie together attended a performance of 'The Importance of Being Earnest' on March 7th. A friend called Charles Goodhard met Oscar in Piccadilly and wished him luck. Oscar replied: "Don't distress yourself. All is well. The working classes are with me – to a boy."

On March 9th, the Marquess of Queensberry was remanded on bail for trial at the Old Bailey. He was advised by his solicitor to brief the eminent barrister, Edward Carson, for his defence.

SIR EDWARD CARSON 1854-1935

Wilde once said that his bete noir was 'a thorough Irish Protestant'. In Edward Carson, he came up against a man who exactly fitted that description. Strangely enough, as children on holiday at Dungarvan, Co. Waterford, they had once shared the same nanny and played together on the beach. (This incident later led the actor Michael MacLiammoir to comment that their animosity must have started when 'Oscar kicked over Edward's sand castle'.)

They also knew each other at Trinity College, Dublin, where Wilde said they would 'walk about together arms around each other's necks'. On the other hand, Carson said that he disapproved of Oscar's 'flippant approach to life', and any friendship faded. In 1895, when he heard that his cross-examiner was to be Carson, Wilde remarked: "No doubt he will perform his task with the added bitterness of an old friend".

(Despite being at the Old Bailey, the first trial had a distinctly Irish flavour to it. Apart from Oscar himself, Carson, his junior counsel Charles Gill, and the trial judge, Mr Justice Henn Collins, were all Irish and ex-Trinity men. It reminded *GB Shaw* of the old adage: 'If you want to baste an Irishman, you can always get another Irishman to turn the spit'.)

During Wilde's trial, Carson's cunning cross-examination fell into two parts. During the first, his questions concerned Wilde's published works, a subject on which Oscar was more than capable of holding his own and, on occasion, of dominating his inquisitor. Some exchanges reduced the court to hilarity:

Carson: "Do you drink champagne yourself?" Wilde: "Yes. Iced champagne is a favourite drink of mine, strongly against my doctor's orders". "Never mind your doctor's orders!" "I never do".

In such a verbal duel, Oscar was always going to win the day. However, Carson was content to allow him this triumph as it led Wilde into over-confidence and to underestimate his opponent. When Carson changed tack and began his real assault, that of questioning Oscar over his sex life, Wilde was off guard.

In one fatal exchange, Carson led Wilde to destroy his own case. When asking about Wilde's dealings with one of Bosie's servants, Walter Grainger, Carson suddenly asked: "Did you ever kiss him?" Oscar, probably hoping for another laugh, airily replied: "Oh, dear no. He was a peculiarly plain boy. He was, unfortunately, extremely ugly. I pitied him for it". Carson immediately pounced: "Was that the reason why you did not kiss him?"

No amount of bluster from Oscar could repair the damage and his prosecution of Queensberry collapsed. The Judge, Henn Collins, sent a note to Carson at the end of the trial: 'Dear Carson, I have never heard a more powerful speech nor a more searching crossXam. I congratulate you on having escaped the rest of the filth'.

During the two later trials though, when Oscar had become the defendant, Carson refused to accept the role of prosecutor and, indeed, suggested that the case should be dropped as Wilde had suffered enough.

Their only later meeting reputedly occurred in 1899 and the neatness of its symbolism suggests that it might be apocryphal. As Carson was hurrying along a Paris street he happened to knock a man aside into the gutter. As he apologised, he realised that the man was Wilde.

The politician *Henry Labouchere* once said of Carson that: "Nature has so fashioned his face that any theatrical manager to whom he applied for an engagement would at once cast him for the part of Iago".

Born in Dublin, Carson became a lawyer in the boisterous world of the Irish courts. (He recounted that, at one trial, after the jury had been selected from the well of the court, the judge asked them: "Gentlemen, will you take your seats?" All twelve jurymen immediately tried to squash into the dock.) After a few well publicised murder cases, Carson began to establish his reputation.

His real rise began in 1887, when *Arthur Balfour* appointed him as a tough Crown prosecutor against the Irish Home Rule movement. His ruthless legal campaign, (which included the jailing of *Wilfred Blunt*), led to his nickname of 'Coercion Carson'. Seen as a Dublin Castle hack, he was stoned in the streets and needed constant protection from assassins. He received his reward when in 1889 he became the youngest Queen's Counsel in the country.

Over the following twenty years he became a Member of Parliament, a very successful London barrister, and consequently a wealthy man. One of his most famous cases occurred in 1909 and the story was later dramatised by Sir Terence Rattigan and filmed by Anthony Asquith with the title of 'The Winslow Boy'.

The case concerned a 13-year-old cadet called George Archer-Shee who, while attending the Royal Naval College at Osborne, had been accused of stealing a five-shilling postal order and expelled from the college. His family, convinced of his innocence, asked Carson to fight the case and, after interviewing the boy for three hours, he agreed to proceed against the Crown by petition of right, ('Let Right Be Done').

It was a cause célébré that captured the attention of the nation and, in a highly charged atmosphere, Carson finally won the case against the Admiralty and vindicated the boy. Carson was not normally a demonstrative man but when, amidst the cheers of the spectators, he rose to leave the court, tears were streaming down his face.

The most extraordinary episode of his life happened four years later in 1913, when the British Government under *HH Asquith* was moving towards a policy of granting Home Rule to Ireland. As the political leader of the Unionists, Carson was so determined to prevent this that he went to the lengths of, in effect, fomenting armed rebellion against the Crown.

The Ulster Unionists attempted to create a state within a state by recruiting 100,000 men into a unit known as the Ulster Volunteer Force. They were short of arms but succeeded in smuggling 20,000 rifles and 3 million rounds of ammunition into the province. Now known as 'the uncrowned king of Ulster', Carson was often to be seen, blackthorn stick in hand, reviewing these troops.

Many British figures on the right approved of these actions. Lord Rothschild, *Rudyard Kipling*, *Lord Desborough*, and Sir Edward Elgar all backed Carson, while the leadership of the British Army wavered in their allegiance to the Government. In an incident known as the Curragh Mutiny, the officers at the army camp there threatened to resign if ordered to suppress the agitation in Ulster.

The future Prime Minister, Bonar Law, declared that 'opposition would not necessarily depend on being kept within the law', while Lord Milner advised encouraging strikes to disrupt the movement of government-supporting army units, adding that resistance should not involve actual rebellion – 'or at least not beginning with it'.

[LORD ALFRED MILNER (1854-1925) had been a student friend of Wilde's at Oxford and a member of *Ruskin's* ill-fated Hinksey road gang. Later Oscar had invited Milner to his wedding in 1884. As one of *Benjamin Jowett's* 'prancing pro-consuls', Milner became British High Commissioner to South Africa where he was arguably more responsible for the outbreak of the Boer War than any other single figure.

He unsuccessfully wooed *Margot Asquith* before her marriage, but had more luck as the occasional lover of *Lord Curzon's* girlfriend Elinor Glyn, the romantic novelist. Elinor rather overstated her case when she said of Milner that: "I always thought he must be the reincarnation of Socrates"]

Ranged against the rightists were the Liberal Government itself, (led by Asquith, Lloyd George, and Winston Churchill), the Irish Home Rule Party under John Redmond, (plus their Irish Volunteers raised to counterbalance the UVF), and the emerging Labour Party.

The issue split Britain into two camps. Where normally politics had not been allowed to disturb the cosy social consensus, hostesses now found that opposing factions would not attend the same dinners – it was described as being 'war to the knife and fork'.

Winston Churchill, who dismissed his right-wing opponents as 'a self-elected body composed of persons who, to put it plainly, are engaged in a treasonable conspiracy', planned to overwhelm the UVF militarily by sending troops to take vantage points, while Navy destroyers appeared in Belfast Lough.

After a defiant speech to the House of Commons, Carson left for Ulster giving orders that, if he was arrested, his men should attack and disarm the Royal Irish Constabulary.

By July 1914, not just Ireland, but Britain itself was as close to civil war as it had been since the 18th century. Then news broke of the start of the First World War. Immediately, Carson and Redmond offered the services of their volunteers to the defence of Britain. Carson made one last inspection of the UVF, (now known as the Ulster Division), before they left for the future horrors of the Battle of the Somme.

Carson also rejoined the colours inasmuch as he became Asquith's Attorney-General and then, in 1917, First Lord of the Admiralty. In 1922, although he ensured that Protestant Ulster was kept out of the newly independent Ireland, Carson felt that the Tories and Ulster Unionists had betrayed his own people, the Southern Unionists. He left government after lacerating them with one of the bitterest speeches ever heard in the House of Lords.

Irrespective of his political stances, Carson was regarded as a man of integrity who never sought an easy life. As he said himself: "I have always walked up hill with the collar hurting".

On March 13th 1895, in an act of surprising insouciance, instead of preparing their defence, Wilde and Bosie Douglas decided to take a short holiday in Monte Carlo, returning to London to stay again at the Avondale Hotel ten days later.

On March 25th, Oscar and Bosie had lunch with Frank Harris and Bernard Shaw at the Café Royal where Harris urged Wilde to abandon the case and leave immediately for France. Under pressure from Bosie, Oscar rejected this advice.

On March 30th, Queensberry's defence Plea of Justification was revealed, accusing Wilde of soliciting ten young men for sodomy.

Wilde and Bosie were forced to take the case more seriously, paying several visits to the solicitor, Charles Humphreys, where, as Oscar put it, 'relying on him to misrepresent us', they 'would sit with serious faces telling serious lies to a bald man, until I really groaned and yawned with ennui'.

The highly regarded barrister, Sir Edward Clarke, was briefed to lead the prosecution on Wilde's behalf against Queensberry. The son of Wilde's solicitor, Travers Humphreys, was appointed junior counsel.

SIR EDWARD CLARKE 1841-1931

Sir Edward Clarke had never met Wilde before and knew of him only as a fashionable playwright. During the preliminary interview, he asked Oscar to assure him on his honour 'as an English gentleman' that there was no truth in Queensberry's allegations. As an entirely Irish gentleman, Oscar declared that there was not.

This lack of background information may have led Clarke to defend Oscar's character, (in Bosie's words), 'as if he had been the Archbishop of Canterbury'. As the trial unfolded, Clarke was to receive some nasty surprises.

During the lunch interval on the second day of the trial, his faith in his client was shaken when Wilde admitted to him that, on one occasion, he and a boy had been turned out of the Albemarle Hotel in the middle of the night. Oscar: "It might be awkward if they found out about that".

After Edward Carson's devastating cross-examination of Wilde, Clarke realised the case was hopeless. Before the trial reopened on the third morning, he decided to warn Oscar that not only was he going to lose but that the judge could, and indeed might, order his arrest in open court. Wilde agreed to abandon the prosecution.

Clarke added, in a heavy hint to run for it, that there was no need for Wilde to remain in court while the case was halted. Another of the solicitors, a Mr Matthews, told Oscar: "If you wish it, Clarke and I will keep the case going and give you time to get to Calais".

Clarke later wrote that: 'I hoped and expected that he would take the opportunity of escaping from the country, and I believe he would have found no difficulty in doing so'.

With this in mind, Clarke entered court on the third day and slowly prepared his statement while his opponent Carson continued his speech. Finally he tugged on Carson's sleeve and indicated that the case was over. This delaying tactic was to no avail as Wilde had remained in the court precincts. The judge, however, took no action.

Although he left the court remarking to Carson, (as a fellow barrister): "What a filthy business. I shall not feel clean for weeks", Clarke agreed to continue as Wilde's defence counsel throughout the next two trials. He fought a dogged and, at times, moving battle against Wilde's prosecutors – Oscar himself was reduced to tears by one great defence speech by Clarke. Ultimately, though, Clarke lost what he described as 'the most painful case which I have ever been engaged in'.

It was indicative of Clarke's character that he continued to defend a man who was the object of violent public disapproval, who was not personally known to him, and who had deliberately deceived him. He also refused to accept any fee for his services. Such behaviour was typical of a man whose overriding sense of fair play and chivalry led to his nickname of 'the Bayard of the Bar'.

In addition to his legal career, he entered politics as an MP in 1880 and stayed in the House of Commons till 1900. Although a colleague commented that: "Clarke's parliamentary speeches seldom erred on the side of brevity", his ability was obvious. During the Tory administration of 1886 to 1892, *Lord Salisbury* appointed him to be the Solicitor-General.

[Clarke relished the story of a predecessor called Sir Frederick Pollock. As a newly fledged Government Law Officer, Pollock had applied to the College of Heralds for his own coat of arms. When he saw the enormous bill that accompanied the honour, Pollock spluttered: "You tell the Garter King-of-Arms to go to the devil sable; in flames guiles, with a pitch-fork ardent in his backside proper".]

Clarke's career in the law spanned fifty years and made him a rich man, (his overall earnings topped £500,000).

Among his many famous cases, he was involved in the *Lady Colin Campbell* and the *Charles Parnell* divorce suits, and the conviction of *Robert Cunningham-Graham* for the Trafalgar Square 'Bloody Sunday' riot.

In 1886, he defended a young woman called Adelaide Bartlett on a charge of murder. It transpired that Adelaide's husband, Charles, having given up intercourse with her, had been in the habit of 'lending' his wife to other men for sexual purposes, in particular to a young curate called Dyson. When Charles then again demanded sex, Adelaide objected and avoided his advances by using chloroform to send him to sleep. Charles, a healthy man aged 40, was found dead next morning.

Clarke defended Adelaide and, after a magnificent speech lasting six hours, secured her acquittal. The result was very popular, but doubts lingered over her guilt. The Lord Chief Justice sent a letter of congratulation to Clarke, but added: 'Mrs Bartlett was no doubt quite properly acquitted, but now it is to be hoped in the interests of science she will tell us how she did it'.

When Lord Salisbury's Tory government was restored in 1895, Clarke was the obvious choice to resume the role of Solicitor-General. He was ignored, however, owing mostly to his role in the 1890 Tranby Croft case.

After an argument over cheating in a baccarat game involving Bertie, Prince of Wales, the man accused of deception, Sir William Gordon-Cumming, had sued for slander. As his advocate, Clarke had been duty-bound to question the Prince of Wales's honesty, thus incurring deep royal displeasure.

Another case in 1897 not only destroyed Clarke's chances of ministerial office but his entire parliamentary career. After the 'Jameson Raid' in 1896, Clarke accepted the brief to defend the leader of the attack, Dr. Leander Starr Jameson, who had been charged under the Foreign Enlistment Act. This murky South African escapade had been secretly backed by Cecil Rhodes and even more secretly backed by the British Cabinet Minister, Joseph Chamberlain.

THE JAMESON RAID

[The Jameson Raid had been a fairly blatant attempt to provoke war with the Boer Republics. On December 29th 1895, Jameson led a small group of men into Boer territory, ostensibly to rescue British subjects from tyranny, but secretly to capture control of the government and therefore the diamond mines of Johannesburg for the imperialist entrepreneur Cecil Rhodes.

Rhodes had fabricated a telegram purporting to come from the women of Johannesburg, (a town described by a contemporary as 'Monte Carlo superimposed on Sodom and Gomorrah'), pleading for help against the Boers. Sir James Sivewright: 'That telegram was written in Rhodes's office in Cape Town and sent from there to the Times in London'. Hoping that the Uitlanders, (the British migrants already resident in the Transvaal), would rise to join him, Jameson set off and was captured ignominiously after the death of 25 of his men.

After the debacle, Cecil Rhodes was forced to resign temporarily as Prime Minister of Cape Colony. Chamberlain, (after a visit to the imprisoned Jameson to tell him to keep his mouth shut), was exonerated by a parliamentary select committee, of which he was himself a member. Chamberlain publicly described the Raid as 'a flagrant piece of filibustering for which there is no justification', (Rhodes said privately that Chamberlain was 'up to his neck in it'). The unfortunate Jameson suffered fifteen months in Wormwood Scrubs Prison, but received the consolation of having *Rudyard Kipling* compose the famous poem 'If' about his predicament.]

Clarke's case for Dr Jameson was hobbled from the outset because he had received instructions that 'he was to follow no line of defence which might cause embarrassment to Her Majesty's Government', (and especially to Joseph Chamberlain). Forced to defend only on technicalities, Clarke lost the case.

However, in the course of preparing the defence, Clarke had seen secret documents proving that government ministers had known and approved of the raid. When, in 1899, the machinations of Rhodes, Chamberlain and the High Commissioner to South Africa Lord Milner eventually succeeded in promoting a conflict, Clarke, knowing the true causes, wrote to the Times that 'it would be a disgrace to the country to enter war'.

When the Boer War began, he attacked Chamberlain and Milner in the House of Commons: "This lamentable war is absolutely unnecessary". As a result he was pressured to resign his position as a Tory MP and stepped down 'for health reasons'.

JOSEPH CHAMBERLAIN (1836-1914) became deeply unpopular in many quarters due to his incessant machinations. Starting as a Radical Lord Mayor of Birmingham and ending as an imperialist warmonger, he was largely responsible for wrecking both of the political parties to which he belonged. He split Gladstone's Liberals over Irish Home Rule, and then divided the Conservatives over Free Trade.

In addition to fomenting the Jameson Raid and the Boer War, he was very likely to have engineered the downfall of *Sir Charles Dilke*, and was definitely involved in the attempts to destroy *Charles Parnell*. As *Henry Labouchere* said: "If Chamberlain were alone on a desert island, he would intrigue against himself".

Chamberlain was an admirer of Wilde's plays and attended several of the first nights. He harboured illusions about his own abilities as a playwright and once sent a script to *Sir Herbert Beerbohm Tree*, insisting that the authorship should be kept a secret. (Tree rejected it as mediocre.)

Chamberlain married an American girl called Mary Endicott, 30 years his junior and the daughter of the US Secretary of State for War. When they honeymooned in New York, the local press hailed the event as the 'Wedding of Joseph and Mary'.

The couple went on to produce something of a political dynasty with Neville, one of his sons, becoming British Prime Minister in the 1930s. (The Chamberlain family's political foe, David Lloyd George, regarded himself as a perceptive phrenologist and was fascinated by the smallness of Neville's head. When Neville became PM, he never forgave Lloyd George for habitually referring to him as 'Pinhead'.)

Joseph Chamberlain also received something of an albeit unintended rebuff when he was the guest of honour at an important civic dinner. When the main courses had finished and the coffee was being served, the chairman leant over to him and whispered: "Shall we let the people enjoy themselves a little longer, or had we better have your speech now?"

CECIL RHODES (1853-1902), having arrived as a mature student in 1877, had been a contemporary of Wilde at Oxford. Although a highly effective imperialist adventurer who established the De Beers diamond monopoly and carved what amounted to a personal empire in Southern Africa, Rhodes remained an enigmatic personality.

Frank Harris wrote: 'His private life no one knew much about. He had a secretary once who told me stories of his erotic tendencies, worthy of Oscar Wilde; but I never believed in them whole-heartedly'.

Despite being known as a ruthless man when in pursuit of his goals, he puzzled many of his acquaintances. *Genevieve Ward* called him: 'a very absent-minded man – also very nervous, and sensitive'. *Lady St Helier* recounted a strange experience when she and a young girl friend accompanied Rhodes to see a slightly risqué new play called 'The Gay Lord Quex'.

At the end of the show, Rhodes suddenly turned on Lady St Helier and roundly rebuked her for allowing her young companion to witness such depravity. Amazed at such offence being taken over what was a very mild production, she tried to defend herself. St Helier: 'He got extremely argumentative – so much so that, even after leaving our box, he sat down on a sofa in the corridor, and continued the conversation… I do not know how long it would have lasted had not the manager of the theatre at last appeared and asked us to leave, and even then I had great difficulty in escaping an adjournment to the Bristol Hotel'.

The trial of Queensberry on a charge of criminal libel against Wilde lasted from April 3rd 1895 till April 5th and ended in the acquittal of the Marquess.

THE EVENTS OF APRIL 5TH 1895

Wilde once wrote in his play 'Vera': 'One can live for years sometimes without living at all, and then all life comes crowding into a single hour'. And so it proved on this pivotal day of his life.

11.30am. As the courtroom erupted into a hubbub of congratulations for Queensberry, (which the judge did nothing to subdue), Wilde, accompanied by *Bosie Douglas* and *Robbie Ross,* slipped out of a side door of the Old Bailey. They were able to avoid the cheering crowds outside and the sight of several prostitutes, pleased to see some of the rent-boy competition temporarily eliminated, dancing in the street.

11.45am. Although the authorities had taken no action, Queensberry and his solicitor, Charles Russell, immediately sent the transcripts of the trial to the Public Prosecutor to force his hand over the prosecution of Wilde, 'so that there may be no miscarriage of justice'.

12 noon. Queensberry sent a characteristic message to Wilde: 'If the country allows you to leave, all the better for the country! But if you take my son with you I will follow you wherever you go and shoot you!'

12.30pm. Wilde, with Bosie and Ross, arrived at the Holborn Viaduct Hotel, not far from the Old Bailey, to have lunch.

The afternoon newspapers were filled with the news of the sensational outcome of the trial. The National Observer was typical of the reaction: 'No one possessed of a wholesome mind is not under a debt of deep gratitude to the Marquess of Queensberry for destroying the High Priest of the Decadents'. A friend pointed out the placards to Wilde and said: "Well, you have got your name before the public at last'. Oscar nodded: "Yes, nobody can pretend now not to have heard of it". (Perhaps reflecting his comment in 'Dorian Gray': 'There is only one thing in the world worse than being talked about, and that is not being talked about'.)

1pm. Wilde scribbled a letter to the Evening News for its later editions and handed it to a reporter. In the note he explained that he had withdrawn from the case so that Bosie would be spared the ordeal of having to testify in the witness box against his father.

2pm. After discussing the advisability of Oscar's departure for France, Ross left to cash a cheque for £200 to aid the escape.

2.15pm. Wilde and Bosie went to Ely Place to visit the offices of the solicitor *Sir George Lewis* to ask for advice. Lewis told them that they were too late now, but that: "If you had had the sense to bring Lord Queensberry's card to me in the first place, I would have torn it up and thrown it into the fire and told you not to make a fool of yourself."

3.30pm. The application for Wilde's arrest warrant was placed before Sir John Bridge, the Chief Magistrate at Bow Street. According to Travers Humphreys, Sir John asked what time the last boat train to Calais departed, (5.30pm from Victoria Station). He then delayed the hearing till 5pm, thus allowing time for Wilde to catch it. As Sir John later proved himself strongly prejudiced against Wilde, it was unlikely that he would have tampered with the course of justice on his own initiative. The delay must have originated with the Home Secretary, *HH Asquith*. Oscar's flight would have been a great relief to the authorities.

3.45pm. Wilde and Bosie arrived at the Cadogan Hotel in Sloane St. where Bosie had previously checked into Room 53. Ross joined them with the £200 in cash and advised immediate departure to France, (which at the time had no extradition treaty with Britain). Oscar remained in a state of chronic indecision, muttering that: "it is too late. The train has gone". He began drinking a large amount of hock and seltzer.

3.55pm. Oscar despatched Ross with a letter for his wife, *Constance*, to ask her that no one should be allowed in his rooms at Tite St. and to give her the news of the outcome. Shocked by the trial's revelations, (of which she had been ignorant), she told Ross to urge Oscar to flee.

She herself packed some luggage and, taking her two boys, left to stay with her aunt, Mary Napier. The Wilde's butler Arthur remained behind to pay off the servants and to safeguard the house.

4pm. Bosie's cousin, the influential politician *George Wyndham*, arrived at the Cadogan. Fearing recriminations, Oscar sent Ross down to see him. Wyndham also urged immediate departure, before Bosie persuaded him to leave for Westminster to find help.

Upstairs, Wilde had settled back into an air of tipsy fatalism: "I shall stay and do my sentence, whatever it is".

5pm. Thomas Marlowe, a reporter for the Star newspaper, arrived with the news that a warrant for Wilde's arrest had been issued.

Bosie left for the House of Commons to see if George Wyndham had succeeded in finding any political support for preventing a new trial. Wyndham, though, had been met from all sides with a reluctance to intervene. The possibility of Rosebery's involvement had silenced any potential aid.

5.15pm. Oscar waited at the Cadogan with Ross and *Reggie Turner*. He had been drinking heavily in an effort to steady his nerves and by this time was half drunk.

6pm. Wilde was arrested at the Cadogan Hotel and taken by cab firstly to Scotland Yard, and then to Bow Street where he was charged. Bail was refused.

7.30pm. Ross returned to Tite St and, with the aid of Arthur the butler, broke into Oscar's study. He gathered many manuscripts, including the half-finished new play 'La Sainte Courtesane', and also some more clothes for Oscar.

8pm. Ross attempted to deliver the clothes to the Bow St cells but was refused entry. He had to dodge his way into the police station through a mob shouting abuse outside. Another mob was busily attacking the offices of the Bodley Head, while others were smashing the windows of bookshops that had a Wilde title on display.

Overnight, there was an exodus of homosexuals on the trains and early morning ferries to France. Henry Harland probably exaggerated when he claimed that 600 gentlemen were to be found on boats normally carrying 60, but the refugees did include Ross, Reggie Turner, and *Lord Ronald Gower*. Of the people most at risk through their association with Wilde, only Bosie remained in London.

SIR GEORGE LEWIS 1833-1911

Wilde was unfortunate in not obtaining the services of the most influential and shrewdest solicitor of the Victorian age. In his youth, Oscar had been close to both Sir George and his wife Elizabeth. It had been Elizabeth Lewis who, in 1881, had suggested to *D'Oyly Carte* that Oscar would be a good choice to lecture in the USA, and George Lewis who had provided him with letters of introduction there, and who later persuaded *Archibald Forbes* to cease his attacks on Wilde.

Oscar had a genuine admiration for the lawyer: "George Lewis does many a thing that is not remunerative. He is the best I know", adding that: "He knows about us all and he forgives us all". This last statement was only true up to a point. Although Lewis, at Wilde's request, was instrumental in extracting *Bosie Douglas* from a blackmail scandal at Oxford, his realisation of Oscar's involvement in the homosexual underworld led to a distinct cooling of their friendship.

In 1895, when *Queensberry* approached him to act against Wilde, Lewis initially accepted the case, but due to his former regard for Oscar decided to withdraw after the first magistrates' court hearing. He later overcame this reluctance when approached to act for *Constance Wilde*, to whom he gave the strong advice to divorce her husband.

Lewis came from a family of Jewish lawyers. His father, James Lewis, was famous among the criminal classes of London, and was said to have inspired the character of 'Mr Jaggers' in Charles Dickens's 'Great Expectations'. Despite having great legal ability, his son George decided to remain a solicitor, realising that often it was the solicitor who controlled a case and not the barrister.

Once described as looking like 'a Jewish Voltaire', George Lewis was highly recognisable from his trademark apparel of a long fur coat and a monocle. (In *Gilbert and Sullivan's* 'Trial by Jury', the 'Solicitor' was always made up to look like Lewis.)

He was known as 'Society's solicitor' and in *Burne-Jones's* words: "knew enough to hang half the Dukes and Duchesses in the kingdom". He was the epitome of discretion and on his retirement in 1909 burned all his papers. The *Prince of Wales*, a frequent client, said of him: "George Lewis is the one man in England who should write his memoirs – and of course he never can".

Much of his usefulness lay in his ability to keep matters outside the courtroom, (mostly to the benefit of all parties), but, once negotiation failed, Lewis was a bulldog. He believed in 'My client, right or wrong' and played a rough game. He relied on a team of private spies and informers, mainly recruited from the ranks of professional criminals who Lewis had successfully defended. One legal observer, a Mr Smalley, commented that Lewis's methods of investigation made: "the processes of Sherlock Holmes seem like the efforts of a beginner". He was also incorruptible: "A man whose only vice was a liking for good cigars could not be got at".

The list of his cases was exhausting, but they included handling several embarrassing episodes for the *Prince of Wales*, (including the Tranby Croft incident), most of *Labouchere's* endless libel suits, all *D'Oyly Carte's* legal affairs, the Valentine Baker indecent assault case, the *Lady Colin Campbell* divorce case, the *Charles Dilke* affair, and the Archer-Shee five shilling postal order case. His clients included *Ellen Terry*, Daisy, Countess of Warwick, *Mrs Patrick Campbell*, Kitty O'Shea, *Lily Langtry*, and *Jennie Churchill*. Together with Labouchere, Lewis also helped to expose the Times forgeries against *Charles Parnell*.

Lewis had also been involved in one of the most notorious sex scandals of the period when, in 1884, the Irish editor and MP William O'Brien was sued over an article alleging that the centre of British power in Ireland, Dublin Castle, was a hotbed of homosexual activity. O'Brien found that the local police were too intimidated to investigate the allegation.

Acting for O'Brien, Lewis employed one of his own spies, a former London police inspector called William Meiklejohn, to make inquiries. Meiklejohn found a wide circle of homosexuals, centred on a brothel in Golden Lane near the River Liffey, that included important British officials and 'men of all ranks, classes, professions, and outlawries – from aristocrats of the highest fashion to outcasts in the most loathsome dens'.

The discovery led to a high profile court case in which some of the accused received twenty-year sentences. Some Dublin wits suggested that the Lord Lieutenant of Ireland, Earl Spencer, should change his title to 'the Duke of Sodom and Begorrah'.

In 1893, the Prince of Wales insisted that Lewis, despite his Jewish background and relatively humble profession, should receive a knighthood. It was a sign of the changing character of society that Wilde noted in a line in 'The Importance of Being Earnest': 'Markby, Markby, Markby and Markby? A firm of the very highest position in their profession. Indeed I am told that one of the Mr Markbys is occasionally to be seen at dinner parties'.

The Lewis family not only attended dinner parties but their home in Portland Place became a centre where Society met the Arts. In particular they welcomed visiting musicians such as Anton Rubenstein and Ignace Paderewski. Paderewski's first ever recital in a private home was at the Lewis's.

It was a period of great enthusiasm for foreign pianists in London. As Wilde put it: 'Even those that are born in England become foreigners after a time'.

GEORGE WYNDHAM 1863-1913

Wilde had met *Bosie Douglas's* influential cousin, George Wyndham, previously in 1894. When Oscar attempted to stave off *Queensberry's* harassment by issuing a solicitor's letter, Bosie's mother had sent Wyndham to dissuade him from further action. Oscar later wrote that 'plausible George Wyndham with his pliant tongue' had suggested that Oscar 'gradually drop' Bosie.

Wyndham, although a great-grandson of the famous 18th century Irish rebel, Lord Edward Fitzgerald, was a thoroughbred Tory aristocrat. He was also exceptionally good-looking – *Sarah Bernhardt* said he was 'the handsomest man I have ever seen'. He was a member of *Wilfred Blunt's* Crabbet Club, where *Herbert Vivian* recalled him: 'dancing a can-can very gracefully on the dinner table without breaking a single glass'.

In his youth, he served in the Sudan campaign of 1885 and was attached to the Suakin expedition that attempted to reach Khartoum from the Red Sea. Wyndham described the experience of being under fire as: 'very much like not being under fire and the 'whit-ping' of the bullets and little puffs of dust sound and look very harmless'.

In 1887, Wyndham married the wealthy and beautiful widow of the Duke of Westminster, the 34-year-old Sibell Grosvenor. (Before the Duke's early death, Wilde once visited their magnificent home and breathed: "Ah! This is how a gentleman should live".)

Wyndham married Sibell in the teeth of intense rivalry, as over eighty men had declared themselves in love with her. The Marquess of Hartington said of her that: "Lady Grosvenor was by far the most dangerous siren in London and that he would not answer for any man keeping his head or his heart when with her". However, within four years, Sibell was having a clandestine affair with Wilfred Blunt.

[Bendor Grosvenor, Sibell's eldest son from her first marriage, succeeded his father as Duke of Westminster. On one occasion in the 1920s, Bendor was dining in the Café de Paris when he spotted an old flame, the American actress Tallulah Bankhead. Not having seen her for ten years, he greeted her enthusiastically. She gave him a haughty glare and barked: "I thought I told you to wait in the car!"]

Wyndham enjoyed the usual pastimes of the landed gentry but was unusual in that he also attempted to become a man of letters. By 1890, he was regularly writing literary pieces for *WE Henley's* 'National Observer' and expressed great admiration for Henley's verse. *Frank Harris* said that Wyndham always called Henley a remarkable poet 'mainly, I think, because Henley's poetry, second-rate though it was, was better than his own.'

In 1889, Wyndham became a Tory MP, but failed to win the trust of the old guard of his party who regarded him as effete. One grizzled fellow Tory said of George: "Damn the fellow! He pirouettes like a dancing master".

His colleagues also found fault with Wyndham's excruciatingly convoluted speech patterns. One of them, Sir Henry Robinson, said that when discussing quite ordinary subjects like local government: "Wyndham used to frighten me sometimes by speaking so incomprehensibly that I thought I had got a migraine, as I had been quite unable to take in what he said'. Wyndham's great friend, Arthur Balfour, once exhorted him: "My dear George, dilute!, dilute!, dilute!"

The previous Prime Minister, *Lord Salisbury*, had ignored Wyndham for high office, but when Arthur Balfour succeeded Salisbury, Wyndham's time had arrived. In fact, Wyndham's sister, Lady Mary Elcho, promised to make Balfour's life a misery if George was not promoted to the Cabinet.

In 1900, Wyndham became Chief Secretary for Ireland where at first he carried out a repressive policy of coercion. By 1902, eleven sitting Irish MPs had been imprisoned. (The Irish leader John Redmond privately congratulated George for imprisoning one MP, as the incarceration had forced the man to halt his suicidal drinking habits).

But in 1903 Wyndham enacted a remarkable change of policy towards Ireland. Aided by his cousin, Wilfred Blunt, George introduced a Land Act that, backed by a Treasury grant of £150 million, allowed the Irish peasantry to purchase smallholdings from their landlords. By 1908, this monumental scheme had enabled over 240,000 Irish tenants to buy their own farms.

Wilfred Blunt, who persuaded Irish opinion of Wyndham's good faith, called the Land Act 'the most advanced move since Catholic Emancipation'. By fatally weakening the (partly absentee) landlord control, Wyndham had disinherited the ruling ascendancy in Ireland and so removed one of the most intractable problems that had dogged Ireland for centuries.

Lord Charles Beresford said of it: "Mr Wyndham with his Land Act did more for Ireland than any Government that ever was. And I say it as one who has lost a great part of my income under the operation of the Act".

The two cousins – Blunt, a fiery leftwing romantic, and Wyndham, a forthright Tory imperialist – had pulled off an extraordinary coup that changed Ireland from a land of great estates owned by the few to one of small farms owned by the many.

However, by 1905, the strain of office proved too much for Wyndham. Noting his insistence on watching a pavement Punch and Judy show every time he walked down Whitehall, his friends became concerned. Balfour wrote to Sibell Wyndham: 'George is really hardly sane'. Wyndham suffered a nervous breakdown and resigned from the Cabinet. It was said that his career was destroyed 'by drink and Ireland'.

In his last years, Wyndham became an intense Tory utopian, believing that only the monarchy, the Anglican Church, and the landed gentry could provide proper governance. When the Tory party were defeated in the 1906 election, he wrote: 'I am glad we are so soundly beaten. We have shed our financiers and brewers. We stand, by our names and our breeding, for a tradition of one thousand years'. He later added: 'If all England were like Sussex, Kent, Wiltshire and Hampshire, what an earthly Paradise for a happy people'.

The American poet TS Eliot said of Wyndham that he was an example of 'a peculiar English type, the aristocrat, the Imperialist, the Romantic, riding to hounds across his prose, looking with wonder upon the world as upon a fairyland.'

In his earlier parliamentary days, the Tory squires had seen George Wyndham as suspect partly due to his literary interests and connections. They especially distrusted his close friendships with such people as the writer Hilaire Belloc, and the Liberal politician and member of the Crabbet Club, **CHARLES GATTY** (1852-1928).

Wilde also knew Gatty and wrote to Bosie Douglas in 1894: 'I saw Gatty, by chance, as I was driving through Pall Mall. He stopped my cab and we had a long chat about you. He is one of your many admirers'.

In 1892, Gatty stood as a Liberal and Home Rule candidate in the general election but lost after his Tory opponent claimed that Gatty had been expelled from Charterhouse School for homosexuality. Gatty won the resulting libel action and received £2,500 in damages. It is possible that Gatty's success encouraged Wilde to pursue his later court case against Queensberry.

George Wyndham's friend **ARTHUR BALFOUR** (1848-1930) was an old acquaintance of Oscar Wilde, having first met him in 1879. When Balfour had been at Cambridge University, (where he knew *Oscar Browning* well), he had also been a collector of blue china and had suffered similar jibes to those Oscar later received at Oxford.

Aged 21, Balfour inherited over £1 million, and, with the aid of his uncle *Lord Salisbury*, became a Tory MP in 1874. Described as 'looking like a sick vampire bat', at first he was regarded as an ornament even by his own side. Lord Randolph Churchill held him in contempt and nicknamed him 'Postlethwaite' in reference to his aesthetic interests.

The fact that he was a leading member of 'the Souls', a movement Balfour regarded as 'imponderable as gossamer and dew', added to his image as a debonair but ineffectual drone. But even at this early stage he occasionally showed some spirit. When asked if the rumour was true that he intended to marry his fellow 'Soul', Margot Tennant (later *Asquith*), he murmured: "No, I rather thought I'd like to have a career of my own".

His only real romantic attachment was with Mary Elcho, the wife of Lord Hugh Elcho. Their affair appears not to have been fully consummated and Mary herself confessed bewilderment over Balfour's lacklustre coolness towards her: "He is not like other men". The only incident that seems to have upset Balfour's sang froid was when he discovered that Mary was pregnant by *Wilfred Blunt*.

Whatever sexuality there was in their relationship appears have found expression in flagellation. Mary once sent Balfour a Valentine card with a birch rod drawn on the cover and, in another letter, wrote: 'I felt a mass of impertinence and just longed to smack your bottie'.

Balfour had a deep interest in the arts and published several books on philosophy, including 'A Defence of Philosophic Doubt', (of which Wilde reported: 'one of the dullest books we know'). He also enjoyed music and played some instruments. *Dame Ethel Smyth:* "Balfour's passion for Handel was so great that he used to play the solos from 'The Messiah' on a concertina".

He had an abiding interest in spiritualism, (becoming the President of the Society of Psychical Research), and held many séances at his home. During one such session, Balfour was contacted by a spirit who, in his previous human manifestation, had been an irascible army major. It transpired that the major was extremely annoyed by conditions in the afterlife, complaining that: "If this is Hell it has been greatly exaggerated, and if it is Heaven I don't think much of it".

The journalist *Frank Harris* once attended a lunch with Balfour. Harris opened the conversation by saying: "The fact is that all the faults of the age come from Christianity and journalism". Balfour yawned: "Christianity, of course. But why journalism?"

When, in 1887, Balfour was appointed Chief Secretary for Ireland, the Irish Nationalists thought that the governance of Ireland was going to be in the hands of, (in the words of a leading Nationalist, TP O'Connor), 'a more than usually mild member of the mild race of curates'. They had completely misread their man.

Frank Harris wrote that: 'Balfour had been called 'Miss Arabella' at Eton till people found out that he was as autocratic and hard as Nero'. In a policy designed to crush Irish resistance, Balfour brought in his 'Coercion Act', which proved to be as repressive a measure as any in the previous forty years. When he learnt that his new nickname was 'Bloody Balfour', he was privately gratified that his resolute methods had been recognised.

(Wilde remained unimpressed: 'Resolute government – that shallow shibboleth of those who do not understand how complex a thing the art of government is'.)

When his uncle, Lord Salisbury, retired in 1902, Balfour became the new Tory Prime Minister, (giving rise to the colloquial expression 'Bob's Your Uncle'). In spite of his now recognised 'razor within the velvet' quality, he retained his air of languid detachment. Balfour: "Nothing matters very much, and few things matter at all".

The actor Fred Kerr wrote that Balfour's attitude could be summed up as: 'When a boy, it had been my ambition to be a bus driver. Then I discovered that bus drivers didn't choose their own routes and their own stopping places, but were merely servants, and what they had to do was to get through the traffic with the minimum of accidents. Government was very like bus driving'.

Unfortunately for Balfour, his semi-detached view of leadership did not work. The deep divisions of the Tory Party over the economics of Free Trade versus Imperial Preference led, in 1906, to the worst general election defeat until that of John Major's government in 1997.

Balfour's opponent, David Lloyd George, said that 'Balfour was not a man but a mannerism', adding that his place in history would be 'just like the scent on a pocket handkerchief'. Lloyd George's estimation proved wrong for, in one important way, Balfour's influence still resounds a century later.

ZIONISM

Perhaps the only political cause for which Balfour showed any real passion was that of the necessity for a Jewish homeland. He said of Zionism that: "It is a great cause and I understand it".

The Zionist pressure group, the ITO, had been formed in 1895. After *Lord Rosebery* secured Uganda as a British protectorate in 1894, it became the declared intention of the ITO to establish the homeland in that country. In 1918, though, Britain and France were granted a League of Nations mandate to govern the territory previously held by the now defunct Turkish Empire.

With Britain now in control of Palestine, the Zionists turned their attention from Uganda towards what they saw as the country of their biblical origin. Balfour, now British Foreign Secretary, strongly agreed and, in a letter to Lord Rothschild, laid out the principles of what became known as the 'Balfour Declaration'. It promised that the new Jewish homeland should be Palestine.

Balfour: 'Zionism, be it right or wrong…. is of far profounder importance than the desires and prejudices of the seven hundred thousand Arabs who now inhabit that ancient land'. *Lord Curzon*, on the other hand, was deeply worried by this development, prophesying endless upheaval: "One cannot expel the present Moslem population". In the event, Curzon's advice was ignored and Jewish immigration began in earnest.

Balfour's last major government office was that of Foreign Secretary, a post he held from 1916 till 1919. During the First World War, he visited the USA to gain support for the Allied cause. While in New York, his hosts proudly showed him a huge new skyscraper, telling Balfour that it was completely fireproof. Raising an eyebrow, he muttered: "What a pity".

HERBERT H ASQUITH 1852-1928

When Wilde was allowed the few hours on April 5th 1895 in which to make his escape, (and later given two weeks bail), the official who permitted the delay was the Home Secretary, Herbert Asquith. The two men had known each other for ten years and had been friendly enough for Wilde to read Asquith the first draft of his story, 'The Portrait of Mr WH' – Asquith had advised against publication 'lest it corrupt English homes'.

In June 1894, Wilde had lunched at Asquith's home with *Wilfred Blunt*, who reported that Oscar had 'made special fun of his host that day', rendering the politician speechless with a flood of epigrams. Ten months later, as a Government minister, it was Asquith's duty to prosecute his luncheon guest.

Throughout his early career as a lawyer, Asquith was acknowledged as having a strong intellect, tempered by a sentimental streak. *Henry James* called him: 'good, kindly, and easy', while his wife Margot said that, when her husband heard of the sinking of the Titanic: 'his eyes were full of tears and he could not speak'. Blunt said that he was 'a good preacher but distinctly bourgeois'.

Asquith finally attained the pinnacle of his career in 1908, when he became Prime Minister of an aggressively radical Liberal government. Over the next six years, he had secured the rights of trade unions, introduced old-age pensions, destroyed the un-elected House of Lords veto over the House of Commons, and pushed forward his plans for Home Rule in Ireland within an imperial framework. In so doing, he gained some bitter enemies.

All his efforts were eclipsed by the onset of the First World War. He was so unaware of the danger that he sent his daughter Elizabeth to Holland in July 1914, just four days before the declaration of war between Germany and Russia – she had to make a speedy departure for home.

(Asquith was not alone in his lack of diplomatic foresight. *Frank Harris* reported that the German Kaiser had never intended war with Britain; when he realised that she would indeed be among Germany's enemies, he desperately tried to stop the conflict.)

As a war leader, Asquith lacked military experience and relied greatly on the War Office under *Lord Kitchener*. However, Asquith became disillusioned with their efforts, claiming that the War Office worked with three different sets of figures: 'One to mislead the public; another to mislead the Cabinet; and the third to mislead itself'.

By 1916 the war had settled into a murderous stalemate and, on both sides, efforts were made to secure peace. (The German General Ludendorff later admitted in his memoirs that his high command realised that the war was lost by the end of that year.)

In November 1916, the British peer, the Marquess of Lansdowne, issued a secret memorandum advocating negotiation because: 'we are slowly killing off the male population of these islands'. He suggested that the allies should make it clear that they did not intend 'annihilation of the enemy' as a war aim, and to appeal to the German peace party that the ruin of Europe should be avoided.

A month later, on December 12, the Germans responded: 'Germany, together with her Allies, conscious of her responsibility before God, their own nation and humanity, have proposed this morning to the hostile powers peace negotiations'.

When news of these moves reached the British newspaper lords, they reacted with fury. The Marquess of Lansdowne was vilified by the Harmsworth Press, (attacks that did not relent until Lansdowne's death). Asquith, who had said of the German offer: 'How I wish I could believe that someone would have the wits to keep this door ajar', came under equal condemnation.

A conspiracy led by Lord Northcliffe, Lord Beaverbrook, and *Edward Carson* sought to impeach Asquith, using a press witch-hunt to destroy him. Margot Asquith said of the attack: 'If 20 or 30 newspapers keep repeating the same thing day after day they will be believed'. Asquith was undermined even within his own party when David Lloyd George joined the Northcliffe camp. Margot seethed with indignation against 'that little parvenu, Lloyd George': "He could not see a belt without hitting below it".

On the 7th December 1916, Asquith was forced to resign as Prime Minister. As Margot said: "Large fortunes were being accumulated and it is surprising how easily non-combatants get acclimatised to death".

For the rest of his life, Asquith remained aggrieved over his political destruction and it exacerbated his already heavy drinking. Another factor in his departure had been that the British people were well aware of his enjoyment of alcohol, and the word 'squiffy' had been added to the synonyms for 'drunk' in honour of their Prime Minister.

Asquith's first wife, Helen, had died of typhoid fever in 1891, leaving him with five children. In 1894, he married Margot Tennant, by whom he had another son. This marriage did not prevent him from gaining a reputation for minor sexual harassment of women, his wandering hands under tablecloths at dinners becoming especially notorious. The politician and socialite Alfred Duff Cooper said of him: "He is oblivious of young men and lecherous of young girls".

In 1912, he began a possibly unconsummated affair with the 24-year-old Venetia Stanley, forty years his junior, whom he described as 'the pole and lodestar of my life'. This ended, to his deep sadness, in 1915. His wife Margot remained complacent about the situation: 'No woman should expect to be the only woman in her husband's life'.

Wilde had known **MARGOT ASQUITH** (1864-1945) even longer than he had known her husband. He was friendly with the Tennant family and when, in 1874, the ten-year-old Margot began a schoolroom magazine, he promised to contribute two stories. In 1891, he dedicated another story, 'The Star Child', 'To Miss Margot Tennant'. As an adult, Margot was less fond of Oscar, saying that there was 'something monstrous and unreal' about him.

Margot was a headstrong, indiscreet young woman, known for shrilly blurting out her views regardless of general opinion. The daughter of a rich Liberal industrialist, she was raised in Peebleshire, Scotland, and, with her sister Laura, arrived to live in London in 1882. Arthur

Benson described them as 'screaming themselves into society', adding primly that 'there is something vulgar about the Tennants'.

Margot enjoyed the company of elderly men and became a favourite of several well known ones. She visited the writer *JA Symonds* in Davos, sat on *Gladstone's* knee while he read her poetry, (a habit she repeated with *Lord Tennyson*), and became *Benjamin Jowett's* unofficial 'hostess' during his last years as Master of Balliol.

She chose her younger friends from the group called 'The Souls', a social network mostly related to each other, who were interested in literature and the arts, rather than the usual country pursuits of hunting and fishing. Although mostly liberals, they were politically promiscuous, providing a common ground where all shades of opinion could mix.

(While Wilde was never seen as a member of the Souls, they admired him for his intellect. *Wilfred Blunt*: "The Souls ran after him, because they knew he could always amuse them, and the pretty women allowed him great familiarities, although there was no question of love-making'.)

Many of the 'Souls' were also members of Blunt's Crabbet Club, and they generally met at weekend parties at such country houses as Stanway, Clouds, Taplow, and Gosford. In the words of Blunt's daughter Judith, Margot 'burst on the Souls like a bomb on a lily pond'.

Margot also mixed in some less rarefied environments. Temporarily sobered by the death of her sister Laura in childbirth, she spent some time attempting social work in a factory in the East End of London. She was there during the 'Jack the Ripper' episode and once accompanied the workers to the scene of the latest murder. Margot: 'It was strange watching crowds of people collected daily to see nothing but an archway'.

One day, she ended up with some factory girls in a grubby Whitechapel pub called the Peggy Bedford. When one of the girls got into a fight with another woman, Margot attempted to help. 'Before I could separate the combatants, I had given and received heavy blows. Unexpected help came from a factory packer who happened to come in; we extricated ourselves as best we could and ran back to the factory'.

When it came to marriage, Margot again seemed to prefer men at least ten years older. She became romantically involved with Alfred Milner, (later to be the High Commissioner for South Africa), and accompanied him to Egypt. On a moonlit ride near the Pyramids, he swept her off her horse, kissed her, and proposed marriage. She turned him down.

(While in Cairo she also met *Lord Kitchener* who she thoroughly disliked, and ever after associated Egypt with 'bed bugs, dysentery, lumpy mattresses, and Kitchener'.)

Back in England in 1892, rumours spread that she was engaged to the now widowed *Lord Rosebery* – to his great annoyance. Although she never mentioned the incident herself, it appears that it was (the inevitable) Wilfred Blunt who finally relieved her of her virginity.

Eventually, Margot turned her attentions to the rising politician, Herbert Asquith. Asquith was warned by his friend Lord Rosebery that: "If you want to know what Miss Tennant is like, read 'Dodo'." *EF Benson* had caricatured Margot in his 1892 satirical book as 'a pretentious donkey with the heart and brains of a linnet'.

Ignoring this advice, Asquith married Margot in 1894, (the register was signed by four current and future Prime Ministers – Gladstone, Rosebery, Balfour and Asquith himself.) Having previously led a humdrum lawyer's life, Asquith found his new bride to be a dazzling experience.

Both sets of their friends were puzzled by their relationship. Asquith's Liberal political colleagues grumbled about his new taste for country houses, while Margot's friends could not understand why a first rate rider should become involved with a man who did not hunt. For her part, Margot decided that Asquith's first name, Herbert, was too plebeian, and insisted that he call himself by his second name, Henry.

Margot's instincts about her husband's potential proved correct and Asquith's political reputation spread internationally. On one occasion, Margot was introduced to the South African gold mine millionaire, JB Robinson.

Margot: 'He was tall and deaf and, as he offered me his arm to take me in to dinner, he paused on the stair, looked at me and said in a voice of thunder: "What is your name?" To which I replied almost as loud: "Asquith!" He thought for a moment and bellowed: "Any relation to the famous Asquith?" I screamed back "Wife!"'

In 1902 Margot gave birth to her only child Anthony, (nicknamed 'Puffin'), but after a further miscarriage the couple abandoned marital relations on medical advice. She became an uneasy stepmother to Asquith's children from his first marriage. The cessation of her sex life did not appear to have fazed Margot; although her enemies always claimed that she was highly sexed, this appears not to have been the case.

When in 1908 Asquith became Prime Minister, the family moved into Number 10, Downing Street. Margot complained: 'The King's peacocks in St James Park were an infernal nuisance – they woke everybody up in the early hours with their cries'.

Throughout the many crises of her husband's premiership, Margot was his combative supporter, and her dominating personality grated on many members of his cabinet. Also, her outspoken defence of the artistic world aggravated the tacit philistinism of the right.

When her friend *Robert Ross* became involved in a 1914 court case involving his homosexuality, Margot not only backed him but invited him to Downing Street during the trial. After he lost the case, Margot pushed Asquith into arranging for a testimonial on Ross's behalf, (an extraordinary reversal of attitudes as compared to the Wilde affair).

However, this tolerance encouraged her enemies to stir surmise about her own lifestyle. During the notorious 'Black Book' trial of 1918, when it emerged that she had allowed the dancer Maud Allen to perform a semi-nude dance at Downing Street, the rumour spread that Margot was a lesbian.

She shared her husband's bitterness at their underhand removal from power in 1916, a bitterness deepened by the fact that, as ex-premiers received no pension, they were now relatively poorly off.

She restored some wealth to the family by publishing her autobiography, a volume about which the American reviewer Dorothy Parker wrote: 'the affair between Margot Asquith and Margot Asquith is one of the prettiest love stories in all literature'.

Her advancing years did little to bridle her acerbic tongue. Through her son Puffin's cinema contacts, she met many film stars including Mary Pickford and Douglas Fairbanks. On one occasion she met the actress Jean Harlow who made the error of addressing her as 'Margot' as if her name rhymed with 'dot'. Margot corrected her pronunciation: "My dear, the 't' is silent. As in Harlow".

Margot enjoyed high fashion and particularly favoured the creations of the most popular couturier in Europe, Monsieur **CHARLES WORTH** (1825-95). Worth was, in effect, the founder of Paris high couture and held court in his fashionable salon at No 7, rue de la Paix.

He had risen to prominence after Pauline Metternich, daughter-in-law of the Austrian Chancellor, had recommended him to the Empress Eugenie. He persuaded the Empress to abandon the crinoline and provided sixty dresses for her trip to Egypt to open the Suez Canal. He also inveigled *Lily Langtry* and *Patsy Cornwallis-West* into posing for advertisements.

(Wilde did not approve of Worth's concept of fashion: 'If one could fancy the Medicean Venus taken from her pedestal in the Louvre to Monsieur Worth's establishment to be dressed in modern French millinery, every single beautiful line would be destroyed, and no one would look at her a second time'.)

406

Although Margot was much more appreciative, it did not prevent her arguing over the gowns with the chubby little designer, arguments that often ended with both screaming at each other in voluble French.

In truth they were both British. Worth was born in Lincolnshire and began his career as a shop assistant in the London emporium of Derry and Toms.

Margot's only child, **ANTHONY ASQUITH** (1902-1968), developed into as heavy a drinker as his father had been. This habit did not prevent him from becoming one of the best-known British film directors of the mid 20th century.

His most famous films included 'The Way to the Stars', (voted the most popular film of the Second World War years), 'The Winslow Boy', (based on *Edward Carson's* Archer-Shee case), and versions of three *Bernard Shaw* plays. He continued the Asquith family connection to Oscar Wilde by directing the first cinema adaptation of 'The Importance of Being Earnest', starring Edith Evans.

The arrest of Wilde was followed by an outburst of public moral indignation against not only Oscar but also anybody or anything associated with him. Amongst the leaders of this crusade were two redoubtable literary ladies, Mrs Humphrey Ward and Mrs Alice Meynell.

MRS HUMPHREY WARD 1851-1920

The novelist and social worker Mrs Ward, (born Mary Augusta Arnold), took on the task of writing to the publisher *John Lane* demanding the dismissal of the Yellow book illustrator *Aubrey Beardsley*, whom she wrongly assumed to be a confederate of Wilde. She told the writer *Edmund Gosse* that: "my position before the British public makes it necessary for me to write".

Gertrude Atherton wrote of Mrs Ward: 'She took herself with portentous seriousness', while Wilde alluded to her type in 'Lady Windermere's Fan: 'A man who moralises is usually a hypocrite, and a woman who moralises is invariably plain. There is nothing in the whole world so unbecoming to a woman as a Non-conformist conscience'.

The granddaughter of Dr Arnold of Rugby School fame, Mrs Ward had been born in Tasmania. The family returned to England in 1856, and in 1872 she married a tutor and fellow of Brasenose College, Oxford, Thomas Humphrey Ward.

In 1884, she published her first novel, 'Miss Bretherton'. Her uncle, *Matthew Arnold*, commented: "Written a novel, has she? No Arnold can write a novel. If they could, I should have written one long ago". Nonetheless, he was quietly rather proud of her efforts.

Her 1888 book, 'Robert Elsmere', was a novel about the moral doubts of a young Anglican curate, and represented the peak of her achievement. While it proved very popular at the time, Oscar Wilde did not share the general view: 'A thoughtful young friend of ours once told us that it reminded him of the sort of conversation that goes on at a meat tea in the house of a serious Nonconformist family. It is only in England that such a book could be produced. England is the home of lost ideas.'

Oscar added fuel to the flames of her resentment when he wrote that, while travelling by train across the American West in 1882, many of his fellow passengers were reading paperback copies of the book. 'As each page is finished, it is torn out and flung through the window, so that in the end the American prairie will get a top dressing of 'Robert Elsmere'.' (Sadly, this anecdote was invented, as the book was not actually published till 1888).

Her interest in the moral improvement of the lower classes led Mrs Ward to involve herself in social work in the East End of London. (Wilde: 'As for that great and daily increasing school of novelists for whom the sun always rises in the East End, the only thing that can be said about them is that they find life crude, and leave it raw.')

The Victorian ruling class strongly opposed the idea of government intervention when it came to the problem of poverty, and preferred to deal with it through private charity. (Henrietta Stanley: "Charity is the calling of a lady").

Wilde was not the only one to argue that this paternalistic method only perpetuated the status quo. The Weekly Dispatch wrote: 'The way in which women of fashion help the poor by travelling 200 miles to sing at a concert or dance at a ball, instead of sending the amount of their first class ticket to a soup kitchen, is one explanation of why so little is really done'.

Mrs Ward continued to write novels, such as 'The Testing of Diana Mallory', with decreasing success until her death in 1920. She spent much of her later life fighting against the introduction of 'votes for women' and in 1908 founded the Women's National Anti-Suffrage League.

MRS ALICE MEYNELL 1847-1922

Another figure who became morally outraged by the revelations about Wilde was the poet and journalist, Mrs Alice Meynell. She led a delegation to *John Lane's* office demanding that Oscar's work should be removed from the Bodley Head publishing list. Discovering that Lane had already done so, she then insisted that *Aubrey Beardsley* was sacked as art editor of the Yellow Book.

Having converted to the Roman Catholic faith in 1872, Mrs Meynell, (born Alice Thompson), married the genial raconteur and fellow journalist, Wilfred Meynell, in 1877; (she gave birth to eight children between 1879 and 1891). Together, they edited the Catholic literary magazine, 'Merry England' from 1883 till 1895. She wrote a considerable amount of Catholic poetry that was highly regarded by many critics.

Gertrude Atherton met Alice on a visit to England and described her as 'perhaps the properest woman in London'. Atherton: 'At first meeting, one assumed impatiently that she was a mass of affectation, and had to keep a sharp rein on one's facial muscles. She spoke slowly and dreamily, her eyes far away'.

Max Beerbohm found Alice to be much too relentlessly cultivated for his taste. When she published an essay entitled 'De-civilised', he scribbled on a copy: 'If only she could have been – just a little!'

Given the level of refinement in the Meynell home, one of their house-guests, (at one point a permanent fixture), was a surprising choice. **FRANCIS THOMPSON** (1859-1907) had been raised in Preston, Lancashire, and became a medical student in Manchester. After a quarrel with his father, Thompson tramped to London where, (having enjoyed Thomas De Quincy's book 'Confessions of an Opium Eater'), he swiftly became addicted to opium.

For three years he led a life of total destitution, sleeping rough on the main rubbish tip in Covent Garden and under the Charing Cross arches. He scratched a bare living by selling matches and opening cab doors for the gentry. One rare episode of employment in a shoe shop ended because of Thompson's inept habit of trying to ram right boots on to left feet.

Finally, he abandoned hope and managed to save enough opium to supply himself with a lethal dose. When he attempted his suicide bid, he had only swallowed half of the required dose before he fell under a bus. A kind-hearted prostitute took pity on Thompson and allowed him to stay in her room for six months.

A further suicide attempt was thwarted when, (Thompson claimed), the ghost of the 18th century poet Thomas Chatterton appeared and persuaded Thompson not to swallow the fatal dosage on the grounds that money would arrive the following day. Amazingly, 'Chatterton' proved to be correct, when payment for a poem that Thompson had written arrived from the offices of Wilfred Meynell.

Meynell had received these scraps of Thompson's poetry six months previously, but only recognised their quality at this late stage. He set out to find the mysterious correspondent, finally traced him to a chemist shop in Drury Lane where Thompson was in the habit of buying opium, and left a message for the poet to contact him. Weeks later, the ramshackle Thompson lurched into the offices of 'Merry England'.

Taking pity on the gaunt bard, the Meynells invited him to make his home with them. Although Thompson never entirely shook off his opium habit, this domestication worked well. His religious verse, in particular 'The Hound of Heaven', soon won him a wide audience.

Wilde, (who had occasionally met Thompson drinking in the Crown pub during his vagrant years), heard Thompson's 'Sister Song' read aloud and exclaimed: "Why can't I write poetry like that? That is what I've wanted to do all my life".

In his last years, Thompson found some solace in his poems and some cash in writing book reviews, but found that the greatest release from his demons came from watching cricket.

Although he had been rescued from suicidal penury, he remained a despondent figure. *Richard Le Gallienne* called him: 'a rather ineffective personality, sitting silent and shrunken within himself'. When Thompson and Alice Meynell visited *Wilfred Blunt's* home, Blunt wrote afterwards: 'They made a lugubrious pair, she with her tearful voice, he weak-eyed and red-nosed'.

Following his overnight stay at Bow Street police station, Wilde was removed to Holloway Prison on April 6th 1895 to await his trial three weeks later.

Meanwhile on April 24th Wilde's creditors insisted on an enforced sheriff's sale of his entire possessions. The auction was held inside his Tite Street home in a scene that bordered on semi-controlled looting. In an early poem, 'On the Sale by Auction of Keats's Love Letters', Oscar had written a prophetic, if understated, description of what now occurred in reality:

'And now the brawlers of the auction mart, Bargain and bid for each poor blotted note, Ay! For each separate pulse of passion quote, The merchant's price. I think they love not art, Who break the crystal of a poet's heart, That small and sickly eyes may glare and gloat.'

Wilde's first trial began on April 26th and lasted for five days. Sir Edward Clarke remained as his defence barrister, while Charles Gill, (Edward Carson's junior counsel at the Queensberry trial), took over the prosecution. The judge was Sir Arthur Charles.

Together with his co-defendant, Alfred Taylor, Oscar was charged with 'indecent behaviour with other men', (a sodomy charge had been considered but, being difficult to prove, had been dropped).

This trial was notable for the conspicuous fairness with which both the judge and the prosecutor treated Wilde.

Clarke, for the defence, demolished the evidence of several of the state's rent-boy witnesses, and Oscar again displayed his ready wit when questioned by Charles Gill.

Gill: "Did it strike you that this place was at all peculiar?" Wilde: "Not at all". Gill: "Not the sort of street you would usually visit in? You had no other friends there?" Wilde: "No, this was merely a bachelor's place". Gill: "Rather a rough neighbourhood?" Wilde: "That I don't know. It was near the Houses of Parliament".

When asked to describe 'the love that dare not speak its name', Oscar replied with one of the most magnificent speeches ever heard from a dock, and one that drew loud applause from the public gallery.

At the conclusion of the trial, the jury was split, eleven for conviction, and one against. (Given the judge's sympathetic treatment of Wilde throughout the trial, many observers thought that, even with a *conviction, the sentence would have been light. Bosie Douglas later wrote: 'I know that Justice Charles would have given Wilde six months jail at the first trial rather than two years. There was no corruption of minors, or brutality, or master and pupil scenario. The victims were all accomplices'.)*

Pending a decision about a re-trial, Wilde was released on bail from Holloway Prison on May 1ˢᵗ 1895. The sureties were provided by Percy Douglas and the Rev. Stuart Headlam.

REV. STUART HEADLAM 1847-1924

Stuart Headlam was an unlikely guarantor of Wilde's bail, as Oscar had only met him twice. Nevertheless, when approached by Oscar's friend, Ernest Leverson, Headlam agreed to put up the £1,250, as he believed that no man should be pre-judged.

During the final trial he insisted on accompanying Oscar each day to the Old Bailey in the teeth of public disapproval. As a result, some of Headlam's servants left his employ, and his house in Bloomsbury was stoned by an anti-Wilde mob.

When Wilde was released from Pentonville jail in 1897, he reluctantly allowed himself to be taken to the, by now, safe haven of Headlam's house. Oscar felt uneasy with the clergyman, telling a friend: 'I do not like the idea at all. If you really wish it, I will go to his house, but I would sooner not'.

Headlam later said of their 1897 meeting: "I like to think of him as I knew him for those six hours on that spring morning, and to hope that somewhere and somehow the beauty of his character may be garnered and the follies and weaknesses burnt up."

Headlam was an unusual man whom Wilde called 'the heresiarch', the press called 'the Dancing Parson', and who **Bernard Shaw** used as the model for his character of 'Reverend Morell' in his play 'Candida'. Impetuous and hot-tempered, Headlam revolted against the concept of the traditional parson: "I have never been a believer in the literal inspiration of the Bible. I pin my faith to a Person, not to a Book".

When a boy at Eton in the 1860s, Headlam had supported views that bordered on socialism, then at Cambridge University had chosen the church as a career.

Between 1870 and 1882, Headlam was a curate at Drury Lane, then at Bethnal Green, and then in two prisons. He became particularly fond of Bethnal Green – an area of London that an American visitor described as 'the most appalling place on earth'. (When the novelist Olive Schreiner told Wilde that: "I live in the East End because there people do not wear masks", Oscar replied: "And I live in the West End because there they do".)

When Headlam's rector, Septimus Hansard, (who shared Headlam's radicalism), attempted to establish a Free Library in Bethnal Green to be funded from the rates, the slum landlords insisted on a poll amongst the ratepayers. Headlam was incensed when he heard that the landlords had threatened to raise the rents by sixpence a week if the library was built. "Damn them all! The actual cost to them would be no more than a shilling a year". When Hansard and Headlam lost the vote, the anti-library churchwardens decided to ring a peal of church bells to celebrate their victory, until they discovered that Hansard had hidden the key to the church.

Such incidents fuelled Headlam's choleric denunciations of the rich and he was soon regarded as a liability by the ecclesiastical authorities. His pastoral homilies included an unorthodox view on temperance. He told one group of workmen to abstain from alcohol on the grounds of avoiding waste: "Every one of you who takes more beer than he needs is guilty of a sin because he is wasting a good thing. He is wasting good liquor".

He was removed from Bethnal Green after advising the young women of the parish to attend the theatres and music halls, (then seen as the haunts of Satan). Eventually he was asked to leave even his prison chaplaincy after making a speech in Trafalgar Square advocating the abolition of the House of Lords. The Bishop of London, Frederick Temple, revoked his licence for eleven years.

Headlam wrote to a friend: 'Just got the sack for being political', and mused over the possible wording of a newspaper advert: 'Reverend Stuart Headlam sacked for the fourth time. Wants work.'

One of his lasting achievements was the creation of the Church and Stage Guild, an attempt to break down the prejudice against theatre in general, and ballet in particular. Predictably it was ridiculed by the press as 'the society for administering weak tea to reluctant ballet girls'. Far from indulging in weak tea, Headlam preferred to accompany young actresses to such venues as the Crown public house where he mingled with the cream of the Decadents.

By 1900, Headlam and the Guild had accomplished their aim and the theatre world was included among 'the respectable'. *Sir Henry Irving*: 'People sometimes maintain that the stage is indebted to me for the greater esteem in which it is now held, but really, did they but know it, actors owe far more to that man Headlam'.

In 1886, Headlam joined the Fabian Society and continued to needle the rightwing by his support for the Bryant and May matchgirl strike. He helped form the Guild of St Matthew to develop Christian Socialism, and spent seventeen years on the London County Council championing the poor.

As a further affront to the abstemious, he started the Anti-Puritan League, a society dedicated to conviviality whose members included the rotund bon vivant, GK Chesterton.

Frederick Temple, the Bishop of London, (Headlam's nemesis during his curate days, and with whom Headlam had had an especially fraught debate about whether ballet dancers were entitled to wear short skirts), had an intimidating reputation. When he later became the Archbishop of Canterbury, he sometimes examined candidates for the clergy himself, a nerve-wracking experience for the aspiring applicants.

During an interview, Temple tested one young hopeful on his ability to comfort the afflicted by asking him to role-play the part of a vicar visiting the sick. "I will lie down on that sofa and pretend to be ill. You leave the room, come in again, and 'hospital-bedside' me". The young man followed the instructions and approached the prone archbishop. Tut-tutting censoriously, he sighed: "Why, Reggie, you've been on the booze again".

Headlam engaged in a series of heated religious debates with **CHARLES BRADLAUGH** (1833-1891), the radical politician who advocated free thought. (Headlam: 'Bradlaugh does not know God, but God knows Bradlaugh'.) In spite of their opposed attitudes, the impeccably fair-minded Headlam had great respect for his opponent's integrity: "How much nearer to the Kingdom of Heaven are these men in the Hall of Science than the followers of Moody and Sankey", (American Christian evangelists who toured Britain in 1874-5).

In 1880, Bradlaugh won a parliamentary seat but was refused admission to the Commons because of his refusal to swear an oath on the Bible. When he tried to force a second entry, he was kicked and thumped by other MPs, then frog-marched away into custody in the Clock Tower of the Houses of Parliament. Headlam sent him a telegram reading: 'Accept my warmest sympathy. I wish you good luck in the name of Jesus Christ, the Emancipator, whom so many of your opponents blaspheme.'

Bradlaugh was eventually allowed to take his seat in 1885 and became a popular member of the House. (It is likely that he was the father of the illegitimate fraudster, Horatio Bottomley).

After his release on bail from Holloway Prison, Wilde travelled by cab to the Midland Hotel, St Pancras, where a room had been booked for him by Percy Douglas. After a few hours, the hotel manager asked him to leave as a gang of thugs, hired by Queensberry, had followed him there and were causing trouble.

Oscar retreated to further hotels in Kilburn and Notting Hill, where the same thing happened. Desperate, he arrived at Oakley Street, Chelsea, the home of his mother, 'Speranza' Wilde, and his brother Willie.

WILLIE WILDE (Second Part – cont. from page 260)

While Oscar's career had spiralled, his brother Willie had been sinking ever deeper into alcoholism. After the end of his disastrous marriage to Mrs Leslie in 1892, he had moved to Great Malvern, Worcestershire, where he lived with a Dublin born woman called Sophia 'Lily' Lees. The rift with Oscar was so great that, when Willie married Lily in January 1894, Oscar did not attend the ceremony.

The newly weds moved back into London to take up residence at the rented Chelsea home of Lady Wilde. 'Speranza', after initial reluctance, welcomed her new daughter-in-law and, after Lily gave birth to a daughter *Dolly* in July 1895, was delighted by her new grandchild.

Although they had not spoken to each other for two years, when Oscar began his action against the *Marquess of Queensberry* Willie was at first supportive. He wrote to Oscar to tell him that he was defending him 'all over London'. Oscar was dubious about the value of such a defence: "My poor dear brother could compromise a steam engine!"

Oscar was right to have doubts. *Bernard Shaw* was amazed at Willie's 'inconceivable want of tact' in stating that: "Oscar is *not* a man of bad character! In fact, you could trust him with a woman anywhere."

When Oscar arrived seeking refuge at Oakley St, Willie said that despite the ill feeling between them: "he came to me like a wounded stag and I took him in". Oscar fell ill for several days and was put on a camp bed near the fireplace. Willie's sympathy apparently started to fade. As he sat drinking, he muttered grudgingly to Oscar: "At least my vices were decent".

Both Speranza and Willie were adamant that Oscar should not flee the country. Willie: "Oscar is an Irish gentleman and he will face the music, like Christ". He told *WB Yeats* that, if it had been in Oscar's best interests, he would have helped him to escape: "Yes, even if I had to inflate a balloon in the back garden myself!"

However, *Frank Harris* told a different story. He said that Oscar feared that, if he tried to run, Willie would turn him in to the police. Oscar: "You don't know Willie. He has made my solicitors buy letters of mine, he has blackmailed me". After a couple of weeks, Oscar left to find a more congenial haven.

During Oscar's imprisonment, the relationship between the brothers collapsed completely. Lily Wilde did visit Oscar in Wandsworth Prison, but over the two years Willie never came, claiming that: "for many reasons Oscar would not want to see me".

One of these reasons was that Oscar was livid with fury because Willie had pawned or sold Oscar's expensive fur coat. Lily later disclaimed all knowledge of Willie's mismanagement of Oscar's possessions, but by 1897 Oscar referred to both his brother and sister-in-law as 'those people'.

After 1895, Willie's life disintegrated further in a series of alcoholic binges and brainstorms. His professional and social career, already insecure, was ruined because of his connection to Oscar. The name of 'Wilde' was now so notorious that any chance of a job vanished.

One night, after the manager realised who he was, Willie was refused entrance to a restaurant. The ensuing fistfight ended with Willie in the dock himself. In an effort to prevent

412

more bad publicity, he offered the court reporters £5 each to keep his name out of the papers. Annoyed at what they considered to be an insult, they went out of their way to report the case as prominently as they could.

Tired of Willie's drinking and abusive behaviour, Lily left him in 1896 and returned with their daughter Dolly to Malvern. Willie sank into an alcoholic depression. In March 1899, he died of hepatic liver failure and was buried in Kensal Green Cemetery in a common grave.

Oscar greeted the news philosophically: 'Between him and me there had been wide chasms for many years. Requiescat in pace'.

Meanwhile, London was gripped by rumour and moral panic, stoked by the press. A Frenchman recalled that, as a boy, he had been brought to London during May 1895. His father allowed him to go for a walk in Hyde Park, with the warning that: 'if any man with a sunflower in his coat and carrying a lily speaks to you, run back to the hotel as fast as possible'.

At the St James Theatre, Wilde's formerly very successful play, 'The Importance of Being Earnest', was forced to close. On May 11th it was replaced by a play by Henry Arthur Jones entitled, with grotesque coincidence, 'The Triumph of the Philistines'.

HENRY ARTHUR JONES 1851-1929

Together with Sir Arthur Pinero, Henry Arthur Jones and Oscar Wilde were the three leading playwrights of the early 1890s. However, there was little love lost between the latter pair. Jones felt a distinct dislike of Oscar, as did Jones's intellectual mentor, the sociologist and philosopher of evolution, Herbert Spencer. (In 1882, Spencer had said: "Oscar Wilde is an outlandish person who attempts to reconcile idiocy with art".)

For his part, Oscar called Jones 'a stage carpenter' with the literary skills of 'a grocer's assistant'. Wilde: 'There are three rules for writing plays. The first is not to write like Henry Arthur Jones; the second and third are precisely the same.'

One day, while rehearsing his new play in a theatre where a Jones show was still running, Wilde was interrupted by a reverberating crash in the wings. Oscar calmly reassured his cast: "Pray do not be alarmed, ladies and gentlemen. The crash you have heard is merely some of Mr Jones's dialogue that has fallen flat".

Coming from humble origins, Jones spent his early adult years working as a commercial traveller until, falling in love with the stage, he decided to become a fulltime playwright. After his first real success in 1882 with 'The Silver King', he wrote over ninety plays, including hits such as 'The Dancing Girl' (1891), 'Michael and His Lost Angel' (1896), and 'The Liars' (1897).

(Bizarrely, this last play was thought to have been ghost-written by Wilde. In 1898, a Californian reviewer reported: 'It is well known that Mr Henry Arthur Jones did not write 'The Liars', but only fathered it. After his seclusion, Oscar Wilde pulled himself together and wrote one supreme masterpiece, 'The Liars'.')

In spite of his success, Jones became the butt of considerable snobbery over his plebeian background and Cockney accent. After the actor *Charles Brookfield* had listened to Jones's first reading of 'Michael and His Lost Angel', he sneered: "But, Mr Jones, it is so long. Even without the 'H's".

In his later years, Jones was famous as a voluble conservative, deeply opposed to the suffragettes, and passionately supportive of the First World War. He viewed the writer *Bernard Shaw* as the epitome of socialist pacifism and saw it as his patriotic duty to launch a vitriolic campaign against him. Shaw remained unmoved. After Jones had described England as his mother and accused Shaw of kicking her on her deathbed, Shaw wrote: 'it is so enormously funny that it deprives me of all power of taking him seriously'.

Jones also clashed with another of his contemporaries, the actor *Sir Herbert Beerbohm Tree*, who played a leading role in Jones's 'The Dancing Girl'. Jones had an ill temper when crossed and, during the rehearsals, his quarrels with Tree became legendary, with Jones rushing out to the street to calm down, while Tree retired to his dressing room to quaff restoratives.

One of their rows became famous in the theatre. One day, Jones exploded: "No! No! No!" Tree replied: "Don't repeat yourself". Jones: "I must if you don't listen". Tree: "Repetition breeds listlessness. By the time you said your last 'no', I've forgotten what the first was about". Jones: "Very well. I'll be content with one. NO!" Tree: "No what?"

As the rehearsals continued, one of Jones's friends inquired: "How are you getting on with Beerbohm Tree?" Jones answered earnestly: "Oh, very well indeed! I had to send him my solicitor this morning, but otherwise things are quite smooth".

Tiring of the oppressive atmosphere of his family home at Oakley Street, Wilde accepted the invitation to move to the house of some close friends, Ada and Ernest Leverson, at 2, Courtfield Gardens, South Kensington.

He arrived on May 18 and, as the Leverson children were away, was installed in the nursery. Amidst the dolls' houses and rocking horses, he held meetings with such visitors as his solicitors and WB Yeats.

Oscar whiled away the time by re-reading his hosts' copies of Dickens and one evening informed them that: "One would need a heart of stone not to laugh at the death of Little Nell".

ADA LEVERSON 1862-1933

The comic writer Ada Leverson, (whom he nicknamed 'the Sphinx'), had known Wilde since 1892 and had parodied him affectionately in Punch and other magazines. They appreciated each other's wit, and Oscar had borrowed Ada's line – "Nothing spoils a romance more than a sense of humour in a woman and the lack of it in a man' – to insert into 'A Woman of No Importance'. When he told her that in Paris he used to be followed by a devoted rent-boy 'with a knife in his hand', Ada remarked brightly: "I'm sure he had a fork in the other".

The Leversons stayed loyal to Wilde throughout his life. Considering Ernest's position as a City businessman, it was an act of considerable courage. On the morning of his release from prison, Ada was present when Wilde arrived at *Rev. Stuart Headlam's* house. Oscar greeted her with the words: "Sphinx, how marvellous of you to know exactly the right hat to wear at seven o'clock in the morning to meet a friend who has been away. You can't have got up, you must have sat up".

Ada was the daughter of the affluent Jewish Beddington family and was raised in the heart of cultured London society. She married the wealthy diamond dealer Ernest Leverson in 1881 but their union had its problems. Ernest was twelve years her senior and she found his company dull; their relationship was also strained by his indulgence in several extra-marital affairs.

Ada responded by taking lovers herself, including a torrid romance with the writer *George Moore*, who encouraged her literary ambitions. It appeared that she made unsuccessful attempts to seduce *Max Beerbohm* and *Aubrey Beardsley.*

(Her sister Sybil also enjoyed affairs, especially one with the libidinous composer Puccini – with whom she discussed the possibility of adapting Wilde's 'The Duchess of Padua' as the libretto for a new opera. In later years, when Ada's daughter Violet asked how on earth they managed the hurried practicalities of sex in the 1890s, given such impediments as the then fashionable layers of corsets, Sybil replied with a twinkle: "Oh, we could get them off quickly enough when we wanted to!")

In 1902, as the result of bad investments, Ada and Ernest lost much of their money and decided to split up. Ernest went to Canada where he died of a heart attack in 1922. (The manner of his death mirrored that of his father who had died of fury at Victoria Station. In the words of Ada's daughter Violet, 'it was an incident which should serve as a warning to those who feel too deeply about a shortage of porters, the loss of luggage, or the missing of a train'.)

Ada remained in London working in journalism and producing six books between 1907 and 1916. The novels gave full range to her light-hearted wit – 'When I talk to Mr Raggett I feel as if he had arrived at Paddington, and I had gone to meet him at Charing Cross' – and also her capacity to suggest character in a single phrase.

She encapsulated the nature of one marriage by saying that 'the couple had gone to Oberammergau for their honeymoon'. Another of her characters announced that he had been to see *Gilbert and Sullivan's* 'The Gondoliers' 31 times, to which the reply came: "Wonderful how a man can describe himself in one sentence'.

After a period of severely reduced circumstances, Ada's last years were relieved by a legacy from Ernest's will and, from 1922, she spent her springs and autumns in Florence, Italy, and her summers and winters in London hotels. As she remarked: "I don't much like the English winter – but it's a nice change after the English summer".

Ada's greatest friend was Ernest's cousin, Marguerite, who was married to the actor and playwright **BRANDON THOMAS** (1850-1914). Thomas had been raised in a poor suburb of Liverpool and had to work hard to achieve note. He finally found international fame after writing the superlative farce 'Charley's Aunt' in 1892, (the 'Charley' of the title was named after Ada's brother, Charles Beddington).

Thomas was just as proud of his other plays and his songs, (which he based on the Negro spirituals he had heard from black seamen in his Liverpool youth), and died depressed in the knowledge that he would only be remembered for 'Charley's Aunt'.

Although he lost his Scouse accent when he decided to become an actor, he remained a blunt Liverpudlian. One day, after a conversation between Thomas, Oscar Wilde, and *Charles Brookfield*, Brookfield said to Wilde: "These northern men are so earnest". Wilde replied: "An interesting subject – the importance of being earnest", and scribbled the phrase down on his sleeve-cuff.

Meanwhile, as the legal pursuit of Wilde built to its climax, the various Douglas family factions had not been idle.

BOSIE AND THE DOUGLAS FAMILY
(Third Part – cont. from page 384)
Bosie Douglas, eagerly relishing the prospect of battle with his father, had spent the weeks after the delivery of Queensberry's 'somdomite' card influencing Wilde with what turned out to be a an almost unrelieved succession of bad advice.

Having incorrectly stated that the Douglas family, in order to remove the 'incubus' of Queeensberry, would provide the financial backing for the prosecution, he then, instead of preparing the case, persuaded Oscar to holiday in Monte Carlo, (Oscar: 'of all revolting places on God's earth').

Dismissing the excellent counsel from *Frank Harris* and *Bernard Shaw* to abandon the whole idea, Bosie exhorted Oscar to stand firm, being 'terribly afraid that Oscar would throw in the sponge'. He assumed, quite wrongly, that the prosecution of Queensberry would allow him to reveal in court the true extent of his father's brutality to his family, not realising that the only real legal issue was the question of Oscar's sexual misconduct.

Whatever doubts could be placed on his judgement, Bosie's courage in remaining in England after Wilde's arrest could not be questioned. As he himself wrote years later: 'Perhaps you will pause to consider whether or not it is consistent with cowardice to do what I did – remain for three weeks in London with the daily and momentary expectation of being arrested and consigned to a fate like Mr Wilde's.'

During his first trial, Oscar was fortunate in that the old (public) school tie masonry came to his aid. (His co-defendant, Alfred Taylor, was offered immunity if he testified against Wilde. Having been educated at Marlborough, he obeyed the schoolboy code and refused to 'snitch', thereby suffering the same sentence as Oscar.) Bosie successfully managed to suborn a further witness, Sidney Mavor, with a similar appeal to his upbringing: 'Don't testify against Oscar. They can't do anything to you. Remember you're a gentleman and a public schoolboy. Lie!'

Finally both Wilde and his barrister *Sir Edward Clarke* persuaded Bosie to leave Britain, fearing that he might be forced into an embarrassing court cross-examination. He travelled to France to stay with *Robert Ross* and *Reggie Turner* in Calais, and then Rouen.

It is likely that Bosie was in much less danger than he feared, as Queensberry appeared to have struck a deal with the prosecution to avoid, as much as possible, involving Bosie in the case. The judge in the final trial, Mr Justice Wills, announced in court that: 'I am anxious to say nothing in the case of a young man like this who is just on the threshold of life, which might to a great extent blast his career'.

From the safety of Rouen, Bosie boiled with rage over the whole affair, despatching a stream of indiscreet letters to such editors as *Labouchere* and *WT Stead*, defending Wilde and claiming that he knew 'at least fifty men at the top of society who practise these acts, MPs, peers, and members of the smartest clubs. On my word of honour'.

While the **MARQUESS OF QUEENSBERRY** might have been in rare agreement with his son on this last point, in the meantime he had been preoccupied with the pursuit of Wilde.

Through the use of private detectives, he had uncovered the vice ring around the Alfred Taylor set, and also found a copy of an Oxford magazine called 'The Chameleon' in which Bosie had published, in Queensberry's words: 'two so-called poems, if filthy gibberish strung together can be called poetry, by Alfred, and signed with his name... the last ending up with the words 'I am the love that dare not breathe its name', meaning Sodomy!'

Armed with this evidence Queensberry had survived his own trial and now revelled in turning the tables on Wilde. Having suspected that, with *Lord Rosebery's* reputation possibly in the balance, the authorities might be laggard in arresting Oscar, he insisted that the trial transcripts should be sent immediately to the Public Prosecutor.

During both of the succeeding trials, Queensberry attended the court assiduously, 'sucking the brim of his hat' and staring at his enemy. Wilde said that throughout the proceedings he felt that the walls of the courtroom: 'seemed to me at times to be hung with multitudinous masks of that apelike face'.

After the end of the final trial, with Wilde securely in prison, Queensberry celebrated his triumph by dining with a group of his supporters, including *Charles Brookfield* and *Sir Charles Hawtrey*. *Frank Harris* was appalled at the sadistic pleasure with which Queensberry's backers greeted the news of Wilde's downfall.

When one gentleman said that he was sorry that the sentence had not been longer, another replied: "No, two years imprisonment with hard labour usually results in death or idiocy. Fifty per cent fail to win through. It begins with starvation and solitary confinement and

416

that breaks up the strongest. I think it will be enough for our vainglorious talker". Harris: 'This must have been the way they talked in Jerusalem after the Crucifixion'.

When Wilde was released at the end of his first trial, Bosie's brother, **PERCY DOUGLAS**, (together with *Rev. Stuart Headlam*), put up the bail surety. As doubts began to rise as to whether Oscar might be convicted during the next trial, Percy said: "It will practically ruin me if I lose all that bail money at the present moment but, if there is even a chance of conviction, in God's name let him go".

Queensberry continued his campaign of vilification against his eldest surviving son, suggesting that Percy had bribed the juror who had prevented conviction during Wilde's first trial. Among the many obscene letters and telegrams with which he bombarded Percy's wife Minnie, Queensberry suggested that Percy's appearance should appeal to the homosexual community: 'white-livered smoothed face, sicked-up looking creature, as if he had come up the wrong way. When he was a child it made me sick to think that he could be called my son!'

Two days before the final trial, Queensberry, while searching for the already flown Bosie, attempted to force his way into Minnie's house. Percy, now roused to real anger, caught up with his father during the trial. When they met on the corner of St James Street and Piccadilly, Percy bellowed: "Are you going to cease writing those filthy letters to my wife?" whereupon Queensberry punched him in the eye.

A cheering crowd gathered as the two men settled into a free-for-all fight, which ended with both being arrested and charged with disorderly conduct. Next morning, forced to their great embarrassment to stand at either end of the same dock together, they were each bound over to keep the peace for six months.

On May 21st, as Wilde's last trial neared its end, an unrepentant Queensberry sent another telegram to Minnie: 'To Lady Douglas – Must congratulate on verdict – Cannot on Percy appearance – Looks like dug up corpse – Fear too much madness of kissing – Taylor guilty – Wilde's turn tomorrow – Queensberry'

[See Bosie and the Douglas Family – Fourth Part – Page 445]

Over the following years, much attention was focussed on why Wilde, given the window of opportunity allowed by the authorities, did not flee from Britain on April 5th 1895.

Even more odd was his refusal to flee during the two weeks' grace allowed on bail between the first and second trials, from May 7th till May 22nd.

TO FLEE OR NOT TO FLEE – WHY WILDE STAYED.

Wilde: 'Whenever a man does a thoroughly stupid thing, it is always from the noblest motives'.

There can be little doubt with hindsight that Wilde's escape from England could have been accomplished easily. Many of his friends urged this course, and indeed a yacht was ready on the Thames at his disposal, to be crewed by the impetuous *Frank Harris.*

In previous situations such as this, (Lords Henry and Arthur Somerset, for example), the authorities had turned a blind eye when the accused had skipped to the Continent. Both of his barristers, *Sir Edward Clarke*, (a former solicitor-general), and Travers Humphreys, (later a High Court judge), assumed that Oscar would jump bail and leave. Humphries: 'The authorities would, I believe, have been quite willing that he should go abroad'.

Sir Seymour Hicks said that the Home Office offered him the opportunity because they 'were anxious that the country should be spared a trial devastating to the last degree'. The deeply unsympathetic Ford Madox Ford wrote that: 'There was no reason for his going to prison and the last thing that the British authorities wanted to do was to put him there'.

The reasons why Wilde remained, against all expectations and common sense, fell into three groups. The first was simply practical. He may have harboured some hopes that he might still be acquitted; the success rate for the defence on homosexual charges was quite high. The Earl of Euston and Charles Gatty had recently won their cases and damages, (and Winston Churchill was soon to win his case).

Wilde also dreaded the idea that he might be caught during the escape itself: "And think of the headlines then!" Neither did he relish the idea of being on the run. He told *Robert Sherard:* "I could not bear life if I were to flee. I cannot see myself slinking about the Continent, a fugitive from justice"; and wrote to *Bosie Douglas:* 'I did not want to be called a coward or a deserter. A false name, a disguise, a hunted life, all that is not for me'.

He rejected the idea of breaking his bail mostly because of the effect on his guarantors, Percy Douglas and *Rev. Stuart Headlam,* neither of whom were rich men. Headlam: 'More than once he said to me – 'I have given my word to you and to my mother, and that is enough'.'

Also, the three weeks he had already spent on remand in Holloway Prison had given him an entirely false idea of just how bad jail could be. He had been refused bail three times during that time, (possibly to impress the realities of confinement upon him).

However, remand conditions did not expose him to the full rigour of prison life. He was allowed to have his meals sent in from a nearby restaurant, he was permitted his own clothes, books, and newspapers, and he could receive visitors. *Paul Verlaine,* during his incarceration, had been allowed a proper bed, his own library, and the means to write; he later wrote a poem in gratitude for the austere tranquillity that had allowed him to readjust his life.

Wilde probably expected a similar Bunyonesque situation and had a quite unjustified spirit of optimism about the prospect of a prison sentence. As he had written fifteen years earlier in his play 'Vera': 'A prison where one's allowed to order one's own dinner is not at all a bad place.'

The second main reason stemmed from family and background. The extended Wilde family had fought several court cases over the years. His father, *Sir William Wilde,* had been charged with rape, his mother, *Speranza,* had risked imprisonment as an insurrectionary during the case against the Irish rebel leader, Gavin Duffy, and *Constance Wilde's* grandfather had been charged with indecent exposure.

The idea of running away was anathema to both Oscar's mother and brother. *Willie Wilde* declared resolutely that: "Oscar is an Irish gentleman and he will face the music". More seriously, Speranza told Oscar: "If you stay, even if you go to prison, you will always be my son, it will make no difference to my affection, but if you go, I will never speak to you again".

Moreover, Oscar's upbringing in revolutionary Ireland had led him to see imprisonment as not necessarily a disgrace but possibly as a badge of honour. Many people he deeply respected had served terms of imprisonment – for example, *Wilfred Blunt, John Boyle O'Reilly,* and *Charles Parnell.* There was little shame in being imprisoned for one's beliefs. Wilde: 'A patriot put in prison for loving his country, loves his country. A poet put in prison for loving boys, loves boys.'

The last group of reasons why Oscar decided to stay were more personal. Pride certainly seemed to have played a part. His social, intellectual, and professional success of recent years had lulled him into a feeling of lofty invulnerability, and fuelled an obstinacy that led to his refusal to run from Queensberry or the law. *Sir Seymour Hicks:* 'His attitude most probably was born of his utter disdain for a system for which he had an almost Neroesque contempt.'

As a youth at Portora School in Ireland he once stated that his great wish was 'to go down to posterity as the defendant in such a case as Regina versus Wilde'. Now he realised the possibility of playing the centre stage character in a great real-life drama partly of his own creation, and to be etched into history by suffering his own 'monstrous martyrdom'. If he ran away, his life would merely be sordid; by going to prison he could achieve magnificence.

On a less grandiose level, as Frank Harris commented: "His will was paralysed and he'd lost his nerve". Wilde: 'I admit I lost my head. I was bewildered, incapable of judgement' – ('It is what we fear that happens to us'.)

Wilde's strong sense of fatalism may have been one of the reasons for this collapse of will power. Firstly he believed in a woefully mistaken prediction of the palmist, Mrs Robinson, who had prophesied 'complete triumph' in his trials. But, more importantly, Wilde felt that there was no way to avoid his destiny: 'The gods mark out a path for us which we must follow to its conclusion'. As he said to *Andre Gide* after his release: "Of course, of course, I knew that there would be a catastrophe, that way or another. It had to end that way".

This theme coincided with Wilde's view that in order to complete his life he had to undergo tragedy. Having always walked in the sun, it was important also to endure the shade.

The final coup de grace to any thought of Wilde's escape remained that he was, of course, still deeply in love. As *Huysmans'* friend Villiers D'Isle Adam put it: 'The secret of the medieval troubadours was that romantic love was really a concealed death wish'.

Wilde's final trial began at the Old Bailey on May 22 1895. As he had forced a confrontation by his refusal to leave Britain, the government was now determined to crush him completely. Sir Edward Hamilton, Gladstone's former private secretary, wrote: 'A verdict of guilty would remove what appears to be a wide-felt impression that the Judge and Jury were on the last occasion got at, in order to shield others of a higher status in life.'

If Judge Charles had erred on the side of leniency in the first trial, Judge Alfred Wills had no intention of repeating the mistake in the second trial. (Wills had been a pioneer Alpine climber in the 1850s, helping to form the world's first mountaineering organisation, the London Alpine Club in 1857. When Bosie Douglas's uncle, Lord Francis Douglas, had been killed on the Matterhorn, it had been Wills who questioned the expedition's leader, Edward Whymper, about the incident. By coincidence, Wills lived on Tite Street and was a near neighbour of Wilde.)

Throughout the trial, Wills barely concealed his hostility towards the now haggard and lacklustre Oscar. He was especially revolted to hear that some of the sexual encounters had taken place at the Savoy; (Wills: "It is a condition of things that one shudders to contemplate in a first-class hotel")

To make sure of gaining the desired result in this new trial, the Solicitor-General himself took over as prosecutor. Although Sir Frank Lockwood had known Wilde socially before the trials, it made no difference to the savagery of his advocacy. (It did not help matters that Maurice Schwabe, the nephew of Lockwood's own wife, had been named in court as one of Oscar's bedfellows.)

One journalist said that Lockwood 'fought like a tiger to secure conviction'. The attack was so extreme that Wilde's counsel, Sir Edward Clarke, was forced to remonstrate with the prosecution. Wilde: 'I remember as I was sitting in the dock on the occasion of my last trial listening to Lockwood's appalling denunciation of me ... and being sickened with horror at what I heard. Suddenly it occurred to me – how splendid it would be, if I was saying all this about myself!'

On May 25th Wilde was found guilty of gross indecency, in private, with four men. Passing sentence, Judge Wills announced: "It is no use for me to address you. People who can do these things must be dead to all sense of shame, and one cannot hope to produce any effect upon them. It is the worst case I have ever tried".

Wilde and his co-defendant, Alfred Taylor, both received sentences of two years in prison.

The news of Wilde's downfall unleashed what Frank Harris called 'an orgy of Philistine rancour', a wave of triumphal anti-artistic jingoism that was to last for five years. Oscar: 'The masses were shocked beyond their highest expectations'. Street mobs regularly taunted and beat up men who looked even remotely effeminate.

In 'An Ideal Husband', Wilde had described the press reaction to scandal as: 'Think of the hypocrite, of his greasy smile, writing articles, arranging foulness for the public's pleasure'. And so it proved.

The News of the World trumpeted: 'Society is well rid of these ghouls and their hideous practices. He got off too lightly'. The Daily Telegraph opined that: 'The grave of contemptuous oblivion may rest on his foolish ostentation, his empty paradoxes, his insufferable posturing, his incurable vanity', while the St James Gazette added: 'What we need now is a dose of wholesome bigotry'.

In the USA, Wilde's name was removed from the theatre posters, (as in London), while public libraries removed his books from their shelves. Between 1895 and 1900 over 900 sermons were preached against Wilde throughout America.

Even in Paris, it was regarded as dangerous to have known Oscar, and such past acquaintances as Marcel Schwob and Jean Lorrain challenged their accusers to duels to deny their involvement. The Parisian journalist Bauer went so far as to claim: 'The darling sin of Wilde does not find any practitioners here!'

Violet Leverson said that, for years afterwards, Wilde was only referred to by his initials, while Wilde's son, Vyvyan Holland, pointed out that from 1895 until 1911 no male child in Britain was registered with the first name of 'Oscar'.

After his conviction on May 25th 1895, Wilde was taken first to Newgate Prison, then to Holloway, and finally on June 9th to Pentonville. He was later to spend a further five months in Wandsworth, and his last eighteen months in Reading.

PRISON CONDITIONS

In a regimen that was to last till 1948, prisoners were divided into three divisions. In the first division, a prisoner could wear his own clothes and have food sent in; in the second, he was allowed to write and receive extra visits; while the third division, to which Wilde was sentenced, was called hard labour.

The first month of hard labour was designed to break the spirit of an incoming prisoner, and consisted of spending six hours a day grinding flour on a treadmill. After each twenty minutes on the mill, prisoners were allowed five minutes rest before continuing; on his first day Oscar climbed 6000ft on this task. ('We banged the tins, And bawled the hymns, And sweated on the mill' – Wilde in 'Ballad of Reading Gaol'). After three days, he collapsed and was moved to the infirmary.

After the first month, hard labour prisoners were taken off the mill and set to work on tailoring, postbag-making, or oakum picking. Wilde was employed on the latter task, which involved untwisting old rope to re-use the hemp. ('We tore the tarry rope to shreds, With blunt and bleeding nails' – Ballad).

To destroy any sense of personal dignity, each prisoner had his head shaved and was given ill-fitting clothes marked with broad arrows. To disorientate a new prisoner, for the first fortnight he was forced to sleep on a plank bed with no mattress, thus inflicting insomnia.

To additionally weaken a prisoner's physical ability to resist, the prison food was of deliberately poor quality, doled out 'ounce by ounce', and consisting of 'skilly', (oatmeal porridge with bits of mouldy meat) and a small loaf. This diet soon induced nausea and diarrhoea, with accompanying hunger. Wilde, a much larger man than normal, suffered greatly from this minimal nutrition.

In order to prevent prisoners communicating with each other by tapping, the sewage pipes were removed from the cells, and replaced with slop buckets. As prisoners were locked into the cells from 5pm till the morning, the diarrhoea often overflowed the bucket. On three occasions, warders vomited after encountering the stench of Wilde's cell. ('Each narrow cell in which we dwell, Is a foul and dark latrine' – Ballad).

One hour's exercise a day was allowed, with the prisoners walking in Indian file and forbidden to speak, together with daily attendance at chapel, (twice on Sundays).

Whereas later on solitary confinement became the ultimate sanction in jail, in Wilde's day it was the norm. No prisoner was allowed to speak and the prisons were places of perpetual silence and solitude. Wilde and his fellow convicts wore caps with face flaps that had to be lowered if they encountered one another.

No communication was allowed with the outside world for the first three months. Then each prisoner was allowed to write four letters a year, and to receive four visits a year. These visits were restricted to twenty minutes, in the presence of a warder, and with prisoner and visitor separated by wire.

No pictures or books were allowed, and any request for pen and paper, other than the standard annual four letters, refused.

The slightest infringement of these rules was disciplined by the offender being locked into a darkened cell and fed on bread and water for a week or more. Wilde was punished in this way on several occasions.

On June 12 1895, while Wilde was in Pentonville, he received his first visitor, Richard Haldane.

LORD RICHARD HALDANE 1856-1928

Richard Haldane, (created Viscount in 1911), was able to gain access to any prisoner as he was a member of the Home Office committee reporting on the prison service. Haldane: 'I used to meet Wilde in the days of his social success and, although I had not known him well, was haunted by the idea of what this highly sensitive man was suffering under ordinary prison treatment.'

His kindly manner on this first meeting reduced Oscar to tears. Haldane suggested that prison might provide him with the material for a great new work and promised to try to obtain writing materials and books. (Although it took time, Haldane's proposal bore fruit. In 1898, Wilde was able to send him a copy of 'The Ballad of Reading Gaol'). After this first visit, Haldane went to see Oscar's mother, Speranza, to give her some reassurance.

Haldane remained something of a guardian angel and his timely interventions possibly saved Wilde's sanity. He was able to transfer Oscar firstly from the tough Pentonville Prison to Wandsworth and, when that also proved too much, to the relatively easier regime at Reading.

Raised in Edinburgh, Haldane spent his early years as a lawyer before becoming a Liberal MP in 1883. As a close associate of *Herbert Asquith*, he was appointed as Secretary of War in the Liberal Government of 1906, and became famous for his radical reform of the Victorian army. He turned the old militia into a Territorial Army reserve, created the British Expeditionary Force, and formed the Officer Training Corps, all measures that enabled Britain to fight on equal terms in any future European wars.

This patriotic forethought did little to save him when the First World War broke out. Now Lord Chancellor, he was attacked by the rightwing jingo press, in particular the Harmsworth group, for being too sympathetic towards Germany. On the grounds that he had attended a German university in his youth and spoke fluent German, he was hounded from government office in 1915, and was further smeared in the 'Black Book' trial.

After the war, he joined the Labour party and, during the short-lived government of Ramsay Macdonald in 1924, again was appointed Lord Chancellor.

Max Beerbohm described Haldane as a 'purring big cat' in whose presence it was impossible to bicker – 'He spreads like treacle'. Haldane was often teased over his considerable weight and his habit of chain-smoking black cigars. Piqued by the implication that he was unfit, one evening he set out in his dinner jacket and walked the sixty miles to Brighton, sending a telegram to his dining companions in London to inform them that he had reached his destination.

He was known to enjoy good living and related how one day he had arrived at the War Office feeling rather tired. "I asked the tall ex-Guards officer for a glass of water. He replied: "Certainly, sir. Irish or Scotch water, sir?"

Wilde's life continued with little to break the brutal monotony other than the rare visitor and the occasional change of prison. On July 4th he was transferred from Pentonville to Wandsworth Prison, where he was visited separately by Robert Sherard, Constance Wilde's brother Otho Lloyd, and on September 21st by Constance herself, (when she withdrew the threat of divorce proceedings).

On September 25th, Wilde was taken on his first trip to the Bankruptcy Court. His total debts had reached £6000, but it was the Marquess of Queensberry's insistence on payment of his £700 court costs that ensured the action for bankruptcy went ahead.

During October, Wilde suffered a physical and mental breakdown. Already suffering from dysentery, he fell and damaged his ear on a paving stone, (an injury that was to plague him for the rest of his life). He lay ill in the prison infirmary for a month, which at least gave him some respite from the hard labour regime. His ear, on the other hand was never properly treated; the doctor accused him of malingering. His sister-in-law, Lily Wilde, made a trip to see him during this time.

After a second visit to court on November 12, Wilde was finally declared bankrupt.

On Haldane's advice, the Home Secretary Herbert Asquith gave instructions that Wilde be moved from Wandsworth to what was seen as an easier prison at Reading. Despite their intervention, he still received no special treatment. To do so would have been too difficult, given the prevailing public sentiment against him.

On November 21st Wilde was transferred by train to his new jail. From 2pm till 2.30pm, he had to stand, handcuffed and in prison uniform, on the platform of Clapham Junction railway station. A crowd formed to laugh and jeer at the convict. Then one man recognised Wilde and spat at him. Wilde: "For a year after that was done to me, I wept every day at the same hour and for the same space of time.'

422

> Reading Gaol itself may have been an improvement on Wandsworth, but the Governor, Lieutenant-Colonel Isaacson, turned out to be, in Oscar's words, a bloated, drunken, 'mulberry-faced dictator' with 'the eyes of a ferret, the body of an ape, and the soul of a rat', who could not sit down to breakfast without punishing someone. Isaacson publicly boasted that he was 'going to knock the nonsense out of Wilde'.
>
> In his own view, Oscar, having been ruined by the attentions of one anthropoid psychopath in the shape of Queensberry, was now at the mercy of another.

1896

> [A boundary dispute in Venezuela caused a crisis that threatened war between the USA and Britain; it was settled after a few months of sabre-rattling.
>
> In Africa, British forces began preparations for the re-conquest of the Sudan, while the Italians were defeated at the Battle of Adowa in their failed attempt to colonise Ethiopia.
>
> In France the Dreyfus Affair rumbled on, dividing the country into antagonistic factions.
>
> In Britain, AE Houseman published his poem 'The Shropshire Lad', and Thomas Hardy published his novel 'Jude the Obscure'.
>
> In Greece, the first modern Olympic Games took place in Athens.]

> Following the death of Alfred, Lord Tennyson, the post of Poet Laureate had fallen vacant. (The poet Sir Lewis Morris had earlier expressed a desire to obtain the job. Wilde: "He was a rather bad poet, who kept complaining long and vigorously that there was a conspiracy of silence against him. My advice to him was to join it".)
>
> On January 1st, 1896, in what seemed like an almost calculated snub to Parnassus, the Prime Minister Lord Salisbury appointed Alfred Austin, a very minor bard, to the position. It was viewed as the promotion of 'Alfred the Little, after Alfred the Great', (Tennyson).

ALFRED AUSTIN 1835-1913

The Yorkshire born poet Alfred Austin had first come to notice when in 1861 he published a satirical poem called 'The Season' in which he set out to expose the immorality of society, using *Wilfred Blunt's* lover, 'Skittles' Walters, as the main target – 'With slackened rein swift Skittles rules the Row, Though scowling matrons champing steeds restrain, She flaunts Propriety with flapping mane', etc. 'The Season' was not well received.

When the *Prince of Wales* fell ill with typhoid in 1872, Austin plunged into patriotic verse on the subject, creating some of the worst lines ever written – 'Across the wires, the electric message came, He is no better, he is much the same'. In spite of this, the *Prince of Wales* recovered.

From 1866 until 1896, Austin worked as a vehemently imperialist leader-writer for various newspapers, dispensing opinions on such subjects as Garibaldi, ('an unmitigated nuisance'), etc.

Wilde commented on the type in 'The Decay of Lying': 'Lying for the sake of a monthly salary is, of course, well known in Fleet Street, and the profession of a political leader-writer is not without its advantages. But it is said to be a somewhat dull occupation, and it certainly does not lead to much beyond a kind of ostentatious obscurity.'

In which Austin may well have remained had it not been for *Lord Salisbury's* eccentric decision to appoint him as Poet Laureate in 1896. When asked why he had done so, Salisbury replied: "I don't think anybody else applied for the post". *Frank Harris* pointed out that: 'Austin had no more poetry in his composition than a housefly. He had other merits, however. For years he had praised Lord Salisbury in and out of season.'

The appointment was unanimously criticised. When Margot Asquith asked George Meredith what he considered Austin's thoughts might be about his new elevation, Meredith grunted: "It is very hard to say what a bantam is thinking when it is crowing".

Austin was unaffected by the derision and went on to blithely deliver his considered views on his rivals. He dismissed *Tennyson, Browning, Matthew Arnold,* and *Swinbourne* as 'indifferent poets', and stated that too much attention had been shown to Keats and Shelley.

Soon after gaining the laureateship, he was inspired to write the stirringly jingoistic 'Jameson's Ride' after the eponymous leader of the Raid in South Africa. It contained some gloriously inept verse, 'They went across the veldt, As hard as they could pelt', being one of the best.

Even in jail Wilde heard about 'Jameson's Ride' and, in need of amusement, requested a copy. When a friend asked him how anybody could remain Laureate under such a tide of ridicule, Oscar replied: "Vanity, the invulnerable breast-plate of man".

Austin expressed his own philosophy when he announced that his idea of heaven was: 'to sit in a garden receiving constant telegrams announcing alternately a British victory at sea and a British victory by land'. When an acquaintance had the temerity to point out some grammatical errors in Austin's verse, the Laureate sighed deeply and told him: "I dare not alter these things. They come to me from above".

As the Philistine triumph was crowned by Austin's appointment as Laureate, Wilde continued to fester in Reading Prison. He received a visit on November 30th from More Adey.

[The English translator of Ibsen's 'Brand', MORE ADEY (1858-1942), was a discreet homosexual, friendly with Ross, who drafted a petition for clemency and helped to look after Wilde's business affairs while he was in prison. Oscar, while praising Adey's many qualities, said that in business: 'he was the most solemn donkey that ever stepped'. Later, Adey became the co-owner of the Carfax Gallery with Ross, and in 1918 became the executor of the Wilde estate after Ross's death. He died insane in 1942.]

One glimmer of good news reached Wilde when he heard that his play 'Salome' had been given its first performance at the Théâtre de l'Oeuvre in Paris on February 11th. However, any relief he gained from this was dashed when on February 19th Constance Wilde herself arrived at Reading to tell him that his mother, 'Speranza' Wilde, had died two weeks earlier.

From February till June of 1896, his friends, Adey, Robert Sherard, Robert Ross, and Frank Harris visited him in prison. They were growing seriously concerned about his health. Sherard: 'His hair was unkempt and a small straggly beard had been allowed to grow. His face was so thin that I hardly recognised him'. Ross: 'Physically he was much worse than anyone had led me to believe'.... 'His eyes were terribly vacant and he cried the whole time'.

His hair had gone grey, (he later dyed it), with an increasing bald patch. In addition to anaemia, gout, and the pain from his untreated ear, his eyesight had been blurred by the permanent gaslight. The fear of going blind and deaf was augmented by the fear of insanity – a common result of these prison conditions. As Wilde wrote later, 'treated like an intelligent animal' in 'this tomb for those who are not yet dead', 'the wretched man who is confined in an English prison can hardly escape becoming insane'.

Wilde: 'As one reads history, one is absolutely sickened, not by the crimes that the wicked have committed, but by the punishment that the good have inflicted'. He told Frank Harris: "If you resist, they drive you crazy'.

Religion brought no comfort at all. When Wilde mentioned to the prison chaplain that he regretted that his cell window offered no view of the sky, the chaplain answered that he would be better employed letting his mind rest not on the clouds, 'but on Him who is above the clouds'. Oscar's reply to this pious observation was: "Get out, you damned fool!"

The chaplain retaliated by reporting to the authorities that Wilde's main consolation seemed to be masturbation. Wilde: 'And all, but Lust, is turned to dust, In Humanity's machine', (Ballad).

To add to the mental stress, Oscar blamed himself for much of the disaster. 'Misfortunes one can endure; they come from outside, they are accidents. But to suffer for one's own faults – ah! There is the sting of life'.

[On July 7th, 1896, Trooper Charles Wooldridge was executed at Reading Gaol for the murder of his 23-year-old wife Laura. Three months earlier on 29th March, Wooldridge, racked by jealousy, had waited on the road between Windsor and Clewer in Berkshire, and slit her throat with a razor.]

By July 1896, Oscar's situation began to change for the better. Frank Harris, appalled by Wilde's appearance and the conditions at Reading, had reported his findings to the chairman of the Prison Commission.

[Described by his boss, Herbert Asquith, as 'a splendid little fellow', SIR EVELYN RUGGLES-BRISE (1857-1935) had just been appointed to the post, (and was to keep it until 1921). He was partly responsible for the reforms of the 1898 Prison Act that abolished the treadmill and the prohibition of speech, (and in 1901 for the removal of children from the prison system into Borstals). These reforms, however, came too late to help Wilde.]

Ruggle-Brise, advised by Harris, decided to remove Isaacson and appoint a new governor at Reading. He also ordered that Wilde should finally be allowed books and writing materials. Under the new regime, Oscar was taken off hard labour and allowed to work in the prison library and the garden.

On their first meeting Major Nelson, the new governor, endeared himself to Wilde by offering him a book: "I have just been reading it myself". A deeply moved Oscar later said that Nelson was: "the most Christ-like man I ever met", and in 1898 sent him a copy of 'The Ballad of Reading Gaol' 'in recognition of many acts of kindness and gentleness'. The respect was mutual. In 1905, when Nelson read Wilde's 'De Profundis', he commented: 'One has to read but little to recognise what literature has lost in the death of a man like poor Oscar Wilde'.

1897

[In Britain, Queen Victoria and the country celebrated her Diamond Jubilee.
War was declared between Greece and Turkey, a short campaign in which Greece was routed.
Spurred on by the Dreyfus case, anti-Semitic riots broke out in France and Algeria.]

Wilde continued to receive visits from Ross, More Adey, and Ernest Leverson.

Under Major Nelson's benign rule, he was now given meat once a day and was allowed a light in his cell as late as he wished. But Nelson also predicted that the treatment that Wilde had received previously meant that his life would be shortened. Nelson: "He looks well. But like all men unused to manual labour who receive a sentence of this kind, he will be dead within two years'.

The imprisonment had to some extent also affected Wilde's mind. As the day of release approached, he became petulant and aggressive towards his friends, particularly over money matters. He completely cut his admittedly unhelpful brother Willie, but also attacked such blameless intermediaries as Ernest Leverson, Percy Douglas, Frank Harris, and Robert Ross. But, most of all, the blame fell on the man he now saw as the fount of his misfortunes – Bosie Douglas.

Four months before his release, Oscar was allowed an unlimited supply of writing materials. He used his new freedom to compose a lengthy letter to Bosie.

DE PROFUNDIS
Written between January and March 1897, the 'letter' was in fact a major literary piece consisting of eighty close-written pages, which Major Nelson allowed Wilde to revise. Originally named 'Epistola – In Carcere et Vinicus', ('Letter – in Prison and in Chains'), Robbie Ross later changed the title to 'De Profundis', ('Out of the Depths').

The letter fell into roughly two parts, one being a damning diatribe against Bosie, the other a cathartic self-exploration in semi-biblical prose which, given the circumstances in which it was written, was an extraordinary achievement. In this second part, Wilde came to terms with his life, confessing his follies but finding forgiveness for himself in the process. Oscar: 'When we blame ourselves we feel that no one else has the right to blame us. It is the confession, not the priest, that gives us absolution'.

On his release, Wilde was allowed to take the manuscript with him but, realising that delivering it to Bosie would mean its destruction, instead handed it over to Ross with instructions to make two copies. This decision became a legal bone of contention for many years to come.

In essence, Ross kept the letter secret until 1905, (when the copyright was removed from the hands of the Official Receiver). He then published the sections that did not mention Bosie Douglas, and presented the complete manuscript to the British Museum to be kept under lock and key.

During a later court case, Bosie insisted on examining the entire document and read, to his horror, the previously unpublished attack upon himself. 'De Profundis' was not published in its entirety until 1960.

In February 1897, Oscar's wife Constance, accompanied by her solicitor Hargrove, visited Reading Prison so that Wilde could sign the Deed of Arrangement to sort out the future of his sons and the family financial affairs.

This agreement handed over custody of the children to Constance and her cousin Adrian Hope, gave Constance a legal separation, and provided Oscar with an annual £150, (his entitlement by the marriage settlement), on the proviso that he did not live 'disreputably'.

Oscar and Constance did not meet in prison but Constance asked a warder if she could take a look at her husband through a spy hole as he signed away his rights to his children. According to the warder, she 'cast one long, lingering glance inside', then 'she drew back apparently labouring under deep emotion'. She left with her solicitor soon afterwards.

CONSTANCE WILDE (Second Part – cont. from page 185)
When she had received the unexpected and devastating news of Oscar's imminent arrest on April 5th 1895, Constance had fled immediately to the refuge of her cousin Mary Napier's house. Attempting to make sense of her predicament she begged the palmist Mrs Robinson for information as to her future: "My life has all been cut to pieces".

She remained with Mary Napier until April 19th, but having been taunted in the streets and horrified by the hatred she encountered, she left to stay with her friend Lady Mount Temple in Babbacombe, Devon.

When the news came that creditors were about to move into Tite St, Constance returned to London on May 20th to try to save some possessions. She gathered what she could and paid off their last servant, Arthur the butler, who had remained to guard the house.

(Arthur had been with the Wildes since their marriage. When Oscar was writing 'The Importance of Being Earnest' he told a friend: "The play is not shaped yet. It lies in Sibylline leaves about the room, and Arthur has twice made a chaos of it by 'tidying up'." Arthur was profoundly upset by the trials and, unable to find new work because of his connection with Wilde, committed suicide in July 1895.)

Before the last trial, Constance went to see Oscar at the Leverson's house to plead with him to escape – she was prepared to go with him if necessary – but Oscar, for his own reasons, refused. When she heard about her husband's imprisonment on May 25th, Constance decided that: 'flight was not just a consideration but a necessity'.

Luckily she was not without friends. Her brother Otho lived in Switzerland, the *Rani of Sarawak* on the Ligurian coast in Italy, *Princess Alice* in Monaco, and another friend Carlos Blacker and his family resided at Freiburg in Germany. Also both *Robert Sherard* and *Robbie Ross* rallied round her.

Accompanied by her two sons, *Cyril* and *Vyvyan*, Constance travelled to Paris, then to Geneva, then to Glion in Switzerland. In Glion, they were recognised by the manager and turned out of their hotel; they moved on to refuge at Otho's house in Bevaix. Realising her outcast status, Constance decided to change her name to 'Holland', (as her brother had done before in similar circumstances).

After spending time with the Blackers in Freiburg, Constance settled at Sori on the Italian Riviera where the Rani had found an apartment for her. She mostly remained on the Ligurian coast for the rest of her life.

Although pressed by her legal advisors, she refused to go ahead with a divorce case: 'My poor misguided husband, who is weak rather than wicked, repents most bitterly all his past madness and I cannot refuse to him the forgiveness that he has asked'.

But she did agree to their suggestion that she should not immediately meet with Oscar on his release, thinking that he needed time to readjust before any attempt at reconciliation was made: 'I think his fate is rather like Humpty Dumpty – quite as tragic and quite as impossible to put right'.

To give Oscar some consolation for not having access, she sent him photographs of the boys taken at Heidelburg. Oscar: ' Such lovely little fellows in Eton collars'. In September 1897, he wrote: 'Had Constance allowed me to see my boys, my life would, I think, have been quite different'.

However, she left it too long and, in the interim, Oscar re-met 'that appalling individual', Bosie Douglas – an act that certainly came under Constance's definition of 'disreputable living'. It shattered any chance of a family reunion.

Despite the wreck of her marriage and the problems after Oscar's release, Constance never deserted her husband. She wrote that if they were ever to meet again she would forgive him everything. In early 1898, she restored his allowance, (stopped because of the Bosie entanglement), and wrote him a friendly letter that hinted at a future meeting.

She had been suffering ill health ever since her fall at Tite St in 1895 had damaged her back. She was diagnosed as having spinal paralysis and went into hospital to relieve the pain. She died during an operation on 7th April 1898.

Neither her sons nor Oscar, (who was not informed until too late), attended her burial service at Campo Santa in Genoa. Oscar eventually did visit the grave in 1899: 'I brought some flowers. I was deeply affected – with a sense, also, of the uselessness of all regrets'. In his last years, Oscar wrote the scenario for a play, 'Mr and Mrs Daventry', about a self-sacrificing woman – its original name was 'Constance'.

Notwithstanding the adaptability of childhood, Oscar's children, **CYRIL and VYVYAN WILDE**, were also deeply affected by the events around them. Prior to April 1895, (when they were aged respectively nine and seven), the boys appear to have enjoyed a carefree existence. They had been given the same sort of freedoms that Oscar himself had been allowed as a child.

Far from being the dignified Victorian paterfamilias, Oscar delighted in joining his sons in their nursery games and, on seaside holidays, helping to build sand castles and teaching them to swim. They were fortunate in that Oscar thought that: 'It is the duty of every father to write fairy tales for his children' – and even more so in having a father whose offerings were tinged with genius.

In 1894, Cyril was sent away to boarding school at Bedales House in Haywards Heath, Sussex, while Vyvyan went to a prep school in Broadstairs, Kent. In 1895, as the publicity storm about Oscar reached the schools, both children were sent home.

Swept up in the chaos, they were rushed out of England to begin a new life abroad. Not surprisingly they were confused about the situation. Vyvyan: 'For months after we had to leave, we kept asking about our toys. Many years later I saw a catalogue of the 'sale', (the auction at Tite St.). Lot No. 237 was 'a large quantity of toys' – they fetched 30 shillings'.

Constance and her advisors considered it to be crucial that the identities of the children should be kept secret. As with their mother, their names were changed to 'Holland' and the distinctive spelling of Vyvyan's name was altered to 'Vivian'.

A few days after they had been installed in a German school in Heidelburg, the boys realised to their dismay that some of their clothing still bore nametags bearing the inscription 'Wilde'. They spent a frantic half hour ripping them out. Vyvyan: 'It was a terrible burden that at any point we might be discovered. To have known our father when he was feted – and now having to deny him was awful'.

As a further precaution, their guardians decided that the children should be split up; the names Cyril and Vivian were a rare combination and might lead to discovery. As Cyril was more amenable to the German system of education, it was Vyvyan who was sent away to a Jesuit college in Monaco. Princess Alice was ready to keep an eye on him and he was able to visit the palace on half-day holidays.

Their mother's death in 1898 completed the cycle of disruption and tragedy. The boys now came under the complete control of Adrian Hope, a distant unsympathetic figure. Vyvyan said that he only met Hope three times in six years and never received letters from him. Mary Napier acted in a foster-mother capacity but appears to have been reluctant and remote.

All attempts to contact the boys by Oscar and his friends were resolutely blocked by the extended Lloyd family. At one point, Oscar wrote to Hope asking if he could write letters to his children that they could open when they came of age. The reply came that any such letter would be destroyed. Wilde: 'Is there on earth a crime so terrible that in punishment of it a father can be prevented from seeing his children?'

The separation of the two brothers was completed when it was decided that Cyril should be sent to board at the Protestant Radley College, while Vyvyan should go to the Catholic Stonyhurst.

On May 18th, the day before Wilde's release from imprisonment, he was taken in the company of two warders from Reading Jail to Pentonville. Taking a cab from the jail at Reading, the three men travelled the few miles to Twyford railway station.

Oscar was so overwhelmed by his first sight in two years of a blossoming bush that he threw open his arms and exclaimed: "Oh, beautiful world! Beautiful world!" Fearful of attracting unwanted attention from reporters, one of the warders asked him to stop. "Now, Mr Wilde, you mustn't give yourself away like that. You're the only man in England who would talk like that in a railway station".

They caught a train to Westbourne Park station in west London. While in transit, Oscar asked if he could look at the copy of the Morning Chronicle that a warder was carrying. (Newspapers had been forbidden in prison). This was refused. Oscar: 'I suggested that I might be allowed to read it upside down. This they consented to allow. So I read the Morning Chronicle upside down, all the way, and never enjoyed it so much. It's really the only way to read newspapers'.

From Westbourne Park, they hired another cab and arrived to stay the night at Pentonville Prison. At 6am, May 19th 1897, Wilde was taken from the prison courtyard by private carriage to freedom.

After a few hours at Stuart Headlam's house, where he was greeted by the loyal Ada Leverson, Wilde and More Adey left, again by cab, to catch the Newhaven train at West Croydon. (They avoided Victoria station to avoid recognition.) That evening Wilde left Britain forever on the overnight ferry to Dieppe.

Arriving at the French port at 4am on May 20th, Wilde was met by Reggie Turner and Robbie Ross, to whom Oscar entrusted the manuscript of 'De Profundis'. The next few days were spent staying at the Hotel Sandwich and celebrating release.

Turning down Frank Harris's suggestion of a trip to the Pyrennees, on May 26th Wilde decided to move to a small village about five miles from Dieppe called Berneval-sur-mer, where he stayed at the Hotel de la Plage.

Before he began to re-arrange his life, Oscar felt that he had to pay off a debt of honour to those who remained behind in Reading Jail.

Before his release two incidents at the prison had especially shocked him. One was the horrific appearance of an insane prisoner named Prince who had been brutally flogged for a minor offence. The other was the imprisonment of three young children, roughly the same age as his own boys. They had been apprehended for poaching rabbits and, as their parents were too poor to pay their fine, they were jailed. One of them was so small the authorities could not find prison clothes to fit him.

Thomas Martin, a humane warder who had admired and helped Wilde, pitied the children and gave them some biscuits to cheer them up. He was dismissed for this offence.

Oscar arranged for the children's fine to be paid off, then wrote the first of two long letters to the newspapers to expose the conditions in prison and the treatment of Warder Martin in particular. On May 28th the first letter was published in the Daily Chronicle.

The letter caused enough stir to provoke the MP Michael Davitt to ask a question in the House of Commons. The new Home Secretary, Sir Matthew Ridley, replied that the Martin's dismissal was 'fully justified' and 'a proper step'. Wilde wrote to Davitt thanking him for his intervention.

[A colleague of Charles Parnell, MICHAEL DAVITT (1846-1906) was a socialist, a journalist, and an Irish nationalist politician. He had been forced into employment in a factory and had lost an arm in a machinery accident when he was aged only 12. Davitt was knowledgeable about jail conditions, having spent seven years himself in Dartmoor Prison convicted of arms smuggling. After years of political struggle, he became an MP in 1895, though he resigned from Parliament in 1899 in protest against the Boer War.]

A friend suggested to Wilde that his experience of both sides of life might now prove to be very valuable. Oscar replied: "Yes, artistically it is perfect; socially most inconvenient". One problem was the reaction of other people to his presence. Oscar: 'The cruelty of a prison sentence starts when you come out'. When the proprietor of a Dieppe restaurant realised who Oscar was, he immediately asked him to *leave the premises. Wilde was subjected to many such insults and snubs, particularly by English visitors to the town.*

After witnessing a similar incident, the English writer Mrs Arthur Stannard crossed the street and taking Oscar by the arm, announced loudly and defiantly: "Come on, Oscar, take me to tea".

JOHN STRANGE WINTER 1856 – 1911

Mrs Arthur Stannard, who wrote under the pen name of 'John Strange Winter', not only went to tea with Wilde but also brought him home for a meal and later visited him in Berneval.

Born Henrietta Palmer, she had married Arthur Stannard, an engineer, in 1883. Suspecting that Arthur's engineering skills might not be enough to sustain a family, she turned to writing and had some success with tales of military life, (her publisher gave her a male nom de plume to encourage sales).

It was her forty-second novel, 'Bootle's Baby', in 1885 that brought her renown, sold two million copies, and gained her the friendship of *John Ruskin*. When the book was successfully dramatised in 1889, *Ernest Dowson* became fixated on its 7-year-old star, Minnie Terry, and collected souvenirs of the child.

Wilde had not been one of the book's admirers. Oscar: "Bootles Baby is une oeuvre symboliste: it is really only the style and the subject that are wrong. Pray never speak lightly of Bootles Baby. Indeed, pray never speak of it at all. I never do".

When the popularity of the 'shilling novel' waned at the turn of the century, Henrietta's career waned with it. She avoided bankruptcy by turning to the production and endorsement of 'toilet preparations', and thrived on the resulting sales.

Her name had cropped up in Reading Jail one day, when a warder asked Wilde what he thought of John Strange Winter. Oscar replied: "A charming lady, he is a charming lady; but I would rather talk to her than read his books".

Having decided to stay in Berneval for the foreseeable future, Wilde was able to offer hospitality to a variety of friends and acquaintances. On June 3rd 1897, he recorded that: 'Ernest Dowson, Charles Conder, and Dalhousie Young came out here this afternoon to dine and sleep – at least I know they dine, but I believe they never sleep.'

CHARLES CONDER 1868-1909

Charles Conder, an artist who specialised mostly in landscapes and decorative fans, had painted a portrait of Oscar back in 1892. Their initial meeting this time in Dieppe had been embarrassing, as Oscar had noticed Conder turning down a side street to avoid meeting him. Conder soon overcame his reservations and fraternised with Oscar again. (Although never a close friend, in 1898 he invited Wilde to stay with him at Chantemesle, near La Roche Guyon, and his name appeared on a wreath at Oscar's funeral.)

Wilde was a particular admirer of Conder's painted fans. When Conder, in a rush to acquire ready cash, was busily selling off his collection, Oscar commented: "Dear Condor! With what exquisite subtlety he goes about persuading someone to give him a hundred francs for a fan, for which he was fully prepared to pay two hundred".

Although born in London, Conder had been sent to Australia when he was aged 15. He acquired a job as a surveyor in the New South Wales bush country that allowed him time to practise his real vocation of painting. (On one occasion, after he had just completed a picture of a bush farmstead, he returned to find a calf had licked half the paint from the canvas.)

His companions, having discovered that Conder's heart was not in surveying, made him the camp cook. This was not a good idea, as he used condensed milk as the staple of every meal, including boiled kangaroo. After he had overdosed one dinner with Eno's salts, the results convinced the survey team that they had all got cholera, and in a panic they broke up the camp.

Returning to Melbourne, Conder became an art teacher for a short period before losing his job. He explained that, having been involved himself in several sexual escapades in the city: 'Of course, I wasn't the person to stop the boys and girls getting fond of each other – so they got into trouble and I got into trouble'.

Agreeing with the observation that: 'The Australians stand pretty well alone in being a people who have never invented a new dish or a new drink', in 1890 Conder left in search of artistic and gastronomic inspiration in Paris.

Settling into Montmartre, he became friends with the artists *William Rothenstein*, Phil May, and *Henri Toulouse-Lautrec*. The latter introduced Conder to the renowned dancehall, the Moulin Rouge, and like his mentor Conder became fascinated by the exotic female dancers.

Having had his taste for sensuality whetted in Melbourne, Conder gleefully launched himself into bohemian Paris. When in funds, he would retreat to his studio with a couple of girls and enough wine to last for several days in bed. It was said that Conder might often be without a franc but he was never without a girl.

Very unusually, Condor actually worked better when drunk than when he was sober, and rapidly passed through the stages of an hourly brandy and soda, then on to Pernod, finally to absinthe. During the Pernod period, he not only drank it but also painted with it, despite a tendency to hallucinate yellow-striped cats as he worked. The youthful artist *Augustus John* was impressed by these habits but added that, if he was ever inclined to alcohol, Conder served as a warning.

Conder became a habitué of Dieppe in the 1890s, becoming very friendly with the artists *J-E Blanche* and Fritz von Thaulow.

[FRITZ VON THAULOW (1847-1906), the Norwegian landscape artist and designer, lived a bohemian life in a house overlooking Dieppe with his wife and their tribe of fair-haired children. He was a large jovial man, (Wilde: 'a giant with the temperament of Corot'), who delighted in hosting vast feasts for his friends and neighbours – Oscar attended one of these banquets on June 27th 1897. J-E Blanche described Fritz's wife Alexandra as: 'of Russian extraction, a nihilist with no nationality, and a howling humanitarian and pacifist'.]

Many friends made the crossing to Dieppe to carouse with Conder – his advice to them if their Channel crossing was rough was: "Get drunk and stay drunk".

Conder's closest companion on these debauches was the London publisher *Leonard Smithers*, who would arrive on holiday to enthusiastically encourage Conder to greater excess. Conder: 'the Crown descended on me last Saturday augmented by two whores from the East End and did a great deal to shatter that pillar of respectability, to wit, myself' – on this occasion they were ejected unceremoniously from the casino.

Conder's friend William Rothenstein was bewildered to receive one cryptic telegram from Conder during this period: 'If you see a man wandering about Chelsea with an enormous wedding cake in the shape of a Bombay temple, you will know he is my uncle looking for me and I hope you will be very kind to him'.

With the growing popularity of his decorative fans, Conder moved to London in 1899, but found his usual practice of living at night and sleeping by day inhibited by the lack of all-night establishments in England. He became an artistic guru to the Slade School students and dazzled them with his ability, when drunk, to plunge a pin up to the head into his deadened muscles. (When Wilde observed this trick, he murmured: "How interested Baudelaire would have been".)

When he met *Max Beerbohm*, Conder was so impressed that he determined to make a good impression on the debonair man-about-town. Unfortunately Max arrived one morning at Condor's lodgings to find the painter still in bed and nursing an appallingly blood-shot hangover. Condor, aghast at having his true lifestyle exposed, stumbled out of bed and gabbled: "I was up very late last night with some friends, and, as young fools will, I suppose, we – er – over-ate".

Condor finally received a proper income when *Robbie Ross* agreed to regularly exhibit his paintings at the Carfax Gallery. In a drunken gaffe one night, Conder implied that the rigorously honest William Rothenstein had cheated him over a deal at the Carfax. Hearing about the accusation, the normally pacific Rothenstein stormed round to Conder's flat and knocked him to the ground.

Now nursing a black eye in addition to his usual hangover, Conder complained that it was not the done thing to punch a man in his own house. Rothenstein responded: "Well, you could scarcely expect me to invite you to mine to do it, could you?"

In 1900, Conder met a young, comparatively wealthy, Canadian widow called Stella MacAdams. Their marriage completely altered Conder's life, making him in Rothenstein's words: 'happier, gentler and more sober', and their house in Cheyne Walk, Chelsea, became a decorous social centre

One weekend, the newly respectable Conder found himself invited to a shooting party in the country. Despite his past in the Australian bush, Conder was a dreadful shot and winged several members of the hunt. Conder: "The rabbits alone were safe".

One unlucky side effect of marriage and sobriety was that Conder's talent dwindled and his work became noticeably inferior. He finally succumbed to syphilis aged 41.

One of Conder's most dedicated drinking companions was **PHIL MAY** (1864-1903), a caricaturist who worked mostly for Punch magazine. May also drank with *Willie Wilde* during the 1880s, and painted Oscar's portrait in 1892.

Born in Leeds, May first met Conder in Australia, where May had been working as a cartoonist on the Sydney Bulletin. In 1890, May returned to England where he came to be acknowledged as a recognised artist.

May was one of the original members of the Chelsea Arts Club, (and acquainted with *James Whistler*, the first membership secretary). The other members soon grew accustomed to May's spectacular drinking bouts.

One evening, when May had become incoherent at the bar, one member helped him to a cab and drove with him back to May's home in Hampstead. Having deposited May in bed, the Good Samaritan decided that, as it was a pleasant night, he would walk the five miles back to the club. When he arrived at the bar at 1am, he was astounded to find Phil May, having woken up and taken advantage of the vacant cab in Hampstead, once more propping up the counter.

May was an interesting raconteur who entertained the members with many stories. One of the most bizarre concerned a visit he had made to a country church. As he leaned on the altar rail, an attendant rushed up and, indicating a pair of ornate golden orbs on the rail, gasped out: "Sir, you must take your hands off them balls, sir. They are Holy".

A surprised May asked why. The attendant explained: "Well, sir, last Sunday there was a Confirmation Service held here and the Bishop who conducted it was short-sighted. He was so short-sighted that he mistook them balls for two bald heads and confirmed them both".

Phil May died of cirrhosis of the liver, aged 39.

*Under his newly assumed, but quickly abandoned, alias of 'Sebastian Melmoth', Wilde
continued to hold court in the Dieppe restaurants. After one especially uproarious meal, he was
threatened with expulsion from France if such behaviour was repeated.*

*He continued to receive visitors at Berneval, including one fellow ex-prisoner from Reading
called Arthur Cruttendon, to whom Oscar gave hospitality and then references to help Cruttendon in
England. Other visitors during June and July 1897 included William Rothenstein, Aurelian Lugne-
Poe, Andre Gide, Aubrey Beardsley, and Charles Wyndham.*

*Oscar now rented a small house called the Chalet Bourgeat in Berneval, and on June 22nd
celebrated Queen Victoria's Diamond Jubilee with the schoolchildren of the village.*

*He half-heartedly planned two new plays on Biblical themes, one about Pharoah and the Jewish
captives, the other about Jezebel; he also continued to dabble with the idea of his new modern play called
'Mr and Mrs Daventry'.*

*Although he had benefited from the efforts of friends, notably Ross, to raise money for his
upkeep, his usual extravagance re-asserted itself once he was back in circulation. On leaving prison, he
had been offered £1000 by an American paper to write of his jail experiences, but majestically turned it
down: "One shouldn't take one's sufferings to market".*

*He resolved to lead the simple life: 'Really, I am rich when I count up what I still have; and as
for money, my money did me horrible harm. It wrecked me. I just hope to have enough to enable me to
live simply and write well'.*

*However, in practice, he came to appreciate one of his earlier epigrams from 'Dorian': 'Young
people nowadays imagine that money is everything. When they grow older they know it'.*

*Financially, he was fortunate to meet one of his next visitors. On July 26th 1897, Wilde wrote:
'I saw Aubrey Beardsley at Dieppe on Saturday – Leonard Smithers the publisher was with him: very
intoxicated but amusing'.*

LEONARD SMITHERS 1861-1907

After 1895, Leonard Smithers had become the shabby saint of the embattled Decadent
movement. *Robbie Ross* called him 'the most delightful and irresponsible publisher I ever knew;
Arthur Symons described him as a cynic who habitually wore a 'diabolical monocle'; *Charles
Conder* said that his face was 'like the death mask of Nero'; while *WB Yeats* grumbled that
Smithers was 'a most disreputable man'.

His true value lay in the fact that, as he boasted himself, "I publish anything that the
others are afraid of", which much of the time involved pornography. Wilde: "Smithers is so
accustomed to bringing out books limited to an edition of three copies, one for the author, one
for himself, and one for the Police".

But, unlike most pornographers, Smithers also revered poetry to such an extent that it
threatened his livelihood. Oscar ruefully commented on this trait: "The fact is, my dear
Smithers, I really don't think you are business-like: it is a painful thing to have to say of anyone:
but in your case it is sadly true".

Luckily for Oscar, Smithers stayed faithful to his artistic instincts when he agreed to
publish Wilde's poem, 'The Ballad of Reading Gaol', (written between July and October 1897).
Smithers suggested bringing out an edition for Christmas but Oscar demurred: "I think after
Christmas would be better for publication. I am hardly a Christmas present".

'The Ballad' was published in February 1898 and sold remarkably well. Smithers was
emboldened to place an advertisement in the Athenaeum magazine reading: 'Three thousand
copies sold in four weeks!" Oscar: "I feel like Lipton's Tea".

Smithers later published the play-scripts of 'Ideal Husband' and 'The Importance', but
these were largely ignored. Oscar was correct in suspecting that the public would not: 'welcome

me again in airy mood and spirit, mocking at morals', adding that they would probably prefer him to 'edit prayers for those at sea'.

Wilde had an ambivalent attitude towards Smithers. Oscar: 'He is rather dreadful. I suppose many of us are rather dreadful now, and do not realise to what we have come. But the other night he was speaking to me of his son, and we wept together.'

(Smithers's son, Jack, grew up to revile the memory of Wilde, describing him as 'utterly selfish, idle, a thief and cadger to boot'. He recounted an extraordinary story – almost definitely untrue – that Oscar had returned to London in 1898, stayed at the Smithers's residence, then, having declared an irresistible carnal desire for Mrs Smithers, had been thrown unceremoniously out of the house.)

Leonard Smithers started his career as a solicitor in his native Sheffield and married a pretty and petite Yorkshire girl called Alice Oldham in 1882. He soon became convinced that his real path lay in publishing superior erotica. In partnership with a Sheffield publisher called Harry Nichols, he created a company with the erudite but fictitious name of 'The Erotika Biblion Society of Athens', (to send the police off on a false trail).

As they shared the same interests, he contacted the explorer *Sir Richard Burton* and the two men worked together on various texts. When Burton died, Smithers was forced to work with Burton's widow, Lady Isabel. This unlikely pair – one striving for maximum erotic effect, the other desperate to bowdlerise her husband's writings – managed to publish 'The Perfumed Garden' and 'The Kharma Sutra'.

The now thriving Smithers moved to London in 1891, but dissolved his partnership with Nichols when the latter moved into downmarket hardcore pornography. Nichols, (having regularly supplied hardcore to such luminaries as *Lord Rosebery* and the American industrialist J. Pierpont Morgan), was arrested in 1900 after a raid on his shop. He absconded to Paris while on bail.

Smithers, on the other hand, prospered despite the risks attached to his trade. To minimise the danger, he kept his pornographic stock in bags under the counter so that, if threatened by a raid, they could be whisked away to a railway station and stored in the left luggage office.

Business was so good that Smithers was able to install his family in a Bedford Square mansion and to move his premises to the fashionable Royal Arcade in Old Bond St. (*Aubrey Beardsley* suggested that Smithers should compete with *John Lane's* 'Bodley Head' by calling his new shop 'the Sodley Bed'). Smithers did toy with the idea of putting a notice in the window: 'Smut is cheap today!''

The business attracted some unusual customers. The widow of a famous but recently deceased High Court judge privately asked Smithers to remove a store of pornography from her husband's effects. Smithers realised on collection that most of it had been purchased at his shop in the first place.

However, Smithers retained a deep desire to become a legitimate publisher. The opportunity fell his way when, in the wake of the Wilde trials, John Lane abandoned his commitment to the Decadents. Smithers eagerly jumped at the chance to take over.

From 1895 till 1900, Smithers became publisher, protector, and friend to many of the major artistic figures of the Nineties. He replaced the defunct 'Yellow Book' with a new magazine called 'The Savoy', with Beardsley as art editor and Arthur Symons as literary editor, and employing such contributors as WB Yeats, *Bernard Shaw* and the sexologist Havelock Ellis. Joseph Conrad was able to publish one of his first stories, 'The Idiots', in the Savoy. Smithers insisted on the finest production values for the magazine, drawing the compliment from *Ernest Dowson*: "May the hair of John Lane grow green with envy".

Following the publication of the first edition of the Savoy in January 1896, Smithers held a celebratory dinner. Under the influence of alcohol, Smithers's brash character clashed with the social standards of his more aesthetic contributors. When Symons read aloud letters from various Irish literati complaining of WB Yeats's involvement in the magazine, Smithers grabbed the notes from Symons's hands, bellowing: "I'll sue 'em".

Determined to keep the party going, Smithers invited selected guests back to his house for more refreshment. A very reluctant Yeats was persuaded to come along. When they reached the house, Smithers proudly unveiled his latest acquisition, a hurdy-gurdy piano, operated by electricity. Unconcerned by the failure of the electricity supply, Smithers insisted on cranking the machine by hand, exclaiming with delight at the ensuing racket. Yeats sat listening in a rictus of distaste.

In the midst of this performance, Aubrey Beardsley suffered a minor haemorrhage and sat spitting blood into a bucket. Yeats was distracted from this sight by Smithers's wife Alice taking him to admire her new bamboo-covered walls. Oblivious of any problem, the sweating Smithers continued to grind out a tinny but thunderous version of 'Goodbye, Dolly Grey'.

Next day, Yeats agreed to continue writing for the Savoy but only on the condition that he need never enter Smithers' house again. Their precarious collaboration ended when the Savoy itself folded in December 1896, as a result of a ban placed on its distribution by the booksellers WH Smith.

Smithers continued to provide incomes for the remaining Decadents by farming out translation work, (notably of the works of *Emile Zola*), and remained a central figure in their bohemian excesses. One night in Paris in 1896, he accompanied Beardsley and Dowson to *Toulouse-Lautrec's* apartment in Montmartre, where Beardsley partook of hashish for the first time.

The drug appeared to have no effect until later in a restaurant when Beardsley was overcome by irresistible giggling. He infected the rest of the party to such a degree that they were threatened with removal by the management. Dowson: "We all behaved like imbeciles".

Smithers did not restrict his interest in sex simply to pornography, being in Vincent O'Sullivan's words: 'always accompanied by some appalling Venus with sagging breasts, pouched jaw, varicosed legs, rheumatic ankles, and wall-eyed'. He also admired younger girls – Wilde: 'Smithers loves first editions, especially of women; little girls are his passion'.

Smithers was rumoured to have a set of photographs depicting himself in the act of sodomising his long-suffering or complicit wife Alice. Beardsley reported that, after a man had expressed appreciation of Alice one night at the Brussels opera house, Smithers arranged for him to purchase her services for the night.

By 1900, Smither's reckless existence and his refusal to compromise over the extravagant production of uneconomic books, led to his bankruptcy. He tried desperate, and often illegal, methods to recoup his losses, swindling nearly every bookseller in London. After the deaths of Beardsley and Wilde, he began manufacturing forgeries of Beardsley's drawings, and pirating many books under such fake publishing house names as 'Melmoth and Co' or 'The Maturin Press'. He became an outcast even among the remnants of the Decadents.

[One of Smithers last remaining friends at this time was the strikingly named **REGGIE BACCHUS** (1858-1921), who had also known Wilde. He was an Oxford educated theologian and pornographic novelist, who married Isa Bowman, (the first actress to play Lewis Carroll's 'Alice' on stage). Bacchus was a robust supporter of erotica, once defending another friend, Thomas Wirgham, who had been arrested for possessing 'an obscene toothpick' – a carved instrument depicting a man and a woman indulging in mutual oral sex.]

As the family fortunes collapsed, Smithers and Alice took to heavy drinking, sending their son Jack out to pawn the last household goods, until finally even Alice had had enough and left her husband.

By 1907, Smithers was a drink and drug addled wreck, addicted to an opiate-based concoction known as Dr Collis Browne's Chlorodyne. He died of cirrhosis of the liver aged 46, and his naked body, (even his monocle had been stolen), was found in a house in Fulham. The building had been entirely stripped of everything except fifty empty bottles of Chlorodyne. *Bosie Douglas* paid the funeral expenses.

One of Smithers's more gifted and certainly more attractive mistresses was the English poet and painter **ALTHEA GYLES**, (1868-1949), a rare example of a woman among the Decadents. She designed book covers for WB Yeats and Ernest Dowson, and also illustrated 'The Harlot's House' for Wilde, who described her as 'an artist of great ability'.

In 1899, to the horror of her friends, the demure Althea fell for the dubious charms of Smithers – in many people's eyes it was the mating of a virgin with a satyr. A disgusted Yeats wrote: 'she gave an 'At Home' the other day and poured out tea with his arm around her waist and even kissed him at intervals'. The affair ended within a year.

Althea remained a devout admirer of Wilde. In an act of real personal sacrifice, she refused to allow her publisher to remove the dedication, 'To the beautiful memory of Oscar Wilde', from her first book of poetry. This resulted in the publisher withdrawing the book and Althea's chance of publication being lost for good.

For the next fifty years, she led a half-life in a series of London bed-sits, casting horoscopes. She died aged 81, an eccentric old woman in a nursing home.

In his last desperate years, Smithers was forced into 'vanity publishing' for unrecognised authors. One of these works was by **ALEISTER CROWLEY** (1875-1947). Entitled 'White Stains', it was essentially hardcore pornography and failed to do well, as most of the copies were destroyed by the British Customs.

Formerly a fellow member, (with WB Yeats), of the Order of the Golden Dawn, Crowley became a rather self-conscious Satanist. As he told *Herbert Vivian*: "Everybody is delighted to make my acquaintance, but usually no one cares to meet me a second time".

(Crowley enjoyed bisexuality, including a relationship with a young man called Herbert 'Jerome' Pollitt whom he introduced to black magic. Wilde also knew Pollitt and once wrote to him asking: 'When you come to Paris pray be golden entirely'.)

Considering his own unusual lifestyle, Crowley was strangely nervous of Smithers. After they met in 1897, Crowley said of his publisher that he was: "an abominable creature of high intelligence and no morals', and nicknamed Smithers 'The Beast'. Ironically, this was exactly the same soubriquet bestowed on Crowley in later years.

On July 8ᵗʰ 1897, Wilde began to write what was to be his final real work, 'The Ballad of Reading Goal'. Although he had finished the first draft by July 20ᵗʰ, he continued to revise it until Christmas.

THE BALLAD OF READING GAOL

Based on the real events at Reading Prison surrounding the execution of Trooper Wooldridge for the murder of his wife, the Ballad was a major departure from Wilde's normal subject matter and style. As a High Court judge declared many years later in reference to the poem: "Wilde owed his inspiration to Her Majesty's Government".

Oscar wrote that the poem was: 'terribly realistic for me, and drawn from actual experience, a sort of denial of my own philosophy of art in many ways. I hope it is good.' He was even proud of managing to insert the word 'latrine' into a serious work – 'It looks beautiful'.

Bosie Douglas remarked that Oscar had worked harder on this piece than at anything he had tried before, considering each word with exceptional care. Bosie: 'I had the Ballad for breakfast, dinner and tea'.

Given this amount of application, Wilde was irritated when a critic pointed out that the line, 'Hanged in his scarlet coat' was wrong, as Trooper Wooldridge had belonged to the Blues regiment. Oscar immediately offered to re-write it as: 'He did not wear his azure coat, For blood and wine are blue'.

Later Bosie pointed out that the derivation of the famous line, 'For each man kills the thing he loves', could be found in Shakespeare's 'The Merchant of Venice'. (Bassanio – 'Do all men kill the things they do not love?' Shylock – 'Hates any man the thing he would not kill? Killing might be loving, loving might be killing'). When Bosie asked him what he meant by the line, Oscar murmured: "You should know".

Under the pseudonym of Oscar's prison number, 'C.3.3.', the poem was published in February 1898 and sold extremely well. Wilde: 'The Ballad of Reading Jail' was very well received. Its popularity, of course, could be increased enormously by my painful death from starvation. The public love poets to die that way. It seems dramatically correct.'

Wilde justified his unusual change to the ballad form: 'The ballad is the true origin of the romantic drama, and the true predecessors of Shakespeare are not the tragic writer of the Greek or Latin stage, but the ballad-writers of the Borders'.

During Wilde's imprisonment, the writer AE Houseman had sent him a copy of his own ballad, 'The Shropshire Lad'. Oscar learnt parts of it by heart and described it as 'a lovely lyric poem'.

[AE HOUSEMAN (1859-1936), possibly by intention, was the least poetical looking of poets. Rothenstein: 'Houseman neither looked nor talked like a poet. He prided himself on this, I think. He was grim and dry and seemed to disdain the artist in himself.' A contemporary said of him that: 'So far from believing that man wrote the Shropshire Lad, I shouldn't have thought him capable of reading it'.

His brother, Lawrence Houseman, met Wilde in Paris in 1899 and wrote admiringly of Oscar's still extraordinary conversational powers. In 1905, Lawrence wrote: 'Perhaps before we die a tablet will be up in Tite Street on the house where he used to live, and a Rodin statue up on the Embankment'.]

Also Oscar was influenced by the work of a man who appeared to be the antithesis of everything that Wilde stood for. The arch-imperialist Rudyard Kipling had recently published a ballad called 'Danny Deevor'. In a reference also to Kipling's fellow jingo, WE Henley, Oscar commented: "I am out-Henleying Kipling".

RUDYARD KIPLING 1865-1936

Wilde was an admirer of Rudyard Kipling – 'He revealed life by superb flashes of vulgarity' – and the last present that he gave to his children was a copy of Kipling's 'The Jungle Book'. This appreciation was not reciprocated, as Kipling despised Oscar and his followers. Kipling's sister Trix was even more disparaging, saying that Wilde seemed to be 'roughly modelled in suet-pudding' and that his lips 'resembled big brown slugs'.

Although the Decadents often appear to represent the 1890s, it is sometimes forgotten that the decade also saw the rise of such writers as AE Houseman, Thomas Hardy, *Bernard Shaw*, Joseph Conrad, and, of course, Kipling, none of whom could be said to typify the aesthetic school.

In Kipling's case, he actively poured scorn on the movement, describing its adherents as 'long-haired things' whose preoccupation with psychology was explained by 'lack of liver pill'. In his poem 'The Mary Gloster', Kipling specifically seemed to target Wilde: 'And the things I knew was rotten you said was the way to live' – 'And your rooms at college was beastly – more like a whore's than a man's.'

(*Max Beerbohm* always harboured suspicions about Kipling's vehemence against aesthetes, and its corollary of over-sycophancy towards the 'manly man' as displayed in Kipling's: 'It's Oh to meet an Army man, Set up and trimmed and taut'.)

Enormously popular for such works as the two 'Jungle Books', 'Barrack Room Ballads', Stalky and Co', 'Puck of Pook's Hill', and his masterpiece 'Kim', Kipling was a divisive figure among his contemporaries. To *Henry James* he was 'the most complete man of genius', while *Mark Twain* said that between them: 'We cover all knowledge; he knows all that can be known, and I know the rest'.

On the other hand, Bernard Shaw called him: 'a romantic schoolboy, who never grew up', adding that he 'was sick of Kiplingesque brutalitarianism'. *Frank Harris* said that: 'Kipling has done more to stir up hate between the nations than any other living man'. And Max Beerbohm thought that Kipling's position in literature would be seen to correspond to President Theodore Roosevelt's position as a statesman.

Owing to his father's appointment as an instructional sculptor at the Bombay School of Art, Kipling was born in India. His mother Alice was one of four extraordinarily well-connected daughters of a Wesleyan minister named George Browne Macdonald.

Of Alice's sisters, Georgina married the artist *Sir Edward Burne-Jones*, Agnes married the President of the Royal Academy Sir Edward Poynter, while Louisa became the mother of the future British Prime Minister Stanley Baldwin. (During their schooldays, Kipling was mildly shocked when his cousin Stanley was expelled from Harrow School for distributing pornographic books.)

Having been sent back to England in 1871 to endure a horrific childhood at a school in Southsea, Hampshire, then a happier time at the United Services College at Westward Ho! in Devon, Kipling returned to India aged 16 to take up a job in journalism.

Unlike most of his compatriots in the British Raj, he was fascinated by Indian life and immersed himself in the local culture. He studied India from the courts of the maharajahs, ('all palaces in India are full of eyes'), to the ordinary existence of the bazaars and villages. During a cholera outbreak, Kipling discovered that opium was an effective medicine: 'It is possible to work with a temperature of 104F even though next day one has to ask the office who wrote the article'.

He found life back in the British compounds just as interesting, though on occasion more crass than he might have wished. Despite his love of realism he had a fastidious streak, recording in his diary: 'Wish they wouldn't put married couple next door to me with one half-inch plank between. Saps one's morality'.

In 1888, he combined his observational skills with his gift of story-telling to produce 'Plain Tales From the Hills', about the Anglo-Indian society in Simla. It was an instant and huge success.

The following year he left India on a meandering journey home. He visited Burma, (the inspiration for his great poem 'The Road to Mandalay'), then arrived in China. Feeling repelled after attending a waxwork exhibition of torture methods and sensing contempt towards the white races, he took a dislike to the Chinese. Japan was much more to his taste, in particular the city of Nagasaki which he described as: 'entirely inhabited by laughing children. The grownups exist on sufferance!"

Aged only 22, Kipling was already famous when he returned to London, and was seen as a worthy rival to *Guy de Maupassant* in the art of the short story.

For a short period he rented a flat over a sausage shop in Villiers St, near Charing Cross. Possibly encouraged by the proximity of Gatti's Music Hall, he began to write songs, one of which was called 'And That's What The Girl Told The Soldier'. He was inordinately proud when it was performed at Gatti's. Kipling wrote: 'Afterwards, the dark street was vocal with various versions of what the girl had really told the soldier, and I went to bed murmuring 'I have found my destiny'.'

While in London, Kipling made the acquaintance of the American Wolcott Balestier, (who, with William Heineman, had published Wilde's 'Intentions' in Leipzig in 1891). In 1892, he married Balestier's sister Caroline, and the newly-weds moved to the USA, where they settled at Brattleboro in Vermont.

He spent an unhappy four years in Brattleboro, quarrelling with his neighbours and his wife's family. One of his few distractions was golf, but found that the frequent snow was a problem as he continually lost his white golf balls. His solution was to paint the balls red.

By 1896, he had not only fallen out with Brattleboro, but with America in general. Owing to the border dispute between Venezuela and British Guyana, the USA and Britain teetered on the brink of war. Kipling now saw the USA as a hostile country and he and Caroline moved back to England.

This did not prevent him from later advising the USA in his poem, 'The White Man's Burden', on how to deal with 'Your new-caught, sullen peoples, Half-devil and half-child' who inhabited the new American empire in Cuba and the Philippines. (At one time, Oscar Wilde suggested that the White Man had carried his burden only as far as the Stock Exchange.)

The Kiplings settled in Sussex, firstly at Rottingdean, then in 1902 moving to a 17th century house called 'Bateman's' at Burwash. Although he was now a revered author who in 1907 was awarded the Nobel Prize for Literature, the tide of public opinion had swung away from the trumpeting imperialist values that he had espoused.

In the light of the badly mismanaged Boer War and unease over European tensions, Kipling's work came to be seen, sometimes unfairly, as blowsy, brutal, and seeped in lethal rightwing romanticism. To add to his problems, he suffered continual pain from an undiagnosed duodenal ulcer.

With the commencement of the First World War, Kipling at first threw himself gleefully into stoking patriotic fervour. He visited the trenches on the Western Front for two hours, declaring afterwards: "It's a grand life and does not give you a dull minute".

However, after the death of his soldier son, his mood changed and he began to write savage attacks on what he now saw as the bungling of the politicians in charge: 'They died because their fathers lied'. After the war, he gave much of his time to serving on the War Graves Commission – due to his endowment, the Last Post is still played every evening at the Menin Gate memorial in Ypres.

He continued to write but his work became less popular, his later books often being referred to as 'the Kipling that nobody reads'. He still remained friends with many of his great contemporaries, especially the author Thomas Hardy.

With the idea of possibly purchasing a house in Dorset, Kipling once accompanied Hardy to view an isolated house in the rural depths of the county. They were shown around by an elderly lady who regarded the two men, who had arrived by bicycle, with disfavour.

In an attempt to allay her suspicions, Thomas Hardy took the lady aside and whispered that his companion was none other than _the_ famous Rudyard Kipling. Never having heard of him, she remained unconvinced. Kipling decided to take a hand and quietly but impressively informed their guide that the gentleman with him was _the_ Thomas Hardy. The old lady's face stayed blank: "Who?"

When Hardy died, Kipling, accompanied by fellow-writers Bernard Shaw, Sir James Barrie and John Galsworthy, acted as pallbearers at his funeral. Shaw: "We must have made a curious procession. Galsworthy and I were six feet tall, while Kipling and Barrie were about five feet. As we marched, Kipling bobbed about continuously right in front of me and kept changing step. Every time he did so, I nearly fell over him'.

Kipling found one consolation for old age in a strong enthusiasm for the motorcar. He said that it opened up England for him as: 'a land full of stupefying marvels and mysteries'. Once, after his Rolls Royce had broken down, he was surprised to find that he had not received a bill for the repairs. When he enquired the reason, the firm replied: 'Our cars never break down, sir'.

He was aware of one disadvantageous aspect of motoring and that was the growing death toll on the roads. He complained: 'All England is out killing each other on the road. We saw five smashes by the roadside between Chelmsford and Colchester. One was a large Rolls copulating with an embarrassed bus'.

Two other writers who vied with Kipling in the patriotic school of literature also had connections to Wilde. **SIR HENRY NEWBOLT**, (1862-1938), had been an undergraduate at Oxford when the University Union had requested a copy of Oscar's poems. He had been one of two speakers to demand that the gift be rejected; their objections were carried and Oscar's poems returned to him.

In 1887, Newbolt heard Wilde give a speech on the lesser-known Elizabethan and Jacobean dramatists. 'His quotations seemed to me to bear out all that he claimed for them. But when I searched the plays afterwards I found not a word of any of the lines. My feeling was chiefly one of almost awed surprise at his wonderful powers'.

Newbolt himself became most famous for his poem 'Drake's Drum' and another poem which, in reference to the Sudan debacle of 1885, bemoaned the fact that 'the Colonel's dead and the Gatling's jammed', before exhorting the reader to: 'Play up, play up, and play the game'. _Arthur Symons_ acidly foretold the fading of such poetry: 'Soon Newbolt's drum-taps will die away like the Salvation Army brass band as it turns the corner'.

Kipling's lifelong friend, **SIR HENRY RIDER HAGGARD**, (1856-1923), met Wilde on several occasions, notably in Homburg, Germany, in 1892. Haggard wrote of the encounter: 'Oscar is here, certainly he is an amusing man, though I wish he'd drop his affectations! ... He tells me that he feels the sneers at and attacks on him. Still, I must say that, if half what one hears is true, he has done a good deal to bring them on his head'.

Rider Haggard became well known for his adventure stories, 'King Solomon's Mines' and 'She', both based on his knowledge of Africa. Wilde: 'He writes like a man playing football, and as long as he confines himself to blood and bruises he does well; but immediately he begins to moralise, he gets outside his natural sphere and becomes absurd'.

Although visits from friends provided Wilde with some diversion, he soon found himself growing bored with village life in Berneval. The nearby town of Rouen began to take on the aspect of an enticing metropolis.

Hearing that his old acolyte, Reggie Turner, was staying in Rouen, Oscar contacted him and suggested that Turner came to stay in Berneval semi-permanently.

Reggie was reluctant and confided his doubts to a fellow guest at his Rouen hotel, the writer Gertrude Atherton. According to Atherton, Reggie told her that: "I now regret bitterly that I ever knew him. He was an evil influence for any young man". Atherton replied: "I see no reason why you should wreck your life for the sake of an old sinner like that", and advised him to leave. Reggie retreated to London without meeting Oscar.

GERTRUDE ATHERTON 1857-1948

The American novelist Gertrude Atherton did not meet Wilde, but on one occasion she had visited his mother Lady Wilde at her home in London. She wrote a rather catty report about Speranza's evident poverty but admitted that she was 'a leaning tower of courage'. When Speranza suggested that she met Oscar, Atherton declined. She had spotted his photograph and was repelled by 'the most lascivious, coarse, repulsive mouth I have ever seen'.

She had been in London during Wilde's trials in 1895 and commented that: 'Lucifer had hurtled from Paradise into the abyss; and if a gigantic bomb had exploded in the middle of London it could not have created more excitement'.

Unaware of Atherton's hostility, in November 1900 Wilde read her book on Washington politics called 'Senator North' and praised it highly. "This is a fine study of the American politician and possesses the quality of truth in characterisation." It was probably the last book he ever read.

Born Gertrude Franklin in San Francisco, Atherton was educated in California and Kentucky where she admitted that she had spent 'an insurgent and heedless youth'. When she married, this was a description with which her husband, George Atherton, might well have agreed.

George endured a stormy courtship, during which Gertrude, irritated by his attentions, had trained her dog to attack him. After five proposals, Gertrude reluctantly consented to the wedding, mostly to get some peace: 'but I preferred Plato!'

The marriage was in trouble from the outset, given their lack of mutual interests. Gertrude adored literature while George struggled to read even a penny shocker. Gertrude: 'He still hadn't finished it when he died nine years later'.

George, frustrated by his lack of success in business, attempted to change his fortunes by establishing a ranch in the Californian backwoods. The episode turned into a nightmare. Their first Chinese cook went mad and tried to kill the family, the second cook was permanently out of action due to opium, the temperature stood at 104F, lightning struck their telephone and hurled Gertrude across the room, and George turned to drink. Finally the money ran out and they returned home.

Despite the birth of two children, Gertrude became bored by the monotony of marriage and flirted outrageously with other men. Gertrude: 'I accumulated four devoted admirers, and, taking a firm stand with my husband, permitted them to call in the afternoon and evening. Whenever they were there, George stalked up and down the hall, looking coal-black, or hung over the banisters muttering.'

She had no intention, though, of exchanging one man for another. Matters threatened to take a serious turn when an admirer decided to challenge George to a duel. Gertrude nipped the idea in the bud by telling the admirer that her only interest in him had been as a human specimen: "You are not interesting in yourself, but through you I have learned something of the world outside of California. Now, you've become a bore" – 'I thought he would assault me'.

She poured her energies into writing and continued to ignore her husband. 'I locked the door against George at night, no matter how much he pounded on it'. She justified one flirtation by telling him: "He's worth two of you, for he is somebody and you are nobody. If you have any pride you would make something of yourself".

Finally, goaded beyond endurance, George took her at her word and left to carve a fortune in Chile. Unfortunately he died on the voyage out.

Even in death he was unlucky, as, given the tropical heat, his body had to be embalmed in a barrel of rum. The sailors, angry over the contamination of their liquor ration, refused on superstitious grounds to travel with a corpse. It finally had to be smuggled on board and brought home camouflaged under a pile of coconuts. Gertrude: 'It was years before I could even look at coconuts again'.

In 1882, she published her first book, 'The Randolphs of Redwoods'. Leaving her surviving child Muriel behind with her husband's family, Atherton left California to begin a life of international travel and to acquire the experiences that gave her the material for over forty novels.

Some of her contacts with American literati lacked decorum. Having survived attempted rape by *Ambrose Bierce*, she was apprehensive about encountering *Walt Whitman*. 'I had been told I would have to kiss him, but he was very hairy and averse to soap and water. A friend had written me that she had searched in vain for a clean spot before performing the rite'. A week before the arranged meeting, Atherton was greatly relieved to pick up a newspaper 'and read that Whitman had gone to his eternal rest'.

By 1890, she had become a regular at the hotels of Paris and London, meeting many of the leading European writers, and observing that 'Englishmen are sentimental and romantic under their impassive exteriors'.

While in Pont Aven, Brittany, Atherton came across the drink-sodden poet *Ernest Dowson* and spent a few days trying to restore him to some semblance of sobriety. She found that she enjoyed the role of reformer – 'Nothing inflates the ego more' – but soon abandoned the job as hopeless. She later used this experience as the plot of her 1908 novel, 'The Gorgeous Isle'.

Although interested enough to research it for a novel, Atherton had little sympathy with the British suffragette movement. She regarded its supporters as 'detestable as women, but as scientific martyrs they were a commanding success'. She met their leader, Mrs Emily Pankhurst, who 'fixed me with a glacial eye and permitted me to understand that she had no use for mere novelists who gave little evidence of being eager to die for the cause'.

In 1906, Atherton witnessed the San Francisco earthquake and subsequent fire, boarding the ferry from Berkeley to check the damage before being driven back by flames. Safely back on shore, she watched the dynamiting of the city to halt the spread of the conflagration. Atherton: 'It is absolutely de rigueur in California to treat an earthquake as a joke (after it is over!)'.

Despite her total inexperience as an orator, in 1912 she was persuaded to give political speeches on behalf of the Democrats and surprisingly her efforts were said to have aided Woodrow Wilson to the White House. Her lack of interest in politics, (and her habit of evading Republican queries by briskly declaring: "Oh, that doesn't matter. Nothing matters much, you know"), charmed the voters of California.

Before the entry of the USA into the First World War in 1917, Atherton went to France to inquire into the harrowing conditions of the French military hospitals. Shocked by her investigations, she worked hard to raise charity money back in America.

In recognition of these efforts, the French government offered her a medal. With her characteristic lack of tact, Atherton replied in a statement that caused a predictable quarrel:

442

"You know, there is only one way left in this world to be distinguished and that is not to be decorated by France".

During August 1897, Oscar's sojourn in Berneval was relieved by more visits from Leonard Smithers and Charles Wyndham. The Francophile American novelist and poet Vincent O'Sullivan, (1868-1940), also befriended Wilde at this time and remained a sympathetic occasional companion in his last years.

On August 1ˢᵗ, Robbie Ross arrived, together with a young architect called John Fothergill.

JOHN FOTHERGILL 1876-1957

Fothergill was a dandyish young painter, who in 1897 was a student at the London School of Architecture. For a short period Wilde toyed with the idea of building a half-timbered chalet in Berneval, 'like, I regret to say, Shakespeare's house'. He discussed the possibilities with Fothergill but, like many building projects before and since, the idea foundered in practicalities. Oscar: "Fothergill has me waiting for him, as he is waiting for me".

The 21-year-old architect found Wilde to be a confusing acquaintance. Fothergill: 'Wilde used to kiss the servant before leaving the Normandy inns round Berneval; he told me it was expected and I timidly followed suit.' Oscar always referred to him as 'the architect of the moon'.

In 1898, Fothergill, in partnership with the solicitor Arthur Clifton, opened the small Carfax Gallery in Ryder St, London; *William Rothenstein* provided artistic advice.

[ARTHUR CLIFTON, (1862 – 1932), looked after the business side of the Carfax. Years earlier, Clifton had happened to mention to Wilde that he could not afford to marry his fiancée Marjorie. Oscar, flush from play profits, immediately sat down and wrote him a cheque for £150, thus enabling the marriage to go ahead. It was a gesture that echoed Wilde's short story, 'The Model Millionaire', when the 'beggar' provides the money for the hero's wedding.]

In 1900, the Carfax was taken over by Robbie Ross and More Adey with variable fortune. One day, Fothergill asked Ross how the business was doing. Robbie replied: "Well, dear John, we are just about keeping our heads below water".

Later, Fothergill spent twelve years working as an archaeologist. By the 1920s, the relatively mild mannered youth had turned into a formidably cantankerous middle-aged man. Ross commented: "John Fothergill is the worst-mannered man in London, but when you know get to know him well – he's far worse".

Now married to his wife Kate, and in need of an income, Fothergill decided to run a pub and searched England looking for something suitable. (He rejected one tavern called 'The Jolly Gardener' on the grounds that: "Who ever knew or even heard of a gardener that was jolly".)

In 1922, he bought the Spread Eagle Inn at Thame, Oxfordshire, and proceeded to rule the establishment by his own extremely individual code. He insisted that the Spread Eagle should be a high-class hotel where only the finest food and drink be served in the best furnished and decorated surroundings.

His insistence on only the best, however, also applied to his clientele. With Oxford University so close, Fothergill announced that he 'merely wished to encourage the right kind of undergrad and better class of don' and refused to serve 'under-bred folk' or 'inferior females'.

Fothergill: "On the whole I've decided that it's not good to scrap with your clients – but certain people have to be tamed". He utterly refused to accept that his role of innkeeper implied that he was a servant of the public in any way, telling one customer: "My name is Fothergill. But 'sir' would be shorter".

To rub home his insistence on gentility, he had the words 'Manners Makyth Man' carved on to the back of the dining room chairs and, to discourage the ill-educated, the menu consisted of erudite crossword clues. This latter habit had to be abandoned, due to the resulting chaos.

His unusual attitudes extended to money making, which he dismissed with: 'Prosperity is a bad word – it smacks of grabbing from others'. Fothergill basically charged what he felt was appropriate. When the poet John Betjeman was an Oxford student, he visited the Spread Eagle and was delighted to find that he had been undercharged for his meal. Fothergill had written on Betjeman's bill: "Less fourteen shillings and sixpence for extravagance'.

This cavalier approach could also work to the detriment of some customers. Fothergill overcharged one group because he considered them to be physically ugly – 'the first time in history seven people without knowing it have left an inn having paid an extra sixpence each for not being beautiful'.

Once, after he had received some Greek honey sent specially from Athens, he proudly offered it to his guests at teatime. One couple politely refused the honey, whereupon Fothergill turned to the rest of the company and snarled: "Aren't they bastards!"

When one old lady insisted on inspecting his bedrooms before staying at the Spread Eagle, a fuming Fothergill sent his wife upstairs to accompany the woman, shouting after them 'Oh, and, Kate, don't show her the room with the vermin!'

True to his Oxford roots, he told one supercilious Cambridge don that Oxford University had now by and large given up rowing, but that once a year they hired a vessel for the inter-university Boat Race, just to be sociable.

One thing that was guaranteed to rouse Fothergill's ire was the practice of non-customers using his toilet facilities. This would draw a torrent of abuse on the head of an offender. Even bona fide guests were not immune. When one guest complained about the state of the lavatory, Fothergill told him that, if he ever returned, he should bring his own lavatory with him.

Sex was another red rag that could be relied on to enrage the Fothergill bull. Fothergill: 'The age around twenty is the young man's only chance of being chaste in his life and he ought to take it' – 'After all, sex won't occupy the child later more than a few minutes a week, so why should there be such a fuss about it?'

Fothergill was determined not only to regulate the sexual lives of his clients but also their choice of partner. Although he considered them to be 'squits', he was upset when two undergraduates arrived for a drink with two shop girls. Having found out that the girls were neither sisters nor fiancées, Fothergill told the students: "Then I don't think I should bring them here again as they are not in keeping with the place, nor indeed with yourselves".

The sight of a girl sitting on a student's knee in his bar roused Fothergill to fever pitch. 'I attacked the four of them like a fury, telling them to go out, never to come again, and to tell their friends not to'.

Adults were not immune to judgement either. When a couple asked for a double room, Fothergill insisted that they had single rooms: "Because you're not married and I discourage indiscriminate coupling here". In one case, Fothergill's morality campaign received a bad rebuff. Having spotted a man entering a woman's room, Fothergill rebuked him: "Isn't this a little unfair on me when I specifically asked you not to enter ladies' rooms?" It turned out that the lady genuinely was the man's wife.

Fothergill was far more at home with the people he regarded as the 'right sort'. When the Maharajah of Lahore stayed for a night at the Spread Eagle, Fothergill begged him for a photograph. The Maharajah took out a letter from home, ripped off the stamp and handed it over. Fothergill admired some elements among the country gentry and treasured a copy of a book written by an elderly acquaintance called 'Our Dumb Friends – How to Kill, Skin, and Stuff Them'.

Occasionally, Fothergill made attempts to soften his irascible image but invariably got it wrong. When he congratulated a guest on how well his mother looked for her age, the man replied sourly that she was his wife.

Having been very impressed by hearing of a tobacconist who, after a fifteen-year gap, had still remembered which cigars a client preferred, Fothergill decided to try to emulate this feat of service. One evening, he approached a guest and, with a encouraging smile, said to him: "You've been here before, haven't you?" The man nodded. Fothergill crinkled his brow, then came up with: "Now, let me think. It must have been about two years ago, wasn't it?" "No" replied the guest, "It was at tea-time".

In 1932, after nine years hard work at the Spread Eagle, Fothergill, having started with a capital of £500, was £1,400 in debt. Aged 56, he moved on to open new ventures at the Royal Ascot Hotel and at the Three Swans at Market Harborough, though neither achieved the eccentric élan of his Thame days.

He retired eventually, 'my accountant having showed me that men were made for accounts and not accounts for men'. In the 1970s, a television film was made of his life starring the British actor Robert Hardy as Fothergill.

Also in August 1897, Wilde received another visit from Robbie Ross and Robert Sherard.

ROBERT SHERARD (Second Part – cont. from page 165)

During Wilde's trials and later during the years in jail, Robert Sherard had travelled from France on several occasions to visit his old friend. Loathing the idea of homosexuality, (and in the face of all evidence and reason), he continued to believe in Oscar's complete innocence. Oscar eventually grew quite irritated by Sherard's block-headed defence.

On this particular occasion in Berneval, Sherard was forced to confront reality when he accidentally spotted Wilde and Ross kissing. When he recovered from the shock, he consoled himself with the idea that Oscar's homosexuality was a symptom of epilepsy induced by over-eating and drinking.

He remained convinced that Oscar's reconciliation to Constance would be the best course for the future, and spent much of 1898 imparting good advice to an increasingly bored Wilde. However, by this time Sherard himself began to have personal problems caused by alcohol and a rabid anti-Semitism, partly fuelled by the then current Dreyfus scandal.

In May 1898, Oscar reported that, in Paris, Sherard had 'created a horrible scene in Campbell's Bar by bawling out 'a bas les juift',' and starting a fight with a Jew who knocked him out cold.

Oscar: 'Yesterday he turned up again and had to receive a rather insolent lecture from Campbell who told him he preferred Jews to drunkards in his bar'. The owner told Sherard that he was only allowed back because he knew Wilde: 'rather amusing after I had been subjected to Robert's monstrous moralising'.

Oscar: 'He was much depressed, so of course I gave him drinks and cigarettes and all he wanted. To show his gratitude he insisted on reciting The Ballad of Reading Jail at the top of his voice'.

Gradually the two men drifted apart until *Bernard Shaw* reported that 'Sherard and Wilde eventually cut one another'. Oscar: 'I hope he will get better. Years ago he was a very good and dear fellow'.

445

After Wilde's death, Sherard became one of his stoutest supporters, indignantly rejecting *Andre Gide's* (essentially accurate) description of the antics in Algeria in a pamphlet called 'Oscar Wilde Twice Defended against Andre Gide's Wicked Lies'. Sherard: 'Heavens! The task of shooing hyenas away from the graves of the illustrious dead!'

He proceeded to write four books on Wilde, about which *Bosie Douglas* commented: "I think his devotion to Oscar is really touching. Of course, as I have frequently told him, he knows nothing at all of at least half of Oscar's life and character".

By 1900, the impoverished Sherard and his wife Marthe had moved into a small house in the deeply unfashionable London suburb of Catford. In his last days, *Ernest Dowson* came to stay with them. At the time, Sherard's only employment was writing a leaflet about new developments in the making of white lead. Marthe was very amused at the sight of the arch-decadent poet solemnly discussing white lead production with her husband. Dowson died in Catford soon afterwards.

After the Sherards divorced in 1906, Robert went through two more unsuccessful marriages. Being 'alcoholic, violent, and syphilitic' did not aid his chances of domestic harmony. After he published several biographies of French writers he had known, his services were recognised in 1929 when the French government made him a Chevalier of the Legion of Honour. In 1943, he died in London aged 83.

His wife Marthe also declined into poverty. Three years before her death in 1942, she was reported to be in a Poor Law Hospital in Poplar, London. A nurse said that, in her ravings, she had cried: "I have known great poets. Ernest Dowson died in my arms".

> *Wilde's renewed correspondence with Bosie Douglas led to a meeting in Rouen on August 28th 1897. Bosie: 'Poor Oscar cried when I met him at the station. We walked about all day arm in arm, or hand in hand, and were perfectly happy'.*
>
> *After staying overnight, Oscar returned to Berneval – but not for long. Oscar: 'I simply cannot stand Berneval. I nearly committed suicide there last Thursday. I was so bored'.*
>
> *On September 15, he left the village and travelled to Paris where Vincent O'Sullivan gave him the money to continue his journey to Aix-les-Bains. In Aix he met Bosie and the pair left on the overnight train for Naples in Italy.*
>
> *Arriving there on September 20th, they stayed first in the Hotel Royal, before moving on to the rented Villa Giudice in Posillipo, north of Naples.*
>
> *Oscar realised the consternation that he had caused by this decision to return to Bosie but justified it: 'I feel that it is only with you that I can do anything at all', (a reversal of his former claim that, while in Bosie's company, he had never been able to write a word). He informed the dismayed Robbie Ross: 'My going back to Bosie was psychologically inevitable'.*

BOSIE AND THE DOUGLAS FAMILY

(Fourth Part – from page 416)

The decision was even more surprising to his friends in view of Oscar's furious denunciations of Bosie while in prison. He had been appalled by Bosie's ham-fisted efforts to defend him by claiming that homosexuality was rife in the ex-public school classes and that there was little to get upset about in any case. This dangerously subjective claim could well have sunk Oscar's chances of seeing his children again.

By the end of his sentence, Oscar was raging: 'I curse myself night and day for my folly in allowing him to dominate my life. If there was an echo in these walls it would cry 'Fool' forever.' However, in the cooler light of freedom Oscar, never one to nurse a grudge, was writing letters to Bosie addressing him as 'My dearest boy'.

Having disregarded Wilde's maxim in 'Dorian Gray' – 'In London, one should never make one's debut with a scandal. One should reserve that to give an interest to one's old age' – Bosie had been advised to stay out of England for two years, (in fact he absented himself for three years).

The Marquess of Queensberry, in an unlikely paternal gesture, offered to restore his allowance if he renounced Wilde. He suggested that Bosie would be better off in the South Sea Islands where he would find 'plenty of beautiful girls'.

Bosie's response was to hire a small yacht in Le Havre, France, and invite several boys on board. The resulting rumours of nude parties attracted the attention of the local press and he was attacked for corrupting the youth of the district.

In 1896, Bosie moved on to rent a villa on the Isle of Capri, Italy, where he reported a 'slight domestic tragedy' involving his servants. 'The boy has complained that the advances of the cook have been insupportable, the cook on the other hand declares that life is insupportable to him without love, both are now weeping. What am I to do? I sympathise with the cook, but I am in a responsible position'.

Oscar and Bosie's 1897 sojourn in Posillipo lasted for two months. It was a period of re-assessment for them both. Their romantic and sexual life had ended but they shared the deep bond of having survived a storm together. There was also the bitter-sweet realisation that this short interlude could not last; they had both changed too much over the intervening years.

On a more practical level, any long-term relationship became impossible when their only means of support, the allowances from Oscar's wife Constance and from Bosie's mother Sibyl Douglas, were stopped.

In November 1897, when their money finally ran out, Bosie decided to leave. He explained his actions to his mother: 'If I hadn't rejoined him and lived with him for two months, I should never have got over longing for him'. He mentioned that Oscar had accepted this decision with equanimity.

(The possibly apocryphal story spread that Oscar had attempted to expand his talents while at Posillipo. After taunts from Bosie that he had none of the usual social skills except talking, Oscar admitted that he could not sing, play an instrument, or dance. In an attempt to rectify the latter, he downed some absinthe and began to practice 'the Oscar Wilde Gallop', while Bosie picked out the tune on an ancient piano.)

Although they never again lived together, they met occasionally in Paris, Bosie making a point of calling on Oscar to sympathise over the death of Constance. In November 1898, (having received private notification from *Herbert Asquith* that no prosecution would be brought against him), Bosie returned to London.

Meanwhile, things had not gone well with Bosie's father, the **MARQUESS OF QUEENSBERRY**. Still obsessed by the feud with Wilde, he despatched a private detective to spy on Oscar's movements once he had left prison. One day, noticing the detective lurking on the beach at Berneval, Oscar said that he felt sorry for the man. 'It must be tedious work. I have sometimes thought of talking to him and trying to cheer him up, for he has a sad countenance; but then, you see, the romance of secrecy would be gone, and I am sure he has nothing else to live for.'

Although Queensberry had triumphed in court in 1895, his success had fallen flat. Enough rumours of his vindictive personality and violent domestic life had circulated to discredit him in society. To his amazement, he found himself cold-shouldered; even his oldest friend, Lord Robert Bruce, whom he had known since childhood, refused to speak to him.

Ignored by his peers, the disgruntled Queensberry spent his time living in hotels and drinking with racecourse touts. He also became subject to delusions, claiming that each night gangs of 'Oscar Wilders' would stand beneath his windows and wake him by shouting abuse.

In 1897, he sold all his estates, including the family home at Kinmount in Scotland; by 1900, he had spent over £400,000. The only one of his children with whom he remained on speaking terms was his daughter Edith.

[EDITH DOUGLAS, later FOX-PITT, (1874 – 1963), had sided with her siblings during the family rows but, having neither been involved in a homosexual scandal nor been married to an overt Christian, the breach with her father was repaired more easily. In 1899, she married a respectable scientific inventor, St George Fox-Pitt, 18 years her senior. She later became a Buddhist.]

In late 1899, after Queensberry had suffered a stroke, his two elder sons visited him on his deathbed at Bailey's Hotel in Kensington. Queensberry tearfully embraced Bosie, but ruined the reconciliation by then sending him another abusive letter relating to 'the beast Wilde'. When Percy arrived, his father sat up and spat at him.

Queensberry died of a brain tumour on January 31st 1900, aged 53. Bosie and Percy attended the funeral at the family burial ground at Kinmount, (the only surviving Scottish patch of land left to the Douglases), then travelled on to Paris. Wilde wrote: 'Bosie is over here with his brother. They are in deep mourning and the highest spirits. The English are like that.'

Bosie's mother, **SIBYL DOUGLAS**, had been deeply affected by the traumatic events surrounding the Wilde scandal. An observer, Desmond McCarthy, wrote that: 'She looked as though she had been struck and was still quivering from the blow'. This did not prevent her husband from continuing his usual habits of sending obscene letters, delaying alimony, and beating on her front door.

Wilde had been angered by Sibyl's refusal to honour what he considered to be the promise to back him financially during the trials. Oscar: 'The Queensberry family can hardly allow people whom they ruined so completely to go to the workhouse'. After his release, he remained upset, rejecting the suggestion that Sibyl had paid him to abandon Bosie in Naples: 'I have had no communication with that mischievous foolish woman'.

(In later life, Bosie lived with his mother firstly in Lewes, Sussex, then in Hove. She died aged 91 in 1935, and was buried at the Franciscan Monastery at Crawley, Sussex. The attendant monk told Bosie: "We have just buried a little saint".)

Wilde's annoyance over the lack of Queensberry family financial support extended to Bosie's brother, **PERCY DOUGLAS**. In 1897, Ernest Leverson contacted Oscar in prison to explain that Percy was not in a position to help: 'He is more to be pitied than blamed. He is completely without means for the present. Things have gone against him financially'.

It was a description that could act as a motif for Percy's life. Despite inheriting the bulk of Queensberry's remaining cash, within 18 months Percy was broke again. After paying off moneylenders and given his own boundless generosity, (he regularly handed out bank notes to beggars), Percy proved incapable of stemming the family collapse. Between them Queensberry and Percy ran through £700,000 – roughly £40 million in modern money.

In 1896 his wife Minnie gave birth to a son called Francis, thus incidentally depriving Bosie of the chance to inherit the title of marquess. *Ada Leverson* made the sardonic quip: "For once I think Bosie would have preferred a girl".

In 1911, Percy tried his luck in the USA, and acquired a job on the Chicago Tribune as a boxing correspondent. Although he knew nothing about the sport, he was given the post on the strength of being the son of the inventor of 'the Queensberry Rules'.

Minnie's death soon after their return to England in 1917 ended a particularly happy marriage. Percy recovered and married Mary Morgan, the widow of a Welsh fish trader.

In 1920, the ever-optimistic Percy went off to search for diamonds in South Africa. After what seemed like a promising survey in the Transvaal, he became the managing director of the Kalahari Diamond Company, but within ten days he was found dead. In a welter of speculation, a CID investigation was launched. The suspicion was that Percy had been deliberately poisoned.

Certainly the most popular of the Douglas clan, his Requiem Mass at Westminster Cathedral was attended by hundreds of mourners, including the London beggars whom he had helped so often. Percy, true to form, died penniless.

One figure who had managed to stay aloof from the Douglas family disasters was Queensberry's fourth son and Bosie's younger brother, **SHOLTO DOUGLAS**, (1872-1942). This appears to have been more by accident than design, as Sholto proved to be more than capable of creating disasters of his own.

After his involvement in numerous scrapes in London, in 1894 the family decided to send him off to seek his fortune in California. He ended up running a fruit farm at Bakersfield in the San Joaquin valley. Bakersfield at the time had become something of a centre for dissolute British aristocrats down on their luck, (although their appearance as authentic rough-riding frontiersmen was let down by their exquisitely English accents).

In spite of their assimilation into Californian life, these English cowboys still attempted to maintain certain standards and, when Sholto announced his intention to marry Loretta Mooney, the barmaid and chanteuse at 'Big Frank's Bar', his friends decided to act fast.

They applied for a warrant and on April 25th 1895 Sholto was arrested and locked up in the county jail on a charge of incapacity through insanity. (His brother Bosie, coincidentally, was in danger of imminent arrest in London at the same time, and his father Queensberry and brother Percy found themselves in a magistrates' dock on a charge of public affray a month later.)

Despite this set back, (and the fact that, as Loretta was just underage, her brother had sworn to kill them both), the lovers married. Sholto was considered to have sunk beneath the social radar, even of Bakersfield.

A few months later, in an extraordinary change of fortune, Loretta's long-lost and presumed destitute father died, leaving her a large estate in Canada and half a million dollars.

The couple settled in Ontario and raised two children, including a son named Bruce. By 1911, though, Sholto had managed to lose the money. Leaving his family behind in Canada, he returned to London.

Faced with bankruptcy, he gained a divorce from Loretta and married Georgina Barnard, the daughter of a wealthy Dutch merchant. His wary new wife, however, kept a close eye on her money and would only allow Sholto the occasional pocket money.

Finding this situation most unsatisfactory, Sholto settled for a second divorce and married a wealthy widow called Mrs Mendelssohn Pickles. Sholto ended his days living peacefully in Putney.

As his father had died too suddenly to carry out his intention to cut **BOSIE DOUGLAS** out of his will, in February 1900 Bosie inherited £20,000. From having to count every franc, he was now in a position to lease an apartment on the fashionable Avenue Kleber in Paris.

His largesse did not extend to helping out his old lover and friend. He turned down Ross's suggestion that he discharge Wilde's bankruptcy and refused to allow Oscar a settled income, explaining that: "I can't afford to spend anything except on myself". Oscar commented sadly: "He really is, now that he has money, become mean, and narrow, and greedy" – "Boys, brandy, and betting monopolise his soul".

For his part, Bosie replied that: "After Wilde came out of prison, he was quite unscrupulous about money". He gave Oscar an occasional handout but described him as 'wheedling like an old whore' for such favours.

Instead, Bosie bought a racing stable at Chantilly, which rapidly drained his resources. Oscar: "He has a faculty of spotting the loser which, considering that he knows nothing at all about horses, is perfectly astounding".

In October 1900, Wilde and Bosie had one last dinner together before Bosie left for a holiday. Wilde was depressed by a sense of foreboding: "If another century began and I was still alive, it would really be more than the English could stand". His instinct proved to be correct.

Bosie arrived back in Paris two days after Oscar's death. He was the chief mourner and paid for the funeral expenses.

[See Bosie Douglas – Fifth Part – Page 499]

During the two months that Wilde and Bosie spent together in Posillipo, they occasionally went into Naples to visit the Teatro Mercadante, one of the local theatres. On several nights they were among the audience for Pinero's 'The Second Mrs Tanqueray', starring the great Italian actress, Eleanour Duse.

ELEANOUR DUSE 1858-1924

Wilde, anxious to generate some money, had been hoping to find a producer for his play 'Salome'. Oscar: 'Unfortunately most of the tragic actresses of Italy – with the exception of Duse – are stout ladies, and I don't think I could bear a stout Salome'. He did not even consider Duse to be ideal: 'She is a fascinating artist, though nothing to *Sarah Bernhardt* '. Nonetheless, he gave her the script to read. Duse, although slim enough, did not like the role and turned it down.

Normally excelling in parts portraying listless neurastheniacs, Duse divided critical opinion. Charlie Chaplin enthused that: 'Bernhardt was always studied and more or less artificial. Duse is direct and terrible'. But *Max Beerbohm* found her dreary: 'Age cannot wither her, nor custom stale her endless uniformity'.

Duse was brought up as a child actress in a North Italian family of travelling players. Despite working under the draconian anti-nationalist censorship of the Austrian government – one local playwright who referred to the 'beautiful Italian sky' was forced to change his script to 'the beautiful Lombardo-Venetian sky' – Duse's career prospered. Aged 14, she played the part of 'Juliet' in Verona, 'the right age in the right town', and by 1884 she was the leading actress in Italy.

By 1889, she had created her own theatre company and began what was to be, with one interval, a lifelong world tour. She arrived in New York in 1893 where, in spite of the problem that she performed in Italian and was therefore incomprehensible to the audience, she was still cheered to the echo. (Though a New York critic claimed that after the show 'most of the audience crept away silently to the Vaudeville Club to listen to 'Daddy Wouldn't Buy Me A Bow-wow' as a sort of refresher'.)

She became as famous for her sex appeal as for her acting abilities. When she was leaving California, she bade farewell to her press representative, one Sam Davies, by kissing him on both cheeks, then on his mouth, declaring: "The right cheek is for the Carson Appeal", (one of his papers), "the left is for the San Francisco Examiner", (another), "and the third, dear friend, for yourself". Davies thanked her, then added with a glint in his eye: "I also represent the Associated Press, which syndicates to three hundred and forty seven newspapers west of Missouri".

Much to her rival Sarah Bernhardt's chagrin, Duse became the leading actress of the 1890s, performing before President Cleveland at the White House, and Queen Victoria at Windsor Castle. Her personal life reached a climax when she met the Italian writer, Gabriele D'Annunzio, in 1894.

Although they each enjoyed numerous lovers before and afterwards, their relationship was a high water mark for both partners. Duse encouraged D'Annunzio to write the plays that she then could interpret on stage. They shared a tumultuous nine years together before D'Aunnuzio destroyed Duse's trust by writing a outrageously heartless account of their affair in a novel called 'The Flame of Life'. She was portrayed as a fading older woman, while he represented himself as a dauntless Adonis.

Devastated by these revelations about her private life and by D'Annunzio's desertion, Duse retired from the stage. She consoled herself by having a series of lesbian affairs, most notably with the dancer Isadora Duncan. Isadora said that, when Duse embraced her, she felt: 'like Dante must have felt when encountering the Divine Beatrice'.

When Italy entered the First World War, Duse, always a staunch patriot, visited the front several times to comfort the wounded. Financially, though, the conflict had a profound effect on her. All her savings had been deposited in German banks and therefore lost during the soaring inflation that followed the armistice. Discarding her own maxim – 'I possess the greatest wealth which consists of not wishing for any' – Duse was forced to return to the stage.

By 1924, she was back touring in the USA, though her health had deteriorated to the point where oxygen tanks had to be present at all times in her theatre dressing rooms. One evening in Pittsburg, she arrived in pouring rain at the door of the theatre to find that it was still locked. The soaking she received brought on the pneumonia from which she died soon afterwards.

A few days prior to her death she had been interviewed by a local newspaper. Asked for her opinion of the city, Duse replied in Italian: "Pittsburg is the most hideous town in the world". When this was translated, the newspaper reported her words as being: "Pittsburg is an ideal vacation spot".

Duse's lover, **GABRIELE D'ANNUNZIO** (1863 – 1938) was a poet and novelist who helped found the tradition of realism in Italian fiction. Arthur Symons called him 'a sensualist at once cold and calculating', while Sir Edmund Gosse dismissed him as 'the most odiously immoral and disgraceful of modern authors'.

D'Annunzio also led a life of extraordinary adventure, both sexually and politically. He told the journalist Herbert Vivian that he would rather kill himself than be condemned to lead a humdrum life: "I have lived a violent life and I mean to die a violent death". To this end he always carried a ring containing poison.

D'Annunzio was a short man, whom an acquaintance, Simone Le Bargy, described as having shoulders narrower than his plump hips. His prominent eyes, (with no lashes or eyebrows), reminded Le Bargy of 'soapy water', and Sarah Bernhardt of 'little blobs of shit'.

He indulged in hundreds of affairs. Women found him irresistible, waiting in line outside his bedroom and ready to offer him anything. A puzzled Le Bargy assumed this success with women must be due to his melodious voice: 'Must I yet again denounce the diabolical hold that language has over those of my sex – their animal need to be tamed by the music of words'.

Vernon Lee, one of the few women to whom, (perhaps wisely), he did not make advances, said that: "He has good manners. Still I suspect him rather of being – well – a Neapolitan".

His affair with Duse disintegrated into a series of cataclysmic splits and tearful reunions. *Robert Hichens* reported visiting a hotel where the main hall carpets were being replaced. The manager explained that, during a blazing row, his previous guest Duse had ruined the foyer by hurling a full inkpot at D'Annunzio.

The main cause of dissension was D'Annunzio's inability to remain faithful. On the disastrous opening night of his play 'La Gioconda' in Naples, while Duse was out on stage attempting to rescue the evening, he was busy in the wings pleasuring another actress.

When he had returned to Duse's bed one night, having just had two young music pupils – 'sisters both expert in perverse games' – he explained his three-hour absence by telling her that 'the fleeting infidelity gave love an intoxicating novelty'.

On another occasion in a Zurich hotel, Duse mistakenly thought that D'Annunzio was lusting after her friend Simone Le Bargy, (one of the few women immune to his charms). Losing her temper she grabbed Simone, dragged her into a nearby bedroom then, flinging her onto the bed, screamed at D'Annunzio: "There you are, you want her, so there she is!" Stalking out of the room, she locked the door behind her and hurled the keys out of a window. The embarrassed couple were obliged to escape by climbing down a ladder provided by a puzzled Swiss management.

After being forced to flee Italy in 1910 due to unpaid debts, D'Annunzio returned to enlist in the Italian forces in the First World War. He joined the Air Force and, after losing an eye during a series of daring exploits, was acknowledged as Italy's greatest flying ace.

At the conclusion of the war, he took advantage of a border dispute between Italy and Yugoslavia to lead a force of 12,000 men into the Adriatic port of Fiume and declare himself the uncrowned king of a new principality. He managed to hold on for two years before the Italian authorities sent a ship to shell the port and to remove him from power.

To some degree the forerunner of Benito Mussolini, he became a vociferous supporter of the Italian Fascist movement and applauded Mussolini's takeover of power. (Commenting on this event, *Bernard Shaw* made the wry observation: 'Did you hear about Mussolini's famous March on Rome? He actually went by train!') As a reward for his assistance, Mussolini named D'Annunzio as Prince of Monte Nevoso in 1924.

He lived out his final years on an elegant estate, surrounded by dozens of servants. Even in advanced old age, he would send for girls to be brought to him from the neighbouring villages – 'whose novelty might stimulate his fancy'.

D'Annunzio made some of his literary reputation out of his stirring poetry about, and in honour of, the sea. Duse obtained a small revenge for his past misdemeanours when she let slip that on one voyage that they had shared together, D'Annunzio had been violently seasick.

[In October 1897, Wilde and Bosie had dinner with the Swedish doctor, AXEL MUNTHE (1857-1949), writer of the famous 1929 novel 'The Story of San Michele'. Wilde later stayed for three days at Munthe's home on the Isle of Capri, describing his host as 'a wonderful personality'. (The Irish heiress, Charlotte Payne-Townsend, had an affair with Munthe when she was in Rome in 1894 and was 'broken-hearted' when it ended. She went on to marry Bernard Shaw).]

With the collapse of their finances, Oscar and Bosie decided that they had to part and Bosie left Naples by December 2nd.

Wilde also left the city and went to stay in Taormina, near Messina in Sicily, at the home of Baron Wilhelm von Gloeden, (1856-1931). Von Gloeden was an elderly homosexual who eked a living by selling erotic photographs of naked Sicilian youths to gentlemen of similar tastes.

1898

[The Spanish-American War culminated in the American capture of Cuba and the start of their conquest of the Philippines.

In Africa, British forces under General Kitchener invaded the Sudan to overthrow Mahdist rule. Kitchener triumphed at the Battle of Omdurman.

In France, the Dreyfus Affair came to a climax with the publication of Emile Zola's denunciation of Dreyfus's imprisonment in a pamphlet entitled 'J'Accuse'.]

Wilde arrived back in Posillipo in January 1898, to find that his house had been burgled. He moved into further rented accommodation at 31, Santa Lucia, in Naples itself.

For the first time, he began to feel the bite of real poverty, writing: 'The Paris Journal has a sympathetic paragraph to say I am starving in Naples, but French people subscribe nothing but sonnets when one is alive, and statues when one is not' – 'It is proposed to leave me to die of starvation or to blow my brains out in a Naples urinal'.

Wilde: 'There is only one class in the community that thinks more about money than the rich, and that is the poor. The poor can think of nothing else. That is the misery of being poor' – 'A hole in the trousers may make one as melancholy as Hamlet and out of bad boots a Timon may be made'.

On February 13, he returned to Paris and stayed at the Hotel de Nice on the rue des Beaux-Arts. On the same day, 'The Ballad of Reading Gaol' was published in England, bringing a welcome influx of cash.

Several observers commented on the deterioration of his appearance. Now going slightly bald, Oscar had lost his decayed front teeth and was unable to afford a dental plate to replace them. Frank Harris: 'Oscar no longer took pleasure in the vanities'.

Oscar: 'The tragedy of old age is not that one is old, but that one is young.'

Wilde arrived back to a Paris agog with the political upheavals associated with the Dreyfus Affair and, almost accidentally, became entangled in the periphery of the scandal.

THE DREYFUS CASE

In 1894, a French spy masquerading as a cleaning lady found a crumpled note, (a 'bordereau'), in a waste-paper basket at the German Embassy in Paris. On examination, the note appeared to be information coming from somebody spying for the Germans. It was decided that the handwriting was that of a Jewish officer in the French Army, Captain Alfred Dreyfus. Dreyfus was convicted by court-martial and was sentenced to the penal settlement on Devil's Island in the French West Indies.

Doubts arose as to Dreyfus's guilt and, after a long period of investigation and further court hearings, the true blame was attached to another officer, a Major Esterhazy. The evidence against Dreyfus had been faked by an army official named Colonel Joseph Henry, who subsequently confessed and committed suicide. Dreyfus was released and reinstated in the army in 1906, while Esterhazy fled to England.

While a minor matter in itself, the Affair took on huge implications in French society as it pitted the military, ecclesiastical rightwing against the republican left, and unleashed a wave of anti-Semitism. In an atmosphere not far from civil war, both sides of public opinion became bitterly entrenched.

[Although lionised by the left as a martyr and undoubtedly innocent, Dreyfus turned out to be a rather unpleasant man. The feeling among most of his backers when they actually met him was regret that they couldn't have chosen a more amenable martyr. After his release, Dreyfus himself became irritated by the attentions of his supporters, grumbling: "I've never had a moment's peace since I left Devil's Island". On one occasion he snapped: "Shut up, the lot of you, or I'll confess!"]

During his now habitual sojourns in the Paris cafes, Wilde met the real culprit in the Dreyfus Case, Major Marie-Charles-Ferdinand Walsin-Esterhazy (1847-1923). One evening in August 1898, he was 'dragged out' to have dinner with Esterhazy and his mistress, a prostitute named Marie Pays, also known as 'Four-Fingered Margaret', (whom Oscar found to be 'very clever and handsome').

Oscar enjoyed Esterhazy's company and they met on several occasions: 'The Commandant was astonishing. Of course he talked nothing but Dreyfus'. To Oscar's amusement, Esterhazy freely admitted his guilt. Wilde: 'He is much more interesting than Dreyfus who is innocent... To be a criminal requires imagination and courage'.

The passions aroused by the Dreyfus Affair also led to the breakdown of a long friendship between Wilde and Carlos Blacker.

CARLOS BLACKER (1859-1928)

Oscar had often socialised with him during the 1880s, describing him as 'the best dressed man in London' and dedicating 'The Happy Prince' – 'To Carlos Blacker'. His wife Caroline became a close friend of Constance Wilde and the Blackers provided refuge for the Wilde family when they fled to Germany in 1895. According to the *Rani of Sarawak*, during 1897/8 Carlos Blacker had been delivering messages between Oscar and Constance 'like a bookie's runner'.

Blacker was an Englishman of independent means who possessed an amazing talent for learning languages; (in his old age he learnt Hebrew, so he might talk to God when he died). He spent most of his life in Europe, having had a chequered career in England. In 1890, Blacker had fallen out with the Duke of Newcastle, who accused him of cheating at cards to the tune of £10,000. According to Wilde, Blacker had also ditched a mistress, leaving her penniless after pawning her jewellery, (Oscar helped her out with £50).

Given Blacker's own dubious past, Wilde became annoyed when Blacker took a disapproving moral stance over Oscar's renewed friendship with Bosie Douglas. As a passionate supporter of Dreyfus, Blacker was angered at Oscar's insouciant attitude to the Affair.

When certain tactical plans of the Dreyfusards were exposed in an American newspaper, Blacker assumed, quite wrongly, that Wilde had been the informant. The Dreyfusards, also incorrectly, assumed that Blacker himself was the spy. As a result, they smeared Blacker by publicising his past misdeeds. Wilde: 'His whole dossier is paraded and he has tumbled into the mud in Paris as completely as he did in London'.

In yet another misunderstanding, Blacker accused Wilde of providing the dossier. Oscar: 'He has behaved like a hypocritical ass.....I need hardly say I never read the paper, or saw the attack...I was so angry, I wrote him a very strong letter'.

Commenting on the incident, (and possibly reflecting the poisonous enmities swirling through Paris), Wilde wrote: 'So Tartuffe goes out of my life. Of course the fact of his being a Jew on his father's side explains everything. I hope on the day of St Hugh of Lincoln there will be a general massacre.'

This unguarded (and probably light-hearted) observation ran counter to Wilde's usual sympathies. On his deathbed he remarked to the Jewish *Reggie Turner*: "Jews have no beautiful philosophy of life, but they are sympathique". An acquaintance, Percival Almy, said of him: "He likes Jews. He has many friends among the Hebrews". This was during a period when anti-Jewish sentiments were expressed freely not only in France, but also in America, Britain, and the rest of Europe.

Yet, with the exception of an unflattering portrait of a Jewish theatre manager in 'Dorian Gray', there is no trace of anti-Semitism in the whole of Wilde's works. Oscar displayed his more characteristic side when he said: "Hostility to Jews is vulgar and ungrateful: they are the only people who lend money".

Wilde's blithe neutrality over the Dreyfus Affair was not calculated to inspire the approval of the man who, with the exception of the actual protagonists, became the most famous participant in the imbroglio.

EMILE ZOLA 1840-1902

Previously, Wilde had met the novelist Emile Zola at a dinner in Paris in 1891, when the French author had proposed a toast to the Arts with the words: "Unfortunately, Mr Wilde will be obliged to respond in his barbaric language". Oscar replied, (in French), "I am Irish by birth, English by race, and as M. Zola has said, condemned to speak the language of Shakespeare". They met again when Zola visited London in 1893. After a short chat at the Alhambra Theatre, Zola said of Oscar that he was 'charming and remarkable'.

This attitude changed abruptly when Oscar was jailed. Zola's disgust at his crimes was so pronounced that *Robert Sherard* said that: "one might have fancied him to be the editor of a religious magazine". (Zola had a lifelong hatred of homosexuals that stemmed from being sexually molested by a family servant called Mustapha when he was seven years old.)

A workaholic whose motto was 'No day without a sentence', Zola was the leading figure in French realist fiction. He propagated the naturalistic theory that man's existence was dominated by heredity and environment. After the success of his first book 'Therese Raquin', he constructed a series of twenty novels, based around a fictional family called 'Rougon-Macquart', to illustrate various aspects of French life.

Between 1869 and 1893, he produced such masterpieces as 'Nana', 'Pot-Boule', 'Germinal', 'La Terre', 'La Bete Humaine', and 'La Débâcle'. Often attacked for obscenity, (his English publisher served a prison sentence for publishing Zola's work), Zola replied: "If they knew how much worse life is, they would stop talking such nonsense".

His critics attacked him mostly for his preference for reality over artistry. They ranged from *Victor Hugo*, who claimed to have mistaken Zola 'for an Italian novelist who had been badly let down by his Swiss translator', to *George Moore*, who wrote that he thought of Zola 'as a striking instance of the insanity of common-sense'.

Unsurprisingly Wilde was thoroughly out of sympathy with the relentless realism of Zola's novels: 'M. Zola's characters have their dreary vices, and their drearier virtues. The record of their lives is absolutely without interest' – 'M. Zola is determined to show that, if he has not got genius, he can at least be dull'.

[Reviewing an unrelated work called 'The Chronicle of Mites', Oscar allowed himself an excruciating pun: 'The style is at times so monstrous and so realistic that the author should be called the Gorgon-Zola of literature'.]

In his early life, Zola had experienced extremes of poverty. His bourgeois childhood had been marred by the premature death of his father and the subsequent severe reduction of the family income. Prior to his breakthrough into literature, his early days in Paris as a young man were desperately poor. He found shelter in den-like lodgings frequented by the most derelict of prostitutes and the most inept of pickpockets. He reputedly survived by trapping and eating sparrows.

After his success as a novelist, he became an influential figure among the French literati. When a dramatised adaptation of his work was howled off the stage, (together with *Goncourt*, Daudet, Turgenev, and Flaubert, whose plays had all suffered the same fate), he formed a club known as 'the Dinner of Booed Authors'.

In 1870, he married Alexandrine Meley and for eighteen years remained a faithful husband in a relationship that provided him with stability and affection but very little passion. In 1888, now aged 48 and distinctly fat, Zola became overwhelmed with sexual urges. He told a friend that he was obsessed with the desire to sleep with a young girl: "It scares me. I see myself hauled trembling before a jury".

He found the solution when he met a 21-year-old chambermaid named Jeanne Rozerot, who consented to become his mistress. Zola: 'Youth caught up with me late in life'. To keep up with Jeanne's demands he went on a health cure that reduced his weight considerably, ('Perfection is so dull that I often regret having gotten over tobacco'). He installed her in a Paris apartment and she later bore him two children.

For years he managed to keep his two households separate, until a 'well-wisher' sent an anonymous note informing Alexandrine of her rival. The next few months proved tempestuous for Zola, following his wife's threats to douse him in acid as he slept, and to murder Jeanne. Alexandrine's rages were so loud that Zola was forced to attach padding to the bedroom walls. Eventually, the storm abated and Alexandrine became reconciled to the situation.

As the Dreyfus Affair reached its climax, Zola, who hated anti-Semitism, became a fervent believer in Dreyfus's innocence. Egged on by *Sarah Bernhardt*, he wrote a pamphlet entitled 'J'Accuse' in which he hammered the rightists. He was arrested and, after being found guilty of libelling the War Office, sentenced to one year in prison. During the appeal process, Zola fled to England where he eventually settled in Upper Norwood, London.

He spent much of his exile grumbling about English cooking, ('Boiled potatoes are the only thing they do well'), and puzzling at the strange turn his life had taken: 'What an extraordinary adventure for a methodical, sedentary sort like myself, in the last lap of an existence devoted to writing'.

In 1899, after the sentence had been rescinded, Zola returned to France. He was still the target of rightist rage and received dozens of death threats. One night in 1902, he and Alexandrine retired to bed in their apartment on the rue de Bruxelles. While they slept, the room filled with carbon monoxide. As a result Zola died of asphyxiation; Alexandrine, although dangerously ill, survived.

Despite a verdict of accidental death, there was a strong suspicion of foul play, increased by an examination of the bedroom that showed that the chimney flue was free of obstruction. (Fifty years later, an anti-Dreyfusard stove fitter claimed that he had blocked the chimney deliberately while repairing an adjacent roof, and unblocked it the next day before the investigation began. There is, however, no proof to confirm this story.)

Even Zola's funeral was eventful. Although the Senate voted for his body to be buried in the Pantheon next to the memorial to Victor Hugo, the procession was attacked by rightist mobs and one of the chief mourners, the unlucky Captain Dreyfus, was wounded by a would-be assassin.

> *During April 1898, Wilde, short of money, spent his time hanging around Parisian cafes, on two occasions meeting an embarrassed Andre Gide. He changed his lodgings to the Hotel d'Alsace on the rue des Beaux Arts.*
>
> *Oscar's wife Constance died in Italy on April 7th. The news arrived in Paris a week later.*
>
> *Also in April, Wilde dined at the home of the Belgian Symbolist poet and playwright Maurice Maeterlinck and his long-term mistress, the actress Georgette Leblanc.*

MAURICE MAETERLINCK 1862-1949

The accounts of the meeting between Wilde and Maeterlinck varied. Georgette Leblanc said that, having received an effusive letter of congratulation over one of her performances, she invited Oscar to dinner. Leblanc: 'Maeterlinck finally agreed although he did not like Wilde, whom he considered an altogether superficial human being'. Oscar, on the other hand, wrote: 'Maeterlinck has conveyed to me his desire to meet me'.

It seems to have been an awkward occasion. Leblanc: 'After having shaken hands, they remained standing, speechless and motionless. I was bored all through dinner by watching these two interesting minds applying themselves to not giving each other anything interesting'. However, after Maeterlinck offered him a wine not available in England, Oscar enlivened the conversation by observing: "The English have the miraculous power to change wine into water".

Although claiming that no other 19th century playwright had been an influence on him, Wilde admitted being 'interested' by *Victor Hugo* and Maeterlinck. However when Oscar first read the script of 'Salome' aloud to W. Graham Robertson, Robertson assumed that Oscar had written a burlesque of Maeterlinck and laughed approvingly.

When Oscar realised Robertson's mistake, he was not amused, observing: "How perfectly odious you are sometimes". Robertson did not change his opinion: 'Take Maeterlinck and Flaubert from Wilde's 'Salomé' and what remains?'

Maeterlinck began his career in the Belgian legal system, but soon abandoned it in favour of writing, ('I inevitably send my clients to prison'). He published his first play, 'La Princesse Maleine', in 1889, and his greatest work, 'Pellêas et Mélesande', in 1892. Later this was set to music by Claude Debussy.

(The British publisher, William Heineman, asked Wilde to write an English introduction to 'La Princesse Maleine' in 1891. On the grounds of 'waiting for inspiration', Oscar dawdled until Heineman asked *Hall Caine* to complete the task instead).

Georgette Leblanc had been born into a wealthy family in Rouen but at the age of fifteen she ran away to join the theatre. With the aid of *Sarah Bernhardt*, her stage career flourished, while her Paris apartment became a bohemian social centre.

Basing her concept of the character as 'a gypsy who had taken hashish', Georgette gave her finest performance as 'Carmen'. Wilde was deeply impressed, describing her as: 'full of quick sympathies – the mind mobile, the whole temperament sensitive to the colours of life as they pass'.

Before Maeterlinck met Georgette in 1895 he was known to live a life of plain regularity, 'a bear who never left his native town of Ghent'. Georgette used her influence to extract him from Ghent and install him in Paris. Neither partner expressed any desire to marry but they remained in love, despite Maeterlinck's alarming personal habits.

Georgette's main complaint was Maeterlinck's capacity for epic sulks. Losing her patience after one such episode had lasted three days, she burst into his study to find him, not in the throes of tortured poetic composition, but inspecting row after row of folded paper hens on his desk.

He insisted on rigid punctuality and would brook no interruption of his meals. During one lunch, a guest arrived five minutes late and began to burble out some important news. Without speaking, Maeterlinck rose to his feet, picked the man up, carried him to a window and dumped on the pavement outside. When Georgette's cat irritated him one day, Maeterlinck shot it dead between the eyes.

Georgette always ignored Maeterlinck's practise of keeping several other mistresses to tow – "It was a pastime like any other" – but in 1911, he introduced an 18-year-old actress into their household to share a ménage a trois. Georgette accepted the situation and acquired a Russian lover of her own, ('It was exhausting satisfying two men at once'). In 1919, Maeterlinck married the new girl, thus ending his long association with Georgette.

He became wealthy and famous from his work, being awarded the Nobel Prize for Literature in 1911. Georgette, after a few years in the USA, returned to spend her remaining life, poverty-stricken in Paris.

In 1898, Maeterlinck had gone through a period of rejecting Art in favour of machinery. Wilde commented that: "He rests his hope of humanity on the Bicycle".

Georgette reported one 'terrifying' incident that occurred when Maeterlinck graduated from a bicycle to a motorcycle. On a test run, he assured Georgette that he would be away no longer than five minutes. Georgette: 'Half an hour later, he suddenly burst through the front gate, passing before me at high speed and without a word. Alarmed, driven to safety against a tree, I had not the strength to move".

One minute later, Maeterlinck appeared for a second time. 'He made elaborate gestures, trying to make me comprehend something incomprehensible. I thought he had gone mad because he drove back again and again with more incoherent signs'.

Over two hours later, a dusty, breathless, Maeterlinck reappeared at the gate, dragging the now lifeless machine. He shouted to the deeply worried Georgette: "I couldn't make the brake work! So I had to go round and round until I'd used up all the petrol!"

> *Another of Wilde's café companions was the playwright Alfred Jarry. In May 1898, Oscar reported that: 'Jarry has sent me a complete collection of his works. He is a most extraordinary young man, very corrupt'.*

ALFRED JARRY 1873-1907

Seen as the forerunner of the surrealist Theatre of the Absurd, Jarry's anarchic eccentricity was apparent even in his formative years. At his school in Rennes, Brittany, one of his favourite tricks was to disguise himself as a monk, then stroll through the streets of the town swearing obscenities at passers-by.

In 1891 he arrived in Paris and, being recognised as highly intelligent, was allowed into such salons as Stephane Mallarme's 'Tuesdays'. He was not so welcome at the café where one day he began to lecture the patrons about the joys of masturbation 'from his own experience'.

As a youth Jarry's sexual experiences had been confined to prostitutes but, aged 20, he became the lover of *J-K Huysman's* ex-mistress, the notoriously lecherous 40-year-old Madame Berthe de Courriere, whose usual speciality was the seduction of priests. (One of Berthe's less attractive habits was her refusal to wash, preferring to smear Vaseline over her body instead).

In 1894, Jarry was horrified when he was called up for service in the French Army. The military training was meant to involve the breaking of the individual, not a task easily accomplished in Jarry's case. He set out to stir anarchy in the ranks by lampooning target practice and parade ground drill with ludicrously inaccurate shooting and robotic clowning.

458

Suspected of being insane by the military authorities, they tried to punish him by forcing him to sweep the parade ground. Jarry set to work with his broom and managed to draw several highly suggestive patterns in the dust before being stopped by his outraged sergeant. He was reduced to latrine duties, potentially an even more dangerous outlet for Jarry's inventiveness.

Finally he injected himself with an acid that turned his skin yellow, thus allowing the army doctors to grant him a honourable discharge. It seems his departure was a welcome relief on both sides.

Returning to Paris, Jarry met the French theatre producer Lugne-Poe who asked him if he would like to do some odd jobs around the Theatre de L'Oeuvre. Jarry helped to paint scenery with *Henri Toulouse-Lautrec* and the Norwegian artist Edvard Munch.

[AURELIEN LUGNE-POE, (1869- 1940) – originally just 'Lugne', he had added 'Poe' to his surname in honour of Edgar Allan – was the most courageous of the avant-garde. In 1896, he had produced the first performance of Wilde's 'Salome' at his Theatre de l'Oeuvre. Wilde wrote to Ross from prison: 'Please let Lugne-Poe know that I am sensible of the honour he has done me. He is a poet himself.' In May 1897, Oscar met him in Dieppe, remarking that: 'I had no idea he was so young, and so handsome.']

In December 1896, Lugne-Poe really chanced his arm by producing Jarry's first play, the grotesque satire 'Ubu Roi'. The opening word of the play was 'Shit!' ('merde'), after which the audience exploded in a righteous uproar that lasted over fifteen minutes. Finally the lead actor managed to restore enough order to be able to deliver the second line. Unfortunately this also was 'Shit'. The show closed after the second night and was not performed again till 1908.

Jarry's appearance at this time varied. Sometimes he preferred a top hat and a black cape on top of a cyclist's leotard, at other times he favoured women's clothing, declaring it to be less restrictive. The only items of dress that he insisted on at all times were a carbine over his shoulder and two revolvers in his belt.

When he took up target practice in his garden, his neighbour begged him to stop in case he accidentally shot her children. Glancing over the neighbour's svelte form, he replied that if such an event occurred he would provide her with some more.

In a restaurant one day, Jarry was talking to a lady when he realised that she was not listening but instead was admiring herself in a wall mirror. To regain her attention, he pulled a pistol from his belt and shot the mirror. Smiling soothingly, he returned the weapon to its holster and continued: "Now that the mirror is gone, perhaps we can concentrate on talking to each other?"

His last years were spent in grinding poverty and increasing alcoholism, despite which he always retained the respect of the younger generation. The Spanish artist Pablo Picasso was a particular admirer and painted Jarry's portrait.

In 1904, Jarry built a shed on stilts beside the River Seine where he lived by fishing – mostly for fish, but occasionally using his rod to hook hens out of his neighbours' chicken coops. His shed was rat-infested and regularly flooded. He later became paralysed in both legs and died of malnutrition.

Jarry was only five feet tall but aspired to greater things. One female visitor to his rooms noticed a sculpture of a huge phallus on the mantelpiece. When she asked if it was a plaster cast, Jarry roared back: "No, madam, it is a reduction!"

Another of Wilde's acquaintances was the French painter Henri de Toulouse-Lautrec. In a sketch by Ricardo Opisso, the two men were depicted as sitting together with the singer Yvette Guilbert at a Paris café table in May 1898.

HENRI DE TOULOUSE-LAUTREC 1864-1901

It was reported that, when Lautrec was in London in May 1895, he had visited Wilde at the Leversons but had been refused permission to paint a portrait of Oscar, (then under pressure over the outcome of the trials). Later, when Lugne-Poe produced 'Salome' in Paris in 1896, Lautrec designed a programme cover, probably from memory or photographs, depicting an aged Oscar framed by a London fog.

When Lautrec was aged ten, the bones in his legs atrophied with the result that as an adult he only reached the height of 4ft 11ins. His facial ugliness combined with this deformity led Lautrec to describe himself as 'a thoroughbred hitched up to a rubbish cart'.

However, he possessed two qualities that outweighed his disadvantages. He had a witty charisma that delighted his friends, and he had a huge penis that delighted his bedfellows. He said that he looked like 'a coffeepot with a big spout', while the Parisian prostitutes whom he frequented gave him the candid nickname of 'Prick on Wheels'.

Lautrec was born into the highest ranks of the French aristocracy, his ancestors being the formerly very influential Counts of Toulouse. The family's power had dwindled – as Lautrec's father Alphonse once ruefully reminded an appalled archbishop at a dinner table: "Alas, the days are over when the Counts of Toulouse could bugger a monk and hang him afterwards if it pleased them".

Lautrec's parents' marriage was unhappy, a state of affairs that had been obvious from its outset. During the honeymoon in Nice, Alphonse had disappeared, leaving his bride Adele distraught with anxiety and convinced that her new husband was dead. Having returned home alone, she received a telegram from Alphonse bearing the laconic message – 'Send ferrets'.

Later on, Alphonse left the family home to live in a tower, from which he would lower a basket to be filled with his everyday needs.

In 1881, Lautrec left his home in Albi to live in Paris and, breaking away from the well meant but suffocating attentions of his mother Adele, moved into the raucous underworld of Montmartre. Bolstered by a generous allowance from his family, he plunged into the life of the art student, and soon became a familiar sight in the bars and the ateliers of the suburb. He became an enthusiastic drinker and a willing participant in the orgies that often followed when students and models relaxed together after painting sessions.

It was a way of life of which he never tired. In 1894, a friend called Jules Renard related how, with a companion, he had visited Lautrec's studio one afternoon. Lautrec answered the door dressed only in his shirt; behind the painter, Renard spotted two naked women lying on a sofa, 'one showing her stomach, the other her behind'. While his companion went forward to introduce himself and shake their hands, Renard found himself 'too embarrassed to look at the models and wondered where to put my hat and dripping umbrella'.

Working in a studio on the Rue Lepic, (the same street on which his fellow artist Van Gogh had lived), Lautrec discovered much of his subject matter in his observations of the Parisian theatre world. Although he enjoyed the classical work of the Comedie Francaise, his favourite destinations were dancehalls such as the Folies Bergere.

In May 1898, Wilde wrote: 'A kind friend took me to the Folies-Bergere last night. The acrobats were more wonderful than ever, but the audience was dreadfully mulierastic', ('mulierist' being a word invented by *Robert Ross* to describe heterosexuality).

One reason for the excessive 'mulierism' was the recent dance craze known as the cancan. Originally it had been a high-kicking chorus line in which the female participants threw up their skirts to reveal their underwear. This evolved into the quadrille erotique, which was the same dance but without the underwear. This proved so scandalous that a police supervisor, (nicknamed 'Daddy Decency'), patrolled the dancehalls inspecting the girls and expelling any not wearing panties.

But it was at the Moulin Rouge that Lautrec found his main inspiration. The most famous event at the dancehall had occurred in June 1893 at the Bal des Quatz'Arts, when the ball degenerated into a debauch. Most of the young women present were stripped naked, and some of them subjected to public sex. (The publisher Grant Richards reported on a similar occasion: 'I saw a poor girl set about by some score of tormentors who tore all her clothes from her limbs'.)

The revellers then burst into the surrounding streets, threatening to destroy any café that refused to serve them free alcohol. Although Montmartre generally treated it as a joke, the police were called and made many arrests. Accused of moral corruption and indecent exposure, the ball's organisers were found guilty and fined. The following day, student protestors took to the streets and in the ensuing riot, the police killed an innocent bystander. The students then barricaded the Latin Quarter and battle raged until the National Guard were called out and restored order six days later.

Lautrec revelled in the anarchy of the Moulin Rouge. The writer *Arthur Symons* reported: 'He was the only painter who absolutely adored it', and partly in return for the pleasure he had received he drew advertisements for the establishment. His first poster, which appeared in September 1891, was a triumph, and made him famous overnight.

As more posters appeared, they became prized souvenirs, often being peeled from the walls before the glue had dried. Ignoring the snobbery that attached itself to technically reproduced advertisements, Lautrec made it his speciality: "The poster, that's all there is!"

During the next seven years, he made over thirty paintings of the Moulin Rouge world and became part of it himself. He became very close to the dancer Jane Avril whom he drew dozens of times. Her particular attraction as a performer was to combine prudery with prurience, (Arthur Symons called it: 'a depraved virginity'). She slept with Lautrec just once as 'a favour to a friend'. He was also on excellent terms with the singer Yvette Guilbert.

[YVETTE GUILBERT, (1869-1944) half-spoke, half sang bawdy songs and was the best performer of her style. *Herbert Vivian* said she was 'wonderfully plain and wonderfully agreeable', while *Bernard Shaw* promised to write a play for her, (sadly it was never written). She became annoyed when Lautrec insisted on consistently portraying her as ugly: "Really, Lautrec, you are a genius at deformity". He replied: "Well, of course I am".]

Other friends realised his interest in decay when he insisted on taking them to a dingy tenement to meet a time-ravaged, almost hairless old woman. Lautrec greeted her with great courtesy and presented her with chocolates and flowers. He explained afterwards that the woman was Victorine Meurent, who in the 1860s had been the beautiful teenage model for Manet's 'Olympia'.

Aside from the dancehalls, Lautrec's other great interest was in brothel life. Considered too ugly to contract a marriage with a woman from his own class, he had been introduced to brothels at an early age. He liked the honesty of the sexual transactions as opposed to the pretences of bourgeois convention. He was open about his activities and aware of their dangers: "I'm digging my grave with my cock".

Eventually he decided to rent a room in a brothel and stayed for months fraternising with, and drawing, its inhabitants. As he explained: "They're the only places in Paris where you can still get a good shoeshine".

His other great passion was for alcohol to which he became increasingly addicted. In case he felt in need of a drink between cafes, he carried a hollow cane filled with brandy. To encourage his dinner guests to drink wine, he used to drop goldfish into the water carafes.

Contradicting the prevailing French disgust over the idea of American cocktails, Lautrec became a fan. However, rather than mix a cocktail according to taste or strength, he preferred to mix it to produce an interesting colour. To popularise the drink, he held a party for over 300 people and, wearing an American flag as a vest, acted as barman. After 2000 glassfuls had been served up, his brain-damagingly awful cocktails caused mass intoxication and put several former teetotallers in bed for days.

By 1897, his indulgences got the better of him and he began to suffer from delirium tremens and the first stages of syphilis. In 1899, his mother Adele reappeared in his life and forced him into a private asylum.

He recovered quickly on a diet of water, but realised that he might be trapped there. The asylum doctors, being privately and expensively paid, had a vested interest in his remaining a patient. The artist *Charles Conder* commiserated: 'It is very sad about poor Lautrec – shutting him up when he is no more mad than you and I'.

Lautrec managed to extract himself from the asylum and, for a time, travelled around the French provinces. In June 1899, he visited Le Havre, where he met Oscar Wilde again, and also fell for and painted an English barmaid called Dolly.

Back on the drink again, his condition worsened. In 1900, he attended the World Fair in Paris but was so debilitated by alcohol that he was forced to use a wheelchair. Ordered to avoid drink and women, ("Both Bacchus and Venus are barred"), he did neither, and died in September 1901, aged 36.

ARISTIDE BRUANT, (1851-1925), was not only one of Toulouse-Lautrec's friends but also one of his most renowned models. He was a tall man who, with his distinctive garb of black wide-brimmed hat and cape, and long red scarf slung over his shoulder, became immortalised in Lautrec's posters of the Moulin Rouge.

He was a hugely popular cabaret singer who specialised in abrasively comic songs that expressed the experience of Parisian slum life. Wilde and *Andre Gide* had a meal with him at a café in 1891, after which Bruant presented Oscar with a book bearing the inscription: 'Pour Oscar Wilde le joyeux fantasiste anglais'.

When Bruant first acquired his own concert-café, he had the disconcerting experience of an opening night with only three customers. As he had borrowed 1000 francs to open up, disaster loomed. Without much hope, he proceeded to bawl out one of his songs in his distinctively harsh tones. Sensing a lack of rapport with his tiny audience, he rasped out threateningly: "Who the hell's complaining?"

The next night, Bruant gloomily reopened only to find the trio from the previous night returning accompanied by a gang of friends. Bruant perked up slightly and sang again. He finished to desultory applause, until one audience member shouted out: "What, no bouquets today?" It dawned on Bruant that they had arrived, not for his singing, but for his abuse.

From then on, his café became a roaring success, with fashionable crowds packing in to hear themselves described as 'pigs', to be outrageously overcharged, and to be forced to sing the choruses of Bruant's atrocious dirges.

462

Another less welcome member of café society was the journalist **ERNEST LA JEUNESSE**, (1874-1917). Wilde mentioned in November 1898 that he, the poet Jean Moreas, and La Jeunesse gathered on occasion at the American Bar: 'I see a great deal of La Jeunesse, who is more intolerable than ever.'

At one time *Anatole France's* secretary, La Jeunesse was a grimy goblin with a shrill falsetto voice. He once overheard his publisher claiming that La Jeunesse's voice was the result of impotence. La Jeunesse responded by impregnating the publisher's wife, an act of vengeance that Wilde described as: "The greatest repartee in history".

On one occasion, La Jeunesse spotted Toulouse-Lautrec in a restaurant and, teasingly grabbing him from behind, attempted to lift the painter from his chair. Arthur Symons: 'What blows from the furious short cane were rained on the skinny thighs of La Jeunesse, who cleared out, howling and hopping like a monkey'.

In late 1900, La Jeunesse was present at a café when Wilde recounted some of his greatest stories, in La Jeunesse's words: 'like a last display of fireworks'. Soon afterwards he attended Oscar's funeral.

His judgement on Wilde was that: 'In exile he remained always English. An Irishman by birth, an Italian in his inclinations, Greek in culture, and Parisian in his passion for paradox and humbug, he never could forget London'.

In May 1898, Wilde re-met a young acquaintance, the Russian Sergei Diaghilev, who provided him with a restaurant meal.

SERGEI DIAGHILEV 1872-1929

Wilde's first meeting with Diaghilev had been in Dieppe earlier in 1898, when they had discussed *Aubrey Beardsley's* art with a view to Diaghilev purchasing a painting. Back in Paris, the young Russian had sought out Oscar, dined with him (during which Oscar went out of his way to be 'rather wonderful'), and then, according to Diaghilev, strolled the boulevards arm-in-arm to hoots of derision from local prostitutes.

Raised in a wealthy St Petersburg family, Diaghilev had been fascinated by the artistic world but uncertain of his own place in it. Having been told by the composer Rimsky-Korsakov that he had no talent for music, Diaghilev, (now richer by a 60,000 rouble inheritance), left Russia for a Grand Tour of Europe in 1895. Acquiring a top hat and monocle, he consciously took on the appearance of a Russian plutocrat, a role he never abandoned no matter what straits he might find himself later.

Returning to Russia in 1899, he used the new ideas that he had gleaned from Wilde and Beardsley to start a new magazine, partly funded by the Tsar, entitled 'The World of Art'. It was effectively a Russian version of the Decadents' 'Yellow Book', and espoused the same values of 'Art for Art's Sake', etc. The magazine folded in 1904, as the failure of the war with Japan had caused an embarrassing shortfall in the Tsar's spare cash.

Diaghilev's life changed when he left Russia in 1906 and moved to Paris with the idea of promoting his native country abroad. He finally hit on his true metier as an active patron of the arts. He produced exhibitions of Russian painting, and concerts of Russian music, (including a resounding hit with a revival of Modest Mussorgsky's 'Boris Gudunov' in 1908).

In 1909, he made the decisive move of founding the Ballet Russe, a company that revolutionised the art form and electrified audiences across Western Europe. Influenced by Isadora Duncan, choreographed by Michel Fokine, starring Vaslav Nijinsky and Anna Pavlova, and set to new music by Ravel, Richard Strauss, Debussy, and Prokofiev, the Ballet Russe could hardly fail.

When the composer Igor Stravinsky joined the ranks of collaborators, Diaghilev was able to launch three of the greatest hits of his career – 'The Firebird' (1910), 'Petrushka' (1911), and 'The Rite of Spring' (1913).) The first night of the latter work produced a virtual riot in the Paris theatre as fistfights broke out between traditionalists and the avant-garde. One critic called it 'Le Massacre de Printemps'. Diaghilev purred: "Exactly what I wanted".

However, with the start of the First World War, the European ballet world collapsed and Diaghilev was in trouble. He extricated himself by taking the Ballet Russe to the USA in 1916. It was a successful tour, despite some problems. In Kansas City, the local police chief heard that some Russian called 'Dogleaf' was promoting smutty sex shows. He threatened to close down the theatre at gunpoint if he found 'Dogleaf's' work to be personally offensive. On inspection, he decided that the public morality of Kansas City would not suffer as a result and allowed the show to go ahead.

In 1917, after the abdication of the Tsar and during the short interregnum of the moderate Kerensky government, Diaghilev was offered the job of Russian Minister of Fine Arts. (His collaborator Stravinsky was asked to write a new Russian national anthem based on the 'Song of the Volga Boatmen'). But the rise of the Bolsheviks and the start of the Civil War put paid to any return to his homeland.

In 1918, now a stateless exile and with prospects for the ballet in France looking bleak, Diaghilev managed to restart his company in London. Through his great supporter Lady Lonsdale, (the ex 'Professional Beauty'), he met and befriended many leading British artistic figures, including the Sitwell family.

(Sacheverall Sitwell loved the ballet but, still being a Grenadier Guard at the time, constantly missed the last acts of performances because of the need to catch the last train back to Aldershot. Diaghilev, irritated by these enforced absences, was heard one night demanding to know: "Who is this Aldershot?" under the impression that a mistress was involved.)

Diaghilev was ruthless over his productions and had no compunction about sending out his ballerinas to seduce rich men on behalf of the company. One such girl, Alice Nikitina, was given the job of sweetening Lord Northcliffe of the Daily Mail. Although she always claimed their relationship was platonic, the money arrived in time to rescue the company finances.

Diaghilev staked his future on a London production of 'The Sleeping Beauty'. Although later acknowledged to be a great ballet, the show flopped badly. A desperate Diaghilev considered everything in the effort to increase ticket sales, including trying to induce *Bernard Shaw* to write a comic inter-act piece, and strapping a naked ballerina onto the scenery to represent the figurehead of a ship. It was all to no avail and, following the worst failure of his career, Diaghilev fled almost penniless to France.

After a period in Paris when he lived in a dingy attic and was forced to haggle over the price of soup at slum cafes, Diaghilev moved to Monte Carlo and recouped his losses by presenting 'safe' productions.

(Despite his promotion of avant-garde music, Diaghilev had no sympathy with the emerging jazz world. He thought that Cole Porter was overrated and dismissed George Gershwin's Piano Concerto as 'good jazz and bad Liszt'.)

Having emerged thankfully from debt, Diaghilev discovered and promoted a new stable of ballet stars including the Irish Anton Dolin, (born Patrick Healy-Kay), the Anglo-Irish Ninette de Valois, (born Edris Stannus), and the Londoner Alicia Markova, (born Alice Marks).

After one last brilliant season at Covent Garden in 1929, Diaghilev, now suffering from diabetes, went on holiday to Venice. He died there at the Grand Hotel des Bains, and was buried on the island of San Michele.

Diaghilev discovered he was profoundly homosexual in his teenage years. He habitually fell in love with his male ballet stars and suffered greatly because of it. A pattern emerged whereby the star would have a strong relationship with the possessive Diaghilev, then leave him to marry a female dancer from the company, leaving a hysterical and bereft Diaghilev to search for a new love.

The most famous of such partners was **VASLAV NIJINSKY**, (1890-1950). In 1911, when dancing 'Giselle' in St Petersburg, Nijinsky had outraged the Dowager-Empress by dancing in such revealing tights that the Empress assumed he was nude. After refusing to apologise, he was dismissed from the Imperial Ballet and joined Diaghilev. (Nijinsky possibly had an anti-Romanov axe to grind, as he had been knouted by a Cossack during the 1905 Bloody Sunday march, in which Tsarist forces had killed over 2,000 protestors.)

Diaghilev proved to be a suspicious lover. The decidedly heterosexual sculptor *Auguste Rodin* called on the bisexual Nijinsky with a view to making a marble statue of the dancer. After an extended lunch both men fell asleep. Diaghilev happened to walk in, drew his own conclusions, and banned Nijinsky from seeing Rodin again.

> *In May 1898, Wilde underwent an operation on his throat: 'The operation itself was all right, as I was drenched with cocaine, but afterwards it was very painful'.*
>
> *He spent a miserably penurious June and July in Paris, and wrote to Ross: 'For two days I had not a penny in my pocket, so had to wander about, filled with a wild longing for bock and cigarettes: it was really like journeying through Hell. I was in the 'Circle of the Boulevards', one of the worst in the Inferno'.*
>
> *It was during this period that the opera singer, Nellie Melba, alleged that she was walking on a Paris street, when: 'a tall shabby man lurched around a corner, his collar turned up at his neck. "Madame Melba, you don't know who I am? I'm Oscar Wilde, and I am going to do a terrible thing. I'm going to ask you for money". Thrusting all she had into his hands, Melba watched the broken man stagger away into an alley. (Melba was prone to embellishment and, sometimes, even invention.)*

DAME NELLIE MELBA 1861-1931

Wilde and Melba had met back in 1892 at Lady Lonsdale's house in Paris. Oscar had declared himself to be 'the Lord of Language' and Nellie 'the Queen of Song', and suggested writing a sonnet to that effect. Melba reported that Wilde delivered 'a brilliant fiery-coloured chain of words' – 'If only he had had a Boswell, what a treasure we might have inherited'.

Born Helen Mitchell, she was the daughter of a well-to-do building contractor in Melbourne, Australia. She grew up as a tomboy but one who, from an early age, was aware that she possessed musical genius. In 1882, aged 21, she married a handsome young Irishman called Charles Armstrong and moved to Brisbane.

(Charles Armstrong, also known as 'Kangaroo Charlie', was a magnificent horseman. When the *'Buffalo Bill' Cody* Wild West Show was in Britain, it was their custom to offer $100 prize money to any European who could ride a bucking bronco; they had never had to pay out. Then, at one show, Cody's men guffawed when then saw an immaculately dressed young fop step out to mount the wildest bronco they possessed. Cody: 'He rode the animal hands down'. The man was, of course, Charlie.)

Notwithstanding her husband's equestrian talents, Nellie grew frustrated in the rural backwater of Queensland and decided to leave Charlie to start her singing career. (Later, after Charlie discovered his wife's affairs with the French Duke of Orleans and others, he divorced her in 1900 and left for the USA to raise their only child, George, in Texas).

Nellie arrived in London in 1886 but was not immediately successful. After she had auditioned for *Sir Arthur Sullivan*, the composer said that she was 'all right', but needed more lessons, after which: "in a year's time, there might be the chance of a small part in 'The Mikado'."

Accepting Sullivan's advice, she went to Paris to take tuition from a first-rate teacher, Madame Marchesi, who realised that Nellie's talents were best suited to Verdi and Puccini's work. (When she later attempted to perform Wagner, the effort nearly wrecked her voice). Also, in honour of her hometown, she changed her name to Nellie Melba.

Now fully prepared, Melba triumphed on stage, firstly in Brussels, then in London, then, (with the backing of *Sarah Bernhardt*, who described Melba's voice as 'pure crystal'), in Paris. By 1889 she was the undisputed star of her true artistic home, Covent Garden in London, and began a series of spectacular international tours to Russia and the USA.

The Italian composer Puccini chose Melba to play the part of 'Mimi' in his opera 'La Boheme' in 1896. It became a high point of her career. One observer, Haddon Chambers, reported that when she sang the high 'C' right at the end of Act One:

'It was the strangest and weirdest thing I have experienced in my life. The note came floating over the auditorium of Covent Garden; it left Melba's throat, it left Melba's body, it left everything, and it came over like a star and passed us in our box, and went out into the infinite. I have never heard anything like it in my life, not from any other singer, ever. It just rolled over the hall of Covent Garden. My God, how beautiful it was!'

Melba appreciated having a tenor of the Italian Enrico Caruso's class to play opposite her as 'Rudolfo' in 'La Boheme'. However, she was not so fond of Caruso's earthy sense of humour. While singing the aria 'Your tiny hand is frozen' at one performance, he suddenly pressed a hot sausage into her hand. With a squawk of surprise, she tossed the object away across the stage. Still singing, Caruso whispered insinuatingly during a breath-pause: "Eh, pretty lady, you lika da sausage?"

As she became more famous, Melba's own antics on stage could be embarrassing. *Bernard Shaw* told of one occasion when Melba's superb performance as 'Desdemona' in the deathbed scene in 'Otello' drew a storm of applause from the audience. Melba rose from her 'deathbed' and signalled for a piano to be trundled in from the wings.

Shaw: 'She then accompanied herself for an encore by singing the hit 'Home, Sweet, Home' with the audience joining in. When the ovation following the encore had died down, she collapsed again upon the bed and the unfortunate Othello was allowed to finish the act.'

Dame Ethel Smyth observed the renowned prima donna while on a yacht cruise off the west coast of Scotland. Melba had only agreed to come on the cruise on the understanding that she should not be asked to sing. The other voyagers scrupulously honoured her wishes, until Melba began to look so miserable that, in Dame Ethel's words, 'she resembled a Jewish barmaid'. Finally, unable to stand her self-imposed silence any longer, Melba announced that she would be prepared to sing. Thereafter, she was quite happy.

Although she had become a major international figure, Melba was conscious also of being the first genuine Australian star. (Wilde gently satirised the patronising European attitude towards Australia in 'Lady Windermere's Fan': 'Dear Agatha and I are so much interested in Australia. It must be so pretty with all the dear little kangaroos flying about. Agatha has found it on the map. What a curious shape it is! Just like a large packing case'.)

It took a long while for Australia to develop a separate nationalism but for many Australians Melba's success came to embody this new sense of patriotism. She responded to their enthusiasm by insisting on tours even of the remotest outback, and on visiting all of the Australian state governors. Her regal progress was resented by some, one hostess commenting sourly: "She does allow you to feel so much at home in your own house."

Despite her iconic status, some Antipodean newspapers launched attacks accusing her of meanness and sexual misbehaviour. When a local critic gave her a foul review during her tour of New Zealand, Melba stormed into his editor's office, demanding that the critic be publicly thrashed. The critic sent her a message agreeing to her demand, providing that it take place in a public hall, that she herself should carry out the thrashing, and that he would receive the entire box office takings.

Melba also came under criticism for her increasing weight, exacerbated by her fondness for food and alcohol. (In fact, two new dishes, Melba Toast and Peach Melba, were named in her honour.) The British cartoonist David Low later delivered a withering judgement: 'a bullying woman who ate a good deal and swore a lot'.

Known to be a supreme egotist, she was ruthless when it came to destroying younger rivals. Melba: 'It's when you are the diva that you have to be nervous. When you are climbing up, you just do your best. When you are the diva, you have to be the best always'. One rising star, the Irish tenor John McCormack, referred to her as 'an interfering bitch'.

During a performance of 'La Boheme', Melba became angry when the audience applauded Fraulein Fritzi Scheff, a young soprano playing the secondary role of 'Musetta'. When Fritzi reached the climax of her Act Two appearance, her solo aria became a duet, as Melba joined in from the wings. An incandescent Fritzi stormed off stage, tried to scratch Melba's face, then broke down in hysterics.

With Fritzi now hors de combat, Melba compensated the audience for the disappearance of the last two acts by regaling them with an operatic selection including 'Home, Sweet Home'.

During the First World War, Melba plunged herself into fund-raising and, in recognition of her efforts, she was made a Dame Commander of the British Empire in 1918. During a welcoming speech, the mayor of one Australian city kept referring to her as 'Dame Melba'. Through gritted teeth, she whispered that he should call her 'Dame Nellie', (the correct address). He gave her a slow grin and a conspiratorial wink, then whispered back: "Well, thanks, but isn't that a bit intimate?"

Melba gave the first of many 'final' performances in 1926, before retiring to live near Melbourne. For many years though, she suffered a largely undeserved reputation as a drunk in her native state, particularly in the town of Ballarat. This canard was due to an event that followed her concert there. The audience had been so overwhelmed by her performance that afterwards they trooped en masse to the street outside her hotel and, joined by other Ballarat citizens, began to thunder out the message: "We want Melba! We want Melba!"

Three Melbourne reporters also happened to be staying at the hotel and had spent the evening drinking whisky. Hearing the racket outside, one of them decided to take action. Slipping into a floral dressing gown and adjusting a toque-style towel on his head, he lurched tipsily out on to a balcony. Seeing what they assumed was Dame Nellie, the huge crowd roared out its approval, but fell silent as the figure on the balcony raised its hand for silence.

Then, after gazing round the expectant multitude, in a slurred falsetto voice, 'Dame Nellie' hiccupped: "Why don't all of you buggers piss off home and let me get some bloody peace!"

Although there was no question of living together again, Wilde occasionally met up with Bosie Douglas during the summer of 1898, and visited the village of Nogent-sur-Marne, a few miles to the east of Paris, with him. In August, Oscar stayed in the almost twin village of Chevennieres-sur- Marne.

When asked if he was going to write again, Oscar was pessimistic: 'I have written all that I was to write, I wrote when I did not know life; now that I do know the meaning of life, I have nothing left to write. Life cannot be written, life can only be lived – I have lived'.

He wrote to Robert Sherard with gallows humour: 'One has to do something. I have no taste for writing now. It is a penance for me; but, as was said of torture, it always helps to pass an hour or two'.

As he pointed out, any future income from writing would have to go first to the Official Receiver to settle his bankruptcy – not the most inspiring of grails.

Left to his own devices in the deserted boulevards of an August Paris, Oscar derived some amusement from watching the English tourists.

Wilde: *'Paris is hot and empty. Even the charming people of bad character have gone away. Perspiring English families are all that can be seen.' 'Even the criminal classes have gone to the seaside, and the gendarmes yawn and regret their enforced idleness. Giving wrong directions to English tourists is the only thing that consoles them'.*

In September, Wilde stayed for a few days with Charles Conder at Chantemerle, near La Roche Guyon, 30 miles northwest of Paris.

On his return to Paris, Oscar and Bosie Douglas were given dinner by Frank Harris at Maire's Restaurant – 'the bill was terrific'. Wilde: 'Rostand and one of his mistresses were dining at another table. He listened so attentively that I feel sure he does not understand a word of English'.

[EDMUND ROSTAND, (1870-1918), was the author of the enduring romantic 1897 play, 'Cyrano de Bergerac'. (Anatole France: 'Rostand has the incontestable glory of having written the worst verse of the century since Victor Hugo'.) Rostand later talked with Oscar and accompanied him to the theatre to see the famous actor Benoit Coquelin in the play 'Poil de Carotte'.]

On October 18th 1898, Wilde corresponded with the English eccentric, Georgina Weldon.

GEORGINA WELDON 1837-1914

In 1887, *Constance Wilde* had written a short gossip column item about Georgina Weldon, informing her readers that: 'The palm of beauty was perhaps borne off by Mrs Weldon, radiant and young-looking as ever'. Obviously, this description was not mere flattery as the next year Weldon was chosen as the Face of 'Pear's Soap', bearing her endorsement: 'I am 50 but my complexion is 17 – Thanks to Pear's Soap'.

(Oscar Wilde was a convinced supporter of advertising, both generally – he himself had fronted publicity for 'Madame Fontaine's Bosom Beautifier' – and personally, explaining: 'Self-advertisement is utterly vital. Why is 'Pear's Soap' successful? Not because it is cheaper or better than any other soap but because it is more strenuously puffed. The journalist is my John the Baptist'.)

In 1898, Georgina wrote to Oscar saying that she saw no reason why she should not visit him in Paris now that he had given up his 'insane and unnatural penchants'. Oscar replied politely but added that, as people at one time had accused her of being 'insane and unnatural', 'do not you, of all people, commit the same error'. Georgina replied belligerently: 'I wished I knew one person who had said that of me, I'd have at them'.

Georgina Weldon was the daughter of a non-practising but wealthy barrister called Morgan Thomas. She took an ironic view of her father, recording in her diary during the Crimean War: 'Papa has no boils at present.... What a dreadful disappointment about the taking of Sevastopol! We had drunk to the memory of the departed and the glory of the living in a bottle of champagne. But Papa had given himself a headache all for nothing, as the next day the news of the surrender of Sevastopol was contradicted'.

When she married an indolent army officer, Harry Weldon, in 1858, 'the dirty old Governor cut me off within 24 hours'. The newly weds lived in Beaumaris, Anglesey, for some years, but built up strong social links in London.

Georgina had an excellent singing voice and in 1870 persuaded Harry, (now in possession of an inheritance), to move to London so that she could set up a music school. Accordingly, Harry leased a small mansion in Tavistock Square. Under Georgina's tenacious guidance, he acquired the job of Rougedragon Pursuivant at the College of Arms, (later becoming Garter King of Arms).

In 1871, Georgina met the French composer, Charles Gounod, (1818-1893), well known for his operas, including his 1859 'Faust'. Gounod had fled to England to avoid the Franco-Prussian War and Georgina determined to give succour to a genuine musical genius. The zeal with which she carried out her self imposed task turned Gounod's life into a nightmare.

Having installed him in Tavistock Square for a three-week visit, she proceeded to entomb Gounod in a domestic tyranny that lasted for two and a half years. (Harry Weldon, having acquired a new mistress, abetted the situation, possibly because it relieved the pressure on his own life.)

Gounod was subjected to a regimen of enforced exercise, a strict bedtime, incessant nagging over the regular taking of medicines, and Georgina's refusal to allow him to read late at night, etc. She patrolled his life like a prison warder, referring to him constantly as 'the old man', despite his being only 53.

Gounod appears to have become enfeebled by this ruthless ministration but occasionally rebelled, pretending deafness as a ruse to escape Georgina's advice. One evening, in a desperate attempt to avoid another dosage of Georgina's homemade medicinal broth, he made a run for it.

Georgina: 'I heard the hall door slam to! I uttered a piercing cry: "Harry! The old man has gone out again in this weather; for God's sake, run after him and bring him back!" My husband rushed to the garden, and before Gounod had got as far as the railings, had got him safe under his arm, as in a vice. My husband took Gounod upstairs.'

After another escape attempt, Georgina summoned the police. 'The old man came home quietly. Tears in the evening'.

Even musically Gounod found himself trapped in a world of banality, being bullied into writing the music to a hymn composed by Mary Gladstone's aunt.

When Gounod became involved in a legal battle with the Novello publishing house and was fined £2 (with £100 costs), Georgina was adamant that he should refuse to pay and instead go to prison, claiming it would be marvellous publicity. To her fury, Gounod's family paid the fine.

In 1874, Gounod faked an illness while on a visit to Blackheath and engineered Georgina's temporary absence. A pre-contacted friend arrived and managed to smuggle the composer back to France, leaving Georgina to rage in vain. The French journalist, Albert Woolf, likening the situation to Samson and Delilah, wrote: 'Gounod believed he had loved an angel, and in reality he had sacrificed his best years to a lodging-house keeper'.

Having tired of Harry Weldon's infidelities, Georgina separated from him on the understanding that she should receive £1000 a year and the continued use of the Tavistock Square house. She invited a French married couple called Anacharsis and Angèle Ménier to move in and help her with her singing school.

The Méniers proved to be a problem from the start, as Anacharsis promptly installed a self-navigating hot-air balloon in the front garden, much to the annoyance of the neighbours. Angèle was a fat, masculine woman, who had thoroughly earned her nickname of 'the human cormorant'. During an absence, Georgina discovered that the villainous Anacharis had filled her house with cronies and was threatening to take it over.

Georgina now started a campaign to force Harry to restore her conjugal rights; he retaliated by trying to have her committed to a private lunatic asylum. In the court cases that followed, Georgina was accused of adultery with Anacharsis, lesbian sex with Angèle, and madness by Harry's medical team. She fought back and was declared innocent.

However this brush with the courts gave her an appetite for litigation that continued for the rest of her life. Although she had never studied law, she turned out to be a most effective advocate. In 1882, she acquired a tiny office in Red Lion Court, and the services of a writ-server called Captain Harcourt.

(Harcourt was known as 'the greatest rogue in London'. While serving with the British Army during the Crimean War, he had got bored with life in the trenches besieging Sevastopol. With a couple of comrades, he switched uniforms with some dead Russians and sneaked into the city where they had 'a jolly good time'. Later, as the British Army marched into Sevastopol through one gate, Harcourt slipped out of another. His name appeared on the casualty lists, until he appeared in London to deny his death. He later spent seven years in prison on a variety of charges.)

By 1884, Georgina was personally conducting seventeen simultaneous legal actions. In one involving the Lunacy Laws, (her particular crusade), Judge 'Hanging' Hawkins was so impressed by her performance that he summed up entirely in her favour. She won the case and £1000 damages and was cheered from the court.

Unfortunately in 1885, she lost a criminal libel case after she showed gross disrespect to the court, (and Harcourt was discovered to have tried to bribe the jury). She received a six-month sentence in Holloway Prison, but found that she actually rather enjoyed jail, (the cell was larger than her office in Red Lion Court). On her release, she sent a card: "To my dear Governor, in grateful remembrance of six happy months in Holloway'.

After further trouble from the Méniers, in which she lost possession of her Tavistock Square home, Georgina went to live in a convent in France, finally moving back to England and dying in Brighton in 1914. It was said that: 'the Courts of Law were very dull without her'.

> *Bored by his life in Paris, Wilde jumped at Frank Harris's suggestion that he spend three months down on the French Riviera.*
>
> *On December 20th Oscar moved into the Hotel des Bains at La Napoule, about ten miles from Cannes. He enjoyed 'the wonderful pine-woods all about, making the air pungent'. 'The fishermen have the same freedom from morals as the Neapolitans – they are very nice'. He said later: "I was very happy on the Riviera".*

1899

> *[The First Hague Peace Conference was called at the instigation of Tsar Nicholas II.*
> *In March the Fashoda crisis that had developed between France and Britain abated.*
> *In October the Boer War broke out in South Africa between Britain and the Boer Republics.*
> *In France the Dreyfus Affaire rumbled on, while the French President Fauré died of a stroke after entertaining his young mistress in the Elysee Palace.]*

> *Wilde spent January on the Riviera, visiting Cannes where he was reunited with Sarah Bernhardt, and Nice, where he was snubbed by Sir George Alexander. Oscar said of Nice that: 'Romance there is a profession plied beneath the moon'.*
>
> *In February, the script of his play 'The Importance of Being Earnest' was published by Leonard Smithers to a resounding silence from the English newspapers and a corresponding lack of sales to the public.*
>
> *In mid-February, Oscar left La Napoule and moved to the Terminus Hotel in Nice. He was plagued with money problems and eventually was turned out of the hotel. Oscar: 'My last week at the Terminus Hotel my bill was left every night by my bedside, and another copy brought up with my coffee in the morning. You can fancy my state of nerves'.*

To compound his woes he was told that he was neurasthenic. 'My doctor says I have all the symptoms. It is comforting to have them all, it makes one a perfect type'. He was also forbidden champagne on account of his gout.

In March, Wilde travelled on through Italy, where he stopped in Genoa to see the grave of his wife Constance. He also learned of the death of his brother Willie on the 13th March.

He moved on Gland, on the north shore of Lake Geneva in Switzerland, to stay as a houseguest of Harold Mellor.

HAROLD MELLOR 1868-1925

Harold Mellor was the highly-strung son of a Lancashire factory owner, who had been expelled at the age of 14 from Harrow School for "having been loved by the captain of the first eleven'. When his father died in 1893, Mellor inherited considerable wealth and decided to live abroad.

He had met Wilde the previous winter at the hotel in La Napoule, where Mellor was staying with his mother and his Italian boyfriend Eolo. They had spent Christmas together eating plum pudding and drinking Pommery-Greno. Oscar: 'I kept Christmas pleasantly'.

However, this agreeable inaugural meeting was not repeated when Wilde arrived in Gland. Oscar found Switzerland and Mellor to be 'a rather dreadful combination'.

Oscar: "The fringes of the Lake are fledged with pines, but I don't like Switzerland: it has produced nothing but theologians and waiters'. Neither was there any consolatory romance: 'The chastity of Switzerland has got on my nerves' – 'The Swiss are so ugly to look at that it conveys melancholy into all my days' – 'Swiss people are carved out of wood with a rough knife, most of them; the others are carved out of turnips. Their cattle have more expression'.

Oscar found Mellor to be an appalling host who was mean to the point of insanity. As well as being refused wine and offered only Swiss beer, Oscar complained that: 'I have had no cigarettes for three days. Mellor keeps his own carefully locked up!'

'Every day I discover some new fault in him…. I am philosophic about it now; indeed we only meet at meals. In the evening he reads the Times or sleeps – both audibly'. Oscar left as soon as he could.

In spite of this, in April 1900, Wilde's ennui had reached such a state that he accepted an offer from Mellor to accompany him on a tour of Italy, staying in Palermo, Naples, and Rome. Mellor informed Oscar that he had a strict spending limit of £50. Wilde: 'When that gives out I shall have to walk home'.

Wilde again stayed at Gland for ten days in May 1900. On this occasion, Mellor drove Oscar back to Paris by motorcar. It was Oscar's first experience of the new machine. After it had broken down for the sixth time, Oscar commented: 'They, like all machines, are more wilful than animals – nervous, irritable, strange things'.

Wilde: 'My last visit to Mellor has given me melancholia. I must go no more'. They did not meet again. Mellor lived on in a villa at Cannes, until he committed suicide in 1925.

With some relief, Wilde left Switzerland on April 1st 1899, and went south to the Ligurian coast where he stayed at Santa Margherita, 20 miles east of Genoa, Italy. He visited the coastal towns of Rapallo and Portofino.

Oscar was now intensely bored by his life, and Robbie Ross, worried by his letters, arrived to rescue him. They returned to Paris on May 7th, where Wilde stayed at a couple of small Right Bank hotels, the Hotel de la Neva and then at the Hotel Marsollier. Worried by a doctor's warning, Ross managed to persuade Wilde to stop drinking for six months.

Oscar's health was affected by a skin complaint that produced a red rash on his arms and torso. Oscar: 'It is impossible not to scratch myself – I feel more like a great ape than ever'. Also he had an occasional recurrence of the malaria that had plagued him for almost 20 years, acquired during 'a visit to Provence at vintage time'. (Oscar: 'An aesthetic disease but a deuced nuisance'.)

His spirit, though, was unaffected by these irritations. One day, he boarded a Parisian tram to visit Bosie Douglas. Realising that he had forgotten his money, he asked his fellow passengers if they could loan him a franc for the fare. His request being met by a stony refusal, he stopped the tram and climbed off. Then, (knowing that Bosie would pay the fare at the other end), Oscar flagged down a taxi and drove off with a lordly wave to the gaping tram passengers.

During June, Wilde had a peripheral encounter with events linked to the major crisis that had developed between Britain and France over an incident in the Sudan.

THE FASHODA AFFAIR

During the 1890s, the scramble for African colonies had led to a desire by the British government to link up its existing control on a north to south route called 'Cairo to the Cape'. Simultaneously, the French wished to link its colonies on a west to east route from West Africa to the Red Sea.

After General Kitchener's victory in the Sudan in 1898, his troops advanced south to the Upper Nile town of Fashoda where in September they met a small French force under Colonel Marchand who were advancing east. Kitchener demanded their withdrawal; Marchand refused. The standoff was only resolved when the heavily outnumbered Marchand agreed to retreat. By March 1899, diplomatic pressure forced an uneasy French quiescence.

The confrontation produced deep ill feeling between the two nations. At one point the French had been determined to go to war over the incident, until it was discovered that, owing to long-term theft, there were practically no stores left at their main naval base at Toulon.

The palmist Cheiro reported that in Paris the patriotic fervour against the English was so strong that, when visiting Americans walked along the boulevards, they carried prominently displayed American newspapers so that they would not be mistaken for English people. Queen Victoria was advised not to visit Nice because of the antipathy.

On June 2nd, Wilde went to the local office of Thomas Cook's Travel Agency to collect a letter containing £10 from Robbie Ross. On the way he became entangled with a large crowd listening to a fiery speech by Colonel Marchand from the balcony of the Military Club in the Avenue de l'Opera.

Wilde: 'I had to fight my way to Cook's, but by the aid of patriotic cries I succeeded in forcing a passage through the patriots'.

Wilde had never regarded the English with great respect, ('He is a typical Englishman, always dull and usually violent'), and his experiences since 1895 had not increased their attraction. However, in a thoroughly contradictory mood, Oscar now claimed to support the idea of British imperialism and regarded Marchand's opponent, Lord Kitchener, as a hero.

LORD KITCHENER 1850-1916

Herbert Kitchener became the most influential and emblematic of all British military men during the turn of the century period. Outwardly a bluff, honest soldier, he was in fact an unscrupulous intriguer whose rationalisation of total war concealed a borderline psychopath. That said, his ability and courage enabled him to rise from lieutenant to Field-Marshal, while possessing neither the wealth nor the social connections then thought vital to such a career.

He was born near Listowel, Co. Kerry, Ireland, and raised in an unforgiving family atmosphere. Once, when he had committed some childhood misdemeanour, his father tied him spread-eagled in the blazing summer sun for several hours as punishment. Kitchener did not complain.

Having been commissioned in 1870, he went in search of action, firstly in the Russian-Turkish War, (when he joined Valentine Baker at the Battle of Plevna), then on Lord Cromer's staff in Egypt, then in 1884 on attachment to the Gordon relief expedition. Having learned fluent Arabic, he disguised himself as a Bedouin and, on an appallingly dangerous mission, spied out the northern Sudan for Wolseley's army. Notwithstanding the debacle that followed, Kitchener's reputation as a soldier was established.

His character, though, came under question. His closest companion in these years, *Fenwick La Terriere*, wrote that: 'Kitchener was a very likeable fellow and we got on very well up to a certain point; but after that point came a certain blank'. Margot Asquith, who met him in Egypt, called him cold and ruthless: 'he was a natural cad and a remarkably clever liar'. She also noted that his troops hated him and, after wondering whether this was a sign of power or weakness, decided that it was a sign of brutality. Kitchener was reputed to have never spoken to an ordinary soldier in his entire career.

This disdain also applied to the native peoples amongst whom he spent much of his life. When asked for his opinion of the Egyptians, he replied that he did not think much of a people who had painted the same cat for 4000 years.

In 1897, he was given command of the British forces sent into the Sudan to destroy Mahdist rule, (and to avenge the death of General Gordon). He succeeded brilliantly, building a railway across the desert and, in the summer of 1898, defeating a vast army of Dervishes at the Battle of Omdurman. He was created Lord Kitchener of Khartoum in recognition of his victory.

For many observers, though, the triumph was marred by his savagery towards his enemy. After capturing one Emir, he had the man roped to a horse and lashed by guards while being dragged through streets full of jeering mobs. After capturing Khartoum, he disinterred the corpse of the Mahdi, (who had died ten years previously). The severed skull was presented to Kitchener as a drinking cup, while the body was flung in the Nile. (Several fingernails were removed as mementoes destined for White's Club in St James St.)

Winston Churchill, who witnessed the event, particularly objected to the killing of the Dervish wounded after the battle: 'The victory at Omdurman was disgraced by the inhuman slaughter of the wounded and Kitchener was responsible for this'. The pro-Arab Wilfred Blunt called Kitchener: 'a big brutal fellow fitly representing modern British soldierdom'. Kitchener defended himself by saying that the only way to impress barbarians was to be even more barbaric.

At the start of the Boer War in 1899, Kitchener arrived in South Africa as Chief of Staff to the British commander Lord Roberts, and again his character came into question. The High Commissioner Lord Milner admitted to friends that Kitchener 'was not straight', while Lord Roberts said that: 'He can't even learn: he is a fool'.

After the strictly military victory against the Boers and the capture of their capitals, Roberts returned home believing the war to be at an end and his mission accomplished. However, with 50,000 armed Boers still in contention, Kitchener, as the new commander, found himself faced with a guerrilla insurgency that threatened to drift on for years.

Kitchener solved the problem by rounding up the Boer families, placing them in what became known as 'concentration camps', and destroying their farms and crops. This scorched earth policy removed the supplies that were vital to the Boers and slowly the resistance dwindled. Kitchener was acclaimed for this new victory, receiving a viscountcy and being made a full general.

Again, the method of his conquest proved controversial. The camps he had created proved to be death traps and over 20,000 Boer women and children died in the epidemics that swept through them. In his defence, it must be emphasised that, other than the name, in no way did his concentration camps have the same motivation or conditions as the later infamous Nazi camps.

The deaths were due entirely to incompetence and lack of medical foresight. Sickness was endemic throughout the war and the casualty lists gave some idea of the proportions. For instance, the British Army lost roughly 6,000 men in battle, but another 16,000 to disease.

Kitchener was blasé about the death toll caused by his policy and described his liberal detractors as purveyors of 'defeatist propaganda'. He stated that the epidemics had been caused by the unhealthy personal habits of the Boers, and contemplated charging some Boer mothers with manslaughter, claiming that their children had died as a result of their own negligence.

In 1902, his arrival in India as military commander caused endless trouble with the Viceroy, *Lord Curzon*. Curzon loathed his new subordinate, describing him as: 'standing aloof and alone, a molten mass of devouring energy and burning ambition, without anybody to control or guide it in the right direction', adding that it was more difficult to govern Kitchener than it was to govern India. Their personal battle led Curzon to a virtual nervous breakdown and his retirement to England.

One observer, *Rennell Rodd*, said of him: 'Many admired Kitchener. Very few really liked him. He walked by himself'.

However, such was his standing in public opinion, that at the start of the First World War he was appointed Secretary of War and became the public face of the military effort. His critics again included Winston Churchill, ("Kitchener may be a general – but never a gentleman"), and also *Sir Edward Carson* who called the new Secretary: "that great stuffed oaf".

Ignoring the 'all over by Christmas' optimists, from the outset Kitchener realised that it was going to be a long war and would need a large supply of fresh soldiers. With his ubiquitous advertising campaign, he managed to recruit and train millions of civilians and thus provide the armies of 1915 onwards. On the debit side, his reputation began to shatter as the blame for the failures on the Western Front and at the Dardanelles fell on his shoulders.

In 1916, while on a diplomatic trip to Russia, Kitchener's ship, the 'Hampshire', hit a mine off the Orkney Islands. He was seen, phlegmatic to the end, pacing the deck before the stricken ship sank beneath the waves. His body was never found.

The chilly front he displayed in his public life seems to have extended to his private life as well. His only lapse into humanity appears to have occurred in 1885 in Egypt, when he fell for Valentine Baker's teenage daughter, Hermione. This ended when she died of typhoid fever aged only eighteen; for many years he kept her portrait in a locket round his neck.

Although denied by some biographers, there is a strong case for suspecting that Kitchener was homosexual. He admitted that he was 'untroubled by sexual desire', and it is possible that he was just naturally celibate.

On the other hand, *Bosie Douglas* told his own biographer (Rupert Croft-Cooke) that he had slept with Kitchener when he met him in Cairo in 1893. They also met later at the London home of Lord Henry Gordon-Lennox, (whose relative Cosmo Gordon-Lennox had a brief fling with Oscar Wilde), and strolled together in Hyde Park. Kitchener was known to interrogate potential young staff officers to find 'men of ceaseless energy and iron will who could be relied upon to carry out their part as far as flesh and blood could permit'. In that case, it is to be wondered what on earth he was doing with Bosie?

The notoriously unreliable *Sir Edmund Backhouse* claimed that while in Constantinople, he had slept with a woman who had compared his carnal efforts favourably with Kitchener's. When he mentioned this to the general, Kitchener told Backhouse that that his tastes lay elsewhere and that: "Where there's no will, my boy, there's no way". Although probably an inventive lie, Backhouse always based his stories on the probability of being believed, (as with his claims about *Lord Rosebery*).

Kitchener also employed military aides, such as 'Brat' Maxwell and 'Kitchener's familiar' Oswald Fitzgerald, whose relationships with the general were regarded as unnaturally close.

Kitchener's biographer George Cassar rejected the assumption by pointing out that his enemies in 1915 would have used such an accusation to smear him, but failed to do so. This did not automatically follow as, in the deepest throes of the war, even Kitchener's most virulent opponents would hardly have wanted Britain's leading soldier to be exposed publicly as a homosexual.

Kitchener had one human failing that he took no trouble to conceal – his lust for porcelain. He gathered a huge collection, often from the houses of friends. During one visit from the general, Rennell Rodd was on tenterhooks that Kitchener might spot a rare Rhodian plate that Rodd treasured. Kitchener set Rodd's mind at ease by telling him that he already possessed one.

On other occasions, his hosts were not so fortunate. If a desired object was not presented freely to him, Kitchener had no scruples whatever when it came to stealing porcelain.

During his campaigns, Kitchener was fortunate to be able to rely on the services of such officers as **GENERAL SIR HECTOR MACDONALD** (1853-1903). Born and raised in the Highlands of Scotland, Macdonald left his job as a draper's assistant in Dingwall and in 1870 enlisted in the army as a private.

During the Second Afghan War of 1878, his outstanding bravery earned him the army nickname of 'Fighting Mac'. Two years later in the First Boer War, although he was captured at the Battle of Majuba Hill, his courage in battle so impressed the Boer commander General Joubert that, when Macdonald was released, Joubert insisted that his sword be returned to him.

He rose through the ranks until, in 1898 when Kitchener set out on his advance into the Sudan, Macdonald was placed in charge of a brigade. During the Battle of Omdurman, Kitchener, thinking that the enemy was beaten, set off to enter the city. He did not realise that a large section of the Dervish army was still intact and about to attack.

Macdonald's rearguard brigade was suddenly subjected to a ferocious charge by this new force. His Sudanese troops began to panic and fired wildly at the oncoming foe. Macdonald coolly strolled along in front of his soldiers knocking up their barrels with a swagger stick, and then performed the extremely difficult manoeuvre of redeploying his troops while under fire. He then directed his new defence and fought off the deadly danger to the British army. Many observers considered that he had saved Kitchener and was the real hero of the Battle of Omdurman.

During the Second Boer War of 1899, he led the Highland Brigade in several actions and was instrumental in the relief of Kimberley. By 1900, he had been made a general and had received a knighthood. He reached a pinnacle of fame when his portrait as a Highland officer was used, (and still is), to illustrate the 'Camp Coffee' brand.

In 1902, he was sent to command the British troops in Ceylon, (now Sri Lanka). During his tenure, Macdonald was accused of homosexuality and returned to London to discuss the situation with the War Office. His old commander Kitchener, on hearing of the scandal, thought that 'Fighting Mac' should be court-martialled and shot.

When he heard that his superiors had decided to hold a court of inquiry, Macdonald travelled to the Hotel Regina in Paris, where the next day he shot himself dead.

(When asked about homosexuals in the 1920s, King George V, probably with Macdonald in mind, grunted: "I thought men like that shot themselves".)

Wilde spent the summer of 1899 based in Paris but with occasional short trips into the French countryside. In late June he visited Le Havre where he met Toulouse-Lautrec, and in July stayed at a local inn at Fontainebleau.

The publication of the script of 'An Ideal Husband' brought him very little extra money. On one occasion, a waiter reported seeing Oscar sheltering from a storm under a café awning. The waiter wished to close and rolled back the awning. Oscar, unable to pay the bill, was forced to remain sitting in the rain.

In August, he moved back into the Hotel d'Alsace, owned by the sympathetic Jean Dupoirier.

Oscar had various encounters with old friends and enemies. Ellen Terry shared a café meal with him, as did JEC Bodley, William Rothenstein and Cheiro. Edward Carson literally bumped into him, though they did not speak, while Oscar Browning spotted him in the distance from a cab. James Whistler pointedly ignored him in a restaurant.

Wilde also met some new acquaintances including, in September 1899, the young artist Augustus John.

AUGUSTUS JOHN 1878-1961

The 21-year-old Augustus John was introduced to Wilde by their mutual friend *Charles Conder*, and spent ten days in the company of what John called 'the distinguished reprobate' and 'great man of inaction'. John: 'There was nothing lugubrious or sinister about Wilde. He fancied himself as a kind of 'Happy Prince', or, admitting a touch of vulgarity, the genial although permanently overdrawn millionaire'.

Although flattered by Oscar's interest, John felt intimidated by the wave of wit that flowed over him. John: 'I could think of nothing whatever to say. Even my laughter sounded hollow'. He escaped to 'easier if less distinguished company'.

In later years, John recalled Wilde with affection: 'My memory of him isn't of a middle-aged man at all, but will always evoke the frank, open, friendly, humorous face of a young one, for the fact is he had too much sense to grow old'.

Augustus John was born and raised in Tenby, West Wales. He was an unremarkable youth who, on his entry to the Slade School of Art in 1894, was seen as a neat and timid student who produced 'methodical' work. Then, in the summer of 1897, an incident occurred that changed his life completely.

While swimming in the sea off Pembrokeshire he struck his head against a hidden rock. On recovery, the mediocre boy metamorphosed into an untidy, wild man of genius. His Slade teacher, Henry Tonks, was startled by the brilliance of the paintings that his pupil now produced, and John left the Slade in 1898 already famous among his peers.

Over the next decades, he became a legendary bohemian artist and lover who could claim with accuracy to be 'the sort of person our fathers warned us against'. In particular, his overpoweringly intense persona proved irresistible to women.

In 1901, he married Ida Nettleship, but this arrangement soon expanded when another girl, Dorelia McNeill, joined the couple in a ménage a trois. Between them, (up until Ida's premature death in 1907), the two women provided John with a brood of children. The family maid also announced she was pregnant by him. As an additional outlet for his energies, John established a second ménage a trios with another lover, Alick Schepeler, and her friend Frieda Bloch.

Not content with this impressive seraglio, John acquired a new lover called Euphemia Lamb, (later rejected by the sexual mystic Aleister Crowley as too wanton). John was fascinated by Euphemia's previous exploits that included entertaining six men in one night – each one representing a different European nation.

During her association with John, Euphemia cut her hair and dressed as a boy. One evening, after a drinking session in France, they made love and fell asleep underneath a caravan. The local police arrived and arrested them for public homosexuality – Euphemia secured their release by stripping in the police station.

John became profoundly attached to the Romany gypsy life, wearing earrings, growing his hair to his shoulders, and taking his ever-expanding family to roam Western Europe in a caravan. They spent one summer camping by the river in Grantchester, Cambridge, where the poet Rupert Brooke became a friend and confidante. The Cambridge sojourn ended after John, (a first-rate boxer), beat up an opponent during a drunken brawl in the city.

In 1911, the clan settled down at Alderney Manor near Wimborne, Dorset, where they spent the next sixteen years in a carefree rural bear-garden, (that bore a strong resemblance to HE Bates's 'Larkin' books). A series of eccentric guests joined the almost feral children romping through the gardens and consuming vast meals at a communal table. Any attempt at domestic order failed – when one guest absent-mindedly left his hat behind, he returned months later to find it, strewn on the floor, in exactly the same position. The sexual merry-go-round revolved under the paternal, if libidinous, eye of Augustus himself.

(The easy atmosphere of concupiscence appeared to radiate even to the most peripheral of acquaintances. John's two daughters once saved a youth from drowning by giving him the 'kiss of life'. As the young man struggled back to consciousness, the girls noticed that their efforts had given him an erection.)

When the First World War broke out, John was found unfit for duty 'owing to knee trouble', but was attached as a war artist to the Canadian Army with the rank of major. He refused to shave off his beard and so became the only bearded Allied officer except for King George V. This caused endless problems as most units panicked at the sight of John, thinking they were about to be inspected by the monarch.

Eventually, John spoiled his military record by knocking out an infantry captain during a quarrel. He was rushed out of the trenches to avoid an embarrassing court-martial and refused re-entry to France for the duration of the war. He was perhaps the only man to be banned from World War One for the offence of fighting.

After the war, John spent some of his time in Ireland, a country that he loved and where he became a close friend of the multi-talented surgeon and writer Oliver St John Gogarty. Despite Gogarty's tendency to monopolise the conversation, (John found that the only way to stop him was to throw a bowl of peanuts in his face), John was impressed by Gogarty's garish waistcoats and his ownership of the first yellow Rolls-Royce.

At the opening event of the Taillteann Games in 1924, the two men were subjected to an unending monologue in Gaelic by an Irish official. During the speech the electricity failed, leaving the hall in total darkness. The official, undeterred, droned on. When the ordeal finally ended, Gogarty apologised to his friend, whereupon John gasped: "Oh, thank God. That's what it is! I thought I'd gone mad".

Gogarty had a devilish sense of mischief which he employed when another friend, Lord Dunsany, invited John to stay at his home, Dunsany Castle. Dunsany barely knew John; Gogarty, on the other hand, was well aware of both men's fondness for liquor.

Realising the comic possibilities, Gogarty told John that Lord Dunsany was bitterly opposed to alcohol in any form and that Augustus should on no account ask his host to supply any. He then phoned Dunsany and told him that Augustus was a fanatical teetotaller who would be mortally offended if offered any drink. He sat back contently to await the result.

The two thwarted imbibers spent three days utterly sober in each other's company. On the fourth night however, Augustus cracked, having been driven nearly insane by his host's attempts to teach him how to play the harp. At midnight, he clambered over the castle wall and walked the twenty miles back to Dublin.

In 1923, John made the first of several visits to the USA, a country he regarded as being chiefly under the control of 'a villain named Randolph Hearst who owns most of the newspapers'. His unsympathetic view of the American mind as being 'a jungle of platitude and bluff' was not tempered by the fact that he arrived as Prohibition was being introduced. He soon discovered the illegal drinking clubs and noted that the greatest supporters of prohibition were the bootleggers themselves. He declared that: 'prohibition is more than a farce – it is a tragedy – it breeds disrespect for all laws'.

After 1918, John's abilities as a painter started to wane. He began to restrict himself mostly to portraits and, in this capacity, met a strange variety of subjects. On one occasion, he painted *Bernard Shaw* who later explained: "I went to sleep while I was sitting, and John, fascinated by the network of wrinkles made by my shut eyes, painted them before I awoke. It turned a most heroic portrait into a very splendidly painted sarcasm. He entitled it 'Shaw Listening to Someone Else Talking'. It made me look like an inebriated gamekeeper".

In the 1940s, John was commissioned to paint the prudish World War Two hero, Field-Marshal Bernard Montgomery. Montgomery treated the artist with some suspicion, asking an aide: "Who is this chap? He drinks, he's dirty, and I think there are women in the background!"

It has to be admitted that Montgomery was correct on all counts, especially the latter. Having re-located the clan at a new home at Fordingbridge, Hampshire, John bought another house in Mallord Street in Chelsea. This became a base from where he held sway as the acknowledged leader of bohemian London, and at which he was the host of some extraordinary parties. One guest reported that: 'a remarkable feature was that there was not one ugly girl, all wonderfully beautiful and young. They always ended in the most dreadful orgies I have ever seen'.

Another of John's parties began in Haverfordwest in Wales on a Friday evening, and finished the following Tuesday in Hungary.

His list of lovers was phenomenal. John: "I am discharging my mistresses at the rate of about three a week". One of them was Eve Fleming, (the mother of the 'James Bond' creator Ian Fleming). Another was an Irish girl called Caitlin Macnamara. They met when she was 16 and he was 60. Caitlin: 'Augustus leapt on me, ripped my clothes off, and penetrated me like some mindless old goat'.

(John introduced her to the young Welsh poet, Dylan Thomas. Despite a fistfight between the two men in a Carmarthen car park, John remained a friend even after their marriage and was godfather to the Thomas's first child.)

John also had an affair with Frieda, the Austrian ex-wife of the Swedish playwright August Strindberg, and lived to regret it. Having spent ten years as a nun, then two with Strindberg, Frieda was now sexually insatiable. Not content with John's usual conveyor belt conception of relationships, she tried to retain his attention through a series of well-publicised 'suicide' attempts. On one occasion, he was forced to hide out in the Welsh mountains as she raged around his usual London haunts. On another, she pursued him onto the platform of Charing Cross Station with a loaded pistol. John referred to her as 'the walking hell bitch of the Western World'.

John rarely failed to snare his prey but his attempt to seduce one of his portrait sitters came to naught. She was an American girl called Hope Scott, (later the inspiration for the heroine of 'The Philadelphia Story' and the musical 'High Society'). Having evaded John's energetic advances in the studio, she was almost trapped when he drunkenly lurched into her bedroom. To his chagrin, John dimly perceived another man already in Hope's bed and left. He never realised that the 'man' was actually a spare bolster.

478

Dorelia McNeill, the nearest person to a constant in John's domestic life, was sublimely indifferent to his incessant infidelities, being far more upset about his habit of arriving late for meals. But John was not unaware that his libido was out of control. One day, his secretary found him beating a desk with his erect penis shouting: "No, no, no, no, NO!"

His reputation as an artist sank as the century wore on – Pablo Picasso: "Augustus John is the best bad painter in Britain". He began to see himself as: "just a legend – not a real person at all", but found consolation with the thought that he was the only anarchist to have been awarded the Order of Merit.

Even in his eighties, John was still a resolute drinker and indefatigable lover. When strolling around his home turf of Chelsea he fell into the avuncular habit of patting the head of every child that he met – "just in case one of them is mine".

In November 1899, after a six-month respite, Wilde began to drink alcohol again. In a very short time, his intake had risen to five bottles of Courvoisier brandy a week, plus wine, advocaat, and absinthe.

Throughout his life, Wilde had an exceptionally high tolerance for alcohol and could consume a huge amount without showing ill effects. Bosie Douglas wrote: 'He drank more than any man I ever knew, but till the debacle he never showed a sign of it'. Robbie Ross agreed: 'Owing to his extraordinary constitution he was able (unfortunately perhaps) to take a great deal too much without being affected'.

It was not for nothing that Oscar coined the motto: 'Work is the curse of the drinking classes'. His usual euphemism for 'drunk', (which he borrowed from Ibsen's play 'Hedda Gabler'), was 'having vine leaves in your hair', though on occasion he varied this to 'having vine yards in your hair'.

At the end of December 1899, Oscar wrote that he had spent 'a very pleasant Christmas'.

1900

[In China, the Boxer Rising led to the siege of the Foreign Legations in Peking.
In Britain, a new political force came into play with the formation of the Labour Party.
Australia was re-defined as a Commonwealth.]

On January 31, the Marquess of Queensberry died. Wilde saw Queensberry's two sons, Percy and Bosie, in Paris 'in the highest of spirits'.
Oscar spent some of February laid up in his hotel room with a throat infection.
In March he visited the studio of the French sculptor, Auguste Rodin.

AUGUSTE RODIN 1840-1917

Wilde was a great admirer of the sculptor: 'Rodin has a pavilion to himself and showed me anew all his great dreams in marble'. He also perceived that Rodin had a strong literary streak in his nature: 'He is by far the greatest poet in France, and has, as I was glad to tell myself, completely outshone Victor Hugo'.

The sculpture that particularly dazzled Wilde was Rodin's provocative statue of the writer Balzac: 'It is superb' – 'the leonine head of a fallen angel, with a dressing gown… People howl with rage'. (In 1883, Wilde had adopted Balzac's habit of wearing a monk-like dressing gown while he was writing.)

Prior to 1880, the art of sculpting the human being had nearly died out, until Rodin, almost accidentally, discovered a new form of representation. While at work sculpting 'The Man with a Broken Nose', his studio had been so cold that overnight the back of the head broke off. Next morning, Rodin examined the piece and realised that the remaining fragment was more suggestive of reality than the completed work would have been. His future art was inspired by this insight. Rodin: 'I choose a piece of marble and chop off what I don't want'.

Over the next thirty years, influenced by the Indian and Japanese traditions, he virtually single-handedly restored sculpture to a new height. He found dancers and dancing to be an especial stimulus, befriending some of its greatest practitioners like Vaslav Nijinsky and Isadora Duncan

(In 1900, after Duncan had danced privately for him, she described how: 'He ran his hands over my neck, breast, stroked my arms and ran his hands over my hips, my bare legs and feet... from him emanated heat that scorched and melted me. My whole desire was to yield to him my entire being and indeed, I would have done so had not been for my upbringing'.)

It took Rodin many years before he was accepted as a modern master and it was in England that he first found appreciation, his main supporters being the editor *WE Henley* and the writer RL Stevenson. A version of his sculpture 'The Burghers of Calais' was positioned behind the House of Lords on the River Thames, and a cast of his famous work 'The Thinker' was purchased for the British nation.

His resulting fondness for the English was proven when he was invited over for a series of dinners to celebrate his success. At one such event, it was discovered that the beef provided for the meal had gone rotten. The other guests pushed their plates away in disgust, but Rodin continued to chomp his way through the meat, declaring to his appalled hostess: "No, no, madame, it is superb! The true roast beef of England!"

Aside from food, Rodin's other great passion was for women. He told *William Rothenstein*: "People say I think too much about women. Yet, after all, what is there more important to think about?" In his work, he refused to accept the prevailing view of the 'purity' of women, and insisted instead that female sexuality was just as powerful as that of the male.

In the 1860s, he was fortunate to meet a young seamstress called Marie-Rose Beuret. For the next fifty years, she remained his faithful companion and nurse, (he married her one month before her death). However, he did not allow this attachment to have any bearing on his sexual conduct and became notorious for his incessant womanising.

Once, when he dined at the painter Monet's house, he perused Monet's four daughters so obviously that, red-faced with embarrassment, they each left the table. It seemed, though, that Rodin simply had no idea that such behaviour could be seen as objectionable. *Frank Harris*: 'There was no venom in him and no exclusions. He accepted life as it was, lived it to the fullest, and had few regrets'.

He found one woman who entirely agreed with him. She was the painter Gwen John, *Augustus John's* sister. Their affair began in 1906 when he was sixty-six and she was a thirty-year-old 'with an admirable body'. However, when she insisted on having a two-hour sex session every day, Rodin's ability to satisfy Gwen began to flag. His predicament worsened when she invited a friend, a sculptress called Hilda Flodin, to join in.

(Even Augustus John was dumbfounded by Gwen's antics, declaring that 'her passions for both men and women were outrageous and irrational'. One of her sexual partners was Augustus's girlfriend and second wife, Dorelia McNeill, who Gwen seduced while on a walking tour of France.)

By 1900, Rodin was honoured not only internationally but also in his own land. *Dame Ethel Smyth*, commenting on his wealth and businesslike mind, wrote: 'The peasant cunning of a Rodin, aware of the market and for all his genius never forgetting it'. He achieved his greatest triumph in June 1900 at the Paris Universal Exhibition when he sold nearly 200,000 francs worth of art. He was feted at a large dinner at the Café Voltaire attended by the cream of the artistic world, including Oscar Wilde.

480

As far as his sitters were concerned, Rodin's one great failing was his inability to complete a sculpture. *Bernard Shaw* said of him: "A strange thing about Rodin was that he never regarded a portrait bust finished while the sitter was still alive". Rodin was amazed when Pope Benedict XV, after posing for yet another interminable session, suddenly burst out: "Finish, Monsieur Rodin, finish!".

Shaw claimed that Rodin's sitters became so fed up of posing for him that: 'they would send forged telegrams to themselves, calling them away on pressing business, just to escape.'

On April 2nd 1900, Wilde left the Hotel d'Alsace in Paris for a holiday in Italy as the guest of Harold Mellor.

They stayed for eight days in Palermo, Sicily, (Wilde: 'the most beautifully situated town in the world'), where Oscar met a doe-eyed Seminarist: 'Every day I kissed him behind the High Altar'.

After three days in Naples, Wilde and Mellor moved on to spend Easter in Rome, where Oscar claimed that his rash disappeared after receiving the Easter Sunday blessing from the Pope.

After seeing a photograph of himself taken in Rome, Wilde commented that he looked 'like an unfrocked Lateran bishop'. He had taken up photography as a hobby, suggesting that in moments of depression he sometimes thought that he should have made a career as a photographer. Oscar: 'Cows are very fond of being photographed and, unlike architecture, don't move'.

Mellor allowed him enough cash to purchase the services of a series of Roman rent-boys. Oscar: 'How evil it is to buy Love, and how evil to sell it. And yet what purple hours one can snatch from that grey slow-moving thing we call Time'. One boy, Amando, was especially insistent on frequent presents. Oscar: 'He really bayed for books, as a dog'.

After Mellor's departure, Wilde stayed on for a return visit to Naples where he had sex with 'a triton'. He went back to Rome for a couple of days to reflect on his options: 'The Cloister or the Café – there is my future. I tried the Hearth, but it was a failure'.

He spent a further ten days at Mellor's home in Gland, Switzerland, before returning to his Paris refuge at the Hotel d'Alsace in May 1900.

Back in Paris, Wilde resumed an affair with a young Anglo-French marine called Maurice Gilbert, who shared his favours with many of Oscar's circle, including Bosie Douglas, Ross, and Reggie Turner, (the latter installed Maurice for a period at Clement's Inn, London). Oscar bought Maurice a bicycle, (with Frank Harris's money), and took him to visit Rodin's studio.

In June 1900, Oscar wrote: 'Maurice was pale, and sweet, and gentle. He now forms part of a ménage a trois: none of the members sleep: the girl – a rose-like thing I hope – lies in the middle, and knows the pleasure and insecurity of the Via Media. Maurice won't tell me the name of the other partner, but admits he has a slight moustache'.

(Maurice proved to be more than a rentboy and remained a loyal friend of Wilde to the end.)

When the International Exhibition opened in Paris in June 1900, Wilde was enthusiastic, strolling around the exhibits almost every day. He wrote that the English visitors, seeing him 'so happy and well dressed', were most depressed at the sight.

In July, the actor-manager Sir George Alexander, compensating for his former behaviour, arrived in Paris to discuss making voluntary payments to Wilde for any future productions of his plays.

On October 25th 'Mr and Mrs Daventry', the play for which Wilde had sketched the scenario, opened at the Royalty Theatre in London.

The play itself had been written by Frank Harris, (who had been understandably annoyed to discover that Oscar already had sold the outline to a long list of trusting purchasers, including Leonard Smithers, George Alexander, Herbert Beerbohm Tree, Ada Rehan, Louise Nethersole, Mrs Cora Brown-Potter, and an agent called Horace Sedger. Harris was forced to buy back the rights.)

'Daventry' starred Mrs Pat Campbell, Fred Kerr, and George du Maurier's son, Gerald du Maurier. The critics reacted badly, Clement Scott describing it as 'the drama of the dustbin'. However, the rumours circulating that the play was really by Wilde produced enough notoriety to secure a box office success and the production ran till February 23rd 1901. Bernard Shaw was not deceived: 'If Oscar had written it, it would now be a classic'.

FRANK HARRIS 1856-1931

Wilde: 'Frank Harris has no feelings. It is the secret of his success just as the fact that he thinks other people have none either is the secret of the failure that lies in wait for him somewhere on the way through life.' Despite this chilly, if accurate, prediction, and their huge differences in character and background, Oscar enjoyed Harris's company.

After they had been introduced at one of *Lady St Helier's* parties, initially Harris had been cautious about Wilde, but by 1891 the two men were close allies. He admired Oscar's wit and his 'gift of enthusiastic admiration', while Wilde felt refreshed by Harris's fearlessly buccaneering mentality.

Wilde: 'Frank is comic really. Fancy a jeremiad preached by a man in a fur coat. But he's really kind and fights for his friends. Sympathy is a sort of religion with him'.

It was this quality that came to the fore during Wilde's downfall. Before the first trial began, Harris, (accompanied by *Bernard Shaw*), met Oscar at the Café Royal, where he accurately explained the probable outcome of Oscar's actions, and suggested immediate flight to France.

Harris was not deterred when Wilde ignored his excellent advice. When Oscar was out on bail prior to his last trial, Harris tried to save him again. In an effort to persuade him to flee, Harris took him for a walk on Parliament Hill, Hampstead Heath, to ponder the benefits of freedom. Harris: 'The beauty of the view from the Heath seemed to revive him'.

On a more practical level, he moored a borrowed yacht at Erith in Kent, and placed it at Wilde's disposal. Oscar, however, refused to take advantage of the escape plan: "Frank has the mind of a schoolboy's annual. I think he rather wanted to hoist the flag of the skull and crossbones above it".

Although he had prophesied the trial verdict correctly, Harris was still shocked by the savagery of the public reaction to the case. Harris: "The hatred shown to Oscar Wilde taught me for the first time what Shakespeare meant when he spoke of this 'all-hating world'." He was one of the few people to visit Wilde in Reading Jail.

After Wilde's release, they continued to meet regularly and in 1898 Harris arranged for Oscar to stay on the French Riviera. Admittedly Wilde now found Harris's companionship rather tiring: 'Frank insists on my being always at high intellectual pressure. It is most exhausting. I am going to break the news to him that I have softening of the brain, and cannot always be a genius'.

In 1899, Wilde dedicated the published edition of 'An Ideal Husband': 'To Frank Harris, a slight tribute to his power and distinction as an artist, his chivalry and nobility as a friend'. When Harris read of Oscar's death he wrote: 'The world went greyer to me'.

Frank Harris, although short sighted and only 5ft 5ins tall, was a powerfully muscular man and possessed a voice that could shatter brass. Bernard Shaw: 'The trouble with Frank was his appalling and ruthless candour delivered in a voice which filled the largest theatres and dominated the noisiest dinner parties'.

Described by *Elizabeth Robins* as 'bumptious and conceited but somehow interesting' and by Vernon Lee as 'a strange sort of cad of genius', Harris cut a swathe of embarrassment through London society. When he announced that: "There is not a great house in London at which I have not dined", Wilde murmured: "Yes, Frank – but only once".

Harris also had a dominating personality that left witnesses breathless. Wilde said that at Harris's lunch parties: 'the remains of the guests were taken away with the debris of the feast'. For all his abounding self-confidence though, it was easy to spot the raffish adventurer beneath. Once, as he boasted of his schooldays at Rugby, someone noticed that he was wearing an Old Etonian tie.

He had, in fact, been at neither establishment. Born in Galway, Ireland, to Welsh-Jewish parents, he had attended a boarding school at Denbigh in North Wales. In 1871, aged fifteen, he ran away and joined a ship bound for America.

In New York, he supported himself first as a street shoeblack, then as a 'sandhog' building the foundations of the Brooklyn Bridge. Moving on to Chicago, he became a hotel clerk. (He recalled an incident from this experience when later he was challenged to define 'tact'. One of the hotel waiters once entered a female guest's bathroom and accidentally found the lady naked. Backing out, he apologised: "Excuse me, sir". Harris: " 'Sir' – now that's tact!")

He travelled on into the West, where he met Wild Bill Hickok, became a cowboy, and participated in a rustling raid into Mexico. On the return journey his party was attacked, firstly by irate Mexicans, and then by a Red Indian war party. Harris said that he managed to break away from the battle and, after riding for five nights to Fort Dodge, brought the US cavalry to the rescue of his companions. (Critics dismissed this version of events as 'a blatant farrago of lies'.)

Nonetheless, Harris could claim he was 'the only cowboy-rustler who carried a copy of JS Mill's 'Political Economy' in his saddlebag.'

Tiring of cowboy life, in 1874 Harris settled in Lawrence, Kansas, where he attended university, and in 1875 bamboozled his way into being accepted as a lawyer at the Lawrence bar.

In 1876, he returned to Europe where he drifted for several years. During the Russo-Turkish War of 1878, he witnessed and sent newspaper reports of the Battle of Plevna, before attending and being expelled from the University of Heidelburg. (After he had knocked a fellow student unconscious in a fight, he was imprisoned in the university jail.) By 1881, he was living in Paris.

It was a tribute to Harris's indomitable bounce that, within three years and without the backing of contacts or wealth, he had risen from this dubious early life to become the most successful newspaper editor in London.

In 1884, through a mixture of bluff and bravado, (and possibly seducing the wife of the proprietor, Lord Folkestone), he was appointed as editor of the Evening News. He astutely decided to pitch the paper to appeal to the imagination of a fourteen-year-old boy, the mental age that he regarded as the norm of the British public.

Remembering that his own interests at fourteen were 'kissing and fighting', he virtually invented sex and violence sensationalism, raising the paper's circulation from 7,000 to 70,000 copies. However, after he had printed the sleazier details of the *Lady Colin Campbell* divorce case and involved the Evening News in a case of obscene libel, the directors decided to dispense with his services. Unfazed by the sacking, Harris joined the Fortnightly Review as the new editor.

In 1887, Harris married Mrs Edith Clayton, a wealthy widow who owned a house on Park Lane. His career reached its zenith when he was asked to stand as the prospective Tory Member of Parliament for Hackney. For a short period it seemed that all Harris had to do was to reach out to grasp the reins of office. Unfortunately that entailed patience and respectability, not his strong suits.

His wife proved to be a problem in that she suspected Frank of having a roving eye, (a not unreasonable misgiving). One of her methods of frustrating him was to deliberately choose a corner table in restaurants, so that Frank would be forced to face two blank walls rather than letting his gaze wander to the nearest pretty girl. (For once, Harris was blameless, as his myopia and vain refusal to wear spectacles meant that, rather than seeing pretty girls, all he saw was a blur.)

This curtailment of his normal freedom, combined with the strain of having to pretend to be a high-principled parliamentarian, created a state of seething rebellion in the volatile Harris. Finally the cauldron of his resentment overflowed. At a reception, he picked on a demure young lady and loudly proceeded to discuss prostitution with her. Spotting a bishop wearing gaiters, he trumpeted across the company: "Tell me, Bishop, did Jesus Christ wear gaiters?" His wife Edith burst into tears and fled.

While lunching at the Savile Club, Harris gazed around the members and suddenly bellowed: "I suppose that one cannot expect in this assembly of faded prigs to find a glass of good wine".

His final act of political self-destruction occurred during the *Charles Parnell* and Kitty O'Shea sex scandal of 1892. While at a Tory dinner, he became intensely irritated by the tide of anti-Parnell condemnation that he heard on all sides. Having drunk a considerable amount of brandy, Frank let rip.

Smashing his huge fist down on the table, he roared: "What's wrong with Kitty O'Shea? She's a woman, and she has a lover! Like a lot of other women I know!" Downing his remaining brandy in one gulp, he barged his way out of the dumbstruck gathering. Still raging, he went on to Hackney where he delivered a violently pro-Parnell speech to a political meeting: "I am not fighting under the flag of Kitty O'Shea's petticoats. I am fighting under the flag of adult common sense".

This was the final straw. His invitation to represent the Tory Party was withdrawn, his wife separated from him and, after he had published an article advocating anarchism in the deeply conservative Fortnightly Review, he lost his job as editor.

With his usual resilience, Harris rebounded to become the owner and editor of the Saturday Review, (having borrowed the necessary cash from the author of 'Charley's Aunt', Brandon Thomas). Having sacked the existing staff, he appointed *Bernard Shaw* as the new drama critic, *Robert Cunningham-Graham* to write travel sketches, *Max Beerbohm* as satirist, HG Wells as the book reviewer, and Thomas Hardy, Joseph Conrad, and *Rudyard Kipling* to write poems and short stories. This policy turned the Saturday Review into possibly the best magazine ever produced in London.

Aside from its spectacular literary scope, Harris also used the journal to investigate current affairs. He personally travelled to South Africa to report on the Jameson Raid of 1896, and his exposure of Cecil Rhodes's bogus claims created a sensation.

While in the region, Harris took a trip north to see the Victoria Falls. One night, an African tribe visited his campsite and Harris was intrigued to see an almost-white half-breed girl amongst their number. Years later, Harris infuriated the explorer – and rescuer of Dr Livingstone – HM Stanley, when he suggested that Stanley must have tracked Livingstone via a trail of partly white offspring left in the distinguished missionary's wake. Harris: "Stanley had no sense of humour and seemed to resent the imputation".

In 1898, Harris sold the Saturday Review for £20,000 and invested the sum in two hotels on the French Riviera. This proved to be a disastrous move and by 1900, Harris was living in very reduced circumstances.

He spent the next fifteen years in London running small magazines, indulging in petty swindles, and promoting suspect financial schemes. His editorial offices were enlivened by repeated scenes of bailiffs breaking down the front door, while Harris lowered his most valued possessions to safety by rope from a rear window.

When Harris was reduced to editing a staid journal called 'Hearth and Home', *Bernard Shaw* was highly amused to watch Harris having to deal with the strait-laced spinsters who were his main contributors. When one such lady arrived at the office, she was met by a glowering Harris, bawling: 'There's only one use for a woman! Get out of here before I show you!"

On another occasion he was able to get the better of even such an experienced hustler as Horatio Bottomley. Soon after Bottomley had attacked a famous man in his newspaper 'John Bull', Harris noticed the same man leaving Bottomley's house. He immediately demanded that Bottomley pay him £500 or 'he would tell all'. Bottomley paid up, then asked Harris how he knew. Harris pocketed the money and smiled: "I didn't".

In 1914, while editing a gossip magazine called 'Modern Society', Harris printed some scurrilous remarks about a court case that was still in progress and therefore sub judice. He was outraged when he was sentenced to three weeks in prison for the offence.

In the same year, his position in England became untenable when he came into possession of some very revealing correspondence between the late King Edward VII and his sometime lover, Daisy, Countess of Warwick. He helped Daisy in her successful plot to blackmail the Palace by threatening to publish these incriminating documents, while trying to blackmail her in turn for a cut of the proceeds.

Finally bankrupt, he left England in 1915 and went to the USA, where he publicly supported Germany during World War One, writing a series of what were regarded as treasonable articles attacking the English aristocracy for their decadent indulgence of 'bed and board'. (This was seen as a bit rich coming from Frank Harris). Neither were the American plutocrats pleased to learn that they were 'a class plundering a nation'. In 1919, Harris left for France, where he settled in Nice.

Throughout his roller coaster of fortune, Harris had remained a deeply committed lover of literature, in particular of the works of Shakespeare. *Bernard Shaw*: 'It is hardly an exaggeration to say that he ultimately quarrelled with everybody but Shakespeare'.

Once at the Café Royal he had been asked his opinion of homosexuality. He announced deafeningly: "Homosexuality! No, I know nothing of the joys of homosexuality. My friend Oscar can no doubt tell you all about that. But I must say that, if Shakespeare had asked me, I should have had to submit". (A gleeful Max Beerbohm seized on the remark and drew a cartoon of a naked Frank Harris peeping coyly over his shoulder at the horrified Bard of Avon.)

Wilde himself suggested that Harris should write on a book on the subject: "Fancy a western cowboy teaching Oxford how to discover new beauties in Shakespeare". In 1899, he witnessed the result of his advice: 'Frank Harris is upstairs, thinking about Shakespeare at the top of his voice'.

In 1910, Harris finally produced his work 'The Man Shakespeare' and received generally good reviews. Encouraged by this reception, he then wrote 'The Life of Oscar Wilde', which Shaw called 'the best literary portrait of Wilde in existence'.

When he was accused of inventing much of the dialogue for this biography, Harris snarled: "Any damned son of a bitch can put down what he's heard. I'm an artist, not a reporter". (He often came under attack for his cavalier approach to veracity. When Max Beerbohm was asked if Harris had ever been known to tell the truth, Max replied: "Sometimes – when his invention flagged".)

The Wilde book was successful in the USA, but was excoriated as a travesty by Wilde's friends *Robbie Ross* and *Robert Sherard*. Oscar Wilde's niece Dolly said that Harris's prose style reminded her of 'a broken ashtray full of chewed up and badly-smelling cigar ends'.

Bosie Douglas, whom Harris had accused of leading Oscar into homosexual excess and then abandoning him, was livid with fury and his threat of legal action prevented the book's publication in Britain. (In a more reflective moment, he also said of Harris's book that: 'I think Harris makes Oscar out much too soft and weak. He really wasn't like that. He had a ferocious will about many things.')

From his base in Nice, the poverty-stricken Harris decided to make money by writing an explicit account of his intimate sex life entitled 'My Life and Loves'. He defended his book by saying that no autobiography could be honest unless it dealt with the subject's sexual life. He undermined this reasonable assertion by including nude photos of professional models in the first edition.

The reaction to what was seen as pure pornography out-moralised any previous response to Harris's escapades. The Nice police raided his house in a search for more pornography, while his US agent was arrested.

Harris certainly had a great deal of experience from which to compose his memoirs. Women had always been attracted to his energetic and demanding character. One anonymous female friend explained: 'His great voice penetrated your personality, vibrated inside you, and his boldness, the swift stroke towards the very heart of you, got you in its grip, and from then on you were hypnotised and there wasn't much choice'.

Harris claimed to have discovered sex at an early age. He wrote that in 1890: 'I had dinner with George Meredith, *Walter Pater* and Oscar Wilde in Park Lane and we talked about the age of sex awakening. Pater thought it began about 13 or 14 and Wilde to my amazement set it at 16. Only Meredith put it earlier. I told them it was 4'. He later added that by the age of 12 virtually all boys and girls had discovered masturbation.

Shocked by the rampant homosexuality he found in the English boarding schools, he plunged into a series of childhood sexual experiences with what appeared to be, (from his writing), a series of complacent young ladies. He went on to detail over seventy carnal encounters with a cast of innkeepers' daughters, maids, artists' models, café-dancers, governesses, etc.

He was inhibited by an initial racism until a black American girl opened his eyes to the possibilities of international sex: 'I am glad of it, for else I might have closed my heart against the Hindu and so missed the best part of life's experiences'.

After his disastrous dalliance with respectability with his first wife Edith, in 1898 he married a beautiful young woman named Helen 'Nellie' O'Hara. He remained with Nellie for the rest of his life, faithful in spirit if not in body. Harris: 'A man's character is supplied by the nature of the woman he really loves'.

Probably his most spectacular exploits occurred at his French Riviera hotels, when he organised orgies for his friends and local girls. (In the interests of work, he restricted these events to Wednesdays and Sundays only). He introduced one game based on 'Musical Chairs' that consisted of plying his guests with drink, then stationing a girl at a gramophone while the rest of the party danced. Whenever the girl stopped the music, everyone had to remove a piece of clothing before changing partners. Eventually, when there was no clothing left to remove, the party was left to develop as it might.

Things took a more serious turn as he encouraged his Italian gardener-pimp to invite younger girls to indulge his 'liking for the immature'. The ensuing nude 'beauty contests' were judged by Harris and his friends. Bosie Douglas later claimed that Harris was nearly lynched by the outraged local population.

Throughout his encounters, Harris denied any wrongdoing: 'Rape is almost unthinkable to me. I always prefer to leave a good deal to the initiative of the woman'. In his many dealings with women, he combined rapacity and reverence: 'There are some women nobler than men and thank God I have met one or two of them that have heightened my estimate of the possibilities of human goodness.'

Harris spent his last years with Nellie in Nice. One brilliantly sunny Riviera day, shortly before his death aged 75, he was sitting with her on the promenade when a resplendent young blonde in a revealing swimsuit sauntered past. Harris's rheumy eyes popped open and he gave an inaudible whisper. Nellie asked him what he had said. Fixing a stare of infinite sadness on the horizon, he sank back into his chair and breathed: "Nothing – nothing".

MRS PATRICK CAMPBELL 1865-1940

Wilde had long admired the star of 'Daventry', Mrs Patrick Campbell. In 1893, he introduced her to the artist *Aubrey Beardsley*, and Beardsley's resulting portrait of the actress adorned Oscar's wall at Tite Street. Although never closely connected to the Wilde set, she breezily dismissed the uproar over homosexuality in a famous line: "I don't care what people do, as long as they don't do it in the street and frighten the horses".

(Years later, in 1908, Mrs Pat performed in Wilde's play 'The Florentine Tragedy', but decided against playing 'Salome'.)

Born Beatrice Stella Tanner to Anglo-Italian parents, she grew up in genteel but reduced circumstances in Dulwich, London. It was a world she found intensely boring, ("Is your mother entertaining this Season, Beatrice?" "No, not very.")

In 1884, aged 19, she married Patrick Campbell, only a year older than herself and with no appreciable income. After the birth of their two children, Alan (nicknamed 'Beloved One' or 'Beo' for short) and Stella, the pleasant but hapless Patrick decided to leave for South Africa to try to build the family fortune.

Mrs Pat, driven by ambition and necessity, poured her energies into a stage career. At first, it was a desperately unglamorous life. One manager instructed her to sit for some publicity photographs. She arrived at the studio where she met a Cockney photographer called Mr Downey. Mrs Pat: "I had got into the position and the expression that I wanted when Mr. Downey announced: "Right, darlin'. Look 'appy, fink of 'im and don't spit".'

Bernard Shaw later said that Mrs Pat was not a professional actress, but an inspired amateur. This natural gift, combined with her 'wind in the chimney' voice, was enough to create a sensation when she triumphed in Sir Arthur Pinero's plays, 'The Second Mrs Tanqueray' (1893), and 'The Notorious Mrs Ebbsmith' (1895), and also in *Maeterlinck's* 'Pelléas et Mélesande' in 1898.

Her success gave her an introduction to the country house elite of 'The Souls', where she became a particular friend of *George Wyndham* and his wife Sybil. This social elevation did not endear her to the theatrical world where she was known as 'the queen of snobs'.

When the still financially floundering Patrick returned home on a visit in 1894, he was bewildered to find that his young wife was now a major London celebrity. Mrs Pat also found the situation awkward: 'Patrick and I were lunching at a smart restaurant when Oscar Wilde passed. I introduced them. "Your husband, Mrs. Campbell? How dreadfully suburban".'

Patrick returned to Africa, leaving the field free for Mrs Pat to acquire a string of well-publicised lovers, including her theatrical co-stars, *Johnson Forbe-Robertson* and Gerald Du Maurier, (and possibly even the portly financier Horatio Bottomley).

News of her entanglements reached South Africa, where Patrick had enlisted in the British forces during the Boer War. Mrs Pat: 'One night, around the campfire, all the soldiers were reading their letters from home and one of them held up an illustrated paper with my photograph in it. "Sergeant Campbell, I don't suppose this actress is any relation of yours, eh, ha ha?" Pat did not look up. He just muttered: "She's my wife". The whole mess grew silent.' Patrick was shot dead in battle soon afterwards.

In 1901, Mrs Pat arrived in New York where, aided by the efforts of a press agent named A. Toxen Worm, (Mrs Pat: "I refused to believe it"), she had a resounding success playing 'Hedda Gabler'. She became the darling of American society and was made guest of honour at innumerable dinner parties.

Her fellow diners were not always to her taste. Mrs Pat: 'At one party I was seated next to an elderly scientist who droned on endlessly about ants. "They are wonderful little creatures, Mrs. Campbell. They have their own police force and they have their own army". I couldn't stand it any longer. "No navy, I suppose?" '

She met her match one night when she was assigned to accompany an inoffensive-looking little man into dinner. Mischievously, she gazed down with her most languorous 'come-to-bed' stare and gurgled: "Tell me, which would you prefer? To love passionately or to be loved passionately?" The little man fingered his tie, cleared his throat, and then replied: "Well, I guess I'd rather be a canary". To which, Mrs Pat admitted, there was no answer.

As her career ballooned, so did her self-esteem. *WB Yeats* complained that she had 'an ego like a raging toothache'. After he had directed one fraught play rehearsal with her, she snapped at him: "What are you thinking?" He took a deep breath and replied: "I'm thinking of the master of a wayside Indian railway station who sent a message to his Company's headquarters saying – 'Tigress on the line: Wire instructions'."

During rehearsals for another play, the long-suffering author shouted up at her: "Really, Mrs Campbell, you seem to have lost your memory!" Glaring back, she rasped: "Indeed! Looking at the jokes in your script, you don't seem to have lost yours".

Her acid tongue extended to other members of the cast. When she heard that a rival was suffering from housemaid's knee, she replied: "Oh, really. I always thought she had two". She had an equally dismissive attitude to her many fans. When one of them sent her what she considered to be a 'hideous' vase inscribed with the words 'Made in Bulgaria', she hurled it over her shoulder muttering: "Smashed in Belgravia."

In spite of Bernard Shaw's earlier description: 'Mrs. Pat resembles a rather attractive bullfinch', when he actually met her, he was entranced. Baffled by his late-flowering experience of sexual desire, he admitted: 'I haven't been quite the same man since'.

Whether they actually consummated their attraction was left in doubt, and Mrs Pat soon jilted the uncharacteristically agitated Shaw. He gave up his quest with a majestically wounded diatribe: 'Go then; the Shavian oxygen burns up your little lungs; seek some stuffiness that suits you.' (He later used the incident as the basis for his play 'The Applecart', in which Mrs Pat was recognisably the character 'Orinthia')

In 1914, Shaw overlooked this tiff when he cast Mrs Pat as 'Eliza Doolittle' in his play 'Pygmalion'. The combined egos and demands of Mrs Pat, Shaw, and Beerbohm Tree, (playing 'Professor Higgins'), produced a rehearsal period of legendary discord. Later, when she decided to write her memoirs, Shaw was horrified to find that she meant to include intimate sections of his love letters: 'The divorce court is not worse than you playing Lady Godiva with me as the horse'. The letters were finally published in their entirety in 1952.

Meanwhile, in 1912 Mrs Pat married for a second time, after seducing the young man-about-town *George Cornwallis-West* away from his wife *Lady Jennie Churchill*. Mrs Pat remarked that she appreciated: 'the deep, deep peace of the double bed after the hurly-burly of the chaise longue'. While the bed may have been peaceful, the marriage wasn't, and George abandoned her in 1920.

As her career declined in the 1920s, ("London wants flappers and I can't flap"), and her once sylph-like figure expanded into obesity, she courageously fought on. Now employed in more humble venues, at least she was able to meet some of the rising young stars such as the black singer Paul Robeson, (whom she predicted correctly would one day play 'Othello'), and the English actor John Gielgud.

When she performed with Gielgud in Ibsen's 'Ghosts', he reported that she was 'beguiling, casual, wayward, petulant, disagreeable – but glamorous'. (Oscar Wilde had been a friend of Gielgud's grandparents, Aniela and Adam, after they had emigrated from Poland to England in the 1860s).

In the 1930s, Mrs Pat, now in her late sixties, arrived in Hollywood intent on a new career in films. She was asked to fill out a studio publicity form, detailing name, height, colour of eyes and hair, etc. In answer to the question 'Experience?' she wrote 'King Edward VII'.

Unfortunately, her sense of mischief ran away with her. Her main trick when being introduced to world-famous film stars was to pretend to have no idea who they were. The American critic Alexander Walcott despaired of her 'unwavering and ingenious rudeness to everyone there who could possibly have been of assistance to her. She was like a sinking ship firing on her rescuers'.

Her Hollywood screen test proved her downfall. Aged almost 70, she played the 14-year-old Juliet in Shakespeare's balcony scene. On seeing the test, she ruefully agreed that: 'I looked more like Mussolini's mother'.

She finally retired to the resort town of Pau in the French Pyrenees where she died in 1940 aged 75.

Back in the days of her triumphs, on the first night of 'Pygmalion', an actor called Philip Merrivale was waiting for his cue in the theatre wings. A stagehand beside him gazed out at Mrs Pat on stage and whispered: "That there Patrick Campbell, he was a lucky man".

Merrivale nodded: "Yes, she's still a handsome woman". The stagehand shook his head: "No, no, I don't mean that. What I mean is, he got himself killed in the Boer War".

Mrs Pat's co-star in 'Mr and Mrs Daventry' was **FRED KERR** (1858-1933). *Frank Harris* had made it a condition that Kerr, who he regarded as 'one of the best character actors on the English stage', should play the role of 'Mr Daventry'. After sixty nights, to Harris's annoyance, Mrs Pat got rid of Kerr – 'and so spoilt the whole cast'.

Fred Kerr went on to become a veteran actor in both theatre and cinema. His experiences ranged from being manager of the Vaudeville Theatre, London, in 1895, through a considerable film career playing support roles in 'Raffles' (1930) and 'Waterloo Road' (1931), to fathering a theatrical dynasty, (his grandson John Kerr starred in the Hollywood film of the musical 'South Pacific').

In 1931, he published his highly entertaining reminiscences, ('Recollections of a Defective Memory'), among which he described his experiences with various theatrical types of the 1890s.

When he was playing in 'Camille' on tour in Leeds, the company hired a local extra to take the tiny role of the footman who announces the arrival of 'Mademoiselle Camille and Monsieur the Comte de Varville'. The man they hired happened to despise all actors on principle.

On the opening night, the extra arrived on stage, gave Kerr a glare of surly resentment, and announced: "Mad Mossel Camel and Moosoo the Condy Var Vil". Kerr, following the script, replied: "Who?" The extra snarled: "You 'eard" and made his exit.

Kerr also played at Toole's Theatre next door to the Charing Cross Hospital in London. The stage door keeper was a taciturn old man who rarely spoke to anybody. One evening Kerr tried to engage him in conversation, remarking that he must find it dull sitting alone all day.

The old doorman shook his head and answered with relish: 'No, it's a lively place. I sits 'ere mornin', noon and night. I sees 'em took in that hospital next door, I 'ears 'em a'ollerin' and a'shriekin' when the knife goes in. Sometimes they comes out, sometimes they doesn't. It's a lively place.' It was the only remark Kerr ever heard him make.

When the well-known Victorian actor Sir John Hare retired, Kerr inherited his dresser. The dresser had been with Sir John for decades and regarded himself as integral to Hare's success. One day, he extracted a decrepit pair of trousers from a laundry basket and waved them at Kerr, crying rapturously: "That's what we wore as Lear!"

Kerr also attended many dinners at the invitation of the City of London livery companies. He reported attending one dinner at the 'Leathersellers Company' where the speaker was an elderly colonel. Kerr: 'I could not tell whether the colonel had a keen sense of humour or no humour at all'.

Kerr was particularly baffled at one extract from the colonel's speech. "Ladies and gentlemen, whenever I find myself dining with the Leathersellers Company, I am always reminded of my poor dear father, who has been dead and gone for many years. When I was a boy, he used to say to me, 'Alfred, my son, whenever you find yourself in any position of doubt or perplexity, whenever you are unable to distinguish between right and wrong, pause and ask yourself the question. What would the Leathersellers Company have done under similar circumstances?"

Perhaps the story that Kerr treasured most was one that he heard from a journalist friend who had been to visit Madame Tussaud's Waxwork Museum during the First World War. Looking for a story, the journalist asked the Museum's laundress whether the waxworks wore underclothes. She replied anxiously: "Well, as a matter of fact they don't. But I'd rather you didn't make it public, because nobody knows except me – and a few Australian soldiers".

Meanwhile, Oscar had settled back into life in Paris. His hotel proprietor, Jean Dupoirier, reported that Oscar's daily routine rarely altered – at noon, a late breakfast of mutton chop and two hard-boiled eggs, then a period of reading, then a trip to the cafes, returning home at two or three am.

Oscar's alcoholism was causing more concern among his friends. Frank Harris reported that he was now drinking spirits between meals as well as wine with them. When Robert Ross took Oscar out driving in a cab, Oscar insisted on stopping at café after café for shots of absinthe. His main drinking cronies during August were the poet Jean Moreas and the journalist Ernest La Jeunesse.

By September 1900, Wilde was partly bedridden and under medical supervision. Oscar: "I only care to see doctors when I am in perfect health; then they comfort one, but when one is ill they are most depressing".

On the advice of Dr Tucker of the British Embassy, on October 10th, Wilde underwent an operation to relieve the pain in his right ear, (the result of the fall in Wandsworth Prison that had not been treated properly at the time.) He recovered in his hotel room, where he received visits from his brother's widow Lily Wilde and her new husband Texeira de Mattos.

He also sent a telegram begging his old friends Robbie Ross and Reggie Turner to visit him. Reggie arrived on October 16th and Robbie on the 17th.

ROBERT ROSS (Second Part – cont. from page 212)

When Wilde had been finally convicted in 1895, the situation also seemed fairly bleak for Ross. He was reported by several newspapers to have been in Oscar's company during the arrest. As a result, he was forced to resign from his London clubs, including the Savile.

While in France in 1895, he attempted to raise the money needed to stave off Wilde's bankruptcy but failed by a margin of £400. Then, in an act of remarkable bravery, he ignored the danger of arrest and returned to London to attend Wilde's bankruptcy hearings on 25th September 1895.

While Ross waited in the court corridor, Oscar was led past in convict dress and handcuffed. As Oscar later wrote: 'before the whole gaping crowd, whom an action so sweet and simple hushed into silence, he gravely raised his hat to me'.

Soon afterwards, Ross became seriously ill and had to have a kidney removed; (the operation was carried out by Sir Frederick Treves of 'Elephant Man' fame). Although Ross was despised by society in general, several influential people admired his behaviour. *Wilfred Blunt*: 'Ross is a good honest fellow as far as I can judge, and stood by Oscar when all had abandoned him'. *Sir Edmund Gosse* called Ross's actions 'quixotic and silly, but honourable' and found him employment with the Society of Authors.

In 1897, when Wilde emerged from prison, Ross was there to meet him in Dieppe. For a short time Oscar was interested in aliases and wrote: 'I am staying here as 'Sebastian Melmoth' – I have thought it better that Robbie should stay here under the name of 'Reginald Turner' and Reggie under the name of 'Robert Ross'.'

Ross said that throughout Oscar's remaining years he felt a sense of responsibility for him, 'like an adopted prodigal baby'. He realised that Oscar's best interests lay in a reunion with his wife Constance Wilde and, when instead Oscar took up again with Bosie Douglas, it caused a partial rift with Ross that lasted for two years.

Whatever temporary estrangement might have occurred, Ross always respected Wilde: 'Among the fine qualities Oscar showed in his later years was that he never blamed anyone but himself for his own disasters. He never bore any ill will to anybody, and in a characteristic way was really surprised that anyone should bear any resentment against him'.

Overcoming his irritation, Ross again saw Oscar in Paris in 1900. Wilde nicknamed him Saint Robert of Philimore, (after Ross's home area in Kensington, London), and in April wrote: 'Do you observe that I have fallen in love with you again? Our Indian winter.'

Oscar: "Natures like his are not found twice in a lifetime".

[See Robert Ross – Third Part – Page 495]

In all, Wilde stayed intermittently at the Hotel d'Alsace-Lorraine for sixteen months. Oscar described the place as 'a poor little Bohemian hotel' in which he was fighting a duel to the death with the wallpaper – "One or the other of us has to go".

However, he was exceptionally lucky in having Jean Dupoirier as his proprietor. Dupoirier ignored the non-payment of rent and supplied both necessities and luxuries, including champagne, out of his own pocket. By Wilde's death, Dupoirier was owed over £190.

When asked why he allowed so much credit, Dupoirier replied: "Well, you know, in those days, people never paid regularly, and then, besides, the gentleman was ill. He was confined to bed for six months. I couldn't throw him into the street".

Robbie Ross said of him: "I can scarcely speak in moderation of the magnanimity, humanity and charity of Dupoirier", and in 1901 Oscar's friends clubbed together to pay off the debt.

Years later, Dupoirier was still proud of his guest. He showed a visitor Oscar's false teeth that he had kept as a souvenir, and, when on a minor charge in 1910, he announced to the court that: 'the great poet Oscar Wilde was once my lodger'. An unimpressed judge replied: "There is no need to boast about it".

Wilde was now almost bedridden, but on October 29th he insisted that Ross took him out to a café. When he ordered absinthe, Ross warned that it might kill him. Oscar answered: "And what have I to live for, Robbie?"

Wilde's thoughts began to dwell on mortality. His comments ranged from the morbid: 'The drama has lasted too long', to the magnificent: 'Robbie, when we are dead and buried in our porphyry tombs, and the trumpet of the Last Judgement is sounded, I shall turn and whisper to you, Robbie, Robbie, let us pretend we do not hear it'.

On October 30th Wilde and Ross went for a carriage ride in the Bois de Boulogne, but returned to the hotel when Oscar complained of giddiness. He was in great pain from an abscess that had formed on his ear.

Ross, not realising how serious Wilde's condition had become, left for a holiday on the French Riviera on November 12th. Reggie Turner took over the nursing duties.

Oscar continued to brood on impending death. When, in a particularly dark mood, he whispered to Turner: "Last night I dreamt that I was dining with the dead", Reggie cheered him up enormously by chirpily replying: "My dear Oscar, you were probably the life and soul of the party".

Oscar himself continued the atmosphere of deathbed banter when he overheard his doctors surmising gloomily about the possibility of receiving their fees from their impecunious patient. He failed to reassure them: "Gentlemen, I am afraid that I am dying, as I have lived, beyond my means".

In response to a anxious telegram from Turner, Robbie Ross returned to Paris on November 29th. He found that Reggie had become 'a perfect wreck' as the result of two weeks of constant attendance and sleepless nights.

Now realising that the end was very close, the strongly Catholic Ross went in search of a priest and returned with a Father Cuthbert Dunne. Dunne asked Oscar whether he wished to convert to the faith. Unable to speak, Oscar gestured with his hand. Assuming consent, Dunne received him into the Catholic Church and rapidly gave him conditional baptism, absolution and anointment.

Ross commented: 'He was never able to speak and we do not know whether he was altogether conscious'. Later Ross was troubled by the thought that what they had thought was Oscar's gesture of assent might really have been Oscar trying to find his cigarettes.

Then, on November 30th 1900 at 5.30am, Wilde's condition worsened considerably. Blood and foam trickled from his mouth throughout the morning.

At 1.50pm, in Turner's words: 'Robbie and I went together to the head of the bed. Oscar was breathing quite regularly and quietly: suddenly he exhaled a long, deep breath, and then nothing more; silence absolute. I said to Robbie in awe: "He's dead," and Robbie nodded his head. That was all'.

There has been much conjecture over the cause of death, with a strong case being put forward for tertiary syphilis. The main body of medical opinion though has swung towards cerebral meningitis, caused by infection of Wilde's right ear.

Ross later told Frank Harris that, as he and Reggie sat by the body: "there was a loud explosion and mucus poured from every orifice of the body – even the bedding had to be burned". (When Augustus John heard about this, he enthused: "What a brilliant idea! What a perfect exit!")

Harris assumed that this reaction must have been caused by a build-up of absinthe in the body. Reggie Turner, on the other hand, said that nothing of the sort happened and that: "The whole scene was an invention of Robbie's".

On December 2nd Bosie Douglas arrived in Paris and the following day acted as chief mourner at Wilde's funeral. The service was conducted in part by Father Dunne at the church of St-Germain-des-Pres on the rue Bonaparte.

The funeral party, including Robert Ross, Reggie Turner, Jean Dupoirier, Maurice Gilbert, Ernest La Jeunesse, and Pierre Louys, then travelled by carriage to Bagneux Cemetery, about four miles from Paris, where Oscar's coffin was buried.

Ross: 'Oscar was very unhappy and would have become more unhappy as time went on. Apart from personal affection, the terrible commonplace, 'It was for the best', is really true in his case'.

The international press generally reacted to the news in unsurprising fashion, one Canadian paper editorialising that: 'He was convicted of a nameless crime and all those who had known him tried to blot out his memory from their minds forever'.

PART FIVE

EPILOGUE

Robert Ross to Vyvyan Holland

The three most conspicuous mourners at Wilde's funeral – Reggie Turner, Robbie Ross, and Bosie Douglas – left Bagneux cemetery to continue lives that remained influenced by Oscar's unforgettable shadow.

REGGIE TURNER (Second Part – cont. from page 360)

As a known associate of Wilde, Reggie Turner spent much of 1895-7 out of harm's way in France. He was present at Dieppe to greet Oscar on his release but thereafter, as he was dependent on handouts from his rich family, he tended to avoid Oscar's compromising company. Wilde complained: 'It's ages since I saw Reggie'.

Instead, Turner occupied his time with occasional legal work and by writing the 'London Day By Day' column for his family's newspaper, the Daily Telegraph. In February 1900, he became involved in a bizarre incident involving the Boer War.

When news of the Relief of Ladysmith arrived in London, Reggie and Bosie Douglas celebrated the event long into the night. In the early hours they announced that they were volunteering for the front but, as the dawn air sobered him, Reggie decided that the better part of valour was to remain at the Daily Telegraph. (Bosie actually did apply but was informed brusquely that the British Army could cope without him).

Wilde wrote to Reggie: 'I hear you volunteered for the front at 5am at the Cecil Hotel, intoxicated by Bosie and Perrier-Jouet '89, but subsequently felt that duty called you to stay in the Fleet Street kopje. Quite right – the pen is more dangerous than the sword'.

Turner still dabbled in the homosexual underworld – Wilde once called him 'the boy-snatcher of Clement's Inn' – and in June 1900 was lucky to survive a court case over homosexuality. He left his job at the Telegraph and removed himself to France where he was able to render assistance during Wilde's last illness. Reggie was saddened by Wilde's death: "Oscar was a great man – a very great man".

After 1900, he stayed on in France, mostly in Paris and Nice, before settling permanently in Florence, Italy, where he became a popular member of the expatriate British set. Aided by funds from his faithful half-brother Frank Lawson, (who left Reggie a legacy of £20,000 in his will), Turner abandoned the idea of regular work and settle down to write.

His efforts met with some mockery among the Anglo-Florence literati; his 'old maid' persona tempted some to claim that Reggie had exhausted his talent years previously under the nom de plume of 'Jane Austen'.

After he had published twelve novels that were greeted with almost total public indifference, Reggie laughingly admitted that his critics might be correct: "Other people's first editions are rare. With me it's the second editions that are rare; in fact they don't exist".

"My twelve novels have long since been pulped. There was one of them in a tramp steamer library plying between Brindisi and the Piraeus, so that when anyone told me they had read one of my novels I could always tell them where they had been. But the boat was sunk during the war and my sole surviving novel went down with the crew and passengers; I hope not before the reader had finished it".

After the First World War, Turner remained in Florence among his many friends, including the novelist DH Lawrence, (who shocked Reggie by reading him the first draft of 'Lady Chatterley's Lover'), and the writer Norman Douglas. (Reggie described Norman Douglas as 'a mixture of Roman emperor and Roman cab driver'. One of Turner's favourite stories concerned Douglas returning to a restaurant and asking in a loud voice: "Has anyone found a toothpick that tastes of ham?")

During the 1920s, Turner became a surprising fan of the Italian dictator Benito Mussolini, (Norman Douglas: "Reggie is doing very well and becoming very Fascist").

Previously Turner, deeply conscious of his Jewish roots, had been vehemently opposed to the anti-Semitism exposed by the infamous Dreyfus Affair.

However in 1929, his finances were threatened by the Wall Street Crash and, when Mussolini prevented the collapse of the Italian banks and returned 80% of deposits to account-holders, Turner was immensely impressed. Later, when he realised the scale of Hitler's antagonism to the Jews, he repented of his enthusiasm and attacked the Pope as a collaborator: 'He may be the Vicar of Christ but he's certainly the Vicar of Bray'.

Determined never to leave Florence, ('I am at home here, and I couldn't go to a strange place where I knew nobody – I am keeping that for Heaven'), Reggie perhaps was fortunate to die in 1938, before the looming storm of World War Two broke over his cosy world.

ROBERT ROSS (Third Part – cont. from page 490)

Troubled by the thought that his initial seduction of Wilde might have been the cause of the whole disaster, Robbie Ross determined to ensure that Oscar's estate was taken out of bankruptcy and that any future profits should accrue to his two children.

Disproving the Official Receiver's assurance in 1901 that Wilde's works were worthless, Ross spent the next six years settling claims and collecting copyrights until he managed to provide full payment, (plus 4% interest), thus discharging the bankruptcy. He also issued the abridged edition of 'De Profundis' and later published the first collected edition of Wilde's writings.

Ross found that, although Wilde's work was still largely ignored in Britain, it had become very popular in Europe, especially in Germany. The play 'Salome' was a runaway success and had been translated into eleven languages, including Yiddish, Greek, and Catalan. In 1901, Ross learnt to his surprise that 'The Soul of Man Under Socialism' was selling in four different languages in the bazaar at Nijni Novgorod, Russia. Ross commented: "It seems that Oscar's name is a household word wherever the English language is not spoken".

As Oscar's representative on earth, Ross also had to cope with persistent rumours that Oscar was still alive and had been spotted in a number of unlikely places. Ross: 'I have received 378 letters from different sources asking me if the reports are true'.

Years later, he made a return visit to the Hotel d'Alsace where he found that the new proprietor had decided to cash in on the notoriety of the famous guest and was now charging a franc to tour the establishment. Ross joined the tour 'out of curiosity and with three Americans and a German as companions'. He was intrigued by the new proprietor's account of Oscar's demise and Ross's own participation during the last days.

Ross: 'I have nothing to complain of in the narrative. He provided me with a halo, under the weight of which I still totter. I was given the undreamed honour of a title. I had become 'the Vicomte de Rosse'. We were then ushered into the wrong room and shown the wrong bed, in which 'le pauvre poete' had breathed his last. It was the best franc's worth I ever had'.

In 1908, as a mark of admiration for his efforts, Ross was given a testimonial dinner at the Ritz, London, attended by 200 guests. The mood was summed up by *Sir George Alexander* who told Ross: 'No one knows better than I do what a heroic role you have played in the Wilde drama, and what your unselfish devotion has done for his memory, and for his children'.

Ross not only provided the income and security for *Cyril* and *Vyvyan Wilde*, (now living under their assumed name of 'Holland'), but also the friendship and the introduction to society that they had been denied throughout their childhood years of exile and neglect by their official guardians.

(Vyvyan recounted one occasion when Ross took him to meet the famous writer HG Wells at his home in Church Row, Hampstead, in London. Before they arrived for dinner, Ross warned Vyvyan that Wells knew nothing about wine and on his last visit had offered Ross a bottle that had been corked. Ross: "I hadn't the heart to tell him as it was almost certainly the only bottle he had in the house and in any case I don't suppose he would have understood what I meant; so I had to drink a couple of glasses."

Vyvyan: 'When we arrived, HG announced: "I've got a treat for you, Robbie. You remember that wine you liked so much the last time you were here? Well, I wouldn't let anyone else have it and I have kept the rest of it for you." And he pointed proudly to the offending bottle standing on the mantelpiece and which was of course by this time the finest corked vinegar'.)

Aside from his involvement with the affairs of the Wilde family, Ross made his living as a proprietor of the Carfax art gallery, (which *Bosie Douglas* always referred to as 'Robbie's unsuccessful little picture shop'). He sold the Carfax in 1908, becoming art critic of the Morning Post until 1912, when he was appointed as an Inland Revenue advisor on picture evaluation for estate duty.

Ross's personal beliefs altered considerably when he lost faith in his previously devout Catholicism and veered towards atheism. Living in rented rooms at 40, Half Moon St, London, he practised an almost openly homosexual lifestyle; one long relationship was with a young actor called Freddie Smith.

In 1914, Ross's life came under considerable strain when Bosie Douglas launched a vicious personal campaign against him. The basic bone of contention was Wilde's letter written in jail called 'De Profundis'. Bosie had never seen the complete letter, and in fact had applauded the bowdlerised version that Ross released in 1905.

However, when a young writer, Arthur Ransome, (of 'Swallows and Amazons' fame), told Ross that he was writing a biography of Wilde, Ross allowed him to see a copy of the complete letter. On the basis of this new material, Ransome's book included pointed references to the part played by 'a young nobleman' in Wilde's downfall.

Bosie, annoyed at what Ransome had written, issued a writ for libel; under court rules he was able therefore to read the complete version of 'De Profundis'. If what Ransome had written had irritated him, what Wilde had written sent him into berserk fury. Searching for a culprit, Douglas rounded on Ross, describing him as 'a filthy bugger and unspeakable skunk' and threatening to horse-whip Ross 'to within an inch of his life'.

In an extraordinary scene, Douglas arrived at a society party, attended by the Prime Minister *HH Asquith* and his wife Margot, and immediately began to shout at Ross. Ross moved out of the room but was followed by a raging Bosie screaming abuse at him. One witness, (Hilaire Belloc's sister), said later that: "certain of the words which Lord Alfred shouted were quite unknown to me". Ross tried to hide behind a table, only to be pursued around it by Bosie. Eventually, Ross was hurried to safety by a 'livid' Margot Asquith, who took him back to No 10 Downing Street to recuperate.

When Ransome was found not guilty of libel, the vengeful Bosie, (abetted by a new associate and henchman, *TWH Crosland*), determined to ruin Ross. Using the same tactics that his father, the *Marquess of Queensberry*, had employed against Wilde twenty years earlier, Bosie and Crosland hired a private detective to spy on Ross's sex life, and then constantly goaded Ross by letter.

A typical Crosland missive read: 'For years past, you have succeeded in foisting Wilde on the public in the figure of a repentant saint, and incidentally you have obtained for yourself a literary credit thereby which would not otherwise have come your way. From my point of view, it is one dirty Sodomite bestowing lavish whitewash upon another.' They then went further by alleging that Ross had indulged in illegal acts with male prostitutes.

Goaded beyond endurance, in 1914 Ross finally sued both Bosie and Crosland separately for libel. It was a situation that almost exactly mirrored the Wilde versus Queensberry case, (this time with Bosie playing the defendant Queensberry and Ross playing the complainant Wilde – tragedy repeated as farce). Even the result of the trials was the same, with first Crosland, then Bosie being found not guilty.

(HG Wells, *Sir Edmund Gosse*, and Oscar's son, Cyril Holland, spoke up for Ross, Cyril saying that: "He was like a second father to me". But a Scotland Yard detective, Inspector West, wrecked Ross's case by testifying that Ross was notorious for associating with 'sodomites and male prostitutes'. Ross's ex-boyfriend, Freddie Smith, was brought into the witness box where he admitted that he 'painted and powdered' his face. When Ross's lawyer pointed out that, as Smith was a member of a amateur dramatic group, it was usual for actors to paint their faces, Smith admitted: "Well, not when they come to church".)

The one area that did not mirror the Wilde-Queensberry case was the reaction of the authorities. Although the papers relating to Ross's homosexual activities were sent to the Department of Public Prosecutions, there was no attempt to indict Ross over what would have been an open and shut case. One indication of how far things had changed since Wilde's day was that, during the trials, Ross dined several times at 10, Downing St.

Not only did Ross escape prosecution but he also received a public testimonial recognising 'the generosity with which you have put yourself at the disposal of all those who claimed your sympathy or your help.' It was signed by the Asquiths, *Bernard Shaw*, HG Wells, *Sir Herbert Beerbohm Tree*, and the Bishop of Birmingham. In 1917, Ross was made a trustee of the National Gallery and worked for the Imperial War Museum on the Commission for War Memorials.

Notwithstanding these tributes, the trials had damaged his reputation and he never regained his poise. He came under additional pressure because of his determined opposition to the First World War, (Bosie Douglas tried again to destroy Ross by implicating him in the notorious anti-pacifist Black Book trial).

Ross's house at Half Moon St became a centre for the anti-war group of young soldier-poets, led by Siegfried Sassoon, Robert Graves, Charles Scott-Moncrieff, and Wilfred Owen; (Owen stayed with Ross to recuperate from shell shock).

(Ross found himself enjoying the black humour of the time, particularly a Robert Graves story concerning a letter that he had sent to a colleague and which had been returned from the Western Front marked with an official stamp: 'July 22. Died of Wounds. Present location uncertain.')

In 1917, a friend reported an incident that seemed to sum up Ross's character. One evening, the friend observed him walking along Piccadilly during a German air raid. Ross noticed a confused old lady standing in the middle of the street, gazing in terror at the sky. Taking her by the arm, Ross raised his umbrella over her head and steered her to safety under the Ritz Hotel arches.

In 1918, Ross died suddenly of heart failure in his rooms at Half Moon St. His last visitors were Siegfried Sassoon, Charles Scott-Moncrieff, and the young Noel Coward.

The tributes that followed were warm, Vyvyan Holland calling him 'the dearest man I have ever known', and the Times obituary recording that: 'It was his foible to pretend to be a trifler in all things. In acts of kindness, he was always in earnest'.

Ross said that his true epitaph should read: 'Here lies one whose name was writ in hot water'.

SIEGFRIED SASSOON (1886-1967) became one of the most influential of the First World War poets. His war record had been exemplary – just before the Battle of the Somme, armed only with a few hand grenades he had attacked a German outpost single-handed. After the Germans fled, Sassoon sat down in the now corpse-strewn outpost and read a book until support arrived.

When he later received a head wound, a convalescent Sassoon became convinced of the insanity of the conflict and began to attack it in his verse. The authorities found his opposition all the more galling as it came from an obvious war hero.

(Oscar Wilde dined with Siegfried's older relatives on several occasions. The Sassoons were an eccentric but hugely wealthy family, originally from Baghdad, and known as the 'Rothschilds of the East'. One member, Reuben, lived at a house in Belgrave Square, London, where he situated his stables on top of the roof. Every time he wished to go out, the carriage and horses had to be conveyed to the ground by lift. Reuben also employed a servant called Hassan whose main claim to fame was that his father had been eaten by a sheep.)

CHARLES SCOTT-MONCRIEFF (1889-1930) was a student at Edinburgh University when he first met Robbie Ross. He was a diffident, rather awkward, young Scot with poetic ambitions, as Ross pointed out in a letter: 'Moncrieff is due to come here Monday, or Tuesday. He has told me the hour of his arrival and the method of his arrival, everything except the date of his arrival. He is obviously a real poet'.

Scott-Moncrieff volunteered for the British army in the first month of the First World War and fought on the Western Front until he was badly wounded in April 1917, wounds from which he never fully recovered. As with Sassoon, he was a highly regarded soldier. Surprised that Scott-Moncrieff had only received a Military Cross, one of his corporals commented: "If ever a man earned the VC, Captain Scott-Moncrieff earned it over and over again. On one occasion he brought back a German sandbag as a souvenir."

(Later, speaking of his experiences in the trenches, Scott-Moncrieff recalled that his troops had kept a parrot that had learnt to imitate the whine of a spent bullet to perfection. "It was the only lower animal I saw that seemed to take an interest in the war'. His men once managed to keep an unpopular staff officer buried face down in the mud for twenty minutes by encouraging the parrot to perform every time the officer raised his head.)

After the war, Scott-Moncrieff, still partly incapacitated by his wounds, decided to settle in Italy and devote the remainder of his life to the translation of *Marcel Proust's* 'A La Recherche du Temps Perdu' into English. As light relief, he also translated Stendhal and Pirandello.

Proust himself was highly doubtful about Scott-Moncrieff's efforts: "I cherish my work and I won't have it ruined by Englishmen". When Scott-Moncrieff chose 'Remembrance of Things Past' as the Anglicised title for the book, Proust's suspicions increased. He was only placated when told that this title was a quote from Shakespeare's sonnets.

> *Before he died, Wilde suggested that eventually he would like to be buried in Pére Lachaise cemetery in Paris, possibly recalling lines from 'The Importance of Being Earnest': 'He seems to have expressed a desire to be buried in Paris'. Chasuble: 'In Paris? I fear that hardly points to any serious state of mind at the last'.*
>
> *(The choice of this famous burial ground did not appeal to all – Victor Hugo sneered at the pretensions of Pére Lachaise's family vaults, calling them 'the ultimate bourgeois chest-of-drawers')*
>
> *In 1909, Robbie Ross arranged for the transfer of Oscar's body from Bagneaux cemetery to Pére Lachaise. (In 1950, honouring his wishes, Ross's own ashes were placed in Wilde's grave).*
>
> *Ross also commissioned the American sculptor Jacob Epstein to construct a suitable memorial over Oscar's new resting place.*

SIR JACOB EPSTEIN 1880-1959

Thanks to Epstein, Wilde remained as controversial in death as he had been in life. Inspired by the Ancient Egyptian Sphinx, Epstein created a modernist monolith that squatted like a concrete tank amidst the more subdued shrines surrounding it. The designer W. Graham Robertson's first reaction was that: 'the incongruity of it struck me with such force that I laughed out loud. The most ephemeral of triflers weighed down by all the gigantic symbols of eternity'.

But what really upset the authorities was Epstein's choice of a pair of giant testicles to adorn the tomb. Before the unveiling in 1914, the cemetery officials insisted that Epstein cover them up with a plaque. When the sexual mystic *Aleister Crowley* spotted this fig leaf, he counter-attacked by ripping it off to allow full display of the offending glands.

When finally the testicles went missing, theories abounded as to the culprit. Local Catholic students were blamed, then a pair of elderly English ladies, then the head-keeper of Pére Lachaise was accused of hacking them off and using them as a paperweight. Robbie Ross at one time suspected *Bosie Douglas* of castrating the monument, but on reflection dismissed the idea: "I don't think Douglas has anything to do with that".

Whether Wilde himself would have approved of his memorial is debatable: 'If a man needs an elaborate tombstone in order to remain in the memory of his country, it is clear that his living at all was an act of absolute superfluity'.

This furore was nothing new to Epstein. Born in the Jewish quarter of the Bowery in New York City, he moved to Europe and in 1905 settled in London. Although he never lost his American accent, he became a British national in 1911.

In 1908, he displayed his ability to outrage when the British Medical Council commissioned him to create a set of symbolic figures on the side of their building in the Strand, London. Epstein sculpted eighteen large nudes depicting human life from cradle to grave. (*Augustus John* said that Epstein was 'going around borrowing babies' as models for the cradle stage.)

The unmistakable nudity of the figures caused an uproar in the press and Parliament. When it was claimed that Epstein was 'turning London into a Fiji island', a police inspector was deputised to examine the statues. He returned a verdict that they were 'rude'.

Finally, the future Archbishop of Canterbury, Cosmo Gordon Lang, was persuaded to climb the scaffolding to inspect the work. He declared that the sculptures were innocent of offence and the row subsided.

It flared up again in 1935, when one of the larger phalluses detached itself from its owner and fell twenty feet into the street below, almost killing a passer-by. The new controllers of the building, the Southern Rhodesian government, decided that the remaining sexual organs should be removed on health and safety grounds.

In 1925, Epstein was commissioned to construct a memorial to the poet WH Hudson in Hyde Park. The Prime Minister, Stanley Baldwin, was asked to perform the unveiling. Normally the etiquette of the occasion required the dignitary to pull the cord, gaze reverently at the sculpture, then turn and bow to the artist.

According to witnesses, on this occasion, Baldwin pulled the cord, looked at the memorial, and then, open-mouthed in horror at what was revealed, forgot completely about any further acknowledgements.

BOSIE DOUGLAS (Fifth Part – from page 449)

Bosie Douglas quickly recovered from the shock of Wilde's death. As the money from Queensberry's legacy ran out, he decided that he should capitalise on his recent conversion to heterosexuality by marrying a wealthy American heiress. (As one of Wilde's characters in 'A

Woman of No Importance' put it: 'The English aristocracy supply us with our curiosities. They are sent over to us every summer, regularly, in the steamers, and propose to us the day after they land'.)

When he arrived in the USA in 1901, Bosie became briefly engaged to, (and apparently slept with), an immensely rich girl called *Natalie Barney*. However, none of his courtships succeeded and Bosie returned to Britain still unmarried.

Back in London, he met an attractive young poetess called **OLIVE CUSTANCE** (1876-1944), a friend of *John Gray* and *Richard Le Gallienne*. She was engaged already to a young aristocrat named Freddie Manners-Sutton, (later Viscount Canterbury), but, a wild child herself, was attracted by Bosie's romantic past.

During a holiday in Paris with Freddie Manners-Sutton, she came across Bosie's ex-lover Natalie Barney. Dumping Freddie, the two women left for Venice where they engaged in a passionate lesbian dalliance. When Olive admitted that she was in love with Bosie, Natalie suggested that the three of them could live together in a ménage a trois. Olive rejected the idea and returned to London.

When in 1902 Bosie and Olive eloped together, their marriage produced a storm of recrimination. Even *King Edward VII*, (who previously had sent his congratulations over Olive's engagement to Manners-Sutton), expressed his disapproval. On hearing this, Bosie snapped: "What the devil's it got to do with him!"

Olive's father, a redoubtable Boer War veteran called Colonel Custance, attempted to query the marriage by demanding to see the Scotland Yard police records on Bosie. When told that there were none, he barked: "Look, there can't be more than a dozen homosexuals in the country and they must all be known to the police".

An inspector replied: "Well, sir, we know of about twenty thousand and Lord Alfred hasn't got a record". Custance's eyes bulged as he gasped: "Twenty thousand! Good God!!"

Only the politician *George Wyndham* kept a sense of proportion about the matter. When told that Bosie had eloped with a woman, he remarked: "Let's face it – anything short of murder in the Douglas family is a source of congratulation".

By 1909, Bosie had become the editor of a magazine called 'The Academy', where he hired a pugnacious Yorkshireman called TWH Crosland as his right hand man. 'The Academy' soon became the mouthpiece for their numerous prejudices. Bosie's views had swung to the right: 'I ran my papers as a die hard Conservative and I consider that Messrs *Asquith*, Lloyd George, and Churchill are jointly responsible for the ruin of the country and the smash up of everything that makes England worth living in.'.

Given Bosie's hereditary intemperance of language, (Wilde: 'his mania for writing revolting and loathsome letters'), the editorship of a national magazine was a dangerous weapon. Even more hazardous was his love of litigation – Bosie was drawn to the libel courts like a gambler to a betting shop.

His first skirmish occurred in 1909, when two student magazines printed articles about himself and Wilde that Bosie considered to be libellous. After he threatened them with court actions, both papers caved in, paid him £50 each, and sacked their editors. A gratified Bosie had tasted blood.

Then, in 1910, during one of the regular financial emergencies at 'The Academy', Bosie tried to borrow ready cash from Olive's ex-suitor, the jilted Freddie Manners-Sutton. When Freddie turned him down on the grounds that Bosie overpaid himself as editor, Bosie blazed: 'I beg to inform you that neither I nor Olive will ever speak to you again. Furthermore, I will tell you quite plainly that I consider you to be a low, huckstering, Jew-minded pimp.'

Crosland poured petrol on to the flames by writing an article that suggested that Freddie, while publishing religious books, also owned shares in a firm that published erotic novels. Predictably Freddie sued. Bosie: 'That little beast Freddie has summoned Crosland for libel.'

During the trial, Bosie managed to destroy Freddie's reputation by revealing a 1905 incident when Bosie had introduced him to a London brothel. While there, Freddie had been to bed with a girl called Maggie Dupont. Later, a man contacted Freddie claiming to be the girl's father and saying she was under the age of consent. Although the allegation was unlikely, Freddie, on Bosie's advice, had paid £1000 hush money. This information convinced the jury of Freddie's guilt and Crosland was acquitted.

Bosie's next court case stemmed from yet another of his attacks on the Liberal Prime Minister. In 1910, Asquith ordered that a Catholic ceremonial procession to Westminster Cathedral should be diverted as it might lead to Protestant protests. Bosie ridiculed the decision in 'The Academy', causing a clergyman, Dr Robert Horton, to write an article in the Daily News advising that: 'the public should know that the paper has become an organ of Catholic propaganda.'

An over-confident Bosie sued the Daily News, lost the action, and was forced to sell 'The Academy' to pay the court costs. Dr Horton's claim was proved to be correct when in 1911 Bosie fully converted to Catholicism. Bosie's relative, *Wilfred Blunt*, fumed: 'That scoundrel Alfred Douglas has become a Catholic, after bringing a libel action not a year ago against a parson who stated that he had done so'. Bosie dismissed the rebuke by informing Blunt: 'What are you but a contemptible cad'.

In 1914, after a minor legal tussle with GK Chesterton, two further court clashes for non-payment of rates on his Hampstead home rendered Bosie bankrupt. This caused his automatic suspension as a member of White's Club, and he remained an un-discharged bankrupt all his life.

His domestic life also crumbled, partly as a result of his conversion to Rome. Bosie and Olive had produced one child called Raymond, and Olive's father Colonel Custance was horrified by the thought that his grandson might be brought up as a Catholic. He altered his financial allowance and will to ensure that Olive and Raymond stayed under his control.

An enraged Bosie responded with a campaign of abuse conducted mostly by telegram, 'scoundrel and thief' being two of the milder epithets. Custance issued a writ for criminal libel and, unusually, Bosie's nerve failed him. He accepted an Old Bailey court sentence to be bound over.

Trapped between her father and her husband, by 1913 Olive began to detach herself from Bosie although they continued to correspond and occasionally to reconcile. In 1914, Bosie's patience snapped again and he resumed the attack on Custance. He wrote to his father-in-law's circle of acquaintances, including the new king George V, to inform them of the 'foul way' that Custance had 'broken up my home and deprived me of the society of my wife.'

As a result, Bosie was refused entrance to the Duke of Richmond's box at the Goodwood races, (Richmond having been an army colleague of Custance). Bosie answered the Duke's snub by letter: 'I do not possess the prestige enjoyed by your Grace of being descended from the bastard son of a French whore'.

Having thus broken the conditions of his Old Bailey sentence, he was ordered to return to court in March 1914. Bosie refused to obey the order and left for France, declaring that he had 'no chance whatever of obtaining justice or fair treatment at the hands of the Central Criminal Court.'

However, the Custance case was not the only reason for Bosie's precipitate flight to Paris. In addition to his newly acquired but fervent Catholicism, Bosie had repudiated his homosexual past and turned against his old comrades. Chief amongst them, of course, was

Robbie Ross. Although Bosie had refused to attend the testimonial dinner given in Ross's honour in 1908, their animosity stayed in check till 1913.

Then, the publication of Arthur Ransome's biography of Wilde and Bosie's discovery of the complete 'De Profundis' shattered the truce, (see Ross – Third Part). Bosie's libel suit against Arthur Ransome collapsed after the jury read Wilde's denunciation of Bosie in 'De Profundis', and heard the icy demolition of his case by the defence lawyer, (and politician), FE Smith.

When Bosie claimed in court that he had been reconciled with his father, the Marquess of Queensberry, FE Smith revealed that after Queensberry's death Bosie referred to him as 'Jack the Ripper', (surely the least likely of all the multiple candidates for the role).

Bosie, seeing Ross as the architect of his defeat, wrote: 'I swore the day after the Ransome trial that I would never rest till I had publicly exposed Ross in his true colours.' The now celibate Bosie managed to convince Crosland that he had never had a sexual relationship with Wilde, and the two men began a rancorous campaign against Wilde's memory and 'Ross, the High Priest of the Sodomites'.

In their co-written book, 'Oscar Wilde and Myself', they accused Oscar of a catalogue of sins, including 'persistently pretending to noble birth', having 'a shallow and feeble mind, incapable of grappling unaided with profound things', and of repeatedly splitting his infinitives in his writings, (a particularly glaring fault in Crosland's eyes).

Having taken great care to find credible witnesses before publishing his views, Bosie issued pamphlets attacking Ross as 'a habitual debaucher and corruptor of young boys', and declaring that: 'I no longer care to associate with people who are engaged with every kind of wickedness from Sodomy to Socialism'.

In 1914, declaring that 'Douglas has become a real danger to the community,' the embattled Ross finally sued his tormentors for conspiring to bring a false charge of immorality against him. Facing libel charges from both Ross and Colonel Custance and under threat of arrest, Bosie retreated to France, leaving Crosland to defend himself in court.

The case was heard in June 1914 and resulted in Ross's prosecution being rejected and a not guilty verdict for Crosland. Bosie was delighted to hear that Ross's barrister, FE Smith, had been bested and gloated in verse that: 'Never was such complete disaster, The great F.E. had met his master!'

Emboldened by this result and pestered by the outbreak of the First World War, ('This war business is rather upsetting, is it not?'), Bosie returned to England. On arrival at Folkestone he was arrested on Ross's criminal libel warrant and, to his surprise and chagrin, spent a week on remand in prison, before being released on bail.

Although one jury failed to agree, at Bosie's second trial, his phalanx of witnesses won the day and Bosie, like Crosland, was acquitted. After the authorities failed to follow up the case and arrest Ross for homosexuality, Bosie was infuriated and blamed this laxity on Ross's 'rich and powerful friends' in the government.

When, instead of prosecution, Ross was presented with a testimonial and a gift of £700, Bosie lashed out in a derisive sonnet: 'Out there in Flanders all the trampled ground, Is red with English blood.... Who will count the cost?, Since here at home sits merry Margot, crowned, With Lesbian fillets, while with front of brass, 'Old Squiffy' hands the purse to Robert Ross'.

Meanwhile, his domestic legal actions were not faring well. Although he avoided Colonel Custance's libel action, his application for full custody of his son Raymond was refused. Inflamed by the decision, in 1915 Bosie abducted Raymond from his boarding school at Ampleforth and removed him to Scotland, (outside the Chancery Court's jurisdiction). Raymond was placed in the Benedictine College of Fort Augustus, on Loch Ness, where Wilde's old Oxford friend *Sir David Hunter-Blair* was the Abbot.

Within weeks, Raymond disappeared while away on a fishing expedition. Fearing that he had drowned, Bosie and Hunter-Blair spent a distraught couple of days before receiving a telegram from Olive telling them that Raymond was safely back in England. Colonel Custance had been in secret communication with the boy and had sent a private detective to pick him up by car from Loch Ness.

Immediately Bosie applied for a warrant to arrest Colonel Custance for kidnap, but, as he explained, the Scottish Lord Advocate was a friend of Asquith, 'so I didn't get it'. Bosie was himself lucky to avoid arrest for contempt of court in England. Disgusted by what he saw as Raymond's 'betrayal', Bosie refused to speak to his son for another ten years.

By 1916, although over-age, Bosie decided that he should offer his services to the British military effort. His application to join the Army was dismissed without comment, (as had his offer during the Boer War), and instead he determined to join the French Foreign Legion. After reluctantly supplying a letter of introduction, his friend Colonel 'Taffy' Lewis finally convinced Bosie that he would not thrive in the Legion. A frustrated Bosie abandoned his martial aspirations and went fishing instead.

During 1916, he fired a couple of desultory legal shells, firstly at the writer *George Moore* who had published what Bosie considered to be a blasphemous book, 'The Brook Keriff', in which Moore denied the divinity of Christ. Not impressed by Bosie's Catholic zealotry, a magistrate turned down the case.

Secondly he considered bringing an action when Aleister Crowley attacked him in print. On reflection, though, not even Bosie fancied a battle with 'The Beast' Crowley and withdrew his complaint.

There was no repeat of this caution when in 1918 his next legal battle loomed.

ORIGINS OF THE BLACK BOOK TRIAL

[The 'Black Book' affair was possibly the most extraordinary trial ever heard at the Old Bailey. It took place against a background of four years of stalemated war, horrendous casualty lists, and the apparent breakthrough of the German army in France. The case itself was an attempt by British rightwing extremists to discredit the left and particularly any pacifist elements within the establishment.

The attack was led by a maverick Tory MP called Noel Pemberton-Billing, (1880-1948), who, under the guise of defending 'purity in public life', blamed the failures of the War on what he asserted was the moral decadence and 'Germanic influence' of the former political leadership, in particular the Asquiths and their allies. He based his campaign mostly on two issues.

The first was his claim that the Germans had in their possession a 'Black Book' containing the names of 47,000 leading British figures who were 'practitioners of vices all decent men thought had perished in Sodom and Lesbos'. Therefore, he said, these people were open to blackmail.

The second issue concerned the relationship between the Asquiths and Maud Allen. Allen, (1872-1956), was an American dancer who had bolstered her career by creating a near-naked routine called 'Visions of Salome', based on Oscar Wilde's play, (she had met Oscar in Paris shortly before his death). The show was advertised as 'a delicious embodiment of lust'.

She performed this dance publicly before King Edward VII, (and apparently repeated it later in his bedroom). But it was her friendship with the Prime Minister and his wife Margot Asquith that provided Billing with his ammunition. When it was learnt that, as well as inviting Maud to official functions at Downing St, Margot paid the rent on Maud's expensive apartment, rumours circulated that the two women had a lesbian relationship.

Billings realised that by associating the Asquith circle with the 'cult of Wilde' he could discredit both and, in Maud Allen, he found an ideal link.

He began his assault by printing an article about the Black Book announcing that: 'The names of Privy Councillors, youths of the chorus, wives of Cabinet ministers, dancing girls, even Cabinet Ministers themselves, diplomats, poets, bankers, editors, newspaper proprietors and members of His Majesty's household follow each other with no order of precedence'.... 'Wives of men in supreme position were entangled. In lesbian ecstasy the most sacred secrets of State were betrayed'.

When his revelations failed to produce any reaction other than lubricious amusement, Billings turned his attention to Maud Allen and in an article entitled 'The Cult of the Clitoris' condemned her performance as 'Salome' and implied that she was a lesbian. This was treated more seriously and Maud brought a private prosecution for criminal libel against Billing.]

To Bosie, the trial was a heaven-sent chance to wound his enemies. He had already had crossed swords with Maud Allen in 1908. He had learnt from his brother Sholto Douglas, that Maud's brother, Theo Durrant, had been executed for the murder of two young girls in California. When Bosie met Maud at a garden party, an argument started between them which culminated in Bosie sneering: "Your brother was a murderer", and Maud slapping him in the face with a fan. Bosie actively backed Billing, advising him that: "Maud Allen is the stalking horse for the Ross gang view of life".

(Although too ill to attend the trial, Robert Ross made a perceptive comment upon it: 'The English enjoyed kicking Oscar's corpse to make up for the failure of the 5th Army'.)

What became known as the Black Book trial opened at the Old Bailey in May 1918 and lasted five days. It provided some of the most farcical scenes ever witnessed in a British court. The unfortunate Judge Charles Darling, who presided over the events, lost control of the case partly because Billing represented himself and therefore could not be ejected from the proceedings.

Billing orchestrated the trial to achieve the maximum amount of xenophobic hysteria, even selecting a gallery audience composed of disabled soldiers encouraged to applaud or catcall when necessary.

Some of the court exchanges bordered on the surreal, particularly when it came to terminology. The word 'clitoris' caused special problems. When Maud Allen admitted knowledge of the word but "only because of my amateur reading in medicine", Billings seized on this evidence of moral turpitude to thunder: "Are you aware, Miss Allen, that out of twenty-four people who were shown that libel, including many professional men, only one of them, who happened to be a barrister, understood what it meant?"

One of Billings' witnesses, a clinically insane army officer called Captain Harold Spencer also claimed knowledge of the offending appendage. Spencer: "I have been informed it is a superficial organ that, when unduly excited or over-developed, possesses the most dreadful influence on any woman, that she will do the most extraordinary things". He further clarified his explanation with: "An exaggerated clitoris might even drive a woman to an elephant."

Judge Darling also became puzzled when Spencer opined that an actress performing 'Salome' might experience 'an orgasm' when kissing the severed head of John the Baptist. Judge Darling: "Repeat the word you used." Spencer: "Orgasm". Judge Darling: "Some unnatural vice?" Spencer: "No, it is a function of the body".

The anarchic atmosphere in court increased when Billing announced that a telephone threat had been made that if one of his witnesses, a Mrs Villiers-Stuart (Billing's secret mistress, later imprisoned for bigamy) took the stand, she would be shot from the court gallery.

Mrs Villiers-Stuart's evidence was indeed inflammatory, as she claimed to have been shown the Black Book by another lover, the now deceased Neil Primrose, (*Lord Rosebery's* son). Amongst the names already leaked was that of the British Ambassador to Rome, Wilde's old friend *Sir Rennell Rodd*, but Villiers-Stuart went much further.

In an increasing hubbub of excitement, Billing ignored Judge Darling's calls for silence and started banging his fist on a table as he thundered out questions to his witness.

Billing: "Is Mrs Asquith's name in the book?" Mrs Villiers-Stuart shouted back: "It is!"

Billing: "Is Mr Asquith's name in the book?" Mrs Villiers-Stuart: "It is!"

Billing: "Is Lord Haldane's name in the book?" Mrs Villiers-Stuart's voice rose higher: "It is!"

Billing: "Is Judge Darling's name in the book?" Mrs Villiers-Stuart's voice reached a crescendo: "It is!"

Judge Darling: "Hey, just a moment".

The court dissolved in uproar as ushers rushed around attempting to restore order.

Towards the end of the trial, Bosie Douglas entered the fray as a witness for Billing. (Bosie already had a grudge against Judge Darling as he had presided over Bosie's court defeat against Arthur Ransome. This was a chance for revenge.)

First, he delivered a bitter onslaught against Wilde and his works: "Wilde was the agent of the devil in every way. It was his whole object in life to attack and sneer at virtue and to undermine it in every way"... "He was the greatest force for evil in Europe for the past 350 years".

Then, when Judge Darling made an innocent slip of the tongue by describing Bosie not as the translator of 'Salome' but as its writer, Bosie erupted: "You have no right to say that I wrote it. You are a liar, a damned liar. If you say it outside Court, I will prosecute you".

As a storm of cheering burst out from Billing's claque of old soldiers in the gallery, Judge Darling ordered Bosie to be removed from court. He was hustled to the door by ushers, accompanied by an old lady who also had been thrown out for brandishing her umbrella at the judge. The audience were entertained further by the sight of Bosie outside the glass doors loudly demanding the return of his hat that he had left in the witness box.

The closing stages of the trial brought yet more attacks on the memory of Wilde. Billings: "This social leper, Oscar Wilde, had founded a cult of sodomy in this country, and travelled from end to end of it perverting youth wherever he could". Even Judge Darling in his summing up took up the cudgels, declaring that 'Salome' was 'a play written with the vilest possible intention' and dismissing Oscar as 'the writer of filthy works, as you know'.

Billings was found not guilty of libelling Maud Allen, a verdict that was greeted with scenes of such uproarious jubilation that Judge Darling was forced to call the police to clear the court.

Bosie was hailed as one of the heroes of the hour by the jingoist press, although the applause was not unanimous. Cynthia Asquith remarked: "Why that lunatic is still at large, Heaven only knows".

(Later Noel Pemberton-Billing became involved in efforts to promote British fascism. In 1934 he was suspended from Parliament after being carried out drunk from the House of Commons. He moved to Mexico where he became co-owner of a casino with the American boxer Jack Dempsey.

Maud Allen's career, in spite of the gross unfairness of the verdict, was wrecked. She was viewed publicly as the lesbian sister of a murderer. She spent much of the rest of her life teaching poor children, and died penniless in Los Angeles aged 84.)

Bosie's next foray into the courts occurred in 1921. One day he was walking in a London street when to his astonishment he saw an Evening News placard reading: 'Sudden Death of Lord Alfred Douglas. Found Dead in Bed by Maid. Heart Failure after a Chill'.

After indignantly phoning the paper to insist that he was perfectly healthy, he then read his own obituary. Written by a journalist called Arthur Machen, it was a less than fulsome tribute which concluded that Bosie: 'might have done anything, and, his poetry excepted, he did nothing, and worse than nothing'.

Spotting an open goal, Bosie rushed to his lawyers and, in the resulting successful prosecution for libel, the Evening News was forced to pay him £1000 and costs. Machen was sacked.

[The Welsh writer **ARTHUR MACHEN** (1863-1947) was the author of the short story 'The Bowmen', a fantasy in which he suggested that the ghosts of the archers from the 1415 Battle of Agincourt had materialised to aid the British troops on their retreat from Mons in 1915. This rumour swept the ranks and the phenomenon of the 'Angels of Mons' became accepted as fact. When Machen tried to set the record straight, he was accused of conspiring to hide the truth.]

During the 1920s, Bosie became convinced that worldwide conspiracies were afoot. They consisted on one hand of financiers, ('a clique of rich Jews'), and on the other of socialists, ('a threat to all I hold dear'). Although not advocating violent anti-Semitism in the later Nazi sense, Bosie was decidedly suspicious of Jewish influence in the corridors of power.

Having now become the editor of 'Plain English', and later 'Plain Speech', he used these magazines to promulgate his views, publishing mild but potentially dangerous jibes such as: 'How odd, Of God, To choose, The Jews.'

However, in 1923, he extended his attack and suggested that during the First World War Winston Churchill deliberately delayed news of the true result of the Battle of Jutland so that his Jewish financier friends could manipulate the New York Stock Exchange to their, (and his), advantage.

Churchill ignored the charge, but the editor of the Jewish Chronicle published a letter in the Morning Post protesting that 'it should not be a paying proposition for Lord Alfred Douglas to invent vile insults against the Jews.' Buoyed up by his recent run of legal triumphs, Bosie sued the paper.

In court, Bosie's case was demolished, mostly by written evidence from *Arthur Balfour*, (First Lord of the Admiralty at the time), who stated that Churchill had nothing to do with the Jutland communiqués. Although his argument was destroyed, the jury decided in Bosie's favour on the grounds that he had acted in good faith and had not invented the story deliberately. But they only awarded him damages of one farthing, leaving him liable for court costs.

Unable to abandon his obsessions, Bosie delivered a barnstorming speech at a public meeting in Farringdon Street, London, in which he not only repeated his accusation that Churchill had falsified the Jutland report, but also added that Churchill's Jewish friends had engineered the death of *Lord Kitchener*.

Bosie's theory was that Kitchener had set off for Russia with the intention of undermining the efforts of the Jewish Bolsheviks; if he had succeeded, the Russian Revolution would have been stymied. Therefore the worldwide Jewish socialist conspiracy had decided that

Kitchener should be assassinated. Bosie claimed that Kitchener's ship had not been blown up by a mine but by time bombs planted on board by Jewish agents. He published these opinions in a pamphlet.

This time, Churchill had had enough and sued for criminal libel. Both he and Balfour appeared in the witness box to deny the accusations, and Bosie's case collapsed. After the jury took only eight minutes to find him guilty, the judge declared that Bosie was 'absolutely reckless in what he wrote and published', and sentenced him to six months in prison.

Bosie was jailed at Wormwood Scrubs Prison for five months, (receiving one month remission for good behaviour). For the first seven weeks he was engaged in shovelling coal, but the labour proved too hard and he spent the remainder of his sentence in the prison hospital.

During the latter months the chaplain employed him to play the harmonium at the Roman Catholic church services. This proved somewhat embarrassing, as the vast majority of Catholic inmates were Irish Sein Feiners, (an organisation that Bosie had consistently reviled in the pages of 'Plain Truth').

Bosie was released in May 1924 and, in contrast to Wilde, his jail experiences seemed to have had a therapeutic effect. In a conscious acknowledgment of Oscar's 'De Profundis', Bosie wrote a sequence of sonnets entitled 'In Excelsis', and described prison as being: 'the obvious goal for any self-respecting English poet, and I never rested till I got there'.

Jail also seemed to cure him of his 'raucous anti-Semitic fury' and of his obsessive hatred for Wilde. (In 1944, Bosie sent a letter of apology to Churchill. Churchill replied: 'Time ends all things'.)

However, despite this more mellow view of the world, in 1925 Bosie showed that he had not quite lost his appetite for litigation. His last opponent was *Frank Harris*.

Their paths had crossed before in 1913, when an argument between them had resulted in violence. Bosie complained that Harris: 'grabbed me by the collar and forced his thumb into my windpipe, thereby reducing me to impotence.'

On this occasion though the casus belli was Harris's biography, 'The Life and Confessions of Oscar Wilde'. Bosie: 'Frank Harris, not content with attacking my character with foul lies and misrepresentations, then used his foul book to make spiteful attempts to run down my personal appearance. This is all part of the modern Bolshevik hatred of beauty in any form'.

The book proved so defamatory that Harris was only able to publish it in America. When the London shop Harrods unwittingly sold a copy of the American edition, Bosie made a beeline to his lawyers. On his nineteenth separate court action, Bosie sued for libel, and won the case and damages.

In the more peaceful period of his later life, Bosie concentrated on his poetry. In 1927, he sent a copy of his 'Collected Satires' to the Prince of Wales, (the future King Edward VIII). When it was returned, the now more conciliatory Bosie, (while bearing in mind Lord Rosebery's dictum that: 'The English nobleman is an enlarged squire, the Scottish nobleman is a reduced king'), sent a reply:

'Remember that though you are the Prince of Wales, I am quite as well born as you are and that my ancestors refused a kingdom which yours subsequently usurped. All the same, I forgive you'.

His attitude to his fellow bards was less lenient. When *WB Yeats*, as editor, omitted Bosie's poems from a new edition of the Oxford Book of Modern Verse, an irate Bosie released an open telegram to the press declaring that this was a typical example of the attitude of the inferior muse to the superior. Bosie: 'But then WB Yeats is a very minor poet and TS Eliot and WH Auden are simply not poets at all.'

Although an Adonis in his youth, Bosie's looks faded as he grew older; his nose in particular became more pronounced. *Augustus John* reported that when the painter Wyndham Lewis was asked to paint Bosie's portrait, Lewis was apprehensive over how to depict this aspect of his notoriously touchy client. John: 'I told him, of course, to make it a bit bigger; but Lewis demurred. He said he had to draw the line somewhere'.

Bosie always claimed that, after 1913 and his conversion to Catholicism, he remained celibate for the rest of his life. However, a professor and writer called Samuel M Steward stated in his 'Chapters from an Autobiography' that in 1937, when he was in his twenties, he had visited the 67-year-old Bosie at his home in Hove, Sussex. Steward said that, after a considerable amount of alcohol, he and Bosie had ended up in bed together and Steward's lips 'were where Oscar's had been'.

Bosie died in 1944. His last act was to place a bet on a horse – the horse lost. His wife Olive, who had remained in contact in the intervening years and indeed lived close to Bosie's house in Hove, had died a few months previously of a cerebral haemorrhage. Their only child, Raymond Douglas, after spending almost forty years in and out of mental institutions, died in 1964.

Bosie's hostile attitude to Oscar Wilde changed radically in his last years. He told a friend that: "Oscar cared more for my little finger than he did for all the Rosses, Sherards, and Harrises put together, body and soul". When it was suggested that Wilde had been heartless, Bosie smiled and shook his head: "No, no, he was the kindest chap. The kindest chap."

In one of his final statements on the whole Wilde imbroglio, Bosie mused: "I was a spoilt and selfish little beast then. The thought which has only recently occurred to me is a terrible one. Did my father really love me all the time and did he only do as Oscar said – and killed the thing he loved. Didn't we all three, Wilde, my father and myself do it, more or less?"

One of the most distinguished legal personalities with whom Bosie crossed swords was the Conservative barrister and politician **FREDERICK EDWIN SMITH, later LORD BIRKENHEAD**, (1872-1930). A tall dandy who always wore his hat tipped jauntily on the back of his head, Smith was invariably known by his initials, F.E. His air of aggressive cynicism and his barbed tongue won him many enemies; Margot Asquith said that he was: "very clever but his brains go to his head"

Bosie's ally, *TWH Crosland*, first met Smith in court in 1911, (when Crosland sued the financier Horatio Bottomley for libel). Having won his case, Crosland sneered that Smith's vaunted courtroom prowess was 'all crackle and no pith'. During the *Robert Ross* trials of 1914, Smith consistently acted on Ross's behalf and, when Bosie and Crosland finally won their cases, Bosie published a derogatory epic against Smith called 'The Rhyme of F Double E'. It contained such observations as: "His sentiments are so much tripe, And he'll be rotten before he's ripe', etc. Smith ignored the attack.

FE Smith had been born and raised in Liverpool, where his obvious talents promoted him first to the bar in 1899, then as Member of Parliament for the constituency of Walton in 1906. As a Tory MP in the Liberal landslide of that year, Smith was not to reach government office until 1915.

Instead he concentrated on his legal career. He was involved in many notable cases, including the defence of Ethel Le Neve, (the accomplice of the murderer Dr Crippen), and later the prosecution of the Irish rebel Sir Roger Casement. Smith became known for his lacerating clashes with judges. On one occasion, after he had explained a complicated legal argument, the judge growled: "I'm sorry, Mr Smith, but I am none the wiser". Smith replied: "Possibly, my lord, but you are now much better informed".

At another trial, the judge snapped at Smith: "You are being offensive, sir!" Smith shot back with: "We both are. The difference is that I'm trying to be, and you can't help it."

Occasionally he came off worse in these exchanges. One day, he teased Lord Chief Justice Hewart about his huge stomach, asking Hewart if he was expecting a boy or a girl. Hewart gazed across bleakly and replied: "If it's a boy, I'll call him John, and if it's a girl I'll call her Mary. But, if as I expect, it's only wind, I'll call it F.E. Smith."

When the Conservatives finally returned to share power in 1915, Smith was made Attorney General with a seat in the Cabinet. In this new role he visited the USA to promote the Allied cause. When he met President Woodrow Wilson, during the conversation Wilson asked him: "And what, in your opinion, is the trend of the modern undergraduate?". Smith answered: "Steadily towards women and drink, Mr President".

When in 1919, Smith was made Lord Chancellor, his promotion to the Lords meant that he could chose his title. A colleague called Bigham was created a peer at the same time. Bigham chose the title of Lord Mersey, adding: "That'll leave the Atlantic for F.E." Smith, in fact, restricted himself to becoming Earl of Birkenhead.

TWH CROSLAND 1868-1924

Bosie Douglas's colleague during his days as editor of the Academy and the legal attack on *Robbie Ross* was the journalist Thomas William Hodgson Crosland. Although Crosland never actually met Wilde, he despised homosexuality and became an implacable detractor of Oscar's memory. After reading even the bowdlerised 'De Profundis', he denounced Wilde as one: 'whose soul was all a sin, whose heart was all a lust, whose brain was all a lie' – 'In fifty years time no one will care a straw about Wilde and his posturing admirers'.

Later in 1912, he delivered another broadside in his poem 'The First Stone': 'Thou, The complete mountebank, The scented posturer, The flabby Pharisee…. The Lord of Language, With the bad teeth, The whining convict, And Prince of Hypocrites', and much more in the same vein.

Crosland was not unaware of the dangers of court actions, ('The man who goes before an English judge and jury with a request for damages for libel must have milk-white hands and exceedingly well-washed milk-white hands'), but nonetheless eagerly set about destroying Ross through legal methods. After he won the case, he announced in 1915 that: 'It is just as important to civilization that literary England should be cleansed of sex-mongers and peddlers of perversity as that Flanders should be cleared of Germans'.

Crosland was a very recognisable figure, tall and pot-bellied, with a food-encrusted beard, a decayed top hat, 'Presbyterian' boots, and a permanent scowl, who excused his own habitual rudeness as 'being blunt'. One acquaintance said that he looked 'like an inspired bus conductor'.

He was not a popular man among his contemporaries. GK Chesterton: 'Crosland has a right to be regarded as the representative Englishman – he has prejudices rather than principles'. Even the shady financier Horatio Bottomley had doubts: 'In the journalistic world Crosland is regarded as the most disreputable member of the profession'.

Crosland was raised in relatively poor circumstances in Leeds, Yorkshire. In 1888 he became a teacher but soon fell out with the Schools Inspectorate. One inspector criticised him over the fact that his pupils were incapable of pointing out 'Hill' on the map of England. When Crosland explained that in the Yorkshire accent the town was pronounced as 'Hull', the inspector shrugged: "So much the worse for Yorkshire", and refused to upgrade his marks.

Crosland decided to become a journalist and moved to London. Without money or contacts, at first he was forced to sleep rough in Green Park. Gradually he fought his way into the newspaper world but spent years involved in hack work. By 1894 he was secure enough to marry a girl called Annie Moore, who provided him with three sons.

He finally made a breakthrough in 1902, when, stimulated by an intense dislike of the Scottish journalists he had met in London, he published a diatribe against their entire nation – it was called 'The Unspeakable Scot'. To his surprise the book became a huge hit in Scotland; the Glasgow Herald reviewed it as 'highly diverting'.

(In 1909, Crosland was returning by train from Scotland when he was taken ill at Hawick and carried to a local hotel. Crosland: 'I had wanted to get as far as Carlisle because I hated the idea of dying in Scotland'. On his recovery the next morning the hotel landlady eyed him beadily: "Ye'll be the mon that wrote the buik?" Crosland nodded. The landlady walked off, sighing: "Aye, aye, it's a funny auld world".)

Encouraged by his success, Crosland went on to write a series of cheerfully racist volumes attacking the English, the Japanese, the Irish, the Welsh, with additional swipes at 'Women' and 'Suburbia'.

In 1905, he met Bosie Douglas. Wrongly assuming that Bosie, being a lord, would inherit 'stacks of boodle', Crosland ingratiated himself by deluging praise upon Bosie's poetry. The flattery worked and, when Bosie acquired the Academy magazine in 1907, Crosland was appointed as assistant editor.

Their editorial collaboration became an eccentric double-act, just about held together by a long-suffering secretary called Miss Alice Head, (later to become editor of 'Country Life' magazine). She sometimes slaved for forty-hour stretches to enable an edition to appear.

One of Crosland's methods of writing was to stride around the office roaring dictation to Miss Head, while downing mugs of beer. Bosie would drop in for about an hour around lunchtime and sometimes invite Crosland out to the Café Royal. In an effort make his bedraggled assistant more presentable, Bosie had to brush Crosland's hair and clothes before venturing outside.

Crosland's fifty-a-day cigarette habit got on Bosie's nerves and he tried to introduce an office ban. However, the sound of Crosland mechanically chewing tobacco as a substitute became even more grating. Finally Bosie roared out: "Crosland, for God's sake, smoke!"

The Academy finances were a continual source of worry – Bosie was horrified by the 'terrifying mound of bills'. Crosland, (a dedicated gambler who made over sixty trips to Monte Carlo), suggested that the magazine bet its way out of trouble. Surprisingly, this dangerous proposal worked quite well – Bosie once had eleven wins in four days. On one occasion though, it failed, and it took five people to restrain a raging bookmaker while Bosie made his escape.

With as volatile a pair as Bosie and Crosland in control, life at the Academy involved constant quarrels. They usually ended when Crosland would appear to have a heart attack and a contrite Bosie would ply him with brandy until he recovered. During one argument, Crosland accused Bosie of upsetting his wife Annie with a poison pen letter. Bosie, amazed at the suggestion, spluttered: "This is absurd! I'd forgotten that you'd even got a wife!"

Crosland used the magazine to pursue some of his own hobbyhorses. When the new licensing laws came in, he was shocked to find that public houses would not be allowed to open until 11.30am. He wrote a scornful dismissal of the law: 'Fancy holding up the entire business of the country till eleven-thirty!'

Crosland sometimes indulged his odd sense of humour by standing on Fleet Street with a pocketful of half crowns. He approached several passers-by to ask: "Excuse me, but are you by any chance the Reverend William Robertson Neill?" When those questioned replied that they were not, Crosland gasped: "Thank God", and pressed a half crown into their hands.

He now acquired a dislike of Irishmen and, as Fleet Street was home to many of them, found himself in regular fistfights. He asked a professional boxer called Charlie Mitchell for advice on self-defence. Mitchell told him that the best defence in the world was 'a decanter aimed low'.

When Bosie was forced to sell the Academy, it was announced that the next editor would be one 'Cecil Cowper, Esq., Justice of the Peace, Barrister-at-Law'. The news that a lawyer was to succeed the notoriously litigious former editors produced guffaws of laughter around the Fleet Street pubs.

Unsurprisingly given their respective natures, the alliance between Bosie and Crosland ended in a storm of abuse. Crosland called Bosie 'a dirty Scotchman', while Bosie replied with: 'You were a brute and more than half a knave'.

Crosland continued his career as a journalist on various publications and also by writing his distinctive style of polemical poetry. He issued a calling card describing himself as "TWH Crosland. Jobbing Poet (by Road, Rail, or Sea). Editors' own material made up. Distance no object. Satisfaction guaranteed. Neatness, Promptitude and Despatch. Cashiers waited upon in their own apartments. NB – Funerals Attended'.

At one point, he worked for the Sunday Chronicle, owned by Sir Edward Hulton. Whenever he found himself short of an article, Crosland would fill the space by inserting sonnets by John Keats. One day, Hulton complained to Crosland that: "We're getting too much of this damned fellow Keats's stuff. Fourteen lines – what do you pay for the like of that?"

Crosland replied that Keats was one of England's great poets. Hulton was unimpressed: "That may well be, but it's only fourteen lines. Make it three and sixpence". Crosland grunted: "We don't pay him. He's dead".

Crosland was dogged by ill health, having suffered from diabetes for twenty years. Neither did his lifestyle help; a friend commented: "He lived on a diet of gin and vermouth which I verily believe kept him alive'. During his final illness, he found time to complain: "Why do they always send grapes to invalids? Look at this place – it's like a bloody vineyard".

Throughout his career, Crosland hated the newspaper proprietor Lord Northcliffe and was proud that he had never written a line for the Daily Mail or any other of the Northcliffe Press stable. Crosland: 'It can be said with truth of Northcliffe that he has touched nothing which he has not degraded'.

After Crosland died he was buried at Finchley cemetery on a cloudless sunny day. As the mourners stood around his open grave, they heard the roar of an aeroplane flying overhead. Then, behind the plane, they spotted a trail of smoke that slowly printed out across the sky the words: 'Daily Mail'.

Wilde's death left only four members of his immediate family still alive – his two teenage sons, his sister-in-law Lily Wilde, and her small daughter Dolly.

In spite of the anger that Wilde had felt over his brother Willie's behaviour during his incarceration, Oscar soon reconciled with his widow, Lily Wilde (1859-1922). When she married Texeira de Mattos in 1900, he commented: "I am very glad my sister-in-law is to be married to Texeira: it is an excellent idea". He was proved correct; the pair enjoyed a long and happy marriage.

Alexander Texeira De Mattos (1865-1921), who Lily always referred to as 'Tex', had been the best man at Lily's first wedding to Willie Wilde. He was a multilingual Jewish Dutchman who had been raised in England, and used his gift for languages to become a well-paid translator of such writers as Maeterlinck and Zola. He supplemented this income by card playing, particularly bridge, and reputedly said that he was disappointed if he made less th an £400 a year at the game.

512

DOLLY WILDE 1895-1941

Wilde's niece, Dolly Wilde, was so fascinated by her uncle's memory that, as she grew up, she began to model herself on him. She claimed that: "I am more Oscar-like than he was himself". The writer HG Wells: "It was delightful to meet a feminine Wilde". Unfortunately, Dolly lacked Oscar's talent.

With the commencement of the First World War in 1914, she left her family to join a group of young Anglo-American women ambulance drivers in Paris. During the war, she reached the rank of lieutenant and received a medal for her services. It was in the company of this hard-living set that she indulged in her first lesbian love affair. Her companion was the seventeen-year-old 'Joe' Carstairs, (heiress to the Standard Oil fortune).

As the Twenties began to roar, Dolly was in her element. She became a fixture on the wild Parisian party scene, mixing with Scott and Zelda Fitzgerald, and involving herself in numerous lesbian liaisons. (Later the social commentator Nancy Mitford wrote that: 'Paris still harbours many an old mistress of Miss Wilde – most Lesbians seem to live forever'.)

Amongst her many lovers were *Natalie Barney*, Gwen Farrar, (the daughter of a baronet turned Variety actress), Monica Morris, (a rapacious girl-hunter known as 'the Stage Door Ferret'), and Alla Nazimova. During the 1920s, Nazimova was the highest paid Hollywood actress, who produced a film of Wilde's 'Salome' in 1922. (She was also the godmother of Nancy Davis, later to enter the White House as Mrs Nancy Reagan).

Dolly's partying instincts also extended to drugs. She became notorious for exiting lavatories while nonchalantly brushing white powder from her nose. At one dinner, she injected heroin into her thigh while the other guests politely continued with the main course.

By the 1930s her lifestyle caught up with her and she spent most of her time in sanatoriums. Shortly before her death, she was discovered dead drunk on a public bench in London. Suffering from a combination of breast cancer, alcohol-related diseases, and heroin addiction, she died aged 46, (the same age as her father and uncle), in a house just across the square from the Cadogan Hotel in London.

Dolly Wilde was not the only lesbian in Paris to have had connections with Oscar.

Elizabeth Marbury (1856-1933), his American literary agent who remained a stalwart supporter all his life, was also a member of a Sapphic ménage a trois who later lived in a pavilion in the Boulevard de la Reine, Versailles. The other two members of the trio were Elsie de Wolfe, a celebrated interior designer, and Anne Morgan, daughter of the renowned American financier, John Pierpont Morgan, (known in the English music halls as 'Pinpoint More Gain).

But by far the most famous of Wilde's lesbian acquaintances was Natalie Barney.

NATALIE BARNEY 1876-1972

Natalie Barney met Wilde in 1882 when she was six years old. While holidaying with her parents on Long Island, New York, she had been tormented by some small boys. Oscar, relaxing from his American tour, had rescued her, sat her on his knee, and told her 'a wonderful story'. She claimed that this incident inspired her with the desire to become a writer. Aged 11, she insisted on having her portrait painted as Wilde's 'Happy Prince'.

Born in Dayton, Ohio, and raised in Cincinnati, Barney was an attractive girl with long blonde hair and striking blue eyes. She was also the heiress to 'the fabulous Barney fortune' inherited from her railway magnate family.

Under the impression that American writers needed Paris to complete their education, she arrived in France and over the years became a minor poet and epigrammatist.

However, her real fame came from the salons held at her Paris home at 20, rue Jacob. For more than sixty years, it was a meeting place for the cream of international culture. Among her hundreds of guests, she entertained Ezra Pound, Thornton Wilder, *Anatole France*, Gertrude Stein, *Andre Gide*, Scott Fitzgerald, *Pierre Louys*, Nancy Cunard, Somerset Maugham, Sinclair Lewis, Harold Acton, Isadora Duncan, and TS Eliot.

Although her looks and money attracted many men, (leading to her short-lived engagement to *Bosie Douglas*), Barney was not interested. She said that she was: 'the friend of men, the lover of women', (proving it by seducing Bosie's future wife Olive Custance in 1902, and twenty years later, Dolly Wilde). Barney: "People call it unnatural – all I can say, it's always come naturally to me".

In the teeth of male opposition, in 1898 she managed to bed Liane de Pougy, the most beautiful courtesan in Paris. At a party, *Robert de Montesquieu* announced loudly that: "Natalie could have married Lord Alfred Douglas but she prefers Liane de Pougy!' (As a result, Liane wavered towards bisexuality before, much to Barney's annoyance, renouncing it all to enter a nunnery. Barney: 'Jesus Christ has seduced many more women than Don Juan'.)

She quickly got over her disappointment and spent the rest of her life in the pursuit of women. She met most of her casual lovers in the changing rooms of chic Parisian department stores and consummated these encounters anywhere she could find, theatre boxes and secluded areas of parks being her favourites.

She preferred her conquests to look feminine, explaining: "Why try to resemble our enemies?" and particularly enjoyed multiple sex. It was said that: 'three was Natalie's favourite number'.

She included among her harem at the rue Jacob, the painter Romaine Brooks, the poetess Renee Vivien, the sewing-machine heiress Wineretta Singer (later the Princesse de Polignac), and the screenwriter Mercedes de Acosta, (a lady who also achieved the difficult feat of becoming the lover of Marlene Dietrich and Greta Garbo simultaneously). Even in old age Barney managed to bed a beautiful American college girl and, aged 82, she seduced the formerly heterosexual wife of a Romanian ambassador.

Her garden parties became notorious, often being followed by complaints by neighbours objecting to the sight of nude women having sex on the lawn. Dolly Wilde once reduced the guests to tears of laughter when she suddenly gasped: "Oh, Natalie, you forgot to put the hermaphrodites in the bushes." Another lover, Mata Hari, arrived at one party, stark naked, on a prancing white horse.

Nicknamed 'the Pope of Lesbos', Barney was curious about the Greek home of Sappho, the most famous of all lesbians of antiquity. In 1903, accompanied by Renee Vivien, she set off to the island determined to start a lesbian community there. The plan fell through when the two women discovered that Lesbos appeared to be inhabited solely by 'hirsute, short, male shepherds'.

One of Natalie Barney's more exotic girlfriends was the Dutch-born Gertrude Margaretta Zeller, better known as **MATA HARI** (1876-1917). After a troubled marriage spent living in the Dutch East Indies, Margaretta broke with her husband and arrived in Paris in 1904. ("I thought that all women who ran away from their husbands went to Paris".)

She changed her name to Mata Hari, (Malay for 'eye of the day') and soon became the toast of Europe as an exotic oriental dancer. She admitted that she could not dance well but explained: "People came to see me because I was the first who dared to show myself naked to the public". She supplemented her income by becoming an exceptionally highly paid prostitute.

In 1917, after being spotted visiting the German trenches at Verdun, she was arrested by the French authorities on the suspicion of spying. She protested her innocence, and the real truth still remains obscure. According to the palmist *Cheiro* with whom she lived for a while,

514

Mata Hari told him that: 'a woman's acting powers, love of intrigue, intuition, gift of credible lying, innate curiosity, and use of sex made them perfect spies'.

(Wilde earlier expressed the view in 'An Ideal Husband': 'Spies are of no use nowadays. Their profession is over. The newspapers do their work instead.')

Mata Hari was sentenced to death and executed, at her own request, without a blindfold. Unsurprisingly, this combination of sexuality and violent death gave rise to legend. She was reputed to have flung her coat open at the last minute to reveal her naked body, thus causing the firing squad to misfire. Also, an aviator boyfriend was meant to have strafed the execution party to save her. Sadly, none of these rumours were true.

One of Natalie Barney's girlfriends who achieved lasting fame was the writer (Sidonie-Gabrielle) **COLETTE** (1873-1954). Barney once received a message from Colette: 'Natalie, my husband kisses your hands, and I the rest.'

Born and raised in the provincial village life of Burgundy, Colette arrived as an innocent ingénue in 1890s Paris. This soon changed when she married the libidinous music critic of 'L'Echo de Paris', Henry Gauthier-Villars, known as 'Willy'. (Willy knew Oscar Wilde from café society and during the 1895 trials had expressed his amusement over the contortions of English embarrassment.)

Colette: 'Monsieur Willy was not huge, he was bulbous. It has been said that he bore a marked resemblance to Edward VII. To use a less flattering comparison, I would say that in fact the likeness was to Queen Victoria'.

Willy lost little time in introducing his young wife to sexual sophistication, (Colette: 'No sooner married than deceived'), and encouraged her to write about her erotic thoughts and experiences as a schoolgirl, (Willy: "Don't be afraid of the spicy bits. Money's short"). The resulting four 'Claudine' novels were a huge success, although Willy insisted on publishing them under his own name.

In 1906, she separated from Willy and found solace with a lesbian lover, the Marquise de Belboeuf, (the niece of *Napoleon III*), known as 'Missy'. Missy was often mistaken for a man, an impression she did little to dispel. One of Willy's jokes was to sit in 'Ladies Only' train compartments and, when questioned, claim to be 'the Marquise de Belboeuf'. When *Ada Leverson* and her lover Frank Richardson met Missy and Colette in Dieppe, Richardson huffed: "I don't like your friends. Who is that old pederast?"

Still unknown as a writer due to Willy's machinations, Colette became a dancer specialising in semi-erotic mime. In 1907, in a ballet called 'Dream of Egypt', Missy performed the male role to Colette's near-naked heroine. Their full-blown stage embraces caused such audience outrage that the second performance was cancelled. Colette and Missy had to leave Paris until the scandal cooled down.

After six years with Missy, Colette met the editor of the Paris newspaper Le Matin, Henri de Jouvenel, who fathered her only child, then married her. Under his tutelage she became the literary editor of Le Matin, (and discovered the detective fiction writer Georges Simenon – who prospered from her advice to 'cut all the literary stuff').

Finally publishing under her own name, she became a popular success, writing seventy-three books in all, including 'Cherie' in 1920 about the affair between a young gigolo and an aging woman.

Divorcing Henri, in 1925 she married her third husband Maurice Goudeket. He was seventeen years her junior but their union remained a happy one. (Maurice had one phobia that Colette found inexplicable – a fear of the countryside. It stemmed from his father's belief that trees absorb oxygen, thus starving human beings. His father once looked at Colette disapprovingly, saying: "You don't look well. I bet you've been to the Bois de Boulogne again".)

By the 1930s, Colette was a revered author, living with Maurice and her beloved cats in their St Tropez house and their Paris apartment overlooking the Palais-Royal gardens.

Then in 1940, Paris was occupied by the invading German army. Colette decided to stay, even after Maurice was arrested and interned. When he escaped, she hid him in the attics of the Palais-Royal building and helped him to dodge the searches. Colette: 'Like other districts of Paris, the Palais-Royal had its maquis. It held its hidden parachutists, its Englishmen sheltered in risk and silence, its protected Jews, its children rescued from a stern fate'.

By 1943, Colette was aged seventy, in constant pain from arthritis, her husband in daily danger of capture and death, her city occupied, and her friends and neighbours disappearing under the Nazi rule. In this desperate situation, she decided on her own individual act of resistance. She wrote 'Gigi', a book suffused with the youthful insouciance and the high spirits of 'La Belle Epoch'. It was an affirmation of happiness, and a magnificent defiance of the horrors that surrounded her.

'Gigi' was hugely successful as a book and in 1958 was made into a Hollywood musical starring Leslie Caron. When Colette died, she was given the rare privilege of a state funeral and buried in Pere Lachaise cemetery.

After their guardian, Adrian Hope, died in 1904, Wilde's two sons, Cyril and Vyvyan, were relieved to be free of his austere control. They came instead under the benign guidance of Robbie Ross, who introduced them to the remaining members of their father's circle. The artist Charles Ricketts said that Ross was: 'the one generous and kindly influence that Cyril had met in his life'.

CYRIL WILDE 1885-1915 (Second Part – cont from 427)

Unlike his brother, Cyril was aware of the nature of his father's offences right from the start of the 1895 trials. Vyvyan later wrote: 'Cyril knew and was profoundly and permanently distressed' – 'he became a taciturn pessimist'. The brothers never mentioned Oscar to each other again.

(Wilde: 'Children begin by loving their parents. After a time they judge them. Rarely, if ever, do they forgive them.')

Cyril decided that it was up to him to restore the family honour. He told Ross later that: 'I became obsessed by 15 that I must retrieve what had been lost. I must be a *man* – with no signs of decadence.'

In pursuit of his aim, he trained himself to be an outstanding athlete, rowing for Radley School at the Henley Regatta, becoming (like Oscar) an excellent swimmer, and being appointed head of his house. On leaving school he entered the Royal Military Academy at Woolwich, and in 1905 was commissioned as a second lieutenant in the Royal Artillery. Although the truth remained secret, Cyril was constantly worried by the possibility of his real identity being discovered.

Cyril spent several years in India with his regiment, went tiger shooting, and in 1913 took six months leave to trek across Tibet. The journey turned into a physical ordeal and a mental exploration.

He walked 400 mountainous miles from Srinagar to the capital of Western Tibet, Ladakh, (where he met 'the Buddhist Reincarnation' – 'not half-witted exactly, but quite childish'), then travelled on into Chinese Tibet, where he 'suffered on that terrible plateau.' Cyril: 'Here may a man muse awhile on the great world.... Here we may take upon us the mystery of things, as if we were God's spies'. He ended up in Peking, (modern-day Beijing).

Despite these experiences, Cyril remained haunted by the memory of his father. Writing to Ross, he explained: 'I am fitting myself for the world, Robbie. They shall not say 'a talker, the son of a talker'. I will hold my own with the best of them. I too have something to inscribe on the pages of that little history book'.

In 1914, his regiment was transferred from India to the trenches of the Western Front. On May 9, 1915, Cyril, now promoted to Captain, was involved in the disastrous attack on the Aubers Ridge during the Battle of Neuve Chapelle. While duelling with a German sniper, Cyril was shot dead. He was buried in a military cemetery at the village of Richebourg-Avoue, six miles northeast of Bethune.

VYVYAN WILDE, (HOLLAND) 1886-1967 (Second Part – cont from Page 427)

Wilde's second son, Vyvyan, was aged 13 when his father died in 1900. His reaction to becoming an orphan was to attempt suicide by freezing himself to death in a snowstorm. (Although he failed, the incident left him permanently deaf in one ear.)

While he knew that Oscar had been in jail, Vyvyan was left in ignorance of the reason for his father's imprisonment. When he found a copy of 'The Happy Prince' at his guardian's house, he was puzzled about why Wilde's name had been scratched off the title page.

Throughout his teenage years, Vyvyan's ambitions were thwarted by the perceived need to protect him from his family past. When he was 14, he was forced to stop studying Greek on the grounds that Ancient Greek influence might lead to homosexuality; (Oscar had been a Greek scholar).

His desire to become a doctor was blocked also, as such a career might reveal Vyvyan's relationship to his grandfather, the surgeon Sir William Wilde. Similarly, he was forced to apply to Cambridge University rather than his real choice of Oxford, because Oscar had been a student at the latter.

When, aged 19, he finally learnt the real reason for Oscar's disgrace, he commented: "Is that all? I thought he had embezzled money".

The death of his guardian, Adrian Hope, and Vyvyan's introduction to Oscar's old friend *Robbie Ross* in 1906 opened an entirely new world. Not only had Ross sorted out the Wilde family finances, but he also introduced Vyvyan to such characters as *Max Beerbohm*, *Reggie Turner*, and *Ada Leverson*. When his nominal protectors, the Lloyd family, ignored Vyvyan's twenty-first birthday, it was Ross who ensured that he had a party; the guests included many of Oscar's old friends and even the writer *Henry James*.

Vyvyan attended Trinity Hall, Cambridge, for two years, where he became friends with the poet Rupert Brooke. He then left to take up a desultory career in law.

In 1914, he married Violet Craigie at a church ceremony presided over by Father Maturin, (a descendant of Speranza's muse, the writer Charles Maturin). Robert Ross was best man, (and also provided several detectives to guard the building against a possible attack by *Bosie Douglas*). Vyvyan and Violet had a difficult time financially as Vyvyan's income from the law dwindled to a trickle.

Initially he found the onset of the First World War something of a relief, finding army life preferable to the bar. His attitude soon altered as the reality of the trenches became apparent. The killing of his brother Cyril in 1915 came as 'a bitter blow' – Vyvyan had been on the front line only three miles away when it happened.

The following year, during the Battle of the Somme, he found himself face to face with a German officer in a captured trench. Vyvyan: 'He took a shot at me with his Luger and his bullet went through my cap. Then his Luger jammed and I, taking careful aim with my brother Cyril's revolver, dropped him. And I felt that in some way I had avenged Cyril's death'.

Vyvyan was wounded twice during the war, was decorated, and mentioned in despatches for bravery under fire.

(As the war came to an end in 1918, he accompanied Allied forces on their drive into Belgium. When he reached the town of Tournai, he was surprised to see that nearly every inhabitant had been able to find a Union Jack with which to applaud their arrival. He later found out that a German officer, seeing which way the wind was blowing, had imported a large collection of the flags and sold them off to the townsfolk before retreating rapidly towards Germany.)

Vyvyan's grief at the death of Cyril, and in 1918 of his surrogate father Robbie Ross, was compounded when he received news, (also in 1918), that his wife Violet had died of burns caused after her dress had caught fire. (It was a hideous re-enactment of the deaths of his aunts Emily and Mary – Oscar's illegitimate sisters – in 1871).

In 1922, against the advice of his close friend, Charles Scott-Moncrieff – "It will obsess you and you will never do anything else" – Vyvyan became a professional translator, and later worked for the BBC.

He once explained the problems of translation and cultural differences by referring to the experience of a China specialist called Albert Gervais. Gervais told Vyvyan that one day a very puzzled Mandarin had approached him with a query about a Christmas card that he had received from an English businessman.

"I quite understand the importance to the Christian religion of the birth of its founder", the Mandarin conceded, "and I quite understand why it should be commemorated by Christians sending cards to their friends. But can you explain to me the connexion between the birth of Christ and three cats on a bicycle throwing snowballs at an old gentleman in a top hat?"

In 1943, Vyvyan married again, this time to an Australian, Thelma Besant. In December 1945, she gave birth to Oscar's grandson, Merlin Holland. Vyvyan went on to write two moving autobiographies, 'Son of Oscar Wilde' and 'Time Remembered', before his death in 1967, aged 80.

'Let us remember that art is the one thing which death cannot harm': Wilde

Oscar Wilde's climb back to tolerance, then acceptance, finally to reverence, took almost one hundred years. It is possible to trace this progress via the various tributes to his memory. Although in 1925 a tentative plaque was placed on the Parisian hotel where he died, it was still possible in 1938 for an American publisher to inform Bernard Shaw that there was no interest in Wilde in the USA, (and not much in Britain either).

In 1954, (the centenary of his birth), a plaque was unveiled at his Dublin birthplace of 21, Westland Row by the Irish playwright Lennox Robinson. Simultaneously, another plaque was unveiled at his old home in Tite Street, London, by the novelist Sir Compton Mackenzie. Also in attendance at Tite Street were Vyvyan Holland, the actors Michael Redgrave and Rachel Kempson, and Michael MacLiammoir, the man who six years later created 'The Importance of Being Oscar'.

(The more-Irish-than-the-Irish Englishman Michael Macliammoir (1899-1978), was born Alfred Willmore in Willesden, London, and performed his famous one-man show on Wilde across the world from 1960 till 1975. At his last performance, there was a standing ovation and a tribute from the Irish President. MacLiammoir was once asked: "How do you remember all those words?" He replied: "By forgetting everything else".)

Soon after its unveiling, the Tite Street plaque was vandalised with white paint by moralists.

However, by the 1990s, the mood had changed enormously. In 2000, (the centenary of his death), statues were erected near Trafalgar Square in London, and in Merrion Square, Dublin. They were received with great enthusiasm, although the first soon suffered damage when Oscar's trademark cigarette was hacked off, while the second was given the usual Dublin treatment accorded to statues, receiving the nickname of 'The Fag On A Crag'.

In 1995, Oscar was given probably the greatest accolade when his name was inscribed in Poets Corner, Westminster Abbey, just below the memorial to Alexander Pope. It is unfortunate perhaps that Oscar's companion in immortality happens to be the poet of whom he wrote: 'There are two ways of disliking poetry – one is to dislike it and the other is to read Alexander Pope'.

THE GREAT WAR

In 1915, *Sir William Rothenstein* witnessed the ceremony of conferring degrees at Oxford University. He wrote afterwards: 'The sight of a number of youths, booted and spurred, with their gowns over their khaki, kneeling before the Chancellor to receive their degrees, put me in mind of the age of chivalry'.

This illusion was to be destroyed in the most horrific fashion. In Britain alone, nearly one man in ten under 45 was killed in the war, and one in five wounded. In percentage terms, the aristocracy lost more than any other class – of the House of Lords, over 200 peers or eldest sons were killed.

Oscar Wilde's friends and acquaintances suffered with the rest. The exclusive St James club White's, the one-time haunt of *Bosie Douglas* and his cousin Algernon Bourke, lost 56 members dead and 150 wounded.

The Liberal Prime Minister, *HH Asquith*, who had both dined and prosecuted Wilde, lost his eldest son Raymond on the Somme in 1916. His mother Margot Asquith wrote: 'When Raymond lay dying on the battlefield he gave the doctor his water flask to give to his father; it was placed by HH's bedside and never moved till we left Downing Street.'. Their second son was shell-shocked, and the third lost his leg at the Battle of the Ancre in 1917.

Lord Lansdowne, Asquith's political ally and the man who, against a venomous press attack, advocated peace moves in 1916, lost his second son in the trenches.

Five of the former Tory Prime Minister *Lord Salisbury's* grandsons were killed, while his successor *Arthur Balfour's* nephew Oswald was severely wounded.

Neil Primrose, the second son of the former Liberal Prime Minister *Lord Rosebery*, was killed fighting the Turks in Palestine in 1918, as was his cousin, Evelyn de Rothschild, in the same battle.

Lord Kitchener, Britain's leading soldier and acquaintance of Bosie Douglas, died when his ship hit a mine off the Orkneys.

The sons of the politician and member of the Crabbet Club, *George Wyndham*, and his wife Sibell (formerly Grosvenor) were killed, as were Ego and Yvo, the two sons of *Wilfred Blunt's* mistress, Lady Mary Elcho.

In 1915, Wilde's hosts at the country house of Taplow, *Willie Grenfell* and his wife Ettie, (Lord and Lady Desborough), lost both of their sons; William (aged 28) and, at the first Battle of Ypres, the poet Julian Grenfell (aged 25).

The writer GK Chesterton's brother Cecil was killed in the trenches, while *Sir Arthur Conan-Doyle*, creator of 'Sherlock Holmes', lost both his brother Innes and his son Kingsley in the subsequent flu epidemic.

WB Yeats's friend and patron Lady Gregory's nephew, Sir Hugh Lane, was drowned after his ship, the Lusitania, was torpedoed, while her son, Major Robert Gregory, was killed when his plane was shot down on the Italian front in 1917, (an incident recalled in Yeats's poem 'An Irish Airman Foresees His Death').

The friend of *Augustus John* and *Vyvyan Holland*, the poet Rupert Brooke, died in 1915 on his way to Gallipoli. The publisher *John Lane's* protégé Hector Hugh Munro, (the writer 'Saki'), was killed at the Battle of Beaumont Hamel in 1916.

Rudyard Kipling's only son was killed at the Battle of Loos in 1915. (When Kipling later visited a war cemetery near Boulogne, he noticed a headstone bearing the name of an Indian dooly-bearer who had been killed in Flanders – it read: 'Gunga Din').

Bernard Shaw's great friend, the drama critic *William Archer*, lost his son in France, while Beo Campbell, the son of the actress *Mrs Patrick Campbell*, was killed in 1917.

Richard Mansfield, who produced Shaw's play 'The Devil's Disciple' in America, lost his son in the trenches.

Eric Benson, the son of the actor and athlete *Sir Frank Benson*, was killed in 1916; Sir Frank also lost ten actors from of his Stratford Memorial Company, the 'Old Bensonians'.

Charles Frohman, the producer of many of Wilde's plays in the USA, died in the sinking of the Lusitania. The actor *Sir Seymour Hicks* lost his two brothers, Percy and Stanley, in France.

Sir Henry Irving's son, Henry Jun., was drowned when his passenger ship was torpedoed in the St Lawrence River, Canada; while the old woman who had sold apples for decades outside Irving's theatre, the Lyceum, was killed in a bombing raid.

Lucas King, the nephew of the newspaper magnate Lord Northcliffe, was killed in action, while the owner of the Daily Telegraph (and *Henry Labouchere's* enemy), Edward Levy-Lawson, lost his two grandsons. *Reggie Turner's* nephew, (and son of Frank Lawson), also called Frank, joined the Royal Bucks Hussars but died of self-inflicted gunshot wounds.

Robin Blacker, the son of Constance Wilde's friend and fervent Dreyfus supporter *Carlos Blacker*, was killed in battle in 1915.

The young naval cadet George Archer-Shee, (Rattigan's 'Winslow Boy'), whose 'postal order' trial had been won by *Sir Edward Carson*, died of his wounds after the First Battle of Ypres. He was aged 19.

Philip Crosland, the son of *TWH Crosland*, Bosie Douglas's right hand man, was killed in action in 1917. Guy du Maurier, the eldest son of the Punch satirist *Sir George du Maurier*, was killed in France in 1915.

Alan and Rex, the two sons of Alice Liddell, (the 'Alice' of Lewis Carroll's 'Alice in Wonderland'), were both killed in France.

Frank Harris's wife Nellie lost her three brothers in battle. Charles Lister, the son of 'the Cordial Aunt' Reggie Lister, was killed at Gallipoli.

Violet Hunt's friend, the sculptor, Henri Gaudier-Brzeska, (creator of the 'phallic head' of Ezra Pound), was killed in June 1915.

Prince Maurice of Battenburg, grandson of *Queen Victoria* and nephew of *Princess Louise*, was killed at the Battle of Ypres.

The translator *Charles Scott-Moncrieff*, as well as being badly wounded himself at the Battle of the Scarpe in 1917, lost nearly all of his Winchester School friends by the end of the war.

The son of the music hall star Sir Harry Lauder, (the colleague of Marie Lloyd), was killed on the Somme.

The palmist *Cheiro* was to be proved tragically correct in some of his predictions. As he foretold, the VC winner, Captain Lionel Bowles, was killed at home, aged 44, when a zeppelin bomb fell on his house. Cheiro also predicted the death of the American journalist Lena Guilbert Ford, (authoress of the song 'Keep The Home Fires Burning'); her Maida Vale, London, home was hit by a bomb, killing Lena, her elderly mother, and her crippled son.

Robbie Ross's nephew, Edward Jones, was killed in battle in 1916, and Ross's friend, the poet Wilfred Owen, died in action in 1918.

Sholto Douglas's son, (and Bosie's nephew), Bruce Douglas, aged 17, was killed on the Western Front in 1915.

Oscar Wilde's son Cyril was killed at the Battle of Neuve Chapelle, also in 1915.

APPENDIX 1 – LORD ROSEBERY

A recent biographer, Leo McKinstry, ('Rosebery – Statesman in Turmoil'), has cast revisionist doubt on the homosexual allegations against Rosebery, dismissing them as 'weak and nebulous'. However, rather than producing any new 'smoking gun' evidence to the contrary, he bases his arguments on alternative explanations for the known facts.

He argues that the main witnesses against Rosebery, (Queensberry, Backhouse, and Bosie), were unreliable; a true observation but not automatic proof that they were lying.

He quotes examples of Rosebery's letters in which Rosebery displays a heterosexual appreciation of girls, and mentions the fact that Rosebery acted as escort to many glamorous women; again true, but the same could be said of Oscar Wilde.

McKinstry suggests that, on hearing of Drumlanrig's death, Rosebery acted as a 'detached observer' and did not subscribe to Drumlanrig's memorial; McKinstry sees this lack of open grieving as proof that there was no relationship. Rosebery was an exceptionally reserved man in any case and, given the circumstances and rumours, it was not surprising that Rosebery was undemonstrative in his grief. He would have wished to distance himself from the scandal as much as possible.

Mckinstry also suggests that if Rosebery was guilty then he would not have treated Queensberry's attacks with 'humorous contempt' – again, Wilde did just that, (at least at first).

He states that the Public Prosecutor, Ham Cuffe, said that he had 'read through every word of the case' and found no mention of any name of interest. This is correct in '*the case*', but takes no account of the surrounding furore or of the efforts to keep 'interesting' names out of the courtroom.

Another of Mckinstry's points is that Rosebery's bitter political enemies, Sir William Harcourt and his son Loulou, did not use the rumours to bring down their rival – hence Rosebery was not guilty. This was not surprising as, much as they might have desired Rosebery's downfall, they were hardly likely to destroy the Liberal Party and convulse the country in a homosexual scandal involving the Prime Minister – and possibly other highly placed figures.

(When Rosebery was thought to have been involved in the Jameson Raid, Harcourt did not use this useful stick with which to beat him either. It was too damaging to the Liberal Party, which Harcourt hoped to lead.)

Dismissing the argument that the Liberal Party was afraid that the Wilde affair might bring down the government, Mckinstry suggests that the Liberals were already resigned to defeat before the Wilde trials. Possibly true – but surely not in a political holocaust.

He points out that the Government, via Harcourt of the Treasury, refused to reimburse Queensberry for the costs of his investigations. But then Queensberry's campaign had not been instigated or desired by the Liberal government.

George Ives mentioned that the CID chief Dr McNaughten had ordered the Hyde Park police never to arrest Rosebery 'because too big a fish often breaks the line'. Mckinstry simply fails to answer the point.

Whether Rosebery had a sexual dalliance with Drumlanrig is debateable but Mckinstry's arguments, while interesting, are certainly not conclusive.

BIBLIOGRAPHY

ADAMS / Madder Music, Stronger Wine – Jad Adams 2000
ALLEN / Hall Caine: Portrait of a Victorian Romancier – Vivien Allen 1997
ALVARADO / Thomas Edison – R V Alvarado 2002
AMOR / Mrs Oscar Wilde – Anne Clark Amor 1983
ANDERSON / A Few More Memories – Mary Anderson 1926
ANSTRUTHER / Oscar Browning: A Biography – C Anstruther 1983
ANTHONY / Louisa May Alcott – Katherine S Anthony 1977
ARCHER / William Archer: His Life, Work, and Friendships – C. Archer 1931
ARONSON / Prince Eddy and the Homosexual Underworld – Theo Aronson 1994
ASQUITH / The Autobiography – Margot Asquith 1920
ASQUITH / More Memories – Margot Asquith 1933
ATHERTON / Adventures of a Novelist – Gertrude Atherton 1932
AUSTIN / Alfred Austin – His Autobiography 1911
BADE / Degas – Patrick Bade 1991
BADENI / The Slender Tree: A Life of Alice Meynell – June Badeni 1981
BADLEY / Memories and Reflections – JH Badley 1955
BAKER / A Question of Honour – Anne Baker 1996
BALDICK / The Life of J-K Huysmans – Robert Baldick 1955
BAMFORD / Vicious Circle – F Bamford and V Bankes 1965
BANCROFT / Empty Chairs – Squire Bancroft 1925
BANCROFT / The Bancrofts: Recollections of Sixty Years 1909
BARING / Sarah Bernhardt – Maurice Baring 1933
BATCHELOR / John Ruskin, No Wealth But Life – John Batchelor 2000
BEATTY / Lillie Langtry, Manners, Masks and Morals – Laura Beatty 1999
BECKSON / Arthur Symons, A Life - Karl Beckson 1987
BECKSON / The Oscar Wilde Encyclopaedia – Karl Beckson 1998
BECKSON / London in the 1890s – Karl Beckson 1993
BEER / The Mauve Decade – Samuel Beer 1926
BEERBOHM / Letters to Reggie Turner – Max Beerbohm, ed. Rupert Hart-Davis 1964
BEERBOHM / Max Beerbohm – A Peep into the Past 1972
BEHRMAN / Conversation with Max – SN Berman 1960
BEHRMAN / Portrait of Max – SN Behrman 1960
BELFORD / Bram Stoker – Barbara Belford 1996
BELFORD / Violet – Barbara Belford 1990
BELFORD / Oscar Wilde: A Certain Genius – Barbara Belford 2000
BENNETT / Margot – Daphne Bennett 1984
BENNETT / Annie Besant – Olivia Bennett 1988
BENSON EF / As We Were: A Victorian Peep-show – EF Benson 1930
BENSON EF / Mother: Mary Benson – EF Benson 1925
BENSON, FRANK / My Memoirs – Sir Frank Benson 1930
BENSON, LADY / Lady Constance Benson – Mainly Players 1926
BENTLEY / The Importance of Being Constance - Joyce Bentley 1983
BERESFORD Memoirs, (2 vols) – Lord Charles Beresford 1914
BETTANY / Stewart Headlam – FG Bettany 1926
BIERCE / The Devil's Dictionary – Ambrose Bierce 1911
BIGGS-DAVISON / George Wyndham: A Study in Toryism – John Biggs-Davison 1951
BILLY / The Goncourt Brothers – Andre Billy 1960
BINGHAM / The Great Lover: The Life and Art of Herbert Beerbohm Tree – Madeleine
          Bingham 1978
BIRNBAUM / Oscar Wilde, Fragments and Memories – Martin Birnbaum 1920
BLANCH / Pierre Loti – Lesley Blanch 1983

BLANCHE / Portraits of a Lifetime – Jacques-Emile Blanche 1937
BLOCH / Sexual Life in England: Past and Present – Ivan Bloch. 1938
BLUNT / My Diaries – Wilfred Scawen Blunt 1919/1920
BLYTH / The Pocket Venus – Henry Blyth 1966
BLYTH / Skittles, The Last Victorian Courtesan – Henry Blyth 1970
BODLEY / The Bodley Head Bernard Shaw: Collected Plays and Prefaces (7 Vols) 1970
BODLEY / The Bodley Head Bernard Shaw: Shaw's Music (3 Vols) 1981
BORNAND / The Diary of WM Rossetti – Ed. Odette Bornand 1977
BOWEN / Seventy-Two Years at the Bar – Ernest Bowen-Rowlands 1924
BRANDON / Being Divine: Sarah Bernhardt – Ruth Brandon. 1991
BRASOL / Wilde: The Man, The Artist, The Martyr – Boris Brasol 1938
BRAYBROOKE / Oscar Wilde: a Study – Patrick Braybrooke 1930
BREMONT / Oscar Wilde and His Mother – Anna de Brémont 1911
BRENT / The Edwardians – Peter Brent 1972
BROAD / The Friendships and Follies of Oscar Wilde – Lewis Broad 1954
BROOKFIELD / Random Reminiscences – Charles Brookfield 1902
BROOKS / The Destruction of Lord Rosebery – David Brooks 1986
BROOME / Frank Harris – Vincent Broome 1947
BROUSSON / Anatole France Himself – Jean-Jacques Brousson 1925
BROWN / Zola, A Life – Frederick Brown 1995
BROWN / George Bernard Shaw – G.E.Brown 1970
BROWN / John Addington Symonds – Horatio Brown 1903
BROWN / Shaw In His Time – Ivor Brown 1965
BROWNING / Impressions of Indian Travel – Oscar Browning 1903
BROWNING / Memories of Sixty Years at Eton, Cambridge, and Elsewhere – Oscar
            Browning 1910
BROWNING / Memories of Later Years – Oscar Browning 1923
BUCKLE / Diaghilev – Richard Buckle 1979
BURDETT / The Beardsley Period – Osbert Burdett 1925
BURNAND / Records and Reminiscences (2 Vols) – Sir Francis Burnand 1904
BUSHELL / Great Eccentrics – Peter Bushell 1984
BUTLER / Thomas Hardy – Lance St John Butler 1978
BYRNE / The Wildes of Merrion Square – Patrick Byrne 1953
CALLOW / Oscar Wilde and His Circle – Simon Callow 2000
CAMPBELL / FE Smith: First Earl of Birkenhead – John Campbell 1983
CARDWELL / The Man Who Was Mark Twain – Guy Cardwell 1991
CARTER / Buffalo Bill Cody: The Man Behind the Legend – Robert Carter 2000
CASSAR / Kitchener – George Cassar 1977
CECIL / Max: A Biography – Lord David Cecil 1964
CHARTERIS / Life and Letters of Sir Edmund Gosse – Evan Charteris 1931
CHEIRO / Confessions: Memoirs of a Modern Seer – Cheiro 1932
CHESTERTON / George Bernard Shaw – GK Chesterton 1909
CHESTERTON / Robert Browning – GK Chesterton 1936
CHURCHILL / Reminiscences – Lady Randolph Churchill 1908
CHURCHILL / Jennie, Lady Randolph Churchill – Peregrine Churchill/Julian Mitchell 1974
CLAYTON / Selected Reviews of Oscar Wilde – ed. Anya Clayton 2004
CLEATHER / Helena P Blavatsky: As I Knew Her – Alice Leighton Cleather 1923
CLIFFORD / The Asquiths – Colin Clifford 2002
CLIVE / Pierre Louys – HP Clive 1978
COAKLEY / Oscar Wilde: The Importance of Being Irish – Davis Coakley 1994
COATES / Patsy – Tim Coates 2003
COHEN / Rider Haggard: His Life and Works – Morton Cohen 1960
COLBOURNE / The Real Bernard Shaw – Maurice Colbourne 1949

COLEMAN / Fair Rosalind: The American Career of Helena Modjeska – Marion Coleman 1969

CONAN DOYLE / Memories and Adventures – Sir Arthur Conan Doyle 1924

CONNELL / WE Henley – John Connell 1949

COMYNS CARR / Some Eminent Victorians – J Comyns Carr 1908

COOK / Thomas Hardy – Cornelia Cook 1989

CORDOVA / Mr Lewis Waller: A Biography – Rudolph De Cordova 1909

COREN / Conan Doyle – Michael Coren 1995

CORK / Jacob Epstein – Richard Cork 1999

CORNWALL / Portrait of a Killer – Patricia Cornwall 2002

CORNWALLIS-WEST / Edwardian Hey-Days – George Cornwallis-West 1930

COWARD / The Noel Coward Diaries – ed. G Payne and Sheridan Morley 1982

COWELL / WB Yeats – Raymond Cowell 1969

CREWE / Lord Rosebery, (2 vols) – Marquess of Crewe 1931

CROFT-COOKE / Bosie – Rupert Croft-Cooke 1963

CROFT-COOKE / Buffalo Bill The Legend, the Man of Action, the Showman – Rupert Croft-Cooke
    and W.S. Meadmore 1952 (reissued 1975)

CROFT-COOKE / The Unrecorded Life of Oscar Wilde – Rupert Croft-Cooke 1972

CROFT-COOKE / Feasting with Panthers – Rupert Croft-Cooke 1967

CROSLAND / Collected Poems of TWH Crosland 1917

CROSLAND / The First Stone – TWH Crosland 1912

CROWELL / Alfred Austin: Victorian – NB Crowell 1953

CUMBERLAND / Written in Friendship – Gerald Cumberland 1923

DALY / Life of Augustin Daly – J.F. Daly 1917

D'AUVERGNE / Pierre Loti: The Romance of a Great Writer – Edmund B D'Auvergne 1926

DAVIS / Sherman's March – Burke Davis 1980

DENT / Mrs Patrick Campbell – Alan Dent 1961

DESBOROUGH, Lady / 'Pages from a Family Journal' 1916 (privately printed)

DONALDSON / The Actor Managers – Frances Donaldson 1970

DONALDSON / Great Disasters of the Stage – William Donaldson 1984

DONOGHUE / Walter Pater – Denis Donoghue 1995

DOUGLAS / Autobiography – Lord Alfred Douglas 1929

DOUGLAS / Oscar Wilde and Myself – Lord Alfred Douglas 1914

DOUGLAS / Oscar Wilde: A Summing Up – Lord Alfred Douglas 1940

DOUGLAS / Without Apology – Lord Alfred Douglas 1938

DOUGLAS / The Sporting Queensberrys – FAK Douglas 1942

DU CANN / The Loves of Bernard Shaw – CGL du Cann 1963

DUFF / Eugenie and Napoleon III – David Duff 1978

DU MAURIER / Selected Letters of George du Maurier, 1860-67 – ed. Daphne du Maurier 1951

ECKENRODE / Jefferson Davis – HJ Eckenrode 1924

EDEL / Henry James – Leon Edel 1960

EDWARDES / Death Rides A Camel – Allen Edwardes 1963

EDWARDS / The Grimaldis of Monaco – Anne Edwards 1992

EGREMONT / Balfour – Max Egremont 1980

EGREMONT / The Cousins – Max Egremont 1977

ELLIOTT / Uncle Sam Ward and His Circle – Maud Howe Elliott 1938

ELLMAN / Oscar Wilde – Richard Ellman 1987

ELLMAN / The Identity of Yeats – Richard Ellman 1954

ERVINE / Bernard Shaw: His Life, Work and Friends – St. John Ervine 1956

ERVINE / Oscar Wilde: A Present Time Appraisal – St John Ervine 1951

EVANS / Fanatic Heart: A Life of John Boyle O'Reilly – AG Evans 1997

EVANS / The A-Z of British History – Eric Evans 1998

FABER / Jowett: A Portrait with background – Geoffrey Faber 1957

FADIMAN / The Faber Book of Anecdotes – Ed. Clifton Fadiman 1985

FANE / Chit Chat – Lady Augusta Fane 1926
FARSON / The Man Who Wrote Dracula: A Biography of Bram Stoker – Daniel Farson 1975
FARROW / George Moore – Anthony Farrow 1978
FARWELL / 'Queen Victoria's Little Wars' – Byron Farwell 1973
FAUSSET / Walt Whitman: Poet of Democracy – HI Fausset 1942
FAWKES / Dion Boucicault – Richard Fawkes 1979
FERGUSON / Mark Twain: Man and Legend – Ferguson 1943
FINCH / Wilfred Scawen Blunt – Edith Finch 1938
FINCH / Gilbert and Sullivan – Michael Finch 1993
FINDLATER / Six Great Actors – Richard Findlater 1957
FITZGERALD / Edward Burne-Jones – Penelope Fitzgerald 1975
FLANDERS / A Circle of Sisters – Judith Flanders 2002
FLEMING / Lady Colin Campbell: Victorian Sex Goddess – GH Fleming 1989
FLEMING / Whistler, a life – G.H. Fleming 1991
FLETCHER / Walter Pater – Iain Fletcher 1959
FORBES / Camps, Quarters and Casual Places – Archibald Forbes 1896
FORBES / Barracks, Bivouacs, and Battles – Archibald Forbes 1891
FORBES / Glimpses Through the Cannon-Smoke – Archibald Forbes 1880
FORBES / 'Tsar and Sultan' – Archibald Forbes 1894
FORBES-ROBERTSON / A Player Under Three Reigns – Sir Johnson Forbes-Robertson 1925
FOSTER / Charles Stuart Parnell: The Man and His Family – RF Foster 1976
FOTHERGILL / An Innkeeper's Diary – John Fothergill 1931
FOTHERGILL / Confessions of an Innkeeper – John Fothergill 1938
FRAZIER / George Moore – Adrian Frazier 2000
FREEMAN / Life of Lord Alfred Douglas – William Freeman 1948
FREY / Jefferson Davis – Herman S Frey 1978
FREY / Toulouse-Lautrec – Julia Frey 1994
FROST / Joaquin Miller – OW Frost 1967
FRYER / Andre and Oscar – Jonathan Fryer 1997
FYFE / Sir Arthur Pinero's Plays and Players – Hamilton Fyfe 1930
GARDINER / Life of Sir William Harcourt (2 vols) – AG Gardiner 1923
GARRETT / General Gordon – Richard Garrett 1974
GARRISON / A Treasury of Civil War Tales – Webb Garrison 1988
GERSON / Lillie Langtry – Noel Gerson 1971
GIBSON / Charles Conder – Frank Gibson 1914
GIBSON / The Erotomaniac – Ian Gibson 2001
GIDE / 'L'Immoraliste' – Andre Gide 1902
GIDE / Journals – Andre Gide 1939
GIDE / Oscar Wilde – Andre Gide 1938
GILBERT / Patience – WS Gilbert 1881
GILBERT / Iolanthe – WS Gilbert 1882
GILLIES / Marie Lloyd: The One and Only – Midge Gillies 1999
GILMOUR / Curzon – David Gilmour 1994
GILMOUR / The Long Recessional: The Imperial Life of Rudyard Kipling – David Gilmour 2002
GLOVER / Jimmy Glover: His Book – James M Glover 1911
GODWIN / Gilbert and Sullivan – AH Godwin 1926
GOGARTY / As I Was Going Down Sackville Street – Oliver St John Gogarty 1937
GONCOURT / Journal, (4 vols) – Edmond and Jules Goncourt 1956 – trans. MA Belloc
        and M Shedlock 1895
GOWER / Records and Reminiscences – Lord Ronald Gower 1903
GRANT / Emile Zola – Elliott M Grant 1966
GRANT / Private Woman, Public Person – Mary H Grant 1994
GRIBBLE / Life of the Emperor Francis-Joseph – Francis Gribble 1914

GRIERSON / Storm Bird: The Strange Life of Georgina Weldon – E Grierson 1959
GROSSKURTH / John Addington Symonds – Phyllis Grosskurth 1964
GUNN / Vernon Lee – Peter Gunn 1964
HACKETT / Shaw: George Versus Bernard – JP Hackett 1937
HALDANE / An Autobiography – RB Haldane 1929
HALL / Max Beerbohm: A Kind of Life – N John Hall 2002
HALLS / Maurice Maeterlinck: A Story of His Life and Thought – WD Halls 1960
HANSON / Verlaine, Prince of Poets – Lawrence and Elizabeth Hanson 1958
HARDWICK / An Immodest Violet – Joan Hardwick 1990
HARE / Story of My Life – AJC Hare 1900
HARE / Swinburne – Humphrey Hare 1949
HARRIS / My Life and Adventures – Frank Harris 1947
HARRIS / My Life and Loves – Frank Harris 1925
HARRIS / Contemporary Portraits, Series 2 – Frank Harris 1919
HARRIS / Oscar Wilde, His Life and Confessions – Frank Harris 1916 (New York, 1932)
HARRIS, WALTER / Morocco That Was – Walter Harris 1921
HART-DAVIS / The Complete Letters of Oscar Wilde – Hart-Davis and Holland 2000
HASLIP / Parnell: A Biography – Joan Haslip 1936
HASKELL / Ballet Russe: The Age of Diaghilev – Arnold Haskell 1968
HASTINGS / Sir Richard Burton: A Biography – Michael Hastings 1978
HAWKINS / Reminiscences of Sir Henry Hawkins, (2 Vols) – Ed. Richard Harris 1904
HAWTREY / Truth At Last – Charles Hawtrey 1924
HAYNES / The Lawyer – ESP Haynes 1951
HETHERINGTON / Melba – John Hetherington 1967
HIBBERT / Queen Victoria: A Personal History – Christopher Hibbert 2000
HICHENS / Yesterday – Robert Hichens 1947
HICHENS / The Green Carnation – Robert Hichens 1894
HICKS / Vintage Years – Seymour Hicks 1943
HICKS / Between Ourselves – Seymour Hicks 1930
HICKS / Me and My Missus – Seymour Hicks 1939
HOARE / Wilde's Last Stand – Phillip Hoare 1997
HODSON / Portraits and Reflections – Stuart Hodson 1928
HOFF / Charles Condor – Ursula Hoff 1972
HOGAN / Dion Boucicault – RG Hogan 1969
HOLLAND / Son of Oscar Wilde – Vyvyan Holland 1954
HOLLAND / Time Remembered – Vyvyan Holland, 1966
HOLROYD / Bernard Shaw, (3 vols) – Michael Holroyd 1988-1991
HOLROYD / Augustus John – Michael Holroyd 1975
HOPKINS / The Life of Oscar Wilde – RT Hopkins 1913
HOUSEMAN / Echoes of Paris – Laurence Houseman 1923
HUNT / The Flurried Years – Violet Hunt 1926
HUNTER-BLAIR / In Victorian Days – David Hunter-Blair 1939
HUNTER-BLAIR / A New Medley of Memories – David Hunter-Blair 1940
IRVING / Henry Irving, The Actor and His World – Lawrence Irving 1951
JACOB / Our Marie – Naomi Jacob 1936
JACKSON / The Eighteen Nineties – Holbrook Jackson 1913
JACKSON / Gertrude Atherton – JH Jackson 1940
JAMES / Lord Randolph Churchill – Robert Rhodes James 1959
JENKINS / Gladstone – Roy Jenkins – 1995
JENKINS / Churchill – Roy Jenkins – 2001
JENKINS / Sir Charles Dilke, A Victorian Tragedy – Roy Jenkins 1958
JOHN / Elizabeth Robins – Angela John 1995
JOHN / Finishing Touches - Augustus John 1964

JOHN / Chiaroscuro – Augustus John 1952
JONES / The First Lady of the South: The Life of Mrs Jefferson Davis – Charles C Jones 1958
JONES / The Shadow of Henry Irving – Henry Arthur Jones 1931
JONES / The Life and Letters of Henry Arthur Jones – Jenny Doris Jones 1930
JOPLING / Twenty Years of My Life – Louise Jopling 1925
JUDD / Radical Joe: A Life of Joseph Chamberlain – Denis Judd 1977
JULIAN / Oscar Wilde – Philippe Julian 1969
JULIAN / Robert de Montesquiou – Phillippe Julian 1965
JUMP / Matthew Arnold – John D Jump 1978
JUXON / Lewis and Lewis – John Juxon 1983
KAPLAN / Henry James – Fred Kaplan 1992
KAPLAN / Mark Twain and His World – Justin Kaplan 1974
KEMEN / Rambles with Anatole France – Sandor Kemen 1927
KENILWORTH / A Study of Oscar Wilde – WW Kenilworth 1912
KENYON / Hall Caine, the Man and the Novelist – C. F. Kenyon 1901
KERNAHAN / In Good Company – John Coulson Kernahan 1917
KERR / Recollections of a Defective Memory – Fred Kerr 1930
KINGSMILL / Matthew Arnold – Hugh Kingsmill 1928
KINGSMILL / Frank Harris – Hugh Kingsmill 1932
KOCHANSKI / Sir Garnet Wolseley: A Victorian Hero – G Kochanski 1999
KURTZ / The Empress Eugenie – Harold Kurtz 1964
LABELLE / Alfred Jarry: Nihilism and the Theater of the Absurd – Maurice Marc LaBelle 1980
LANG / My Darling Daisy – Theo Lang 1966
LANGTRY / The Days I knew – Lily Langtry 1925
LANGTRY / All at Sea – Lily Langtry 1913
LAVER / The First Decadent, Huysmans – James Laver 1954
LAWRENCE / Collected Letters of Bernard Shaw, (4 vols) – Ed. Dan H Lawrence 1965
LEBLANC / Maeterlinck and I – Georgette Leblanc 1932
LEECH / Stuart Headlam and the Guild of St Matthew – Kenneth Leech 1968
LEEVES / Leaves from a Victorian Diary – Edward Leeves 1985
LE GALLIENNE / The Romantic 90s – Richard Le Gallienne 1926
LEIDER / California's Daughter – EM Leider 1991
LEJEUNE / The Gentlemen's Clubs of London – Anthony Lejeune 1979
LEJEUNE / White's: The First 300 Years – Anthony Lejeune 1993
LENNON / Alfred Jarry, The Man with the Axe – Nigey Lennon 1984
LERNER / Maupassant – Michael Lerner 1975
LESLIE / Jennie: A life of Lady Randolph Churchill – Anita Leslie 1969
LESLIE / J.E.C. Bodley – Shane Leslie 1930
LEVERSON / Letters to the Sphinx from Oscar Wilde, with Reminiscences of the Author – Ada
     Leverson 1930
LEVERTON / Through the Box Office Window – WH Leverton 1932
LEWIS / Sherman: Fighting Prophet – Lloyd Lewis 1932, (reissued 1960)
LEWIS / Augustus John – Mark Lewis 1995
LEWIS MAY / John Lane and the Nineties – J Lewis May 1936
LEWIS / Oscar Wilde Discovers America – Lloyd Lewis and Henry Smith 1936
LHOMBREAUD / Arthur Symons: A Critical Biography – Roger Lhombreaud 1963
LIDDELL-HART / Sherman – BH Liddell Hart 1933
LILLY / Sickert, The Painter and His Circle – Marjorie Lilly 1971
LONGAKER / Ernest Dowson – Mark Longaker 1944
LONGFORD / A Pilgrimage of Passion, Wilfred Scawen Blunt – Elizabeth Longford 1979
LONGFORD / The Oxford Book of Royal Anecdotes – Elizabeth Longford 1989
LONGFORD / Victoria – Elizabeth Longford 1964
LOUYS / The Songs of Bilitis – Pierre Louys, trans. MS Buck 1966

LUCIE-SMITH / Toulouse-Lautrec – Edward Lucie-Smith 1983
LUDLAM / A Biography of Dracula: The Life Story of Bram Stoker – Harry Ludlam 1962
LYTTON / Lord Lytton's Personal and Literary Letters, (2 vols) – ed. Lady Betty Balfour 1906
MACDONALD / The Long Trail: Kipling – Meryl Macdonald 1999
MACHEN / Far Off Things – Arthur Machen 1922
MACHEN / Things Near and Far – Arthur Machen 1923
MACKAY / Allan Pinkerton – James A Mackay 1996
MACKAY / Balfour: Intellectual Statesman – Ruddock F Mackay 1985
MACMANAMIN / The American Years of John Boyle O'Reilly – Francis Macmanamin 1959
MAGNUS / Gladstone – Philip Magnus 1954
MAGNUS / Kitchener: Portrait of An Imperialist – Philip Magnus 1958
MAGNUS / King Edward VII – Philip Magnus 1964
MACLIAMMOIR / W.B.Yeats – Michael MacLiammoir/ Eavan Boland 1971
MARBURY / My Crystal Ball – Elizabeth Marbury 1923
MARBERRY / Splendid Poseur: Joaquin Miller, American Poet - M. Marion Marberry 1953
MARCOSSON / Charles Frohman: Man and Manager – Isaac Marcosson and Daniel Frohman 1916
MARJORIBANKS / The Life of Lord Carson – Edward Marjoribanks 1932
MARLOWE / Cromer in Egypt – John Marlowe 1970
MARLOWE / Milner: Apostle of Empire – John Marlowe 1976
MASON / Sir George Alexander and the St James Theatre – AEW Mason 1935
MASON / Oscar Wilde: Art and Morality – Stuart Mason 1915
MASTERS / The Life of EF Benson – Brian Masters 1991
McCLURE / Gertrude Atherton – Charlotte S McClure 1976
McCORMACK / The Man Who was Dorian Gray – JH McCormack 2000
McCORMICK / Dion Boucicault – John McCormick 1987
McKINSTRY / Rosebery: Statesman in Turmoil – Leo McKinstry 2005
McLYNN / Burton, Snow Upon The Desert – Frank McLynn 1990
McMULLEN / Degas: His Life, Times and Work – Roy McMullen 1985
MELBA / Melodies and Memories – Dame Nellie Melba 1925
MELTZER / Mark Twain Himself – Milton Meltzer 1960
MELVILLE / Mother of Oscar – Joy Melville 1994
MELVILLE / Ellen and Edy – Joy Melville 1987
MEYNELL / Alice Meynell: A Memoir – Viola Meynell 1929
MIKHAIL / Oscar Wilde, Interviews and Recollections (2 vols) – EH Mikhail 1979
MILLER / Memories and Rimes – Joaquin Miller 1884
MILLER / His California Diary – Joaquin Miller 1936
MILLER / Kropotkin – Martin A Miller 1976
MILNE / Esher, The Enigmatic Edwardian – James Lees Milne 1986
MINNEY / The Bogus Image of Bernard Shaw – H.J.Minney 1969
MITCHELL / Colette – Yvonne Mitchell 1975
MODJESKA / Memories and Impressions – Helen Modjeska 1910
MONEYPENNY / Life of Disraeli – WE Moneypenny and GE Buckle 1929
MONTGOMERY-HYDE / Lord Alfred Douglas – H Montgomery-Hyde
MONTGOMERY-HYDE / Henry James at Home – H Montgomery-Hyde 1969
MONTGOMERY-HYDE / Their Good Names – H Montgomery Hyde 1970
MONTGOMERY-HYDE / The Other Love – H Montgomery Hyde 1970
MONTGOMERY-HYDE / Aftermath – H Montgomery-Hyde 1963
MONTGOMERY-HYDE / Oscar Wilde – H. Montgomery Hyde 1975
MONTGOMERY-HYDE / The Trials of Oscar Wilde – H Montgomery-Hyde 1948
MOORE / E. Nesbit: a biography – Doris Langley Moore 1967
MOORE / Confessions of a Young Man – George Moore 1904
MORLEY / Oscar Wilde: An Illustrated Biography – Sheridan Morley 1976
MOSLEY / Curzon: End of An Epoch – Leonard Mosley 1960

MOSLEY / Efforts at Truth – Nicholas Mosley 1994
MUDDIMAN / The Men of the Nineties – Bernard Muddiman 1920
MURPHET / Blavatsky: When Daylight Comes – Howard Murphet 1975
MURRAY / Bosie – Douglas Murray 2000
MURRAY / A Life of Matthew Arnold – Nicholas Murray 1997
NELSON / Out of the Silence – Edith Nelson
NELSON / Publisher to the Decadents, Leonard Smithers – James G Nelson 2000
NEVILL / My Own Times – Lady Dorothy Nevill 1912
NEWMAN / The Life of Richard Wagner – Ernest Newman 1976
NEWBOLT / My World as in My Time – Sir Henry Newbolt 1932
NICHOLLS / The Lost Prime Minister: A Life of Sir Charles Dilke – David Nicholls 1995
NICHOLSON / Paul Verlaine – Harold Nicholson 1921
NORRIS / Two Men of Manxland – Samuel Norris 1947
NOYES / William Morris – Alfred Noyes 1908
O'BRIEN / Oscar Wilde in Canada – Kevin O'Brien 1982
O'CONNOR / Ambrose Bierce – Richard O'Connor 1968
O'CONNOR / Memoirs of an Old Parliamentarian (2 vols) – TP O'Connor 1929
ORMOND / George du Maurier – Leonee Ormond 1969
O'SULLIVAN / Aspects of Wilde – Vincent O'Sullivan 1936
PAGE / Tennyson – Ed. Norman Page 1983
PAINTER / Andre Gide – George Painter 1951
PAINTER / Marcel Proust (2 vols) – George Painter 1959, 1965
PAKENHAM / Sixty Miles from England: The English at Dieppe 1814-1914 – Simon Pakenham 1967
PALMER / E F Benson, As He Was – Geoffrey Palmer and Noel Lloyd 1988
PARRIS / Great Parliamentary Scandals – Matthew Parris 1995
PARTRIDGE / A History of Orgies – Burgo Partridge 1958
PATCH / Thirty Years With G.B.S. – Blanche Patch 1951
PEARCE / The Unmasking of Oscar Wilde – Joseph Pearce 1997
PEARSON / Dizzy – Hesketh Pearson 1951
PEARSON / Bernard Shaw – Hesketh Pearson 1942
PEARSON / Gilbert and Sullivan – Hesketh Pearson 1935
PEARSON / The Last Actor-Managers – Hesketh Pearson 1950
PEARSON / Conan Doyle: His Life and Art – Hesketh Pearson 1943
PEARSON / The Man Whistler – Hesketh Pearson 1952
PEARSON / Labby – Hesketh Pearson 1936
PEARSON / Beerbohm Tree – Hesketh Pearson 1956
PEARSON / Life of Oscar Wilde – Hesketh Pearson 1946
PEARSON / Edward the Rake – John Pearson 1975
PELLING / Winston Churchill – Henry Pelling 1974
PEMBLE / J.A. Symonds: Culture and the Demon Desire – Ed. John Pemble
PENNELL / The Life of James Mc Neill Whistler – ER and J Pennell 1911
PENNELL / The Whistler Journal – ER and J Pennell 1921
PERRY / Alfred Tennyson – Seamus Perry 2005
PERUGINI / Victorian Days and Ways – Mark Perugini 1932
PETERS / Mrs Pat – Margot Peters 1984
PETERS / Bernard Shaw and the Actresses – Margot Peters 1980
PETERSON / Joaquin Miller – Martin S Peterson 1937
PHILLIPS / Solomon J Solomon – Olga Phillips 1933
PILE / The Book Of Heroic Disasters – Stephen Pile 1979
POPE-HENNESSEY / The Years of Promise, Monckton Milnes – James Pope Hennessy 1949
POPE-HENNESSY / The Flight of Youth, Monckton Milnes – James Pope-Hennessy 1951
POULSON / William Morris – Christine Poulson 1996
PRICE / A History of Punch – RGG Price 1957

QUEENSBERRY / Oscar Wilde and the Black Douglas – Marquess of Queensberry and Colson 1949
QUENNELL / Ruskin – by Peter Quennell 1949
RABY / The Cambridge Companion to Oscar Wilde – Ed. Peter Raby 1997
RADIC / Melba: The Voice of Australia – Therese Radic 1986
RAFFALOVICH / A Willing Exile, (2 vols) – Marc-Andre Raffalovich 1890
RANI OF SARAWAK / Good Morning and Good Night – Ranee of Sarawak 1934
RANSOME / Oscar Wilde – Arthur Ransome 1912
RAYMOND / Life of Lord Rosebery – ET Raymond 1923
REID / Life, Letters and Friendships of R. M. Milnes, first Lord Houghton – Sir TW Reid 1890
REYNOLDS / The Vision of Simeon Solomon – Simon Reynolds 1984
RICHARDS / Memories of a Misspent Youth – Grant Richards 1932
RICHARDS / Seven Years of Eton – James Brinsley Richards 1883
RICHARDS / Julia Ward Howe (2 vols) – Richards and Eliot 1916
RICHARDSON / Verlaine – Joanna Richardson 1971
RICHARDSON / Victor Hugo – Joanna Richardson 1976
RICHARDSON / Colette – Joanna Richardson 1983
RICKETTS / Oscar Wilde: Recollections – Charles Ricketts and Jean Paul Raymond 1932
RICKETTS / Self-Portrait, Letters and Journals of Charles Ricketts – T. Sturge Moore 1939
RIDEING / Many Celebrities and a Few Others – William Rideing 1912
ROBB / Victor Hugo – Graham Robb 1997
ROBB / Rimbaud – Graham Robb 2000
ROBERTS / Salisbury: Victorian Titan – Andrew Roberts 1999
ROBERTS / The Mad Bad Line – Brian Roberts 1981
ROBERTSON / Life of Longfellow – E.S. Robertson 1887
ROBERTSON / Time Was – W. Graham Robertson 1931
ROBINS / Both Sides of the Curtain – Elizabeth Robins 1940
ROBINSON / Fifty Years of Fleet Street – Sir John Robinson 1904
RODD / Social and Diplomatic Memories, (3 vols) – Rennell Rodd 1922-5
RODRIGUEZ / Wild Heart: A Life – Suzanne Rodriguez 2003
ROLFE / Without Prejudice: 100 Letters from FW Rolfe to John Lane – F Rolfe 1963
ROOKSBY / A.C. Swinburne, a Poet's Life – Rikky Rooksby 1997
ROOT / Frank Harris – EM Root 1947
ROSE / Daemons and Angels: A Life of Jacob Epstein – June Rose 2002
ROSS / Robert Ross, Friend of Friends – Margery Ross 1952
ROSS / Aubrey Beardsley – by Robert Ross 1909
ROTHENSTEIN / Augustus John – Sir John Rothenstein 1946
ROTHENSTEIN / The Life and Death of Condor – Sir John Rothenstein 1938
ROTHENSTEIN / Men and Memories, (3 vols) – Sir William Rothenstein 1934-6
ROY / James Matthew Barrie – James A Roy 1937
ROYLE / The Kitchener Enigma – Trevor Royle 1985
RUEFF / I Knew Sarah Bernhardt – Suze Rueff 1951
RUSSELL / The Lives and Legends of Buffalo Bill – Don Russell 1960
RUSSELL / Cheer, Boys, Cheer – Henry Russell 1895
SALA / The Life and Adventures of George Augustus Sala – by Himself 1896
SALTUS / Oscar Wilde: An Idler's Impression – Edgar Saltus 1917
SAUNDERS / Ambrose Bierce – Richard Saunders 1984
SAXTON / Louisa May – Martha Saxton 1978
SCHENKAR / Truly Wilde - Joan Schenkar 2000
SCHROEDER / Additions and Corrections to Richard Ellman's Oscar Wilde – Horst Schroeder 2002
SCOTT / Old Days in Bohemian London – Mrs Margaret Scott 1919
SCOTT-MONCRIEFF / Memories and Letters – CK Scott-Moncrieff 1931
SEWELL / In the Dorian Mode – Brocard Sewell 1983
SEYMOUR-SMITH / Rudyard Kipling – Martin Seymour-Smith 1989

SHAPLEN / Free Love and Heavenly Sinners – Robert Shaplen 1956
SHARLAND / A Theatrical Feast – Elizabeth Sharland 2002
SHARP / Life of Robert Browning – William Sharp 1890
SHAW / Our Theatres in the Nineties, (2 vols) – Bernard Shaw, 1932
SHAW / Bernard Shaw and Alfred Douglas, A Correspondence – Ed. Mary Hyde 1982
SHAW / Bernard Shaw: Collected Letters, (4 vols) – Ed. Dan H Lawrence 1965-1988
SHERIDAN / Andre Gide – Alan Sheridan 1998
SHERARD / Twenty Years in Paris – Robert Sherard 1905
SHERARD / The Life of Oscar Wilde – Robert Sherard 1906
SHERARD / Bernard Shaw, Frank Harris, and Oscar Wilde – Robert Sherard 1937
SHERARD / Oscar Wilde: The Story of an Unhappy Friendship – Robert Sherard 1902
SHERARD / The Real Oscar Wilde – Robert Sherard 1916
SHERRIN / Theatrical Anecdotes – Ned Sherrin 1991
SINCLAIR / Death By Fame – Andrew Sinclair 1998
SINFIELD / The Wilde Century – Alan Sinfield 1994
SMITH / Psychic Messages From Oscar Wilde – Hester Travers Smith 1924
SMYTH / Impressions That Remained (2 vols) – Ethel Smyth 1919
SMYTH / Beecham and Pharoah – Ethel Smyth 1935
SMYTH / A Final Burning of the Boats – Ethel Smyth 1928
SMYTH / As Time Went On – Ethel Smyth 1936
SMYTH / What Happened Next – Ethel Smyth 1940
SMYTHE / The Life of William Terriss, Actor – Arthur Smythe 1898
SPEEDIE / Wonderful Sphinx, Biography of Ada Leverson – Julie Speedie 1993
SPENDER / The Life of Herbert Henry Asquith – JA Spender 1932
SPROULE / Thomas A Edison – Anne Sproule 1990
SORLEY-BROWN / Life and Genius of TWH Crosland – W. Sorley-Brown 1928
SOUHAMI / Wilde Girls: Paris, Sappho and Art – Diana Souhami 2004
STAMP / Royal Rebels – Robert Stamp 1988
STANFORD / Mahaffy – WB Stanford and RB McDowell 1971
STARKIE / Arthur Rimbaud – Enid Starkie 1938
STARRETT / Ambrose Bierce – Vincent Starrett 1920
ST AUBYN / Edward VII: Prince and King – Giles St Aubyn 1979
STEAD / My Father: Personal and Spiritual Reminiscences of WT Stead – Estelle Stead 1918
STEELE / Lord Salisbury: A Political Biography – David Steele 1999
STEEN / A Pride of Terrys: Family Saga – Marguerite Steen 1962
STERN / Louisa May Alcott – Madeline Stern 1952
STEVENS / The Voyage of the Catalpa – Peter Stevens 2002
STEWART / Edward Carson – A.T.Q. Stewart 1981
ST HELIER / Memories of Fifty Years – Lady St Helier 1909
STILLMAN / Alfred Jarry – Linda Klieger Stillman 1983
STOKER / Personal Reminiscences of Henry Irving – Bram Stoker 1906
STOKES / In The Nineties – John Stokes 1989
STRACHEY / Eminent Victorians – Lytton Strachey 1918
STURGIS / Aubrey Beardsley – Matthew Sturgis 1998
SUTTON / Rodin, Triumphant Satyr – Denys Sutton 1966
SUTTON / Walter Sickert – Denys Sutton 1976
SWANN / Ernest Dowson – TB Swann 1964
SWANWICK / 'I Have Been Young' – by Helena Swanwick 1935
SWEET / Inventing the Victorians – Matthew Sweet 2001
SYMONS AJA / The Quest For Corvo – AJA Symons 1934
SYMONS AJA / Aubrey Beardsley – AJA Symons 1966
SYMONS / Horatio Bottomley: A Biography – Julian Symons 1955
TARNES / The Life and Works of Auguste Rodin – Richard Tarnes 2001

TAYLOR / Richard Wagner – Ronald Taylor 1979
TERRIERE / Days That Are Gone – B. De Sales La Terriere 1924
TERRY / Memoirs – Ellen Terry, ed C St John and Edith Craig 1933
THOMAS / Sam Ward; King of the Lobby – Lately Thomas 1965
THOMPSON / Imperial Vanities – Brian Thompson 2001
THORPE / Phil May – James Thorpe 1948
THOROLD / The Life of Henry Labouchere – Algar Thorold 1913
THWAITE / Edmund Gosse – Ann Thwaite 1985
TOLLEMACHE / Benjamin Jowett, Master of Balliol – Lionel A Tollemache 1895
TRAUBEL / With Walt Whitman in Camden – Horace Traubel 1914
TREE / Herbert and I – Maud Tree 1920
TREHERNE / A Plaintiff in Person – Apsley Philip Treherne 1923
TREVOR-ROPER / A Hidden Life: Sir E Backhouse – Hugh Trevor-Roper 1976
TROUBRIDGE / Life Among the Troubridges – Laura Troubridge, ed Jacqueline Hope-Nicholson
     1966
TROUBRIDGE / Letters of Engagement – Troubridge and Hope 1999
TSCHIFFELY / Don Roberto – AR Tschiffely 1937
TWAIN / Greatly Exaggerated: Wit and Wisdom of Mark Twain – Ed. Alex Ayres 1988
VANBRUGH / To Tell My Story – Irene Vanbrugh 1948
VERE WHITE / The Parents of Oscar Wilde – T de Vere White 1967
VIVIAN / Myself Not Least – Herbert Vivian 1925
VIVIAN / The Reminiscences of a Short Life – Herbert Vivian 1889
VON ECKHART / Oscar Wilde's London – Wolf Von Eckhart 1988
VYVER / Memoirs of Marie Corelli – Bertha Vyver 1930
WAGENKNECHT / Longfellow: A Full-Length Portrait – Edward Wagenknecht 1955
WALFORD / Memories of Victorian London – LB Walford 1912
WALKER-SMITH / Life of Sir Edward Clarke – Walker-Smith and Clarke 1939
WALKOWITZ / City of Dreadful Delight – Judith Walkowitz 1992
WALLACE / Guy De Maupassant – Albert H Wallace 1973
WALLACE / The Intimate Sex Lives of Famous People – Irving Wallace
WARD / Both Sides of the Curtain – Genevieve Ward and R Whiteing 1918
WARD / A Writer's Recollections – Mrs Humphrey Ward 1918
WARE / Life and Times of Colonel Burnaby – Ware and Mann 1882
WATERHOUSE / 'Cafe Royal: Ninety Years of Bohemia' – G Deghy and K Waterhouse 1955
WATERS / Burne-Jones: An Illustrated Life – William Waters 1973
WEAVER / Duse: A Biography – William Weaver 1984
WEINTRAUB / Private Shaw and Public Shaw – Stanley Weintraub 1963
WEINTRAUB / Reggie, A Portrait of Reginald Turner – Stanley Weintraub 1965
WELLESLEY / Democratic Despot: A Life of Napoleon III – Sir Victor Wellesley 1934
WHISTLER / The Gentle Art of Making Enemies – JM Whistler 1904
WHITE / Proust – Edmund White 1999
WHITELEY / George Du Maurier: His Life and Work – Derek Pepys Whiteley 1948
WHITTINGTON / The Quest for the Golden Boy: The Life and Letters of Richard Le Gallienne –
     Richard Whittington-Egan and Geoffrey Smerdon 1960
WHYTE / The Life of WT Stead – Frederick Whyte 1925
WHYTE / William Heineman – Frederick Whyte 1928
WILBERFORCE / Backsettown and Elizabeth Robins – Octavia Wilberforce 1921
WILDE / Collected Works of Oscar Wilde – Collins edition , general editor JB Foreman 1948
WILLIAMS / Henry Wadsworth Longfellow – Cecil Brown Williams 1964
WILLIAMS / PGT Beauregard: Napoleon in Gray – TH Williams 1955
WILLIAMSON / Murray Marks and His Friends – GC Williamson 1930
WILLIAMSON / WE Henley – Kennedy Williamson 1930
WILSON / The Victorians – AN Wilson 2002

WILSON / Bernard Shaw: a Reassessment – Colin Wilson 1969
WILSON / Victorian Doctor – TG Wilson 1942
WINSTEN / Days With Bernard Shaw – Stephen Winsten 1951
WINSTEN / Jesting Apostle – Steven Winsten 1956
WINWAR / Wilde, and the Yellow Nineties – F. Winwar 1940
WOODCOCK / The Anarchist Prince – by George Woodcock 1950
WOODCOCK / The Paradox of Wilde – George Woodcock 1950
WORTHAM / Oscar Browning – HE Wortham 1927
WRATISLAW / Oscar Wilde: A Memoir – Theodore Wratislaw 1979
WRIGHT / The Life of Walter Pater, (2 vols) – Thomas Wright 1907
WRIGHT / Table Talk – by Thomas Wright 2000
WYNDHAM / The Sphinx and her Circle – Horace Wyndham 1963
WYNDHAM / Speranza, A Biography of Lady Wilde – Horace Wyndham 1951
YEATS / Memoirs – W.B.Yeats 1972
YEATS / WB Yeats – Autobiography 1965
YOUNG / Arthur James Balfour – Kenneth Young 1963
ZWEIG / Walt Whitman: The Making of the Poet – Paul Zweig 1985

'Intentions' magazines – The Oscar Wilde Society - ed. Donald Mead
'The Wildean' magazines – The Oscar Wilde Society – ed. Donald Mead and Michael Seeney

ALPHABETICAL CHARACTERS

ADEY, WILLIAM MORE - English translator, 423
ALCOTT, LOUISA MAY - American writer, 132
ALEXANDER, SIR GEORGE - English actor, 315
ALICE, PRINCESS OF MONACO - French-American socialite, 188
ALMA-TADEMA, SIR LAWRENCE - Anglo-Dutch artist, 123
ANDERSON, MARY - American actress, 163
ARCHER, WILLIAM - English theatre critic, 327
ARNOLD, MATTHEW - English author and poet, 126
ASHBEE, HENRY - English pornographer, 70
ASQUITH, ANTHONY - English film director, 406
ASQUITH, HERBERT H - English statesman, 402
ASQUITH, MARGOT - Scottish wife of HH Asquith, 403
ATHERTON, GERTRUDE - American writer, 440
AUSTIN, ALFRED - English poet, 422
BACCHUS, REGGIE - English academic and pornographer, 434
BACKHOUSE, SIR EDWARD - English fraudster, 347
BADEN-POWELL, ROBERT - English soldier, 385
BAKER, VALENTINE - English soldier, 199
BALCOMBE, FLORENCE - Irish girlfriend of Oscar Wilde, 53
BALFOUR, ARTHUR - English statesman, 400
BANCROFT, SIR SQUIRE - English actor, 98
BARLAS, JOHN - Scottish poet and anarchist, 286
BARNEY, NATALIE - American social hostess, 512
BARRIE, SIR JAMES - English playwright, 343
BEARDSLEY, AUBREY - English artist, 336
BEARDSLEY, MABEL - English actress, 338
BEAUREGARD, GENERAL PIERRE - American soldier, 159
BEECHER, HENRY WARD - American religious preacher, 160
BEERBOHM, JULIUS (jun.) - English dandy and financier, 347
BEERBOHM, SIR MAX - English writer and cartoonist, 344
BELL, LAURA - Irish courtsean, 35
BENSON FAMILY - English family of writers and ecclesiastics, 357
BENSON, EDWARD F. - English writer, 357
BENSON, SIR FRANK - English actor, 111
BERESFORD, LORD CHARLES - Anglo-Irish admiral, 206
BERNHARDT, SARAH - French actress, 327
BESANT, ANNIE - English politician and mystic, 251
BIBI LA PUREE - French street thief, 174
BIERCE, AMBROSE - American writer, 150
BISMARCK, OTTO VON - German statesman, 67
BIZET, GENEVIEVE (STRAUSS) - French salon hostess, 292
BLACKER, CARLOS - English linguist, 453
BLANCHE, JACQUES-EMILE - French writer, 166
BLAVATSKY, MADAME HELENA - Russian mystic, 249
BLUNT, WILFRID - English poet and adventurer, 303
BODLEY, JOHN EDWARD COURTENAY - English student friend of Wilde, 45
BOOTH, JUNIUS - American actor, 317
BOTTOMLEY, HORATIO - English fraudulent businessman, 186
BOUCICAULT, DION(ysus Lardner) - Irish-American actor, 144
BOUCICAULT, DOT Junior - Irish-American theatre promoter, 146

540

INDIVIDUAL TOPICS